The Ministers Manual for 1995

By the same editor

Best Sermons 1
Best Sermons 2
Best Sermons 3
Best Sermons 4
Best Sermons 5
Best Sermons 6
Best Sermons 7
Biblical Preaching: An Expositor's Treasury
God's Inescapable Nearness (coauthor with Eduard Schweizer)
A Guide to Biblical Preaching
Learning to Speak Effectively
Minister's Worship Manual (coeditor with Ernest A. Payne and Stephen F. Winward)
Preaching
Surprised by God
The Twentieth Century Pulpit, Volumes I and II

SEVENTIETH ANNUAL ISSUE

THE MINISTERS MANUAL

1995 EDITION

Edited by

JAMES W. COX

HarperSanFrancisco
A Division of HarperCollins*Publishers*

Editors of THE MINISTERS MANUAL

G. B. F. Hallock, D.D., 1926–1958
M. K. W. Heicher, Ph.D., 1943–1968
Charles L. Wallis, M.A., M.Div., 1969–1983
James W. Cox, M.Div., Ph.D.

Translations of the Bible referred to and quoted from in this book may be indicated by their standard abbreviations, such as NRSV (New Revised Standard Version) and NIV (New International Version). In addition, some contributors have made their own translations and others have used a mixed text.

Other acknowledgments begin on page 351.

 For information, address HarperCollins Publishers, 10 East 53rd Street, New York, NY 10022.

FIRST EDITION

Library of Congress Catalog Card Number
25–21658
ISSN 0738–5323
ISBN 0–06–061621–0 (cloth)

94 95 96 97 98 HAD 10 9 8 7 6 5 4 3 2 1

This edition is printed on acid-free paper that meets the American National Standards Institute Z39.48 Standard.

CONTENTS

PREFACE

I would like for you to read the following words from my textbook on preaching. They definitely relate to the materials presented in *The Ministers Manual.*

> Preaching is here to stay. From time to time observers and critics have questioned its value. They have noted popular preference for other means of communication. They have witnessed the failure of preaching at times to deal effectively with certain important issues. Yet the return of people again and again to the word of the pulpit, as they seek answers to at least some of their questions, demonstrates the durability of preaching.
>
> The chief factor in its favor is its content, not its practitioners. Unworthy, uninformed, and unskilled preachers have not been able to put preaching out of business, for its message has always stood in judgment on even the best preachers. In this way, preaching has maintained a kind of independence of the forces that would diminish its role in society. (*Preaching: A Comprehensive Approach to the Design and Delivery of Sermons,* San Francisco: HarperCollins, 1985, 1993, p. xi.)

The biblical text inspires and—if the preacher takes the text seriously—regulates what is said in the sermon. To that end, the lectionary text can be a creative and controlling force.

Please note that for the first time in *The Ministers Manual* a number of the lectionary messages in Section II are based on the Old Testament or Epistle lesson, rather than on the Gospel lesson. This change should highlight the often-overlooked possibilities in other lectionary texts. In the Sermon Suggestions in Section II, I have presented brief outlines on texts not treated in the Lectionary Message.

I have attempted to bring together some of the finest homiletical materials from excellent preachers of the past and present times. It is hoped that what is presented here will stimulate thought; provide inspiration and ideas for sermons; and highlight examples of noteworthy sermonic structure, illustration, and style.

Many individuals have contributed to this volume. From their reading and from their pulpit ministry they share with you their discoveries and their own thoughts and creations as well. I continue to be grateful for the secretarial support provided by The Southern Baptist Theological Seminary, and I wish to thank preachers and publishers for permission to quote from their material. Clara McCartt, C. Neil Strait, and Lee R. McGlone over many years have made special contributions behind the scenes, and to them I offer my hearty thanks. I owe profound gratitude also to Laura Allen, Tonya Vickery, and Bev Tillman, word processing operators who typed the manuscript, and to Alicia Gardner, office services supervisor. I am most appreciative of the faithful attention and careful work of the editorial staff at HarperSanFrancisco.

James W. Cox
The Southern Baptist Theological Seminary
2825 Lexington Road
Louisville, Kentucky 40280

SECTION I.
General Aids and Resources

Civil Year Calendars

1995

JANUARY

S	M	T	W	T	F	S
1	2	3	4	5	6	7
8	9	10	11	12	13	14
15	16	17	18	19	20	21
22	23	24	25	26	27	28
29	30	31				

FEBRUARY

S	M	T	W	T	F	S
			1	2	3	4
5	6	7	8	9	10	11
12	13	14	15	16	17	18
19	20	21	22	23	24	25
26	27	28				

MARCH

S	M	T	W	T	F	S
			1	2	3	4
5	6	7	8	9	10	11
12	13	14	15	16	17	18
19	20	21	22	23	24	25
26	27	28	29	30	31	

APRIL

S	M	T	W	T	F	S
						1
2	3	4	5	6	7	8
9	10	11	12	13	14	15
16	17	18	19	20	21	22
23	24	25	26	27	28	29
30						

MAY

S	M	T	W	T	F	S
	1	2	3	4	5	6
7	8	9	10	11	12	13
14	15	16	17	18	19	20
21	22	23	24	25	26	27
28	29	30	31			

JUNE

S	M	T	W	T	F	S
				1	2	3
4	5	6	7	8	9	10
11	12	13	14	15	16	17
18	19	20	21	22	23	24
25	26	27	28	29	30	

JULY

S	M	T	W	T	F	S
						1
2	3	4	5	6	7	8
9	10	11	12	13	14	15
16	17	18	19	20	21	22
23	24	25	26	27	28	29
30	31					

AUGUST

S	M	T	W	T	F	S
		1	2	3	4	5
6	7	8	9	10	11	12
13	14	15	16	17	18	19
20	21	22	23	24	25	26
27	28	29	30	31		

SEPTEMBER

S	M	T	W	T	F	S
					1	2
3	4	5	6	7	8	9
10	11	12	13	14	15	16
17	18	19	20	21	22	23
24	25	26	27	28	29	30

OCTOBER

S	M	T	W	T	F	S
1	2	3	4	5	6	7
8	9	10	11	12	13	14
15	16	17	18	19	20	21
22	23	24	25	26	27	28
29	30	31				

NOVEMBER

S	M	T	W	T	F	S
			1	2	3	4
5	6	7	8	9	10	11
12	13	14	15	16	17	18
19	20	21	22	23	24	25
26	27	28	29	30		

DECEMBER

S	M	T	W	T	F	S
					1	2
3	4	5	6	7	8	9
10	11	12	13	14	15	16
17	18	19	20	21	22	23
24	25	26	27	28	29	30
31						

1996

JANUARY

S	M	T	W	T	F	S
	1	2	3	4	5	6
7	8	9	10	11	12	13
14	15	16	17	18	19	20
21	22	23	24	25	26	27
28	29	30	31			

FEBRUARY

S	M	T	W	T	F	S
				1	2	3
4	5	6	7	8	9	10
11	12	13	14	15	16	17
18	19	20	21	22	23	24
25	26	27	28	29		

MARCH

S	M	T	W	T	F	S
					1	2
3	4	5	6	7	8	9
10	11	12	13	14	15	16
17	18	19	20	21	22	23
24	25	26	27	28	29	30
31						

APRIL

S	M	T	W	T	F	S
	1	2	3	4	5	6
7	8	9	10	11	12	13
14	15	16	17	18	19	20
21	22	23	24	25	26	27
28	29	30				

MAY

S	M	T	W	T	F	S
			1	2	3	4
5	6	7	8	9	10	11
12	13	14	15	16	17	18
19	20	21	22	23	24	25
26	27	28	29	30	31	

JUNE

S	M	T	W	T	F	S
						1
2	3	4	5	6	7	8
9	10	11	12	13	14	15
16	17	18	19	20	21	22
23	24	25	26	27	28	29
30						

JULY

S	M	T	W	T	F	S
	1	2	3	4	5	6
7	8	9	10	11	12	13
14	15	16	17	18	19	20
21	22	23	24	25	26	27
28	29	30	31			

AUGUST

S	M	T	W	T	F	S
				1	2	3
4	5	6	7	8	9	10
11	12	13	14	15	16	17
18	19	20	21	22	23	24
25	26	27	28	29	30	31

SEPTEMBER

S	M	T	W	T	F	S
1	2	3	4	5	6	7
8	9	10	11	12	13	14
15	16	17	18	19	20	21
22	23	24	25	26	27	28
29	30					

OCTOBER

S	M	T	W	T	F	S
		1	2	3	4	5
6	7	8	9	10	11	12
13	14	15	16	17	18	19
20	21	22	23	24	25	26
27	28	29	30	31		

NOVEMBER

S	M	T	W	T	F	S
					1	2
3	4	5	6	7	8	9
10	11	12	13	14	15	16
17	18	19	20	21	22	23
24	25	26	27	28	29	30

DECEMBER

S	M	T	W	T	F	S
1	2	3	4	5	6	7
8	9	10	11	12	13	14
15	16	17	18	19	20	21
22	23	24	25	26	27	28
29	30	31				

Church and Civic Calendar for 1995

JANUARY

1 New Year's Day
The Name of Jesus
5 Twelfth Night
6 Epiphany
7 Eastern Orthodox Christmas
16 Martin Luther King Day
18 Confession of St. Peter
19 Robert E. Lee's Birthday
25 Conversion of St. Paul

FEBRUARY

1 National Freedom Day
2 Presentation of Jesus in the Temple
Groundhog Day
3 Four Chaplains Memorial Day
12 Lincoln's Birthday
12–19 Brotherhood/Sisterhood Week
14 St. Valentine's Day
20 Presidents' Day
22 Washington's Birthday
28 Shrove Tuesday

MARCH

1 Ash Wednesday
4 World Day of Prayer
5 First Sunday in Lent
6 Eastern Orthodox Great Lent begins
12 Second Sunday in Lent
16 Purim
19 Third Sunday in Lent
Joseph, Husband of Mary
25 The Annunciation
26 Fourth Sunday in Lent

APRIL

2 Fifth Sunday in Lent
Passion Sunday
Daylight Saving Time begins
9–15 Holy Week
9 Palm Sunday
Passion Sunday (alternate)
13 Maundy Thursday
14 Good Friday
Pan American Day
15 Pesach (first day of Passover)
16 Easter
23 Eastern Orthodox Pascha (Easter)
25 St. Mark, Evangelist

MAY

1 Law Day
Loyalty Day
May Day
St. Philip and St. James, Apostles
7–13 National Family Week
14 Mother's Day
Festival of the Christian Home
21 Rural Life Sunday
22 National Maritime Day
Victoria Day (Canada)
25 Ascension Day
29 Memorial Day

JUNE

4 Pentecost (Whitsunday)
First day of Shavuot
11 Children's Sunday
Trinity Sunday
St. Barnabas, Apostle
Eastern Orthodox Pentecost
14 Flag Day
18 Father's Day
29 St. Peter and St. Paul, Apostles

JULY

1 Canada Day
4 Independence Day
22 St. Mary Magdalene
25 St. James the Elder

AUGUST

6 The Transfiguration
7 Civic Holiday (Canada)

14 Atlantic Charter Day
15 Mary, the Mother of Jesus
19 National Aviation Day
24 St. Bartholomew, Apostle
26 Women's Equality Day

SEPTEMBER

3 Labor Sunday
4 Labor Day
8 Birth of Virgin Mary
10 Grandparents' Day
Rally Day
17 Citizenship Day
17–23 Constitution Week
19 International Day of Peace
21 St. Matthew, Apostle and Evangelist
23 Native American Day
24 Christian Education Sunday
Gold Star Mother's Day
25 Rosh Hashanah
29 St. Michael and All Angels

OCTOBER

1 World Communion Sunday
2 Child Health Day
World Habitat Day
4 Yom Kippur
8 Laity Sunday
9 Thanksgiving Day (Canada)
First day of Sukkot
9 Columbus Day
16 World Food Day
18 St. Luke, Evangelist
Hanukkah
24 United Nations Day
28 St. Simon and St. Jude, Apostles
31 National UNICEF Day
Halloween
Reformation Day

NOVEMBER

1 All Saints' Day
2 All Souls' Day
4 Sadie Hawkins Day
7 Election Day
11 Armistice Day
Veterans Day
Remembrance Day (Canada)
12 Elizabeth Cady Stanton
Stewardship Sunday
19 Bible Sunday
Thanksgiving Sunday
21 Presentation of the Virgin Mary in the Temple
23 Thanksgiving Day
30 St. Andrew, Apostle

DECEMBER

3 First Sunday of Advent
10 Second Sunday of Advent
15 Bill of Rights Day
17 Third Sunday of Advent
Wright Brothers Day
21 Forefathers' Day
24 Fourth Sunday of Advent
Christmas Eve
25 Christmas
26 Boxing Day (Canada)
26 St. Stephen, Deacon and Martyr
27 St. John, Apostle and Evangelist
28 The Holy Innocents, Martyrs
31 New Year's Eve
Watch Night

The Common Lectionary for 1995

The following Scripture lessons are commended for use in public worship by various Protestant churches and the Roman Catholic church and include first, second, Gospel readings, and Psalms, according to Cycle C from January 1 to November 26 and according to Cycle A from December 3 to December 31. (Copyright 1992 Consultation on Common Texts.)

Jan. 1: 1 Sam. 2:18–20, 26; Ps. 148; Col. 3:12–17; Luke 2:41–52 (Holy Name); Num. 6:22–27; Ps. 8; Gal. 4:4–7 (alt.);

Phil. 2:5–11 (alt.); Luke 2:15–21 (New Year); Eccles. 3:1–13; Ps. 8; Rev. 21:1–6a; Matt. 25:31–46

EPIPHANY SEASON

Jan. 6 and 8 (Epiphany): Isa. 60:1–6; Ps. 72:1–7, 10–14; Eph. 3:1–12; Matt. 2:1–12 (Baptism of the Lord); Isa. 43:1–7; Ps. 29; Acts 8:14–17; Luke 3:15–17, 21–22

Jan. 15: Isa. 62:1–5; Ps. 36:5–10; 1 Cor. 12:1–11; John 2:1–11

Jan. 22: Neh. 8:1–3, 5–6, 8–10; Ps. 19; 1 Cor. 12:12–31a; Luke 4:14–21

Jan. 29: Jer. 1:4–10; Ps. 71:1–6; 1 Cor. 13:1–13; Luke 4:21–30

Feb. 5: Isa. 6:1–8 (9–13); Ps. 138; 1 Cor. 15:1–11; Luke 5:1–11

Feb. 12: Jer. 17:5–10; Ps. 1; 1 Cor. 15:12–20; Luke 6:17–26

Feb. 19: Gen. 45:3–11, 15; Ps. 37:1–11, 39–40; 1 Cor. 15:35–38, 42–50; Luke 6:27–38

Feb. 26: Sir. 27:4–7 (alt.); Isa. 55:10–13 (alt.); Ps. 92:1–4, 12–15; 1 Cor. 15: 51–58

LENT

Mar. 1 (Ash Wednesday): Joel 2:1–2, 12–17 (alt.); Isa. 58:1–12 (alt.); Ps. 51:1–17; 2 Cor. 5:20b–6:10; Matt. 6:1–6, 16–21

Mar. 5: Deut. 26:1–11; Ps. 91:1–2, 9–16; Rom. 10:8b–13; Luke 4:1–13

Mar. 12: Gen. 15:1–12, 17–18; Ps. 27; Phil. 3:17–4:1; Luke 13:31–35 (alt.); Luke 9:28–36 (alt.)

Mar. 19: Isa. 55:1–9; Ps. 63:1–8; 1 Cor. 10:1–13; Luke 13:1–9

Mar. 26: Josh. 5:9–12; Ps. 32; 2 Cor. 5:16–21; Luke 15:1–3, 11b–32

Apr. 2: Isa. 43:16–21; Ps. 126; Phil. 3:4b–14; John 12:1–8

HOLY WEEK

Apr. 9 (Palm/Passion Sunday): Luke 19: 28–40 (palms); Ps. 118:1–2, 19–29 (palms); Isa. 50:4–9a; Ps. 31:9–16; Phil. 2:5–11; Luke 22:14–23:56 (alt.); Luke 23:1–49 (alt.)

Apr. 10 (Monday): Isa. 42:1–9; Ps. 36:5–11; Heb. 9:11–15; John 12:1–11

Apr. 11 (Tuesday): Isa. 49:1–7; Ps. 71:1–14; 1 Cor. 1:18–31; John 12:20–36

Apr. 12 (Wednesday): Isa. 50:4–9a; Ps. 70; Heb. 12:1–3; John 13:21–32

Apr. 13 (Thursday): Exod. 12:1–4 (5–10), 11–14; Ps. 116:1–2, 12–19; 1 Cor. 11:23–26; John 13:1–17, 31b–35

Apr. 14 (Good Friday): Isa. 52:13–53:12; Ps. 22; Heb. 10:16–25 (alt.); Heb. 4:14–16, 5:7–9 (alt.); John 18:1–19:42

Apr. 15 (Holy Saturday): Job 14:1–14 (alt.); Lam. 3:1–9, 19–24; Ps. 31:1–4, 15–16; 1 Pet. 4:1–8; Matt. 27:57–66 (alt.); John 19:38–42 (alt.)

SEASON OF EASTER

Apr. 15–16 (Easter Vigil): Gen. 1:1–2:4a; Ps. 136:1–9, 23–26; Gen. 7:1–5, 11–18; 8:6–18; 9:8–13; Ps. 46; Gen. 22:1–18; Ps. 16; Exod. 14:10–31; 15:20–21; Exod. 15:1b–13, 17–18 (resp.); Isa. 55:1–11; 12:2–6 (resp.); Bar. 3:9–15, 32–4:4 (alt.); Prov. 8:1–8, 19–21; 9:4–6 (alt.); Ps. 19; Ezek. 36:24–28; Ps. 42–43; Ezek. 37:1–14; Ps. 143; Zeph. 3:14–20; Ps. 98; Rom. 6:3–11; Ps. 114; Luke 24:1–12

Apr. 16 (Easter Sunday): Acts 10:34–43 (alt.); Isa. 65:17–25 (alt.); Ps. 118:1–2, 14–24; 1 Cor. 15:19–26 (alt.); Acts 10: 34–43 (alt.); John 20:1–18 (alt.); Luke 24:1–12 (alt.)

Apr. 16 (Easter Evening): Isa. 25:6–9; Ps. 114; 1 Cor. 5:6b–8; Luke 24:13–49

Apr. 23: Acts 5:27–32; Ps. 118:14–29 (alt.); 150; Rev. 1:4–8; John 20:19–31

Apr. 30: Acts 9:1–6 (7–20); Ps. 30; Rev. 5:11–14; John 21:1–19

May 7: Acts 9:36–43; Ps. 23; Rev. 7:9–17; John 10:22–30

May 14: Acts 11:1–18; Ps. 148; Rev. 21:1–6; John 13:31–35

May 21: Acts 16:9–15; Ps. 67; Rev. 21:10, 22–22:5; John 14:23–29 (alt.); 5:1–9 (alt.)

May 25 (Ascension Day): Acts 1:1–11; Ps. 47 (alt.); 110; Eph. 1:15–23; Luke 24:44–53

May 29: Acts 16:16–34; Ps. 97; Rev. 22:12–14, 16–17, 20–21; John 17: 20–26

SEASON OF PENTECOST

June 4 (Pentecost): Acts 2:1–21 (alt.); Gen. 11:1–9 (alt.); Ps. 104:1a, 24–34, 35b; Rom. 8:14–17 (alt.); Acts 2:1–21 (alt.); John 14:8–17 (25–27)

June 11 (Trinity Sunday): Prov. 8:1–4, 22–31; Ps. 8; Rom. 5:1–5; John 16: 12–15

June 18: 1 Kings 21:1–10 (11–14), 15–21a; Ps. 5:1–8; Gal. 2:15–21; Luke 7:36–8:3

June 25: 1 Kings 19:1–4 (5–7), 8–15a; Ps. 42–43; Gal. 3:23–29; Luke 8:26–39

July 2: 2 Kings 2:1–2, 6–14; Ps. 77:1–2, 11–20; Gal. 5:1, 13–25; Luke 9:51–62

July 9: 2 Kings 5:1–14; Ps. 30; Gal. 6:(1–6) 7–16; Luke 10:1–11, 16–20

July 16: Amos 7:7–17; Ps. 82; Col. 1:1–14; Luke 10:25–37

July 23: Amos 8:1–12; Ps. 52; Col. 1:15–28; Luke 10:38–42

July 30: Hos. 1:2–10; Ps. 85; Col. 2:6–15 (16–19); Luke 11:1–13

Aug. 6: Hos. 11:1–11; Ps. 107:1–9, 43; Col. 3:1–11; Luke 12:13–21

Aug. 13: Isa. 1:1, 10–20; Ps. 50:1–8, 22–23; Heb. 11:1–3, 8–16; Luke 12:32–40

Aug. 20: Isa. 5:1–7; Ps. 80:1–2, 8–19; Heb. 11:29–12:2; Luke 12:49–56

Aug. 27: Jer. 1:4–10; Ps. 71:1–6; Heb. 12:18–29; Luke 13:10–17

Sept. 3: Jer. 2:4–13; Ps. 81:1, 10–16; Heb. 13:1–8, 15–16; Luke 14:1, 7–14

Sept. 10: Jer. 18:1–11; Ps. 139:1–6, 13–18; Philem. 1–21; Luke 14:25–33

Sept. 17: Jer. 4:11–12, 22–28; Ps. 14; 1 Tim. 1:12–17; Luke 15:1–10

Sept. 24: Jer. 8:18–9:1; Ps. 79:1–9; 1 Tim. 2:1–7; Luke 16:1–13

Oct. 1: Jer. 32:1–3a, 6–15; Ps. 91:1–6, 14–16; 1 Tim. 6:6–19; Luke 16:19–31

Oct. 8: Lam. 1:1–6; 3:19–26 (alt. resp.); Ps. 137 (alt.); 2 Tim. 1:1–14; Luke 17:5–10

Oct. 15: Jer. 29:1, 4–7; Ps. 66:1–12; 2 Tim. 2:8–15; Luke 17:11–19

Oct. 22: Jer. 31:27–34; Ps. 119:97–104; 2 Tim. 3:14–4:5; Luke 18:1–8

Oct. 29: Joel 2:23–32; Ps. 65; 2 Tim. 4:6–8, 16–18; Luke 18:9–14

Nov. 5: Hab. 1:1–4; 2:1–4; Ps. 119:137–144; 2 Thess. 1:1–4, 11–12; Luke 19:1–10; Dan. 7:1–3, 15–18; Ps. 149; Eph. 1:11–23; Luke 6:20–31

Nov. 12: Hag. 1:15b–2:9; Ps. 145:1–5, 17–21 (alt.); 98; 2 Thess. 2:1–5, 13–17; Luke 20:27–38

Nov. 19: Isa. 65:17–25; 12 (resp.); 2 Thess. 3:6–13; Luke 21:5–19; Jer. 23:1–6; Luke 1:68–79 (resp.); Col. 1:11–20; Luke 23:33–43

Nov. 23 (Thanksgiving): Deut. 26:1–11; Ps. 100; Phil. 4:4–9; John 6:25–35

Nov. 26: 1 Kings 8:22–23, 41–43; Ps. 96:1–9; 1 Kings 17:17–24; Ps. 30

ADVENT

Dec. 3: Isa. 2:1–5; Ps. 122; Rom. 13:11–14; Matt. 24:36–44

Dec. 10: Isa. 11:1–10; Ps. 72:1–7, 18–19; Rom. 15:4–13; Matt. 3:1–12

Dec. 17: Isa. 35:1–10; Ps. 146:5–10 (alt.); Luke 1:47–55 (alt. resp.); James 5:7–10; Matt. 11:2–11

Dec. 24: Isa. 7:10–16; Ps. 80:1–7, 17–19; Rom. 1:1–7; Matt. 1:18–25

CHRISTMAS SEASON

Dec. 25 (Christmas Day): Isa. 9:2–7; Ps. 96; Tit. 2:11–14; Luke 2:1–14 (15–20); or Isa. 62:6–12; Ps. 97; Tit. 3:4–7; Luke 2:(1–7) 8–20; or Isa. 52:7–10; Ps. 98; Heb. 1:14 (5–12); John 1:1–14

Dec. 31: Isa. 63:7–9; Ps. 148; Heb. 2:10–18; Matt. 2:13–23

Four-Year Church Calendar

	1995	1996	1997	1998
Ash Wednesday	March 1	February 21	February 12	February 25
Palm Sunday	April 9	March 31	March 23	April 5
Good Friday	April 14	April 5	March 28	April 10
Easter	April 16	April 7	March 30	April 12
Ascension Day	May 25	May 16	May 8	May 21
Pentecost	June 4	May 26	May 18	May 31
Trinity Sunday	June 11	June 2	May 25	June 7
Thanksgiving	November 23	November 28	November 27	November 26
Advent Sunday	December 3	December 1	November 30	November 29

Forty-Year Easter Calendar

1995 April 16	2005 March 27	2015 April 5	2025 April 20
1996 April 7	2006 April 16	2016 March 27	2026 April 5
1997 March 30	2007 April 8	2017 April 16	2027 March 28
1998 April 12	2008 March 23	2018 April 1	2028 April 16
1999 April 4	2009 April 12	2019 April 21	2029 April 1
2000 April 23	2010 April 4	2020 April 12	2030 April 21
2001 April 15	2011 April 24	2021 April 4	2031 April 13
2002 March 31	2012 April 8	2022 April 17	2032 March 28
2003 April 20	2013 March 31	2023 April 9	2033 April 17
2004 April 11	2014 April 20	2024 March 31	2034 April 9

Traditional Wedding Anniversary Identifications

1 Paper	7 Wool	13 Lace	35 Coral
2 Cotton	8 Bronze	14 Ivory	40 Ruby
3 Leather	9 Pottery	15 Crystal	45 Sapphire
4 Linen	10 Tin	20 China	50 Gold
5 Wood	11 Steel	25 Silver	55 Emerald
6 Iron	12 Silk	30 Pearl	60 Diamond

Colors Appropriate for Days and Seasons

White. Symbolizes purity, perfection, and joy and identifies festivals marking events, except Good Friday, in the life of Jesus: Christmas, Epiphany, Easter, Eastertide, Ascension Day; also Trinity Sunday, All Saints' Day, weddings, funerals. Gold may also be used.

Red. Symbolizes the Holy Spirit, martyrdom, and the love of God: Good Friday, Pentecost, and Sundays following.

Violet. Symbolizes penitence: Advent, Lent.

Green. Symbolizes mission to the world, hope, regeneration, nurture, and growth: Epiphany season, Kingdomtide, Rural Life Sunday, Labor Sunday, Thanksgiving Sunday.

Blue. Advent, in some churches.

Flowers in Season Appropriate for Church Use

January. Carnation or snowdrop.
February. Violet or primrose.
March. Jonquil or daffodil.
April. Lily, sweet pea, or daisy.
May. Lily of the valley or hawthorn.
June. Rose or honeysuckle.
July. Larkspur or water lily.
August. Gladiolus or poppy.
September. Aster or morning glory.
October. Calendula or cosmos.
November. Chrysanthemum.
December. Narcissus, holly, or poinsettia.

Historical, Cultural, and Religious Anniversaries in 1995

Compiled by Kenneth M. Cox

10 years (1985). *March 13:* Mikhail Gorbachev succeeds Konstantin Chernenko as general secretary of the Communist Party of the Soviet Union. *June 21:* Remains of Nazi doctor Josef Mengele are identified in Brazil. *September 1:* U.S. and French explorers identify the wreck of the *Titanic,* which sank in 1912 off the coast of Newfoundland. *September 19:* Earthquakes kill as many as 20,000 in Mexico.

25 years (1970). *April 30:* President Nixon announces he has ordered U.S. combat troops into parts of Cambodia. *May 4:* National Guardsmen open fire on students protesting the Vietnam War at Kent State University in Ohio, killing four. *September 6:* Two armed hijackers force a Pan Am jet to fly to Beirut, then Cairo, where the plane is blown up with no one on board. *September 28:* Egyptian President Gamal Abdel Nasser dies, and Anwar el-Sadat is elected October 14. *November 9:* Former French President Charles de Gaulle dies. *Debuts:* Television's *All in the Family;* Amtrak; Environmental Protection Agency; Alvin Toffler's *Future Shock;* Gray Panthers.

40 years (1955). *April 5:* British Prime Minister Winston Churchill resigns at age 81. *September 6:* Fires in Istanbul, Turkey, destroy 73 churches, eight chapels, two convents, 3,584 warehouses, and 1,954 shops belonging to Armenians, Greeks, and Jews. *Debuts:* Disneyland; Ford Thunderbird; *Guinness Book of World Records; National Review;* polio vaccine.

50 years (1945). *March 16:* U.S. forces take the Pacific island of Iwo Jima. *April 12:* President Roosevelt dies in Warm Springs, Georgia. *April 28:* Italian dictator Benito Mussolini is executed. *April 30:* Adolf Hitler commits suicide in Berlin. *May 8:* VE Day—World War II ends in Europe. *August 6:* United States drops an atomic bomb on Hiroshima, Japan. *August 14:* VJ Day—World War II ends in the Pacific. *Debuts:* CARE; frozen orange juice; *Meet the Press.*

75 years (1920). *January 3:* Babe Ruth signs with the New York Yankees. *January 16:* Prohibition of sales of alcoholic beverages in the United States takes effect. *April 30:* Use of religion in Turkey for political ends is made punishable by death. *May 16:* Joan of Arc is canonized. *August 26:* Tennessee's ratification of the Nineteenth Amendment leads to proclamation of women's suffrage. *Debuts:* American Civil Liberties Union; Chanel No. 5; League of Women Voters; Miss America.

100 years (1895). *May 20:* A four-minute showing of a boxing match in New York becomes the first commercial presentation of a film on screen. Jose Martí leads a rebellion in Cuba, sparked by economic depression and enhanced by U.S. sugar tariff. *Debuts:* Asheville's Biltmore House; London School of Economics; safety razor; wireless telegraph.

125 years (1870). *March 30:* U.S. Secretary of State Hamilton Fish proclaims ratification of the Fifteenth Amendment, which forbids denial of the right to vote "on account of race, color, or previous condition of servitude." *July 18:* Bishops at first Vatican Council, convened by Pope Pius IX, support a decree declaring the pope infallible when defining doctrines of faith or morals. *July 19:* France declares war on Russia. Hiram R. Revels, senator from Mississippi, and J. H. Rainey, representative from South Carolina, become the first black U.S. legislators. *Debuts:* F. A. O. Schwarz; periodic table of elements; post cards.

150 years (1845). *March 3:* Florida becomes the 27th state. *December 29:* Over the objections of Mexico, Texas becomes the 29th state. The Methodist Episcopal Church of America splits into northern and southern conferences after Georgia bishop James Andrews resists an order to give up his slaves or quit his bishopric. U.S. evangelist William Miller founds the Adventist Church. Persian religious leader Ali Mohammed of Shiraz founds

Babism. English cardinal and writer John Henry Newman converts to Catholicism. *Debut:* U.S. Naval Academy.

175 years (1820). *January 17:* Novelist Anne Brontë is born in Yorkshire, England (d. 1849). *January 29:* Britain's King George III dies. *March 2:* Missouri Compromise admits Missouri to the Union and divides Maine from Massachusetts. *May 12:* Florence Nightingale, pioneer of modern nursing, is born in Florence, Italy (d. 1910).

200 years (1795). *October 24:* Russia, Prussia, and Austria partition Poland for the third time. *October 31:* Poet John Keats is born in London (d. 1821). *December 4:* Thomas Carlyle, historian and essayist, is born in Scotland (d. 1881). *Debuts:* Harvard's Hasty Pudding Society; London Missionary Society.

Anniversaries of Hymn Writers and Hymn-Tune Composers in 1995

Compiled by Hugh T. McElrath

50 years (1945). *Birth* Bruce Ballinger, author "We have come into His house," composer WORSHIP HIM; Andrae Crouch, author "Bless His holy name," "The blood will never lose its power," "My tribute," "Soon and very soon," composer BLESS HIS HOLY NAME, THE BLOOD, MY TRIBUTE, SOON AND VERY SOON; Mylon R. LeFevre, author "Without Him I could do nothing," composer WITHOUT HIM; Thomas H. Troeger, author "Our Savior's infant cries were heard," "O praise the gracious power," "Source and Sovereign, rock and cloud," "Silence, frenzied, unclean spirit!" "Wind who makes all winds that blow," "Swiftly pass the clouds of glory," "As a chalice cast of gold," "Let all who pray the prayer Christ taught," and others; Derek Williams, composer SAN ROCCO ("When Christ was lifted from the earth," "Give us the wings of faith to rise"). *Death* Oliver Cooke (b. 1875), author "I know a fount," composer I KNOW A FOUNT; Harper G. Smyth (b. 1873), author "Make me a channel of blessing," composer EUCLID; George C. Stebbins (b. 1846), composer FRIEND ("I've found a friend, O such a friend"), ADELAIDE ("Have Thine own way, Lord"), JESUS, I COME ("Out of my bondage, sorrow and night"), CALLING TODAY ("Jesus is tenderly calling today"), BORN AGAIN ("Ye must be born again"), HOLINESS ("Take time to be holy"), and others; J. Athelstan Riley (b. 1858), author "Ye watchers and ye holy ones"; H. Wheeler Robinson (b. 1972), author "O Thou whose love has brought us here"; John Henry Hopkins (b. 1861), composer GRAND ISLE ("I sing a song of the saints of God"); Dietrich Bonhoeffer (b. 1906), author "By gracious powers" (tr. Fred Pratt Green).

75 years (1920). *Birth* Dave Brubeck, composer POSADA ("God's love made visible"); T. Brian Coleman, composer OASIS ("As water to the thirsty"); Joseph Gelineay, composer LE CENACLE ("By gracious powers so wonderfully sheltered"); Charles P. Price, author "As now the sun shines down at noon," "O Christ, you are both light and day," "O God, to those who here profess," "The fleeting day is nearly gone," "The golden sun lights up the sky," and others; William J. Reynolds, author "Share His love," "People to people," and other texts; composer KEEGAN ("A charge to keep I have"), MORA PROCTOR ("We would see Jesus, lo, His star"), PASCHALL ("Praise Him, O praise Him"), ROBERTSON ("My song is love unknown"), WASHBURN ("People to people"), among others and numerous arrangements. *Death* Eliza E. Hewitt (b. 1851), author "More about Jesus would I know," "There is sunshine in my soul today," "When we all get to heaven," and others; W. Vaughan Jenkins, author "O God of love, to Thee we bow," "O God, our father who dost make us one," "O loving Lord, who art forever seeking"; Arthur H. Mann (b. 1850), composer ANGEL'S STORY ("O Jesus, I have promised"); J. H. Maunder (b. 1858), composer MARTHAM ("O love of God, how strong, how true!"), THE WHOLE WIDE WORLD ("The whole wide world for Jesus!"); Hardwicke D.

Rawsley (b. 1851), author "O God, whose will is life and good."

100 years (1895). *Birth* E. M. Bartlett, Sr. (d. 1941), author "I heard an old, old story," composer HARTFORD; Avis M. B. Christiansen (d. 1985), author "Blessed Redeemer," "Come, come, ye saints"; Gordon Jacob, composer BROTHER JAMES AIR ("The Lord's my shepherd, I'll not want," "How lovely is Thy dwelling place"); Albert Hay Malotte (d. 1964), composer MALOTTE ("The Lord's prayer"); Leo Sowerby (d. 1968), composer PERRY ("The people who in darkness walk"), ROSEDALE ("Come, risen Lord, and deign to be our guest"), and others; Francis Bland Tucker (d. 1984), author "Awake, O sleeper, rise from death," "Christ, when for us you were baptized," "All praise to Thee, for Thou, O King divine," "O all ye works of God," "Our Father, by whose name," "The Lord, my God my shepherd is," and others; translator "Alone, Thou goest forth, O Lord," "All glory be to God on high," "Father, we thank Thee who hast planted," and others. *Death* Cecil Francis Alexander (b. 1818), author "All things bright and beautiful," "Once in royal David's city," "There is a green hill far away," "He is risen! He is risen!", "Jesus calls us, o'er the tumult," and others; J. S. Blackie (b. 1809), author "Angels holy, high and lowly"; Alexander Ewing (b. 1830), composer EWING ("Jerusalem, the golden"); W. S. Rockstro (b. 1834), arr. OMNI DIE ("Jesus calls us, o'er the tumult," "For the bread which you have broken"); Samuel F. Smith (b. 1808), author "My country, 'tis of thee," "The morning light is breaking."

125 years (1870). *Birth* Frank Fletcher (d. 1954), author "O Son of man, our hero strong and tender"; C. B. Jutson (d. 1930), composer THE STORY OF JESUS ("God has given us a book of stories"); May Whittle Moody (d. 1963), composer WHITTLE ("Moment by moment"); Ernest William Olson (d. 1958), tr. "Children of the heavenly Father"; William M. Runyan (d. 1957), composer FAITHFULNESS ("Great is Thy faithfulness"). *Death* William H. Havergal (b. 1793), composer EVAN ("Blest be the door uniting love," "O that the Lord would guide my ways"), PATMOS ("Take my life, that I may be consecrated"), arr. RATISBON ("Christ whose glory fills the skies"); Alexis Lvov (b. 1799), composer RUSSIA ("God, the Omnipotent," "Christ, the Victorious"); G. H. Smyttan (b. 1822), author "Forty days and forty nights."

150 years (1845). *Birth* William Boyd (d. 1928), composer PENTECOST ("Fight the good fight") and others; John D. S. Campbell (d. 1914), author "Unto the hills around do I lift up"; Vincent S. S. Coles (d. 1929), author "Ye who claim the faith of Jesus"; R. F. Dale (d. 1919), composer ST. CATHERINE ("O Jesus, I have promised"); F. W. Goadby (d. 1880), author "O Thou whose hand hath brought us"); Max Landsberg (d. 1928), co-tr. "The God of Abraham praise"; William H. Parker (d. 1929), author "Holy Spirit, hear us," "Tell me the stories of Jesus"; Rebecca J. Weston (d. 1924), author "Father, we thank thee for the night."

175 years (1820). *Birth* George Cooper (d. 1876), composer ST. SEPULCHRE ("From every stormy wind that blows"); Luther Orlando Emerson (d. 1893), har. AR HYD Y NOS ("For the fruit of all creation" and others); Elvina M. Hall (d. 1889), author "Jesus paid it all"; Edwin P. Hood (d. 1885), author "God who made the daisies"; John Henry Hopkins, Jr. (d. 1891), author "We three kings of Orient are," composer THREE KINGS OF ORIENT, COME HOLY GHOST ("Come, Holy Ghost, our souls inspire"); Jean Ingelow (d. 1897), author "And didst Thou love the race that loved Thee"; Richard Redhead (d. 1901), composer REDHEAD 76 ("Go to dark Gethsemane," "Rock of ages, cleft for me," and others); Clarence A. Walworth (d. 1890), tr. "Holy God, we praise your name"; Anna B. Warner (d. 1915), author "Jesus loves me, this I know"; John Freeman Young (d. 1885), tr. "Silent night, holy night." *Death* Lewis Edson (b. 1748), composer LENOX ("Arise, my soul, arise," "Blow ye the trumpet, blow"); Thomas Haweis (b. 1734), composer RICHMOND ("Hark! the glad sound," "Fill Thou my life, O Lord my God," and others).

200 years (1795). *Death* Samuel Stennett (b. 1727), author "Majestic sweetness sits enthroned," "On Jordan's stormy banks I stand," and others.

225 years (1770). *Birth* Ludwig van Beethoven (d. 1827), composer HYMN TO JOY ("Joyful, joyful we adore thee" and others); William Billings's *New England Psalm Singer,* source of "When Jesus wept" and other songs and canons; Edward Cooper (d. 1833), author "Father of heaven, whose love profound"; William Gardiner (d. 1853), compiler *Sacred Melodies* (1815), source of GERMANY ("Where cross the crowded ways of life"); John Wyeth (d. 1858), compiler *Repository of Sacred Melody* (1813), source of DAVIS ("O Thou in whose presence"), MORNING SONG ("O holy city, seen of John," "Awake, awake to love and work," and others), NETTLETON ("Come, thou fount of every blessing").

300 years (1695). *Death* Henry Purcell (b. 1659), composer WESTMINSTER ABBEY ("Christ is made the sure foundation," "God of grace and God of glory").

350 years (1645). *Birth* Johann Loehner (d. 1705), har. ALLES IST AN GOTTES SEGEN ("Come, pure hearts, in joyful measure," "Praise the Lord, rise up rejoicing").

450 years (1545). *Publication:* an ed. of John Calvin's *The Strassburg Psalter,* source of "I greet Thee, who my sure redeemer art" (tr. Elizabeth L. Smith).

Quotable Quotations

1. When the Well's dry, we know the Worth of Water.—Benjamin Franklin
2. What I want is, not to possess religion but to have religion that shall possess me.—Charles Kingsley
3. The greatest dangers to liberty lurk in insidious encroachment by men of zeal, well-meaning but without understanding.—Associate Justice Louis D. Brandeis of the U.S. Supreme Court
4. God prepares the cure before the hurt.—The Talmud
5. It is the heart that is not yet sure of its God that is afraid to laugh in His presence.—George MacDonald
6. To be what we are, and to become what we are capable of becoming, is the only end of life.—Robert Louis Stevenson
7. Swearing was invented as a compromise between running away and fighting.—Finley Peter Dunne
8. A mind all logic is like a knife all blade. It makes the hand bleed that uses it.—Rabindranath Tagore
9. Ah! though I am a Christian, the feelings of a man do not the less burn in my breast.—Molière
10. More die in the United States of too much food than of too little.—John Kenneth Galbraith
11. Traffic signals in New York are just rough guidelines.—David Letterman
12. I do not pretend to know what many ignorant men are sure of.—Clarence Darrow
13. One comes, finally, to believe whatever one repeats to one's self, whether the statement is true or false.—Napoleon Hill
14. Life is full of silly, absurd, ridiculous things, thank God.—Paul Kreeft
15. To educate a man in mind and not in morals is to educate a menace to society.—Theodore Roosevelt
16. Never go to bed mad. Stay up and fight.—Phyllis Diller
17. You may know God, but not comprehend Him.—Richard Baxter
18. Mammon holds the one outpost Christianity has not been able to conquer.—Anonymous
19. Goodness is the only investment that never fails.—Henry David Thoreau
20. Expedients are for the hour, but principles are for the ages.—Henry Ward Beecher
21. Have thy tools ready; God will find thee work.—Charles Kingsley
22. He is happy that can beware by others' harms.—William Camden
23. Generosity gives help rather than advice.—Luc de Vauvenargues
24. Anyone can do any amount of work, provided it isn't the work he is supposed to be doing at that moment.—Robert Benchley

25. The Holy Ghost is certainly the best preacher in the world, and the words of Scripture the best sermons.—Jeremy Taylor

26. A man lives by believing something; not by debating and arguing about many things.—Thomas Carlyle

27. Where there is shame, there is hope for virtue.—German proverb

28. Even if you're on the right track, you'll get run over if you just sit there.—Will Rogers

29. Hypocrisy is the homage which vice pays to virtue.—La Rochefoucauld

30. Avarice walks among us disguised as ambition.—Ezra J. Mishan

31. The most absolutely magical thing of all is that anything at all exists.—Paul Kreeft

32. Give a man a fish and you feed him for a day. Teach a man to fish and you feed him for a lifetime.—Chinese proverb

33. The point is that nobody likes having salt rubbed into their wounds, even if it is the salt of the earth.—Rebecca West

34. The brain is a wonderful organ. It starts working the moment you get up in the morning and does not stop until you get into the office.—Robert Frost

35. The tendency to claim God as an ally for our partisan values and ends is . . . the source of all religious fanaticism.—Reinhold Niebuhr

36. Belief in a cruel God makes a cruel man.—Thomas Paine

37. Every artist dips his brush in his own soul, and paints his own nature into his pictures.—Henry Ward Beecher

38. Certain thoughts are prayers. There are moments when, whatever be the attitude of the body, the soul is on its knees.—Victor Hugo

39. Sin has many tools, but a lie is the handle which fits them all.—Oliver Wendell Holmes

40. Failure is instructive. The person who really thinks learns quite as much from his failures as from his successes.—John Dewey

41. Those who are unhappy have no need for anything in this world but people capable of giving them their attention.—Simone Weil

42. The love of power is oppressive in every sphere, but in the religious most of all.—Romano Guardini

43. Men have become the tools of their tools.—Henry David Thoreau

44. Keep thy eyes wide open before marriage, and half shut afterward.—Thomas Fuller

45. What luck for rulers that men do not think.—Adolf Hitler

46. One thing I know: the only ones among you who will be really happy are those who will have sought and found how to serve.—Albert Schweitzer

47. Work spares us from three great evils: boredom, vice and need.—Voltaire

48. I long to accomplish a great and noble task, but it is my chief duty to accomplish humble tasks as though they were great and noble.—Helen Keller

49. When yu' can't have what you choose, yu' just choose what you have.—Owen Wister

50. Satan, like a fisher, baits his hook according to the appetite of the fish.—Thomas Adams

51. Science knows what it is. It does not know what it ought to be. . . . Science in our day claims more room in the totality of human life than it is entitled to.—Emil Brunner

52. To be wronged is nothing unless you continue to remember it.—Confucius

53. The fear of God kills all other fears.—Hugh Black

54. Whosoever walks toward God one cubit, God runs toward him twain.—Hebrew proverb

55. Habit is a cable; we weave a thread of it every day, and at last we can not break it.—Horace Mann

56. Young men are apt to think themselves wise enough, as drunken men are apt to think themselves sober enough.—Lord Chesterfield

57. History teaches us that men and nations behave wisely once they have exhausted all other alternatives.—Abba Eban

58. Tyranny is always better organized than freedom.—Charles Peguy

59. Let the burden be never so heavy, love makes it light.—Robert Burton

60. They do not love that do not show their love.—William Shakespeare

61. No army can withstand the strength of an idea whose time has come.—Victor Hugo

62. Death is just a distant rumor to the young.—Andy Rooney

63. Love life for better or worse without conditions.—Arthur Rubinstein

64. One cannot be strong without love.—Paul Tillich

65. The church must be reminded that it is not the master or the servant of the state, but rather the conscience of the state.—Martin Luther King, Jr.

66. My way of joking is to tell the truth. It's the funniest joke in the world.—George Bernard Shaw

67. God made meat before mouths.—John Trapp

68. A happy life is one spent in learning, earning, and yearning.—Lillian Gish

69. Life does not cease to be funny when people die any more than it ceases to be serious when people laugh.—George Bernard Shaw

70. There are ten men who will fight for the Bible to one who will read it.—L. R. Akers

71. There is no race so wild and untamed as to be ignorant of the existence of God.—Marcus Tullius Cicero

72. To believe in immortality is one thing, but it is first needful to believe in life.—Robert Louis Stevenson

73. He was the Word that spake it:
He took the bread and brake it;
And what that word did make it
I do believe and take it.

—John Donne:
On the Sacrament (1633)

74. The middle of the road is all of the usable surface. The extremes, right and left, are in the gutters.—Dwight D. Eisenhower

75. Remorse is pride's *ersatz* for repentance.—Aldous Huxley

76. Heaven is the presence of God.—Christina Rossetti

77. The wish to pray is a prayer in itself.—Georges Bernanos

78. Where there is a sea there are pirates.—Greek proverb

79. Never lend your car to anyone to whom you have given birth.—Erma Bombeck

80. It is the very pursuit of happiness that thwarts happiness.—Viktor E. Frankl

81. Justice is the right of the weakest.—Joseph Joubert

82. No one can be perfectly free till all are free; no one can be perfectly moral till all are moral; no one can be perfectly happy till all are happy.—Herbert Spencer

83. Opportunities are usually disguised as hard work, so most people don't recognize them.—Ann Landers

84. It is not enough to make use of ordinances, but we must see if we can find God there. There are many that hover about the palace, and yet do not speak with the prince.—Thomas Manton

85. No matter how old a mother is, she watches her middle-aged children for signs of improvement.—Florida Scott-Maxwell

86. Great emergencies and crises show us how much greater our vital resources are than we had supposed.—William James

87. The Universe is but one vast Symbol of God.—Thomas Carlyle

88. God wishes man to ask forgiveness, and not to see him in his guilt.—The Midrash

89. Snobbery is the pride of those who are not sure of their position.—Berton Braley

90. An unjust peace is better than a just war.—Cicero

91. All you need in this life is ignorance and confidence, and then success is sure.—Mark Twain

92. I am a great believer in luck, and I find the harder I work the more I have of it.—Stephen Leacock

93. We believe not in a creed, but through a creed; we believe in a Person.—Gerald Vann

94. Those who cannot remember the past are condemned to repeat it.—George Santayana

95. The world is divided into people who do things—and people who get the credit.—Dwight Morrow

96. Music hath charms to soothe a savage breast, To soften rocks, or bend a knotted oak.—William Congreve

97. The Church always arrives on the scene a little breathless and a little late.—Rev. Bernard J. F. Lonergan, S.J.

98. Sometimes even to live is an act of courage.—Seneca

99. Human history becomes more and more a race between education and catastrophe.—H. G. Wells

100. It is more important to cure people than to make diagnoses.—August Bier

Questions of Life and Religion

These questions may be useful to prime homiletic pumps, as discussion starters, or for study and youth groups.

1. What can nature tell us about the existence of God?

2. Does the physical world give us a clear picture of the character of God?

3. How should we interpret the biblical accounts of Creation in view of the conclusions of modern science?

4. What are the possibilities and limits of language to tell us of God—his nature, his thoughts, and his purposes?

5. How does Jesus Christ reveal to us all that we need to know about God?

6. Do our sins hinder our getting to know God?

7. What can we do to facilitate our growing knowledge of God?

8. What does it mean to be created in the image of God?

9. Should we consider protecting the environment a religious duty?

10. How can we know the will of God for our lives?

11. Can illness or death frustrate God's purpose for a life?

12. How does one cope with a sense of the absence of God in one's life?

13. What is the place of prayer in the Christian life?

14. Does God punish us in this life for our sins?

15. How can we be assured that our sins are forgiven?

16. What ingredients should go into making important decisions?

17. Is our Christianity more a matter of feeling or of doing?

18. Is "doing what Jesus would do" a helpful guideline for our discipleship?

19. Who is to blame when we sin?

20. Is idolatry a problem in Judeo-Christian cultures?

21. What is our obligation to people who practice non-Christian religion?

22. In what sense are we "free from the Law" in Christ?

23. Can we accept people in Christ without condoning their life-style that rejects biblical teachings on morality?

24. Is there one basic principle for Christian behavior?

25. What can we do to win out in the struggle with temptation?

26. How should we react to unanswered prayer?

27. Does it help to "take a solemn vow"?

28. How secure is our relationship to God once it is established?

29. Does one's being unusually blessed or gifted bring greater accountability?

30. Is poverty a virtue?

31. Should we distinguish between faith and feeling when pondering our relationship to God?

32. What is the place of joy in the life of faith?

33. Why do good people suffer?

34. When is contentment good, and when is it bad?

35. When is hope more than wishful thinking?

36. What is the good of fear?

37. Why did Jesus perform miracles?

38. What are the perils of pride?

39. How do friendships promote the Christian life?

40. How can we distinguish among the different kinds of love?

41. Can we explain the anger of God?

42. What is the biblical teaching on marriage?

43. How can we forgive people who have gravely wronged us or those we especially love?
44. What does it mean to repent?
45. Is restitution appropriate to repentance?
46. Who are the "pure in heart"?
47. Does God reward righteousness?
48. Why does the Bible call God "Father"?
49. Why does the Bible compare God with a mother?
50. What is the baptism of the Holy Spirit?
51. Why is water baptism important?
52. Why did Jesus receive baptism?
53. How does "the Spirit" guide us?
54. Do "angels" have a special ministry to us?
55. How should we think of Satan?
56. What is the relation of the Old Testament to the New?
57. In what sense is "holiness" a proper goal for Christians?
58. Why does the New Testament refer to all true believers as "saints"?
59. Is worship an option for us?
60. What is "the church"?
61. Is pastoral ministry a special calling?
62. How important is ritual in the Christian life?
63. What can new translations of the Bible do for us?
64. How can biblical ethics be lawfully related to government and public policy?
65. Are "law" and "grace" enemies?
66. How can we protect our children from sexual abuse?
67. Is gun control a proper Christian concern?
68. Is world peace possible?
69. What is the "image of God" in humans?
70. Why does the Gospel of John call Jesus' miracles "signs"?
71. How far should we go in adapting biblical teachings to present-day situations?
72. What are the duties of church members toward their pastor?
73. What are the duties of the pastor toward the church members?
74. Is evangelistic outreach the obligation of every congregation?
75. What does Scripture tell us about our relationship as Christians to the government?
76. Does our Christian faith give us guidance for the shape of our economic life?
77. How do you understand the American tradition of the separation of church and state?
78. How can retirement square with our call to Christian service?
79. Is the proper care of our physical self a spiritual duty?
80. What can we do to check the flood of sex and violence in the movies and on television?
81. Should parents blame themselves when their children go wrong?
82. What can the average citizen do to improve his or her community?
83. Despite many differences, what do all Christians have in common?
84. How should we relate to people of other religions?
85. What will help us to learn how to be forgiving?
86. Should we use the Bible for specific and dated predictions?
87. Is humor a normal part of a healthy religious life?
88. What is the role of archaeology in helping us to understand the Bible?
89. How does the experience of the church since apostolic times help us to understand God's will for us today?
90. How can the Psalms help our worship of God?
91. Why did God make Israel his "chosen people"?
92. What is the contribution of psychology and psychiatry to religion?
93. Why do the God of the Old Testament and the God of the New sometimes seem to be different?
94. How does self-esteem affect moral behavior?
95. What resources are available to help us through a difficult time?
96. In simple terms, what is the way of salvation?
97. For what may we pray?

98. Why do good people do bad things?
99. What are some basic guidelines for interpreting the Bible?
100. What is the role of "covenant" in the history of God's people?
101. Are there churches that abuse?

Biblical Benedictions and Blessings

The Lord watch between me and thee, when we are absent from one another.—Gen. 31:49

The Lord bless thee, and keep thee; the Lord make his face to shine upon thee, and be gracious unto thee; the Lord lift up his countenance upon thee, and give thee peace.—Num. 6:24–26

The Lord our God be with us, as he was with our fathers; let him not leave us, nor forsake us; that he may incline our hearts unto him, to walk in all his ways, and to keep his commandments, and his statutes, and his judgments, which he commanded our fathers.—1 Kings 8:57–58

Let the words of my mouth, and the meditation of my heart, be acceptable in thy sight, O Lord, my strength, and my redeemer.—Ps. 19:14

Now the God of patience and consolation grant you to be likeminded one toward another according to Christ Jesus; that ye may with one mind and one mouth glorify God, even the Father of our Lord Jesus Christ. Now the God of hope fill you with all joy and peace in believing, that ye may abound in hope, through the power of the Holy Ghost. Now the God of peace be with you.—Rom. 15: 5–6, 13, 33

Now to him that is of power to establish you according to my gospel and the preaching of Jesus Christ, according to the revelation of the mystery, which was kept secret since the world began, but now is manifest, and by the scriptures of the prophets, according to the commandment of the everlasting God, made known to all nations for the obedience of faith: to God only wise, be glory through Jesus Christ for ever.—Rom. 16:25–27

Grace be unto you, and peace, from God our Father, and from the Lord Jesus Christ.—1 Cor. 1:3

The grace of the Lord Jesus Christ and the love of God, and the communion of the Holy Ghost, be with you all.—2 Cor. 13:14

Peace be to the brethren, and love with faith, from God the Father and the Lord Jesus Christ. Grace be with all them that love our Lord Jesus Christ in sincerity.—Eph. 6:23–24

And the peace of God, which passeth all understanding, shall keep your hearts and minds through Christ Jesus. Finally, brethren, whatsoever things are true, whatsoever things are honest, whatsoever things are just; whatsoever things are pure, whatsoever things are lovely, whatsoever things are of good report; if there be any virtue, and if there be any praise, think on these things. Those things, which ye have both learned and received, and heard, and seen in me, do; and the God of peace shall be with you.—Phil. 4:7–9

Wherefore also we pray always for you, that our God would count you worthy of this calling, and fulfill all the good pleasure of this goodness, and the work of faith with power; that the name of our Lord Jesus Christ may be glorified in you, and ye in him, according to the grace of our God and the Lord Jesus Christ.—2 Thess. 1:11–12

Now the Lord of peace himself give you peace always by all means. The Lord be with you all. The grace of our Lord Jesus Christ be with you all.—2 Thess. 3:16–18

Grace, mercy, and peace, from God our Father and Jesus Christ our Lord.—1 Tim. 1:2

Now the God of peace, that brought again from the dead our Lord Jesus, that great shepherd of the sheep, through the blood of the everlasting covenant, make you perfect in every good work to do his will, working in you that which is well-pleasing in his sight, through Jesus Christ, to whom be glory for ever and ever.—Heb. 13:20–21

The God of all grace, who hath called us unto his eternal glory by Christ Jesus, after that ye have suffered a while, make you perfect, establish, strengthen, settle you. To him be glory and dominion for ever and ever. Greet ye one another with a kiss of charity. Peace be with you all that are in Christ Jesus.—1 Pet. 5:10–11, 14

Grace be with you, mercy, and peace, from God the Father, and from the Lord Jesus Christ, the Son of the Father, in truth and love.—2 John 3

Now unto him that is able to keep you from falling, and to present you faultless before the presence of his glory with exceeding joy, to the only wise God our Savior, be glory and majesty, dominion and power, both now and ever.—Jude 24–25

Grace be unto you, and peace, from him which was, and which is to come; and from the seven Spirits which are before his throne; and from Jesus Christ, who is the faithful witness, and the first begotten of the dead, and the prince of the kings of the earth. Unto him that loved us, and washed us from our sins in his own blood, and hath made us kings and priests unto God and his Father; to him be glory and dominion for ever and ever.—Rev. 1:4–6

SECTION II.
Sermons and Homiletic and Worship Aids for Fifty-three Sundays

SUNDAY: JANUARY FIRST

SERVICE OF WORSHIP

Sermon: The Beginning of Wisdom

TEXT: Ps. 111:10

My dear brothers and sisters, wisdom, our subject this morning, is quite evidently a great thing. Wisdom is the knowledge of life, or, as we might say, the art of living. Knowledge and art both presuppose ability. This is the greatest knowledge as well as the most difficult art: to be able to live! Not to let one's life drift into ill-fated disorder but to give it substance and direction! He who is able to live rightly is a wise man. But how do we get wisdom, this ability to live?

The "fear of the Lord is the beginning of wisdom," we are told. But what is this wisdom, this knowledge of life? What is the connection between wisdom and the fear of the Lord? Let us pursue these questions further.

I. Let me begin by recalling a story from the Old Testament. The name of King Solomon probably sounds familiar to all of you. There is a story about this king in the third chapter of the First Book of Kings. Solomon, when he was very young, had a dream in the city of Gibeon. None other than the Lord himself is said to have appeared to him, saying: "Ask what I shall give you." This sounds like a fairy tale, doesn't it, and yet it was a very serious order. Young Solomon did not answer, "Give me money, honor, victory over my enemies; give me a long life!" Rather, he replied, "I shall now be king over this great people of Israel, although I am but a little child and do not know how to go out or come in. Give me an understanding heart to guide me! Teach me to discern between good and evil! Give me insight to grasp what justice is!" This is the story of Solomon, how he became the wise Solomon, the one who knew the art of living. What may we learn from this story?

(a) Solomon became wise—he proved himself wise already—in that *he did not presume to be wise,* as do so many young people, and even older and old ones. He was not ashamed to confess, "I am but a little child and do not know how to go out or come in," and therefore he begged God, "Give me wisdom!" He is wise, whether young or old, who knows he is a child not knowing how to go out or come in. Wisdom has this characteristic: nobody has it stored away; nobody is *already* wise, not in his mind, and even less in his heart. We may only *become* wise.

(b) Solomon became wise, and was wise, in that he asked for things he needed *not for himself but for others.* To be king was his lot, to reign was his duty, and all his thoughts were centered on this task. He understood his life as a service to be rendered not for his own good but for the good of his people, the people of God. His great problem was how to be a man in the full sense of the word, responsible among, with, and for his fellowmen, willing and prepared to act in their behalf. Solomon was a man who understood that only as a true fellowman could he become a true man. He also understood that he was in need of an understanding and a wise heart in order to be a fellowman to his fellowmen.

(c) Solomon became wise, and was wise, in that he asked for the *ability to discern between good and evil*—between that which is above and that which is below, between what comes first and what comes next, between what may and must by all means happen, and what may and must not happen by any means. How could he serve them without this gift? He would only cause disaster around him! This is why the God-fearing man will again and again stretch out his empty hands. This is why he can only ask. Solomon was wise because he asked God precisely for this capacity to discern between good and evil. He who does not fear the Lord will again act quite differently. He will not bother discerning at all and, constantly confusing good and evil, will wobble like a drunkard on his way. He who fears the Lord will most earnestly want to be able to discern between good and evil, but he will want to learn it from God himself. He will turn to God to be taught.

(d) Solomon became wise, and was wise, in that he wished for one thing, and one thing only: *an understanding heart for his service.* Wisdom brings with it integration of all human faculties, singlemindedness and concentration of the one thing necessary. We heard how Solomon did not get short-changed, how, on the contrary, he even received things he had not asked for. He received them because he had not asked for them! Unconcerned, he had asked for one thing only, for the understanding heart and the discerning mind, which was needed for his service as a king. This was his wisdom. But it takes the fear of the Lord to make such a beginning in wisdom, in the art of living. He who fears the Lord does not seek after many things but singlemindedly seeks after the one thing that is necessary, quite content that he will receive all the rest with it.

II. But what actually is this "fear of the Lord"?

(a) A wrong kind of fear abounds around us and is not to be confused with the right fear of the Lord. It would be better to call it anxiety. We are afraid of bad and dangerous people, afraid of spooks, afraid of death, afraid of the atom bomb, afraid of the Russians, and especially afraid of ourselves, because we do not know how to go out and to come in and refuse to admit it! All this fear, this anxiety, is not the beginning but the end of wisdom.

(b) Moreover, there exists a false, a merely apparent, fear of the Lord, which is even less to be confused with the right fear of the Lord. *Anxiety* would again be a better name for it. We are afraid of God because he is so great and mighty, and we are so small and weak. We are afraid that he will accuse us like an oversized giant prosecutor, and that he will judge us like some skyscraping chief justice. Such reflection about God will almost certainly end up in fleeing, through some kind of a backdoor, to the wrong assurance that things cannot be so bad after all. In the face of this false fear of God we may again be comforted by the gospel word: be not anxious. And wisdom is surely the end of all such false fear of God.

(c) What, then, is the right fear of the Lord?

Let me go back to the 111th psalm. It is worth noting that this psalm, which ends with the fear of the Lord, begins with these words: *Praise the Lord, I will give thanks to the Lord with my whole heart.* And it continues: *He has caused his wonderful works to be remembered; the Lord is gracious and merciful. He provides for those who fear him; he is ever mindful of his covenant.* And later: *The works of his hands are faithful and just; all his precepts are trustworthy.* This leads to the passage on the fear of the Lord; it is born, it is given as soon as man discovers that God is *this* God and does *these* things of which the psalm speaks.

III. When the right fear of the Lord takes possession of our hearts, we are both lost in amazement and struck by awe, even terror.

(a) For we discover that God, since the beginning of time, has not hated or threatened you and me but has loved and chosen us, has made a covenant with us, has been our helper long before we knew it and will continue this relationship. The fear of the Lord springs from the discovery that the high and eternal God gave his beloved Son for us, for you and me, taking upon himself our sin and our misery; he made his Son, our Lord Jesus Christ, to be our brother, for whose sake we may call God our Father and ourselves his children. The fear of the Lord springs from the discovery that I did not merit this gift, that it has been given to me by the pure and free goodness of God, in spite of all I deserved.

(b) This fear of the Lord is the beginning of wisdom, the beginning with which we are all called to begin. Each one of us, even the most evil or most foolish person, may quite simply begin here, today, tomorrow, every day, and may become versed in the knowledge of living. Our text continues, *A good understanding have all those who practice it* and closes with these words: *His praise endures for ever!* Already in this life the wise man lives beyond death. Already here and now he may begin to live eternally.

(c) And now there remains only one question, dear brothers and sisters. I must ask each one of you: "Have you also made the discovery that leads quite inevitably to the fear of the Lord as the beginning of wisdom?" There is not a single person here present who cannot and may not make this discovery, no one who may not experience this fear of the Lord, no one to whom it may not become the beginning of wisdom, and therefore no one who may be denied living in time for eternity. Rely on this: *No one!* As surely as Jesus Christ has died and risen for us all! Amen.—Karl Barth

Illustrations

FAMILY INFLUENCE. The Reverend Martin Niemoller, once a U-boat captain, says:

> When I now think on these eventful and decisive years of my life, the question arises whether my call to the pulpit was not inspired through—if not actually decided by—the traditions of my parents' home.
>
> I am bound to admit that I should scarcely have found my way to it if matters had been otherwise.
>
> One may have one's own ideas concerning the effect of a Christian upbringing, but my experience has convinced me that a spirit of piety derived from the parental home is a decisive factor in a man's life. Indeed, it is becoming increasingly clear to me how strongly the first recollections of my parents' rectory at Lippstadt impressed themselves on my memory and how their influence on me is increasing with the passing years. Every day began with God's Word, and in the evening it was the last thing we heard.

—Benjamin P. Browne

FEAR OF GOD MISUNDERSTOOD. When I was a small boy I had a well-meaning but somewhat foolish Sunday School teacher who thought it right to provide us children with a precise description of hell and of the eternal punishment awaiting evil people. We were of course immensely interested and likewise excited. But surely not one of us children learned the fear of the Lord and the beginning of wisdom from this.—Karl Barth

Sermon Suggestions

WHAT TO DO WITH GOOD NEWS. TEXT: Luke 2:15–21. (1) Enjoy it. (2) Confirm it. (3) Share it.

"NO LONGER A SLAVE." TEXT: Gal. 4:4–7. The timely coming of Jesus Christ (1) has given us a new status with God; (2) has imparted a new attitude in us toward God; (3) has promised us a filial inheritance from God.

Worship Aids

CALL TO WORSHIP. O sing to the Lord a new song; sing to the Lord, all the earth. Sing to the Lord, bless his name; tell of his salvation from day to day (Ps. 96:1–2 RSV).

INVOCATION. We do not know how to pray as we ought, Father. How can we express the depths of our desires, our needs, or our contritions in language that tells adequately what we want you to understand from us? So we pray that you will overlook our struggle with adequate wording and see our hearts, our souls, and hear our thoughts as we worship before you in this sacred hour. As only you can, Lord Jesus, lead us to the high altar of God that we may find ourselves in his purpose and will. Then show us how to return to the world glorifying God and saying with other disciples: (LORD'S PRAYER).—Henry Fields

OFFERTORY SENTENCE. Offer to God a sacrifice of thanksgiving and pay your vows to the Most High (Ps. 50:14 RSV).

OFFERTORY PRAYER. Gracious Lord, let us give this new year as generously as ever before, for we have been given so much for so long, and we would share with others that which sustains us in Christ Jesus, year in and year out.—E. Lee Phillips

PRAYER. Sometimes, Father, we must confess that we have a hard time knowing how you communicate with us. Unlike those whom we read about in the Bible, we do not hear a voice when we feel we need one so much. Neither do we have a pillar of cloud to lead us in our high noons of need or a pillar of fire to guide us through our midnights of the soul. How do you communicate to us, Father? Have we tried so hard to hear you that we have missed you? Can we have the assurance this morning that you speak to us through the channels with which we are familiar and to which we readily tune when we want and need to hear you clearly?

Father, will you speak to us through the Bible today so that we will have no hesitation in declaring that we have heard from you? Can the familiar stories and the marvelous sayings of that grand book be made alive with light and truth for us this morning? O Father, let us hear you speak through the Bible with clarity and compassion and conviction this morning.

Will you speak to us through prayer this morning so that we may understand anew that our God thoughts and life needs uttered to a loving Father are not in vain? Can there be some sense of Presence that kindly engulfs us in these concentrated moments as we struggle to lay our souls bare before one whom we cannot comprehend or understand in every measure? Will you in some manner turn this one-way conversation into a glorious time of encounter with the living God as we wait before you? O Father, this morning make of prayer a two-way street where we know that we have heard from you, even as we pray.

Will you speak to us through relationships this morning, Father? Can you somehow help us to hear the deeper cry of fellow pilgrims as they struggle with pain, loss, fear, confusion, limitations, loneliness, and all the many other emotions and traumas that relationships at their best engender? Can we hear you communicate to our better selves as we encounter the joyful, the sorrowful, the happy and the hurting, the religious and the pagan, the learned and the ignorant, the powerful and the degraded so that we love them, help them, and win them to the way of Christ, who is to be our example in all matters and circumstances? O Father, let us hear you through others. Let us hear you clearly through every channel along which you come, and let us hear you even now.—Henry Fields

LECTIONARY MESSAGE

Topic: God's Perfect Blessing

TEXT: Num. 6:22–27

Many people go through life never receiving the blessings they need. Children long for the blessings of parents who are sometimes too busy. Workers want to be blessed or commended for a job well done. Husbands and wives seek approval and blessings from one another. All of us like to be blessed. We not only feel better emotionally but also have our confidence raised when someone blesses us.

God instructed Moses to convey to the people of Israel a blessing from God so that the people would always look to God for their source of strength and support. God's blessing of his people carries forth in the New Testament as Jesus is born into the world.

I. The Lord bless you and keep you (v. 24). The thrust of this verse seems to point to God's desire to pour out his love upon his people. But the pouring out of his love also contains a note of assurance and promise that his love is not temporary but everlasting as God continues to draw us near him. Galatians 4:5 speaks of God's action in redemption so that we might be drawn near to him as sons. Parents long to keep the bonds of love, communication, and nurture strong even though their children grow to maturity and leave the home in which they grew up. Even so, God longs to continue his blessing of us and to hold us near him.

II. The Lord make his face to shine upon you (v. 25). Nothing brightens up the face of a person like a smile. Certainly the hope of every child is to have the face of his or her parent smile lovingly at him. In the same way, our heavenly Father's attention is directed toward our lives. His desire is to be gracious toward us. Yet that means that we, as his children, are to be obedient, receptive, and intent on pleasing our Father in heaven. Galatians 4:6 tells us that because we are God's children we can address him with the kind of freedom of a child who lovingly relates to his father. What a wonderful concept that we who know him as Savior can call the God of the universe our Father.

III. The Lord lift up his countenance upon you and give you peace (v. 26). No other peace is quite as complete as the peace that comes from God. Nations seek peace. Individuals long for the absence of wars and rumors of wars. Yet there is still strife in the world. The Prince of Peace, Jesus, was celebrated in Luke 2:15–20. His birth brought to earth the quiet assurance that those who live in Christ can weather any storm, yet without panic. Peace can come to the Christian as she realizes that in Christ her hope for tomorrow is assured. Her journey through life today is made easier. She is anchored to the rock of God's salvation. She knows that God watches every step and that God longs to give to his children the kind of peace through life that will sustain in every trial. As a mother looks across the way to watch after her child, God lifts his eye and searches for us and makes provision for peace in our lives. As we struggle in the world, we should be encouraged, for God is a loving and giving God. Our response to him must be one of love and devotion and confidence that he will bless us just as he has promised, with perfect blessings of peace.—Ronald W. Johnson

SUNDAY: JANUARY EIGHTH

SERVICE OF WORSHIP

Sermon: Baptizing Pocketbook and All

TEXT: Luke 19:1–10

This may seem a rather unusual topic, and I want to tell you how I found it. Some time ago Mrs. Z. Demarest Race of our congregation gave me an interesting book entitled *Incidents in the Life of John H. Race.* This book relates biographical incidents in the life of the Reverend John H. Race, a Methodist minister who became a publishing agent of our Methodist Publishing House.

The author tells a delightful story about his father, also a Methodist minister, who, when conducting a revival, was challenged by a leading citizen generally known as the Squire. The Squire dared the minister to preach on a text he would give him. He gave the preacher one of these impossible texts, with difficult proper names and little else, but the preacher handled the matter with such sincerity, earnestness, and agility of intelligence that the Squire remained to listen with deep seriousness and that very night was converted to Christ! A little later it was decided that there would be a general baptism of all those who were converted, and since it was a Baptist community it was decided to have the baptism by immersion in the river. On the day of the baptism the Squire himself came down to be baptized. As he was about to walk into the water, he took his pocketbook out of his pocket and handed it to his wife. But the minister saw it and he said, "Not a bit of it, Squire Conrad. If this minister of the gospel baptizes you today, he baptizes you pocketbook and all." And that is the way it was done. He was baptized "pocketbook and all!"

I. Baptism symbolizes the cleansing, renewing, and revealing grace of God. How completely are we baptized?

(a) We think of the head as being baptized. The life of the mind must be baptized and brought into the service of Jesus Christ. If we should always feed our minds with things that are good and true and right so that our minds would always give glory to Christ, how wonderful it would be! How strange that although we would not put garbage on our table to feed our bodies, yet we put garbage on the library table to feed our minds! If only our minds could be baptized to moral and spiritual vigor in the service of Christ, what a glory would be released into the world! If we could have this mind in us that is in Christ Jesus!

(b) Again, how wonderful if we could baptize our hearts! If our emotions and our enthusiasms could be dedicated to Jesus Christ, we would serve a deep need in the Christian church. Very often we have the form of loyalty to Christ without enthusiasm. We have activity, but our heart is not in it. But the heart must be baptized also, so that when we serve Christ we serve Christ with enthusiasm. We love him because he first loved us. We give ourselves to him heartily because our heart is in it. We need to baptize our hearts. The worst thing that can be said about a church is that it is a cold church. The Christian fellowship was never meant to be a cold fellowship. It is meant to be a warm fellowship, a living fellowship, a lively fellowship, a fellowship of people whose hearts are one, who have mutual compassion and concern and mutual interests, who sustain one another by the very quality of their affection. It is a wonderful thing when the heart is baptized; it is a tragic thing when it is not.

(c) Again, how thrilling when the hand is baptized! When I think of the great amount of talent and ability in almost any Christian congregation that is not dedicated to Jesus Christ I feel sad. For people to have talents and not to dedicate them to Christ, to have hands that are able to do things well, able to serve efficiently, and then not give these talents to the service of the church—this is tragic both for the individual and for the church! And I am sure it strikes sorrow into the heart of God when a person who is able to do something will not do it. How sad when the hands are not baptized. If only we could gather up all the manpower in the laity of the church and make it available to the cause of Christ—the hands baptized so that they work and serve in the name of Jesus Christ—what a glorious thing that would be! It is a wonderful thing when the hands are baptized—dedicated to Jesus Christ. It is a wonderful thing when people who are asked to do something in the church leap to the opportunity with eagerness. When you are offered the privilege of doing something for Christ, can you say, "Yes, I am glad for this opportunity. I serve because my hands are baptized; they are dedicated to Jesus Christ. I will use them, I will serve, I will work in the cause of Christ through this church!"? How wonderful it is if a person is baptized completely—the head, the heart, the hand.

(d) But we cannot stop here, can we? We cannot stop here if we are true to the Bible. We must include something else, something that occupied the mind of Jesus so much that he gave over half of his preaching to it. We have to baptize not only the head and the heart and the hand but the pocketbook as well!

II. And now we are ready for our text. "For the Son of man is come to seek and to save that which was lost."

(a) If you read that verse out of context, you will say that it does not have anything to do with money. But if you read it in the context, you realize it has everything to do with money. For this belongs to the story of Zaccheus, and it tells us something about the purpose, the evangelistic purpose of Jesus Christ, who has come to seek and to save that which was lost. Has he come to seek and to save the head, the heart, the hand? Of course! But he has come to seek something else—the pocketbook! In order to save, Christ seeks not only the person but also the purse! This is the very heart of the story of Zaccheus—what he did about his money. His money was an obstacle, not an opportunity. His ill-gained wealth blocked his way to his true life. It led him astray in ways of selfishness and unconcern and dishonesty.

(b) When Zaccheus dined with Jesus, suddenly he saw himself as for the first time. The thing that needed to be converted was his money! It is not that there was something wrong with money, but there was something wrong in the way he gained and used his money. Not money was the root of his evil but the love of money. Zaccheus cried, "My money has been working against me all my life. In order to get money I have been dishonest. I have accused wrongfully in my office as the tax collector. I have frightened people into giving me more money than they were legally required to give me. I have accused men of smuggling. I have made them pay me money under the counter. Now I see for the first time my money has been my enemy; it has been against my true life. My money has never been baptized; it has been embattled. And all the while I have been surrounded by the world of the poor, the world of people in need. I have not thought anything about them. I have simply thought of myself and how to get more for myself by any manner or means.

I am going to do this with my money. I am going to make restitution for the wrong that I have released into the life of the world. If I have accused people wrongfully, I am going to pay them back four times over. I am going to fling away my money in order that I may find myself. I am going to throw away my purse that I may become a new person. And as for this world of the poor, suddenly I understand that the loneliness that is in my heart is in the hearts of other people too; I can do something about it. I am going to give half of my goods to the poor! It will make this a better world than I found it. I will make my money my friend. It will be my instrument of helpfulness." And Jesus said to Zaccheus the most wonderful words that can be said to any man: "Today is salvation come to this house."

(c) In Zaccheus a person was lost, and the key to finding the person was the purse. This is what the Gospel says to you and me, who have been skirting around the edges of this subject too long. Jesus is speaking home to our hearts. Today we are living in a financial civilization. As the poet Wordsworth said, "The world is too much with us, late and soon, getting and spending, we lay waste our powers." This week I have been asking myself again and again, if we take from our lives the time and energy that we use in "getting and spending," what would be left? Are we making a life, or just a living? This is the challenge of the Gospel: *remember to live*.

(d) The wonderful thing about the purse is that it can help you be a better Christian. It can extend all your powers. Your money can travel for you all around the world and do good. It can go where you do not have time to go personally. It can serve people you will never even be able to meet. It will serve a variety of causes, although you could not possibly have time, strength, or energy to deal personally with all of them. Your money will do so much for you. It will extend your enthusiasm. It will extend what you know and how you feel and your passion to serve. It will become an instrument of God's holy purpose if you give it a chance by dedicating it to Christ!

We who are baptized in the name of Christ—baptized in head, heart, and hand—are we baptized in pocketbook as well? Is the purse saved as well as the person?

The end of the story of the Squire is

interesting too. Twenty-five years after he was baptized pocketbook and all, the Squire attended a church service where the Reverend Mr. Race was serving as guest preacher. A new church had been built. The raising of the money had been something of a problem. People had subscribed all the money they thought they could subscribe, but it was not enough. At the worship service, it was announced that $350 was still needed. The Squire stood up and said, "The man who preached to us today is the man who first taught me that I must be baptized pocketbook and all. Before the service began today I had given all I could possibly give to this new church. At least I thought so. But because I was baptized pocketbook and all, I am going to complete this building fund right now." And he did!

May we all be rich toward God, and may we too be baptized pocketbook and all!—Lowell M. Atkinson

Illustrations

SERVICE THROUGH PRAYER. J. Wilbur Chapman often told of his experience when he went to serve a church in Philadelphia. After his first sermon, an old gentleman met him in front of the pulpit and said, "You are pretty young to be pastor of this great church. We have always had older pastors. I'm afraid you won't succeed. But you preach the gospel, and I am going to help you all I can."

"I looked at him," said Dr. Chapman, "and said to myself, 'Here's a crank!' " But the old gentleman continued, "I am going to pray for you that you may have the Holy Spirit's power upon you, and two others have agreed to join with me."

Then Dr. Chapman related the outcome: "I did not feel so bad when I learned he was going to pray for me. The three became ten, the ten became twenty, the twenty became fifty, and the fifty became two hundred, who met before every service to pray that the Holy Spirit would anoint me. In another room, eighteen elders knelt so close around me to pray that I could put out my hands and touch them on all sides. I always went into my pulpit feeling that I would have the anointing in answer to the prayers of 219 people.

"It was easy to preach, a very joy! Anybody could preach with such conditions." —Fred W. Andrea

SUMMONED TO A FEAST. We are summoned in the Gospel to a plentiful banquet, a marriage supper. For though connected with toil and self-denial, godliness is not a fast but a feast, a feast at which we are invited to partake not only in heaven hereafter but on earth *now.* Pardon full and free—the favor of God—the honor of serving him—the privilege of fellowship with him—joy and peace in believing—the blessed hope of immortality—these are offered *now;* why then defer accepting them?—Adapted from Newman Hall

Sermon Suggestions

WHEN GOD OPENED HIS TREASURE CHEST. TEXT: Matt. 2:1–12. (1) The story: wise men from non-Jewish Eastern territory came to Bethlehem and paid homage to the newborn king of the Jews. (2) The meaning: God's purpose for humankind is achieved when people of all nations and philosophies seek him as his truth goes forth. (3) The contemporary relevance: (a) The Christian mission to go into all the world with the gospel is the will of God. (b) Coercion of belief is ruled out, for God has his own ways of guiding the minds and hearts of those who truly seek him.

"ARISE AND SHINE." TEXT: Isa. 60:1–6 NRSV. (1) The glory of God has now appeared in Jesus Christ and shines forth most brilliantly in his cross ("And I, when I be lifted up from the earth"). (2) The glory of God in Christ has universal drawing power ("will draw all people to myself"). (3) This glory can be seen in the church, when the church arises to its universal mission to proclaim Christ to all the world.

Worship Aids

CALL TO WORSHIP. "Ascribe to the Lord, O mighty ones, ascribe to the Lord glory and strength. Ascribe to the Lord the glory due his name; worship the Lord in the splendor of his holiness" (Ps. 29:1–2 NIV).

INVOCATION. How thankful we are, Father, that we can take refuge in the shadow of your presence. We come to this sacred place in need of refuge from the demands, toils, and wrestlings with life. Still our minds that we may be ready to think on the higher things of God. Calm our nerves that we may for a fleeting moment in time rest in you. Direct our attention that we may push out of our thoughts those many side issues of life that so easily claim us and thus concentrate on the eternal matters that make a difference in what we do in the everyday affairs of living. O Father, in this hour may we truly worship you and, having done so, go from this place spiritually renewed and invigorated to do your will.—Henry Fields

OFFERTORY SENTENCE. "On coming to the house, they saw the child with his mother Mary, and they bowed down and worshiped him. Then they opened their treasures and presented him with gifts of gold and of incense and of myrrh" (Matt. 2:11 NIV).

OFFERTORY PRAYER. God of mercy, keep us from all that is small and narrow when we come to give in thy name. Save us from the stinginess of hoarding and the selfishness that is greed and release us to the generosity of faith and the sacrifice of love, through Christ our Savior.—E. Lee Phillips

PRAYER. May we who would invoke your presence realize that you are already turned toward us in the eternity of your love. That in a universe where there are worlds beyond worlds, galaxies seemingly without number, you would invade *this* planet with so great a love, blows our minds. There is a mystery here—the mystery of your *grace*—out of which the cosmos was created and the ways of life established.

How can we appear before you except in praise: "Lord, you *have* been our dwelling place, in all generations. Before the mountains were brought forth or ever you had formed the earth and the world, from everlasting to everlasting *you* are God."

In the beginning your Spirit brooded upon the depths and order was created out of chaos and so your Spirit hovers over your creation in every generation, seeking to lead your people to that order that leads to life—where there is a waiting according to your Word. We praise you, O Father, that in every generation you have been faithful according to all your promises.

That we have been brought to the knowledge of the gospel and are privileged to share the life of the church in this time and place is of your abounding grace. We marvel at the mustard seed sown in that first century that strangely came to life, and today its branches reach through the whole world. We pray that we may fulfill Christ's commissioning to be the light of the world and the salt of the earth.

Renew us, O God, in such a sense of mission that we do not allow housekeeping duties to keep us from ministry to all the world and all the worlds of people to which you are calling us in the height, the depth, the length, and the breadth of your love in Christ.

In the full dimensions of your love, he was "a man for *others.*" So may we live and love. Where there is any brokenness among us, of mind, of body, of spirit, we pray for the healing to make whole. We pray not only for the ill among us but also for those caregivers who with love, understanding, and patience minister so faithfully. Strengthen and encourage them according to the demand of day-and-night calls.

We pray for the brokenness of this world. You have created a cosmos, but through self-serving ways we often render it a chaos. We pray for those who in the face of much danger seek to bring peace to areas where human and earth's resources are squandered by hostility and armed conflict. Grant to all leaders in church and state the wisdom of your truth and the faith and courage to answer its call according to their opportunity and responsibility.

We pray through him in whom all things cohere and who is among us as living Lord teaching us to pray and live.—John Thompson

LECTIONARY MESSAGE

Topic: Unsearchable Riches

TEXT: Eph. 3:1–12

At one time or the other most of us have dreamed of riches. We have fantasized about discovering a hidden treasure or being included in a wealthy person's estate so that money would flow into our pockets and make it possible for us to have anything our heart might desire. But reality is that there is no genie in a bottle. No magic wand that will produce untold riches for us. Only hard work promises that we can make a living that keeps us out of poverty. And yet, there are many who work hard each day and still live in poverty, not only in this nation but in nations around the world. Hard work cannot guarantee riches. Luck cannot guarantee riches. In economies that fail, even the best efforts may provide only a meager living. Certainly the Apostle Paul knew firsthand the problems of poverty and of suffering. But Paul also knew that those whose life is hidden in Christ can experience the untold riches of heaven.

I. Our riches are found in the grace of God. If anyone knew of grace it was the Apostle Paul. He had persecuted the church and, knowing that, characterized himself as the least of all the saints (v. 8). Yet God had chosen to save him. He had been given grace not only for himself but also for those to whom he would minister. It was a mystery that God would use him so that even as a prisoner he would still be able to relate Christ to persons in such a way that they would also know of God's riches in Christ. Every Christian who walks with God knows of the grace of God in daily life. By grace we live. By grace we share our faith with others. By grace we are encouraged in our Christian lives. By grace we go through the hard times. In our own strength we can do little. But according to the riches of grace in Christ we are equipped and amazed at what God enables us to do in our lives every day.

II. Our riches in Christ assure access to God. Just as money in the bank is of no use to us when the bank is closed, grace without access would mean very little. But the Christian never has to worry about God being inaccessible. In fact, God is always willing to reveal his grace to us through his mighty deeds. Someone has said that most Christians are so subnormal in their spiritual lives that when God does what he deems normal, we think it is the abnormal. God is willing to demonstrate his power in the world. Yet Christians often do not desire that power. We pray little. We praise God usually only once a week. We seldom witness to others about his mighty deeds. We need to stop being timid about accessing the grace of God and pouring it out as we share it with others who need to know him.

III. Our riches in Christ help us be bold. Paul was bold. He had a confidence in Christ that was inspiring. Persons who were around Paul caught his confident spirit. Nothing is so depressing as to be around someone who is negative all the time. Christians need to be confident. Even in the midst of hard times, Christians should never forget that God is there. We stand upon the mighty rock of his power. We might not be able to feel him emotionally, but our faith assures us that he is there. Paul kept his eyes on Christ in the midst of hardship and struggle. He did not lose heart. Neither should we. Those who have earthly riches are confident in them. Even in times of economic distress the wealthy trust their money to carry them through. Christians do not depend on riches that will rust and decay. We know the one who owns the cattle on a thousand hills. Our riches are spiritual. And they are hidden in Christ.—Ronald W. Johnson

SUNDAY: JANUARY FIFTEENTH

SERVICE OF WORSHIP

Sermon: When God Summons

TEXT: Jon. 1:1–2

The Book of Jonah opens upon a note of grave concern. The writer tells us: "Now the word of the Lord came to Jonah the son of Amittai, saying, 'Arise, go to Nineveh, that great city, and cry against it; for their wickedness has come up before me' " (1:1–2). Then there is a word about Jonah's surprising reaction: "But Jonah rose to flee to Tarshish from the presence of the Lord" (1:3a), going west although God had ordered him to go east. Jonah was refusing to accept God's will; he was defying God's order. He did not want to do as commanded, and he did not hesitate to let his feelings be known. He fled Palestine, moving in the wrong direction. In the face of such a refusal, we rightly anticipate that this man will have trouble. We all know that when we differ with God, we do so at great risk of ruin.

After telling what Jonah did, the writer goes on to tell what God chose to do about Jonah's refusal. God set about to rebuke his hard-heartedness. Let us now examine this story and learn from it for the sake of our own lives.

I. When God summons, it is selfish, silly, and sinful to refuse him. Jonah had to learn this the hard way.

Although God had clearly spoken to him, Jonah had other plans for himself. He put his will against God's will. He did not want to go to Nineveh. Being human, he was *free* to refuse, and he did so. He boarded a ship bound for Tarshish, seeking to escape God.

God respects the human will and will not violate it. God honored Jonah's freedom and would not compel it. But he did design a plan to deal with Jonah's refusal. God wanted Jonah to get right, think right, and then act right. So he moved to deal with Jonah's selfish and silly deed: he sent a windstorm to make the sea trip miserable for him.

The words are impressive and informative: "But the Lord hurled a great wind upon the sea, and there was a mighty tempest on the sea, so that the ship threatened to break up" (1:4). That storm was both unexpected and unusual. Nor did it readily diminish, so the crewmen had to lighten the ship, throwing valuable cargo overboard. But even after this their chances for survival seemed slim. Startled, superstitious, anxious for life, every crewman began crying out to the god of his choice. How surprising, then, that Jonah was fast asleep down in the inner part of the ship! How could he sleep during such a crisis? How? Because he was dead tired. Trying so hard to put distance between God and himself, Jonah felt worn out. He was exhausted by hasty, selfish actions of disobedience, unaware that God was doing all this in an effort to reach him.

But Jonah did not remain unaware very long. The shipmaster awakened him with a stinging rebuke: "What do you mean, you sleeper? Arise, call upon your god!" (1:6a). It is a tragic picture: God jeopardized many lives in the attempt to jolt one life. Even the crewmen sensed that this was the case as they valiantly but vainly battled the storm. Casting lots, they discovered that Jonah was the one on whose account it was all happening. And then that question of questions put by them to him: "What is this that you have done?" (1:10). Jonah's answer made the crewmen know what they must do. "So they took up Jonah, and threw him into the sea; and the sea ceased from its raging" (1:15).

"What is this that you have done?" This is the question every hypocrite needs to be asked. This is the question every person who rebels against God needs to answer! This is the question I now raise to those now trying like Jonah to run away from God's will. When God orders, who would be silly and defy him? When God summons, who would be selfish and refuse that call? Will *you* like Jonah have to learn the "hard way"? Always remember that those who run from God will always run into a storm.

It is always true: whoever runs from God always runs into a storm. The storm is God's deed to reach the one who runs. The greater our refusal, the greater is God's rebuke. When God summons, it is selfish, silly, and sinful to refuse him.

II. When God summons, he has a purpose in view for us. God went to such lengths to rebuke Jonah because the purpose behind his call was so great. Thus the storm—and the rescue of Jonah from drowning in the sea. The "great fish" that swallowed him was at first a chamber of horrors, but Jonah soon realized that it was a chamber of hope. That time of felt peril brought about a needful prayer. "Then Jonah prayed to the Lord his God from the belly of the fish" (2:1). Chastened by events, alert now to the higher purpose he had resisted, Jonah finally surrendered to God's concern to use him. "And the Lord spoke to the fish, and it vomited out Jonah upon the dry land" (2:10).

Then God repeated his concern to Jonah: "Arise, go to Nineveh, that great city, and proclaim to it the message that I tell you" (3:1). Summoned this second time, Jonah obeyed—acting in agreement with the will of the Lord. "So Jonah arose and went to Nineveh, according to the word of the Lord" (3:3). And Nineveh heard God's Word from Jonah.

Jonah announced, "Yet forty days, and Nineveh shall be overthrown" (3:4). The Ninevites heard the summons, believed God, and decided to obey, and the city was spared. A great calamity had been averted. How crucial Jonah was as God's messenger!

The God who created us is a God who works with grace, concern, and reasonableness toward us. We need to remember this in a day when judgment appears needed but does not seem to come. God wants first of all to deliver and save us; punishment is always a last word and work. Every storm he sends to stop us is reasonable, no matter how drastic it seems at the time. God summons us because he has a purpose for us—and those whose lives we will touch.

God still seeks those who try to run from him. Will it take a storm to halt you and bring you back into line? God is still concerned about the cities of this world, and he wants to send us to save the people in them. But he can use us best when we work willingly and not reluctantly, when we serve without narrowness, provincial notions, and prejudicial attitudes. These were the obstacles in Jonah's heart and mind from the first. Except for these, Jonah would have responded obediently when first summoned.

Are you ready to work for God? Is your concern strong enough? Is your commitment deep enough? Jonah had a lot to learn; so have we. Jonah learned it the hard way. May we be spared his chastisement and the attitudes that made it all necessary. May the results of our obedience be as fruitful as his. And may the mercy of the Lord continue to prevail toward those who hear his summons through us.—James E. Massey

Illustrations

CHRISTIAN LIVING. To know that we are going back to God . . . keeps our personal integrity and motivation for action on course. If God is both the origin and the ultimate target, then God's character necessarily runs through the dreams, the energy, and the motivations that drive our daily work. So we can expect to have our own dreams and our scheme sanctified by the penetrating light of God's justice, truthfulness, and unconditional love.—Donald M. Joy

GOD ACCEPTS. That God accepts us as we are is the good news; that God is not through with us at this point is the call to discipleship. Here the work of explanatory theology is to depict the devastation of the world and to sketch an alternative vision of what God calls us to. The gift of grace is not merely the coming of a warm interiority but also entrance into the reign of God. Justification and justice are inextricable. Liberation and salvation are finally one. God's transformation of the world is at work like leaven.—Tex Sample

Sermon Suggestions

SOMETHING BETTER. TEXT: John 2:1–11. (1) The satisfactions we seek. (2) The inadequacies we experience. (3) The fullness Christ brings, verse 11 (see also John 10:10).

GOD'S STEADFAST LOVE. TEXT: Ps. 36:5–10, especially 7a. Why is it precious? (1) Because it is all-encompassing, verses 5–6. (2) Because it guarantees our security, verse 7b. (3) Because it satisfies our hunger and thirst for God's good gifts and approval, verses 8–9.

Worship Aids

CALL TO WORSHIP. "How precious is your steadfast love, O God! All people may take refuge in the shadow of your wings" (Ps. 36:7 NRSV).

INVOCATION. How grateful we are that you are present with us in light and in darkness, Father. As we come to this hour, some alive and responsive to your light, others seeking some solace for life's invasions, which blot out the light, we pray for your presence. Enable us to rejoice that we have here in this congregation a family to sustain and support us in all situations. Open your Word to us that we might grasp sufficient truth to guide us as we make our journey along. Meet us in your power that we might be empowered to meet others in your name.—Henry Fields

OFFERTORY SENTENCE. "Moses said to all the congregation of the Israelites: This is the thing that the Lord has commanded: Take from among you an offering to the Lord; let whoever is of generous heart bring the Lord's offering" (Exod. 35:4–5a NRSV).

OFFERTORY PRAYER. Shed the light of thy kingdom a little brighter, Lord, because we dedicate these gifts to thee and are willing to follow our gifts with actions that tell of a Savior, a kingdom, and a faith imperishable.—E. Lee Phillips

PRAYER. O you who are the God who calls—as you called Abraham at the dawn of recorded history, so you are calling *us* out of our history. With the dispatch that Abraham answered, may we respond: "He went out not knowing where he was going."

Your call is always a call to walk by faith, not by sight. You call us to the open road, to "go out not knowing where *we* are going"—to live with expectancy—to embrace the untried, the not yet—to perceive the *new* thing you are doing in our day; you call us to the windswept frontiers of existence—to venture and adventure—to live on the growing edge. You call us to "the road less traveled," for narrow is the gate and disciplined is the way that leads to life.

How we want a faith for the security of the familiar, but you call us to a faith for insecurity, the unknown. We want to tent on the old campground, but you are calling us with the dawn of each new day to break camp and move on. Your call is always to the unknown, to some land of your promise. With Abraham of old, we too are pilgrims "looking for that city whose builder and maker *you* are."

O you who call us again and again—may we hear your call loud and clear in the Word spoken so discreetly in this hour. You are calling us to a renewed sense of mission—to "enlarge the place of our habitation," to embrace the inclusiveness of your love—to proclaim your salvation to those near as well as those afar. We pray for such commitment as to grasp with both hands—with all our mind and heart and person—the new day of opportunity that has dawned upon us.—John Thompson

LECTIONARY MESSAGE

Topic: Spiritual Gifts

TEXT: 1 Cor. 12:1–11

The giving of gifts is a practice that is as old as humankind itself. People love to receive gifts, and many love giving gifts to others. Spiritual gifts are special because God has given them to Christians so that Christians might be a blessing in the lives of others. And these gifts are given so that the body of Christ in the world might mature and reach ever outward to a lost and dying world. Three insights can be gleaned from this passage in 1 Corinthians.

I. Spiritual gifts are from the Lord (v. 3). Spiritual gifts need to be tested to see if they are from the Lord. Lost persons are not able to exercise spiritual gifts since they are given to those who belong to God in Christ. It is the Holy Spirit that reminds us that our gifts are to be used to glorify Christ. There is no room in the Christian life for pride or for glorification of our efforts in ministry. Everything that is accomplished for Christ must be laid at his feet in thankful appreciation for the opportunity to serve him.

II. Spiritual gifts are varied (v. 4). Although there is unity in the Spirit of God, gifts are varied. They are varied according to the kinds of service needed and according to the person to whom the spiritual gift is given. Gifts are not competitive. That is, no one gift is better than another. Rather, the measure of the gift is its use in the kingdom and the faithfulness of the person to whom the gift is given. Paul is careful to illustrate in verse 12 that the gifts given contribute to the whole body. Therefore, each gift should be exercised with humility and a willing spirit.

III. Spiritual gifts are apportioned (v. 11). God gives gifts according to our ability to handle them. He knows the true depth of our spiritual walk. Just as the body is restricted when a member such as a foot or arm is broken or injured, so the body of Christ suffers when a Christian is carnal and is not exercising his gifts in a close walk with the Lord. Christians should understand the serious nature of being given a gift to use for Christ and strive to keep sin from hindering the free exercise of the spiritual gift that God has given.—Ronald W. Johnson

SUNDAY: JANUARY TWENTY-SECOND

SERVICE OF WORSHIP

Sermon: Can We Still Get There from Here?

TEXT: 1 Cor. 1:10–13a; 3:11

To my knowledge the Apostle Paul was the first to scribble out this question: "Has Christ been divided?" I think it somewhat irritating that this troubling question should still be relevant after some two millennia: "Has Christ been divided?" Well—has he?!

It seems to me that everything we know of and experience about human nature mitigates against the possibility of unity. At gatherings like this we talk at great length about the commandment to be one in the Lord; we say prayers, petitioning God to grace us with the common sense to pull it off; we even confess that we've sinned and fallen short of such a high and noble calling in Christ. But we seem to forget that it's the nature of the animal to be divisive.

I. Look at us! We have enough trouble becoming and remaining united within our own households. In less than two decades we've created a society in which the family meal has become a dinosaur. And a recent Gallup poll indicated that, in the average family, one is likely to locate as many different positions on any given issue as there are persons in the household.

(a) And when it comes to the church? Well, we all know how that house of cards has fared in the raging winds of individual choice—don't we?! Mom and Dad are fortunate if their children show a passing interest in the faith. But that's okay, because everyone's entitled to his or her own personal choice—isn't that so?

(b) And then there's the call of culture and society. Even if the family should manage to create something closely resembling unity, the hectic and hassle-producing world soon steps in to drive a deep wedge into the very heart of the "happy home." I tell you—it's a real mess! "I belong to the country club," or "I belong to the racquetball club," or "I belong to the basketball team," or "I belong to the cheerleading squad."

(c) And whenever our so-called outside interests become the priority over anything and everything that goes into making unity a reality on the home front, then it seems to me it's time for a serious family pow-wow. That's because while we can afford to lose out on some extra goodies in this life, we'd best not tamper with the one essential element in the survival of the social fabric: family unity!

II. Okay, already—enough of that. Let's think about our business and working worlds.

(a) There divisiveness is called by a different name. I think we call it something like "competition" or "climbing the corporate ladder." I understand that some have even tagged it "back stabbing on the way to success"! Anyway, call it what you will—it all amounts to pretty much the same thing.

(b) We all want to do well. We're all looking for a raise. We're all riding on the merry-go-round of monetary success, hoping to beat the other guy or gal to that elusive brass ring. And beat them we will—even spill some blood if we have to!

III. So, you see, I wonder if perhaps part of the problem we face on this issue of unity isn't the fact of our fallen human nature. Sure, we'd love to be one with another and others.

(a) But there's always this nagging sense of somehow risking the loss of something important to me if I should compromise on something crucial to you. In fact, if you'll recall, that's exactly what happened immediately following the Fall.

(b) Believe it or not, this was once a united front—Adam, Eve, and God working in harmony with all the other creatures of creation. A veritable paradise of peace and prosperity for all concerned. But just throw in a little self-interest to the point of selfishness; now add a pinch of hunger for personal power and finally some sinful "me against you"—and there you have it: deadly divisions!

IV. Now, maybe you're ready to return to those troubled Christians in Corinth. And even if you're not—I'm going to drag you along. Because they have something very important to teach us.

(a) How easy for us, two thousand years later, to point the finger of shame at those sinful Corinthians! We might even claim to be amazed at the apparent ease with which they held so tenaciously to their destructive divisions. It's even possible that we perceive ourselves to be in the background of this conflict—able to pass judgment on the bad behavior of these brothers and sisters in the faith.

(b) I envision Paul putting down his pen and staring us in the face, saying: "Now, I appeal to *you,* brothers and sisters, by the name of our Lord Jesus Christ, that all of *you* be in agreement and that there be no divisions among *you,* but that *you* be united in the same mind and the same purpose." Ouch!

You see, regardless of the age or place, these words of the apostle are directed at the church's divisions, whenever and wherever they're found.

When we look into the Corinthian church—if we look with eyes open!—we'll see ourselves sitting in the pews, with all our bad behavior and disgraceful divisions hanging all over us like a cheap suit.

V. When the commitment to and the compassion of Christ are sacrificed on the altar of self-interest, then and there the church begins to crumble from within! Apparently, the Corinthian Christians had developed a severe case of self-interest. So, out of love and concern for their survival as a church, Paul admonished them: "Be in agreement . . . have no divisions among you . . . be united in the same mind and the same purpose."

(a) Reading Paul's words while acknowledging the reality of the contemporary church causes me to question: "Can we still get there from here?"

Perhaps the best that we can do is to continue to sacrifice our individual and collective self-interest for the purpose of healing our divisions. Maybe we should step into one another's pulpits and pews more than once a year. I wonder if we'll take the risks required to *truly* repent in order to achieve *genuine* reconciliation and renewal.

(b) The Gospel tells us—in no uncertain terms—that the outcome of the church has never been and will never be dependent upon the feeble and faltering faith of human beings. Paul made that quite clear. He wrote: "*God* is faithful!" And that's what we need to remember in these times of troubled commitments: "*God* is faithful!"

That's certainly not to say that we can sit back and breathe easy! It's a confession that God's grace is always greater than our inglorious behavior. And only God's grace will get us to the coming kingdom!—Albert J. D. Walsh

Illustrations

UNITY. In his letter to the Ephesians, Paul talks about maintaining the "unity of the Spirit" (Eph. 4:3). Sometimes unity can be a difficult thing to maintain, especially if we are willing to settle for something less. Unity necessarily involves giving up our own insistence upon having our way in order that singleness and harmony can thrive. Too often we settle for union instead of unity.

In most of our relationships we have the choice of having union or unity. England and Northern Ireland have union, but they lack a spirit of unity. All marriages have union, but only unity can make a real marriage. Union artificially binds together dissimilar elements, but unity makes dissimilar elements into a single element.

Every organization, even a church, has dissimilar elements. When we come together under one roof to worship, we have union, but God calls us to move beyond that into a deeper spirit of unity.

Whenever we are able to recognize a distinct group in the church that we can refer to as "them," we are settling for union. God help us to change "them" to "us."—Hal Poe

MOTIVES. Once there was a charming village with a picture-postcard church on the central square. A generous family, the Smiths, had provided the church with every benefit. Inspiring stained-glass windows, a majestic pipe organ, and handsome pulpit furnishings carried plaques recognizing the family's donations. Yet, the splendid church building housed a dwindling, rather cold congregation. A wise observer suggested that the church needed one more plaque in recognition of its true spirit: "Dedicated to the everlasting glory of Mrs. Smith and to the loving memory of God."—J. Edward Culpepper

Sermon Suggestions

WHEN THE WORD OF GOD IS SPOKEN. TEXT: Neh. 8:1–3, 5–6, 8–10. The appropriate responses are (1) attention, verses 1–3; (2) a worshipful attitude, verses 5–6; (3) joy and celebration, verses 8–10.

THE BODY OF CHRIST RECONSIDERED. TEXT: 1 Cor. 12:12–31a. (1) The foundational truth is that all of us as Christians are one in Christ. (2) There is a temptation that works two ways: (a) to think less highly of ourselves than we ought; (b) to think less highly of another member than we ought. (3) God's gifts are many and varied and subject to our unfair comparisons, while each and all are important.

Worship Aids

CALL TO WORSHIP. "The fear of the Lord is pure, enduring forever. The ordinances of the Lord are sure and altogether righteous. They are more precious than gold, than much pure gold; they are sweeter than honey, than honey from the comb. By them is your servant warned; in keeping them there is great reward" (Ps. 19:9–11 NIV).

INVOCATION. Father, give us today a new measure of the love that along with faith and hope will remain when other sought-after things are gone. Help us to find in you and in the self-giving of Jesus such an example as will enable us to forgive those who have sinned against us, to care for those who seem undeserving of our time, and to go beyond the call of duty in what we do for you and for one another. Above all, let us experience your forgiveness and salvation here today.—Henry Fields

OFFERTORY SENTENCE. Every animal of the forest is mine, and the cattle on a thousand hills (Ps. 50:10 NIV).

OFFERTORY PRAYER. Give us the wisdom, O Lord, to know how to spend and how to save and how to share a portion of it all in the name of Jesus.—E. Lee Phillips

PRAYER. O you who are in our coming in and our going forth, you who are present not only in the green pastures and beside the still waters but in the valley of the shadow of death. You are here preparing a tale for us not only in the presence of our friends but in the presence of our enemies. You are present not only in the brightness of the noonday sun but when the shadows of evening fall. We thank you that you never give up the chase—that you truly are "the hound of heaven." Your love pursues us to the far country of our own willfulness and also into the darkest night of the soul.

O Love that will not let me go
I rest my weary soul in Thee.

Grant to *us* the understanding of the psalmist to know that you are never so present as when you seem most absent.

You are here this morning present in your Word, calling us as you have so many times before. The question is never your call but our response. Make us sensitive and responsive to your call in our common and uncommon tasks and opportunities "that fail not man or thee."

O Giver of every good and perfect gift, you give us the understanding that to meet you at the throne of grace is to be present with all our brothers and sisters. You so loved the world that you gave your only Son. Love, your love, looks for ways of being constructive, creative, even to dying on a cross. This is our calling, to love all others as you love us. To be faithful to prayer is to commit ourselves to do what we can do—to make love visible.—John Thompson

LECTIONARY MESSAGE

Topic: A Prophet at Home

TEXT: Luke 4:14–21

It has been long taught that a prophet is not without honor except in his own home. Sometimes the hardest people to witness to are those who know us best. They know our weaknesses and are quick to point them out. It is often the inconsistency of our lives that causes others not to believe. But in Jesus' case the situation was entirely different. Jesus was always consistent in his message, his life, and his goals. We can learn from Jesus' visit to his home.

I. He returned in the power of the Spirit (v. 14). Witnessing cannot be effective unless the witness goes in the power of the Spirit. We need to remember that we never win anyone to Christ. It is the Spirit of God that convicts persons and leads them to Christ. All we can do in witnessing is to plant seeds, water them, and seek to keep them growing. It is absolutely vital for the witness to seek the leadership of God in every witness encounter so that he or she may be led to the person in whom the Spirit is actively working. Jesus was always sensitive to the leadership of the Spirit of God. So should we be also.

II. Jesus read from the Scriptures (vv. 18–19). There is precious little that we can do to convince people about God. However, the Scriptures are eternal and are the Word of God. As such they have the power to cause people to interact with eternal truths. Each time we witness to another we should be careful to let them hear from the Scriptures. They need to see the mighty acts of God through the Scriptures and to see how God has moved in the lives of others in the Bible. All of our witnessing should point to the Scriptures. And since the Scriptures point to Jesus, they will get a much clearer picture of the author of their salvation. Jesus often quoted Scriptures to point others to the Father.

III. Jesus gave people time to think about what he had said (v. 20). Instant evangelism can be problematic. When people deal with eternal truths of the gospel, they need time to think and reflect. They need time to hear from the Spirit of God and to ask questions. We are often so busy telling people what they should think that we never give them time to hear from God. Jesus read the Word of God and then sat down. He was ready to let people think about what he had said before he began to teach them further. Give people an opportunity to think on eternal things as you witness to them. And when lost people ask questions of the faith, point them again to the Word of God. Remember, God will not let his Word return void.—Ronald W. Johnson

SUNDAY: JANUARY TWENTY-NINTH

SERVICE OF WORSHIP

Sermon: The Devil, You Say?

TEXT: Luke 4:1–13

The devil, you say? Now you have gone too far. "How do you expect any intelligent, educated person to believe in the devil?" C. S. Lewis was asked a similar question and responded that if by "devil" you meant a power opposite to God, self-existent from all eternity, then the answer is no. I quite agree the Bible knows no such cosmic dualism. Evil is not an absolute; it is an eventually destructive imitation of that which is good, true, and beautiful. What we cannot deny is that through the abuse of God-granted freedom, there is evil in the universe and of such a personal, beguiling nature that it must be named, as it is here, *temptation.* And our aversion to the concept of a power called the devil is not really toward the laughable image of a man with black batlike wings or dressed in a red suit with arrow-tipped tail. It's not even the Hollywood hype of dishes swirling above the table and shutters blinking ominously.

I. John Updike in his novel *Rabbit Run* comes closer to the truth of our distaste for the subject. Harry Angstrom is sitting listlessly through a sermon on the devil's confrontation with Jesus in the wilderness. "Harry has no taste for the dark, visceral side of Christianity, the *going through* quality of it." This talk of going through death and suffering to redemption seems repulsive to us. We, like the character in the novel, want the lighter side of religion. Yet something draws us into this wilderness, this barren plateau of the heart where good and evil meet. According to this story, it's not the power of evil, the shadow side, that lures us. Here Jesus is sent by the Holy Spirit. The Hebrew and Aramaic words for spirit are feminine, and the apocryphal Gospel according to the Hebrews even says, "My Mother the Holy Spirit took me." For indeed, like a loving parent, the Spirit does not seal her children off from the world and its undertow. But then neither is Jesus deserted. Indeed, it is in this setting that we see a compelling account of Jesus' continual battle with the subtle enemy of God.

(a) It is not difficult to see that the basic form temptation takes is that of doubting that he is the Son of God. "If you are the Son of God, prove it." Is not that the poison root of our own temptation? If you were really a child of God, wouldn't you be happier, better taken care of, more consistent . . . the list is endless. So, too, Jesus hears the question spring from within. If the voice was genuine at the baptism, if the call is authentic, if, if, if. . . . Why is it such doubt of who we are is often coupled with a point of physical vulnerability? He was hungry (not the way you and I use the word); his body cried out for food. So comes the first temptation. Turn the rounded, smooth, dark stones into succulent loaves of bread. You heard the voice; you have the power. *If* you do. So the first temptation was to *settle for less* than the high calling of God's creative purpose. But even messiahs have to eat. Psychologist Abraham Maslow's hierarchy of needs will tell you that before you can get to your creative needs, you have to take care of the physical stuff. What good would he be to God dead in the desert? Furthermore, if he could turn rocks into bread, wouldn't he be meeting the primary needs of men and women? Yes, yes indeed. But wasn't the real question whether God would provide all his needs? Why is God so slow? If faith is dealing with God's delays, then you and I know what it is to be of little faith. Unable to wait, we continually settle for less than we've been promised. We, like Esau, sell our birthright for a mess of pottage; like Judas, speed up the action so *something* will happen . . . in our hunger for love and affection, we settle for less than the real thing . . . and the *bread tastes like stone.*

(b) Again, he is asked, "If you are the Son of God, why don't you leap from the pinnacle of the Temple? You have God's Word on your miraculous delivery." The temptation behind a death-defying leap is the demand for conclusive proof for our faith. Jesus is, no doubt, in a period of contemplating what it will take to call all people to himself as Messiah. He is ripe for the suggestion that it must be something spectacular. Not just for a sign for the people, but did not some voice resound within him of his own need for unassailable proof so that his mission would become self-evident? There's the subtlety of temptation. To tempt God to use our prayers, our positive attitude, our sacrificial giving as a down payment for what God has promised to deliver. I have heard television evangelists say that if you do this or sacrifice that, God has to bless. How does that promise differ from the standard television commercial? Closer to home, are we teaching prayer, discipleship, and the life of the Spirit as some kind of God manipulation?

(c) The third temptation was to rule all the country that could be seen with the mind's eye (from the tallest native peak, you could not even see all of Palestine). This is the temptation to secure power over people. The gnawing thought in our wilderness as well as that of Jesus: "Can we trust a God who becomes weak for our sakes?" Shouldn't we take the way of the cross but arm ourselves with something the world respects . . . just in case? Being God's foolish one is OK, but how about something for leverage? Seek ye first the kingdom of God. Yes, but let's have the kind of knowledge that is power, degrees on the wall, speak the language. Let's make sure that we attract enough of the right kind of people, so that at least the world will say all those people can't be wrong. Let's be a light to the nations but stockpile enough arms so that, just in case might does make right, we'll be OK.

II. As Jesus is exhausted, yet victorious in this life-and-death struggle, his story becomes the acting out of a prayer: lead us not into temptation, or do not give us over to the power of temptation's victory. Indeed, he eternally said, "Deliver us from the evil one." Jesus is not hung up on the personal nature of evil. We are in a battle.

So this strange retelling of a lifelong struggle makes its mark on us. First, as Shakespeare said, "It is one thing to be tempted and another to fall." Temptation is a sign we are alive. C. S. Lewis said there is a silly idea about that good people are not tempted. Behold Jesus in the wilderness. Secondly, this was not shadow boxing. He was really tempted in every way that we are: through the physical desire and appetites, in our human productivity, for doubting who we are and *whose we are,* to use our personal power to push ourselves above those who need us as a brother or sister. All of this points beyond itself. This is more than a page from a spiritual autobiography. This is in microcosm the war that was fought between God and the evil one for the soul of humankind. The result is the cross and Easter morning. Death, where is your sting; temptation, who has won the world? The devil, you say? No; Christ Jesus, it is he. In him is our victory.—Gary D. Stratman

Illustrations

MINISTRY OF THE WORD. Too many pastors today suffer from a disgrace. They are disqualified for service, and the reason is simple: they have abdicated their historic role as guardians of the church. They are no longer the spiritual and moral leaders of the church and society. An unfortunately small number of pastors call the church to account or seek to renew and reform it as mandated by Scripture. Instead of working to awaken and revitalize the church, many have accepted its lowered standards and have settled in to enjoy its materialistic lifestyle.—John W. Fowler

SKILLS FOR LIVING. A national news network told the story of a man who received a strange wedding gift. When he was married in 1940, some close friends gave him an alligator from the swamps in Florida. The man moved to a New England state. It was necessary for him to build a large pool for the alligator to live in. As the years went by, the man began to discover that the alligator likely would live longer than the man. He also began to think about what might happen to the alligator when he died. He decided that the best thing to do would be to send the alligator back to the Florida swamp so that it could continue to live after the man died. However, the problem was not easily solved. Allie, the alligator, who for years had lived a sheltered existence, was not prepared to live in the swamps of Florida. The National Forestry Commission, seeing his plight, decided to intervene and retrain the alligator so that it could survive in the Florida swamps. For several months, the alligator was progressively taught those skills essential to surviving within a new environment.

Goals that arise out of our dreams are very worthwhile. However, simply to set goals without seeking to acquire the skills essential to achieving them is to invite despair and failure.—John Ishee

Sermon Suggestions

THE GOSPEL FOR STRANGERS. TEXT: Luke 4:21–30. (1) At first, Jesus pleased the people of his hometown; they were proud of him and could hardly believe their ears. (2) However, when he suggested that God, in some instances, preferred foreigners to Israelites, the people were incensed and ready to kill him. (3) Yet Jesus eluded them, continuing a style of service that led to his Crucifixion—and Resurrection.

THIS THING CALLED LOVE. TEXT: 1 Cor. 13:1–13. (1) Love's imitation, verses 1–3. (2) Love's reality, verses 4–7. (3) Love's future, verses 8–13.

Worship Aids

CALL TO WORSHIP. "In you, O Lord, I take refuge; let me never be put to shame. In your righteousness deliver me and rescue me; incline your ear to me and save me" (Ps. 71:1–2 NRSV).

INVOCATION. In this sacred place this morning, Father, call us to true worship. Help us in this special hour to escape momentarily the things that furrow our brows and burden our hearts and blacken our spirits. Lead us to concentrate on whatsoever things are true, whatsoever things are just, whatsoever things are pure, whatsoever things are lovely, whatsoever things are of good report. (LORD'S PRAYER)—Henry Fields

OFFERTORY SENTENCE. "The silver is mine and the gold is mine, says the Lord of hosts" (Hag. 2:8 NRSV).

OFFERTORY PRAYER. Lord of life, accept now these gifts we bring, in joy and in gratitude. Allow us to be faithful in that which is least, knowing that of small matters great good may come, through the Spirit and the Son.—E. Lee Phillips

PRAYER. Here we have been confronted with the Word—to pray without ceasing—to be responsive to your presence in all the little things of our daily lives. We do not need to wait for special days, but the routine is filled with your glory. In each opportunity, in every relationship, we can discern your glory in the face of Jesus Christ. May we hear your Word in this hour as it calls and recalls us to daily obedience, discipline, and prayer that we may more fully live by the power of your abounding grace.

Often we long for another time—for another place—and miss the wonder of your coming in this time and place. How easy to avoid the challenge to live by procrastinating—tomorrow, tomorrow, tomorrow, but "today" is the day of salvation, and *now* is the timely time. Help us to realize that in our every moment you are present in the greatest way that you can be—you so love the world that you gave your only Son. To love you with all our mind, heart, and strength is to be alert, to be attentive, to be awake to your coming in the here and now of our every day. "Great is thy faithfulness." "Morning by morning new light do I see!"—John Thompson

LECTIONARY MESSAGE

Topic: Confidence to Speak

TEXT: Jer. 1:4–10

In almost every Christian's life there have come doubts. Can I possibly witness to my neighbor? Can I teach Sunday school? Can I live the Christian life at work, where so many do not honor the Lord? Jeremiah knew the burden of doubt. But when he remembered who created him, his doubts were eased. From this passage we can learn some significant insights.

I. We are no surprise to God (v. 5). Jeremiah heard God say that he knew Jeremiah even before his birth. God had plans for Jeremiah's life even before Jeremiah was born. So it is with our lives. God has plans for every person's life. But each person has to respond by faith to God's plan for his life. God does not manipulate us. He gives us freedom to say no to God. But when we say yes to God, he enables us to do things that astound us. Knowing that God has created us and has planned for us to accomplish things for him should give us a confidence that we can do all things in him.

II. Our human limitations should not discourage us (v. 6). The truth is that all of us are limited in one way or another. One is old. One is young. One is blind. One is poorly educated. All of us are limited. But limitations should not remove us from service to God. He is willing to use us if we are willing to be used. The secret is the willing heart. In a way we insult God by saying that we cannot do certain things. He can empower us over any obstacle. He will send us forth. He will give us the confidence we need. So do not be discouraged.

III. His words should be our words (v. 9). We have no business offering our opinions to the lost. We are to offer the good news of the gospel to them—God's Word. Our words have little effect in the lives of others. But God's Word convicts. It corrects and it instructs. We should pray before each witnessing encounter for God to give us his words so that the other person might hear Jesus in all that we say. Too many times we rely on our programs and our procedures in witnessing to others. The programs we use are helpful but should never take the place of confidence to speak the words of God, which comes to us as a result of having spent much time on our knees hearing his instruction.—Ronald W. Johnson

SUNDAY: FEBRUARY FIFTH

SERVICE OF WORSHIP

Sermon: Enthusiasm in Religion

TEXT: Ps. 147:1–20

The last four psalms in the Psalter are psalms of praise. They radiate enthusiasm, joy, gratitude, and thanksgiving. Yet, withal, they are amazingly realistic in lining up reasons for their enthusiasm. The writer of the 147th psalm gathers up some sixteen such reasons, ranging all the way from "healing the brokenhearted" to casting "forth his ice like morsels." They illustrate rather than exhaust the nature of God's loving care for his people and the motif of profound enthusiasm.

I mention this now because it stands in such vivid contrast with that dull, washed-out, faded, timid thing that all too many of us call "our religion."

We want to feel at home with our religion; we want to enjoy it; we want to live it in full sincerity and honesty and with as little hypocrisy as possible. Yet we draw back from its fervor, contagion, and enthusiasm with real concern, and well we might, because enthusiasm comes to us bearing a blessing in one hand and a curse in the other. If we are not careful, she will give us both hands at the same time.

I. The existence of great men and movements should emphasize rather than blind us to the dangers of enthusiasm in religion. Let me, therefore, file as strong a brief as possible against enthusiasm in religion.

(a) Enthusiasm cripples our critical faculties. When we get enthusiastic about something, we tend to exclude from consideration all troublesome questions and contradictory evidence. We tend to forget the facts we do not like. We begin to associate with only those people who agree with us. The British poet Dryden was thoroughly soured on enthusiasts and enthusiasm when he wrote, "Truth is never to be expected from authors whose undertakings are warped with enthusiasm; for they judge all actions and causes by their own perverse principles, and a crooked line can never be the measure of a straight one."

(b) Enthusiasm breeds dogmatism and cruelty. Paul is an eloquent example of this. Raised as a Pharisee, he was zealous to defend the Law against all doubters. When he went to Jerusalem, he was shocked to discover the Christian group openly challenging the Law. His enthusiasm leaped to the conclusion that the Christian group should be exterminated, and he volunteered to take the lead in the effort. He was so successful that he was first known throughout the Christian church as its most relentless persecutor. Years later, looking back on all this, Paul says, "I thought I was doing God's will." So does every other religious enthusiast. Who can measure the damage done in human life by the fanaticism and bigotry that parade as legitimate enthusiasm?

(c) A third indictment of enthusiasm is this: it can gather a crowd and weld that crowd into a mob. If you remember hearing the booming "Sieg Heils" of the Nuremberg Congress of the Nazi party in the late thirties, you know what I mean. And every skillful propagandist knows what I mean, too! The problem of propaganda is not to keep people from thinking or to encourage them to think creatively; it is to encourage them to think about one or two things and then to whip their enthusiasm to a frenzy.

II. Yet a powerful case can be built for enthusiasm, one we tend to overlook.

(a) To begin with, enthusiasm is natural: we are creatures of feeling, of emotion, of desires, fears, and all the rest. We cannot live without our emotions no matter how much trouble we may have with them. Enthusiasm, then, is no alien creation of religion imported into the human enterprise for the purpose of confusing us; it is at home with humanity and has always been. Much as we may deplore its ravages and excesses, we neither can nor would wish to disown it throughout life.

(b) Enthusiasm is not only natural, it is essential to any great effort or achievement. Emerson, about as cold-blooded a thinker as we have ever produced in the life of our country, was exactly right when he said, "Every great and commanding movement in the annals of the world is the triumph of enthusiasm—nothing great was ever accomplished without it." Even a sober treatise on ethics comes up with this gem: "No virtue is safe that is not enthusiastic."

As a way of life and a way toward a new life, religion suggests goals and purposes for us and commends them to us. It urges us to believe in, strive for, and if necessary die for certain great ends. It invites us to share in the life of the Christian church, which is supposed to be a group where contagious enthusiasm for and loyalty to the ends of religious faith are fundamental.

III. Enthusiasm and great religion go hand in hand. How could it be otherwise if we are to take seriously the ideal of a Christian life, a Christian society, and a Christian church?

(a) The case for enthusiasm, I suppose, might be summarized by contrasting it with its opposite number in the scale of human attitudes. Enthusiasm's opposite number is not objectivity, as some think; it is apathy, indifference, insensitivity. That, I greatly fear, is the state in which citizenship and churchmanship are usually found. A country of apathetic citizens is a weak, irresolute country and headed for some form of dictatorship as certainly as the sun rises. A church composed of apathetic members is on its way out and will be replaced by another that is blessed with a contagious enthusiasm throughout its fellowship.

(b) Let us make a covenant now that so far as in us lies, we personally are going to become centers of contagious enthusiasm for this church, the church universal, and the Christian faith, which lies at the heart of our church. Let us make a love of the church, enthusiasm for the church, and a sacrificial loyalty to the church essential parts of all that we think, say, and do. As we do this and to the extent that we are able to do it, there will come into existence here in our common life a sense of joy, peace, and new life that deserves the ancient word "God within."—Harold A. Bosley

Illustrations

FEAR OF THE SPIRIT. Often, mainline Christians are willing to leave the Spirit talk as a special vocation for the Spirit-filled folks. "Let them talk that way," they may say. In such a response, avoidance of Holy Spirit themes or references are intended to defend against what could be exaggerated or distorted claims.

But there is another reason why some of us shy away from the Spirit. Many of us fear being grasped by an invisible presence we cannot control. In this regard, we share the problems of spiritual experience throughout all ages.

We may wonder, "What am I likely to do? How will I behave if I surrender my control to the Divine Spirit? How can I be sure that some other spirit won't actually take over my mind?" Rudolf Otto, in *Idea of the Holy* (pages 12–13), calls this strange feeling of attraction and dread "mysterium tremendum." It is the awe-filled experience of the majesty of God—overpowering and yet enrapturing, both thrilling and chilling. But it nevertheless envelops the longing for the Spirit with deep emotive ambiguity. In any event, respectful distance—not only from the Holy Spirit—may seem to be the better part of wisdom, especially for moderns, who are given to quantification and control. Consequently, the Holy Spirit is less understood, less experienced, and doesn't have a meaningful place in the worldview or the sacred cosmos of most of us.—James Forbes

INTERRUPTING THE FLOW. A certain man was working in his garden, assisted by his little girl. She had undertaken the interesting task of watering the lawn by means of the usual rubber hose. Matters proceeded harmoniously enough until she suddenly cried out in disappointment: "Daddy, the water has stopped." The father looked over and, taking the situation in at a glance, said quietly, "Well, take your foot off the hose." The child had inadvertently placed her foot and most of her weight upon the soft rubber pipe and thus, by her own action, shut off the water that she needed. She, of course, removed her foot at once, whereupon the water again flowed freely.

Five minutes later, she once more cried plaintively: "Daddy, the water has stopped again." Her father glanced across and observed that now she had placed her other foot upon the hose. He replied: "Well, take your foot off." The child did so, and again the stream flowed freely, and, as she had by this time learned her lesson, she did not repeat the mistake and completed the interesting task she had chosen, with much satisfaction to herself.—Emmet Fox

Sermon Suggestions

CHRIST'S CHALLENGES AND THE STAGES OF DISCIPLESHIP. TEXT: Luke 5:1–11. (1) Failure, verse 5. (2) Success, verses 6–7. (3) Fear, verses 8–10a. (4) Promise, verse 10b. (5) Commitment, verse 11.

A MATTER OF IMPORTANCE. TEXT: 1 Cor. 15:1–11. (1) The experience of salvation, verses 1–2. (2) The message of salvation, verses 3–4. (3) The witnesses of salvation, verses 5–11.

Worship Aids

CALL TO WORSHIP. "I give you thanks, O Lord, with my whole heart; before the gods I sing your praise; I bow down toward your holy temple and give thanks to your name for your steadfast love and your faithfulness; for you have exalted your name and your word above everything" (Ps. 138:1–2 NRSV).

INVOCATION. Eternal God, our Father, high above all yet in all, thy children gather in thy sanctuary to worship thee. Thou fillest the heaven and the earth so that none can hide himself where thou canst not see him. Through all the universe thou flowest like the living blood through our bodies, yet there is one spot where we feel the pulse, where, putting the finger, we know the heart is beating. Let thy sanctuary be that to us this day. O God, who fillest all things, here let us feel the beating of the Eternal Heart.—Harry Emerson Fosdick

OFFERTORY SENTENCE. "Jesus sat down opposite the place where the offerings were put and watched the crowd putting their money into the temple treasury" (Mark 12:41a NIV).

OFFERTORY PRAYER. Lord, let this giving affect our finances until it stretches our souls where faith and action meet in salvation and service through Christ our Lord.—E. Lee Phillips

PRAYER. O God, the burden of the world is great and our hands are small; the mystery of life is very deep and our love falters; sin is stubborn and our wills are feeble; without thee, we are lost. Strengthen our hands, empower our love, direct our wills. Though the day be short, help us to lift some burden, bring light to some darkness, and stand firm against the evil one. Open new paths of righteousness for our souls' sake, that we may not grow weary in well-doing; lengthen our sight that we may see farther than this day, even into the eternal vista of thy kingdom; and when the night lays the world away, take our souls into thy keeping and restore them with thy spirit for the work of another day.—Samuel H. Miller

LECTIONARY MESSAGE

Topic: The Worship of the King

TEXT: Isa. 6:1–8 (9–13)

OTHER READINGS: Luke 5:1–11; 1 Cor. 15:1–11

Asked about the greatest need of the world today, William Temple replied, "Worship," and went on to define it: "To worship is to quicken the conscience by the holiness of God, to purge the imagination with the beauty of God, to devote the will to the purpose of God." Isaiah's experience recorded in our text illustrates Temple's definition of worship. Isaiah caught a vision of God's holiness in his temple and responded appropriately to it in worship. He gives us a model for worship in six stages.

I. He sought the Lord (6:1). Isaiah not only recognized his need for God; he sought the place where God dwelt in a special way. He could say with the psalmist, "As the deer pants for streams of water, so my soul pants for you, O God" (42:1), and he fit Jesus' description of those who "hunger and thirst for righteousness, for they will be filled" (Matt. 5:6).

II. He saw the Lord (6:1). How? Probably in a special miraculous vision. But the question is: "How do we see God? How do we catch a vision of him?" Jesus' answer is, "Anyone who has seen me has seen the Father" (John 14:9). Paul said the same thing in different words, for God "made his light to shine in our hearts to give us the light of the knowledge of God in the face of Christ" (2 Cor. 4:6). Isaiah saw God's majesty, God's holiness, and God's glory. Through Christ that revelation is ours.

III. He confessed his sin (6:5). Isaiah's confession is especially important for a future prophet: "I am a man of unclean lips, and I dwell in the midst of a people of unclean lips." This is the response of the saints through the ages. The people closest to God have been the most aware of their sin. What makes our lips unclean? They may be lying lips or surly lips or arrogant lips or filthy lips or cursing lips or lustful lips or even silent lips. "If we confess our sins, he is faithful and just and will forgive us our sins and purify us from all unrighteousness" (1 John 1:9).

IV. He was renewed (6:6–7). Isaiah was told that his guilt was taken away and his sin atoned for. The greatest therapy in the universe is the assurance of forgiveness. Regular, genuine worship renews us through God's grace.

V. He saw God's world as God sees it (6:8). In response to God's call, "Whom shall I send? And who will go for us?" Isaiah replied, "Here am I, send me!" He saw the spiritual meaning of life and his stewardship of it. For him it meant to carry out God's commission to Israel; for us it means to carry out his commission to disciple the nations. We need to see the world as God sees it.

VI. He dedicated himself to serve the Lord (6:8). In the agony of Gethsemane's garden, Jesus dedicated himself to serve God: "Yet not as I will, but as you will" (Matt. 26:39). And Paul dedicated himself on the Damascus road to serve God: "What shall I do, Lord?" (Acts 22:10). Genuine worship always leads a person to dedicate herself or himself to serve the Lord.

Only genuine worship could sustain Isaiah when he faithfully proclaimed the Word of God and people refused to "hear with their ears, understand with their hearts, and turn and be healed" (6:10).

Changed lives mark whether worship has taken place. When Isaiah walked out of the temple, everything was different. The temple was the same, the climate was the same, the flowers and the grass were the same, but Isaiah was different. He had been in the presence of God, and he had worshipped Him. He had begun by seeking the Lord, and he was led through worshipping God to surrender his life to the service of God—and so should we.—Wayne Shaw

SUNDAY: FEBRUARY TWELFTH

SERVICE OF WORSHIP

Sermon: Salt of the Earth?

TEXT: Matt. 5:13–20

What is it that keeps this world from doing what it seems most intent on doing? I don't know how you see it, but when I look at the world around us, it seems to me that we are intent on self-destruction. We can talk about the wonders of the capitalistic system and the evils of the communist systems, and yet one has already destroyed itself and the other seems so open to corruption, greed, selfishness, and bottom-line profit that it is destined to "kill the goose that laid the golden eggs." Our welfare system is said to have now become so monstrous that it must be scrapped and we must start over. There is evidence that our educational system is in need of a massive and major renovation. The street killings and drug wars indicate that the very fabric of society is rotten and tearing apart. Over and over again we hear that the world is "going to hell in a hand basket." Society so easily becomes corrupt. Greed, lust, and indifference lead so quickly to decay and rot. These are the forces of death, and they are not stayed unless something interferes with the process. And yet, somehow, day after day, year after year, century after century, humanity has endured. Something has prevented the inevitability of the process.

I. You and I think we know what it is that protects and preserves society. You and I, as part of a people created, formed, instructed, and guided by the biblical story, know what it is that keeps creation from falling into the abyss completely. It is because of God's judgment and wrath upon all creation for the sake of those who are his people.

(a) We get our first glimpse of this patience of God, this power of a few faithful to save the whole creation, back in the discussion between Abraham and God over the fate of the cities of Sodom and Gomorrah. The sin of those cities is very grave, and God has determined to destroy both cities. But Abraham is not ready to give up on those cities. Abraham has family there. Abraham thinks there are still some faithful and devout people in those cities. "God, will you destroy the cities if fifty righteous people can be found in those cities?" Fifty righteous people will have the ability, the power to preserve Sodom and Gomorrah. Abraham keeps talking and brings the number all the way down to ten. Ten righteous people are worth enough to God that God will withhold his punishment; God will preserve and keep the cities for the sake of ten righteous people. God's love of his people, people who are his faithful followers, is so great that God will renew, restore, preserve, reform, infuse into creation new possibilities, so that creation survives for the sake of those ten.

G. K. Chesterton once observed that men and women can strive for goodness and reach a kind of plateau of goodness and maintain that level, but evil spirals downward and no one reaches a level of evil and remains there. It keeps getting worse and worse. One lie leads to another and bigger lie. And yet something prevents our total disintegration. Something preserves humanity.

(b) The story of Noah is the story of great evil, and yet God out of his great love for one righteous man and his family did not totally destroy creation. God did not destroy all humanity in the Flood. God's love for eight faithful people was enough to preserve human life.

(c) Surely it is something like that that Jesus is saying here in this Sermon on the Mount. He has just described in the Beatitudes those who are happy and blessed in his kingdom. And now he says to his disciples around him, "You are the salt of the earth; but if salt has lost its taste, how shall its saltness be restored? It is no longer good for anything except to be thrown out and trodden under foot by men." Not that they shall be, not that they could be, but Jesus says that his disciples *are* the salt of the earth. They are what preserves and keeps society from spoiling. The community of the faithful has a responsibility in the whole of society. Those few who are blessed and happy are the very thing that keeps and protects society from rot.

II. "You are the salt of the earth."

(a) We must surely look for the grace and guidance of the Holy Spirit in listening to this well-known quote from Scripture, because if we try to take it literally it is an almost stupid saying. You are the salt of the earth, and that is supposed to be good? When Rome and Carthage were engaged in their long Punic wars for the dominance of Africa and the west, at the end of the Second Punic War, the great and horrible punishment that Rome inflicted on Carthage was to plow salt into their fields. The Romans poured salt on all the lands of Carthage because salt ruins the productivity of the land. Plants cannot get water out of salty land. With all the salt water of the oceans, it would be wonderful if we could just use that to irrigate the land, but salt on the earth is not helpful. So if we are called the salt of the earth in any literal sense, it is not a compliment or a blessing.

And the whole idea, from a chemist's point of view, that salt might lose its saltness is strange. The chemical compound of salt does not decompose. It may react with other things and become diluted. Or it may get mixed with dirt and become unfit for use, but salt in the ocean is still salt. Salt piles at the South Park salt barns will stay salt for ages. What does he mean "lose its saltness"?

(b) But salt in the time of Jesus was tremendously important because it was used to keep things from spoiling. Salt was the primary means of preservation of food. Salt was the one thing that stood between rot and health. Jesus says to us as his disciples that you and I are the one ingredient in society that prevents society from going to hell completely. It is the existence of faithful disciples that preserves society from total decay. By our being faithful, by our worship, by our singing our hymns of joy, by our being merciful, by our being poor in spirit, by our being concerned to minister to others, the whole of creation is preserved from the destructive consequences of evil.

(1) What is it that keeps saving history? What is it that keeps God at work preserving and rescuing society? What is it that acts like salt in the world? Jesus says you are that which saves and preserves creation. The fellowship of believers has the high calling of being the force in the midst of creation that prevents society from its natural decay. God's great love for his few faithful people, for two or three together in his name, keeps him working to prevent the powers of destruction from coming to completion.

(2) "You are the salt of the earth" is not a compliment so much as it is a description of work of the church. We are to be the community that preserves and keeps creation from decay. And if we forget what our job is, if we lose our commitment to God in Christ, then we have lost our saltness, our purpose, and are just tossed out on the road.

(3) If we are to be salt, our main opportunity is to provide a place where the continuing impact of Jesus Christ can be felt upon the lives of others, to be a people where the power of the Holy Spirit can be felt. The members of the kingdom of God are to be the ones who activate that dangerous and liberating story of a good and gracious God that is told in Scriptures. If we are to be the salt of the earth, then it is our joy to nurture growing allegiance to Jesus Christ through praise, prayer, a climate of openness and friendship, until the effects of that allegiance to Christ are as obvious to others as the presence of salt is on McDonald's fries.

The world may think of the church as the watchdog of decency, the policewoman of moral and spiritual values, but we are not called to be salt by the expectations of the world. The job we have is to confront head on again this gospel of Jesus Christ, this good news that God so loves one faithful follower that he will spare the whole world in order to give glory and joy, to give life to that one. We are the salt of the earth wherever we try to live in response to God's goodness for us, however we try to live as those who have been given more than they can earn, where we accept this amazing love for us that while we were yet sinners God still loved us. Being salt of the earth doesn't have anything to do with our own goodness or any reward for us. What keeps society from ultimately destroying itself on the rocks of selfishness is the community of believers who live their lives in response to a goodness and love of God that are given without being earned, are offered to those who don't deserve them, and are the sources of delight and surprise because they come and there is nothing for us to do but receive them. Such a community of grace always acts as salt to preserve the world from decay.—Rick Brand

Illustrations

ANTISEPTIC INFLUENCE. If the Christian is to be the salt of the earth, he must have a certain antiseptic influence on life. We all know that there are certain people in whose company it is easy to be good, and that also there are certain people in whose company standards are relaxed. There are certain people in whose presence a soiled story would be readily told, and there are other people to whom no one would dream of telling such a tale. The Christian must be the cleansing antiseptic in any society in which he happens to be; he must be the person who by his presence defeats corruption and makes it easier for others to be good.—William Barclay

TOWARD A DEEPER FAITH. Some years ago one of my students in the seminary remarked, "My classmates and I have been here now for approximately a year and a half, and as a result of the teaching in this seminary many of us have just about lost our faith." He proceeded to ask me what I would do about it! My reply was along these lines: "I would suggest that you go to your room and drop upon your knees and thank God that you have been thought worthy to enter this institution with a view to losing your faith and regaining it at a deeper level." I went on to ask him whether he did not realize that he was to preach the gospel to a world that had lost its faith, and I inquired whether he thought that were possible if he had not gone through a like experience of loss of faith himself and issued victoriously from it.—John Wick Bowman

Sermon Suggestions

LEST OUR HEARTS DECEIVE US. TEXT: Jer. 17:5–10. (1) Mere mortals can lead us astray into a moral desert, verses 5–6. (2) The Lord can plant our lives by nourishing streams of spiritual resources, verses 7–8. (3) The time of reckoning comes, and we shall experience the consequences of our choices, verses 9–10.

THE TOTAL PICTURE. TEXT: 1 Cor. 15:12–20. (1) The problem: many live as if there were no life beyond, whatever they profess to believe about it. (2) The solution: the Resurrection of Christ assures us of our own life to come (a) by the historical evidence of Christ's Resurrection and (b) by the experiential evidence shown in our grateful striving to do Christ's will in this world.

Worship Aids

CALL TO WORSHIP. "Happy are those who do not follow the advice of the wicked, or take the path that sinners tread, or sit in the seat of scoffers; but their delight is in the law of the Lord, and on his law they meditate day and night" (Ps. 1:1–2 NRSV).

INVOCATION. Lord, so speak to us in this hour of worship that we will not leave the same as we entered and the things of God will never have been more precious or more real.—E. Lee Phillips

OFFERTORY SENTENCE. "Like good stewards of the manifold grace of God, serve one another with whatever gift each of you has received" (1 Pet. 4:10 NRSV).

OFFERTORY PRAYER. Lord, let us not withhold what we ought to share, or resent that which we ought to sacrifice, for it all belongs to thee, and others may need what we bring more than we do. Let the Holy Spirit show the way.—E. Lee Phillips

PRAYER. Gracious Father! Thou hast revealed thyself gloriously in Jesus Christ, the Son of thy love. In him we have found thee, or rather are found of thee. By his life, by his words and deeds, by his trials and sufferings, we are cleansed from sin and rise into holiness. For in him thou hast made disclosure of thine inmost being and art drawing us into fellowship with thy life. As we stand beneath his cross, or pass with him into the garden of his agony, it is thy heart that we see unveiled, it is the passion of thy love yearning over the sinful, the wandering, seeking that it may save them. No man hath seen thee at any time, but out from the unknown has come the Son of man to declare thee. And now we know thy name. When we call thee Father, the mysteries of existence are not so terrible, our burdens weigh less heavily upon us, our sorrows are touched with joy. Thy Son has brought the comfort that we need, the comfort of knowing that in all our afflictions thou art afflicted, that in thy grief our lesser griefs are all contained. Let the light that shines in his face shine into our hearts, to give us the knowledge of thy glory, to scatter the darkness of fear, of wrong, of remorse, of foreboding, and to constrain our lives to finer issues of peace and power and spiritual service. And these prayers we offer in Christ's name.—Samuel McComb

LECTIONARY MESSAGE

Topic: The People of the Kingdom

TEXT: Luke 6:17–26

OTHER READINGS: Jer. 17:5–10; 1 Cor. 15:12–20

Jesus is a people person. He cares about people—all kinds of people. He cares for those of us needing direction as sheep without a shepherd. He cares for those of us needing forgiveness for our sins. He sets the example for those of us who need to forgive each other.

Jesus calls us into his kingdom. His kingdom is spiritual, not material; moral, not nationalistic; and actual, not ideal. Where is the kingdom of God? It is wherever a man or woman has made Christ the Lord of life and accepted the rule of God in the heart. It is the other world, breaking through into time, coming above the surface in that person's life. If we enter his kingdom, we have two addresses—where we get our mail and our citizenship in heaven.

Jesus as the king of the kingdom invites all kinds of people into his kingdom. He sets the moral and spiritual standards for the members of his kingdom, which he summarizes in his sermon on the plain. The good news of the gospel is that he accepts us into his kingdom with full benefits and empowers us to carry out the purpose of his reign in the world—to bring his fallen world back into fellowship with God.

In this passage, Luke describes three kinds of people in terms of how they respond to the message of the kingdom.

I. The people interested in the kingdom. Then as now, they came from many different places and backgrounds. Luke specifically mentions the twelve disciples, whose call he has described in the preceding verses. The disciples, learners, and followers who have committed themselves to him are there. So is the crowd who are intrigued by him and want to hear more of what he has to say about the kingdom. They make up a great number, and they come from all over Judea, including the capital city, Jerusalem, and from Tyre and Sidon. It is like Luke to include Tyre and Sidon, symbols of heathenism, to hint at what Acts proclaims—that the gospel of the kingdom is for all the people groups of the earth.

II. The people who inherit the kingdom. Two expressions often heard today are "get real!" and "get a future!" Jesus spoke to both of these in our text. But "get real!" for Jesus meant the very opposite of what the world calls reality. He proclaims that the truly blessed are the poor and destitute, the hungry and the weeping, as well as the hated and excluded because of choosing to follow Christ. Talk about a reversal of values! Why would anyone willingly endure those things? And why would Jesus call them blessed? The answer is in "get a future!" Paul said it well: "If only for this life we have hope in Christ, we are to be pitied more than all men" (1 Cor. 15:19). His disciples who are poor by the world's standards will inherit the kingdom of God, the hungry will be satisfied, the weeping will laugh, and those rejected by the world will rejoice and leap for joy in heaven. The same future belongs to them that belongs to their forefathers, the prophets. And the promised hope makes any present hardship endurable. "Jesus promised his disciples three things," wrote F. R. Maltby, "that they would be completely fearless, absurdly happy and in constant trouble." These are the people who are real because they have a future.

III. The people who bypass the kingdom. These are the people who live for this life only. They may be rich here, but they fall under divine judgment (the four woes) because they are not rich toward God and have received all the comfort they are ever going to get. They may be full now, but they will be eternally hungry. They may laugh now, but many will mourn and weep forever. They may be applauded here, but they will suffer the fate of all false prophets hereafter. The contrast is not only between the physically poor and physically rich. Jesus is addressing the whole person, but his account accents the contrast between the spiritually rich, who follow the Son of man as the people of the kingdom, and the spiritually poor, who refuse to follow him. We are the people of the kingdom not only because he chose us but also because we chose him.—Wayne Shaw

SUNDAY: FEBRUARY NINETEENTH

SERVICE OF WORSHIP

Sermon: Longing for Egypt

TEXT: Num. 14:3–4

The tragedy of a wasted opportunity! How often this is the story of our lives and of the lives of nations and of institutions. We stand on the threshold of a chance to do something good, to better the world or to better ourselves, but for this reason or for that, we let the opportunity slip by.

Such was the case as recorded in our Scriptures. The Israelites had gone to the edge of the Promised Land. The people became frightened and discouraged and began to murmur against Aaron and Moses, saying, "Let's go back to Egypt." They were meant for the Promised Land, and here they were at the edge of it, but they decided that it would be better to go back than to go forward.

Take a look at some of the reasons why they turned back. They are some of the same reasons we often miss our opportunities. There are many opportunities presented to us to better ourselves, to better our lives, but we miss them. We head back for Egypt. Why do we?

I. We long for Egypt because we're too frightened to go forward.

(a) The advance scouts said the land was "a land of milk and honey." But it would be a difficult land to settle. It would require work. But more importantly, there were people already there. Some of them were sons of Anak! Giants! By comparison, the scouts saw themselves as grasshoppers. That scared them. They weren't ready to do battle with any giants. They became frightened and decided that maybe they had better go back to Egypt. At least they would be alive in Egypt.

(b) The same is often true in our lives. In the face of many opportunities, we too are frightened. We are afraid of communism, atomic destruction, pollution, taxes, crime, and cancer. We're afraid of meaninglessness, failure, and what other people think of us. As a church, we are afraid of the new. We seem to define life in terms of what we fear.

(c) There is much to fear. As we look at the future, we are frightened by it. We stand paralyzed, afraid to assault the future. There are so many giants in the land that scare us. While the giants are there, God is too. God brought the Israelites out of Egypt. God had taken care of them in the wilderness. God will provide for them in the Promised Land. God was not too weak for the giants. He could handle their problems. But they did not take the Promised Land. Fear conquered their faith.

II. We long for Egypt because we've forgotten what Egypt was like.

(a) All these people were saying, "Remember how Egypt was? Let's go back there. Remember Egypt?" But the tragedy of that was they *didn't* remember what Egypt was like. Egypt was a place of agonizing slavery and the cruelty of man's inhumanity to man. They would rather have the security of slavery than the responsibility of freedom. How tragic. We will sell our souls for security. They were wanting to go back to Egypt. They had forgotten that Egypt was a literal hell on earth for them.

(b) We are living in a day that worships nostalgia. We collect relics of the past and listen to the music of the past. We are interested in the history of the past and the people of the past. Hardly a week goes by when someone doesn't come up and say, "If only we could go back to those good old days, how good it would be." I always want to say, "What good old days?" Where were they? Since the turn of the century we have been involved in four wars, with the tragedy and inhumanity that come with them. Since the turn of the century we have lived through a terrible depression and a prohibition that was violent and unfruitful. We have seen the rise of organized crime. We have seen spiritual emptiness everywhere.

We need to realistically remember the past like that woman in the nineties did.

She said, "Everybody is talking about how good the gay old nineties were. They weren't any good. There were problems then just as there are now."

(c) The day we are living in could be the best day there ever has been. It depends on whether or not we will have the kind of faith in the goodness and the presence of God to believe that we can do something with this day. It depends not on the time we live in but on the faith we live. The God who led the people out of Egypt to the Promised Land is the God who can do the same thing for us—lead us out of the Egypt of our despair into the joy of abundant life.

III. We long for Egypt because we don't have the commitment to go forward.

(a) The Israelites didn't take the Promised Land because they didn't want to pay the price for it. It would not be an easy task. It would mean work, difficulty, and danger. They didn't want that. They wanted God to deliver them from slavery. They wanted God to provide for them in the wilderness. They wanted it easily. God said no to all: "You can have the Promised Land if you want it. I will help you get it. But you have got to go take it. It's got to be your life given, your commitment shown. You've got to give your life to it." They didn't want to do that. And they didn't!

(b) We would like to have a Promised Land flowing with milk and honey where love is real, where joy and happiness and laughter are the order of the day, where we are confident and hopeful and live in faith. But the problem is that we want God to hand it to us on a silver platter. We don't want to pay the price for it. We want the benefits of the kingdom but not the responsibilities of the kingdom. We want the glories of the cross without the sacrifice and suffering of it. We want faith without commitment. Christ laid down the condition of discipleship when he said, "If any man will come after me, let him deny himself."

(c) We talk about the Promised Lands we want. We want a Christian home. But there's a price to pay—honesty, kindness, patience, long-suffering, unselfishness, and faithfulness.

We want a Christian community. We have to pay the price for that, too. That means involvement in community groups in order to make sure that what needs to be done gets done.

We want a good church, but there's a price for that, too. It's a price of involvement in worship and in the organizational ministry of the church. It means a willingness to serve, to sing in the choir, to visit the nursing home, to be involved in mission work, to visit the sick and the prospects.

If we want the benefits of the Christian life, we have to take the condition of it. "Take up your cross daily and follow me. For if you lose your life for my sake, you will find it." Are we willing to pay the price?

(d) The tragedy of missed opportunities—they are there. The Israelites missed their chance for the Promised Land because they were afraid. We forget that God is with us. Sometimes we don't take God at his word. We don't trust him enough.

The future is before us. God will help us if we're not afraid to try. Head for the Promised Land! If we commit ourselves to taking the Promised Land, we will discover that God is with us.

If we head back for Egypt, we will miss the joys of the Promised Land, the hope of it, the God of it. To miss God is to miss life. The Promised Land or Egypt? Which one will it be? Which one will you head for?—Hugh Litchfield

Illustrations

THE CHOICE. A church lived in a neighborhood that was fast becoming a ghetto. It had a choice to make—would it stay there and try to minister to that community, or would it move? It moved! Where it used to be is now a supermarket, and that area is a place of high crime, high poverty, high drugs, and high despair. The church had a chance to minister to all of that, but it lost its chance.—Hugh Litchfield

WHAT COUNTS AT LAST. If the whole world had applauded him because he had made a concession, however small, to its desires for bread and power, then in the eyes of eternity this would have been only a defeat. But when, lonely and misunderstood by all, he dies, afterward to be loved by a few Galilean fishermen and publicans, then to the world this is a wretched failure, as Celsus says: "a despicable life that ends in a wretched death"—but to God a glorious victory.—Karl Heim

Sermon Suggestions

NOT YOU, BUT GOD! TEXT: Gen. 45:3–11, 15. (1) The Joseph story. (2) The meaning: God works in unpromising circumstances to bring about his will: (a) overruling human will; (b) giving grace to the undeserving; (c) bringing about reconciliation.

OUR FUTURE IS WITH GOD. TEXT: 1 Cor. 15:35–38, 42–50. We can be sure of these things: (1) It will be quite different from this life. (2) It will bear the image of Jesus Christ. (3) It will bring to fulfillment God's purpose for us, individually and as his people.

Worship Aids

CALL TO WORSHIP. "Do not fret because of evil men or be envious of those who do wrong; for like the grass they will soon wither, like green plants they will soon die away. Trust in the Lord and do good; dwell in the land and enjoy safe pasture. Delight yourself in the Lord and he will give you the desires of your heart" (Ps. 37:1–3 NIV).

INVOCATION. Lord, help us in this service of worship to see what so long we have not seen and to experience that which has so long eluded us because we pause to pray and listen and act as the Holy Spirit leads.—E. Lee Phillips

OFFERTORY SENTENCE. "For you know the grace of our Lord Jesus Christ, that though he was rich, yet for your sakes he became poor, so that you through his poverty might become rich" (2 Cor. 8:9 NIV).

OFFERTORY PRAYER. Give us such a vision of your glory that no sacrifice may seem too great as we come to make our offerings before you this morning in Jesus' name.—Henry Fields

PRAYER. Here this morning, Father, we bow our heads but raise our hopes to you. We know that we do not always recognize the riches that we receive from your hand. Yet you allow so many of us to possess a body that functions without pain and a mind that moves out beyond time and space. We know that we enjoy advantages we did not work for and advances we did not make. They are gifts from hands bigger than our own and come to us from minds that have been blessed with insights we do not have. Life has been enriched by the efforts of others; music with all its wonder, drugs that work the miracle of healing, literature that expands our minds, machines that take the strain out of labor, and hundreds of other wonderful things that have come to us as gifts for life. Gratitude wells up in us when we stop and remember our debt to you and the special folks through whom you have worked to make life as meaningful as we know it to be today.

But we also know, Father, that there is much in us that we would have taken away so that we can be more like you would have us become. We nurture our jealousies when we ought to let them go. We cling to our hatreds when we ought to remove them from the furniture of our hearts. We do our sins even while we hate them and allow them to dominate when we should seek the power of your Spirit to eliminate them. We do not care for the needs of others as we do the needs of ourselves. We do not love our fellowman as we love ourselves. We do not often turn the other cheek or walk the second mile. We know that all of this is a part of the Christian walk, but we have not taken these things seriously enough to let them make a difference in our daily lives. Forgive us, Father, and call us to a new commitment to doing your will in the small as well as the great things of life, in the unseen events as well as the spectacular matters in which we are involved. Let this be for all of us an hour of insight and soul searching, even as it is an hour of exhilaration and inspiration, we pray in Jesus' name.—Henry Fields

LECTIONARY MESSAGE

Topic: The Supreme Strategy of the Kingdom: The Kingdom Strikes Back

TEXT: Luke 6:27–38

OTHER READINGS: Gen. 45:3–11, 15; 1 Cor. 15:35–38, 42–50

I. The problem we face. How do we as Christians strike back at those who hate us, exclude and insult us, and treat us as evil (6:20)? We cannot simply roll over and play dead. But if being a part of the kingdom of God and living by the standards taught in the sermon on the plain are God's will for everyone, what is God's strategy for conquest? How do we as Christians respond to those who misunderstand and mistreat us? Jesus says that we are to treat others as we want them to treat us (6:31). We call that principle the Golden Rule.

(a) Many have substituted the Rule of Greed for the Golden Rule. They believe that the way to get ahead is to "get the other person before he or she gets you." Christians who behave like this clearly have their kingdoms confused.

(b) Many Christians, however, think they do well when they practice the Silver Rule: what you do not want others to do to you, do not do to them. Many great philosophers and religious teachers have recognized the nobility of this principle and have taught it to their followers, including Socrates, Philo, Rabbi Hillel, and Confucius. Detractors of Jesus have claimed that the Golden Rule merely copied what all great religions had already taught. But every one of these maxims is negative. They vote for justice; they are silent on mercy. The difference between the Golden Rule and the Silver Rule is vast. It is the difference between the Good Samaritan in Jesus' parable who saved the man's life on the Jericho road and the priest and Levite who passed by on the other side. They did not hurt the injured man, but neither did they help him.

(c) Still others, many of them Christians, secularize the Golden Rule. Recognizing it as a superior way to live, they advocate it as the way to be happy at home, successful in business, productive in society, and popular with friends. Of course, loving one's neighbor as oneself works. It has always worked in the long run when it has been tried. Stephen R. Covey calls it making "emotional deposits." It is a powerful principle because it was given to us by our Creator to tell us how to live with each other. But Jesus means much more than anything contained in the Rule of Greed, the Silver Rule, or a secularized Golden Rule.

II. The solution. The supreme strategy of the kingdom of God is to love our enemies, and that is the context for the Golden Rule. It is not merely an ideal to be dismissed in our normal existence but our working strategy for world missions and church growth. All the methods and techniques of missiology and church growth, as valuable as they are, are spiritually futile without the catalyst of the Golden Rule.

When Jesus commanded us to love our enemies, he did not use the word for natural affection between family and friends. He chose a term of love *(agape)* that is not dependent on the attractiveness of the recipient but rather seeks to imitate the attitude of God, who is love. It has been defined as intelligent goodwill, and it always seeks the other person's benefit.

Jesus applies the Golden Rule specifically to how we respond to our enemies. We are to do good to those who hate us, bless those who curse us, pray for those who mistreat us, turn the other cheek to those who strike us, and give to those who want to take from us. Why would anyone act like that? He gives us several reasons. If you want any credit for good behavior, love your enemies, do good to them, lend to them without expecting to get anything back, and forgive instead of condemning them. By doing these things, you will be loving like God loves, you will please your heavenly Father, you will be blessed both here and hereafter, and you will be an effective witness to those who are your enemies because they are God's enemies.

This is Christ's supreme strategy for impacting a hostile, pagan world for the kingdom of God. This is how God wants us to live and love, and he will reward us. We will be forgiven, not condemned, and we will be given to as we give, but more abundantly by far—good measure, pressed down, shaken together, and pouring over in our lap. And part of our blessing is to know that we have done what we could to meet our enemies in heaven.—Wayne Shaw

SUNDAY: FEBRUARY TWENTY-SIXTH

SERVICE OF WORSHIP

Sermon: Why We Believe in God

TEXT: 2 Cor. 5:18–19

One of the astounding facts about Christ's Crucifixion is that it has been for Christians the supreme revelation of God's love—"God commendeth his own love toward us, in that, while we were yet sinners, Christ died for us"—and yet concentrated in that Crucifixion are all the factors that make it most difficult to believe in God at all, to say nothing of his love. What makes faith in God difficult is life's injustice, its cruelty, what Keats called "the giant agony of the world," and there on Calvary you have all that.

The cross is thus the epitome of our deepest problem. There you have the very worst and the very best—both there—with the question rising, which are we going to put our faith in? Which goes deeper and reveals the more truly the ultimate nature of things? Let us face that issue!

I. Consider, in the first place, that we indeed must choose. I know all about agnosticism and to how many it seems a place of neutral retreat. We neither believe in God nor disbelieve, men say; we do not know. But that is a deceptive neutrality. Real faith in God is a positive matter—either you have it or you don't.

(a) Surely a man can segregate what he calls his mind from the rest of himself and, in his mind alone, can decline to say either yes or no to God. He can hold his judgment in suspense. But he cannot hold his life in suspense; that gets made up one way or the other. Either he lives with a positive, sustaining, triumphant faith in God, or he does not; the agnostic misses that just as much as the atheist.

(b) At Calvary one confronts this forced issue about God. Everything that most makes men disbelieve in God is there; everything that makes men believe in God is there. I can stand before Calvary and, looking at one aspect of it, cry, "How can there be a good God?" And I can stand before Calvary and, looking at the other aspect of it, cry, "Such character, such sacrificial love can be no accidental outcome of ruthless matter; behind such goodness is an eternal source, as surely as behind the sunshine is the sun." But what I cannot do at Calvary is find any neutrality to which I can retreat. Which side then do you take?

II. Some of us have made our choice and do believe in God, in part because that character upon the cross and his sacrifice have done things to us and to the world that we are sure cannot be explained merely by protons and electrons going it blind.

(a) The New Testament is utterly inexplicable without its physical factors—the paper it is printed on, the type it is set in, the presses that print it. The physical is indispensable to the New Testament, but the creative cause of the New Testament, its ultimate fount and origin, go far back behind the physical into the invisible realm of mind and spirit. When a materialist says, as one did say, "All events are due to the interaction of matter and motion acting by blind necessity," my mind cries, "That is childish! That is believing in magic!" To explain Christ and all that Christ stands for by matter and motion acting by blind necessity is like thinking that the waving branches cause the wind.

(b) What troubles most of us, however, is not so much the arguments of skeptical philosophy as the awful facts, shown up in a scene like Calvary—life's cruelty, its brutal torture of the innocent, its senseless, wicked agony such as our eyes look upon today. Well, let's face it! If we start by believing in the best at Calvary, in Christ and his love as the revelation of the Eternal, if we say God is like that, we do face a mystery—the mystery of evil. How explain that? Why does God allow that? But suppose we reverse the process. Suppose we start with the worst at Calvary, the ruthless brutality there, and believe in that as the revelation of the ultimate truth of things—have we escaped mystery? My soul! We have run headlong into it, the most inexplicable of all mysteries: how, in a world with nothing but ruthless physical power at the heart of things, can one explain Christ and all that is Christlike in the world—friendship and beauty and creative intelligence and sacrificial love? There is a mystery—to get such things out of ruthless matter going it blind! Let us stop thinking that if we deny God we escape mystery; we run headlong into it in its most insoluble form.

III. Another factor in the Crucifixion constrains us to believe in God, namely, the astonishing way that scene on Calvary came out. It was appalling then, but now,

In the cross of Christ I glory,
Towering o'er the wrecks of time.

—millions sing that!

(a) Here is a mystery requiring more than a materialistic philosophy to explain: the fact, namely, that so often the worst turns the best in the end, a power and providence appear in life, as though God indeed made even the wrath of men to serve him. I am not pleading for sentimental optimism, as though to say that everything always comes out all right—one cannot get easygoing optimism out of Calvary. But I am remembering how Pilate and Caiaphas went home that night, their vile work done, that troublesome carpenter from Nazareth all finished, slain as a felon, with the imprint of imperial Rome's condemnation on him; and I am facing the fact that long since Rome has fallen and Caesar gone, that Pilate and Caiaphas are the accursed now, that Christ's life divine with its unearthly glory still is here, the most haunting, fascinating figure in man's history, and that cross of shame the symbol of salvation.

(b) History's great agonies that made men deny God have often produced results that made men glorify God. Commonly in retrospect the world's most troubled eras look far different from the way they looked when men were in the midst of them. "No chastening," says the New Testament, "for the present seemeth to be joyous, but grievous: nevertheless afterward it yieldeth the peaceable fruit of righteousness." I have read that verse hundreds of times, but only the other day did the momentous meaning of those two words strike home: "*nevertheless afterward.*"

IV. This, then, is the issue of the matter: on Calvary we come face to face not so much with an argument as with a fact, a personality, a character, and as Dean Inge put it, "A character cannot be confuted." Arguments we can confute. Argument for argument we can debate it out, but when we are all done arguing, a great character is still there, not to be confuted or denied. So Christ confronts us. He is either an accident or a revelation, one or the other.

(a) Some of us have had experiences with him deep within ourselves and in the lives of our friends, not to be confuted or denied. That we too have seen in the spirits of men where Christ has come, a momentary likeness of the king—temptations conquered, evil habits overthrown, trouble surmounted, character transformed, social progress achieved, saviorhood not to be confuted or denied.

(b) Such salvation we and the world we

live in critically need today. It is a humbling experience for men and nations to acknowledge the need of being saved, but we surely face it. Military victory notoriously begets pride. After every victory it is the defeated who are restless, dissatisfied, rebellious, demanding change, while the conquerors are tempted to settle back, proud, self-satisfied, reactionary. America, never noted for its humility, is thus tempted now.

(c) With faith in God, however, one's whole view of life is altered. Fellow workers with the eternal purpose, we can draw on eternal resources. One by one, our inward lives can be reinforced. That is no opiate but hope and power and stimulus and courage!

Take your choice! You can never make a more momentous decision. I believe in the ruthless Pilate and the treacherous Judas as the revelation of the Eternal—no! you do not really believe that. God was in Christ, rather, in Christ there on Calvary, reconciling the world unto himself.—Harry Emerson Fosdick

Illustrations

KEEPING ON COURSE. Some years ago a little church on the coast of England was ruined in a hurricane. The congregation thought themselves unable to rebuild. Then one day a representative of the British Admiralty came to the clergyman to ask if they intended to reconstruct the church. The clergyman explained why they could not do it. "Well," said the representative of the British navy, "if you do not rebuild the church, we will. That spire is on all our charts and maps. It is the landmark by which the ships of the seven seas steer their course." A true parable, that! Never more than now, when the souls of men need divine help, stable and secure, strong, sustaining, and empowering, was the church's message needed.—Harry Emerson Fosdick

AN INSISTENT APPEAL. A few years ago a magazine article about my prison ministry concluded that "prison radicalized the life of Chuck Colson." It is understandable that the reporter might have thought that, but it is simply not so. I could have left prison and forgotten it; I wanted to, in fact. But while every human instinct said, "Put it out of your mind forever," the Bible kept revealing to me God's compassion for the hurting and suffering and oppressed; his insistent Word demanded that I care as he does.

What "radicalized" me was not prison but taking to heart the truths revealed in Scripture. For it was the Bible that confronted me with a new awareness of my sin and need for repentance, it was the Bible that caused me to hunger for righteousness and seek holiness, and it was the Bible that called me into fellowship with the suffering. It is the Bible that continues to challenge my life today.—Charles Colson

Sermon Suggestions

GOD'S POWERFUL WORD. TEXT: Isa. 55:10–13, especially verse 11. (1) In creation, Genesis 1. (2) In prophecy, Jer. 1:9–10. (3) In Scripture, Deut. 30:11–14; Ps. 119:11. (4) In everyday, seasonal, and crucial events, Ps. 119:111 and Isa. 9:8. (5) In ultimate revelation, John 1:1–18.

A FASCINATING MYSTERY: "WE WILL ALL BE CHANGED." TEXT: 1 Cor. 15:51–58. (1) When? "At the last trumpet." (2) In what way? "This mortal body must put on immortality." (3) Why? "Victory through our Lord Jesus Christ." (4) With what implications? "Be steadfast, immovable, always excelling in the work of the Lord." (5) With what assurance? "In the Lord your labor is not in vain."

Worship Aids

CALL TO WORSHIP. "It is good to give thanks to the Lord, to sing praises to your name, O Most High; to declare your steadfast love in the morning, and your faithfulness by night" (Ps. 92:1–2 NRSV).

INVOCATION. Lord of all, hear the joy of our praise, hear our petitions, fill us with grace and truth and the wisdom that is forever humble before the Lord.—E. Lee Phillips

OFFERTORY SENTENCE. "No one has greater love than this, to lay down one's life for one's friends" (John 15:13 NRSV).

OFFERTORY PRAYER. O Giver of every good and perfect gift, in our more perceptive thoughts, we know that you have need of nothing, for "the earth is yours and the fullness thereof, the world and those who dwell therein." But we have need, the need to be saved from our own selfishness—to express your love not only in word but in deed. Consecrate these gifts that through your blessing they may be translated into the Word of life for us who dwell here and for those in distant places and for the healing of the nations that all peoples may know Salaam, Shalom, the health of your coming.—John Thompson

PRAYER. O you who are the Great Dreamer who with unbelievable imagination created this world with its order and life of infinite variety for our habitat, how can we be present before you except as we are "lost in wonder, love, and praise"? We praise you that you have created not only a world but a world filled with all kinds of extras. You did not create a flower with a single hue, but you have created fields of flowers with every color of the rainbow. You did not create one bird—a monotone—but you have created myriads with amazing sounds and incredible repertoire. You not only created a world but also peopled it—you not only peopled it but have given us family and friends.

With what love you do love—the world—creation—with what love you love us that we should be your children, and it does not yet appear what we shall be. You call us to live life on tiptoe to see the wonderful fulfillment of the sons and daughters of humankind. In this place may we catch the vision of the wholeness that you will for each of us, for our families, for the whole human family. May we see the community now present in all relationships in your reconciling love in Christ. In the fullness of your truth and grace in him, we are one.

In this place we may catch the vision of your glory, which fills the whole earth, to see that every common bush is aflame with your glory calling us to the amazing unity present in all the diversity of creation. There is "one Lord, one faith, one baptism, one God and Father of us all, who is above all and through all and in all." Your glory is the singleness of your love, which binds all creation as sister and brother—as family.—John Thompson

LECTIONARY MESSAGE

Topic: The Character of the Kingdom

TEXT: Luke 6:39–49

OTHER READINGS: Isa. 55:10–13; 1 Cor. 15:51–58

In his book *The Jesus of History,* T. R. Glover points to the victory of the church across the centuries, calling it one of the greatest wonders of history. How did the church do it? It was made up of people, he said, who "outlived," "out-died," and "out-thought" the pagan. This is precisely what Jesus is telling his followers to do as he concludes the sermon on the plain.

In polls too numerous to mention, we in the church are told that if we are going to reach unchurched Americans today, we must meet their needs. If we do not address their recognized needs, we will not have the opportunity to address their deeper, unrecognized needs. How then are we to reach them with the good news of the gospel?

Jesus faced the same problem when he preached the sermon on the plain. He spoke to the same three kinds of people that give him a hearing in every generation: the smaller group of serious followers, the larger group of committed disciples, and the still larger company of the interested but uncommitted. It may help us reach our audience if we learn what he said to them.

Jesus has warned his followers that they would be hated and insulted because of him; he has taught them to love their enemies; and he has demanded that they live his standards with absolute integrity. Now, through a series of parables, he emphasizes the integrity that is at the heart of the character of the kingdom.

I. We must have integrity if we are to lead in the kingdom (6:39, 40). Stephen R. Covey reminds us that good leaders have two qualities: character and competence. Jesus recognized the importance of character and competence when he asked, "Can a blind man lead a blind man? Will they not both fall into a pit?" Or when he declared, "A student is not above his teacher, but everyone who is fully trained will be like his teacher." The character and competence of Christ are the standards for integrity of leadership in the kingdom of God.

II. We must have integrity if we are to confront for the kingdom (6:41, 42). Hypocrisy will doom to failure any confrontation in behalf of Christ. We cannot attempt to take the speck of sawdust out of another's eye when we have a plank in our own eye. The tragedy is that it is often easier for us to see the speck in someone else's eye than it is to see the beam in ours. Jesus insists that we get our own life in order so that we can help to bring order to the lives of others.

III. We must have integrity if we are to produce fruit for the kingdom (6:43–45). What we say we believe must agree with what we do if we are to produce good fruit. Across the centuries it has always cost the church to live a straight life in a crooked world. Many of those listening to Jesus that day were going to pay with their lives for their integrity of faith, but they were also going to change the world forever.

Interested inquirers, now as then, look at us to see if we actually produce figs and grapes or thorns and briers (6:44). Jesus taught that a life of Christian integrity—the good life—is lived out of one's inner core, the heart. "The good man brings good things out of his heart, and the evil man brings evil things out of the evil stored up in his heart. For out of the overflow of his heart his mouth speaks" (6:45).

IV. We must have integrity if we are to endure the storms that threaten our lives as people of the kingdom (6:46–49). The critical question of Christian integrity is "Why do you call me 'Lord, Lord,' and do not do what I say?" His searching question applies to the ethical demands of the sermon on the plain. To heed these words of Christ is the only way to build a life that lasts because the storms will come and their torrents will batter us, sometimes when we least expect them. The only protection we have is to build a solid foundation by obeying the words of Christ.

Jesus ends the sermon on a negative note—something preachers are taught almost never to do. Why? He did it because to fail at integrity is to destroy oneself completely. But, fortunately, the one who warns us so strongly is also the one who offers himself so powerfully to us today. That is the good news of the gospel of the kingdom.—Wayne Shaw

SUNDAY: MARCH FIFTH

SERVICE OF WORSHIP

Sermon: Christ and the Meaning of Life

TEXT: Matt. 18:21–35

We cannot determine with any certainty what it was that prompted Peter to ask this remarkable question: "How often shall my brother sin against me, and I forgive him?" But whatever the motive that prompted Peter to ask his question, one thing is certain: he is trying to get Jesus to sanction a limitation upon Christian love of one's neighbor. For, as you know, it is in many ways very reassuring to know when and where one can *stop* loving one's neighbor with good conscience. Generally, to know the answer to this question is of more interest and importance to us than the question of when and where we must *begin* to love our neighbor.

The limit! This is what Peter was asking about. He wanted to know when it is reached.

And this brings us right to the theme of the parable. For here the Lord shows us two things. First, that we are *not* the echo of our environment but rather the echo of what God has done for us. Second, he shows us that we are human beings, not because we can permit ourselves to explode but because we can exhibit and pass on to others what God has given to us.

I. First, what about the relationship to the king, to God? This is a problematical thing. The parable says that "man"—this is the best way to express it—owes the king millions of dollars. In plain terms, this signifies that to be in debt, to be a sinner means that we owe to God everything we are and everything we have. This is a tremendous, a daunting statement.

(a) What happens here is that a man actually stands before God and confesses everything to him, and this turns out to be his death sentence. He not only feels like sinking into the ground; he actually does. No man can stand before God if he takes him seriously.

So when the king looks at this poor, corrupt fellow who has squandered his master's goods in evil machinations, lifts him up from the ground, takes his hand, absolves him, and gives him a new start, we can rightly appreciate this astonishing, incomprehensible reaction of the king only if we see it against the dark foil of the fact that the whole scene should have turned out altogether differently. There is certainly nothing logical about it. What is logical is what the culprit did to his fellow servant: he made him pay back his debt, his incomparably smaller debt. Sin and retribution belong together. This is logical.

But this is the wonderful part of it: God seeks you and me with such an everlasting love that, despite all the calculating and all the objectivity, he sees not the "object" but behind the object his unhappy "child," not only the values but also the person, that when he condemns the sin he does not condemn us, that though he calls sin by its name, he also calls me by my name and calls me his child.

And when his Son dies on the cross, we get some idea of what it costs him to beat down the logic of his holy righteousness and remain our Father. Truly, this is not "kindly God," who covers everything with the mantle of his love; this is no harmless metaphysical concept; this is the holy, subduing God who breaks the cursed spell of relentless logic and gives us the miracle of sonship.

What must have been this man's state of mind when he left this scene of clemency and pardon? A short time before he was a depressed man.

And now all this—the fear, the shame, the pangs of conscience—was gone, blown away without a trace. He learned that it can be nothing short of delight, that it can be simply wonderful to be able to trust someone with one's whole heart and love him in gratitude. To live by forgiveness is actually to experience a transport of joy and relief. Now, for the first time, he knew what life really means.

(b) But now our story takes a sudden and appalling turn. It turns out that man is terribly at odds with himself and that in the very next moment the inspiring, reviving stream of life can be poisoned and turned into a noisome sump. No sooner has the central figure in our parable returned to ordinary life, after leaving the Sunday atmosphere that pervaded that audience at the palace, than the blessed experience is obliterated.

There he meets a poor wretch to whom he had once made a small loan. Mr. X, as we may call the unmerciful servant, is suddenly in the same relation to his fellow servant as the king was in relation to him just a few moments before. But now he treats his fellow servant in exactly the opposite way from that in which his master treated him.

He simply allows the logic of retribution to run its full course. Nobody can blame him, for, after all, when he demands repayment of the money he is acting in accord with the principles of justice.

Mr. X is reacting according to the law of retaliation, the principle of you hit me, so I hit you; you owe me, so I collect. This is human and legal. But Mr. X has forgotten (you have forgotten!) that he has just been accepted by God contrary to all expectation and that now he must live in response to the mercy he has received and stop responding to the injustice that men do to him.

What a terrible self-contradiction, what abominable hypocrisy! It simply makes our Christianity unworthy of belief. God must put up with our despising him, but anybody who despises us must suffer the consequences. We are constantly rebelling against God. We are always judging by two different standards. That we should be given another chance by God, this is only right and proper. After all, this is God's "line"; that's what he's there for. But *we* go on treating our debtors as before. This is *our* line—this is the human, all-too-human element in us, and we are all too ready to flirt with it. But such is the way of the world.

(c) But now it turns out that God won't stand for it. Forgiveness that is not passed on to others is an abomination to him. He takes it back again.

God has affirmed with the blood of his Son, with his heart's blood, that he loves me, that I may be his child, and that my conscience may be free. This is, so to speak, the agreement that he offers me. But now I must ratify the agreement. And the way I ratify it—and the *only* way I ratify it—is by taking what God has given to me and passing it on to others. If I do not do this, I contradict the terms of the agreement by my own life and practice and thereby nullify the agreement. Everything that God has done for me becomes an indictment if I do not allow this act of God to flow through me to others. For then I have embezzled the mercy of God; then suddenly I am millions of dollars in debt; then I have allowed Jesus to die in vain.

II. So Peter has the answer to his question of when the limit has been reached, when a man can stop being patient and forgiving and may with good conscience explode. This answer can be summed up in this way:

(a) First: your question, Peter, is completely wrong. For it starts with the assumption that it is a moral hardship, a colossal exertion of self-control for you to grant pardon repeatedly to another person.

Jesus, however, shifts us completely beyond this level of morality and says to us: if in all seriousness you consider how often you have offended God and how he has forgiven you again and again; if you take seriously the literal fact that every morning and every night you can say, "Forgive us our debts," and that he actually does forgive them; then it is no longer, in any case not primarily, a question of self-control whether you go on repeatedly forgiving your neighbor.

The glorious thing is that with Jesus we become free, at ease, and cleansed of complexes. It is not a matter of exerting great willpower at the cross. Then the will will function of itself. It is "added unto us." Then we shall not so easily grow weary. "As we have received mercy, we do not grow weary." For God has not grown weary of us either.

(b) The second thing we have learned is this: no matter how miserably we fail, no matter how choked with resentment toward our neighbors, our family, our close associates we may become, our first question should not be whether our nerves will fail and whether our self-control will be equal to these trials but rather whether we ourselves have sufficiently availed ourselves of the forgiveness of God. Only he who himself receives forgiveness can pass on forgiveness. One doesn't go far on one's nerves when in reality the spiritual man in us is sick. When a person grows weary of forgiving, he has not yet availed *himself* sufficiently of mercy.

(c) And finally, the third thing we have learned: we receive the liberating gift of forgiveness only if we pass it on immediately. These two things, "forgive us our debts" and "as we forgive our debtors," belong together. Forgiveness is like the wand in a relay race; it must be passed on.

Should there be one among us who is oppressed by guilt and anxiety, who simply cannot find peace and assurance of forgiveness, though he has yearned for it and prayed for it again and again, that person ought simply to forgive his brother and his sister and in the name of Jesus and simply leave off this everlasting spitefulness. Perhaps the only reason for all his peacelessness lies in the fact that he has simply accepted all the sermons and meditations on grace and mercy that he has heard and stored them away in his heart like buried treasure.

III. Look at your neighbor, that neighbor who (as Luther once said) "would become a Christ to you," is standing at your door. Don't you feel your hand in the hand of God? But what is your other hand doing? Is it a clenched fist—or is it stretched out toward your neighbor so that the divine circuit can be closed and thus allow the current of creative power to flow into you? Our left hand is capable of doing something different from our right hand, and this can split and break us. It can send us staggering down the wrong road and make us miss the gates of the Father's house. But to miss those gates means that I shall also lose myself and miss my destiny, that I shall not become what I was intended and created to be. For I was intended to be not merely an echo of the world's evil and its exemplars but rather to be an echo of that unceasing love that comes from the cross.—Helmut Thielicke

Illustrations

THE STRENGTH OF KINDNESS. All ordinary violence produces its own limitations, for it calls forth an answering violence that sooner or later becomes its equal or its superior. But kindness works simply and perseveringly; it produces no strained relations that prejudice its working; strained relations that already exist it relaxes. Mistrust and misunderstanding it puts to flight, and it strengthens itself by calling forth answering kindness. Hence it is the furthest-reaching and the most effective of all forces.

All the kindness that a man puts out into the world works on the heart and the thoughts of mankind, but we are so foolishly indifferent that we are never in earnest in the matter of kindness. We want to topple a great load over and yet will not avail ourselves of a lever that would multiply our power a hundredfold.—Albert Schweitzer

FORGIVING YOURSELF. A mistake is a human error, not a fatal flaw that must be camouflaged forever. Sometimes, certain factors are just beyond our control. If you feel you must hide your mistakes out of shame, then you are trying to appear perfect—better than anyone else. Of course, you should try to do the best you're capable of in your career and in your personal life. You shouldn't stop striving to achieve or settle for something less than you desire. But having to be number one and perfect all the time in everything is a very grandiose aim. You are setting yourself up for disappointment.

Ask yourself how you would respond if a friend told you that he or she had made the same mistake you made. Would you feel your friend was a failure? Would you even care very much about the mistake? How long would it take before you forgot about it? Chances are, it would have little effect on your overall opinion of your friend. You might even like him better for being vulnerable. Treat yourself as reasonably as you would your friend.—Joan C. Harvey

Sermon Suggestions

WHY GIVE TO GOD? TEXT: Deut. 26:1–11. (1) Because of his providential leadership. (2) Because of his intervention for us in a time of crisis. (3) Because of his continuing blessing of us.

HOW WE ARE SAVED. TEXT: Rom. 10:8b–13. (1) By an outward confession (2) that is based on an inner conviction (3) that has its source in a Lord gracious to all.

Worship Aids

CALL TO WORSHIP. "He that dwelleth in the secret place of the Most High shall abide under the shadow of the Almighty. I will say of the Lord, He is my refuge and my fortress: my God; in him will I trust" (Ps. 91:1–2).

INVOCATION. Lord of life, so move among us to instruct and lift and guide that upon leaving we can say we have met God and our hearts are strangely warmed.—E. Lee Phillips

OFFERTORY SENTENCE. "As ye abound in every thing, in faith, and utterance, and knowledge, and in all diligence, and in your love to us, see that ye abound in this grace also" (2 Cor. 8:7).

OFFERTORY PRAYER. Creator of all, help us to be good sisters and brothers in the community of faith so we may reach to those outside the fold and enlarge that family for whom heaven is home and faith in Christ Jesus is joy.—E. Lee Phillips

PRAYER. Eternal God, who without our asking it hast set us in this mysterious scheme of circumstance, widely we would open the doors and windows of our souls to thee. We crave the experience of thy people, who have so felt thy nearness that they have cried, Whither shall we flee from thy presence? Whither shall we go from thy Spirit? In the beauty of nature, in the revealing relationships of friendship and family, in all that is excellent and worthy, courageous and full of hope in human life, in victories of light over darkness, love over hate, good over evil, become thou real to us and in the silence of our souls speak to us quietly that we may be sure of thy presence.

Through another week we have been tempted to be careless and ungrateful. Like streams flowing through our common days, goodness has been richly given, and we have been thoughtless of the fountain. O God, today we thankfully acknowledge thee as the friend behind all friendship, the spring of all beauty, the source of all goodness.

Send us forth to be builders of a better world. Our hearts are burdened in this place of privilege and beauty by the poverty that afflicts the sons of men. Thy providence has been sufficient and the world brings forth abundantly so that all should be fed, but our injustice and our niggardliness have made some rich and many poor. O God, have mercy on us who live in comfort lest we should be selfish in our privilege. Teach us not only to be merciful in overflowing charity but also to be just that we may build a society in which such inequity may be impossible. Open our eyes that we may see; unstop our ears that we may hear the cries of those who call for help. Make our hearts sensitive and our consciences quick. Forbid that we should be among the cursed who stand at ease in Zion and care not for the affliction of Joseph.

In the Spirit of Christ we lift our prayer.—Harry Emerson Fosdick

LECTIONARY MESSAGE

Topic: To Hell with the Devil!

TEXT: Luke 4:1–13

OTHER READINGS: Deut. 26:1–11; Rom. 10:8b–13

Jesus did not seek to avoid any part of human experience. "He was not a kind of divine doll who walked through life without being touched by it." This point is absolutely basic to our Christian faith, that in Christ God became man. He did not become like a man or play the part of a man. He became man, and so he experienced life as it really is. Even Jesus did not escape conflict with evil (Luke 4: 1–13).

I. The reality of evil. The question as to whether or not the devil exists gives rise to many heated debates! Fundamentalists and more liberally minded theologians advance spirited arguments and quote numerous biblical texts in support of their case. It has been said that perhaps the greatest trick that the devil can play is to make men and women doubt his existence! In many ways, of course, the debate is only of academic interest. The really important issue is not whether or not the devil exists but the reality of evil.

Sin and *evil* are words that have dropped out of our everyday vocabulary. Instead, we speak of mistakes, errors of judgment, and indiscretions but not of sin, in the sense of disobeying God or missing the mark. No one can escape the reality of evil and the temptation to sin—not even the Son of God. Evil is real. Look at the cross. We must take it seriously.

II. The value of evil. Often we imagine, to quote from Eliza Doolittle's song in the musical *My Fair Lady,* "Wouldn't it be lovely" if we were to live in a world in which there was no evil, no sin, no pain or suffering. Wouldn't it be lovely? It might not be just as lovely as we imagine! It might not even be in our best interest. Just as steel is tempered by fire in order to make it stronger and more perfect, so too, it is often only through the temptation experience that our faith in God is made stronger and more perfect. Evil can destroy, but with God's help good can come out of evil. Saints are sinners who recognize not only the reality of evil but also the value of evil!

III. The defeat of evil. Evil is a terrifying force. However, at the very center of the Christian faith is the belief that God offers to each one of us not only the power to escape from the clutches of evil—through the forgiveness of sins—but also the power and the confidence to overcome evil. At the very center of the Christian Gospel is the good news that on the cross of Calvary Jesus overcame evil. This is what Jesus meant when he cried, "It is finished" (John 19:30). Evil has been defeated! Of course, skirmishes with evil still occur. Temptations to sin come our way. This should not surprise us, since there is a sense in which the story of the cross never ceases. The truth is that the cross will remain nothing more than a piece of ancient history until the story of the cross is reenacted in our own life. The cross must become for us a personal experience, so that like St. Paul we can say, "I have been crucified with Christ; it is no longer I who live, but Christ who lives in me" (Gal. 20a). So to hell with the devil! Do not let evil overcome you but with God's help use it to grow into the likeness of Christ. You too can become a saint, so to hell with the devil!—Eric Young

SUNDAY: MARCH TWELFTH

SERVICE OF WORSHIP

Sermon: Spoiled Clay

TEXT: Jer. 18:1–4

I. I wonder if you have ever "made a mess of things." I don't mean a complete mess; very few people make a complete mess of their lives. But I wonder if for you there are some things about which you have deep regrets. I'm not talking of some strange experience when I put it like that, am I? I myself have wished that opportunities could have come my way that never did. And then there are opportunities missed. And there are things said that would to God we'd never said. And actions taken—well, looking back they weren't very wise. And some young people have failed examinations. And some young man has married the wrong woman, and some young woman has married the wrong man—you can tell it now when you see them together. For some there are incidents for which they were not responsible—an illness that all but took their strength away; an unhappy home behind them; a makeup that now seems one big bundle of unbound nerve ends. . . .

Am I addressing someone this morning with no regrets of any kind somewhere in the buried past? Then, my friend, I'll leave you behind, just for this morning; but the rest of you I'll take, if you will come, along a narrow street. It is narrow because it is Eastern, but what we are going to see is just the same in principle as in our English potteries—a man sitting at a wheel. And in his hand is clay, and he casts it on the wheel, revolving it with a treadle. Then with his fingers he shapes that clay into a vessel. It stands there before your eyes. You are fascinated; you can scarcely believe your eyes.

And there are more finished vessels on the shelf behind. . . . Then the clay splits. Instantly the potter's foot comes off the treadle. The wheel stops. But the potter doesn't throw the clay away. He uses it again. He presses it into a lump. He starts the wheel once more revolving. And now you see *another* vessel taking shape. Made from the same clay, made by the same potter. And you look at all those vessels on the shelf behind, some of which you long to have; and you say to yourself: "Funny thing, they're probably all made from *spoiled* clay."

Do you know who is in our little group? Oh, you wouldn't recognize him if you knew—but it is the prophet Jeremiah. "Then I went down to the potter's house and, behold, he wrought his work upon the wheels." And Jeremiah's head was full of the great mess that his people had made of their history—but not half so full as his heart, for he was a sensitive man. They'd been given a land, but they'd quarreled over it. They had been granted prophets, men of vision to show God's ways of life and peace; but they only picked up stones to throw at them. Jewry was meant to be a shining example for all the world to see of a nation governed by the laws of righteousness, but she became instead a quarrelsome, bigoted, defeated people, a race without a home.

And with all this in his mind, Jeremiah went down to the potter's home. You know how it is when your mind is filled with something—you don't *see* anything: objects move before you as shapes. And people watching say you have a vacant stare. And that is how Jeremiah stood before the potter's wheel. But the objects clarified. Jeremiah even saw what he was seeing. He saw spoiled clay being remade into beautiful vessels. He saw the potter not casting away the vessel that was marred in his hand but remaking it—and what he saw became to him the very Word of God. God does not throw *us* away when we break in his hands upon the turning wheels of life.

Of course, the interpretation was first of all national. It was national for Jeremiah, for he was thinking of his nation. But the Word still stands for every one of us. A man may have broken up his marriage—I've had a conversation about that this week. A woman may have failed to hold her children's love; any one of us may have felt the wrong thing, or done the wrong thing, or thought the wrong thing. But whatever it is, whether sin or misfortune, failure to rise to an opportunity, or dogged all the way with crippling ill health—God never throws us away when we break in his hands upon the turning wheels of life.

II. That's the first fact, and the second is this—God's sovereignty is not rigid. There are some people who have run away with the idea that God has a rigid plan for every one of us. And they use big words like *determinism* or ordinary words like *fate;* but whatever word they use, they mean the same—God makes out of us what he wants; it's all fixed and settled; we can't do anything about it; we're just clay in the potter's hand. And it isn't true; it isn't one little bit true.

Look at that clay on the floor. The potter does not expect to turn it all to vessels of a certain shape. He makes, and then he makes again upon his potter's wheel. He makes not so much what he wants but what he can. This piece of clay wouldn't make into a jar, so he turns it into a basin. To see the potter doing this is half the fascination.

And don't you see—God is like that. We worry about the mess we made so long ago; we harp back on that failure; we wring our hands over some misfortune that came just when we were getting going, and those times *were* bad; we did get marred upon the wheels of life. But this is the point—God never casts the clay away because it didn't shape the way he wanted. He simply turns it to another shape.

And someone comes and sits in my study: "If only I hadn't got this nervous makeup." But, my friend, that is the very thing about you that can cause you to become a sensitive leader where you work.

And another is dogged by some indiscretion many years ago. But, my friend, you wouldn't know the exceeding love of God as shown in his forgiveness were it not for this grave fault. You'd be a Pharisee, you'd be self-righteous, you'd be too proud to live with—or anyway you might be.

And I can see a young medical student dogged with an illness so that he had no chance to specialize but can only be a plain general practitioner. But you'll go a long way to find a doctor with more tenderness and more tact and more sympathetic insight than he possesses. It is the marring process on the wheels of life that has caused the comely shape that now appears.

III. And one more thought before we leave the little street where works the potter on his wheel—we must accept the vessels that we are. I don't mean by this we cannot improve ourselves. I don't mean by this we cannot by the grace of God achieve a higher standard than once we thought was ever possible; but in the last resort we are as God made us on the wheels of life. And I know no more frustrating attitude than to quarrel with this. It means dropping the "if only's" in our reckoning. *If only* I hadn't been made this way. *If only* I had more skill with my fingers. *If only* I had more brains in my head. But I haven't, and there's an end of the matter. But that doesn't mean God has cast me off from the wheel of life. Nor does it mean a vessel useless and without attraction. We must accept the vessels that we are and then go forward in this confidence.

May I finish with a story? It comes from one of Schiller's poems. When God made the birds, so the story goes, he gave them plumage gorgeous to behold and gave them voices entrancing to the ear; but what he didn't give the birds was wings—they had no wings at all. But this is what God did instead. He laid the wings upon the ground. "Take these burdens," he said, "and bear them." And this they did, folding them over their hearts. But presently, as time wore on, they found the wings had grown fast to their breasts and they could fly. So what they thought were burdens were changed to pinions. Thus Schiller, the German poet, and you smile pityingly at his imagination. But ought you to? And ought I to? When viewed in faith, it is the difficulties of life that raise us higher—or to return where I began, God makes his choicest vessels from spoiled clay.—D. W. Cleverley Ford

Illustrations

OUR ULTIMATE SECURITY. In the arid lands that were the birthplace of monotheistic religion, the desert was a primary symbol of trial and temptation. And water, especially freshly flowing "living" water, became a prominent image of God's grace. Just as fresh water could transform wastelands into gardens, the living water of God's Spirit could cause love to grow within the most parched and willful souls. In the psalms, the soul thirsts for God "as a deer yearns for running waters," "like a dry and weary land." And in Isaiah, God promises grace: "Let the desert rejoice. . . . For waters shall break forth in the thirsty ground. . . . The wasteland will be turned into an Eden. . . . You will become like a watered garden."

Eden, as a garden, becomes symbolic of humanity's rightful relationship with God's grace. It represents both our birthplace and our destiny, our home and our Promised Land, where we rely upon grace as our ultimate security.—Gerald G. May

LEARNING AND RELEARNING. We have all been brainwashed into believing that "if it's worth doing, it's worth doing well." Another equally erroneous version is "if you can't do it right, don't do it at all." If we take these folk wisdoms literally, we are left with nothing but blowing our noses or picking our teeth. How can this reflect reality? Did we not all fumble as we learned to walk, talk, or use a knife and fork? Did we not appear clumsy and self-conscious when first learning to dance?—Paul A. Hauck

Sermon Suggestions

LATE, BUT NOT TOO LATE! TEXT: Luke 13:31–35. (1) An imminent threat, verse 31. (2) A fearless response, verses 32–33. (3) A compassionate apostrophe, verse

34. (4) A possible time for repentance, verse 35.

WHEN GOD IS OUR PROTECTOR. TEXT: Gen. 15:1–12, 17–18. (1) Abraham's vision: God gives the promise of an heir, innumerable descendants, and a place to call home. (2) The timeless meaning: God continually works to bring his purpose to fulfillment. (3) The timely application: (a) God can make a way for us when there is no way. (b) We can expect interruptions and setbacks along the way. (c) Times, circumstances, and fulfillment are in God's hands.

Worship Aids

CALL TO WORSHIP. "The Lord is my light and my salvation; whom shall I fear? The Lord is the stronghold of my life; of whom shall I be afraid?" (Ps. 27:1).

INVOCATION. Lord, here are our minds; shape them. Here are our eyes; open them. Here are our ears; fill them. Here are our hearts; direct them with the power of the Holy Spirit and the presence of our Lord Jesus Christ.—E. Lee Phillips

OFFERTORY SENTENCE. "And whatever you do, in word or deed, do everything in the name of the Lord Jesus, giving thanks to God the Father through him" (Col. 3:17 NRSV).

OFFERTORY PRAYER. Lord, let our gifts reflect what our hearts believe and our souls desire that our lives may reveal the higher counsels of thy will, through Christ our Lord.—E. Lee Phillips

PRAYER. O God of ancient prophets and holy martyrs, pour out thy spirit upon us in this new day, that once again in the hour of our need we may dream dreams and see visions. Drop the plumb line of thy justice beside every wall we have built; weigh in the balances of thy truth all the accomplishments of our skill and science; test with thy consuming fire the permanent worth of our industry and art. If the earth be shaken and the foundations tremble, grant us courage to look beyond the ruins to that which has not fallen. If judgment falls and the hollow vanity of much that passed for the substance of life is revealed as nothing, steady us until we lift up our eyes unto thee and know that our hope is in thee, both now and forever. In the name of him who was steadfast against death and sin, we pray for our own perseverance in all good works.—Samuel H. Miller

LECTIONARY MESSAGE

Topic: Just Visiting!

TEXT: Phil. 3:17–4:1

OTHER READINGS: Gen. 15:1–12, 17–18; Luke 13:31–35

Writing to the Philippians, St. Paul reminds us that as Christians, "our citizenship [*politeuma*] is in heaven." St. Paul was thinking not so much about where he had come from as to where he belonged. In his secondary missionary journey, St. Paul had traveled through many hamlets and villages. As he entered the gates of Philippi, he saw everywhere reminders of Roman rule. Philippi had been given the status of a colony, with special privileges and a constitution modeled on that of Rome. It had become a center of Roman influence. St. Paul was proud of the fact that he was a Roman citizen. An even greater joy to him was the fact that his "true citizenship" was in heaven (Phil. 3:20). He saw the church at Philippi as an outpost of the kingdom of God. He was on earth simply as a visitor. The same is true of all of us. We are just visiting!

I. The purpose of our visit. Visits to a foreign country tend to be for one of two reasons, business or pleasure. A few people are fortunate enough to be able to mix the two!

Many people, since they have no spiritual dimension to their life, regard this life as an end in itself. Their philosophy is "let us eat, drink, and be merry, for tomorrow we die." Death for them is the end. Perhaps not surprisingly, they regard this life and their time on this earth as a time for enjoyment and pleasure. The result is that they trivialize life.

Their own enjoyment and pleasure become the sole aim and purpose of life. St. Paul's admonition that "our citizenship is in heaven" reminds us that we are not just on holiday but that our life here must be seen as a period of preparation for the life to come—when we have returned home. St. Paul warns us also that while we are "just visiting" and living in a foreign land, we must follow his example (v. 17) and not be influenced by the standards, values, and attitudes of those who are the enemies of the cross of Christ (v. 18). Those who regard this life as a time of preparation for the life to come will realize also that while this life is a gift from God and therefore to be enjoyed, we must not trivialize life but treat it seriously—as a time in which to do God's work. We must see all people, regardless of their race, color, or social status, as fellow travelers, in need of help and encouragement.

II. The duration of our visit. Visits abroad vary in length. Usually the duration is dictated by factors beyond our control. The length of our life is in God's hands. One thing is certain: one day we will be called home. Our visit will end. The wise, therefore, will travel light and will not allow themselves to become obsessed by the desire to possess many things. Even our human body is but a temporary dwelling, which at the end of our visit we will leave behind.

III. Going home. There are always mixed feelings! There is the joy in the fact that we are going home, to be reunited with those whom we love. There is also sadness, for it means saying goodbye to people near and dear. It takes a great faith to follow the example of St. Francis of Assisi and welcome death. This is where the Christian gospel outshines all of the other great religions of the world. We have a faith not just by which to live but also by which to die. We can look forward to that day when we go home and find all things made perfect in Christ (v. 21).—Eric Young

SUNDAY: MARCH NINETEENTH

SERVICE OF WORSHIP

Sermon: Simple, and Not-So-Simple, Kindness

TEXT: 2 Pet. 1:3–9

This is a sermon about kindness . . . simple kindness. It is a sermon about those chances that we have—all of us—every day to treat other people with mercy and compassion and kindness. We have many opportunities every day to show a little kindness, and sometimes we do and sometimes we don't . . . but what I am talking about this morning is kindness . . . simple kindness.

Now, I admit that kindness is not a very controversial or daring topic. Even the Boy Scouts are "brave . . . thrifty . . . clean . . . reverent . . . and *kind.*" We all know that kindness is a good thing and that the world needs as much kindness as it can get.

I. But is kindness really all that tame? I'm not looking for controversy or trouble, but I would like to say that if we look at this a bit more closely, we will discover, I think, that kindness is actually a very controversial business, and there are good reasons why Christian people ought to think twice before chirping about the virtues of kindness.

(a) To begin with, kindness can be a coverup for the real problems in life, a way of smoothing over the real issues. Several weeks ago, my wife and I visited a church in New York City. We got there a little early; there was a small park with a pretty fountain next to the church, so we bought a couple of styrofoam cups of coffee and two doughnuts, and we took them over to a bench in the park. No sooner had I gotten the lid off my coffee than a man came up to me and asked if I could spare him any money. Then I noticed behind the man several other men, all watching me to see what I would do, ready to take their turn in line if I had some money. Behind them was a city with thousands who need money, behind them a nation with millions in need, behind them a world with billions in desperate straits . . . and there I was, with thirty-five cents in my hand and kindness in my heart. Could I really believe that my action, for all of its kindness, would make even the smallest dent in the real problem?

(b) The Bible, too, knows about this matter of kindness being a coverup for the real problems. Do you remember where the Letter of James says, "If a brother or sister needs clothes and food, and you say, 'Go in peace, be warmed, be full,' but don't do what is necessary to really help them, what good is it?" And these people James is talking about—the ones who say, "Be warmed, be full, have a nice day"—are not being cynical and callous; they're trying to be kind, but it is a kindness that avoids the problem.

(c) Another problem with simple kindness is that it not only can cover up the point, it can also just plain miss the point. It can be naive, giving people softness and tenderness when they really need firmness and toughness. A parent once told me that he had learned the hard way that when his son called from college saying, "Hey, Dad, listen. I've got a little problem here. I need . . . ," sometimes the best thing he could do was to hang up the phone. Being kind to people can be a way of undermining their responsibility.

(d) So, kindness may not sound at first like a controversial topic, but Christians need to think twice before they start singing the virtues of kindness. That's why, when the Bible talks about kindness, we need to pay close attention, because when we do we see that what the Christian faith means by kindness . . . simple kindness . . . turns out not to be so simple at all.

II. To be a disciple of Jesus Christ is to be able to see ourselves and other people in a different light.

(a) In one of Frederick Buechner's novels there is a character named Leo Bebb who is locked in combat with a university professor named Roebuck. Enraged, Bebb charges into Roebuck's office and confronts him, but right at the point that the battle reaches its peak, Bebb notices the nameplate on Roebuck's desk. It reads "Virgil M. Roebuck."

"All I knew up to then," he said, "was Roebuck." But now he knew that this wasn't just any old Roebuck. This was the Roebuck that his parents had loved and had settled on calling Virgil. "Once you commence to notice the lines a man's got round his eyes and mouth and think about the hopeful way his parents gave a special name to him when he was born into this world, you might as well give up" your anger.[1]

Christians are called to be kind because every person we meet—the tired woman at the cash register, the man asleep on a bench in the bus station, the child who brings home a less-than-ideal report card, the friend who lets us down, even our enemies—every person we meet is a person who is fighting a tough fight and also a person cherished and loved by God as a son or daughter.

(b) Our passage from 2 Peter puts it this way: "Whoever does not show kindness to other people is blind and shortsighted," seeing people only at the surface.

Christians are called to let the future happen in the present. What is this future we have to let happen? What we have been told about the future is a picture of a great feast with Jesus Christ as the host. Gathered around the table are rich and poor, old and young, black and white, all feasting on the grace of God. There is the woman from the grocery store . . . our sister. There is the rude man from down the street . . . now our brother. There is the person we used to call enemy now sharing with us the meal of joy. There we are at this feast table, and how did we get there? Because we deserved it? No, we got there the way every other person gets there, by the rich grace of God in Jesus Christ. People who don't show kindness, says 2 Peter, have simply forgotten that we, too, are sinners cleansed by the grace of God.

III. Second Peter tells us that kindness

[1]Frederick Buechner, *Love Feast,* (San Francisco, Harper & Row, 1984), 156.

is a violation of the world, and I think we should be clear that what Peter is telling us is that Christians are called to be kind not because being kind is sugar and spice, sweetness and light, and everything nice but because kindness is a kind of Christian civil disobedience. The world teaches us to be self-sufficient, get all we can, deal with our own problems, and leave other people to their own devices unless they get in our way. But that is not the way God treats people. Second Peter says that by being kind we participate in the very nature of God. We learn who God is, and the world learns, too.

The world might even end up getting saved . . . through kindness. Through kindness, said Peter, you show the very nature of God. As Henry James once said to his young nephew, "There are three things important in human life. Be kind . . . be kind . . . be kind."—Thomas G. Long

Illustrations

THE FRUIT OF KINDNESS. Nobody is kind to only one person at once, but to many persons in one.—Frederick W. Faber

MULTIPLYING OUR POWER. All the kindness that a man puts out into the world works on the heart and thoughts of mankind, but we are so foolishly indifferent that we are never in earnest in the matter of kindness. We want to topple a great load over and yet will not avail ourselves of a lever that would multiply our power a hundredfold.—Albert Schweitzer

WHAT CONVINCES PEOPLE. If any group of Christians who claims to believe and practice all God has said in his Book will face up to their personal responsibility within the family of Christ and to the real needs of Christians around them, their church will impress its community with the shining goodness of God's love—to them *and* among them. Such a transformation probably would do more to attract others to Jesus Christ than any house-to-house canvass, evangelistic campaign, or new church facility. People are hungry for acceptance, love, and friends, and unless they find them in the church they may not stay there long enough to become personally related to Jesus Christ.

People are not persuaded—they're attracted. We must be able to communicate far more by what we are than by what we say.—Marion Jacobsen

Sermon Suggestions

GOD WAITS—AND WAITS! TEXT: Luke 13:1–9. (1) The need for repentance cannot be explained by selective punishment or accident. (2) All have sinned and all must repent. (3) God is patiently at work in the stubborn soil of human hearts to bring about a harvest of change and fruitfulness.

THE WAY OUT. TEXT: 1 Cor. 10:1–13. (1) The message of history and experience is this: sin does not pay, verses 1–11. (2) We, too, are vulnerable and can bring on ourselves dire results, verse 12. (3) Nevertheless, we can be assured that (a) our testing is a common human experience, (b) God will not test us beyond our strength, and (c) God will faithfully see us through our ordeal, verse 13.

Worship Aids

CALL TO WORSHIP. "O God, . . . because thy lovingkindness is better than life, my lips shall praise thee" (Ps. 63: 1, 3).

INVOCATION. Shepherd God, you know your own, and your own know you. Your sheep recognize your voice and follow you. You are no hireling; the love you share, like the love you inspire, beggars all wealth except the harmonies of the resonant heart.

You come to shepherd us to the pasture of life, not coerced but graced, not alone but in the strength of the called and the joy of the loved. Open our hearts to hear you more clearly, and to see, in sheep not of this fold, and in ourselves, your yearning and your grace.—Peter Fribley

OFFERTORY SENTENCE. "And God, who supplies seed for the sower and bread to eat, will also supply you with all the seed you need and will make it grow and produce a rich harvest from your generosity" (2 Cor. 9:10 TEV).

OFFERTORY PRAYER. Father, we have often failed you, but you have never failed us. Provision for our lives has come to us in abundance from many quarters. In gratitude we come this morning to express something of our appreciation for gifts given as well as to provide means to care for the needs of others. Take these offerings we bring and bless them that they may be used for the glory of your kingdom among people.—Henry Fields

PRAYER. We praise you, O Father, for this privilege to worship among your people. What a joy to experience the unity of the Spirit in the bonds of peace! For this house of the interpreter where your Word is so faithfully taught and preached, we give you thanks. We praise you for a faith for all seasons—a faith that even gives us songs in the night to sing. As John proclaimed hope for the believer in his generation facing the night of persecution, "The Lord God omnipotent reigns," so he assures hope for us whatever our "dark night of the soul" may be.

Today and every day, may we live in the power of Christ's Resurrection:

Loving with a love that perseveres in the face of every estrangement—

Hoping when all but hope is lost—

Trusting in your faithfulness even when life appears to us godforsaken—

Celebrating life in the presence of death.

In this assembly may we affirm and celebrate that we *are* the Body of Christ. May we realize with sensitivity the intimacy of our relatedness to one another—that if one member suffers, the whole Body suffers; that if one member rejoices, the whole Body rejoices. We lift to you, O Father, those persons we have named in special need: give us the love and will to make that call, to speak that word, to send that card, to pray that prayer, that their faith may be deepened and encouraged in the face of precarious health or flagging spirit or haunting loneliness.

For those who have the awe-full responsibility of governing others—full of awe because they have no power except that it comes from you—grant wisdom: the love of truth and justice, that all peoples may know life, not death.—John Thompson

LECTIONARY MESSAGE

Topic: Find Him!

TEXT: Isa. 55:1–9

OTHER READINGS: 1 Cor. 10:1–13; Luke 13:1–9

Simple questions often result in the discovery of profound truths. Isaiah's call (Isa. 55:6) gives rise to deceptively simple questions. Spiritual deafness will prevent many from hearing the question. Sin or a preoccupation with business and worldly affairs will prevent others. Those, however, who are concerned about their spiritual welfare will attempt to answer the questions with sincerity and honesty.

I. Why search for God? Isaiah's call is addressed to those who have no religious or spiritual dimension to their life and who are so preoccupied with worldly affairs that they neglect the worship and service of God and indeed their own salvation (v. 2). Isaiah's warning reminds us of Jesus' admonition: "What does it profit a man [or woman] to gain the whole world and forfeit his [her] life?" (Mark 8:36).

Finding God, however, is everyone's wish. Many people regard religion, and not least the Christian faith, as an unnecessary burden. Finding God, and being found by him, would involve them in obligations and a way of life that they would find tedious and inhibiting. Isaiah reminds us that finding God, instead of bringing us irksome duties and responsibilities, enables us to experience true joy and happiness (v. 2).

II. Where will we find God? The obvious answer, especially from Christians, is in the Bible, in prayer, and in the sacraments. Countless men and women have found God in these ways. God's presence, however, cannot be limited and pin-pointed like this. Until recently, God was thought of as being in "heaven." Indeed, space travel encouraged the belief that when astronauts succeeded in ascending high enough into the sky, they would eventually reach heaven and see God! The Russian astronauts and others have put an end to that expectation. On their return to earth from outer space they reported, "We have seen no sign of God!" No longer does the three-decker concept of earth sandwiched between heaven and hell carry conviction.

God is no longer conceived as "localized" or limited by space and time. The psalmist is much nearer the truth when he exclaims, "Whither shall I go from thy Spirit, or whither shall I flee from thy presence?" (Ps. 139:7). How can the psalmist hope to escape from the presence of God, since God is everywhere? This may be an awesome thought for the psalmist, but it is encouraging news for those who seek God! The truth is that God is everywhere, not least in situations and experiences involving pain and suffering. If you ever doubt this, look at the cross. On the cross, God was in Christ redeeming the world. Perhaps one of the most important tasks for the preacher is to learn how to recognize God's presence in every situation and experience. Not only the preacher needs to develop this "eye of faith"; those who listen to the preacher must also cultivate the ability.

III. When shall we find God? Many people have searched for God without success. This sense of failure has sometimes led them to question God's love and God's existence. This is no new experience. All Job longed for was to feel, for just a moment, the reassuring touch of God's hand (Job 22:3). Given that, he was prepared to bear any pain and face any darkness. Many share Job's anguish. Who does not pray that in the hour of death we may walk with God? Happy is the man or woman or child who can say with sincerity, "Yea, though I walk through the valley of the shadow of death, I will fear no evil for you [God] are with me" (Ps. 23:4).

When will we find God? There is no secret involved, nor is it a matter of luck. We will find God when we are prepared to fall on our knees and pray, "God, be merciful to me a sinner" (Luke 18:13). When we commit ourselves to God's mercy, we find not only God but also the good news that God is a God of love!—Eric Young

SUNDAY: MARCH TWENTY-SIXTH

SERVICE OF WORSHIP

Sermon: Playing to God

TEXT: Matt. 6:1–4, 16–18

Methodist Bishop Gerald Kennedy engaged the issue of hypocrisy in the church with a shocking confession: "Of course there are hypocrites . . . as there ought to be." More than hypocrisy, the bishop feared apathy. When no one cares to make a pretense of religious piety, the church is in real trouble. Kennedy then observed that there are probably more hypocrites at the opera than in church on any given week. His word to the folks who stay away from church because of the hypocrites was, "There is always room for one more. So why don't you come and join them?" Is the sermon of Jesus null and void? If hypocrisy and pretense are essential to life in the church, again it seems that Christ was calling us to the impossible. Jesus had a lower toleration for the hypocrisy of the Pharisees than he did for the gross immorality of the prostitute and the thief. The audience is important—the audience to whom we offer our acts of piety and the audience to whom Jesus addressed the sermon. This is a message to disciples about the righteousness of the kingdom, not to sinners about the need for the church. Jesus was preaching to the choir, but somehow we get the impression that the folks on the inside had room to grow.

I. The world is a stage. Jesus addressed the three primary modes of worship in Jewish life—the offering, prayer, and fasting. The worship of God is not a three-ring circus in which we perform to the thrill of the crowd. Nothing is wrong with giving, prayer, or fasting, but everything is wrong with the purpose and motivation of going on stage every time one enters the worship of God. Shakespeare made hypocrites of all of us: "All the world's a stage, and all the men and women merely players: They have their exits and their entrances; And one man in his time plays many parts." Aren't we all just actors playing out our roles in life?

The word *hypocrite* came out of Greek theater. It was the word for an actor playing a specific role. It did not necessarily imply dishonesty except as it was applied to relationships in daily life outside the theater. A good hypocrite—that is, a good actor—might be so immersed in his role that he forgets that he is playing a part and loses touch with his real identity. In the synagogue, the amount donated and the name of the donor were announced, and perhaps Jesus is referring to the trumpets that called attention to exceptionally large gifts. Others have noted the trumpet shape of the conduit to the offering box. Small coins can make a lot of noise. The motive for giving was to hear the gasp of approval from one's peers. The motive for fasting was to create the hungry look in order to impress the neighbors. Fasting was a significant part of worship, but not as an exercise in ascetic, self-inflicted punishment. Jesus taught self-denial, but his cause was higher than human praise. To keep the actions of one hand from the other is obviously a figurative statement intended to challenge the pious play for reward.

II. What is your role? During an era when the fad of self-discovery created a generation of pilgrims in search of themselves, a popular journal of psychology suggested that our personalities are like onions—layer upon layer of fronts created for the diversity of roles that we play. We live in a superficial world of tinsel and images. If we cannot find a true self under the layers, maybe we ought to look at the superficiality of our world rather than the difficulty of the search. Bishop of Woolwich John A. T. Robinson declared that the world had come of age. *Honest to God* was a bombshell for traditional Christianity. He suggested that we lay aside the use of the word *God* for awhile until we recover the reality behind the word. He suggested that prayer might be interpersonal dialogue and that the new ethics would lay aside law in preference for radical love—a new morality. A parody on the book, *How to Become a Bishop Without Being Religious,* only slightly distorted the bishop's picture of honesty.

As in the call to be salt and light, Jesus asked nothing more or less than that people be who they are. The Pharisees may have been paragons of virtue measured against their peers, but Jesus persisted in preference for the notorious sinners of his day. Was he trying to shock his audience into radical holiness? Jesus must have found a crude kind of honesty and lack of pretense beyond improvement, and they were. However, they were not honest. They had played a role for so long that they lost themselves in the process. As they played to the applause of the spectators, they thought they were worshiping God. Truth got lost somewhere in the shuffle.

III. Who is your audience? Without an audience, the stage has no purpose and the role has no meaning. Jesus addressed the question of rewards. What is the pay for being good? I am gratified to know that "What's in it for me?" is not a modern judgment of value. Rewards center in applause. Who is your audience? For whom do you act out your role? Everyone plays to someone. Playing to peers is indeed rewarding, but not enough. It is far too easy to set our standards on the basis of the neighbors' behavior rather than the high calling of Christ to the perfection of God, but something is wrong at the core of playing for applause. The very moment we begin to play to the approval of our peers, we have lost sight of our audience. Jesus calls his disciples to play only to God.

The very word *pious* drips with that sickening sweet flavor of saccharin. Here is the key to true piety. We are prone to throw out the baby with the bath. In our struggle to be honest to God, we hear a call to give up religion. Not so! The acid test of religion is the audience to whom we offer our gifts, our prayers, and our personal sacrifices. Bishop Kennedy was right. There is a little hypocrisy in every act of worship. We never come before God with absolutely pure motives, but the only audience that matters knows our hearts.—Larry Dipboye

Illustrations

FOR THE LOVE OF GOD. Lucien Coleman tells this story about Nicholas Herman, a seventeenth-century French monk known as "Brother Lawrence." This humble lay brother led an obscure existence among the pots and pans of his monastic kitchen. A personal acquaintance described him as "a great awkward fellow, who broke everything." He experienced no visions and had no remarkable religious experiences, but he was profoundly conscious of the continual presence of God at all times and in every circumstance. He had a natural aversion to kitchen work, but he undertook this task with gladness of heart, for everything he did there was done for the love of God and in a spirit of prayer. His workplace became a worship place. "The time of business," he said, "does not with me differ from the time of prayer, and in the noise and clatter of my kitchen, while several persons are at the same time calling for different things, I possess God in as great tranquility as if I were upon my knees at the Blessed Sacrament." He summed up this basic attitude in a little book entitled *The Practice of the Presence of God* (still in publication today).

GOD DECIDES. For years, when our sons were boys of, say, six to ten, my wife took them every week to an Episcopal Sunday school, even though I got weary of (sometimes really annoyed by) some of the pieties the children brought home. They got quite immersed in that formal religious life—but one of our sons, on a Palm Sunday afternoon, made me forever a fan of such educational experience, because out of it, with wonderful irony, came this considered assertion: "There's religion and there's the Spirit." Whence *that* idea? Our ten-year-old answered, "St. Paul talked about 'the letter and the spirit,' the difference, and the teacher said you can go to church all the time and obey every [church] law, and you're not really right in what you do, you're not spiritual." We asked him how we could know if we were being spiritual, not just religious, and he promptly said, "It's up to God to decide, not us."—Robert Coles

Sermon Suggestions

OF THE FATHER'S LOVE. TEXT: Luke 15:1–3, 11b–32. Religious leaders criticize Jesus for his associating with tax collectors and sinners, and Jesus answers with a parable. The father is the main player in the drama. (1) The father reaches out to a guilt-ridden, down-and-out younger son. (2) The father reaches out to a self-righteous, up-and-out older son. (3) The response of the younger son is clear and full of gratitude; the immediate response of the older son is likewise clear, but it is bitter and resentful, yet the ultimate response remains in doubt.

WHEN THE MANNA STOPS. TEXT: Josh. 5:9–12. There come times when we have to live our lives under drastically changed conditions. (1) Matters may get better, and maturity is required to handle our success. (2) Matters may get worse, and faith and courage are required to work through our struggle. (3) In either case, it can be a new and promising beginning with God.

Worship Aids

CALL TO WORSHIP. "Happy the man whose fault is forgiven, whose sin is blotted out; happy the man who Yahweh accuses of no guilt, whose spirit is incapable of deceit!" (Ps. 32:1 JB).

INVOCATION. Almighty God, enter our worship with authority, speak to our hearts with clarity, and give us over to words and deeds of charity, in Jesus' name.—E. Lee Phillips

OFFERTORY SENTENCE. "And God is able to give you more than you need, so that you will always have all you need for yourselves and more than enough for every good cause" (2 Cor. 9:8 TEV).

OFFERTORY PRAYER. Lord, forgive our blindness in the face of need and our approval in the face of greed. Turn us from that which turns us from thee and bring us to a generous offering and a holy dedication, through Christ our Lord.—E. Lee Phillips

PRAYER. Gracious Lord, here we are again, and it is a weekly miracle, all the things that delight us, all that is comforting and hopeful, all that enables us to start over again and believe. And even if we do not believe, here we are, and how shall we say why? By what means do you draw us toward you even as we run so hard from you? Is it our desperate need to get through the day? Is it habit? Is it the dutiful child within?

It is all these things, but is it all these things only? Is it not your Spirit within our spirit, your life within our life, like the ocean within the rain? Do not our hearts long for you, as the hooded falcon longs for the sky, as the refugee longs to stop running, as all mortals long for the open border of a forgiving heart?

Whatever it is that draws us toward you, it is a miracle, weekly observed, and here we are, and we are glad.—Peter Fribley

LECTIONARY MESSAGE

Topic: Christian Diplomats

TEXT: 2 Cor. 5:16–21

OTHER READINGS: Josh. 2:9–12; Luke 15:1–3, 11b–32

Young people are often asked these questions: "What would you like to be? What kind of job would you like to do in life?" The answer differs enormously. Although in a recession, and at a time of vast unemployment, most people would settle for almost any job, modesty would probably deter most of us from mentioning the diplomatic service as our great ambition in life. To be a diplomat and perhaps represent our country at the United Nations would seem at best a wild dream, or pious hope, or at worst a terrible display of arrogance and pride. Yet, says St. Paul, we have been called to join the diplomatic service, since everyone who has been signed with the cross in holy baptism has been made an ambassador for Christ (v. 20).

I. Our authority. Who gives us this authority to speak on behalf of Christ, to speak on his behalf and preach in his name? Let there be no mistake about this—our authority is from God, given to us by Jesus Christ through the church. There is no such thing as a freelance ambassador. Nor indeed have we volunteered! We are called and sent by Christ. Whatever we say and do is said and done in his name and for his sake. Human instrumentality plays a very important role in God's plan. Generally speaking, God works through people.

II. Our responsibility. It is right that we should pray God's blessing on the work of the United Nations and on all organizations working for peace. The ministry of reconciliation is greatly needed in a world torn apart by violence and bloodshed. Ambassadors have an enormous responsibility, and none more than those of us who have been appointed ambassadors for Christ. In a very real sense, every Christian shares with Christ responsibility for the salvation of the world. Only through the cross can men and women come to experience peace with God and with each other.

III. The art of diplomacy. People disagree, arguments occur, fighting breaks out, and greed takes over. True diplomacy calls for quiet determination, great tact, and not a little charm! These are the qualities required not just for an effective preacher but for every Christian, if we are to bring others to the saving knowledge of Jesus Christ. Angry debate, bullying tactics, and a disgruntled manner have never brought anyone to Christ. Indeed, the best advertisement for the Christian faith is the person who mirrors in his or her life something of the quiet determination, tact, and charm of Jesus Christ—God's great ambassador!

IV. The reward. Most people entering the diplomatic service can look forward to a high salary, splendid "perks," and a delightful house in which to live during their term of office. Christian diplomats—ambassadors for Christ—must not expect such rewards, even for long and devoted service. On the contrary, their lot may be an inadequate income and to live and work in an unpleasant place among difficult and unfriendly people. During his own ministry, Jesus accepted the dignity of reflection. So must every one of his ambassadors. Those, however, who persevere and faithfully proclaim the king's message will be rewarded when on their return home Jesus will commend their diligence: "Well done, thou good and faithful servant." There can be no greater reward than this, as one day you will find out!—Eric Young

SUNDAY: APRIL SECOND

SERVICE OF WORSHIP

Sermon: Who Could Be Against Jesus?

At this time of the year I often find myself wondering about the grim part of the Christian story, the way in which Jesus was treated during the final weeks of his mortal life. What bothers me is the conflict between the clear record that almost everyone turned against him and the modern assumption that nearly everyone admires Jesus and has nothing but good to say about him. If we say that no one is against Jesus now, may it not be that we haven't really understood what it was that brought him to his cross?

I suggest that a careful reading of the story, of the words and actions of Jesus, and of the response of different sections of the population might reveal to us the answer to the haunting question, "Who could be against Jesus?"

I. First, I am struck by the fact that in the early chapters of the Gospels Jesus is shown to be avoiding as much as possible the adulation of the crowds and the leadership role they seem to be thrusting upon him.

(a) An alarming story about the execution of John the Baptist is followed by Jesus' words to his disciples, who had just returned from an exciting missionary tour: "Let us go off by ourselves to some place where we will be alone" (Mark 6:31). But he has trouble shaking off the crowds, and you sense in these passages the tension between his desire to avoid the pressure of the crowd and his tremendous compassion.

(b) Then we find him moving about the country a great deal, never staying long enough anywhere for a mass movement to form behind him. He discourages any talk about his being Messiah. Why?

One reason relates to the Roman authorities, who could easily become his dangerous enemy. But there is a more important reason for the reluctance of Jesus to rouse the crowds. You can be against Jesus, or his church, because you see him as a menace to the established order. You can also be against him when you misinterpret his message and the meaning of his kingdom. He seems to have sensed in the attitude of the crowds what you might call religion for the wrong reasons.

(c) It is during this period that Jesus reveals himself more and more to those who are closest to him. Time and again he takes the disciples apart, and at least three times he tells them of his coming trial and death. At the same time as he speaks of his rejection, there are increasing revelations of the mystery of his being Son of God. It is as though Jesus were telling those who had eyes to see and ears to hear: "Look! Listen! This is the kind of Christ I am—not the political leader that some want, not the miracle worker who satisfies the crowd, not the avenging Messiah who burns up the wicked and sets up his kingdom with invincible force, but the Son of God who is willing to suffer in order to liberate the world." And when Peter would have none of it, Jesus does not hesitate to call him an enemy: "Get away from me, Satan. Your thoughts are men's thoughts, not God's!" (Matt. 16:23).

II. Now I want to turn to a remark of Jesus that comes almost as a parenthesis in the story of the boat and the bread. Under his breath we hear Jesus saying: "Look out, and be on your guard against the yeast of the Pharisees and the yeast of Herod."

(a) Who were these Pharisees, and why were they against him? Mark's use of the word to denote people who were fanatical defenders of the external rites of religion but inwardly corrupt, hardhearted, and proud led to the word *Pharisee* being used in common speech as the equivalent of *hypocrite*. This is unfair to a sect of Judaism that did much to preserve its great traditions during a period of laxity and demoralization. When Jesus warned of "the yeast of the Pharisees," he was talking of one particular group that had resisted him from the beginning, that had attacked him for his compassionate disregard for the Sabbath laws, that had objected to the low company he kept, and that finally saw him as a deceiver of the common people whom they were trying to keep in line.

In attacking this perverted religion of outward forms and rigid rules, Jesus stood in the line of the great Hebrew prophets. Who could actually hate this man who spoke of God's kingdom, who healed, and who banished the demons? Only, apparently, those whose brand of religion was offended by his offer of salvation to all and sundry, by his healing done on the Sabbath day, and by one who was thought by some to be an exorcist in league with the devil to do such things. That is the record. It was the hyperreligious—not the scallywags, the harlots, or the rough Roman soldiers—who were furiously against Jesus.

Is there nothing in us today that, perhaps secretly, corresponds to this hostility to Jesus? Do we never find ourselves longing for a quiet and orderly religion that will not be disturbed by the flaming demands of Christ's love? Are we easily outraged by persons or movements that seem to threaten the religious structure in which we feel secure? Is it possible that we too may let the religious institution or our code of moral behavior at times smother the spirit of Jesus? You and I know the answer to these questions, so once again we must look within.

(b) What was that other yeast working against Jesus, the Herodians? All the Herods were equally obnoxious and corrupt. The one who had John the Baptist's head cut off was Herod Antipas, the tetrarch of Galilee. He was half-Jewish and ruled by favor of the Roman emperor, with whom he was careful to keep on good terms. The political party that supported him in his policy of detente with the Romans had the name "Herodians," and from the Gospels we can derive a rough picture of the kind of people they were. Herod himself stood for a life of personal words; he was privately a rogue and politically a twister. Jesus, according to Luke, once referred to him in passing as "that fox." This puppet king represented a way of life that was totally opposed to that of the Pharisees and also totally opposed to the mission of Jesus.

Those who were against Jesus included not only the fanatically and rigidly religious but also those who cared nothing about the kingdom of God, laughed at the moral demands of the Sermon on the Mount, and carved out for themselves a kingdom of sensuality, profligacy, extravagance, and vice.

III. These, then, are some of the answers to the question, "Who can be against Jesus?" We can follow him on that last journey to Jerusalem and see him on his cross only if we realize the subtle forces around us, and in us, that really oppose him. May we experience this Lent the expulsive power of his sacrificial love in our own hearts and accept the challenge to be always on his side.—David H. C. Read

Illustrations

WHY JESUS CAME. Jesus Christ is come not only to show us the true man but also to tell us God's purpose to remake us in our lost image. That you shall become. Moreover, you shall be like Jesus Christ, who has gone into eternity. "It doth not yet appear what we shall be: but we know that, when he shall appear, we shall be like him."

That is the glad message of the gospel. We suffer most from ourselves, even when we do not realize it, even when we suppose the cause of our grief and suffering is from without. The deepest cause of all that is not right is that we ourselves are not right. And therefore that is the greatest message that we can hear—things will be right with you. Ponder how a blind man must feel when he is told, "You will receive your sight again," or when a cripple is told, "You will be straight and strong again!" And this is only external! We are to become internally right again, straight and strong and fine through God's grace. "Rejoice with exceeding joy." That is the message of the Son of man.—Emil Brunner

JESUS' HARD TRUTHS. See thou how by degrees he withdraws us from the things that now are and at greater length introduces what he hath to say, touching voluntary poverty, and casts down the dominion of covetousness?

For he was not contented with his former sayings, many and great as they were, but he adds others also, more and more alarming.

For what can be more alarming than what he now says, if indeed we are for our riches to fall from the service of Christ? Or what more to be desired, if indeed, by despising wealth, we shall have our affection toward him and our charity perfect? For what I am continually repeating, the same do I now say likewise, namely, that by both kinds he presses the hearer to obey his sayings; both by the profitable, and by the hurtful; much like an excellent physician, pointing out both the disease that is the consequence of neglect and the good health that results from obedience.—St. John Chrysostom

Sermon Suggestions

AN AGE-OLD DILEMMA. TEXT: John 12:1–8. (1) Then: Mary's costly act of devotion to Jesus gave rise to discussion of the priority in the use of money. (2) Always: Debate goes on and on over practicality versus the spiritual or aesthetic. (3) Now: (a) The needs of the poor are forever with us and must be addressed. (b) While exploitation of the needs of the poor by a few dishonest promoters of various charities is a worthy concern, it is no excuse for our doing nothing. (c) There are times and places in which we may have to make painful choices, so as to do sometimes the "practical," sometimes the "impractical."

WHEN GOD DOES "A NEW THING." TEXT: Isa. 43:16–21. (1) It is because he is forever committed to us in covenant. (2) It is in response to a new need. (3) It happens in ways that contradict ordinary human expectation. (4) God is glorified in what he does.

Worship Aids

CALL TO WORSHIP. "Those who sow in tears will reap with songs of joy" (Ps. 126:5 REB).

INVOCATION. In this service of worship, O Lord, grant that we may once again see beyond the difficulties of the days, hours, or moments and catch a fresh vision of the meaning of our lives and rejoice in your glorious purposes working out among us and in us.

OFFERTORY SENTENCE. "Honour the Lord with your wealth and with the firstfruits of all your produce" (Prov. 3:9 REB).

OFFERTORY PRAYER. Lord, you have been gracious to us in providing for our needs and for the needs of others through us. Grant to us the willingness to be partners with you in blessing others and causes beyond our personal pleasures.

PRAYER. Your love is an everlasting love, Father. From the moment we were born, you have cradled and sustained us. And even when we pass from this life into your kingdom, your love will keep us, protect us, and provide for our every need throughout eternity. Teach us how to love each other with that same kind of faithful endurance. We ask for the compassion of our Lord toward those whom we do not even know—those who are hungry and homeless and helpless.

But most of all, we ask that you would help us truly love those with whom we live and work day in and day out. Help us to be patient with people even when they are foolish and silly and annoying. Make us at all times courteous and thoughtful and kind. Help us never to look at another person with contempt or disrespect. Help us never to grudge other people their possessions or successes but to be as glad for them as if they were our own. Lord, keep us from sulking when we do not get our own way. Help us not to be irritable and difficult to live with.

Our life, the world we live in, and the relationships we cherish are gifts, Father, and we thank you for them. Forgive us for the times when we do not see the wonder of it all—when our pride, our self-centeredness, our worries, and our fears blind us to your amazing grace. Mold us more in the image of Christ our Lord, who never lost sight of the gift.

You have loved us without limit, O God. Teach us how to love like that. Through Jesus Christ we pray.—Gary C. Redding

LECTIONARY MESSAGE

Topic: No Waiting!

TEXT: Phil. 3:4b–14

OTHER READINGS: Isa. 43:16–21; John 12:1–8

I. It's a hard life! Many people find it so. The reasons may vary, but the conflict is real. Every day we see on our television screens pictures of people living under the most difficult conditions. Men, women, and children starving to death. Others hounded, raped, and savaged by hostile armies. For them, it is indeed a hard life. Less dramatic, but no less real, are the sufferings of the unemployed, the lonely, and the destitute. Even those fortunate enough to have employment are under stress and pressure. They find the business world nothing more than an updated version of jungle warfare. Domestic violence, greed, and selfishness add to the misery. The reasons may differ, but the conflict is real and often so bitter that many turn to drugs and alcoholism in an attempt to escape from their unhappiness. Too often, suicide is seen as the last resort. Many lose hope, for it's a hard life!

II. Who wants to live forever? The answer is, not many people. Certainly not nearly so many as one might think! It's a hard life, so much so that only a fool would want the pain and suffering to continue forever. For countless people, the possibility of living forever is anything but good news! Instead, it's a frightening and appalling prospect, to be feared rather than welcomed. Little wonder that many people will have nothing to do with the church if this is its good news—if this is all that the Christian gospel has to offer, the possibility of living forever. Many would say no thank you!

III. Victorious living. There is no denying it. The Resurrection of Christ does mean that death is not the end, so through the risen Lord we are offered the possibility of living forever. However, Christ's Resurrection offers us something much more important than the possibility of living forever. It offers us the possibility of victorious living! This is what people are looking for—the power to overcome the trials and pressures of life. Through the power of the Resurrection, we are offered a new kind, a new quality of life. The Bible calls it eternal life. Eternal life is often thought of as something that belongs to the future. Something that begins when this life ends. Eternal life, or the Resurrection life, as it is sometimes called, is not just a mere extension of this present life. It is not something to which men and women pass automatically when their struggle here is over. The Resurrection offers us a new quality of life. It is this kind or quality of life to which St. Paul refers when he says "that I may know him, and the power of his resurrection" (v. 10). Eternal life then is not so much "life forever" as life worth living forever, in other words, the possibility of victorious living. At the very center of the Christian gospel is the belief that through the Resurrection, Jesus conquered sin and evil, even death itself. The risen Lord offers us the power to share in that victory. This was St. Paul's prayer, as it must be ours, that he might know Christ and through fellowship with the risen Lord have the power to live out this new quality of life.

Through fellowship with the risen Lord and through the power of his Resurrection, your life can be transformed, redeemed, made perfect. You can experience victorious living today. There is no waiting! Accept Jesus as your Lord and Savior. It's as easy as that. Try it . . . now!—Eric Young

SUNDAY: APRIL NINTH

SERVICE OF WORSHIP

Sermon: Things That Money Cannot Buy

TEXT: Isa. 55:1

Long ago Isaiah cried to his people, "He that hath no money; come ye, buy, and eat; yea, come, buy wine and milk without money and without price." Long ago Jesus pled for the unpurchasable treasures of the spirit that moth and rust cannot consume or thieves break through and steal. Nevertheless, while this emphasis on the things that money cannot buy is not new, there is urgent contemporary need of its recovery.

It is a good thing to have money and the things that money can buy, but is *that* the emphasis needed here today? "Man," said Jesus, "man shall not live by bread alone"—that thought is crowded out. Treasures that moth and rust cannot consume or thieves break through and steal—they are crowded out.

I. In the first place, then, consider that the deepest differences between persons lie in the things that money cannot purchase.

(a) Here, for example, is a cynic. He sees no sense in life.

Here on the other side is a far different sort of man, who has kept his zest. Life for him has been hard enough, tragic even, but it has had meaning. He might even say with Epictetus, "Bring whatever you please, and I will turn it into *good,*" or with Paul, "To them that love God all things work together for good," and as for his epitaph, it is far different from the cynic's, for at his life's end he says, "I have fought the good fight, I have finished the course, I have kept the faith."

That difference between men who keep their zest and those who lose it is one of the most significant in human experience. You cannot explain that difference in terms of anything that money can buy. A cynic may die in a palace. Paul died a prisoner. The deep faiths, the spiritual insights, the inward resources of personal power, the strong companionships of the soul—these factors that make all things work together for good are not for sale, not listed in any market, not rated on any exchange. They move in the unpurchasable realm.

(b) Despite our exaggerated popular theories of economic determinism, this holds, I think, of all the profoundest differences between people. A life burdened by a sense of guilt and shame versus a clear conscience that can look the whole world in the face—what a difference that is! And always the same truth emerges: you cannot buy in any market a clear conscience or genuine affection or inward spiritual power or deathless hope. They move in the unpurchasable realm.

(c) Jesus cared about the poor and constantly emphasized his concern for them, but Jesus did not worry half so much about the moral estate of the poor as he did about the moral estate of the rich. He feared the possession of money as a major peril. We are all concerned about that portion of the American population lacking money enough for decent livelihood. Were Jesus here, he also would be concerned about that problem of penury. But he would be more concerned about the moral estate of us who do have money enough for a decent livelihood.

If we do not take account of this, all our economic utopias will turn out to be failures. Be sure of that! Imagine, if you can, a world where monetary abundance belongs to all, everything that cash can get in the hands of all, every man and woman able to say to his soul, "Soul, thou hast much goods laid up for many years; take thine ease, eat, drink, be merry," but where the things that money cannot buy have been neglected, forgotten, lost. What a hell it would be! Underscore this: *everything that money can buy depends for its ultimate worth, for the purpose it serves for its final effect on human life, upon the things that money cannot buy.* There, in the unpurchasable realms of the spirit, lie the determinants of human destiny.

II. In the second place, consider that this truth, if we take it in earnest, throws the responsibility for what our lives are to mean inwardly upon ourselves.

(a) Obsession with the economic aspects of life creates the idea that money makes the man, so that if one lacks money one is tempted to think oneself a failure or to blame lack of character on lack of means, or in general to be discouraged and at loose ends. Poverty does profoundly affect character. Who can know anything about slums and doubt that?

But we cannot tell where great character is coming from, from penury or plenty. Gautama Buddha came from a king's palace. Jesus Christ came from a carpenter's shop. Lincoln and Gladstone emerged at the same time, born in the same year, one with very little that money could buy, but both with a strong hold on the things that money cannot buy.

(b) Put it this way: possession is one thing; ownership is another. Some people possess much and own little; some people possess little and own much. Possession concerns things that can be bought and sold; ownership concerns values that money cannot buy. I am not saying these two are unrelated or that possession does not matter. I am saying those two things are different. Happy the man who has been inwardly liberated from the too clamorous insistence of possession and who really lives in the wide ranges of spiritual ownership.

III. Finally, see how straight our truth leads to one of the deepest needs of our generation, the need for a redefinition of success. Our fathers may have cried in earnest, "What must I do to be saved?" but our generation has been reared to cry, "What must I do to succeed?"

(a) Here, I suspect, is the most difficult problem we face when we try to be really Christian. Here in the church we are supposed to be concerned with things that money cannot buy. These unpurchasable treasures of the soul we would get for ourselves and hand on to our children, but out there in the world, what tremendous pressures of ambition and desire move in another direction toward the things that money can buy!

(b) When it is a question of money, all men are not of the same religion. On that point Judas Iscariot and Jesus Christ were not of the same faith. In a long ministry I have known many a businessman to sacrifice gain, position, and sometimes all apparent promise of an economic future for conscience' sake. Yet the temptation is terrific to say, "What must we do to succeed?" and then to define success in financial terms. Wanted, men and women not for sale! More than anything else in the world today, in the pulpit, in business, in public life, wanted, men and women not for sale! But on only one condition can such men and women come. They must be persons who within themselves have centered and grounded their life in the things that money cannot buy.

(c) Stand for a moment before the

cross of Christ! We cannot pay for that. Such a free gift of life moves in the unpurchasable realm. So the whole weight of the gospel presses home our truth. It is a good thing to have money and the things that money can buy, but it is a good thing to check up once in a while and make sure that we have not lost the things that money cannot buy.—Harry Emerson Fosdick

Illustrations

THINGS AND THINGS. I can remember my mother, under economic pressure, weeping because once more she had to lower another notch the level of expenditures in our family, but I had a lovely home. And I see today households with everything cash can get that in comparison awaken my pity or disgust. Granted the importance of purchasable things to the family, yet in the long run it is the things that money cannot purchase, listed in no market, rated on no exchange, that determine what the family will really be.—Harry Emerson Fosdick

WHAT REALLY MATTERS. Once when I had not seen Mother for some time, I made a trip to her home in Florida. I was very happy as I approached the house. Of course she was waiting for me. Before I could get to the house with my bags, she ran out on the lawn, and I expected her to say how glad she was to see me. But no.

"Nels," she said, her first greeting after this long absence, "can I think anything too good about God?"

Surprised, I said, "No, Mother, of course you can't."

"Then," she said, "nothing else matters."—Nels F. S. Ferre

Sermon Suggestions

WHEN WE TEACH FOR GOD. TEXT: Isa. 50:4–9a. (1) We must be first taught by God. (2) We must be prepared for rejection by those we would teach. (3) We must continue our task with assurance of God's help and vindication.

THINKING LIKE CHRIST JESUS. TEXT: Phil. 2:5–11. (1) The problem: envy and selfish ambition. (2) The solution: self-giving, after the example and spirit of Christ Jesus. (3) The reward: the approval of God and the achievement of glory for God.

Worship Aids

CALL TO WORSHIP. "Look on your servant with kindness; save me in your constant love" (Ps. 31:16 TEV).

INVOCATION. Lord, as we walk with Jesus to the cross and view him in his sacrificial love, help us to remember that love did not die with him but was made more alive and universal than the world had ever known.

OFFERTORY SENTENCE. "Do not be troubled, then, and cry, 'What are we to eat?' or 'What are we to drink?' or 'How are we to be clothed?' (pagans make all that their aim in life) for well your heavenly Father knows you need all that. Seek God's realm and his goodness, and all that will be yours over and above" (Matt. 6:31–33 MOFFATT).

OFFERTORY PRAYER. Lord, in thy providence and grace we give what we can as we are able. Take what we bring and make of it all it ought to be because thy providence is best and thy grace is blessing forever.—E. Lee Phillips

PRAYER. Shepherding God, you have called us to be beatitudes: poor in spirit, gentle, mourners, ones who hunger and thirst after what is right, merciful, pure in heart, peacemakers, ones who suffer in the cause of right. You have called us to do such things, you have called us to be such things, and you have promised us your blessing if we do.

But we have not taken you at your word. We have been anything but poor in spirit, and even our humility has been as a security system in a home without warmth or welcome. In the music of our lives has too seldom been heard lamentation, Rachel weeping for her children. We have feared to live lives of labor for right and have not trusted the joys of the fruits of lives so lived. We have not watched eagerly for the coming of your kingdom in every day, nor, like Ezekiel, have we scanned the horizon for whole new worlds aborning, that we might welcome them, prepare their way, link up with them as friendly forces, and share with them the victors' champagne. Purity of heart is to will one thing, but our linoleum may be purer than our hearts, for we have willed many things, and no one higher, brighter thing has held us in its thrall.

Bestow upon us the beatitude of glad and channeled holiness; deliver us from the gothic sadness of anxious goodness; and free us as a church to do and be your blessings, your jaunty, confident troops: poor in spirit, debonair, bearers of the world's sadness through those details most grievous to us; souls with an insatiable appetite for right, merciful, with hearts as windows cleaned, peacemakers; cross bearers; gladly, madly, in love with you and all that is or could be yours.—Peter Fribley

LECTIONARY MESSAGE

Topic: The Response Is Ours

Text: Luke 23:32–43

Other Readings: Isa. 50:4–9a; Phil. 2:5–11; Luke 22:14–31, 44–23:5

They crucified Christ with two criminals, one on his right and one on his left. What a way to have your mission to the world end! No doubt those who had followed Christ for the past three years of his ministry felt this was the end. He had told them what would happen, but they did not understand victory over death would come in a few days. Often we see paintings depicting Jesus' cross taller than the other two crosses, but it is very doubtful there was any difference in their size. However, there was a great difference among those who hung there. Let us think of the experience that prompted the words of Christ to the dying thief.

All four Gospels note the fact that there were two criminals crucified with Christ, but only Luke gives an account of what happened among the three. The crowd shouted contemptuous words at the central figure. "He saved others; let him save himself if he is the Christ of God, his Chosen One!" Soon the lawbreakers joined in the chorus. They wanted to be delivered from their fierce pain and death. One of the criminals said, "Are you not the Christ? Save yourself and us!" The other criminal reprimanded him, saying, "Do you not fear God, since you are under the same sentence of condemnation? And we indeed justly, for we are receiving the due reward of our deeds, but this man has done nothing wrong." Then this man said to Jesus, "Remember me, Jesus, when you come as King!" Jesus said to him, "I tell you this: today you will be in Paradise with me."

There was a contrast in the approach to the men who hung on either side of him. The situation was critical for both. They were no doubt revolutionaries who had turned to stealing. The end was just a few hours away for them. They reacted in a very normal manner as they reached out for some straw of hope.

I. One man made a demand (v. 39). The Greek interrogative used here in the original language suggests a tone of strong affirmation. He wanted Christ to be the Savior for his own sake. He was not repentant, nor did he acknowledge any wrong of his own. He demanded this of Christ with no conditions offered on his part. Individuals today may not be so hostile, but they do seek to deal with God on their terms.

II. One made a request (vv. 40–42). Both men were as close to death as perhaps they had ever been, and yet at the same time they were closer to one who could give eternal life. Like a great beam of light, the answer to the request of the thief broke through the darkness of that hour, and he received much more than he had requested. His plea without any excuse brought forgiveness and grace.

III. The promise (v. 43). Jesus promised the thief that he would be in the presence of God. He was saying that he would experience life after death. This encounter on the cross tells us that it is never too late to find life over death in Christ.

We see from this encounter with Christ there is no formal pattern or procedure in becoming a Christian. Wherever, whenever, and however we respond to Christ's call to repent and believe, he will give us eternal life. We must have the desire and will to let Christ change us with the power of his Resurrection.

A dying man's breath became his saving act as he asked for what only Christ can give. One can begin life with God at any time. It may begin for some in the home. It may begin for some in a worship service. It may begin for some as death draws close. It may begin on the battlefield. God wants it to happen to every one of us and has gone to the end of giving his Son on the cross and raising him from the grave. Now the response is ours to accept the grace of God by faith.—William P. Cubine

SUNDAY: APRIL SIXTEENTH

SERVICE OF WORSHIP

Sermon: Eyewitness News

TEXT: Isa. 65:17–25; Luke 24:1–12

According to Luke, even the disciples at first thought it was an idle tale. So unimpressed were they that they wouldn't get up from what they were doing to see for themselves. It probably should be stated that they wouldn't come out of hiding for fear of being arrested. So, they said, it's an idle tale. Which means their fear was stronger than their faith, which is consistent with what we know of them, and of ourselves. They, like us, had a great difficulty with faith when it involved risk.

I. To tell the truth, one reason they were unimpressed with the message was because of the messengers. They were women.

You must remember that all of this took place in a time characterized by a male-dominated hierarchical society where women were not taken seriously when it came to legal matters such as witnessing important events, such as the Resurrection of our Lord. Nowadays we would call that a sexist age, where women were abused in a number of ways and ignored in many more ways.

So the empty tomb was like one of those good news/bad news jokes. The good news was the tomb was empty; the bad news was the women witnessed it. To tell the truth, the disciples probably concluded it was an idle tale because the women reported it.

But look at this. If that was the case, if women were considered to be unreliable witnesses, how come all four Gospels agree that they were there first? They are who we rely upon as the primary witnesses. Why didn't they change the record? Why didn't they revise history? Everybody does it, especially when they become established and want to make sure their history looks respectable. Most people, most institutions, and all nations do that. It's not considered cheating. After all, you can read history from several points of view. Why didn't they just play down the role of the women and elevate the role of Peter?

There's only one reason. The church knew that it was not here to conform to the world or to please the world. It was here to change the world, and the first thing it did to change the world was to remove these distinctions of class, and race, and gender that allow some people to lord it over other people. In Galatians Paul issues what constitutes a manifesto of this new humanity: "In Christ there is no longer Jew or Greek, male or female, slave or free, but we are all one in Christ Jesus."

II. The church has taught two things about Easter. You can see it in every Gospel account. Every narrative of the Resurrection is divided into two parts: the empty tomb and the Resurrection appearances of Jesus to his disciples.

(a) There is a great variety of testimony on the second point, the Resurrection appearances. Every account is different—different in what happened, when it happened, where it happened, what he said, what he looked like when he appeared, how many were there, where it was. There was this great diversity in the record of the appearances of Jesus to his followers.

(b) But there was great unanimity on the first point, the empty tomb. They all agree. They all say that the women were there first, and then came Peter. And they all say the tomb was empty. It was no idle tale. You may think it's an idle tale, but the church says it wasn't. In fact, the church stakes its existence on the empty tomb. That's why Paul says to the Corinthians, "If Christ be not raised from the dead, our preaching is in vain, and your faith is in vain."

(c) It has always puzzled me that no one seemed to question that he appeared to his disciples. They scoffed at the empty tomb, but they shrugged off reports of Jesus appearing to his followers all over the place.

Then it occurred to me, in the Greek and Roman world where this Christian preaching took place, almost everyone believed in what was called "the immortality of the soul." That's why there was no problem with Resurrection appearances.

The problem was the Resurrection. If we have here a case of immortality of the soul, then the body will still be there. But if we have here a resurrection, there will be no body. That's why the first reaction was, they've taken him away.

III. The difference between the immortality of the soul and the resurrection of the body is no small matter for Christian faith.

(a) The immortality of the soul is about our indomitable spirit. Resurrection of the body is about God's unspeakable love. Our spirits may live on, but only God can resurrect a body. So if what we are talking about is immortality of the soul, then all Christianity is about how wonderful human beings are, and how beautiful their spirits are, and how great a potential we have because of our immortal spirit.

(b) But if we are talking about the resurrection of the body, then we are talking about God, who renews and creates and redeems the world. That's the Christian gospel. God has redeemed the world through Jesus Christ. "The old has passed away. Behold the new has come." God, who from the very beginning of creation made covenants with his people, with Noah, with Abraham, and with Moses, has done it again. Jesus is the sign of a new covenant. The cross, the empty tomb, are its symbols. All who believe in him, all who follow him will know the same victory over the enemies of life that he experienced, even the last enemy, death itself.

(c) Easter is not about the immortality of the human spirit. Easter is about the power of God, who created you to have life in its fullness, who has sent his Son as a promise that God can redeem your life from whatever it is that keeps you from that fulfillment and has resurrected his Son now as a sign that there isn't anything in all creation, not even death itself, that can stop God from keeping his promise. That is why Paul said, "If Christ is not raised from the dead, then our preaching is in vain, and your faith is in vain."

IV. So how will it happen with us, our resurrection? I must say, I don't know. Paul at some points seems to think it will happen at the end, at one time at the end of history, in "some great gettin' up mornin'," as the Negro spiritual put it, "fare thee well, fare thee well." And until then, between death and the Resurrection, we sleep. Which reminds me of all the times I have heard the dying say, "I am so tired."

However, in John he says, "I go to prepare a place for you, that where I am you may be also," which seems to me to indicate an immediate change of address.

So I don't know, and I don't need to know, because I believe that the God who created life can recreate it, and the second creation will be no greater a miracle than the first. The Resurrection is given to us as a promise. So I can trust that though I will not be in charge at that time, God will be. So I have nothing to fear.

V. Easter is told in two parts: the empty tomb, and the Resurrection appearances. There were many reports of the latter. In fact, there were so many of them they kept only the best and threw back the rest. But there was only one report of the former, of the empty tomb. It says the witnesses were the women, and they were told, "Why do you seek the living among the dead?" which is like saying, Why don't you trust that God will keep God's promise?—Mark Trotter

Illustrations

A SPECIAL GREETING. Christ by his death and Resurrection broke the power of evil forever. At Easter we meet together to celebrate a triumph, or we ought to! It is said that the early Christians used to greet one another not with a tame "good morning" or "good day" but with the words "the Lord is risen!" to which the reply was immediately forthcoming, "He is risen indeed!"—John Trevor Davies

CHRISTUS VICTOR! Michelangelo, it is said, once reproached his fellow painters, saying to them: "Why do you paint Christ on the cross so often? Christ suffering. Christ dying. Christ dead. Paint him, rather, risen, with his foot upon the riven rock—paint him victorious and glorious! Paint him the conqueror of sin and death!"—John Trevor Davies

Sermon Suggestions

THE GREAT SURPRISE. TEXT: John 20:1–18. (1) Jesus really died. (2) His followers did not expect his Resurrection. (3) Mary made several mistakes. (a) She misunderstood the significance of the empty tomb. (b) She did not recognize the living Lord when she saw him. (c) She tried to cling to a limited and temporary experience of the Christ. (4) But Mary was granted the privilege of being the first evangelist of the Resurrection.

WHEN GOD AT LAST MAKES ALL THINGS RIGHT. TEXT: Isa. 65:17–25. (1) There will be joy. (2) There will be fulfillment. (3) There will be peace.

Worship Aids

CALL TO WORSHIP. "The Lord is my strength and song, and is become my salvation" (Ps. 118:14).

INVOCATION. Lord of Calvary, let us learn of your ways, follow your precepts, and love as you have taught us to love through the example of Christ Jesus, who left his tomb empty and his hands forever open.—E. Lee Phillips

OFFERTORY SENTENCE. "On the first day of the week, let each of you put aside a sum from his weekly gains, so that the money will not have to be collected when I come" (1 Cor. 16:2 MOFFATT).

OFFERTORY PRAYER. Lord, for all the riches that are ours we express our gratitude: for goods material and truth spiritual and the faith that gives balance to these two in Christ our Lord.—E. Lee Phillips

PRAYER. With thee, O Christ, I would arise indeed to newness of life. I beseech thee to make all things new to me. Let the old duties, the old work, the old burdens, the old friendships be transfigured as thou dost touch them. Let Easter joy lift me from loneliness and weakness and despair to strength and beauty and happiness. I would fain live the risen life, my Jesus. Help me by thy call, by thy message, by thy beauty, by thy goodness, to be thy true child, looking to thee, and serving thee until at last I see thee face to face.—Floyd W. Tomkins

LECTIONARY MESSAGE

Topic: The Victory of the King Beyond the Grave

TEXT: 1 Cor. 15:19–26

OTHER READINGS: John 20:1–18; Isa. 65:17–25; Acts 10:34–43

Eight of the most important words ever written are these: "Christ has indeed been raised from the dead" (15:20). The major reason I am a Christian is that we have the only religion in the world whose leader did not stay in his grave. Jesus rose from a borrowed grave—the tomb owned by Joseph of Arimathea, who saw to his burial. It turned out that Joseph was not as generous as he intended because Jesus only borrowed it for three days and nights.

Jesus not only won victory over the grave when he arose from the dead; he also rules in regal splendor as Lord of the universe, and he gives us hope: confident expectation because of his victory. What the Apostle Paul teaches us in this passage highlights three ways that the victory of the risen king affects our hope.

I. Our hope in the Resurrection of Christ is located beyond the grave (15:19). Paul's point is clear: "If only for this life we have hope in Christ, we are to be pitied more than all men." But someone counters: does not Christianity's old argument hold true that even if, perchance, we are mistaken and this life is all there is, Christianity is still the best way to live? Try telling that to the tortured and the martyred to encourage them while they are being persecuted! And even in a society friendly to the Christian faith, it would be settling for so little when Christianity promises so much. The Resurrection of Jesus says that the center of gravity of the Christian faith is the other side of the grave.

II. Our hope for our resurrection through Christ is located beyond the grave (15:20–23). The central doctrine of the Christian faith is stated in 15:20: "But Christ has indeed been raised from the dead." And Paul gives two pictures from his Jewish past to illustrate the difference Christ's Resurrection has made.

(a) He calls the resurrected Christ "the firstfruits" of those who have died (15:20). The picture comes from the Feast of the Passover. It fell during barley harvest, and so the Jews not only remembered their deliverance from Egypt but also celebrated the harvest (Lev. 23:10, 11). The first sheaves were brought to the Temple, parched in a perforated pan so that each grain was touched by the fire, exposed to the wind to blow away the chaff, and then ground and the flour offered to God. Only after this was done could the new barley be made into flour and used by the people. The firstfruits were a sign of the harvest to come. And the Resurrection of Jesus is a sign of the resurrection of all believers yet to come.

(b) The other picture contrasts Adam to Christ. Because of the disobedience of Adam in the Garden of Eden, sin and death entered into the world. The result was that Adam and all since Adam "return to the ground" (Gen. 3:19). But Christ, who was sinless, broke the cycle. As the sinful children of the first Adam, we all die physically and spiritually, but as followers of Christ, the second Adam, we will all be made alive in him. "For since death came through a man, the resurrection of the dead came also through a man" (15:21), and "each in his own turn: Christ, the firstfruits, then, when he comes, those who belong to him" (15:23).

III. Our hope in the Resurrection reign of Christ is located beyond the grave (15:24–26). Paul goes cosmic on us, as he often does, and he shows us a glimpse of the big picture that stretches across eternity. Listen to his marvelous predictions:

(a) He is certain that Christ will destroy all enemies of the kingdom of God; in fact, all dominion, authority, and power will be put under his feet. Evil in every shape and form will be finished forever (15:25).

(b) He predicts the final coming of Christ and the end of the present age (15:23, 24).

(c) Christ will hand over the kingdom to the Father. The mission impossible will become the mission completed. The kingdom will be intact. All things will be as God intends.

(d) The last enemy he will destroy is death. He has already proved by his Resurrection that death has no more power over him, and he will demonstrate by raising his followers that death has no more power over us because he defeated death by his cross and Resurrection.

IV. Two things seem apparent from

this: (a) If we are Christians, we never have to taste spiritual death. (b) If we have not accepted the Resurrection gospel, we cannot taste eternal life. We have to go through Good Friday to get to Easter Sunday.—Wayne Shaw

SUNDAY: APRIL TWENTY-THIRD

SERVICE OF WORSHIP

Sermon: Thomas: Locked Out by Doubt

TEXT: John 20:19–31

Have you ever been locked out by doubt? Thomas was. The "doors were shut" (v. 19), and he was outside. His doubts kept him from seeing the risen Christ.

How do you deal with doubt? When questions, like ominous thunderclouds, arise in your mind, how do you handle them? When events in life seem to contradict your faith? When the throne of God seems to be vacant, and justice is hanging on a scaffold? When Jesus Christ himself seems like a fairy tale, what then?

Do these doors lock you out? Or have you learned to let them lock you in to renewed faith? Thomas's experience teaches us how to transform doubt into faith.

I. At first Thomas allowed his doubts to lock him out.

We have nicknamed him the "doubting disciple." In all fairness, Thomas's doubts were no different from the other disciples' before they had seen the resurrected Jesus.

Nevertheless, Thomas's questioning spirit kept him away from that first Sunday gathering of the group. There is a hint of this trait in Thomas at each of his appearances in the Gospel of John (11:16, 14:5, 20:25). All three times he expressed some doubt and uncertainty about Christ.

Thomas, like many of us, was a man who wanted proof. He wanted firsthand evidence. His analytical mind demanded more than hearsay; he must witness the truth for himself.

(a) Perhaps this lack of personal evidence allowed his fears to grow. The door of *fear* may have locked him out. Thomas seemed not to lack courage. He was the first who sensed trouble ahead and said, "Let us also go that we may die with Him" (John 11:16 NASB).

Yet the hatred and hostility heaped upon Jesus at the Crucifixion may have cracked the rocklike courage of Thomas. As he pondered all these strange events, he may have decided that to meet with the disciples was too big a risk.

The fear of death and persecution still keeps many would-be disciples in the safe shadows of neutrality today.

Have you failed to believe in Jesus Christ because you feared what it would cost—your friends, your fortune, your fun? What if it cost your life? The door of fear can lock you out of faith.

(b) Another door that shut Thomas out was *pessimism.* Although he seldom lacked courage when he was sure, Thomas was a pessimist. He just knew things were going to go badly. He feared the worst. And it happened.

The enemies of Jesus did what he had feared the most. The arrest, trial, and execution seemed like a bad dream. But they weren't. Their leader was dead. The way Thomas described Jesus in verse 25 indicates Thomas had witnessed the Roman Crucifixion. Christ's death had deeply disturbed him.

Thomas's prophetic pessimism fulfilled, despondency led to a sense of defeat. And defeat led to doubt. This pessimistic doubt led Thomas into stubborn self-sufficiency.

Have you been defeated by your doubts? Has a pessimistic spirit so discouraged you that you have become self-sufficient and cynical? Take heart, my friend. The Bible is your book. It's full of persons plagued by pessimism, whose faith has been hammered out on the anvil of doubt. Don't let the door of pessimism shut you out.

(c) *Grief* was the third door that locked Thomas out of the upper room.

There is no doubt that Thomas loved Jesus. He loved him so much, he was willing to go with him to Jerusalem, at the risk of death, when the others were hesitant. Then when what he feared happened, it broke his heart. Thomas had totally committed his life to Jesus Christ, his Lord and leader. And suddenly they killed him!

So grief-stricken was Thomas that he could not be with anyone. He had to be alone. There are times when sorrow needs silence and solitude. But grief not shared also leads to loneliness. Facing his suffering and sorrow alone, he missed the appearance of Jesus and the supportive strength of his comrades.

Life's mysteries can become doors of doubt that lock us out. Doors of grief, pessimism, and fear did that to Thomas on that first Sunday.

But the same circumstances that seem to shut you out can become doors to usher you in to deeper faith.

II. On that next Sunday, the disciples met again in the upper room. The doors once more were locked, but this time Thomas was inside with the rest (v. 26).

(a) What a difference it makes to be locked in rather than locked out! Thomas discovered some new doors that Sunday, doors that opened the way to renewed faith.

There was the door of Christian fellowship. Thomas realized his first big mistake was withdrawing from the fellowship of the disciples. He sought loneliness instead of togetherness. Isolated, like an iceberg in the Gulf stream, his faith melted. Not present with the apostles that first Sunday after the Resurrection, Thomas missed the appearance of the living Christ.

We miss a great deal when we separate ourselves from the fellowship of other Christians and try to go it alone. Things can happen to us within the community of believers that will never happen to us alone. That is one reason why Christ built his church—to establish a group of loving, caring members of the Body of Christ always ready to give help to the helpless and hope to the hopeless.

(b) Another door the doubting disciple discovered when locked in was the door of truth.

Thomas was uncompromisingly honest. He refused to say he understood what he didn't or that he believed what he couldn't. He would never quiet his doubts by pretending they didn't exist. "Except *I* shall see . . . and put *my* finger . . . and thrust *my* hand . . . *I* will not believe" (v. 25).

Do you have honest doubts? The struggle you are having is a way to deep faith and strong conviction. Like Thomas, find a firsthand faith. Doubt your doubts. Discover that on the other side of the door of honest doubt is the door of abiding truth. Thomas did. A week's reflection and honest inquiry led him to the door of truth.

(c) A third door that locked Thomas in to faith was the door of Jesus Christ himself. Through a personal encounter with Jesus Christ, Thomas discarded doubt and found renewed faith.

Notice in the biblical account that after the doors were locked securely, suddenly Christ appeared in their midst. First Jesus greeted the group; then he turned toward Thomas and said, "Reach hither thy finger, and behold my hands; and reach hither thy hand, and thrust it into my side; and be not faithless, but believing" (v. 27).

Thomas's response was not a mere exclamation of surprise. When he said, "My Lord and my God!" (v. 28), he was expressing a complete commitment to Jesus Christ. Thomas earlier did not air his doubts for the sake of mental gymnastics. He doubted in order to be sure, and when he was sure, his commitment was complete.

(d) Do you have that certainty? Have you had that personal encounter? Have your honest doubts been changed to ultimate faith through an experience with Jesus Christ? The same living Lord Jesus Christ wants to transform your doubts into belief if you will let him.

John the apostle concluded this chapter by saying, "But these have been written, that ye might believe that Jesus is the Christ, the Son of God" (v. 31). Hear Jesus Christ say to you today, "Be not faithless but believing." Don't let your doubts lock you out. Let him change them into ultimate faith.—Joe E. Trull

Illustrations

BEYOND APPEARANCE. Someone tells me a story of a bishop who lost his wife and child in a tragic accident. And he said to his people, "I have been all the way to the bottom. And it is solid."

Yes.

A couple of years ago a friend called me from her hospital bed, demanding, "Madeleine, do you believe everything that you have written in your books?"

I said *yes* then. It is still *yes* today.

But grief still has to be worked through. It is like walking through water. Sometimes there are little waves lapping about my feet. Sometimes there is an enormous breaker that knocks me down. Sometimes there is a sudden and fierce squall. But I know that many waters cannot quench love, neither can the floods drown it.—Madeleine L'Engle

THE QUALITY OF FAITH. Faith is the eye by which we look to Jesus. A dim-sighted eye is still an eye; a weeping eye is still an eye. Faith is the hand with which we lay hold of Jesus. A trembling hand is still a hand. And he is a believer whose heart within him trembles when he touches the hem of the Savior's garment that he may be healed. Faith is the tongue by which we taste how good the Lord is. A feverish tongue is nevertheless a tongue. And then we may believe, when we are without the smallest portion of comfort; for our faith is founded not upon feelings but upon the promises of God. Faith is the foot by which we go to Jesus. A lame foot is still a foot. He who comes slowly nevertheless comes.—George Mueller

Sermon Suggestions

BELIEVING. TEXT: John 20:19–31. (1) The way of evidence, verses 24–28. (2) The way of faith, verse 29; also 2 Cor. 5:7.

AN EVERLASTING DOXOLOGY. TEXT: Rev. 1:4–8. To Jesus Christ: (1) Who loves us. (2) Who freed us from our sins by his sacrifice. (3) Who has given believers a priestly function in reconciling the world to God.

Worship Aids

CALL TO WORSHIP. "Open to me the gates of the Temple; I will go and give thanks to the Lord" (Ps. 118:19 TEV).

INVOCATION. Quiet us in this time of worship, Lord, for we would walk with God and hear the voice of God in the quietness of prayer and the reality of faith.—E. Lee Phillips

OFFERTORY SENTENCE. "Every good gift and every perfect gift is from above, and cometh down from the Father of lights, with whom is no variableness, neither shadow of turning" (James 1:17).

OFFERTORY PRAYER. Gracious God, our lives are in your hands, and your providence gives us day by day such things as we need. We trust your faithfulness to see us through all circumstances. Though many things change, your love is forever the same. Steady our fitful love by the constancy of your own and make us faithful stewards of your good and perfect gifts.

PRAYER. Lord Jesus, make the season of Easter a continuing experience in our lives as well as a day on a calendar. We want our faith to be far more than a memory of past events in a distant land. We want the crucified, risen Lord to be a living presence and a guiding power right now.

The stone has been rolled away; the tomb is empty. The body of Jesus has not been stolen or hidden by anyone. The worst that wicked, sin-led people could possibly do has been done, but their ugly wickedness most assuredly is not the last word or the final deed.

Jesus is here in our midst, right now, knocking at the door of our lives, as he promised. And in worship we celebrate that he who was dead is alive, alive forevermore. We do not celebrate only what has already happened, the pages of faith already written, the miracles that have already occurred. We celebrate as well, in humility and wonder, the promise of what we sinners can yet become when we place ourselves in the care of the living Savior. All of us have a *long* way to go on our journey from sin to sanity, darkness to light, despair to hope, death to life.

Through Christ our Lord we pray.—Gordon H. Reif

LECTIONARY MESSAGE

Topic: Saved to Be Witnesses

TEXT: Acts 5:27–32

OTHER READINGS: Rev. 1:4–8; John 20:19–31

A few days ago we celebrated God's power over death in the Resurrection of Christ from the grave. It is wonderful to experience the joy and power of Easter Sunday. How often our churches so quickly lose that spirit even by the first Sunday after this glorious celebration. The victory we proclaimed last Sunday must be taken by each of us as Christians to the world, which is still in ignorance and darkness concerning the gift of God's grace in Jesus Christ. In our text Peter reminds us that we are witnesses of this gift of salvation in Christ Jesus.

I. What does Christ expect of those who witness? The call of Jesus to his first followers was a call to sacrifice, and he has the same expectations of us today. Jesus does not want individuals speaking for him who are not willing to live a life that reflects him. The world is hearing a lot about the change that Christ can bring in a person's life, but it really wants to see Christ lived in our lives. We are to testify concerning the things we have experienced and personally observed. Witnessing is a means of influencing others through the ministry of friendship. Each Christian needs to survey the daily opportunities of witnessing, beginning with relatives and reaching out into the community. The historian Gibbon said of the early Christians, "It became the most sacred duty of a new convert to diffuse among his friends and relations the blessings that he had received."

II. What authority do we have to be witnesses?

Jesus commissions each of us to be his witnesses (John 20:21). He not only commissions us but also promises us the power of the Holy Spirit as we tell the world about this good news. We must remember that witnessing for Christ is a divine appointment, and we must have the power that only God can give to be effective messengers. God inspires and empowers us.

III. What are we to witness to the world?

We are to bear witness to the Resurrection of Christ because we have experienced his personal presence. Because Christ lives, we too shall live for eternity with God. We are to tell the world that God has done this great miracle through Christ. We are to tell others that redemption through Christ is for all the world and not a limited few. We as Christians are to constantly remind each other that God wants to use us as instruments of reconciliation. We have a part in the great divine plan of God to redeem the world.

IV. Why do we hesitate to witness?

So many of us can find excuses for not accepting certain responsibilities.

This holds true in sharing our witness of what God can do in our lives. Some Christians do not witness because of the inconsistencies in their lives. Others are too polite and do not want to offend anyone. Many Christians are just timid. A very large segment of Christians are ignorant concerning leading a person to Christ.

We are called to be witnesses. Every day we have the opportunity for Jesus to be experienced through us here on earth. Never forget that as Christians we are witnesses, either in a positive manner or in a negative sense. If we call ourselves Christians, we are under a divine imperative to share Christ with others. We do not convert people. It is only when the

Holy Spirit works in persons' lives, convicting them of their need to accept Christ, that conversion can take place. But most of the time God needs us as instruments to accomplish this great act.—William P. Cubine

SUNDAY: APRIL THIRTIETH

SERVICE OF WORSHIP

Sermon: Trust in Spite of Everything

TEXT: Job 13:15

This sermon is addressed especially to troubled Christians who are asking themselves, either secretly or openly, this question: in a world like this, can we keep on trusting God?

A great many serious-minded and thoughtful Christians are going through that dilemma right now.

When we are in a mood like that, and I take it that all of us are at some time or other, we need to remember that there was once a man who kept on trusting God in spite of everything; who, when everything seemed to be against him, could say, "Though he slay me, yet will I trust in him." This sermon is an attempt to set before you for consideration suggestions that may be foundations for that kind of trust. They are suggestions, intimations that, may I say, I have tried to work out myself as I ask the question that I set before you at the beginning of the sermon.

I. To begin with, things in the world are coming out just about as we expected they would.

(a) For example, the world, or at least a large part of it, is in economic chaos. That is exactly what perceiving people expected would happen. When the war first began, one prophetic soul made a statement something like this: "to win the war is one thing, but whether or not the Western world will ever be able to recover itself economically is another thing." How tragically true his words turned out to be. Yes, that is exactly what we expected to happen.

(b) Again we see all around us a kind of tragic moral disintegration. There again is something that we might have expected to happen. You cannot dislocate the greater part of humanity, separate them from their homes and from all domestic and community responsibility, and subject them to all the techniques of terror and cruelty and brutality, and expect them to go on living with moral sensitivity and awareness of all the finer realities of life. If there is moral disintegration after a global war, that is exactly what we expected would happen.

(c) What does this do to our trust in God? For a great many people it tends to weaken it. I submit that in my case it confirms it. For example, if in a cold room you lighted a log fire, you would expect the room to be warm. But if you lighted a fire in the room and suddenly the temperature went down to zero, you would say in utter bewilderment, "What kind of universe is this where such an unpredictable thing can happen?" I say that if we could have gone through this worldwide colossal destruction of everything that is humanly valuable and dear to us, if we could have gone through it and come out with prosperity, and plenty, and happiness, and goodness, then we would say, "What kind of moral universe is this?" Oh, I for one, when I see these things, terrible as they are, coming out just about as we would expect them to in the light of what we know about God, I am prepared to say, "Though he slay me, yet will I trust in him," trust him in spite of everything, for in him there is an integrity that prevails even though to my hurt.

II. Then again, we point out as a second consideration that things are not always coming out the way we want them to.

(a) We want, for instance, peace and plenty, and we seem to be getting strife and starvation in large parts of the world. We all want health and happiness, and a great many of us are getting pain and misery. We all want life, and some of us are getting death. Those facts as some people observe them threaten to weaken their trust in God. Is it not true that to contemplate the fact that we do not always get what we want implies that our God has a will of his own?

(b) If we could only stretch our understanding and imagination of God just enough to glimpse his infinite purpose and some of the concerns that he has on his mind, not only the welfare of the human race but the glory of the furthest star; to appreciate his concern not only with our immediate comfort and happiness but with the total welfare of humanity that he has set before himself! God has a will of his own, and as we see things coming out, not always as we want them, sometimes it seems to me as though God were saying to us, "You cannot have everything you want, willy-nilly." We worship the God who is the Creator of the universe and the Governor of it on his own terms, and I for one, if I should see signs that God suddenly became indulgent and said to us, "You had a hard time; although you have not paid the price and measured up to the cost, nevertheless I will give you what you want just the same"—I should begin to suspect a God like that. But so long as I see a God who has a will of his own, with great purposes that stretch out far beyond my own personal purposes, valuable as they are to me, I can say, "Though he slay me, yet will I trust in him."

III. Furthermore, there are some things that God has little if anything to do with directly.

(a) That is always a dangerous thing to say, especially in the presence of theologians, because it involves the question of the omnipotence of God. We grant that everything that we know ultimately depends upon God. Its existence is derived from him, and yet there seem to be some things that God has given a life of their own and within certain limits lets have their own way.

(b) He is responsible for everything that happens to us, and yet, in his mysterious and loving wisdom, he has given us and other forms of life a share of his creative will, and he lets us go about our way to see what we can make of it. Sometimes we make a mess. We make planes that kill people. God is not responsible for that. We are responsible for the mismanagement of the power that he has given us. We are now in a seething cauldron of postwar hatred, fear, and strife. God is not responsible for that; we are. We have misused some of the precious rights and privileges that he in his generosity gave us, and he is saying to us, at this time, "You are in a mess, to be sure. Do not hold me responsible for it. You are in it because you thought you knew better than I did. I am trusting you to get out of it." A God like that is worthy of our unqualified trust, trust in spite of everything.

IV. Finally, there is nothing that God cannot do something with *in time.*

(a) We who have only a fraction of time in which to work out our lives are often understandably impatient. That was impressed upon me two weeks ago today when I stood as I have wanted for years to stand on the rim of the Grand Canyon. What a spectacle of God's creative power that is! He has been at it for six billion years! He has been working with man about six thousand. You may say to yourself, cynically, "Well, he has had enough time to do better than he seems to have done." It is not for us to stand in judgment on the Almighty. The fact is that God works his way slowly and that it is unfair for us to judge the outcome before he is anywhere near through.

(b) This, as you know, is not entirely a matter of the mind. (No one can rationalize himself into trusting God.) It involves all of a man. The great German theologian whom I quote so often, Baron von Hugel, had a pet dog. When William Temple was last in the United States, he told the story of that dog's end. It came to the time when the dog, after years of faithful companionship with the baron, was no longer able to get around, and the baron took him to the veterinarian to have him put out of his misery. The baron told William Temple that as the doctor was about ready to take away his life, the dog looked up at his master with a kind of implicit trust, doubting nothing, fearing nothing. The baron said, "I knew then what Job meant when he said, 'Though he slay me, yet will I trust in him.' " That is the kind of trust that the baron had. It is unqualified; it is unshakable; it is a trust in God, no matter what, in spite of everything.—Theodore Parker Ferris

Illustrations

THE VITAL PART OF FAITH. The vital part of faith in the New Testament is not the believing of propositions but the trusting of a person. For a man may accept theological dogmas and be not one whit the better or stronger if he does not trust the person about whom he believes these things. And, in contrast, as somebody has said, "many a man has been held fast by his trust in God while in perplexity he has thought out his beliefs *about* God."—Leslie J. Tizard

YET HE TRUSTED. When I look at the cross, I say to myself very quietly—and a strange awe and hush come upon me—"He thought of that." He knew it would cost that. And he went on because he had enough patience to believe that it was worth even that. And he who hung there—he who, so pure and innocent, might have railed at God and called the universe a failure, a devilish fraud, a foul obscenity—called God *Father* and died in unbroken peace. And all the saints in their own way, and so many of them at cost of everything that human lives count dear, followed that lead.—Leslie Weatherhead

Sermon Suggestions

RESTORATION. TEXT: John 21:1–19. (1) Retreat, verses 1–3. (2) Encounter, verses 4–14. (3) Renewal, verses 15–19.

WORTHY IS THE LAMB. TEXT: Rev. 5:11–14. (1) Because of his redeeming sacrifice, Jesus Christ is worthy to receive all worship. (2) Even more, this worship is fitting because it comes from the relationship Jesus Christ shares with God the Father. (See also 11:15.)

Worship Aids

CALL TO WORSHIP. "I will remember the works of the Lord: surely I will remember thy wonders of old. I will meditate also on all thy work, and talk of thy doings" (Ps. 77:11–12).

INVOCATION. For all your wondrous works in ancient times, we give you thanks, O God. For the blessings of this past week, we bless your name. For the promise of your presence in this service, we praise you. Grant that we may so celebrate what you are and what you do among your people that our lives may be a witness to those who do not know you.

OFFERTORY SENTENCE. "And the grace of our Lord was exceeding abundant with faith and love which is in Christ Jesus" (1 Tim. 1:14).

OFFERTORY PRAYER. Lord, you overwhelm us with your grace, loving us when we do not deserve it and forgiving us as we constantly need your mercies. You have given faith, and the love of Christ urges us on. So we bring our offerings to you, believing you will bless them and use them so that others also will know your love.

PRAYER. Amid the beauty of a flowering world we come this morning to worship you, Father. Everywhere we look we see the handiwork of the Creator. Blooming bush, greening grass, budding trees all turn our minds to new beginnings, new possibilities, and new life. Help us not to forget the new life given by a loving Father through the Lord Jesus. Call us again, amid all the splendor of springtime and the wonder of Resurrection, to the need for each of us to be renewed through faith. In this sacred hour let us see again the possibilities for us as we meet the Master and determine to follow him through the maze of life.

You have set our lives in pleasant places, Father. As we enjoy the glories and wonders of life, we pray that you will keep us loyal to the highest traditions of our faith and heritage. Make us worthy of the sacred trust that has been placed in our hands and enable us to guard it against everything that would cheapen, dilute, make ugly, and profane what is high and noble and holy and right. Preserve us from selfish indifference, which dishonors the past and disregards the future. Kindle within us the passion to defend and enrich those sacred values that have been bought and paid for by the tears and sacrifices of others. Give us wisdom and courage to serve our generation faithfully, to work unceasingly for the good of all, so that when we have finished our journey here on this earth we may leave with a clean conscience and a pure heart.

Now let the power of your Spirit come upon us. Let the truth of your Word inspire us. Let the wonder of your redemption claim us. And let our hearts respond to your call to commitment and service, we pray in Jesus' name.—Henry Fields

LECTIONARY MESSAGE

Topic: Two Sides of Conversion

TEXT: Acts 9:1–20

OTHER READINGS: Rev. 5:11–14; John 21:1–19

Throughout the Bible there has always been a two-sided relationship between God and mankind. God gave clear directions in the beginning about how those individuals who occupied this earth would live in peace with their Creator. There was God's side and there was the human side of this new association. Sin entered the world, and a separation took place between Creator and creation. Over the years that followed God gave different instructions concerning atonement for sin. As God had planned from the beginning, a final divine act would take place as restitution for our sins. We call the experience of reconciling Creator with creation *conversion*. The text deals with one of the most outstanding conversion experiences: Saul of Tarsus on the Damascus road. This experience is described at least seven different times in the New Testament. We must focus on what happened in Paul's conversion and not let the form of the experience destroy the real event. Conversion is a divine work. The human part brings to completion what God started.

I. The direct intervention of God (vv. 1–6). Paul was certain he was an instrument being used of God to protect the faith of his fathers. The event that changed his life began with the direct contact he had with Christ on the road to Damascus. It was God who acted in a mysterious way to change his life. With all of our beautiful buildings, fine musical instruments, and moving worship services, we must not forget the great mystery of the divine encounter in reconciling individuals to God. We have the tendency to reduce the conversion experience to a system we have developed. We explain God's grace and in the process leave out the supernatural. Remember, we are dealing with God in our attempts to win others to the Christian way of life. We cannot reveal God; God alone can disclose God. It was God who became flesh and lived in our midst. The same is true in the conversion experience.

II. The human side of conversion (vv. 7–20). God wants to use us in the conversion experiences of others. Usually there are those whom God uses prior to and after the divine redemptive act. Paul was no stranger to the Christians of his day. There were many times that Paul, in anger and hatred for the people of "the Way," was influenced by the unusual behavior of Christians as they faced persecution and death. Paul could not talk with the Sanhedrin guards during the long seven-day journey to Damascus. Perhaps thoughts of those he had already persecuted came to his memory. The way we react to the difficult times of life so many times speaks louder than any words we may utter. Paul was brought to his knees and blinded. Helpless and changed, he depended on the guards to guide him to Damascus. No doubt the Christians there knew he was coming. He was aware of this and wondered what type of reception he would receive. God prepared the way by using others to be a source of support in the new life that had started for Paul. There was another human part in the conversion experience; Paul by faith had to reach out and accept that which was offered to him. Salvation is still primarily the gift of a loving and forgiving God. God gives, and we accept.

The life-changing experience of Paul is offered to all. God wants to use us in witnessing to others by showing them how we are different as Christians. God needs committed Christians on both sides of the human conversion experience. Who knows what Saul might be changed to a Paul? God wants to use us in this process.—William P. Cubine

SUNDAY: MAY SEVENTH

SERVICE OF WORSHIP

Sermon: Home Security

TEXT: Deut. 6:9

All over the world, home-security systems are becoming more necessary. In many countries, private dwellings are surrounded by high walls; iron gates swing open to let in a vehicle or a bicycle and then clang shut, locked to outsiders. Some entire housing developments are behind a fence with an iron gate; a security guard checks people in.

The problem, however, is that no ordinary security system can lock out our most treacherous enemies today. They are not interested in our money, our furniture, our jewelry, or our toys. Our most treacherous enemies are interested in us, personally.

They want to steal us. They want to own us. They want to manipulate our minds. The want to make us their slaves. These cruel enemies want our children. They will kidnap them right before our eyes.

Nowadays a totally new world order is being expressed right within our homes by enemies who laugh at the locks on our doors. It is a world order that encourages sexual promiscuity, exalts materialism, promotes hedonism, and is built on an evolutionistic view of reality. We must protect our homes against this worldview, and the only way we can do that is to take the message of Deuteronomy 6:4–9 very seriously.

These words from Deuteronomy describe the way God's people Israel had to use the commandments he gave them. The people were not to receive these commands, acknowledge their value, and then file them away. The way of life that God revealed was to be remembered. It was to become the primary preoccupation of the people's lives.

I. I find the idea of writing God's Word on the doorframes of our homes intriguing. This deals with the matter of home security, you see, but it is a security that goes beyond what's provided by locks and deadbolts.

(a) It is fascinating that through the years, and even to this day, many of the people of Israel responded to the command to carry God's Word on their foreheads and hands by making little boxes called *phylacteries* and tying them to their arms and heads when they prayed.

And when it came to writing the Word of God on the doorframe, a Jewish person made a little box called a *mezuza,* which contained the very passage we have been looking at, Deuteronomy 6:4–9, and attached it at eye level on the right side of the main doorframe of the house.

(b) Basically, of course, the statement in Deuteronomy requires more than simply making little boxes that we attach to ourselves and to our homes. Put something on the door of your house that will make it really secure. Put the very Word of God there. It counters all the pagan, heathen ideas that have existed since God spoke to his people centuries ago.

When God said the people should bind his commandments to their heads and hands and attach them to the doorframes of their houses, he wanted them to understand that his good words of life should not be hidden away in a book somewhere or filed away for future reference. God wanted his commands to be present in their minds and hearts at all times.

(c) Surely it's important that we counteract the damaging influences that come into our homes and corrupt our families. Terrible things are happening to us as individuals, to our families, and also to our nation. And sometimes we feel helpless because the evil influences are so dominant and so powerful. They take up so much of our time.

II. Now, do you want to do something about this enemy, or don't you? I realize that many of you don't even think there's a problem. But we *are* in danger of a problem that will destroy everything fine and good, so please read on.

(a) First, it's important to realize what is happening in our society today. Talk about it with your spouse. Talk about it with your children. Recognize together that there are influences in your home right now that can ruin everyone in your family.

(b) Second, you have to get what you need to counteract the evil influences that come into your home. You need the influence of God himself, and that will come into your life only if you know the Word of God.

III. As we have seen, God wanted this revelation of himself in these commands to be in people's minds and hearts and homes. A home that expressed God's will and commands would be a truly safe and secure place to live.

(a) This type of home is what you need, too. If you are a parent, you have to work on getting rid of the ignorance you have about God and about the way of life God wants for his people. If you are like most people these days, you don't know very much about God. And one of the main reasons is that people spend hundreds of hours being entertained by the media products that come into their homes.

(b) If you are serious about protecting yourself and your family, you will need a church in which the Word of God is taken seriously. There are some churches, sorry to say, that have become nothing other than social organizations, and they will not help you much if you want to know about the Bible. But there are churches where the Bible is at the center of the people's lives, where the Bible is proclaimed and taught vigorously. Find a church like that so that you can learn about the Word of God.

(c) You will also have to find ways to bring the influence of the Bible into your home. To do this, you as a parent will have to control as well as you can the influences within your home. Talk with your children about the enemies that threaten your home security. If your children are addicted to television, for example, you should do all you can to break them of that habit. Parents and children alike should talk about the enemies within their home and do everything necessary to keep the family from becoming slaves to media products that can destroy a household.

(d) Then, in order to bring the influence of the Bible into your family, you will have to develop some family activities that have something to do with the Word of God. Have you ever heard about family devotions? You might want to have a special time for prayer and Bible reading as a family. Many committed Christian families do this.

IV. Finally, if you are to have a safe and secure home, you really have to have a living relationship with the Lord Jesus Christ. And this is the most important item of all.

(a) The enemies within our homes today are so powerful that we cannot withstand them unless the people within our homes know Jesus as their Savior. If you are a parent, please realize that Jesus Christ wants you to come to him and believe in him. Jesus wants you to have a living relationship with him.

(b) Parents who believe in the Lord Jesus Christ and who have his Holy Spirit can withstand the powerful enemies that threaten us by way of many media products today. Such parents will see that there is something horribly wrong in their home when they identify the enemies that are still present after they have locked all the doors. And such parents will understand that it is absolutely necessary for them to learn about God as he has been revealed on the Bible's pages.

(c) Filling your home with the Word of God can change your life and your family. There is only one way to ward off the enemies that are seeking to destroy us these days. We need the security that God alone can bring. We must repent of our sinful indifference. We must repent of the hours we have spent in trivial pursuits, in some cases actually being involved in activities that are unspeakably damaging. And we must flee to God.

Father, mother, when you lock the doors of your home, do you ever think about the enemies within it? Please think about them. Turn to Jesus, become part of his church, learn the contents of his glorious Word, and make your home truly safe and secure.—Joel Nederhood

Illustrations

HEALING THE HURTS OF LIFE. A woman came to New York from an upstate city. She said to her family, "I will return when I have found the answer to my problem." When she was here three weeks, she began to realize that she had been trying to run away from herself. Of course it was true that life had hurt her badly, but she had been striking back and had hurt others. There were hostility and constant tension in her home.

Then one Sunday morning, for the first time, she came to church. Later she said, "Strangely enough, the moment I entered I felt an atmosphere of quietness and peace, and as the service progressed that feeling deepened. The minister spoke of an occasion when he had heard Dr. Grenfell tell of his work in Labrador, and said that as the physician was speaking his face was so transfigured with the love of Christ that for a moment he seemed to have vanished and in his place stood One 'whose form was like unto that of the Son of God.'

"In that instant," said the woman, "I felt that Christ himself was present in the congregation, moving through our midst, touching men and women one by one and saying 'Peace be unto you.' I felt that his hands had been laid in benediction upon me. Then I knew that my problem had been solved, and that I would take back to my home the answer that I had found."—John Sutherland Bonnell

ULTIMATE SECURITY. When John Quincy Adams, one-time president of the United States, was more than eighty years of age, a friend who called said, "How is John Quincy Adams today?" The ex-president replied, "John Quincy Adams is fine, thank you, but soon he must find a new tenement to live in. This old tenement leaks badly and the foundations are undermined, but John Quincy Adams is fine, thank you."—Benjamin P. Browne

Sermon Suggestions

THOSE WHO BELONG TO CHRIST. TEXT: John 10:22–30. (1) They are attentive. (2) They are obedient. (3) They are immortal. (4) They are secure.

A GLIMPSE OF HEAVEN. TEXT: Rev. 7:9–17. (1) Who? The redeemed—righteous: "robed in white"; victorious: "with palm branches." (2) What? (a) Perpetual worship by the redeemed: "day and night within his Temple." (b) Total peace and happiness: "God will wipe away every tear." (3) How? The continuing work of Christ: "the Lamb at the center of the throne will be their shepherd."

Worship Aids

CALL TO WORSHIP. "Surely goodness and mercy shall follow me all the days of my life: and I will dwell in the house of the Lord for ever" (Ps. 23:6).

INVOCATION. In this place of worship, we pray that you will quicken our minds to understand your truth, Father. Make us aware that we are your children, children in need of a father's love and guidance. Bring us in from the far country; call us from the highways and hedges that we may feast at the banquet that you have prepared for us today. Feed us with the fruit of joy, peace, purpose, challenge, and hope that we may return to the world strengthened in the Spirit to do your will.—Henry Fields

OFFERTORY SENTENCE. "Your life must be controlled by love, just as Christ loved us and gave his life for us as a sweet-smelling offering and sacrifice that pleases God" (Eph. 5:2 TEV).

OFFERTORY PRAYER. Lord, we make these gifts with commitment and dedicate them with gratitude because of our love for God, our compassion for others, and the difference faith in Jesus Christ makes to us every day.—E. Lee Phillips

PRAYER. O God, who art unsearchable in thy judgments and in thy ways past finding out, we bow before the mystery of thy being and confess that we know nothing and can say nothing worthy of thee. We cannot understand thy dealings with us. We have faith, not sight; when we cannot see, we may only believe. Sometimes thou seemest to have no mercy upon us. Thou dost pierce us through our most tender affections, quenching the light of our eyes in dreadful darkness. Death tears from us all that we love, and thou art seemingly deaf to all our cries. Our earthly circumstances are reversed, and bitter poverty is appointed us, yet thou takest no heed and bringest no comfort to the sorrow and the barrenness of our life. Still would we trust in thee and cling to that deepest of our instincts, which tells us that we come from thee and return to thee. Be with us, Father of mercies, in love and pity and tenderness unspeakable. Lift our souls into thy perfect calm, where all our griefs are put to rest, and our wills are in harmony with thine.

O Lord, remember each one of us in our need. Thou wilt not forget our dear ones who are sick. Many whom thou lovest are ill in body or in mind. Heal them, we entreat thee; and grant that after they have been afflicted, they may be comforted and taste of those deeper joys that are purchased only with pain. Graciously bless our children. Lay thy hand upon them and grant that through the coming years, in joy or in sorrow, in health or in sickness, in all the changes of their life, they may live under thine eye and in thy strength and rise into the measure of the stature of the fullness of Christ. Be gracious to those who bear responsibility, the toilers who win bread for wife and child. Let them not be crushed by the burdens that they have to carry. Sweeten every task; lighten every load with a sense of duty done, of love's command obeyed.—Samuel McComb

LECTIONARY MESSAGE

Topic: What Do You Expect?

TEXT: Acts 9:36–43

OTHER READINGS: Rev. 7:9–17; John 10:22–30

In contrast to the record in the Acts of the Apostles, nearly two thousand years later we Christians are counting heads and calculating bank accounts to get the work of the church done. Our church committee meetings and especially our board meetings resemble the meetings of corporate boards or political groups much more than they do the meetings we see described in Acts. If we can't staff it or pay to get it done, we don't try it. In our attempt not to be seen as doing anything foolish or impractical, we put a gag order on God. We plan and work as though everything depended on us. We even pray that God would help us—rarely that God would do something on his own.

Has God retired? Has God taken a vacation? We Christians would hardly put it that way, but we appear to live as though God were not a force to contend with. During the ferment of the 1960s, many movements arose to challenge and plague the academic community. One of these movements that arose among Christians became known as the "God is dead" movement. One of the probable causes of the brief popularity of the idea that God is dead was the way Christians and churches carried out their daily lives. I am afraid that we haven't changed much in thirty years. We still go about our business and our play as though God were not a power to be reckoned with. It is not just the humanistic establishment, which has pushed God to the edge of human existence; it is also the Christian establishment.

How often do you take God's will into account when you make decisions? Does he figure in what you buy? In where you go on vacation? In whom you date or marry? In how you rear children? In the choice of your life's work? As long as we relegate God to a few hours a week in a church building, we are showing that our expectations are quite ordinary. And we tend to get what we expect—rarely more.

But the early church expected the extraordinary—and got it. Look at our text again. The Apostle Peter was making the rounds of the congregations, and in Lydda he became the agent for the healing of Aeneas, who had been bedridden with paralysis for eight years—the extraordinary. He then was called over to Joppa, where a fine, leading woman of the church there had died. Her name was Tabitha. Her sisters and brothers in the faith apparently expected that God could work the extraordinary in that case, too, so they told Peter about her and left him alone with the corpse. Peter prayed, and Tabitha was restored to her friends. The extraordinary had happened again. Not every sick person was healed in the early church; not every dead Christian was raised. But "business as usual" was not their motto, either. Those early Christians expected great things of God, and God was able to accomplish great things through those Christians.

James S. Stewart, in his little book *Thine Is the Kingdom,* writes: "To be alive in the same world with the risen Christ—what a thrilling tension of expectancy this must involve, what a fresh unwearied wonder of discovery! Daily they were 'tasting,' as one of them expressed it, 'the powers of the world to come.' The two ages overlapped; time was shot through with eternity; and gleams of glory were continually piercing and shattering the darkness of sinful history."

That's it! They were aware of being "alive in the same world with the risen Christ." They knew that there was nothing ordinary about the Resurrection of Jesus, and therefore they expected the extraordinary every day.

We, God's people at the end of the twentieth century, need to dedicate ourselves to expect the extraordinary. We need to develop eyes to see and ears to hear the power of God at work in our lives, in our churches, in our communities, and in the world. And we need to find ways of describing God at work so that we can lead others to faith in the risen Christ.

Only then can we truly resonate with the longer view of the early Christians who expected not only the extraordinary to happen periodically in their earthly lives. They expected also the eternal outpouring of praise described in Revelation 7:9–12.

We will celebrate the presence and power of God for eternity. Let us celebrate the presence and power of God today and tomorrow by expecting the extraordinary.—Bruce E. Shields

SUNDAY: MAY FOURTEENTH

SERVICE OF WORSHIP

Sermon: The Mother Who Changed the World

TEXT: Mark 7:24–30

Did you ever go away on a vacation, wanting to get away from the office or the store or your household responsibilities, and you hadn't any more than got your bag unpacked in the motel when the phone rang and it was somebody wanting you to do something? Apparently that's what happened to Jesus in the text.

I. He had been with crowds of people in Galilee and had been teaching in the synagogues and countryside, and he felt the need to get away for awhile; so he went over to the seacoast, on the Mediterranean, and retired to a little house to rest. And this woman who had heard about him found him there and invaded his privacy.

(a) A nameless Greek woman from the coastal region of Syrophoenicia was shopping in the market. Her little daughter, whom she loved with all her heart, was lying in bed in their home on the edge of town, terribly sick with a high, high fever. The woman had already lost one child, who was kicked by a camel, and she couldn't afford to lose this one. Her mind filled with resolve, she went straight to old Michael's house and asked Matthew, who was sitting on the doorstoop whittling, if he was the miracle worker. No, he wasn't, said Matthew; the Master was asleep in the house.

"Then wake him up," said the woman. "I have something for him to do."

Her daughter was extremely sick, she said. She needed a miracle.

(b) Jesus was reluctant.

"Let the children first be fed," he said, "for it is not right to take the children's bread and throw it to the dogs."

He was talking about the Jews; they were the children of God. His ministry had been spent entirely among the Jewish people. To this point, apparently, he understood his mission to be for them. She was Greek, not Jewish. Her daughter had no right to what was ordained for the Jews.

But she was clever, and she was persistent.

"Yes, Lord," she said, "yet even the dogs under the table eat the children's crumbs."

Jesus, apparently pleased with her spirit, granted what she had come for. "For this saying," he said, "you may go your way; the demon [that is, the illness] has left your daughter."

And she went home and found the fever broken and her daughter lying quietly in bed.

II. A sweet little story, but it doesn't seem to justify the extravagance of the sermon title, does it? "The Woman Who Changed the World."

But wait, there's more.

We have to see the story in its fuller context in the Gospel and see how the writer intended it.

(a) If we turn back to the sixth chapter of Mark, verses 30–44, we find the famous story of Jesus' feeding of an immense crowd in the wilderness—five thousand people in all—with a few loaves of bread and two fish. It is a mind-boggling story.

Then if we turn the other way, over to the eighth chapter of Mark, there is another story of a feeding miracle. This time, Jesus feeds four thousand people in a wilderness setting, and again there is much food left over.

But there is another significant difference, aside from the sizes of the crowds and the amount of food left over. In the second feeding, Jesus is in the region of the Decapolis. This was a territory that lay southeast of Galilee, adjacent to the area of Samaria, that was settled largely by non-Jews. The first feeding had been in Galilee—Jewish territory. The second was in the Decapolis—Gentile territory.

(b) Jesus had moved, in other words, from a ministry to the Jews to a ministry among the Gentiles; and his encounter with the Greek mother in the region of Tyre and Sidon, where he was vacationing, or attempting to, was the springboard from one to the other. In the understanding of Mark, the Gospel writer, it was the meeting with this mother that led Jesus to broaden the scope of his activities and include the Gentiles in his work of teaching and healing.

So you can see that she literally altered the history of the world. If she had not interrupted Jesus' rest in the house of old Michael the fishmonger and convinced him of the importance of doing something for her poor daughter with a fever, it is possible that Jesus would never have expanded his mission beyond the Jewish people he had originally planned to go to; and the chronicles of early Christianity, and therefore of the whole world, would have been significantly different than they are.

III. The New Testament, I have to tell you, was not insensitive to woman's role in the creation of our faith. It pays great attention to the beautiful story of Mary, the mother of our Lord. It often shines the light on the several women who traveled with Jesus and the disciples and on certain women whose actions are significant in the biography of Jesus, such as the woman at the well, Mary and Martha, the poor widow who gave her entire living to the Temple treasury, and the women who went to the tomb on Easter. And Paul frequently alludes to various women in the churches of the several cities to which he addressed his Epistles. The women of the New Testament were loving, guiding, nurturing forces in the shaping of our religious understanding, and we owe them an inestimable debt.

(a) This woman in our text today was one of the beautiful women of the Bible. She was beautiful in her love for her daughter. She was a real mother. You have the feeling she would have crawled over splintered glass for that little girl. And her love—her natural, human love, her motherly love—was the pivot on which the entire ministry of Jesus turned. A mother's love is like that.

(b) And Jesus responded to that mother's love and care. It was as if she reminded him of God's love and care for all his children, the Gentiles as well as the Jews, and he turned his ministry to the world because of her love for her child. Her love was the hinge on which all history turned.

IV. And isn't it interesting, we don't even know her name. Such an important woman, and the disciples neglected to learn who she was.

(a) But perhaps there is significance in the fact that she remained nameless, that this wonderful mother has gone down in history as our great unknown benefactress; for aren't most of the wonderful deeds of mothers done in silence and anonymity, without the world knowing who did them? That is part of what being a mother is about—loving without credit, pouring oneself into others for the pure joy of doing it.

(b) How many mothers, like this faithful, ardent mother in our scripture, have really changed the history of the world, and we never acknowledged it? How many are changing the world today, quietly, softly instilling love and human values in their children, praying for their children, making their children whole in a fragmented society and thereby helping to make society itself whole?—John Killinger

Illustrations

JESUS' PUZZLING REPLY. First, he said, the children must be fed; but only first; there is meat left for the household pets. True, Israel had the first offer of the gospel, but only the first; there were others still to come. The woman was a Greek, and the Greeks had a gift of repartee, and she saw at once that Jesus was speaking with a smile. She knew that the door was swinging on its hinges. In those days people did not have knives or forks or table napkins. They ate with their hands; they wiped the soiled hands on chunks of bread and then flung the bread away, and the house dogs ate it. So the woman said, "I know the children are fed first, but can't I even get the scraps the children throw away?" And Jesus loved it. Here was a sunny faith that would not take no for an answer, here was a woman with the tragedy of an ill daughter at home, and there was still light enough in her heart to reply with a smile. Her faith was tested, and her faith was real, and her prayer was answered. Symbolically she stands for the Gentile world, which so eagerly seized on the bread of heaven that the Jews rejected and threw away.—William Barclay

FRUITFUL PERSISTENCE. I remember a similar mother I met once at a spiritual retreat center in Kentucky. Her name was Margaret Howard. Margaret was about sixty-five at the time. She was a good, solid woman of the hills who managed a small bookstore in Richmond, Kentucky, called the Miracle Book Room. Margaret had only an eighth-grade education. She married when she was fourteen. But she was a woman of rare qualities. When one of her daughters had a brain tumor at the age of seven, the doctors removed most of the right hemisphere of her brain. They told Margaret the girl would be a mere vegetable for the rest of her life. Margaret wouldn't accept the judgment. She nursed the girl and prayed for her. She saw an article in the newspaper about a special operation being performed in Canada that might improve her daughter's condition. Pursuing the information, she learned that it would cost seven thousand dollars for the operation. Margaret's family was dirt poor. They didn't have seventy dollars, much less seven thousand dollars. But that didn't stop Margaret. She prayed some more and told some people about her need. An article in the newspaper raised more than ten thousand dollars to send her and her daughter to Canada.

When Margaret and the little girl arrived in Canada, they didn't have the proper papers and were not permitted to deplane. Margaret persuaded the airport officials to get her a phone connection with the Canadian government. She told the government officials that she was from the Commonwealth of Kentucky and needed to get her daughter to the hospital. The officials thought she was related to the governor of Kentucky and sent an ambulance and a limousine to take her and her daughter to the hospital.

Later someone asked her, "Are you from the governor?"

"No," she said.

"Are you a friend of his?" she was asked.

"I didn't even vote for him," she said.

The doctors at the hospital took X rays, studied them, and said they did not want to operate. Margaret said, "There's a power higher than you that obviously wants you to." The doctors operated, and the girl lived an almost normal life until she was a young woman.

Now I almost never read the story of the Greek mother in today's scripture without thinking of Margaret Howard. God invented something pretty special when he invented mothers. They put an awful lot of love and care into the world. In fact, they are a never-ending supply.—John Killinger

Sermon Suggestions

IDENTIFYING A REAL CHRISTIAN. TEXT: John 13:31–35. (1) Not by church membership. (2) Not by correct theology. (3) Not by strenuous activism. (4) But by genuine love.

THE HOME OF GOD. TEXT: Rev. 21:1–6 NRSV. (1) It is a renewed creation. (2) It is among mortals. (3) It is free of death, sorrow, and pain. (4) It is replete with life. (5) It is guaranteed by the One who is the source and perfection of everything.

Worship Aids

CALL TO WORSHIP. "Praise ye the Lord. Praise ye the Lord from the heavens: praise him in the heights" (Ps. 148:1).

INVOCATION. This morning we come to express to you the gratitude we feel, Father, for the manner in which you have established life around the family. We are grateful that we live in families and relationships of friendship. Through the worship of this hour may the bonds of love be drawn closer. May faith and hope and love not be just mighty words in our speech but active functions in our lives with one another in these close relationships of family. And as we learn to love one another, may we do so because we have learned to love you with all our heart and mind and soul.—Henry Fields

OFFERTORY SENTENCE. "My God shall supply all your need according to his riches in glory by Christ Jesus" (Phil. 4:19).

OFFERTORY PRAYER. Your charity toward us has been great, Father. There has been bread upon our tables, a roof over our heads, and necessities for every circumstance. We have experienced the "extras" of life in great abundance. Help us this morning to show our appreciation, our gratitude by becoming agents of charity, dispensers of grace to those who need our care around the world, we pray in Jesus' name.—Henry Fields

PRAYER. In this season we think especially of family and the ones who make it meaningful for us, Father. This morning we pray that you will send your blessing on our homes that in them true love and faith may abide. On this special day we ask that you let honor rest on all mothers. May the day bring rest and peace to those who have grown old. May strength and happiness be given to those who bear the responsibility of growing children. May inspiration and guidance be imparted to those who approach motherhood. Grant that all of us may look back along the paths of memory and gain the inspiration and incentive to walk our future road with wisdom and courage because we have seen these in those who significantly guided us in our formative years. Truly we pray that you will strengthen the bonds that bind us together in our homes and that make us families together.

In this age when so many factors are causing the deterioration of family life, we pray that we will be inspired to deal with the factors and bring stability where we can. We realize that both riches and poverty are disruptive. Help us to use wisely the wealth that we control so that it will be a positive factor in the stability of life not only for us but for all people. Enable us to stem the tide that has caused a loss of decency among us. Open our eyes to the value of truth, goodness, and beauty so that they will not be lost in our times. Enable us to prevent the mists of evil from descending upon us like a stifling cloud. Father, grant that the Holy Spirit will bring us into a new day, and as we see it dawning on the horizon, help us to respond with all our strength and seek with all our hearts the kingdom of righteousness, beginning in the homes where we live, we pray in Jesus' name.—Henry Fields

LECTIONARY MESSAGE

Topic: "Whosoever Will"

TEXT: Acts 11:1–18

Luke, the author of the Acts of the Apostles, obviously considered the conversion of Cornelius and his household vitally important, since he devoted a chapter and a half to the story and its aftermath. In fact, the last twelve verses of chapter 9 detail Peter's route to Caesarea, where our story is set. Then the whole of chapter 10 is his description of the event itself. The passage we are considering today tells of the aftermath, that is, Peter's justification of his permitting this Roman soldier and his family to be baptized.

Why would this story be so important? There are a number of conversion reports in Acts. What makes this one so special? The first verse of our passage clarifies that: "The Gentiles had also accepted the word of God." Up to this time those converted to the Christian faith had been Jews and Jewish proselytes. Cornelius was a highly respected man, but he had not submitted himself to circumcision, which would have marked his conversion to Judaism. He and his household, then, were still outside the realm of God when they suddenly and unexpectedly became Christians. They did not become Christians by being converted from Judaism, as had all other believers up to that time. They came to Christ directly out of the world of Roman paganism.

In other words, they were outsiders, and Peter had let them in. Is it any wonder, then, that the Jerusalem elders demanded an explanation from Peter? The mother church felt responsible for all other congregations and for the proclamation of the good news everywhere. The leaders of the mother church took very seriously their responsibility for checking on such a report.

The thrust of Peter's defense is simple: God made it clear that he chose these people, so we baptized them. The Jerusalem Christians learned a valuable lesson that day—a lesson that the church has too often forgotten since then. In fact, it is a lesson we should be reminded of regularly. God does the choosing of who will join his realm, and he chooses "whosoever will."

Peter's vision of the clean and unclean animals taught him that *God cleanses.* The words must have rung in his ears; even Luke records Peter's exact repetition of them to the elders: "What God has made clean, you must not call profane." Peter says that he heard this three times. There was no escaping God's lesson here. When God chooses to include people who have previously been excluded, it is not that he is lowering his standards. His cleansing power can bring up to standard anybody who wills. Cornelius was not just a Gentile; he was a centurion in the Roman army of occupation! We can hardly imagine anybody who would make good Jewish believers more nervous than a Roman officer. If God could cleanse and include him, he could cleanse and include anybody.

Peter witnessed the coming of the Holy Spirit on these Romans, and he realized that *God blesses.* God's work of cleansing is not limited to secret, interior change; he sends along with it the gift of the Holy Spirit, so that others notice the change. Peter recognized that this blessing was in no way inferior to the blessing he and the others had received on the day of Pentecost. He described it just that way to the elders: "And as I began to speak, the Holy Spirit fell upon them just as it had upon us at the beginning." God does not play favorites. His love is intended for the whole human race, and "whosoever will" can receive it.

Peter and the elders learned from this that *God gives life.* The response of the elders to Peter's report was, "Then God has given even to the Gentiles the repentance that leads to life." The admittance of the Gentiles into the realm of God was not a matter of human strategy; it was a gift of God. And the gift that God gives is life by means of a transformed understanding of reality.

In awe those early Christians tried to take in the significance of God's welcoming the enemy into his realm. There was only one appropriate response—praise. Praise God, from whom all cleansing, all blessing, and all life flow. Praise him and practice his approach, which is put so well in Romans 15:7: "Welcome one another, then, just as Christ has welcomed you, for the glory of God." See to it that no centurion, no stranger, no outsider, not even an enemy is excluded from hearing that God cleanses, God blesses, and God gives life.—Bruce E. Shields

SUNDAY: MAY TWENTY-FIRST

SERVICE OF WORSHIP

Sermon: It's Dynamite!

TEXT: Rom. 1:16–17

When Nobel, the Swedish chemist, invented dynamite, he gave it a name taken from the Greek word that means power. That is the very word that Paul used to describe the gospel in Romans 1:16.

We have in our hands a gospel, the good news that we can have right standing with God. It is dynamite!

I. When you think of the gospel as dynamite, you make an affirmation. Paul said, "I am not ashamed of the gospel" (v. 16). That sounds a bit negative to us. What he meant was that he was proud of the gospel. "For I have *complete confidence* in the gospel" is the way the GOOD NEWS BIBLE translates it.

(a) It is an amazing thing to think of the background of that statement. Paul had been imprisoned in Philippi, chased out of Thessalonica, stoned in Lystra, smuggled out of Beroea, laughed at in Athens. He had preached in Corinth, where his message was foolishness to the Greeks and a stumbling block to the Jews, and out of that background Paul declared that he was proud of the gospel. There was something in the gospel that made Paul triumphantly victorious over all that men could do to him.

(b) But if Paul wrote out of that background, think also of what he had seen:

He had seen the jailer at Philippi fall on his knees asking what he must do to be saved. And he had been saved.

He had seen churches established in Europe and Asia.

He had seen a demented girl turned into a rational creature.

He had seen the cynical intellectuals at Athens, who laughed at him, also yield some people of faith.

He had seen the wicked and corrupt Corinth, known as the prostitute of the world, become the site of a church.

No wonder he had confidence in the gospel! He had seen it work.

And that is our affirmation of the gospel. It works.

II. When you think of the gospel as dynamite, you have an assurance. The assurance is that the gospel is the power of God.

Power was a strange word to use of the gospel when the Roman legions tramped down every road. It would seem that at that time power was with Rome. But where is Rome today? And where is the gospel?

(a) People often search for power.

Is it in military might? Look at the fallen military powers of the world: Carthage, Rome, Germany, Japan.

Is it in political power? Most observers feel that former President Richard Nixon's fall was due to his obsession with power.

Is it in economic strength? Fortunes have been made and lost. And so have people.

(b) In contrast to all of these concepts of power, we have the gospel, going its way, exploding into the lives of people, blowing old ways of life, old patterns, old sins into smithereens. It's dynamite!

III. When you think of the gospel as dynamite, you see an activity. Paul affirmed that it was the power of God unto salvation.

(a) That is the first activity of God's powerful, dynamic gospel: it brings salvation.

Salvation means deliverance. When Christ saves us, he delivers us from our sin.

We had been in the power of sin, self, and Satan. When Jesus is accepted as Savior, he delivers us from that and gives to us salvation.

From the Greek word for power comes dynamite: God breaking into our lives.

(b) But there is another activity of God's powerful gospel: giving us strength every day.

Dynamo also comes from the same word for power. A dynamo continually and constantly pumps out power.

Some of us who have known the power of God in salvation have failed to use the power of God in our daily lives. Professing Christ, we may also make a shambles of the Christian convictions by drinking, lusting, lying, cheating, manipulating. Why? There are two reasons: (1) you may not really try to change, or (2) you have not depended on the power of God to help you change.

But God's power is an activity at work daily in our lives.

IV. When you think of the gospel as dynamite, you come to an acceptance.

Paul showed the inclusiveness of the gospel. It was for all people, both Jews and Greeks.

If it is so inclusive, how do you receive it? By believing.

Everyone who believes in Jesus Christ, who expresses faith in him, can know this power of God working salvation in his life.

It's dynamite! And this power of God can be known in your life if you believe in Christ. Won't you believe today?—James E. Carter

Illustrations

INCONCEIVABLE POWER. Many years ago I spoke at a dinner at a Strategic Air Command (SAC) base in western Oklahoma. During a tour of the base the commanding officer showed me five large bombers loaded with nuclear weapons. He said that even if someone pushed a button in Omaha, Nebraska, in the middle of the night, a signal would sound on this base, and these bombers would be in the air in fourteen minutes.

I commented that I was sure the United States could protect itself. The commander replied, "Well, that is classified information, but I can tell you this much. If the firepower on any one of those five planes were reproduced in terms of World War II explosives, a train five thousand miles long with each freight car holding one hundred thousand pounds of bombs would be required to carry the load." I asked him to tell me no more, for I could not stand it. So much power for destruction!

Yet the explosives on all those five planes were as firecrackers when compared with the infinite power of God. All his power is for benevolent use and is available to God's people if only they will claim and use it.—Herschel H. Hobbs

BEYOND TRAGEDY. "Short of damnation, there can be no Christian tragedy. If a person writes a tragedy of the classic type, Christianity must be kept out of it. . . . Where Christ is, cheerfulness will keep breaking in." So wrote Dorothy L. Sayers in the introduction to her radio plays, *The Man Born to Be King*.—Maxwell Butcher.

FOR THE CHRISTIAN, REALITY IS RESURRECTION. God is the one who cares and rescues, using even death itself as a method and transforming death into life. God is, as Moltmann insists, involved in Jesus' death, as in every tragedy. There is no escape *from* tragedy: there is escape *through* tragedy. The Resurrection is not an avoidance of the cross: it is its natural outcome.—H. Maxwell Butcher

Sermon Suggestions

THE THINGS THAT BRING US COMFORT. TEXT: John 14:23–29; Phil. 4:7. (1) The word of Christ to guide us, verses 23–24. (2) The Holy Spirit to teach us, verses 25–26. (3) The peace of Christ to guard our hearts, verse 27 and Phil. 4:7.

PRESENT AND ABSENT IN HEAVEN. TEXT: Rev. 21:10, 22–22:5 NRSV. (1) Present: (a) "the Lord God the almighty and the Lamb"; (b) the best of this world; (c) total security; (d) "those who are written in the Lamb's book of life." (2) Absent: whatever would contaminate or compromise the security or purity of heaven.

Worship Aids

CALL TO WORSHIP. "God be merciful unto us, and bless us; and cause his face to shine upon us; that thy way may be known upon earth, thy saving health among all nations" (Ps. 67:1–2).

INVOCATION. Move with great power among us, Lord, comforting the sorrowful, strengthening the tempted, inspiring the faithful, saving the lost, and bringing in the kingdom of God.—E. Lee Phillips

OFFERTORY SENTENCE. "Whenever we have an opportunity, let us work for the good of all, and especially for those of the family of faith" (Gal. 6:10 NRSV).

OFFERTORY PRAYER. Lord, we have experienced your providential care for us. May we now possess the magnitude of spirit that will enable us to give liberally and freely.—Henry Fields

PRAYER. O God, who has been our refuge in the hours of the world's travail, accept us we pray thee once again and restore our souls by thy mercy to their strength and peace. We come to thee tired of struggle, our faith weakened, and the sight of thy glory dimmed. Pour out thy Spirit on us, O God, both in forgiveness and in power, that we may be reassured and lifted up with courage to do thy will amid the perplexing circumstances of our lot. Set our feet on a sure rock and, though the storms assail us, keep us steady with an upright purpose and the certain hope of thy kingdom's triumph.—Samuel H. Miller

LECTIONARY MESSAGE

Topic: Who's in Charge?

TEXT: Acts 16:9–15

OTHER READINGS: Rev. 21:10, 22–22:5; John 14:23–29

When we read this text, it's hard not to ask the question, "Who? Who is telling this story, anyway?" In verses 6, 7, and 8 it is "they" who are acting: "they went," "they had come," "they attempted to go." Then verse 9 tells of Paul's vision, and from verse 10 on it is "we": "God had called us," "we set sail," "we went outside," "we sat down." Who is telling this story? Is this the place in Luke's account where he finally enters the picture? It certainly looks that way. We might see this as the beginning of Luke's pilgrimage. Was he from Troas or from Philippi, or did he just happen to run into Paul here? Nobody knows the details. Perhaps he recorded somebody else's personal story here. But it is clear that the account becomes very personal throughout this section of the book.

An even more important "who" question is, "Who is in charge of this mission?" Paul and Silas had been sent out by the believers in Antioch (15:40) to visit the churches he and Barnabas had established on their first journey. But here we find them making a beeline northwest through the province of Asia, turning to neither the north nor the south, and then setting sail for Europe, landing at Neapolis and going overland to Philippi. I fear that if we sent a mission team out to one continent and they went to another we would fire off an indignant letter demanding that they reconsider who was in charge of this mission. We usually assume that those who pay the bills are in charge. "Who pays the piper?" and all that.

But in case we haven't noticed it earlier, Luke makes it clear to us readers now that the one in charge of the Christian mission is God's Holy Spirit. They were "forbidden by the Holy Spirit to speak the word in Asia." "They attempted to go into Bithynia, but the Spirit of Jesus did not allow them." By Paul's night vision they became "convinced that God had called us to proclaim the good news to" the Macedonians. And when they met Lydia and her group, they saw that "the Lord opened her heart to listen eagerly to what was said by Paul."

God had chosen to spread his good news by means of us human beings. But the personalities and human authorities involved in the Christian mission are of secondary importance. As Paul was later to write, "But we have this treasure in clay jars, so that it may be made clear that the extraordinary power belongs to God and does not come from us" (2 Cor. 4:7). Just as Peter had discovered that God was able to include even the Gentiles in the divine community, so Paul discovered that the plan, the power, and the product of the church's mission all come from God.

How often we neglect that simple lesson! God's love was the impetus of Jesus' coming to earth. God's grace links the death and Resurrection of Jesus with our forgiveness. God's Word becomes the source of inspiration and understanding for our testimony. God's presence enlivens our worship and guides our living. God's promise draws us to that future that can be accomplished only by divine power—a future described in Revelation 21:22–22:5.

Knowing that God's Spirit is the principal actor in the unfolding drama of Christ's church, how can we neglect the disciplines of prayer and deep study of the Word? Those are the very disciplines that are the way to a better grasp of God's will for us today and a fuller use of God's power for the mission of the church. The Book of Acts is not out of date; it waits with models of church life and growth to be applied in our congregation. We can be part of that adventure if we look to the One in charge.—Bruce E. Shields

SUNDAY: MAY TWENTY-EIGHTH

SERVICE OF WORSHIP

Sermon: God's People in God's World

TEXT: 1 Pet. 1:22–2:12

I read about a religious organization that voted itself out of existence. When they had vacated their offices, the last members of the group posted a sign on the door. It said, "Gone out of business. Didn't know what our business was."

The quickest way for a church to go out of business is to be cloudy in its concept of its purpose. Every Christian should have a clear concept of what the church is all about. A church cannot fulfill its purpose if it is not sure of that purpose.

Many books have been written about the church and its role in the world. A couple that I read offered some fascinating analogies. One writer compared the church to a wagon train of pioneers. The preacher would be the cook on the train. He is just another pioneer who has learned to cook, and his job is to help the pioneers to pioneer.

The other author compared the church to a football team, and the preacher is to be a playing coach. No analogy is perfect, and you might not like either of these analogies, but keep them in mind. We will refer to them later.

The best book to read on the church is the New Testament, and one of the best writers to consult in the New Testament is the man called Simon Peter. He was there when it all began, and he was a vital part of the church. The inspired apostle would admit that some things about the church change and must change—methods, meetings, organizations. The church should seize every tool that can be used for the glory of Jesus Christ in fulfilling the purpose of the church. But while some things change, other things must never change. The unchangeables were Peter's concern in his recorded concept of the church.

Peter reminded us that as the church we are *God's people,* and that must never change. We are *God's priests,* and that must never change. We are *God's pilgrims,* and that must never change.

I. We are God's people. We are people, human beings. We are sinners who know the frustration and bitterness of defeat and failure. We need one another. God has brought us together as a church to love and help one another. We are not qualified to judge one another. We lost the right to judge when we knelt at the cross to accept God's forgiveness. We have no cause for pride but every cause for rejoicing and thanksgiving.

We are people to whom something indescribably and everlastingly wonderful has happened. God has made us his people. We have been redeemed with the precious blood of Jesus Christ, God's Son (1 Pet. 1:18–19). Peter informed us that in accepting Jesus Christ as our Lord and Savior, we have been born again with incorruptible seed (1 Pet. 1:23). God himself has chosen us and called us out of the darkness of sin and failure to be his people and to declare his praises (1 Pet. 2:9).

God has made us a part of his own family. Alexander MacLaren, that Scottish saint, reminded us that "the world takes its notions of God, most of all, from the people who say that they belong to God's family." They read us a great deal more than they read the Bible. They see us, while they only hear about Jesus Christ.

II. We are God's priests. Again, the zealous apostle declared that we are God's priests. Every child of God is meant to be a priest of God. William Barclay calls to our attention that in Latin *priest* means "bridge builder." Our very lives are to be bridges by which God can cross to give himself to others. We are to be the means of other people coming to know, love, and trust Jesus Christ as Lord and Savior. We are to listen, to witness, to minister, and to pray.

Dr. Stewart Newman tells of a man in his hometown who was to undergo a very serious operation in a large hospital in the state capital. Just before leaving, the man asked a friend of his to tell him about becoming a Christian. "John," he said, "you know I don't go to church. You are a Christian. Tell me how to become a Christian." John stammered and cleared his throat. Finally he said, "I guess you had better go to the preacher." That's something, but not much. John had a wonderful, God-given opportunity to share his faith, but he was not ready. John failed to be a bridge builder.

The writer of Hebrews wrote to some people like John. He said, "For when for the time ye ought to be teachers, ye have need that one teach you again which be the first principles of the oracles of God; and are become such as have need of milk, and not of strong meat" (Heb. 5:12).

After an evening worship service a concerned lady approached her pastor, requesting that he speak to a friend of hers who was not a Christian. She explained that God had given her a great burden for her friend. The pastor agreed to make the call, but then he had another thought. He asked the lady to consider that if God gave her the burden, he must want her to speak to her friend. In asking someone else to do it, she was avoiding her responsibility.

You might be asking, "Well, what are we paying the preachers for?" That question has been asked often. Paul helped us answer the question in Ephesians. He wrote that the risen Christ "gave some, apostles; and some, prophets; and some, evangelists; and some, pastors and teachers; for the perfecting of the saints, for the work of the ministry, for the edifying of the body of Christ" (4:11–12). The pastor is in the equipping ministry of helping God's priests to fulfill their tasks. Remember the cook on the wagon train? God needs the pioneers that they might carry out their tasks.

Yet that is not all of the pastor's responsibility. The other analogy compared the pastor to a playing coach. That reminds the minister that he must get into the game, too. He must listen, witness, minister, and pray as well as help equip others to do so.

III. We are God's pilgrims. The third unchangeable in the church is that we are God's pilgrims. A pilgrim is a temporary resident, a transient, someone passing through. A pilgrim is not a tramp. A tramp does not know where he is going. A pilgrim is someone with a purpose and a destination. He is a citizen of heaven who is moving toward the fulfillment of God's purpose for his life.

A pilgrim travels light. He does not carry this world's valuables. He is not bound by "things." He does not need a bigger house or a bigger car to keep him going. The pilgrim realizes that these things are all but incidental because heaven is his home, and from there he takes his values.

Someone rushed into the study of Ralph Waldo Emerson one day and interrupted the great man to exclaim, "I have just heard that the world is about to come to an end." Without bothering to look up, Emerson responded, "Well, we can get along without it." Indeed, Christian pilgrims can get along without the world.

As a Christian pilgrim, Simon Peter said, you will not need some things. You can strip them off and throw them away. You can leave behind malice, that poisonous, ill-willed spirit of revenge.

We are told that in painting the Last Supper, Leonardo da Vinci sought revenge upon an enemy by painting his face on the figure of Judas. When he came to paint Jesus Christ, the great artist found himself completely frustrated. Only when he painted out the face of his enemy was he able to paint the face of Jesus. Malice had stymied him.

You can throw away guile, that tiresome hypocrisy and deceitfulness, envy, and evil speaking. A little girl proclaimed to her mother that she had been a peacemaker that day. "Oh," inquired the concerned parent, "did you prevent a fight?" "No," came the reply, "but I heard something bad and didn't repeat it." That's fine peacemaking.

There are some essentials that as pilgrims we need to take with us. We will need a daily supply of nourishing food from God's Word (1 Pet. 2:2). We will need a generous supply of love for others because we are called to love everyone (1 Pet. 1:22). That love will be expressed through good works (1 Pet. 2:12) that will glorify God.

IV. A World War I novel related the story of two young men who became inseparable companions. One was from a fine, outstanding family and had lived a decent and wholesome life. The other grew up on the wrong side of the tracks and had been in constant trouble.

An enemy bullet felled the young man from the fine family. As he lay dying in the arms of his friend, he said to him, "Your name has many marks against it. You have no place to go when the war's over. My name has no marks against it. Give me your name, and let it die with me. You take my name and live a new life."

Jesus Christ did that, and more, for us. At the cross he took our names, our lives, and our sins and let them die with him. He came forth from the tomb and gave us his name and a new life to live by his daily grace.

At the cross Jesus made us God's people, God's priests, and God's pilgrims. That's who we are. Isn't it time we lived like it?—Alfred L. Miller

Illustrations

OUR PARISH. Far too little emphasis has been placed on the fact that for the Christian his *work* is the sphere in which he is called to translate his acknowledgment of God into action. . . . It is not just a question of sending into industry, the professions, local government, and the like what perhaps I may be pardoned for calling "private" Christians, men and women who say their prayers, are regular communicants, take their share in parish life. . . . Such men and women carry with them into their daily work a *personal* integrity that is indeed a noble thing. But too often their concern is only to *preserve* that personal integrity, to keep their own hands clean. Their Christian faith does not impel them to consider the far more difficult question of the integrity of the industrial or commercial system in which they work: to ask why it is so easy for others to get their hands dirty.—F. A. Cockin

THE TIME IT TAKES. On several occasions, my wife and I were invited to be present for the Bar Mitzvah of one of our friends' children. This is the time when a Jewish boy, at the age of thirteen, becomes responsible and accepts his personal religious duties. The service is an impressive and memorable one. On one such occasion, my wife and I were present for the Bar Mitzvah for our across-the-street neighbor. In the large synagogue, full almost to capacity, he read the Scriptures in Hebrew with clarity and enthusiasm. Then came the time for him to deliver his message to the congregation. He chose to speak about the family. A sentence captured my imagination. He said, "It takes only a moment to become a parent, but it requires a great deal to be a parent."

This thirteen-year-old lad had hit upon a significant truth. As the service continued, at times in Hebrew, and then in English, I let my mind draw a parallel to Christianity. We were probably the only Christians in that great congregation. I had a burden for them. I thought, "It only takes a moment to become a Christian, but it requires a lifetime to be a Christian."—Harold C. Bennett

Sermon Suggestions

THE WHAT AND THE WHY OF CHRISTIAN UNITY. TEXT: John 17:20–26. (1) The nature of our unity: (a) It is a unity in diversity, as in Father and Son, verse 21a. (b) It is an accomplished gift, verse 22. (c) Paradoxically, it is something to pray for and bring to expression, verses 20–21a, 23a. (2) The goal of our unity: (a) that the world may believe, verse 21b; (b) that Christ may be glorified, verses 22 and 24.

EPILOGUE AND PROLOGUE. TEXT: Rev. 22:12–14, 16–17, 20–21. (1) A solemn truth, verse 16. (2) A potential blessing, verse 14. (3) A sweeping invitation, verse 17. (4) A comforting assurance, verses 20–21.

Worship Aids

CALL TO WORSHIP. "Arise, shine; for thy light is come, and the glory of the Lord is risen upon thee" (Isa. 60:1).

INVOCATION. This morning, Father, make us aware of past blessings and deliverances that have enriched our lives. Having reminded us of what has been, open our eyes that we might see the possibilities of the present and how you are working in the situations that claim us at the moment. Knowing that in your care and keeping all things work together for good to them that love you and are called according to your purpose, give us the courage to entrust every tomorrow and every coming event into your hands that you might direct our lives in accordance with your blessed will. Now let the joy that can be ours as we gather in your house be realized among us, even as we sing unto you in Jesus' name.—Henry Fields

OFFERTORY SENTENCE. "Bear ye one another's burdens, and so fulfill the law of Christ" (Gal. 6:12).

OFFERTORY PRAYER. Reigning God, giver of every good and perfect gift, in whom we live and dwell and have our meaning; appropriate our gifts in redemptive ways that will point to thee, save many, and honor the Christ.—E. Lee Phillips

PRAYER. We would see in the darkness thy light, O Lord, and give ourselves into the charge of thy wisdom, looking to the promise thou has spoken and to the power that will make it to stand fast forever. Let the knowledge of thy redeeming purpose shine in our hearts, and on our path, for a lamp to our feet. We would have thy will to be our will. Strengthen us by thy Spirit, each to his task, and all to the coming of thy kingdom. For Jesus' sake.—Paul Scherer

LECTIONARY MESSAGE

Topic: The Paradox of Power

TEXT: Acts 16:16–34

OTHER READINGS: Rev. 22:12–14, 16–17, 20–21; John 17:20–26

We live in a context of straightforward power. *Military might, political clout, corporate takeovers*—all of these terms and more are often used to describe the age we live in. We claim to know how power works. The powerful people drive the powerful cars, wear power neckties, and eat power lunches. They are the "up and inners," not the "down and outers." Powerful people are at the top; they are the winners in the game of life. They control their own lives and those of many others. That's what power is all about.

And that's what makes the events described in our text today seem so strange. There is power, but its results are not so clear-cut. Paul and Silas are hounded for several days by a slave girl with the power to tell fortunes. Now a slave with power is hard to comprehend, but it seems that her masters made money with her power, and that is understandable. What she was saying about the Christians was OK. She identified them as "slaves of the Most High God," which was true, but which is also surprising coming from a pagan slave girl. However, Paul finally became annoyed by all her fussing, so he cast the "spirit of divination" out of her. In other words, Paul freed the girl from the unclean spirit that had been enslaving her. Paul's power—the power of the Most High God—was obviously greater than hers. And what did Paul and Silas get for their exercise of power? They got thrown into prison! They were severely flogged, and then they were secured in the innermost reaches of the jail, with their feet in stocks. That's a strange story of a power conflict: the winners end up losers. It is a paradox of power.

But the story goes on. At midnight they experienced another working of power. An earthquake happened, so severe that it opened the prison gates and loosed the prisoners' chains. Our understanding of power would lead us to say that this was justice coming. These men should not have been in jail, so God released them. But wait. They stayed put. The jailer thought he understood power, too; so he prepared to take the honorable way out, by committing suicide. He assumed that all the prisoners had run. But he was struck by the paradox when they told him that they were all still there. What was happening here? Paul and Silas were freed by the power of God, but they chose to stay in prison. It is a paradox of power.

What happened next? The jailer was so struck by the implausibility of the situation that he brought out his special prisoners and asked for their power to save him and his household. They told the whole group about Jesus and his salvation, and they were all baptized. Two powerless Jews in the Roman city of Philippi turned down the opportunity to escape from prison and ended up leading a whole group of Romans to faith in Christ. It is a paradox of power. But now it becomes a bit clearer. The power of God is used not to control or enslave people, but to free us and empower us to follow God's lead.

The primary focus of the power of God is the inclusion of people in the reign of God—what Acts calls salvation. The jailer and his household heard this good news and responded with appropriate obedience and joy. The praise of God expressed by Paul and Silas in that prison of powerlessness resulted in even greater praise of God as a Roman family joined God's family. Paul and Silas demonstrated their freedom while in prison, and then their jailer was set free in Christ. The paradox of power is that the way to be free—truly free—and to spread true freedom has nothing to do with human authority and control. The way to be free and to spread freedom is to praise the Lord and preach the gospel.—Bruce E. Shields

SUNDAY: JUNE FOURTH

SERVICE OF WORSHIP

Sermon: According to Your Faith

TEXT: Matt. 9:29

All of us live by faith. To live is to make an evaluative response to the world in which we live, to the universe, to reality. Because all of us live by faith, the question is what kind of faith, how much faith, and how real is our faith.

I. First of all, our faith must be right.

(a) Right faith must be right outside the believer. The blind men of whom we have read came to Jesus. If they had not come to the one who could heal, they would not have been healed. Many of us fail to come to God as he has truly revealed himself and to come to him fully. God's actual presence in human history as unconditional, universal love, the one who can always be trusted, came in Jesus Christ in fullness.

I have come to believe that the kind of God we believe in is our basic choice. God as a living God must be more than a symbol. It is all right to worship God as a symbol if by that we mean that the God we worship is ever more than anything we can understand. God must at least be as much as and more than the symbol.

(b) We cannot stop with a symbol. We must believe that God acts and is a living God. Modern man's greatest offense is prayer, because if we really pray and believe that God will answer our prayer, we must presuppose a God who is real and acts in history.

We must completely pray for God's will. The fundamental and first choice is the acceptance of God's will without any reservations. When we have done that, we can leave everything with confidence in his hands to be done in his way and to follow out our faith as never before.

II. The second thing we must remember is that our strength must be strong. Passion—true passion, Christian passion, a religious passion—comes from passivity. Very often we work up a feverish acceptance that is nothing more than our own rationalizing. When we really accept God's will, we have to learn first of all to be completely passive, to let God be God and God's will reign.

(a) This is Pentecost. A hundred and twenty people passed fifty days praying and waiting. I wonder what would happen today to the Christian church if we really had the grace and the patience to keep waiting for God and God's will and then were willing to do it!

You see, passivity comes from an active God who must become central to our lives if we are going to be effectively active. True passivity is necessary if we are to find God's presence.

(b) If we are going to have a true Christian passion, it must come first of all from being passive. Intensity of faith, however, can never substitute for intelligence of mind. You may have seen a man trying to lift a heavy piece of furniture up some stairs. You come along and ask him if he doesn't know there's an elevator just down the corridor. There are some people who try to lift things when, if only they could let go, they would find that there is a power lifting things from on high, and that power can operate through their intellect when their intellect is used by their faith. Faith never takes the place of study, or of personal or social responsibility. Strong faith, true faith, is always motivated by love.

(c) Why is it, I ask myself over and over again, that we do not live this reality that we know so well? History shows that it is the power of believing love that can change the course of affairs as nothing else can.

If we are going to find the reality and power of God, we must find it insofar as we accept the one who was wholly, unconditionally, universally love in Jesus Christ and surrender ourselves without any qualifications in joy and peace to this love.

III. Christian faith, then, is real, right, and strong when Christ as God's Word becomes central to us as men—universal, unconditional, and our final authority. God is the personal Spirit who is the infinite holy love, and Christ is the Spirit who disclosed this love and in whom it is self-attested.

(a) The Holy Spirit today is waiting for a new Pentecost. Perhaps the deepest thing that I have to say or leave with you is that I believe the Holy Spirit to be God actually available to each person now according to his own need and in his own way; that God is not dead, but that God is available for everyone under every circumstance. I believe that God is here to give us a strong and right faith through the Holy Spirit, to give us an inclusive community and open communications in all areas of life.

(b) I have often thought about this. Are we heading for a final catastrophe, or are we heading for a new age? My own conviction is that we are free and either can happen. My real hope is that as God holds the nations in his hands, as well as our personal lives, he can find enough faith for his purpose to be accomplished. God has shifted the gears of history.—Nels F. S. Ferre

Illustrations

TOO MUCH FAITH? Many of you may remember reading in the paper of a group of hill folk who in their simple faith took the promise of Mark 16:18 literally, that we shall drink poison as Christians and it shall not hurt us. One evening, you remember, the young minister passed a cup of poison to his young, strongly believing deacon, who lifted the cup high, thanked God for the sureness of the promises, drank, and died. When he was buried, his wife said, "My husband died from having too much faith."

Now I believe he died not from too much faith but from a false faith. You may remember, too, reading about a widow in Georgia who copied Abraham and murdered her only daughter because, she said, her daughter stood between her and God. She loved the daughter more than anything else, and God could not be real to her. Whatever the psychological explanations are, the fact is that as far as her conscious, deliberate choice was concerned she could hardly have had more faith, but the faith was not right.—Nels F. S. Ferre

KEEPING GOD IN VIEW. We may indeed pray for material good—for necessities, for health, but always in such a way that our manner of asking redounds to our eternal glory, whatever the answer we receive. In asking, we must make an oblation of our will to that of God. We must pray with a constancy and perseverance that are living proofs of our trust in God's guidance of human affairs; of our hope in a world full of the shadows of death; of a true love for God that is not simply pious self-seeking and does not depend on incessant rewards. Since we are on this earth as "strangers and pilgrims" on a journey to eternity, we must not pray as though we had here "a lasting city." We know that it is through sickness and death that we shall enter into that life that is the final object of all our prayer. As long as we keep our minds raised to God in prayer, even when disappointments and misery crowd about us, we are sustained by the invisible and mysterious, yet true and real, power of God's grace and of participation in the life of God; and, when "this mind is in us," death loses its terrors and become a swallowing up in the abyss of God's everlasting love.—Karl Rahner

Sermon Suggestions

ON KNOWING GOD THE FATHER. TEXT: John 14:8–17 (25–27). (1) By the character of Jesus Christ, verses 8–9. (2) By the words and works of Jesus Christ, verses 10–11. (3) By personal experiences of God in Christ, through "the Holy Spirit," verses 12–17.

THE PROOF OF OUR PARENTAGE. TEXT: Rom. 8:14–17. (1) In our experience of God's leadership, verse 14. (2) In our sense of the intimate fatherhood of God, verse 16. (3) In our willingness to suffer for Christ, verse 17.

Worship Aids

CALL TO WORSHIP. "I will sing unto the Lord as long as I live: I will sing praise to my God while I have my being" (Ps. 104:33).

INVOCATION. Lord, open us to divine principles, holy directives, and undeniable truths, as today we seek the mind of God for a world of need, through Christ, our Savior.—E. Lee Phillips

OFFERTORY SENTENCE. "Ye shall receive power, after that the Holy Ghost is come upon you: and ye shall be witnesses unto me both in Jerusalem, and in all Judaea, and in Samaria, and unto the uttermost part of the earth" (Acts 1:8).

OFFERTORY PRAYER. Lord, we have received through the sacrifices of others. Lead us this morning to make significant monetary sacrifices that others may in turn be blessed by our giving, we pray in Jesus' name.—Henry Fields

PRAYER. Holy Spirit of God, who at Pentecost didst descend with power upon Christ's disciples and didst send them out to preach the gospel and to found the church, inspire us also to sustain what they began. O Most High, mean to us what thou didst mean to them: the grace of our Lord Jesus Christ, the love of God, and the fellowship of the Holy Spirit. Enrich our souls with that threefold experience, that thou mayest be to us the almighty Creator, the Saving Character, the Indwelling Comforter.

Eternal Spirit, mysterious beyond our understanding yet shining clearly in all that is excellent and true, we deeply need thy help. We are not sufficient unto ourselves. As we did not create ourselves, so we cannot sustain ourselves amid life's strains and anxieties, storms and temptations, disappointments and griefs. Here we would lay aside all pride and humbly acknowledge our urgent need. For light enough to walk by through dark days, for inner strength to carry heavy burdens, undertake courageous deeds, sustain personal sorrow, and render faithful service to our generation, we pray to thee. Spirit of the eternal, make us more than ourselves, because we have thee for our ally and reinforcement.

Baptize us with the grace of appreciation. Enlarge our capacities for joy. Forgive us that we miss so many opportunities to be glad and grateful. Open our hearts to happiness in simple things, to mirth that has no bitter springs and no sad aftermath. In the beauty of nature, in human friendship, in family life, in the joys of common tasks and familiar relationships, may we find satisfaction, that we may live not only with integrity but also with radiance.

We thank thee for the heritage that is ours in Christ and for the great tradition that thy church has handed down to us. Make us worthy of our inheritance. Let us not because of any infidelity or lack of character hurt it by our mishandling or rob our children of its full possession. We pray for another Pentecost, another outpouring of thy Spirit on thy church. For still the peoples of the earth wander like sheep without a shepherd. Still earthly riches leave them destitute in soul, and by the very things their ingenious minds invent their spirits are wounded and the hopes of mankind are threatened. Still tyranny oppresses multitudes, the liberty of human souls is taken from them, the hopes of the young are destroyed, and the Spirit and teaching of Christ are trampled underfoot. O God, awaken thy church. Raise up leaders, prophets in thy pulpits, teachers in the schools, statesmen in seats of government, and enlighten and inspire thy church throughout the world.

We pray thee for venturesome and courageous spirits. Save us from our timidities and fears, from the reluctance and paralysis of our uncertainties and doubts. Nerve us, we beseech thee, that with noble tasks to be enterprised and done, we may be strong to endure, to sacrifice, and to achieve. Since thou hast done us this high honor, calling us into an unfinished world to bear a hand with thee in its completion, give us wisdom and strength that we may work while it is day, ere the night comes when no man can work.

We pray in the name of Christ.—Harry Emerson Fosdick

LECTIONARY MESSAGE

Topic: The Day of the Lord

TEXT: Acts 2:1–21

OTHER READINGS: Gen. 11:1–9; Rom. 8:14–17; John 14:8–17 (25–27)

The record of the first Christian Pentecost is fascinating. There are so many details that seem strange to us that we run the danger of missing the grandeur of the scene and its larger significance. As important as it might be to understand something about the nature of the miracles portrayed here or to meditate on one or another aspect of Peter's sermon, we do the text an injustice when we neglect the place of this event in the history of God's dealings with humankind.

Let's step back a bit and try to comprehend the total picture. The scene begins by describing two groups of people in Jerusalem on that first Pentecost after the Resurrection of Jesus. The first of these groups was made up of his disciples, who were meeting together when the promise of Jesus to them was fulfilled. He had said, "But you will receive power when the Holy Spirit has come upon you" (Acts 1:8). As he had indicated, they then became his witnesses. We'll call them messianic Jews.

Group two comprised "devout Jews from every nation under heaven living in Jerusalem." Over the centuries Jewish families had been moved or had chosen to move to other parts of the world. In later generations some of them had moved back to Jerusalem, either permanently or temporarily. At any rate, they represented the whole of what is called diaspora Judaism. We'll call them international Jews.

The two groups got together when the sound connected with the power of the Holy Spirit attracted the international Jews to the messianic Jews. Each foreign Jew heard the gospel in his or her heart language. Anytime we spend even a brief time in a place where the predominant language is not the one we grew up with, we welcome the sound of that mother tongue—that heart language. When we hear in that language, we hear somehow more deeply even when we are fairly comfortable using what is to us a foreign language. Such an experience made a profound impression on those international Jews.

This gave Peter an opening to preach to the whole assembly in their common language. Now that they had heard in a preliminary way the Word of God in their heart languages, they paid close attention as Peter reminded them of their prophetic expectation that precisely what they saw happening had been foretold. He then told them about Jesus and how his death and Resurrection were part of God's plan.

Three thousand were baptized that day, getting the church of Jesus Christ off to an auspicious beginning. But this is more than just an interesting record of the birth of the church. Those three thousand people were more than just an impressively large group. They were a group representing God's chosen people scattered in "every nation under heaven." God was fulfilling many other prophecies that day.

Isaiah (2:2–3) proclaimed that all the nations would stream to Jerusalem to hear the Word of the Lord. Jeremiah (29:11–14) promised that God would gather his people from all nations back to their homeland. Daniel (7:13–14) prophesied that the coming one would be served by "all peoples, nations, and languages."

The preaching of the gospel of Christ and the existence of the church are not just human strategies to get a job done. They are God's chosen means to fulfill his desire to bring all nations into one humanity in Christ. It is therefore appropriate for us to attend to the preaching and hearing of the Word of God with great care. As Paul put it to the Thessalonians (1 Thess. 2:4, 13), preachers should "speak, not to please mortals, but to please God," and hearers of the gospel should "accept it not as a human word but as what it really is, God's word." It is also appropriate for us to handle the work of the church of which we are members with deep reverence and thanksgiving. In so doing we participate in the work of God to unite all of humanity under his reign.—Bruce E. Shields

SUNDAY: JUNE ELEVENTH

SERVICE OF WORSHIP

Sermon: Religion: A Toy or a Power?

TEXT: 1 Thess. 1:5

These words of St. Paul employ one of the most effective devices of teaching and writing—putting a truth in terms of one strong contrast.

It is the way that nature paints. There are the green and yellow of spring, the black and white of winter, the red and brown of autumn. It is the way that Jesus taught, in such large measure. At least three-fourths of all his parables picture a vivid contrast, the Pharisee and the publican, the wise and foolish virgins, the sheep and the goats, the houses built on sand and rock. They are pictures that caught the eye first and then the imagination and the conscience.

I. Life needs power from a source outside of itself. It needs power from a source other than the ingenuities of a mechanical civilization. An individual and a society need invisible means of support. Is there any self to which one can be true that is not in turn true to something beyond itself?

(a) Say to a pilot on a ship, "To thine own self be true." It is a wonderful mouthful. But if a ship is to make any port, he had better be true to something beyond himself, the North Star. Say to the builder of a skyscraper, "To thine own self be true." A good idea! But if the building is to stand, he had better have a plumb line handy. If a life is to stand under the pressures that play upon it, it needs more than a subjective feeling; it needs the objective moral and spiritual reality of God.

(b) There is today an impressive recognition of that need. The confident disdain of religion, which marked so many in the boisterous 1920s, looks awfully thin today.

"Fear and sorrow are no longer major themes of our culture." Say that in a day when fear stalks down every city street and country lane in the world, and sorrow has walked into hundreds of millions of homes! Fear and sorrow, far from being outmoded by our inventions, are the major themes of our culture.

II. The Christian faith has been a measureless power in lives. That is not theory but observation.

(a) Faith, of course, can never be anything but a venture. That is what makes it exciting. It is true of the two greatest experiences of life, falling in love and getting religion. When a young man falls in love, he draws sufficient conclusions from insufficient evidence. Sometimes, to unemotional and tough-minded onlookers, the evidence seems fantastically insufficient. But the conclusion that he draws, that she is a little bit of infinity, is very frequently sufficient for a lifetime.

(b) The evidence of the right of Jesus to be the interpreter and master of life is sufficient for a venture. He meets life's needs at such vital points. Man's sense of not fitting into his environment as other creatures of earth do is met by Jesus' revelation of the larger environment in which his life is set—the great Other in whom his fragments are complete. Man's sense of missing the mark is met by Jesus' assurance of forgiveness and a power to make life over. Our experience of the curiously self-defeating quality of selfishness is matched with Jesus' demand for the fulfillment of life in service.

(c) The surest evidence for Christian faith is people with empowered lives. The crowning evidence of Christianity is a new kind of people. Very few persons are so poor in experience that they cannot reach out mentally and lay their hands on four or five people in whom religion is not a toy but a power, a motive force that turned the wheels of life. The striking thing about them is that the truths of their faith are not what Coleridge called "bed ridden truths which lie asleep in the dormitory of their minds." Their minds are not dormitories but powerhouses. The truth gets up and walks. You can hear the beat of it in their steps: "I am strong for all things in him who strengtheneth me."

III. In the life of the world our Christian faith can be and must be not an ornament or a fair covering for a pagan mind but a power. T. S. Eliot writes, "The search for material remedies to cure our spiritual distresses can have only one end—failure. Only when we accept the truth that man does not live by bread alone will there be laid the foundation stone of a civilization worthy of the name."

(a) But faith is a power only when it finds expression in concrete action. We have had a surfeit of merely verbal Christianity. All too often, in the face of conditions and threats of our frightened world, Christian people and churches have taken refuge in a vague "hope for the best," which is called hope or trust. It deserves neither name. Genuine faith and trust are not in word but in deed.

(b) Faith is reliance, surely. God never gets to the end of his rope. His kingdom is an everlasting kingdom. But faith is also direction and propelling power. To be a power in our world of conflict and wars, hot, medium, and cold, our gospel must be in deed. It demands a sustained effort to bring about human welfare in lands where it does not exist. In that sense, we must be more than conquerors.—Halford E. Luccock

Illustrations

A PERSONAL GOD. I shall never forget talking once with Henry Norris Russell, one of the foremost astronomers of our day. He had been telling us about the size of the universe and fairly splitting our heads with facts about its magnitude, such as that light, traveling 186,000 miles a second, takes a million years to get from one side of the universe to the other. At that time as a young man I was reaching out for divine guidance about the daily decisions of life. As I listened to this man talk, it seemed to me that he had knocked the idea of a personal God into a cocked hat.

"How on earth," I thought, "can a God big enough to create and control such a universe have any time left for the details of my one human existence?" My friend the astronomer was also a profound Christian believer. When I asked him the question above, he replied, "The trouble with your infinite God is that he is not nearly infinite enough. Since God is really infinite, he can dispatch the affairs of this universe in the twinkling of an eye and then have all the time in the world left for you."—Samuel M. Shoemaker

FORGIVENESS AS POWER. We cannot be born anew if the power of the old is not broken within us, and it is not broken so long as it puts the burden of guilt upon us. Therefore religion, prophetic as well as apostolic, pronounced, above all, forgiveness. Forgiveness means that the old is thrown into the past because the new has come. "Remember not" in the prophetic words does not mean to forget easily. If it meant that, forgiveness would not be necessary. Forgiveness means a throwing out of the old, as remembered and real at the same time, by the strength of the new, which could never be the saving new if it did not carry with it the authority of forgiveness.—Paul Tillich

Sermon Suggestions

THE TRUTH ABOUT JESUS CHRIST. TEXT: John 16:12–15. (1) It is not obvious. (2) It is given by the guidance of the Spirit. (3) Its essence is in Jesus' relation to the Father.

WHY LADY WISDOM CANNOT BE IGNORED. TEXT: Prov. 8:1–4, 22–31. (1) Her ubiquitous call. (2) Her prior claim in the nature of things (cf. John 1:1–5, 10–18).

Worship Aids

CALL TO WORSHIP. "O Lord our Lord, how excellent is thy name in all the earth! who hast set thy glory above the heavens" (Ps. 8:1).

INVOCATION. God of grace, enter our worship with such power and justice and holiness that our vision will be opened as never before to the goodness of providence and the spiritual needs of others.—E. Lee Phillips

OFFERTORY SENTENCE. "All along I showed you that it is our duty to help the weak in this way, by hard work, and that we should keep in mind the words of the Lord Jesus, who himself said, 'Happiness lies more in giving than in receiving' " (Acts 20:35 REB).

OFFERTORY PRAYER. Our offerings come from grateful hearts and full lives, Father. May they be used across the world to fill the emptiness in the lives of others as they come to know you because we fulfill the need to give.—Henry Fields

PRAYER. O God most merciful and holy, forgive us our sins. Forgive us for the sin of blindness, which sees so superficially that it sees no sin. More deeply still, forgive the sins that make us blind—the furious haste, weary indifference, hard sophistication, evasive restlessness, covered guilt, and love of comfort. Forgive us and save us from that sin of all sins, of denying thee; forgive us for confessing thy name but avoiding thy presence; most of all for coming into thy presence too well protected by self-satisfaction to be humbled by thy glory or meekened by thy grace. Forgive us, O God, and open our eyes that we may repent and be saved, through Jesus Christ our Lord.—Samuel H. Miller

LECTIONARY MESSAGE

Topic: Shameless Hope

TEXT: Rom. 5:1–5

OTHER READINGS: Prov. 8:1–4, 22–31; John 16:12–15

Hope when it is disappointed results in shame. Only that hope that cannot be disappointed may be described as shameless. The hope of which this passage speaks is so closely related to faith and love as to be firm and fulfilled. For here is the familiar trilogy of which 1 Corinthians 13:13 is the clearest explanation: "Faith, hope, and love abide." The study of hope has become resurgent in post–World War II theology. It is closely related to faith in the New Testament. Hebrews spells it out: "Faith is the substance of things hoped for" (11:1). 1 Peter 1:21 may be translated "so that your faith may be hope in God" as well as "so that your faith and hope might be in God." Christian hope is not disappointed—it is without shame.

I. *Hope is grounded in the grace of God*—as is faith. We stand in this grace, and we rejoice in hope. God's grace provokes both faith and hope. The hope for peace with God is real—whether we translate as a declaration, "We have peace with God," or as an exhortation, "Let us have peace with God." This in itself becomes more personal when we confess ourselves to be justified in consequence of our faith. It is God's grace that is responsible for our being acceptable to God—God's grace in the gift of Jesus Christ. This makes access to God possible. This makes peace a lasting condition. Thus "we rejoice in hope of the glory of God."

II. *Hope is strengthened through exercise under God.* Hope is tried and proved shameless. Against the background of Paul's own experience he has written . . . we rejoice not only in hope, but also in tribulations. It is as if he were saying, "I've lived through that. I can take anything." Here are the stages of a man's life. We rejoice in hardships—in tests of strength. Lift that weight—dig that ditch—up, down, up, down—work, work, work! Much of the apostle's ministry was characterized by hardships. Ah, but they were under God's watchful eye. And hardship makes for steadiness—"tribulation works steadfastness." There was no tremor of indecision. Paul confidently faced the future because of his experience—he had come through hardships. His conviction hammered out in experience made for strength. Steadfastness makes for acceptability—for approvedness. This made him acceptable to both God and man. His access to God was easily translated into acceptability. This approvedness completed the circle: it worked hope. This hope, buttressed by tribulation, steadfastness, and approvedness, was shameless. "Hope putteth not to shame."

III. *Hope is confirmed by the love of God.* No wonder it is without disappointment, without shame. God's love has been poured out lavishly in the gift of his Son. It has become a part of our experience, for it has been ministered through the Holy Spirit. In an upbeat book, Lewis Smedes has treated *Shame and Grace.* There can be no shame of inferior feelings when we recognize ourselves as objects of God's love. How can one be disappointed in the love of God? The initial exhortation, "Let us have peace with God," is fulfilled in verse 11: "We rejoice in God through our Lord Jesus Christ through whom we have now received the reconciliation"—peace with God realized in hope.—J. Estill Jones

SUNDAY: JUNE EIGHTEENTH

SERVICE OF WORSHIP

Sermon: Always in Debt

TEXT: Rom. 1:14–15

Some time ago I was reading St. Paul's letter to the Romans, and these words captured my attention: "I am under obligation both to Greeks and to barbarians, both to the wise and to the foolish." Supposing, I thought, that St. Paul were seeking admission into one of our conferences and this question about debt were put to him. He would answer, "Am I in debt so as to embarrass me? I sure am. I owe everybody from the cultured to the crude; from the wise to the foolish; from the good to the bad. Why," he might say, "if I lived a thousand years I could not pay back what I owe."

He was saying, of course, that a man is always in debt and that no one can ever say he owes no one. We are born owing so much that none of us ever gets clear of obligations.

I. The first thing I want to say is that we fear debt.

(a) On this subject I speak with some authority. I cannot remember a time in my childhood when my family was clear of debt. Although it always seemed that we were just about to make it, we never did. My father would call a family conference and tell us why we could not do what we had set our hearts on. But, he would tell us, we only had so many more payments on this particular debt, and then we ought to have a little more money to give us more spending choices. It never worked out that way, and while it was pleasant to dream and plan, debts were a part of my youth. I hated them, and I feared them.

A friend of mine, who has directed a social agency for young men and boys for forty years in the Elephant and Castle district of London, once told me of his family's fear of sickness when he was a boy. Sickness meant loss of work and going into debt. They were urged to "work it off " when they felt ill. Those of us who are more fortunate must not forget the burden of debt on the poor. It is a very real thing around the world, and it is of concern to all of us.

(b) We are also afraid of being in debt intellectually. We want to be known as men of new ideas and originality, and consequently we are tempted to claim as our own what came from another.

Almost any writer is tempted constantly to minimize his obligations to other writers. Most of our material comes from somebody else, but we ought to think it through, give it the style of our personalities so that it has the stamp of our minds. While few of us will ever be regarded as original thinkers, all of us have something of our own to contribute. To confess our debts makes us not poor but rich, and plagiarism is the sin of a small mind.

II. The second thing to notice is the opposite side of the coin: we seek independence and freedom.

(a) There is a sense in which this is the legitimate process of growing up. The boy wants to arrive at the place where he can be independent of his father and be his own boss. He imagines a time when no one can tell him to be in at midnight or to mow the lawn. The girl thinks it will be wonderful when her mother cannot tell her to use less makeup and to wear her skirts longer. There is a time in life when parents are taskmasters whose chief function is to prevent their children from doing what they want to do and to make them do what they do not want to do. Then it is that to be free to do as one pleases seems like heaven. We learn one day that a man's real troubles begin when he can do as he pleases.

There is the slavery to money. The young couple begin bravely with a budget. It all makes sense on paper, and it is a new adventure to plan just how much can be spent for each need. Of course, it never quite works out that way, and the budget becomes increasingly a burden and an irritation. Someday, says the wife, may we have enough money to spend without having to worry about the budget! Happiness is a situation where an extra hundred dollars is not a matter of life and death. Madison Avenue spends most of its time and skill in persuading us that financial success is the true goal of life.

(b) There is a sense in which independence is the Protestant promise in man's relation to God. We do not have to pray through the priest or by way of the saints. No professional or expert is necessary to represent us before God. Each man is a priest, and every man is confronted by God directly. The hierarchy may be necessary for the housekeeping duties connected with the institution, but it is not necessary to get me introduced to God. We sometimes forget that this means terrifying responsibilities for the individual. But the ability of every Christian to enter directly into fellowship with God is a precious heritage.

III. Let us, therefore, look at a third proposition that will sound like bad news. It is simply that we can never be out of debt.

(a) My parents died before I could do much to repay them what I owed. My father was not alive when the Methodist Church, in a weak moment, no doubt, elected me a bishop. If he had been present when that happened, he would have thought it a greater honor than to have a son president of the United States. My mother, who gave so much that I am just now beginning to realize it, never received any proper recognition of my debt to her. This troubles me many times, and if there were a way to make plain to my parents how much I owe them, it would be joy. One thing is perfectly clear, and that is that I could never come near being clear of my obligations to them. Let any man or woman think two minutes of love and sacrifice invested in them, and they will not talk any more about being self-sufficient.

(b) The man who began with nothing and achieved success is tempted to speak of himself as a self-made man. All this does is relieve the Almighty from a mighty embarrassing responsibility. No man is able to claim that he is a self-made man. Every one of us had friends who strengthened us by believing in us and giving us encouragement. Let us not minimize our own efforts with false humility, but let us not forget how much we owe to other people. When a football player makes a long run, there was a key block that sprung him loose. There are always key blocks when we break away for a big gain, and only small men will forget it.

IV. The last thing to say is that acknowledging our debts brings us a strange joy.

(a) You see, the acceptance of our status as debtors destroys our pride, and that is good. It brings us to the end of a vain search, and finally we accept the truth that we are loved. We are filled with such thankfulness that our hearts overflow with joy. It is the discovery that all our giving is merely a drop in the bucket when it comes to settling our accounts. While it is true that giving is more blessed than receiving, being the object of loving concern brings a blessedness all its own.

(b) One of the amazing things is that people who do the most seem to be least aware of it. There is never the slightest tendency to let others do the difficult work or to regard themselves as excused from the hard jobs. Those whose lives have been models of service never seem to realize they have been making sacrifices. Rather, at the root of their characters is a sense of something owing that is sheer joy to acknowledge.

(c) God has brought us the spirit of joyous obligation through Christ. The gospel is glad announcement that God loves the world and gave his Son for it. We are the ones for whom Christ died. We discover that before we sought him, he sought us. Christianity is a proclamation that we are always in debt and service to our brethren is our privilege. All of the great church festivals have this as their basic theme. For our debt is not one that makes us unhappy and worried, but one that sets us free from arrogance.—Gerald Kennedy

Illustrations

DUTY. Robert E. Lee, though the defeated general in the Civil War, is surely the most remembered military figure of that struggle. Something of the reason for his greatness is suggested by the following quotation from Lee's biography by Douglas S. Freeman: "What was his duty as a Christian and as a gentleman? That he answered by the sure criterion of right and wrong, and having answered, acted. Everywhere the two obligations went together: he never sought to expiate as a Christian for what he had failed to do as a gentleman, or to atone as a gentleman for what he had neglected as a Christian. He could not have conceived of a Christian who was not a gentleman."—Charles L. Wallis

A STAGGERING DEBT. I remember my teachers, especially a young man who taught my Sunday school class when I was about eight years old. We were an ornery bunch, and if anybody has trouble believing the theological doctrine of original sin, let him teach a class of eight-year-old boys. Yet that young fellow was patient and faithful and now and again took us to the river on a Saturday. I have thought since how many things he must have preferred doing on those occasions and how often he must have been tempted to push us in. I wish there were some way to tell him what he has meant to me through the years and how many things he said I still remember. And when I think of all the other fine teachers who have enriched my life with their example and wisdom, the debt is so staggering that I am in despair.—Gerald Kennedy

Sermon Suggestions

GENUINE RELIGION. TEXT: Luke 7:36–8:3. (1) The story: a sinful woman came in and anointed Jesus' feet at a dinner party—questioned by the host and defended by Jesus. (2) The meaning: extraordinary forgiveness produces extraordinary gratitude. (3) The application: (a) Genuine religion may be unconventional in some of its expressions. (b) Genuine religion must make room for those who have failed and are recovering. (c) Genuine religion will initiate the process of recovery.

ON SELLING ONESELF TO DO EVIL. TEXT: 1 Kings 21:1–10 (11–14), 15–21a. (1) The causes of evildoing are complicated, with various motives playing into the action. (2) The consequences of evildoing bring immediate or ultimate disaster upon the perpetrators and/or their deeds.

Worship Aids

CALL TO WORSHIP. "But I, through the abundance of your steadfast love, will enter your house, I will bow down toward your holy temple in awe of you" (Ps. 5:7 NRSV).

INVOCATION. We are forever indebted to you, O God, for your many mercies and forever obligated to extend your mercies to others. Grant us the vision and the willingness to see and to do, even as you have blessed us.

OFFERTORY SENTENCE. "They shall not appear before the Lord empty-handed; all shall give as they are able, according to the blessing of the Lord your God that he has given you" (Deut. 16:16b–17 NRSV).

OFFERTORY PRAYER. Merciful God, if we give with ambivalence or share with hesitation, then turn us around, show us the cross, and change uncertainty to generosity through the reality of the sacrifice of our Savior for all persons.—E. Lee Phillips

PRAYER. O Lord our God, we do not praise thee worthily. We do not understand thee. Our thoughts are fashioning thee like unto ourselves; and when we behold thee, it is not as thou art. Our imagination is both prophet and interpreter. We shall yet stand before thee and see thee as thou art; but now we see thee through a glass darkly, and our best vision is, after all, but a fragment. The highest that we can understand is but the spark of that great orb that thou art. And all those affections that we cull from the best men, and purify in imagination, and ascribe to thee in a wider range and in a grander power—what are these but interpreters of thy real nature?

So vast is the volume of thy being that we cannot by any measure understand thee as thou art. But as the stars lead us; as, though we cannot see what they are, we follow them, safely crossing the trackless deep; as they guide us, though they are so far away that only something of their light falls upon our eye—so, sun of righteousness, we follow thee, because of thy light, and not because we have risen to the orb of thy being with a full understanding.

We rejoice that thou art so great. If thou wert a God that our thought could encircle and compass, how small wouldst thou be! And because thou art always more than our conceptions make thee to be, as thou art exceeding abundantly greater than we can think, thou art the God that we desire. Thou art glorious in holiness. Thou art fearful in praises. If they that are about thee can behold something of thine excellent glory—if heaven is full of testimonies of their pleasure that are in the sweet delight of thy presence—if in that glorious tropic of thy purity all the force of thy nature is developing the riches of theirs—and if they, single or banded, are praising thee, speaking evermore the language not of duty but of ecstasy and love, and of necessity are pouring our their joy, which thou art creating, how grand is that sound! How glorious is that music! And how little do we know of it, whose best thoughts trickle in us as the rills in the mountains that are not yet large enough for streams or rivers! And yet, these thoughts of ours, unimportant as they now seem, shall ere long roll and sound as might thunders in heaven.

It is sweet to praise thee, though we are afar off. It is good to draw near to thee, though we are so imperfect, both in our own character and in our conception of thine. We have taken more internal delight, we have had stronger joys and more cleansing ones, in our communion with thee than in all the things that we know upon earth beside.

How shall we praise thee for thy condescension? How shall we speak thy friendship, that so walks forth from out of its very sphere, and again, and forever in increasing circles, incarnates itself, bows the heavens, and comes down to earth, and maintains its humility for man's sake? How wonderful is that patience, how gracious and tender is that love, by which thou dost nourish, and carry, and forgive, and patiently bear with the sin and imperfection of all the wretched ones upon the earth! For wickedness hath its nest. It spreads abroad its dark wings and broods over desolation, and sorrow and trouble have filled the ages. And still, as men pour wine forth from a goblet, so is trouble poured forth from the lap of earth. Time is but the record of sorrow, imperfection, and misery. And thou hast borne it and art bearing it. Thou art carrying thy creatures, and yet thou art a sacrifice—yet thou art giving thy life.

We cannot enter into the thought of this high mystery of thy way of living without rebuke of our own selfish, self-seeking, and indulgent lives. What in us is there that answers to our calling in thee?

O Lord our God, grant, we beseech of thee, that we may have this knowledge of God, and that we may find in ourselves the beginnings of that self-denial, that meekness, that forbearance for others, that forgiving spirit, carrying healing with forgiveness, which belongs to the divine nature. Grant that we may be, in ourselves and toward our fellows, what thou art, and what thou art toward us. We not only pray that thou wilt forgive our sins—which thou dost forgive already, or ever we speak or ask—but we pray above all that thou wilt lift us above evil. Bear us up in thine hands, lest at any time we dash our foot against a stone. Bear us up, that we may not be carried away captive by that vanity that snares us or spins its films on every side and catches us as the spider catches insects in summer upon the web and would devour them. Lift us up so that pride shall not have dominion over us, that we may walk in a humble and gentle spirit. So lift us up that we shall not fall into the slough of passion. So lift us up that we shall not be given into the jaws and devouring appetites of avarice.

Grant, we beseech of thee, that we may not walk in the way of selfishness. May we seek to be as the king's sons, to be clothed with all the garments of the Lord, and to know how to put on the Lord Jesus Christ. May we know how to put on his garments of humiliation. May we know how to wear his suffering. May we know how, too, in hours apart, when we stand upon the mount of transfiguration, to put on the Lord Jesus Christ and to be clothed with garments of light, whiter than any fuller's soap can whiten them. Grant that we may have an abiding faith in that triumph that we shall have in the kingdom of God's glory.—Henry Ward Beecher

LECTIONARY MESSAGE

Topic: I Died That I Might Live

TEXT: Gal. 2:15–21

OTHER READINGS: 1 Kings 21:1–10 (11–14), 15–21a; Luke 7:36–8:3

Life comes through death. It is spring in Georgia . . . the old dead pine cones produce tiny seedlings. The old dead leaves conceal tender shoots. The old dead bulbs sprout to colorful jonquils. There was a certain deadness about the law in Paul's experience. It was Paul who died, however, not the law. This passage is biographical. It is Paul's testimony.

I. I died due to the law. The confession is preceded by the account of the action by Peter and Barnabas in Antioch. Their fellowship with Gentiles had been interrupted by so-called demands of the law. Earlier they had found it attractive to eat with Gentiles. Paul was disappointed in their action. Not even these loyal Jews, Peter and Barnabas, can live by the law. It was a Jewish problem. Their rabbis had so interpreted the law that it spelled death to anyone who tried to obey it. In any event the law could not bring life. We know this. It became a Gentile problem when the Jews sought to intimidate Gentile converts to the Christian faith. If they should go the route of legalism, they too were marked for deadness. Both Jew and Gentile were marked for deadness if they supposed that life came through the law. Neither Jew nor Gentile could perfectly observe the law. The law itself declared: "Cursed is every one who continueth not in all things that are written in the book of the law, to do them" (Gal. 3:10; Deut. 27:26). When a person is pledged to justification by law, that person is excluded from the grace of God. He dies.

II. I live unto God. Life to God begins with death to law as a source of justification. Justification, acceptance, fellowship with God come through faith—a gift of his grace. By legalistic standards such independence from law constitutes sin. Is Christ then a minister of sin? How logically the apostle draws it out. Of course not! Paul would prove himself a transgressor if he, like Peter and Barnabas, sought to build up again that spirit of legalism that his faith in Christ terminated. His confession is straightforward: "I through the law died unto the law that I might live unto God." If it's a choice between law and God, I'll take God. If it's a choice between works and grace, I'll take grace. It is a choice. Paul made it. He had followed Christ in death that he might live.

III. I live in faith. In his faith he identified himself with the object of his faith. His death and his life were in Christ. It was no longer Paul that lived—"Christ lives in me." This is the essence of faith—to so closely identify with its object as to be indistinguishable from it—how far we fall short! His faith was in the Son of God, who loved him and gave himself up for him. He continually bore witness to the grace of God. He did not presume upon it. He did not deny it. If what he has seen in his own experience is not true, then Christ died in vain. If acceptance with God comes through the law, then all of Christ's suffering and sacrifice was for nothing. As law is overwhelmed by grace, so sin is overwhelmed by faith. The testimony of Paul gets down to the basics. It's a matter of death and life.—J. Estill Jones

SUNDAY: JUNE TWENTY-FIFTH

SERVICE OF WORSHIP

Sermon: The Cure for Depression

TEXT: 1 Kings 19

Depression has been called the common cold of emotional illnesses. It is, without a doubt, one of the most common problems in our time.

"Depression," according to Everett Worthington, "is a downward spiral, begun by loss of control and made worse by lack of energy and negative thinking." The dictionary defines *depression* as "a feeling of extreme hopelessness." This emotion manifests itself in the seeming reactions of: All is lost. I want to quit. I want to give up. I can't make it.

Unfortunately, Christians—even great spiritual leaders—aren't exempt from this painful problem. The psalmist experienced it: "Why are you downcast, O my soul? Why so disturbed within me?" (Ps. 42:5 NIV).

Moses cried out, "I cannot carry all these people by myself; the burden is too heavy for me. If this is how you are going to treat me, put me to death right now" (Num. 11:14–15 NIV).

Jonah was depressed after his rousing success in Nineveh. He prayed, "Now, O Lord, take away my life, for it is better for me to die than to live" (Jon. 4:3 NIV).

Elijah, the great prophet, battled depression after his triumph on Mount Carmel against the prophets of Baal. While in the desert, he said to God, "I have had enough, Lord. Take my life" (1 Kings 19:4 NIV).

Depression is no respecter of persons.

Everybody gets depressed at times. What is God's remedy for depression? The remedy God provided Elijah is one you can use.

I. Realize that depression is not a sin but a symptom. The way we respond to depression may be sinful, but the emotion itself is not. Sin may lead to depression, but all depression does not come from sin. Depression is like a warning light on the dashboard of a car. The way to extinguish it is not to smash the light but to find the problem. When depression sets in, something deep usually is wrong.

II. Restore your physical body. "Then he [Elijah] lay down under the tree and fell asleep. All at once an angel touched him and said, 'Get up and eat' " (1 Kings 19:5 NIV). God's remedy involves rest, food, and relaxation.

I asked a doctor what she does when depressed people who have attempted suicide are brought into the emergency room. Her answer may surprise you: "Well, sometimes the first thing we do is to feed them—often a steak dinner. They are generally low in protein. We often discover that they have not eaten properly for two or three days. Their protein level is low; therefore, their energy level is low, and their depression level is high."

We must never forget the role our bodies play in our emotions. Some people consistently neglect themselves physically and then wonder why they are depressed.

Perhaps depression is God's built-in cruise control. If you're depressed, the first step toward recovery is to get in shape physically. You should get sufficient rest, eat a balanced diet, and exercise regularly.

III. Relinquish your frustration to God. The Lord asked, " 'What are you doing here, Elijah?' He replied, 'I have been very zealous for the Lord God Almighty. The Israelites have rejected your covenant, broken down your altars, and put your prophets to death with the sword. I am the only one left, and now they are trying to kill me too' " (1 Kings 19:9–10 NIV).

Elijah blew off steam to God. He poured out all his inner feelings.

Notice that God did not condemn or criticize him. He just let him vent his frustration.

Regardless of how bad circumstances seem, never stop talking to God. Share your heart. Don't try to be eloquent or creative; just tell God how you feel. Relinquishing your frustration is a catharsis—a cleansing, a venting of all that has been pushed down inside of you and caused your depression.

IV. Refresh your awareness of God's presence. "The Lord said, 'Go out and stand on the mountain in the presence of the Lord' " (1 Kings 19:11 NIV).

Nothing will refresh you like coming into the presence of God and realizing he loves and cares for you regardless of how you feel or act. God never promised this life would be happy, but he did promise to go with us through all our pain.

If you are depressed, spend time alone with your Bible and God. Read your Bible. Let God speak to you and love you. You will find no greater antidepressant than communication and fellowship with God.

V. Redirect your life. God gave Elijah a new assignment. "Go back the way you came, and go to the Desert of Damascus. When you get there, anoint Hazael king over Aram" (1 Kings 19:15 NIV).

The quickest way to defeat depression is to quit drowning in self-pity. Take your eyes off yourself and start looking at the needs of others. Find people who are less fortunate and invest your life in them. When you give yourself to others, God will give to you. Jesus said, "Whoever loses his life for me will find it" (Matt. 16:25 NIV).

Maybe now is a good time for you to start a new project, begin a new hobby, join an exercise club, or enroll in a Bible study.

VI. Renew a friendship. "So Elijah went from there and found Elisha son of Shaphat" (1 Kings 19:19 NIV). Depressed people need true friends. Don't battle depression alone. Find a friend who will provide support and encouragement—someone who will help you see circumstances as they are, not as you perceive them.

Eugene Kennedy said, "The main business of friendship is to sustain and make bearable each other's burdens."

Christ can lift you out of depression. He can help you. He can heal you. You don't have to hobble through life depressed.—William Richard Ezell

Illustrations

PATIENCE. No matter how blue and gloomy you may feel at times, try to remember that this feeling of despair will someday be history. Count on it. You don't have to kill yourself to get over your blues; all you need is patience!—Paul A. Hauck

COURAGE. Life is beautiful, but it is hard for all human beings, very hard even for the majority. It is even harder in misfortune, in the face of deprivation. That requires a lot of courage. I stress the fact because I am well aware that it is something of which I have very little. My own courage revives when I come into contact with courageous people—often my patients, more handicapped than I am, and displaying courage that I admire. For courage is not taught; it is caught. Society is a vast laboratory of mutual encouragement. Each member can give the other only the courage he has himself—doctors as well as patients.—Paul Tournier

Sermon Suggestions

FROM MADNESS TO MISSION. TEXT: Luke 8:26–39. (1) An isolating illness. (2) A healing encounter. (3) A remarkable mission.

HOW GOD SPEAKS TO US. TEXT: 1 Kings 19:1–4 (5–7), 8–15a NRSV. (1) God speaks to us in a time of need. (2) God speaks in unexpected ways: (a) Practically—as with rest, food, and drink. (b) Quietly—as in "a sound of sheer silence." (c) With something specific to do—as in "Go, return on your way."

Worship Aids

CALL TO WORSHIP. "As the hart panteth after the water brooks, so panteth my soul after thee, O God. My soul thirsteth for God, for the living God: when shall I come and appear before God?" (Ps. 42:1–2).

INVOCATION. Our needs are great, O God, and we come to thee, asking thee to fulfill our deepest need, our need of thee. Thou art here: give us the faith to enter the reality of what is ours even now.

OFFERTORY SENTENCE. "The world and all that is in it belong to the Lord; the earth and all who live on it are his" (Ps. 24:1 TEV).

OFFERTORY PRAYER. As your faithful stewards, O Lord, we bring to you a part of what you have placed in our care, so that it may be used in special ways to continue and spread the good news of your love and salvation. Bless what we bring and those who hear and receive and pass on that good news to others.

PRAYER. We invoke thy blessing upon all who need thee and who are groping after thee, if haply they may find thee. Be gracious to those who bear the sins of others, who are vexed by the wrongdoing and selfishness of those near and dear to them, and reveal to them the glory of their fellowship with the sufferings of Christ. Brood in tenderness over the hearts of the anxious, the miserable, the victims of phantasmal fears and morbid imaginings. Redeem from slavery the men and women who have yielded to degrading habits. Put thy Spirit within them, that they may rise up in shame and sorrow and make confession to thee: "So brutish was I, and ignorant: I was as a beast before thee." And then let them have the glad assurance that thou art with them, the secret of all good, the promise and potency of better things. Console with thy large consolation those who mourn for their loved dead, who count the empty places and long for the sound of a voice that is still. Inspire them with the firm conviction that the dead are safe in thy keeping, nay, that they are not dead but live unto thee. Give to all sorrowing ones a garland for ashes, the oil of joy for mourning, and the garment of praise for the spirit of heaviness. Remember for good all who are perplexed with the mysteries of existence and who grieve because the world is so sad and unintelligible. Teach them that thy hand is on the helm of affairs, that thou dost guide thine own world and canst change every dark cloud into bright sunshine. In this faith let them rest, and by this faith let them live. These blessings we ask in the name of our Lord and Savior Jesus Christ.—Samuel McComb

LECTIONARY MESSAGE

Topic: You Are All One

TEXT: Gal. 3:23–29

OTHER READINGS: 1 Kings 19:1–4 (5–7), 8–15a; Luke 8:26–39

What an amazing declaration: you are all one. It was written to the Galatians: Antioch, Iconium, Lystra, and Derbe. The first mission tour was difficult. Paul and Barnabas had been harassed from city to city, principally by the Jews when it became evident that the Gentiles were receiving the gospel. It was written against the background of the demands that the Jewish law made—a law that many of the Jews sought to extend to the Gentile Christians. Faith had made a difference that many of the Jews did not see.

I. Before faith came, there was divisiveness. Paul described it in terms of social customs with which he was familiar. The Jews were kept as wards under the law. Their immaturity was taken for granted. Free expression and association were limited by the requirements of the law. One great division was accepted by all: those who were not Jews were Gentiles. The ancient world was thus divided on the basis of God's covenant. One wonders if God's covenant was intended to be divisive. Social custom for both Jew and Gentile divided the slave from the free. There were only two kinds of people: the bond and the free. One wonders if the revelation of God in the law was intended to perpetuate the division. Social custom and the law and all of ancient society divided the male and the female. And the law kept them in separate dormitories: the Jew and the Gentile, the bond and the free, the male and the female. One wonders if God intended for the divisions to be divisive. Before faith came they were kept for the clear object of faith.

II. Now that faith has come, you are all sons of God. We are no longer limited to the legal teachings of a tutor. Truth is ours for the taking. To be sure, Paul saw that the original end of the law was to lead to faith. His experience with the proponents of the law had been that they had resisted faith. But in his ministry, faith was at the center of the stage. The divisiveness was at an end. The same faith was to be experienced by all—to be expressed by all. The term *sons* of God is hardly sexist in the light of verse 28. It is rather a word of inheritance. Insofar as the promise made to Abraham was concerned, all of us are heirs—"sons" of God.

III. As many of you as were baptized into Christ, you are all one. The reference here is to more than the physical rite of baptism, yet the figure of immersion is clear. You were immersed into Christ—all of your person. It is as if you took off your old clothes and put on new clothes—in Christ. Here then is a new environment—new clothes—a new experience in Christ. The condition is for all—"as many as." There are no divisions. Through faith, and faith alone, you are all one.

IV. There is no difference; you are all one. It is important to read "you are all one" rather than "you are all one man." The former is certainly the preferred translation. There is no word for *man* in the text. It would tend to perpetuate the divisiveness between male and female, which faith came to remove. Now there is no difference between Jew and Gentile, bond and free, male and female. You belong to Christ. You have the promise made to Abraham. You are all one. Faith makes the difference.—J. Estill Jones

SUNDAY: JULY SECOND

SERVICE OF WORSHIP

Sermon: Through to the Better End

TEXT: 2 Cor. 11:19–12:9

My subject is not misprinted, though I did hope that the possibility might occur to you.

The text is 2 Corinthians, the twelfth chapter, at the ninth verse.

I want to take St. Paul's experience for what it is, a parable of the Christian life. You know as I do how often it seems that we too have come to the bitter end of things: of a friendship, of some plan or hope or ideal that we have cherished. But I wonder if you know that nothing can ever alleviate or transform that bitterness until we understand what the source of it is? And for that we've got to look inside, not outside.

I. The ultimate threat to our existence is not necessarily greater when everything outside seems all wrong; it may be just as great, far greater perhaps, when we are so sure everything outside is all right, north, east, south, and west, that it takes God himself to show us how much of it is indeed all wrong. It goes without saying that each of us is surrounded by his own quota of difficulties. We'll tell you that. We'll tell the world! Who doesn't have just about enough—at home, with his friends, in the work he is doing? But just leave us alone. It may be bitter, but it isn't the end. We'll iron it out. We'll get together a few more facts and go over them carefully.

(a) When along comes the good news of this gospel, but always with the bad news, which we have to hear first: that even when everything outside seems all right, matters inside are a good deal worse than we think. The gospel tells us what we do not know about the real source of all bitterness, about the real threat to our existence, come sunshine or shadow. It talks to us about the serpent in Eden, worming its way into the heart of every paradise we stake out for ourselves, turning it into a fool's paradise. And the name of that serpent is I, alias me, alias my or mine—a self so busy with its own claims of priority, its own ceaseless demands on life, that it has little time to do anything more than to look around in the rush and shake its head in deep perplexity about you and yours, about him and her and it—as if something were unaccountably wrong with the whole structure of the universe! The bitterest thing about the end is the bitterness of the defeated and frustrated self, which has brought us there.

(b) Paul saw at last that this was precisely what had corrupted the Jewish religion of his time, and the Jewish religion of his time was the best religion there was. It had corrupted what knowledge he himself had had of piety and virtue, and all his practice of it: until he was caught off his guard at noon one day on the road to Damascus. What was wrong was no more than the self, curved in on itself, and so trying by hook or by crook to establish itself; whether in man's sight or in God's, it was all the same, asserting its primacy somehow.

That's why sin, which preachers talk about so much less nowadays than novelists and dramatists, has to be defined as man's "attempt to attain life through his own efforts." There is no inevitability about it other than the inevitability that the self gives to it when the self gets out of bounds.

(c) But even that is by no means the ugliest face of sin that the self wears. What you and I think is ugly is only the mask that sin puts on. If the mask were ripped off, we could see what God thinks is ugly. He sees sin as more than the self's perversion of some human good: he sees it as the self's perversion of his good. And God's good is the fullness of his grace, his power, and his love pressing in on us; we live under that, and move by it, and have our being in it. So much so that the withdrawal of it would make all the difference between being and not being. It is by his grace that we keep his commandments, if we ever do. But is it not grace, misshapen and misspent, that the murderer is what he is? The grace that keeps the breath in your nostrils and provides the strength for your arm whether you raise it to wield a knife or to pronounce a benediction? Only by God's own power can a man make a hell out of what was intended to be a paradise.

(d) I am afraid of the "cheap grace" that we think we can have for nothing and can keep even when we make no use of it, but I am more afraid of twisting God's grace and distorting it.

Not cheap grace, twisted grace! When you take that for a clue to the meaning of history, you see how hard it is for God to have his way, and what it's bound to cost, from Calvary on "to the last syllable of recorded time." I do not wonder that all his life Camus kept affirming his "vision of cosmic absurdity" and by his death seemed to prove it. The wonder is that in the same breath he could keep passionately avowing, beyond the absurdity, his belief in "human creativity"—with all the evidence we have that human creativity apart from God serves only to provide more cosmic absurdity. The only justice it achieves is the injustice that comes of a grace that shuts itself up, like Camus' Caligula, in the demonic sovereignty of its own freedom, piling tragedy on top of tragedy in the "emptiness that passes understanding." What cosmic absurdity there is can scarcely be blamed on the cosmos.

II. Well now! I'm through with the "bitter end." It's the place where the self, in order to affirm its primacy, overplays its hand and turns in on itself, distorting not so much the grace that God has promised as the grace that he has already supplied. The "better end" is the place where self has learned to renounce the priority of its claims. Let's talk no nonsense about it. You can no more renounce all of the self than you can renounce hunger and thirst. But you can renounce the self that keeps setting itself up at the center of the picture. You can renounce the self that gets out of line once you know where the line is.

And just this is the point of the story Paul tells. Half a dozen times here he sneaks out in front and is on the edge of boasting. Caught up into paradise—the account reads like a kind of fever chart—where he heard unspeakable words. He might well have stayed up in front on that score if God hadn't outflanked him and sent this messenger of Satan to buffet him: a thorn there in the very sinews of his apostleship, and it wouldn't budge. Why in God's name couldn't he be rid of it? But all he got on his lonely island of discontent was the hint and murmur of the sea, God's completeness around his incompleteness—around his restlessness, God's rest. Many a preacher finds that out when one day his old winged words come home to roost. "You have my grace; that's enough. You have my strength; it's being made perfect in your weakness." A man has to fall pretty far out of his own esteem to land there.

III. But then comes a question that is more important still: if he has to fall out of love with his own image, how in the name of common sense does he do it?

(a) You must learn to "think highly of yourself," says some peddler of slightly old and somewhat warmed-over chestnuts. An inferiority complex doesn't come of not thinking as highly of yourself as you ought to think. An inferiority complex is the seatbelt we use when we have to fly slightly lower than the stratosphere where we are sure we rightly belong. Whoever can't tell the difference between that and this that Paul had—"most gladly therefore will I rather glory in my infirmities"—can't tell the difference between anything and anything else.

(b) Just don't make the mistake of supposing that it was trouble that maneuvered him out of his self-esteem into the arms of God, where the power of Christ could rest upon him. Trouble alone can't do it. If only it did speak up, any one of us perhaps could be another what Isaiah called a hiding place from the wind, the shadow of a great rock in a weary land. But it doesn't. Peevishness is what's vocal: not the deeper anguish that like some timid wild thing goes off into the woods with its hurt to be alone. Yet for all that it can never bring anybody to write the self off as Paul did, and write God in! You don't get as far along as that simply by being beaten about from pillar to post by the winds of adversity.

(c) And you don't get that far along because you've suddenly been frightened by the shape of things in the world. "It's all pretty bad. You aren't up to it. Better try God!" There are too many alternatives, too many other live options. He told them it wasn't knowledge they could count on, and it wasn't anything they could do. No use trying to fling yourself with the Greeks into the struggle after virtue, or with the Jews into the hope of earning salvation by slogging down the road from one duty to another. You had to fall out of love with yourself. As far as he was concerned, that was the only way for it to happen.

(d) And he set down very clearly the how of it: "I knew a man in Christ above fourteen years ago." What do you make of that? Mysticism? It was Paul's experience of the patient and holy love of God. If there is any such thing at all, what's so mystical about having it brought home to you? That's how it happened: Christ had got in to wrestle with his weakness and his pride. Unless the long epic of human life in the Bible, with God feeling around in the middle of it to find some Jacob or some Amos, some Peter or some Zacchaeus or some Magdalen, and getting crucified for it that day, they made a man trudge along carrying a sign down the windy street, "Jesus of Nazareth, King of the Jews," then nailed him to a cross, and the sign with him—unless from beginning to end every bit of that is some kind of weird vagary, you don't have to argue that being found can't happen to you. You don't have to inquire where the road to Damascus runs and wish you could get up and walk down it. It runs through your home. It runs wherever you want it to run. "Lord, what wilt thou have me to do?" Ask that, and you're on it. You have come to the place where the self can get itself written off in the margin and God can get himself written down in the text. Call that "mystical" if you like, but you can't be quit of it that way. It is as solid a fact as any of the facts that have sprung from it.

IV. Let me put to you now two of those facts as Paul does, and leave them. They are both right here.

(a) One of them, and you can handle it as you'd handle any other, is this: "My grace is enough for you." I suppose there are people who read those words and are far more sure than they ought to be that Paul actually heard them spoken out loud. They say, "We could manage too, on such terms. He prayed once, and what he wanted didn't happen; so he prayed again, and it didn't happen then either. We'll go along with that. That's exactly how it is. But the third time he got an answer, and we haven't had any." I can't help wondering about that.

(b) And this fact too: "My strength is made perfect in weakness." In weakness it comes into its own, nowhere else, accomplishing even in you what it's meant to accomplish. That's what perfect means: rounding itself out, full statured and complete. It was like the long gesture forward that the cavalry officer used to make when he led his men toward battle. It was like the first moving up along the beach of "a huge inrushing tide with the whole sea behind it." What happens to you then doesn't have to look like strength. There are places in your heart where nothing that looks like strength can get in—only something that seems weaker than any hand you can get to drive a nail but in spite of that shows itself stronger at last than all the generations of mankind. Whatever else the cross means, that's part of it. Maybe we'd better quit casting around for evidence, peering about on top of everything and under everything for proof: wishing there were some other sign than the signs we have—some stone turned into bread, some wild leap from the pinnacle of a temple, some gathering up of all the kingdoms of this world, and the glory of them.—Paul Scherer

Illustrations

LETTING THE SOUL BLOSSOM. I am wondering what most of us would have done with the handicaps of a Helen Keller. If she had ever admitted to herself for a single moment that she was a failure, she would have been through before she started. "The one resolution," she says, "which was in my mind long before it took the form of a resolution is the keynote of my life. It is this: always to regard as mere impertinence of fate the handicaps which were placed upon my life almost at the beginning. I resolved that they should not crush or dwarf my soul but rather be made to 'blossom like Aaron's rod with flowers.' "—Lewis L. Dunnington

OUR FEEBLE EFFORTS. A man once set down all the facts he could remember about his wife and spread them out in front of me. Whereupon she gathered quite a good many about him and in due time spread them out as he had done. They thought they could no doubt set it all straight if they brushed up a little on psychology. Possibly there were strategies that they had never tried. So it is with most of us. We have an idea that maybe if we can just figure out a new approach or another technique we'll be able to muddle through.—Paul Scherer

Sermon Suggestions

WHY PEOPLE HESITATE TO FOLLOW CHRIST. TEXT: Luke 9:51–62. (1) Prejudice, verses 51–52. (2) Hardship, verses 57–58. (3) Materialism, verse 59. (4) Family ties, verse 61. (5) However, the call of God in Christ makes every other consideration of lesser importance, verse 62.

WHERE IS THE LORD, THE GOD OF ELIJAH? TEXT: 2 Kings 2:1–2, 6–14. God is present in power at every significant call to service. (1) We may doubt that the miracle of God's powerful presence will be continued or repeated. (2) We may cling nostalgically to a picture of the fire of God instead of experiencing that fire anew. (3) Or, we may enter by faith upon a new adventure with the living God and witness even in our own lives God's marvelous works (cf. John 14:12, 13, 15–17).

Worship Aids

CALL TO WORSHIP. "I call to mind the deeds of the Lord; I recall your wonderful acts of old; I reflect on all your works and consider what you have done" (Ps. 77:11–12 REB).

INVOCATION. Lord, whenever we ponder what you have done in the past, whether in the unfolding story of salvation or in our personal history, we are encouraged and strengthened for today and tomorrow. Let this be a special time of reflection and commitment for us, as we tune our hearts to sing your praise.

OFFERTORY SENTENCE. "He that hath a bountiful eye shall be blessed; for he giveth of his bread to the poor" (Prov. 22:9).

OFFERTORY PRAYER. Let thy saving goodness be proclaimed by this offering, Lord: thy power to protect, thy mercy to forgive, thy strength to undergird, thy Son to walk beside, to ever walk beside.—E. Lee Phillips

PRAYER. Spirit of the living God, discover us today. Come through the tangled pathways, grown with weed and thicket, that have kept thee from us. We cannot reach to thee; reach thou to us, that some soul, who came here barren of thy grace, may go out singing, "O God, thou are my God!"

Discover us in conscience. Let some moral imperative be laid upon our souls today. Save us from our evasions and deceits and the soft complacency with which we excuse ourselves and let some ennobling word of justice and beauty come to us today. Be stern with us, O living God, and chasten us by strong guidance in righteousness.

Discover us through the experience of forgiveness. Thou seest how many sins here have never been made right—barbed words spoken that hurt another, never atoned for, and still unforgiven; wrongs done against thy laws and man's good, and no pardon sought, no restitution made. Grant us the salvation of thy forgiveness and the pardon of those whom we have wronged. May some fellowship gone awry be put straight today; may some broken relationships be restored to integrity; may some storm-tossed souls find thy peace.

Come to us in the spirit of dedication. Never great until we confront something loftier than our own lives, never happy while we are self-centered, we seek our salvation in thee. Bring thou within our ken some purpose worth living for; remind us of some whom we can help, some cause that we can serve. May we forget ourselves into character and usefulness, because thou hast sought us out.

Come to us in the experience of inner power. We ask not for easy lives but for adequacy. We ask not to be freed from storms but to have houses built on rock that will not fall. We pray not for a smooth sea but for a stout ship, a good compass, and a strong heart to sail. O God, discover us with the resources of thy power, that we may be strong within.—Harry Emerson Fosdick

LECTIONARY MESSAGE

Topic: Freedom to Love

TEXT: Gal. 5:1, 13–25

OTHER READINGS: 2 Kings 2:1–2, 6–14; Luke 9:51–62

Liberty and law and love—the Liberty Bell tolls its message. What is liberty's finest expression? Love! What is liberty's greatest threat? Love's absence. God had freedom to love and loves against the greatest odds. "For freedom Christ set us free . . . stand fast." And freedom is understood in terms of love.

I. You have freedom to love because you feel loved. You can afford to risk it all in loving another. He who holds back a part loves that much less—falls that far short of love. Edgar Allen Poe expressed it in his poem "Annabel Lee"—"this maiden lived with no other thought than to love and be loved by me." And you don't have to be afraid because "perfect love casts out fear"—from A and acrophobia to Z and zoophobia—you have freedom to love. But it is not that you *are* love, for that is God. It is rather that you *do* love both God and man. "Thou shalt love"—and you can forget so much more of the law. "Love and do as you please," wrote Augustine . . . with a great understanding of what love means. Be sure that you fully understand the meaning of love—in a combination of freedom and responsibility. You don't have to hate. You are free to love. You may suppose that love limits your freedom, but it doesn't: ask any husband or wife! It is true that real love disciplines, strengthens, exercises, as any parent knows. It's the loveless one who gives the child the butcher knife simply because he asks for it. And you are free to love because you feel loved.

II. You have freedom to love because a person is worth loving. That person is not necessarily good or beautiful . . . you weren't when God first loved you. But the person is promising in some sense and satisfying to some degree, needing something you have to offer. More important, that person is made in the image of God. You don't have to hate—that person is worth loving. Teenagers don't have to hate their parents. Parents don't have to hate their teenagers. Whites and blacks don't have to hate one another. You don't have to hate the church. You don't even have to hate yourself. You can look at and accept your faults. You can major on your wonderful possibilities. You are free to love yourself. God loves you—why shouldn't you love yourself? You are worth loving.

III. You have freedom to love because love lasts. And in loving you give yourself to a durable quality. And you can love just for the sake of loving—in love with love. He that loveth his brother is in the light—no stumbling. He that loveth his brother is alive—no deadness. To love is a sign of light and life: "We know that we have passed from death to life because we love." Hatred is a sign of darkness and death. The last word is not darkness but light. The last word is not death but life. And this because God who is light loves. And this because God who is life loves. And it bears fruit. In verse 22 the harvest of the Spirit begins with love, and all the other parts of the harvest sprout out from that love: joy, peace . . .

IV. "Thou shalt love." It's the law—the law of freedom. The alternative is not attractive . . . biting and devouring one another. You snap at one another with cruel words—with thoughtless, uncaring words. You bite one another with cruel deeds as well as words—animal-like behavior. Watch out lest you be chewed up by one another. You'll both be eaten up with hatred. You'll both lose your joy and your peace, your witness and your sense of security. But you are free to love God and give yourself to him, to love his church and join with Christian friends in his service. For freedom, freedom to love, Christ set us free. Stand fast therefore!—J. Estill Jones

SUNDAY: JULY NINTH

SERVICE OF WORSHIP

Sermon: The Most Crucial Choice We Make

TEXT: Matt. 22:1–14

Some years ago an old mentor of mine suggested the three most important decisions some of us will make in our lives could be summed up as follows: What do you do? Who do you marry? What do you believe? I don't know about you, but I have found those three questions and the answers to them determinative for my own life. I do not know what three decisions in your life you might rate highest, but those three in my life, surely, have proved the most critical.

I. The passage we read a few moments ago about the king inviting guests to a fabulous wedding banquet confronts us with another critical decision. This parable asks essentially, to what are you going to give your life? When you add everything up, what counts most? An invitation has gone out asking you to join the festival of the reign of God. Can you come? Will you come? It's urgent! It's vital! It's life changing!

(a) Life changing! Do you know why? Do you know to what you are invited? You are summoned to participate in the kind of world we hope for, a world of mutuality and service breaking in upon us right now. The chance to turn our injured cities, our wounded communities, our limping families, our own ragged and torn spirits into citadels of hope and joy and justice—this opportunity—beckons immediately.

(b) We find ourselves immersed in the terrible tragedies of human beings trying to make it together, and failing. We know the terrible plight of human beings trapped by the demons of blood and soil intent on exterminating each other. And heaven knows we want to avoid falling into any sentimental illusions indicating that in this world "all we need is love." But . . . but . . . the New Testament proclaims to us that even amid the virulence, the miscommunication, the moral myopia, the selfish distortions infecting the human community—even amid all this—there lies an opportunity to join with Christ, in all the risk, amid all the dangers, of building a new world. And, yes, maybe even getting crucified for trying. The invitation to the wedding banquet delivered to you and to me implores, "Come now, come through all the proscriptions, the polarizations, the so-called tragic complexities, real as they may be, come throw your life onto the scales, betting on a new humanity. Come, for right now, the preparations for a joyous human festival are complete. Come, I beg you, for all is ready."

II. There is the invitation; will we accept it? There is the summons; it arrives requesting an RSVP; how do we reply?

(a) Matthew indicates some of us may take the invitation lightly. He suggests we may pass off God's invitation as just another piece of junk mail. That's possible.

Ah, we may take it lightly, but the urgency of an invitation to Christ's banquet of peace and joy among us still stands. When Luke tells this parable, he knows the things demanding our time and commitment are difficult and of no small moment. The invitation competes with our most treasured loyalties. In Luke's parable one of the invitees responds with a business card. And heaven knows we have to make a living.

(b) Another begs off with a claim about

family. What could be more important in this world? A third invitee consults a calendar and sees there an important civic appointment, one that might save a neighborhood. Absolutely crucial!

(c) But you know, the real experts at sending "regrets" with a "sorry, I'm busy" on them are we minister types. Talk about business getting in the way of the kingdom! Talk about all kinds of lofty priorities and noble excuses! My soul, have we got them!

For all of us, the gospel knows the tremendous pressures of our daily life. It knows what pulls us this way and that. It knows we live by necessity as well as by choice. It know all the vital and important things we must do. But it asks even amid all this, do you, do I, do we respond with promptness, enthusiasm, and joy to this finally decisive invitation? Our decision literally could make all the difference in the world.

III. Do you remember the character at the end of the parable who attends the wedding banquet without a wedding garment, the clown who shows up at the party in his old clothes? Do you recall the rough treatment that character gets from the host? That joker wants to come to God's party but does not want to change her wardrobe.

(a) Matthew is saying this: the most crucial choice we make is what kind of world we are going to live in; how we are going to treat others in it; how much we understand ourselves to be in solidarity with all of humankind, especially those who get the short end of the stick. Commitment to the kind of community God wants in this world entails a change of attitude, a change of values, a change of goals; it means a different set of loyalties, a different way of apportioning time or money, or relationships, or property, or people or values; it may involve a change of vocation or career, or lifestyle—or whatever—and that if it does not, our professions of faith, our vows of discipleship, our positive RSVPs to the banquet may be empty, fraudulent, and worth no more than a niche in hell.

(b) Have you got it? This crucial choice? I invite us all to treat our Lord's invitation with the urgency it deserves; and for the sake of what God wants for human life on this earth, just as we would for a royal banquet, let us be prepared to accept the invitation, to honor our host and maybe—just maybe—for the high and joyous occasion before us, redesign completely our spiritual wardrobes.—James W. Crawford

Illustrations

THE CALL TO DISCIPLESHIP. When we are called to follow Christ, we are summoned to an exclusive attachment to his person. The grace of his call bursts all the bonds of legalism. It is a gracious call, a gracious commandment. It transcends the difference between the law and the gospel. Christ calls; the disciple follows: that is grace and commandment in one. "I will walk at liberty, for I seek thy commandments" (Ps. 119:45).—Dietrich Bonhoeffer

THE DETOUR AS A WAY OF LIFE. One of the central contributions of the Judeo-Christian faith in God is the persistent expectation that we shall have no other gods before him. We cannot serve two masters, says Jesus. From the vantage point of sustained resistance to the temptation of idolatry, most of the ways in life's pilgrimage that we choose are bound to demand a detour if we discover the larger purposes of the one God. What is at first seen by us as a dead end, a noisome and bothersome detour, is in fact a diversion of our path away from our own petty idolatries to the great highway of the worship and love of God.—Wayne E. Oates

Sermon Suggestions

TEMPTATIONS OF RELIGIOUS WORKERS. TEXT: Luke 10:1–11, 16–20, especially verse 20. (1) To take excessive pride in achievement. (2) To use one's position as an excuse for taking ethical liberties. (3) To forget what is of first and final importance—to be simply a faithful servant of God, enrolled to do God's will.

WHEN THE EASY IS TOO DIFFICULT. TEXT: 2 Kings 5:1–14. (1) Then: Naaman was healed when he finally and simply obeyed the prophet's commands. (2) Always: while God's way for us is demanding, his yoke is easy and his burden light (cf. Matt. 11:28–30). (3) Now: (a) Salvation was costly to God, but it is free to those who will receive it. (b) Service to God may be overwhelming in the aggregate, but it begins and continues and succeeds in simple obedience.

Worship Aids

CALL TO WORSHIP. "Sing praise to the Lord, all his faithful people! Remember what the Holy One has done, and give him thanks! His anger lasts only a moment, his goodness for a lifetime" (Ps. 39:4–5 TEV).

INVOCATION. Accept our worship, O Lord, for though we are imperfect, we confess our sins and seek your cleansing. Do mighty things in us, because we pray and wish more than anything else to do as you lead.—E. Lee Phillips

OFFERTORY SENTENCE. "Think of us in this way, as servants of Christ and stewards of God's mysteries. Moreover, it is required of stewards that they be found trustworthy" (1 Cor. 4:1–2 NRSV).

OFFERTORY PRAYER. God of grace, before whom to stand is awesome, before whom to pray is privilege, and before whom to give is joy, use what we bring today to extend thy kingdom and compound the rewards of faith.—E. Lee Phillips

PRAYER. Each of us brings before thee, in holy remembrance, our heavenly Father, loved ones and friends. Some are in far lands, some upon the sea, some in barren places, enduring loneliness, hardship, and peril, some confronted by perplexities or wearied by monotonous duties, all of them bearing the burdens of this world's struggle, and striving everywhere to do their duty, and to be found worthy of their fellow men. On those who stand in the circle of our heart's embrace, O God, we pray thy most merciful benediction and the outpouring of thy life-giving Spirit, that they may be strong in whatsoever life demands of them, strong of heart to dream, strong of will to dare, strong of hope to endure, and strong of faith to keep their souls against the evil one, through Jesus Christ our Lord.—Samuel H. Miller

LECTIONARY MESSAGE

Topic: Be Not Deceived

TEXT: Gal. 6:(1–6) 7–16

OTHER READINGS: 2 Kings 5:1–14; Luke 10:1–11, 16–20

Two illustrations may be found in the auxiliary passages. Naaman, the Syrian leper, had to realize that the waters of the Jordan with God's help are more therapeutic than more familiar waters. The disciples of Jesus were cautioned to rejoice in the most significant events. Be not deceived!

I. God is not mocked. The words in Paul's letter to the Galatians may be literally translated "God is not to be turned up the nose at." That is, do not turn your nose up at God supposing that you can outwit him. There is a basic law of nature: you reap what you sow. You sow grass; you reap a grassy lawn. You sow turnip seed; you reap turnip greens. You sow corn; you reap corn. How strange that there are some who accept this as axiomatic but fail to relate that basic law to the Creator who legislated it! It is a law of life. If you sow the things of the Spirit, you will reap eternal life. The Spirit, superior to the flesh, is yet under the sovereignty of God, and the same law applies—you reap what you sow. It is also a law of ministry. It is so easy to bog down in weariness—even in ministry. Paul's word of encouragement is clear—let's don't! For in due season we will reap the blessings promised. So then—let us give ourselves to ministry. God knows.

II. God sees below the surface. Circumcision was indicative of submission to all the Jewish law. It is used as an example of legalistic compliance. God sees the true person—male and female. Do not try to camouflage disobedience as obedience. The Judaizers were counting their converts hoping for acceptance by the Jews and thereby avoiding persecution. They might deceive men, but not God. God saw their motivation beneath their movement. Do not try hypocrisy. If you wear a mask of legalism, you may deceive some folks. You may even deceive yourself. You may be accepted in the best circles and respected as a law-abiding citizen, but God sees below the surface: he knows what you really are. Do not subject another to a standard of judgment that you are unwilling to respect yourself. Even those who encouraged circumcision and total compliance with the law did not obey it. Good examples (or bad examples) are described in the persons of Peter and Barnabas in chapter 2:11–14. And they glory in it!

III. God was glorified in the suffering of Jesus. It is interesting that the causes of glorying in men and in God should be so different. Those whom Paul rebuked were glorying in the success of their proselytizing mission. God was glorying in the apparent failure of Jesus' ministry. We ought to accept God's standard here and recognize the triumph of suffering love. The apostle exhorts his readers to glory in the cross of Christ. Neither circumcision nor uncircumcision is the issue, but a new creation. And this is God's business—creating. Here is a rule—a law, if you will, that merits our prime loyalty—the way of a new creation. Walk in it!

That which frequently appears most attractive is apt to be most dangerous. Be not deceived!—J. Estill Jones

SUNDAY: JULY SIXTEENTH

SERVICE OF WORSHIP

Sermon: Pure Religion

TEXT: James 1:27

The Book of James has its feet on the ground, even when it lifts its eyes to the stars. It has nothing to say about those mystical experiences where men are "caught up into the third heaven," whatever that may mean. It shows religion as a way of life. "Pure undefiled religion before God the Father is to care for the widows and orphans in their affliction and to keep one's self unspotted from the world."

From start to finish the Book of James is as practical as the multiplication table. Its main appeal is to those plain people who do the larger part of the world's work. It scorns sham and emphasizes the practice of goodwill. "Doers of the word and not hearers," or talkers, only! Religion is a way of life. It means living a clean life and a kindly one.

I. Let me speak of those two points! "Unspotted from the world"—we think of "a clean life" as one that has steered clear of certain forms of physical immorality.

(a) Here is a boy growing up, but somewhere along the way he has lost something. He is wise and knowing about certain bad things to which he was formerly a stranger. His conscience is no longer keen and tender; it is hard and callous like blistered hands. He was once reverent and hopeful; now he is flippant, scornful, cynical. The texture of his life is not wholesome. We see spots all over him as plainly as if he had leprosy.

Here is a young man who went into business with high purposes, saying to himself, "Business is a social utility to bring together the resources of earth and the needs of human society. 'Diligent in business, fervent in spirit, serving the Lord!' It is a place for the cultivation of honor and fidelity." Now he has become hardboiled, suspicious of other men's motives, laughing at the social ideals he once cherished.

Here is a mature man who goes into politics with high aims, and he is elected to Congress. We meet him a few years later and find that his enthusiasm for good government is all gone.

Here is a woman in society who "came out" years ago radiant with all the fine aspirations of healthy young womanhood. Now her face, her manner, her tone of voice, tell another story.

(b) How unnatural and unnecessary it all is! Those people are all sick. Men do go into politics with the flags of high purpose flying, and those flags are never lowered. Men do go into the thick of business life and maintain their honor and their integrity. Their hands are clean and their hearts friendly. Women do go into society with a capital S, and after years of entertaining and being entertained they still wear the pure white of that finer womanhood that is the hope of the race.

II. It can be done. It is being done now, here and there and yonder, by men and women like ourselves. The Master knelt in the garden and prayed not that his followers should be taken out of the world but that they should be kept from evil. "Sanctify them through thy truth, that they may be one as we"—he and the Father—"are one."

(a) How were they to do it? How did he do it? He knew what was in man. No one ever knew it better. Yet through it all, he never lost his faith that weak men can be made strong, that crooked men can be made straight, that bad men may become good. That radiant faith in the grace of God and in the possibilities of human nature kept him "unspotted from the world."

(b) He was not forever holding his life apart and aloof for fear it should be soiled. He pushed straight out into the forefront of the battle between right and wrong to overcome evil with good. What kept Jane Addams strong, fine, serene, living though she did for many years on Halsted Street, Chicago? Something in her that was not of Halsted Street. It took her there in the first place to minister to the needy and the unprivileged. Halsted Street could not change her, though she did change Halsted Street.

III. Pure religion means also living a kindly life. Caring for the widows and orphans as universal types of human need. Here is that permanent symbol of human need found everywhere! We are to minister to that. The debt of privilege that must be paid if we are to hold up our heads and face society without shame! We are to live kindly lives in all the ways that the spirit of our common humanity can suggest.

(a) "God's in his heaven, all's right with the world." No—Browning was mistaken. God is in his heaven, we trust, but all is not right with the world. We are here to set it right. This is our main business. This is not the best of all possible worlds. We are trying every day to improve conditions and make it a better world. We understand fully why men ask, sometimes with tears and sometimes with sneers, "If there is a being of infinite power and wisdom and goodness, why all this pain and grief?" They cry out sometimes in harsh tones, "Where now is thy God? Is there knowledge with the Most High?"

(b) This is not a perfect world—anyone can see that with half an eye. Would it be better for us if it were? Here is a world where there is pain and distress, but we are learning to relieve it, and we are learning to live by doing just that. Here are disorder and injustice, but we are engaged in setting it right. That plain hard task is greatly to our advantage. Here is evildoing, but we are learning how to change that by heroic effort, self-sacrifice, and honest devotion. We are here to overcome evil with good and to become thoroughly, actively, and genuinely good ourselves in the process.

(c) Millions of plain, everyday people do not know a great deal about theology or care very much about ritual. Yet they have a certain faith, which makes them strong for duty, patient and courageous under trial. It softens their cares, sweetens their joys, makes their whole impress upon the lives of others wholesome. It clothes their lives with a certain dignity and beauty that we rarely find apart from religious faith.

IV. Purity and sympathy! A clean life and a kindly one! These qualities are legal tender worth their full face value the world over. A loaf of bread is a loaf of bread in every land the sun shines on. The heart kept free from malice, grudge, or bitterness is as good as gold coin anywhere. Heaven be praised that the author of this Book of James was wise enough to define the expression of "pure religion" in those universal terms. Not by might or by power, not by statutes or by armies, not by stern creeds or by stately liturgies, but by my spirit, saith the Lord of hosts, shall the kingdom of heaven come.—Charles R. Brown

Illustrations

THE STRATEGY OF JESUS. We take too low views of people. We dwell on their faults and their limitations. Our influence with people is in proportion to our faith in them. A mother can have great faith in a backward child and by her faith in him can make him self-reliant and strong. A friend can have great expectations for another doubting and melancholy friend whose will is weak and flabby and by knowing what is really in him can make that will as taut as a bowstring. A wife can have faith in her husband who is discouraged and irresolute and thus give him initiative and courage. If a teacher cherishes high views of what his pupil can do, he can thereby help him to do it.

If, like Jesus, we can see beneath unpromising exteriors and know what really is in people, like him we can make them what they may be and can be and ought to be.—Raymond Calkins

PURE RELIGION. Kagawa of Japan came of good stock, honest, clean, friendly people. What kept him clean, straight, hopeful through those long hard years of daily contact with the foulest slums of Kobe? Something in him that was not of Kobe. He came up out of it unspotted and ready for a wider service. When one has walked in the open, rejoicing in the sunshine, even though he may go to the bottom of a mine to earn his bread, he feels that he belongs "up there." If you had to leave a well-appointed home to live for a year in the slums, that sense of union with certain higher forces would keep you. "This is the victory that overcometh the world, even our faith. Our lives are hid with Christ in God."—Charles R. Brown

Sermon Suggestions

GOD'S PLUMB LINE. TEXT: Amos 7:7–17. (1) God has a standard by which nations and individuals are measured. (2) God's true prophets disclose the unfaithfulness of those who err from God's standard. (3) The prophetic message is characteristically met with resistance. (4) The predicted consequences of unfaithfulness follow inevitably: (a) unless there is a return to God or (b) unless God intervenes with grace and mercy.

THE SECRET OF CHRISTIAN GROWTH. TEXT: Col. 1:1–14. (1) Hearing and understanding the truth of God's grace, verse 6. (2) Trusting in Christ Jesus, verse 4a. (3) Having love for all of God's people, verse 4b.

Worship Aids

CALL TO WORSHIP. "Arise, O God, judge the earth: for thou shalt inherit all nations" (Ps. 82:8).

INVOCATION. Father, each of us has come to this sacred place this morning with our expectations of what we want to take place. Some have come expecting great release from backbreaking burdens. Some have come expecting forgiveness from deadening sins. Some have come to find the sustaining of their joy and peace. And some have come expecting nothing. Help us to forget what we want and to lay aside our demands, that we might concern ourselves with what you expect for this hour of worship. Make us aware that you expect us to listen, that you may speak; to silence our turmoils, that you may grant us your peace; and to lay aside the cares of the moment, that we might glimpse the care of your love as we wait together before you. In the poignant moments in which we wait, speak so clearly that we cannot but know that it is you whom we hear.—Henry Fields

OFFERTORY SENTENCE. "Therefore, my dear friends, stand firm and immovable, and work for the Lord always, work without limit, since you know that in the Lord your labour cannot be lost" (1 Cor. 15:58 REB).

OFFERTORY PRAYER. As we bring our offering, Lord, we bring it in faith, believing that you will use it and multiply its blessings in ways that we can hardly begin to imagine, for, like your Word, it will surely not return to you empty.

PRAYER. O thou Creator of all that is, was, and shall be, we marvel that you have so created us in your image that we are not left to the loneliness of our finitude but that we can communicate and relate to you as a child to his parent. With what love you love us that this should be our privilege of all creatures of the created order. Whatever our language you hear us. There is a "deep speaking unto deep" that undergirds the elusive and broken words that we attempt to form with our lips.

From the beginning you have been speaking a *life-giving* Word. Your Word was so spoken through the affairs of the people Israel as to reveal your being and purpose to all humankind. Their pilgrimage from slavery, through the trials of the wilderness, to the Promised Land haunts the human race as the likely pilgrimage of every person. Even more presently your Word is here in the flesh and blood of Jesus and dwells among us in the meaning of his life, ministry, passion, living again. May the indwelling gift of your Spirit to illumine and energize call to mind your word from the beginning and quicken our minds and hearts and persons that we may do your will in the flesh and blood of our time and place.

In these moments we have been confronted again that this is our vocation as the *ecclesia*, the called-out ones to be the light of the world, the light on the hill, the salt of the earth, the savor that preserves and gives zest, meaning, to life. When with our preoccupation with religion—its rites, its forms, its practices—we neglect or turn from our high calling as children of Abraham, you are not left without a witness, but you raise up the novelist, the playwright, the artist through whom your Word, the very stuff of reality, breaks through, and we realize there is no hiding place. Your Word is so indelibly written in the fibers and tissues of our creation that we cannot get away from it.

May we so hunger and thirst for your Word that for us it becomes the bread of life and the well of living water springing up into everlasting life. For your Word of grace mediated through forgiveness that makes all things new, we pray, not only for our personal relationships but for the healing of the nations. Deliver us from those who would provoke rather than reconcile—who incite fear rather than inspire brotherhood—who are more concerned to fill the coffers of the merchants of death than to mediate life through peace-loving and life-giving pursuits. Grant us lawmakers with the wisdom and courage to turn from the moral bankruptcy of political expediency to the righteousness that exalts life giving.

Where there is any brokenness among us in illness, in sorrow, in love, in disappointment, in failure, we pray the ministry of your Word of grace that alone makes whole, we pray through him who is your Word from the beginning, is now, and ever shall be.—John Thompson

LECTIONARY MESSAGE

Topic: Love for God and Neighbor

TEXT: Luke 10:25–37 (Col. 1:1–14; Amos 7:7–17)

A lawyer approached Jesus with a general question about eternal life. Prompted by Jesus, he cited the precedent from Old Testament law. Yet his own response, though familiar and comfortable, proved unsettling. Troubled by the semantics, he asked that Jesus define *neighbor*. The stark contrast between the calculated evasion of Jewish insiders and the generous help of an ethnic outsider illustrated how the recipients of eternal life must integrate their love for God with their love for neighbor. Mercy makes a stranger into a neighbor.

I. Looking for loopholes (vv. 25–29). The lawyer tried to test Jesus, but his query backfired, and he was tested instead. After Jesus responded with an interrogative about sources (v. 26), the conniving petitioner adroitly recited a scriptural summary of the law (Deut. 6:5; Lev. 19:18). Eternal life is granted to those who truly love God and thus manifest love for neighbors commensurate with one's own self-interests. When Jesus admonished the practice of what he allegedly understood, provincialism surfaced as the lawyer struggled with conventional stereotypes of neighbor based upon cultural bias.

II. Beaten and bypassed (vv. 30–32). In the more direct and hazardous descent from Jerusalem to Jericho, a lone traveler was brutalized by thieves and abandoned at the point of death. The tragedy of criminal self-interests can be summarized with "what is yours is mine—I will grab it." The probability that the culprits were also Jewish previews the dearth of brotherhood that follows.

Two equally alone travelers avoided the anonymous victim. The priest, whose task was to represent humanity to God, respected ceremonial purity (Num. 19:11). The Levite, whose birthright brought him to the inner sanctum of Temple service, respected compulsory ritual. Neither man was willing to make contact with the victim; both committed a sin of omission by deliberately ignoring the desperate needs of flesh and blood. Excuses always abound as momentary concern deteriorates into idle curiosity. The tragedy of callous indifference can be summarized with "what's mine is mine—I will keep it." Woe to the prideful and complacent (Amos 7:7–17)!

III. Treated like family (vv. 33–35). Yet another sojourner stumbled upon the wounded walker, an unlikely hero. By orthodox and diaspora Jews alike, Samaritans were despised as half-breeds and reviled as heretics.

Hearers know nothing of his own dilemma: was he already pressed by debt? Or was he rushed for time? What burdens was he carrying? The tender details of aid and comfort demonstrated that his compassion was circumscribed neither by legal technicalities nor by cultural precedents nor by personal preoccupations. He did not merely bind the wounds and supply some shelter; he lavished God's love upon a stranger. Such mercy can be summarized with "what is mine is yours—I will share it." Blessings to those living worthy of the Lord and bearing fruit (Col. 1:1–14)!

Although they all three loved God, only the Samaritan loved his neighbor as himself. Without a love for God, the love for others is mere reaction. Without a love for others, the love for God is hypocritical. Thus, Jesus concludes by repeating the mandate to compassionate action (vv. 34, 37).—Daniel E. Hatfield

SUNDAY: JULY TWENTY-THIRD

SERVICE OF WORSHIP

Sermon: Lydia

TEXT: Acts 16:12–15

If you could choose one word and know that that one word would become the motto of your life, the epitaph on your grave, the summation of your personality, what would you want that one word to be? I would like to suggest a word for you to consider. It is the word *faithful.*

I have selected to illustrate the word with one of the least prominent characters in all the Bible. Women were by definition unimportant in the thinking of the ancient East. A scant three verses of Acts tell us all that we know about this woman. And yet I believe a look at Lydia will tell us more clearly than ten thousand words the meaning of faithfulness.

I. Faithful means filled with faith.

(a) It is the end of the day of business in Lydia's shop. She has just waited on the last customer, taken a last look around the shop, instructed her assistant to close up, and, checking her appearance in the looking glass, swept lightly out the door. She is the picture of self-assurance as she walks down one street and then another toward home. Is the picture real?

At last, at the end of a long day, Lydia is alone in her own home. As she stands alone, the fixed smile drains from Lydia's face; her shoulders slump a bit; a great wave of weariness sweeps over her. "Another day ended. And for what? What am I living for? Possessions? They cannot give me what I need. Family? I have had that; it does not satisfy these yearnings within me. Prestige? The respect of others? I do not want it. What is my life for? What is the profit in it all? Death? And what comes after death? Who knows?" On this melancholy note, Lydia moves sadly to her own bed and a restless, dream-filled sleep.

(b) The next day is the Jewish Sabbath. Lydia is of this faith. Her shop will not open today. Instead, she slips early in the morning through the gates of Philippi to the place by the river where those of her creed are accustomed to meet for prayer, there being no synagogue in her city. With the other women Lydia repeats the prayers of her ancient faith. Still there is no answer to her secret prayer. This morning, however, when the prayers are ended, an unusual thing happens. A visiting rabbi from Jerusalem rises to be recognized and to speak to the worshipers. All listen attentively, expecting a lesson on the keeping of the law. But from the very first, Lydia recognizes something different about this speaker.

(c) "My sisters in Israel," says the rabbi, "I had every reason to be confident in our righteousness. I was so zealous in our faith that I persecuted its enemies, especially followers of one Jesus, a Nazarene, who called themselves 'the way.' This same Jesus, I declare to you, is our promised Savior, who can bring forgiveness of sins and set us right with God."[2]

(d) As Lydia hears these words, she realizes that God is answering her prayer. This Paul, the rabbi, must be sent from God. There by the riverbank, the old, old miracle of the Damascus road occurs again. This time there is no blinding light, no audible heavenly voice. But there is a gospel of salvation; there is a believing heart; there is the miracle of the new birth. Lydia is saved. She is "full of faith." This is the first, great meaning of *faithful*—to be filled with, dominated by faith in Jesus Christ. Without faith there is no faithfulness. And Lydia, "whose heart the Lord opened" (Acts 16:14), has become faithful. Has it happened in your life?

II. Faithful means living your faith.

(a) Faithfulness is inward, but it is not merely inward. Lydia expressed her faith with public commitment in baptism. To many of us, to be sure, that does not seem a great thing. It is not so everywhere. I ministered to a Baptist church in a land where Baptists were few in numbers and small in influence. The people regarded Baptist conformity to New Testament practice in baptism with amusement or suspicion. It is in this way that becoming a Christian is regarded in many parts of the world today. It must have been so in Lydia's day. "When she was baptized"—who can know what anguish of spirit, what courage, what sacrifice, personal and financial, that step may have required?

(b) Listen, I think I can hear two of the society matrons talking on the street of Philippi. "My dear, have you heard about Lydia?"

"Why, no, but do tell me!"

"Well, you knew she was Jewish, and a foreigner?"

"Yes."

"Well, now it's worse than that. It seems that these people calling themselves 'Christians' (whatever that is) have come to town. And Lydia, can you believe it, has joined their sect! She even let them take her out in the river one morning and baptize her. Some queer ceremony of theirs."

"I always thought she was a little odd. And her prices are outrageous, though I have found some bargains there."

"My dear, have you shopped at Sylvia's lately? Her prices are perfectly reasona-

[2]Phil. 3:4–6; Acts 26:11–15, partly quoted.

ble, and besides, Sylvia doesn't do queer things like getting baptized!"

(c) No, it was not easy to take a faithful stand for Christ in Philippi. It may not be easy in your town. But Lydia did it in such a way that the record can add three very important words: "when she was baptized, and her household." I believe these words tell us about Lydia's faithfulness in another way. They tell us that after she found Jesus Christ, she went back to her home and to her shop. In many ways, she was the same old Lydia with the same gracious smile, same motherly love, same shrewd business judgment. But there was also a new Lydia present. Now the smile spoke of a new tenderness and warmth. Now the shrewdness was tempered by a new love of honesty and fair dealing.

III. Faithful means serving.

(a) There is a third meaning of *faithful,* and this is the faithfulness of devoted service. Lydia had trusted Christ and had been converted; she had taken a loyal stand for Christ and lived her witness. But that was not enough. She wanted to serve. Now Lydia was not qualified, perhaps, to serve as a Sunday school teacher in Philippi, although they must soon have established a Sunday school or something like one. Very likely she was not ready, upon her conversion, to become an officer of the Woman's Missionary Union of Philippi. It may be that she had no voice for the new church choir. But Lydia did notice that the apostles had no place to stay. There were no decent hotels, even if apostles could have afforded them, which they could not. So Lydia said, " 'If ye have judged me to be faithful to the Lord, come into my house, and abide there.' And she constrained us."

(b) The apostles did not stay long at Lydia's house. They were thrown into jail instead, chapter 16 tells us. Of course, that was not too surprising. Apostles had been in jail before and have been since. And the Lord knew how to care for the preachers of his gospel. There was the matter of an earthquake, a converted jailer, and an embarrassed magistrate who set the apostles free. But now, surely, they will not come back to Lydia's house? Surely she has done enough. It is embarrassing to be hostess to jailbirds, and Lydia has already found her faith costly. Surely she will say, "Well, I believe we should pass the offices around. I entertained the apostles last time. Now it is someone else's time." So we might expect. But look at verse 40: "They went out of the prison, and entered into the house of Lydia." Faithful means that you find a place of service and keep it. And I believe you will agree that little Lydia had discovered the meaning of faithfulness.

(c) It will cost you something to become a faithful Christian. I cannot tell you in advance what it will cost you, except the single, all-inclusive cost—yourself. But I can tell you this—that in faithfulness to Christ you will gain far more than you could possibly give. For in faithfulness you will become the person with *faithful* as his motto. You will become the person you want to be.—James W. McClendon

Illustrations

GIVING VERSUS GETTING. Some time ago a woman spoke quite critically of the church of which I was pastor. She had recently attended that church, but she had sat so far away that she did not recognize me when I called. Therefore, she said, "I attended services at that church, but will never do so again." When I asked the reason, she said, "Not a soul spoke to me—not even the pastor!" What is the real meaning of a declaration like that? She might have stated it in these words: "I went to church today. There were hundreds of friendly people as hungry for fellowship as I, but I dodged them all and ducked out and went my selfish and lonely way because I refused to speak to a single one of them." There are exceptions I know; but generally speaking, if we give the world the best we have, the best will come back to us.—Clovis G. Chappell

DISCIPLINE. If you would find freedom, learn above all to discipline your senses and your soul. Be not led hither and thither by your desires and your members. Keep your spirit and your body chaste, wholly subject to you, and obediently seeking the goal that is set before you. None can learn the secret of freedom, save by discipline.—Dietrich Bonhoeffer

Sermon Suggestions

HOW CAN THERE BE A FAMINE FOR THE WORD? TEXT: Amos 8:1–12, especially verse 11. (1) Is it because there are no Bibles? No. (2) Is it because there are no preachers? No. (3) It may be (a) because teachers, preacher, and Bible readers are too selective in their emphases from the many "words of God" or (b) because they deliberately or unconsciously twist the truth to conform to their sinful desires.

THE WORD OF GOD IN ITS FULLNESS. TEXT: Col. 1:15–28 NIV. (1) That Word is Jesus Christ. (2) Through Jesus Christ all things were created. (3) All things have their unity in Jesus Christ. (4) Because of those truths we have been reconciled to God (a) through Christ's death on the cross (b) to the end that we may be presented to God holy, without blemish, and free from accusation.

Worship Aids

CALL TO WORSHIP. "I will always thank you, God, for what you have done; in the presence of your people I will proclaim that you are good" (Ps. 52:9 TEV).

INVOCATION. Lord, spread the joy of heaven abroad in our hearts because our faith is open and expansive and our hope is in God, Maker of heaven and earth, Father of our Lord Jesus Christ.—E. Lee Phillips

OFFERTORY SENTENCE. "Whoever shares with others should do it generously; whoever has authority should work hard; whoever shows kindness to others should do it cheerfully" (Rom. 12:8b TEV).

OFFERTORY PRAYER. Through these offerings we bring, Father, we seek to give our strength to the weak, our sympathy to the suffering, our provision to the needy, and our hearts to you. Bless the gifts as you did the little boy's offering of fish long ago and through them minister to the multitudes.—Henry Fields

PRAYER. Eternal Spirit, thy servants seek thee not so much to secure what they desire as to open their hearts to the gifts that thou desirest to bestow. Through another week we have imposed imperious wishes on the world to get our will, and we confess before thee the evil and unwisdom of our craving. Give thou to us not what we would ask but what thou wouldst bestow.

We seek easy and fortunate circumstance while thou hast in thine hand courage with which to face ill fortune and win a shining victory against hardship and adversity. Lord, give thy gifts to us—thy will, not ours, be done—courage, let it be, that we may prove ourselves the sons of God and heirs with Christ in overcoming the world.

We seek from thee happiness and like children would stand with open hands to receive life's pleasures, while thou hast a task to give us that will call us out of ourselves and claim all that we are for thee. A task, then, let it be, O God, according to thy wisdom! Give us a duty that will dignify our days that we may join the honorable company of thy true servants who, called of God, have found their vocation and have done it well. We would seek thy sanctuary, not to present our unwise wishes but to put ourselves at thy disposal. Release thy power in us. Reveal thy wisdom through us and grant that in and for and because of us thy will may be done.—Harry Emerson Fosdick

LECTIONARY MESSAGE

Topic: Stop, Look, and Listen

OTHER READINGS: Luke 10:38–42 (Col. 1:15–28; Amos 8:1–12)

After the redefinition of love for neighbor, epitomized by the Samaritan, Luke's narrative then illustrates the love for God in the account of Martha and Mary. Both sisters, first introduced here, appeared to do well in serving and listening, yet only one gave herself in love.

I. Martha's hospitality. More her story than Mary's, Martha received Jesus into her home, a supposedly genuine gesture soon spoiled by resentment. Martha encircled Jesus in a whirlwind of ministry, allowing herself to be overwhelmed with tasks. The industrious hostess became manipulative and petty when she protested Mary's neglect, though no standards of etiquette were breached. Driven by ulterior motives and feeling unappreciated, she made herself a martyr, the victim of self-aggrandizement.

Such activists engender motion devoid of progress in a restless quest for approbation that cannot be satisfied. Worse, they usually regard their way as the only option and resent the failure of others to fulfill their standards. Ostensibly serving, they are self-serving; ostensibly merciful, they are self-pitying; ostensibly pious, they are self-righteous.

Noteworthy is that the work was not condemned, only the complaint, which revealed an absence of focus on the priority of being in the Lord's presence, the very reason for all the domestic activity. Martha's worthy deeds could not substitute for relating to Jesus.

II. Mary's undivided attention. The goal of Mary was hearing the Master's words. Sitting at the feet of Jesus, she was a living portrait of humble meditation and devotion. The Lord had her undivided attention.

Juxtaposed with Martha's servitude, Mary's behavior could be misconstrued as laziness. Still, she is neither idle nor negligent but rather engaged and invested. Having recognized the same logistical necessities as her sister, Mary addressed her spiritual need of being in the Master's presence. She thus responded directly to Jesus, not indirectly like Martha. Mary gave her whole self, not just her best efforts. Ultimately, she did a good work, free from the contaminations of self-interest.

Disciples abide in Christ, dwelling on things of the Spirit, listening to holy Word. Such reverence begins with singular concentration. More convenient are the contributions of time, energy, and resources; less demanding are tokens or gestures. The incarnate image of God comes first before everything else under creation (Col. 1:15, 17).

III. The good part. Shallow readings are distracted by secondary issues, such as sibling rivalry, personality clash, irresponsible sloth, idolatry of deeds, or the contrast between legalism and meditation. Both sisters had good intentions, but only Mary loved the Lord to the extent that she was willing to give herself. Only after hearing the Word could she have rendered useful service in the kingdom of God.

Martha's efforts were ruinous, crushed under the weight of egotism. Mary selected the good portion, equally available to Martha. In giving herself to the Lord, Mary offers a therapeutic example echoed in the kindergarten drill to "stop, look, and listen." Believers accompany the Lord whom they love.—Daniel E. Hatfield

SUNDAY: JULY THIRTIETH

SERVICE OF WORSHIP

Sermon: Sin as a Loss of Perspective

TEXT: Rom. 7:14–25

I. The theme for the Monday morning worship at camp was "God is . . . ." Central to the development of the theme for that first morning was the concept of God as Creator.

(a) To give the junior high campers some feel for what is involved at the emotional level in the act of creation, the worship leader passed out cans of modeling clay. We were instructed to let our creative juices flow and make anything we desired out of the clay. We were given sufficient time to brood over our creation so that by the time the music ended we were quite attached to our works of clay.

(b) The worship leader then asked a couple of younger people to show their creations and put into words something of what their works meant to them. I distinctly recall a finely sculptured clenched fist. Julian Chong explained that the fist represented the manner in which people relate to God: tight, resistant, rebellious, self-sufficient. The fist was particularly meaningful because only that morning we had been asked as a group to spend time in prayer and meditation with our hands open, palms upward, symbolizing our openness to God.

II. The next morning the theme was "God grieves," and we contemplated sin and its effect on God. As we sat in silence, we noticed one or two people get up from their seats, go to the platform, and begin walking slowly back and forth, looking very carefully at our creations. One of the people took a clay work in his hand and squeezed it until it oozed between his fingers. He dropped the remains on the floor. We sat in shock! What was happening should have been obvious to us adults. The "destroyers" had been chosen beforehand and instructed to select several creations and demolish them before the eyes of their creators. The worship leader would then be set up to talk to the group about sin as rebelliousness and destruction and the effect this has on God.

But something happened next that the worship leader could not have predicted. A girl on the front row evidently thought that destroying the clay looked like a lot more fun than sitting there praying, so she left her seat, walked to the railing, picked up a piece of clay, and destroyed it! Immediately several other kids ran to the stage and did likewise. Within minutes the worshipers had become a mob. They were completely out of control. Hands that had been upturned in prayer were clenched in fists.

(a) Our leader had attempted to set up a tightly controlled set of circumstances under which to illustrate the nature of sin, but what happened was much more realistic, much more frightening than anything he could have contrived. *We were not watching a cleverly devised demonstration of sin; we were the demonstration.*

(b) What was being acted out? What was the essence of the sin? Wasn't it that in the excitement of the moment, in the thrill of mob action, *the group lost its perspective?*

A loss of perspective. Under the pressure, in the excitement, the thrill of the moment, doing what you, under more sober moments, would never do, saying what you would never say, thinking what you would never think. Hurt and disappointment inflicted not as a result of a premeditated action, yet not the result of an accident either. Rather, persons hurt because other persons let go for awhile, let go of their values and their commitments. And the name of that letting go is sin.

III. How much pain has been inflicted because a person let go or lost contact with himself and his deepest beliefs?

(a) The idyllic story of Adam and Eve is a paradigmatic illustration of sin as a *loss of perspective.* I have recently noticed something interesting about this ancient story. Eve did not succumb to the temptation as a result of the persuasiveness of the serpent's arguments; rather, she disobeyed God when she "saw that the fruit of the tree was good to eat and that it was pleasing to the eye and tempting to contemplate" (Gen. 3:6 NEB). It wasn't the power of the serpent's theology; it was the strength of her own desires that led to her downfall.

(b) Paul is trying to express his frustrations in Romans 7:14–25. There is no question about Paul's dedication to the law of God. None whatsoever. And he could say with some degree of justifiable pride that at times he did a pretty good job at living by God's standards. But there were other times when other elements within him took control, and he broke God's law as though he had never known God. "The good which I want to do, I fail to do; but what I do is the wrong which is against my will" (vv. 19–20). I do that which contradicts my own higher principles.

(c) There is no better biblical illustration of a loss of perspective than David, who had everything a man could want but was able to see only the one thing he didn't have and couldn't have legitimately. So Uriah must die. Perspective was lost. He couldn't see the forest of goodness for the single tree he couldn't have.

(d) And what of Simon Peter? He knew better. But under the pressure of criticism his perspective became distorted, and he denied the deepest commitment of his entire life.

To paraphrase Paul, "We have all lost our perspective and fallen short of the glory of God, who always keeps his priorities straight and never loses sight of what he values and loves." And the name of that loss of perspective is sin.

IV. During the second day at camp, sometime after our experience of sin and our existential knowledge of God's grief, a young man, still upset by the morning's experience, asked, "*When do we get to the good news part?*"

(a) *We get to the good news part right now.* The good news is: God is a patient, loving potter who molds and remolds broken vases into beautiful pieces of art.

Jeremiah had been instructed by God to go down to the potter's house and simply observe the man at work. "Now and then," Jeremiah observed, "a vessel he was making out of the clay would be spoilt in his hands, and then he would start again and mold it into another vessel to his liking" (18:4 NEB). As Jeremiah watched the potter molding and remolding, the message came to him: "Can I not deal with you, Israel, says the Lord, as the potter deals with his clay?" (vv. 5–6 NEB).

(b) That's the good news: God reclaims wasted lives, rebuilds devastated egos, gives hope where there is only despair, builds up, shapes up. He salvages. He saves. We got to the good news part on the third day of camp. The theme was "God forgives." Our worship leader spoke soothingly of the forgiveness of God and the willingness of the Father to remold destroyed lives into something beautiful. Then he called Julian Chong to the front. In his hands was a new clenched fist, this one much bigger but just as finely shaped as the original, which had been destroyed. But there was something odd about the color. Where the original had been made from a single can of clay and had been totally blue, this one had been made from scraps of clay picked up off the floor and scraped off the walls of the auditorium. Its multicolored appearance spoke eloquently of the recreative work of God the potter.

Let him who has ears to hear, hear the good news!—Richard Groves

Illustrations

JESUS THE CONVINCING EXAMPLE. A young village artist, conceited, of course, has painted a picture that would make a man crawl, and yet he thinks it is beautiful. His mother thinks it is thrice beautiful, his aunts think it is four times beautiful, and they all pamper him. Suppose, now, a professor should come in and undertake to say to him: "This color is hard, and these forms are almost grotesque"? He would not believe it. What would you do? Take another picture, and put it alongside of his. He has a true eye and a true sense of color, and though at first he says, "Well, I don't see anything," he comes in every morning, and looks at that one and then at this, and begins to say to himself, "By George, that is rather harsh, isn't it? Oh, that I could get that graceful curve." Keep that picture, which is beautiful in all its elements, by him, and he will burn up his own in a short time.—Henry Ward Beecher

THE PRAYER FOR PARDON. In castles of the old world, visitors are shown hidden doors leading to secret passages and are told: "This is how help came when the castle was held in unbreakable siege." Mankind is a prisoner to a helpless will and a mind of enmity, but there is a secret way. Any man still has contact with a vast country beyond his beleaguered self, for he can pray: "Forgive us our debts, as we forgive our debtors." Then, as a forgiven man, he can say to his brother, "I forgive you, as I trust you to forgive me." Thus the siege is lifted. "Be ye kind one to another, tenderhearted, forgiving one another, even as God for Christ's sake hath forgiven you."—George A. Buttrick

Sermon Suggestions

CHILDREN OF THE LIVING GOD. TEXT: Hos. 1:2–10, especially verse 10. God's owning of his people is: (1) Not because they belong to God by nature, for they are sinful. (2) Not because they have earned a change of status, for they are not able to make themselves acceptable. (3) But because God is gracious to forgive and restore, for he binds himself to his people in an everlasting love.

A FULL LIFE IN CHRIST. TEXT: Col. 2:6–15 (16–19), especially verses 6–7. (1) By receiving him as Lord. (2) By continuing to live in him. (3) By abounding in thanksgiving.

Worship Aids

CALL TO WORSHIP. "Wilt thou not revive us again: that thy people may rejoice in thee? Show us thy mercy, O Lord, and grant us thy salvation" (Ps. 85:6–7).

INVOCATION. Lord, make us to rejoice in this special day that you have made for rest and gladness. Open our hearts to your love, our minds to your truth, and our wills to your service.

OFFERTORY SENTENCE. "Also he said to them, 'Take care what you hear; the measure you deal out to others will be dealt out to yourselves, and you will receive extra' " (Mark 4:24 MOFFATT).

OFFERTORY PRAYER. We know, O God, that everything we are and have, and everything that we can ever hope to be, ultimately comes from thee. Keep alive in us that sense of dependence upon thee and give us the grace and the wisdom so to cooperate with thy laws, that we may work together with thee to do things that by ourselves we could never accomplish at all.—Theodore Parker Ferris

PRAYER. Almighty and eternal God, we come before you recognizing that you are a God of history. We acknowledge your involvement in the lives of people throughout the corridors of time. We know of your love for your creation and of your desire to share that love with all that you have brought into being. It is you, O God, who have provided strength and hope for our mothers and fathers as well as our grandmothers and grandfathers as they have planted their lives in the rich soil of your being.

We come to this day seeking your help for our very lives. You are the God of salvation! Save us, O God, from our enemies, yes, even ourselves. Deliver us from the evils of our world, that we might live in your victory. Deliver us from the anguish of death. Teach us to recognize that you are the God of life and death. Heal the hurt we experience deep within ourselves. Deliver us, O God, from the reality of loneliness. Aid us in sensing your living presence in our lives. It is you, God, we seek as our companion. Deliver us from the fears of illness. Help us in our struggles with uncertainty. Give us peace in the midst of our doubt. Deliver us from the captivity of our failures. Establish within us the gift of faith. Strengthen our foundation in order that we might fully trust in you.

Almighty and eternal God, we come to you seeking hope for our future. Help us to live in a manner that is mindful of those who are oppressed. Help us to be liberators just as you have liberated us. Give to us strong hearts that we might believe in you and your kingdom and that we might dedicate our lives in total service to you. Stir within us the power of your presence that we might grow in our ability to live and to love just as your Son came and demonstrated to us how to live and to love and in whose name we ask these things.—John W. Neal

LECTIONARY MESSAGE

Topic: Jesus Taught Them How to Pray

OTHER READINGS: Luke 11:1–13 (Col. 2:6–15; Hos. 1:2–10)

The model prayer in Luke, as also the longer Matthean account, Jesus offers to his disciples as a cogent outline for communication with the Lord. The prayer divides into two parts. First, the heavenly Father is praised and his kingdom sought. Second, requests are made for daily provisions, mutual forgiveness, and divine assistance. In the accompanying midrash of parable and proverbs, Jesus promises the loving response of the heavenly Father to the prayers of his children by arguing from the lesser to the greater (v. 13).

I. Model prayer (vv. 1–4). The disciples observed how Jesus prayed and perceived the relationship to his teaching and authority. Still, they did not know the content of his prayers. An anonymous disciple, evidently speaking on behalf of the others, asked that Jesus might instruct them to pray and then cited the (jealous?) example of John the Baptist. Perhaps they originally desired only a perfunctory piety, yet Jesus seized the teachable moment to give them a prayer for the ages.

The name of address is Father. The context and abundant concordant references make clear that familial substitutes are neither offered nor implied. The title indicates intimate accessibility as well as hierarchical authority. Two imperatives follow that offer praise. Divine identity mandates reverence even in the mere citation of the name—sanctified, consecrated. Holy dominion extends from heaven to earth so that eschatological hopes for the kingdom of God anticipate a new world order.

Three petitions target the primary human needs of sustenance, renewal, and guidance. Like the Israelites gathering wilderness manna, disciples seek essential provisions sufficient for the day. This fundamental request also includes intercession for the sake of others. The reception of forgiveness for sins hinges upon the commensurate bequest of pardon for current debtors, friend or foe. Such generous negation is a mere fraction of God's grace already granted. The concluding entreaty is a plea for protection in the midst of testing (cf. James 1:13–15). Contrary to the false independence of rugged individualism, disciples acknowledge innate weaknesses and appeal for divine help.

II. Persistent prayer (vv. 5–11). The parable illustrates the superiority of God's motive to that of someone pestered by a friend at midnight. Likewise, even pagans provide for their children's needs and would not resort to cruel chicanery by substituting stone for bread or scorpion for egg. Thus, the Lord provides.

The Lord awaits legitimate requests from his children. They ask and do not simply tell or lay claim. They seek and do not presume to make divine decisions. They knock and do not demand their own desires. Asking posits an interrogative, seeking features a measure of patience, and knocking entails labor. Perseverance is not tantamount to presumptuous badgering. Good gifts are granted to those who show their willingness to receive through reverent submission, contrary to the shameless impudence of the midnight friend.

III. Effectual prayer. Sometimes prayers deteriorate into begging, as if God were a magician on call for personal rescue. Sometimes prayers degenerate into covetousness, as if God were a benevolent benefactor akin to Santa Claus. The majesty of the passage must not be misconstrued to mean that the limitless scope of prayer is tantamount to a blank check for personal whims or a medium for self-destruction.

Shallowness flourishes in the absence of reflection and preparation. Consequently, prayers suffer from sameness, lameness, and tameness. At times, stones are wanted instead of bread, or poisonous scorpions instead of nutritious eggs. What is the condition of the petitioner? And is it appropriate for asking, seeking, and knocking?

The model prayer for all disciples of Jesus begins with praise that honors God for being Father and professes citizenship in his kingdom. True needs for oneself and others are voiced. Sins are confessed with an understanding that forgiveness follows for the forgiver. The prayer concludes with a recommitment to follow divine guidance in the warfare of witness.—Daniel Hatfield

SUNDAY: AUGUST SIXTH

SERVICE OF WORSHIP

Sermon: One Full of Faith and of the Holy Spirit

TEXT: Acts 6 and 7

The history of the early church as recorded in the Book of Acts leaps out at us as one of the most exciting in the human story. One of Luke's major objectives lies in showing how the Christian church grows from the seed of a babe born in an out-of-the-way Palestinian village into a gospel embracing all the world.

For Luke the spread of the gospel depends upon people. We read about one of those important evangelists just a moment ago. His name is Stephen. Stephen's story is pivotal in Luke's world history of Christianity. This morning we will take a look at Stephen's story as it reverberates for you and for me as well.

I. First of all, Stephen's story seems to emerge from nowhere. Luke never mentions him before chapter 6. And when he does, Stephen pops into view because of a complaint. Someone in the church has a gripe. We get to know Stephen because a faction of church members feels overlooked—no, worse than that, slighted—worse than that, discriminated against. The widows of church members who speak Greek are not getting their share of the church's charity. Widows of church members who speak Hebrew get their share and then some.

So they lodge a complaint: "Your outreach committee is unfair." "Your deacons' fund plays favorites." "Your ministers play footsie with their own kind."

(a) I must say, these kinds of complaints are endemic to churches. Men and women who should be on the same wavelength, molded for common purpose, pointing toward God's promises of wholeness and mutuality tend to serve their own interests, to slight others who perceive things differently, to treat those of differing perspective or styles with benign neglect. Frequently the complaint is warranted. Occasionally it is not. But these things happen—and they have been happening in churches since the very beginning.

(b) But among the most interesting aspects of this complaint and the surrounding situation is Stephen's getting chosen to deal with it. His name arises in almost unpropitious circumstance. Now, in no way do I wish to demean the considerable gifts Stephen brings to this situation. Luke describes him as a man of great spiritual presence, one full of faith and the Holy Spirit. But this unhappy, troublesome occasion, not big by any means, as one would appraise the history of the world—this trivial occasion turns out to be one of enormous historical impact. Stephen, chosen to negotiate widows' pensions, commissioned to a simple work of charity two thousand years ago in Jerusalem, amid a tiny, Jewish messianic sect, turns out to be one of those who revolutionize the world and leave us agog and breathless.

(c) You know how this works, how emergencies, challenges, bad news sometimes call out the very best in us, how doors open for us in ironic and surprising ways. And we know just as well our lives can change because of an encouraging remark from a teacher, a casual conversation at the water cooler, a letter from out of the blue—in any case a door opens; we may not initially even recognize it—and mysteriously God does something in our behalf, calls us out to some new opportunity and responsibility and we, for some reason, in the providence of grace, respond to the invitation. I pray you, like Stephen, make the change, take the plunge.

II. So Stephen comes to our attention through a complaint. But then he gets into trouble—very serious trouble. Stephen preaches his heart out. And he makes some people very, very angry.

(a) Indeed, he tries to tell his fellow Greek-speaking Jews that Jesus of Nazareth, crucified in Jerusalem as a common criminal and raised by God as vindication of a life of love, compassion, and forgiveness, is the true salvation of our world. He tries to tell them a new world order comes into being with the coming of Jesus—a new world order where national chauvinism, religious parochialism, ethnic blinders, all the distinctions we concoct to separate ourselves from one another come tumbling down in the universal grace of Christ binding us into one family of God.

And as usual such an announcement about that kind of new world gets him into trouble. Stephen faces a faction of his fellow religionists who cannot stomach this message. So in frustration, this faction sets up an appointment with the highest religious court in the land. There, sad to say, Stephen's message about a new world order in Jesus Christ is adjudged a fraud and a blasphemy.

(b) My soul! How human nature resists this message of reconciliation and peace. Look across the world. What is this mess, this horror story pounding us daily from Bosnia but national, religious, ethnic contempt, and the wholesale, strategic rape of women and girls, gender contempt, invasion, destruction born of fear and perverse loyalties to blood and soil always poisoning life in our global village? Before the high religious court Stephen launches a passionate, searing polemic laying out the highest aspirations of the biblical faith for human unity, extols the God who grounds this unity, and then in light of those high aspirations indicates how supposedly faithful people betray those aspirations. Stephen lays before his sisters and brothers their proclaimed faith and then demonstrates their gross hypocrisy. And he gets what that kind of harsh, outspoken, scalding courage usually gets: a lynch mob organized to do him in. (And I have to tell you, had I been there he would have made my blood boil, too.)

III. And so Stephen dies. Those who hear his passionate address affirming the New World of God revealed in the crucified Jesus, those who stand confronted and estranged by his accusations of religious betrayal, plug their ears, then rush him and throw him into a pit, where in their fury they crush and bury him with boulders.

(a) As Stephen goes through this terrible ordeal, Luke shows him praying. Praying! He prays for the forgiveness of the lynch mob. He prays God release the mob from the guilt of his execution. Stephen demonstrates the authenticity of his faith. He emulates the character of his Savior. He proves the depth and power of his faith as he serenely invokes God in his hour of torture and petitions for the forgiveness of his executioners. Oh, the grudges *we* hold, the little revenges *we* plot. Here we see the character of one truly fused with the Savior.

(b) All of which leads one to ask the question: is it any wonder that the man who probably instigates this violent ending to Stephen, a fanatic from Tarsus named Saul—Saul who holds the coats of Stephen's executioners—is it any wonder Saul never forgets the radiant face, the fervent prayer, the blanket release? Stephen's gallant martyrdom? Stephen haunts Saul. And it is the haunted Saul—nay, Paul—who turns the world upside down.—James W. Crawford

Illustrations

ASKING WHAT WE WILL. If Jesus dwell at the fountain of my life; if the currents of his life have displaced and superseded all self-currents; if implicit obedience to him be the inspiration and force of every movement of my life, then he can safely commit the praying to my will, and pledge himself, by an obligation as profound as his own nature, that whatsoever is asked shall be granted. Nothing can be clearer, more distinct, more unlimited both in application and extent than the exhortation and urgency of Christ, "Have faith in God."—E. M. Bounds

PRAYER FOR HEALING. The essential thing in prayer for healing is that by its means both the sick person and the intercessor are set within the great saving plan of God. Whether in the process the sick person becomes medically healthy and whether this is brought about through a doctor and his treatment or through some inexplicable cause are less important than the fact that this person has rediscovered his right partnership with God. This partnership may call for him to live on as an invalid or even for his death, but what matters is that these things now come to him "from God's hand" and to his glory.—Theodor Bovet

Sermon Suggestions

HOW MUCH IS TOO MUCH? TEXT: Luke 12:13–21. (1) When possessions become an obsession. (2) When possessions obscure other values in life. (3) When possessions have no valid purpose beyond this life.

SPIRITUAL RENEWAL. TEXT: Col. 3:1–11. (1) Our position—"raised with Christ." (2) Our priority—"the things that are above." (3) Our protection—"hidden with Christ in God." (4) Our purpose—"put to death, therefore, whatever in you is earthly." (5) Our power—"the new self."

Worship Aids

CALL TO WORSHIP. "O give thanks unto the Lord, for he is good: for his mercy endureth for ever" (Ps. 107:1).

INVOCATION. Loving Lord, we do not always know what to expect in worship. Thou art infinite, and there is so much for us to learn. Help us to learn all that we can because first we adore and honor thee, in whom is our security and peace.—E. Lee Phillips

OFFERTORY SENTENCE. "Then he said to them all, 'If any want to become my followers, let them deny themselves and take up their cross daily and follow me' " (Luke 9:23 NRSV).

OFFERTORY PRAYER. Lord, accept now the gifts we bring, that in their giving our capacity to give and our compassion to care might be enlarged and others may be nurtured in the faith of the Son of God.—E. Lee Phillips

PRAYER. Call us, Father, and recall us to the challenge that your love sounds to every person who comes to follow Christ. This morning may we hear clearly the challenge of Christ to take up our cross and follow him. In love we pray that you will strengthen us and lead us to keep pushing back the frontiers of our lives until we are truly your own.

In this world through which we walk we daily find ourselves facing new realities that we would not have chosen for ourselves. As we confront the mysteries of these challenges, make us confident of the grace of Christ to sustain us, that we may be victors and not victims in the struggle. Show us how to transform difficulties into opportunities. Even when we feel broken and battered by life, remind us that you are fashioning eternal glory out of the clay of which we are made when we follow your truth and abide in you in all circumstances. Call us again to the cross, that we may see anew how it makes us whole and heals us of our brokenness. Help us to remember that wholeness does not come without pain and suffering. In the cross of Christ may we find the strength and courage to bear our own as we realize that his is a love that will never let us go.

May the good work that you have begun in us as individuals and as a congregation continue, that this church may be as a light on a hill guiding many to follow Jesus. May we be bringers of healing in your name, Father, healing in the marketplace, healing in the halls of government, healing among the nations, healing the weak and weary. Raise up among us, yea, even from this family of faith, some individual who will be used to make a difference in the world. Let great things be done among us and through us, Father, and let it begin as we wait and worship before you in this sacred hour.—Henry Fields

LECTIONARY MESSAGE

Topic: The Dangers of Freedom

TEXT: Hos. 11:1–12

OTHER READINGS: Luke 12:13–21; Col. 3:1–11

I. Taking advantage of freedom. Freedom is a gift of God. He called his son out of Egypt and set him and his people free. In this passage, Hosea reminds Israelites that they were redeemed because they were God's people. Referred to in Matthew 2:15 as a prophecy applying to Jesus Christ, this passage declares God's liberty granted in love for his people.

Freedom can be lost easily. Those who push freedom to the limits are those who most endanger its survival. Many travelers have taken advantage of freedom and have brought drugs, explosives, and firearms aboard aircraft, endangering hundreds of lives. Because of their violations, it is no longer a pleasure to attempt to board an international airline flight. Security precautions, while necessary and protective of passengers, nevertheless are very annoying. Using freedom irresponsibly is a sure way to destroy it completely. How much longer can we count on being free to enter an office building or a department store without being stopped and searched, if many who enter do so to take human life?

Any freedom can become its own gateway to its loss, to an abuse that soon leads to slavery, to deprivation. Abuse of liberty is followed by holistic effects; the sin of one is passed upon all, because of the solidarity of the human race. If one misuses a specific freedom, soon all others are deprived of it.

II. The freedom to receive love is freedom to reject it. Hosea and Gomer lived a story that applies to all humanity, not only to Israel or Ephraim. As Israel persisted in sacrificing to strange Baals, they lost the fruits of God's love for them—not the love but the joys of it.

We can draw a parallel between Israel as God's son and young people today as children of their parents. Parents' greatest longings are to bestow the gifts of love, experience, hard-won understanding, and the means of successful living upon their children, just as God desired above all else to bestow all the spiritual, moral, and physical gifts of his love on Israel. But the more he called them, the more they went away.

Could we say that each of us relives the fate of Israel, insofar as we spurn the teaching of parents and resent their attempts to keep us from learning in too hard a way the lessons of life? One daily sees some young boy or girl light up and smoke a cigarette and can hardly help grabbing him or her by the shoulders and yelling, "Can't you read? Hasn't anyone told you?" The thought is, surely no one in his or her right mind would launch a habit from which there is no retreat except in deathly illness. But, with freedom as one of that child's gifts from God and from his or her parents and as a citizen of America, no one can force the youth not to smoke or do other harmful things. We can only go on loving and providing, just as God will go on loving and redeeming those who are his people.

III. The wisdom to avoid sin. The effects of sin pass upon the whole nation or society, but the wisdom to avoid it is not natural. "The belief that God is our Father does not come to us with our carnal birth— . . . It is conferred by love, and confirmed by duty."[3] The third verse of the chapter metaphorically likens the nation of Israel to a creeping and falling baby; then verse 4 compares it to hard-working farm animals rewarded with rest and feed. God then inevitably and necessarily reverts to judgment as a preliminary to the justice they deserve, promising further servitude under the Assyrians and further warfare to devastate their cities, because of their apostasy and unfaithfulness.

IV. God's redeeming constancy. Then God does for his people what they cannot or will not do for themselves—love them to the end. The best news for Hosea's Israel and for us is in verses 8 and 9. God asks how he can make his people like those cities destroyed at the time of Sodom's destruction; then he answers that though he must maintain his righteousness, he is still God and may, through his warm and tender compassion, withhold his execution of the sentence. He is the holy one in our midst; he is the one who came as a man to redeem his people by his holy perfection and sacrifice. Shall we persist in our disobedience and willful-

[3]G. A. Smith, *The Twelve Prophets,* vol. 1, 318.

ness, defying God and his love? The answer is that we shall—until his life, given for us, becomes our life. We live as described in Romans 5:20: "Where sin abounded, grace did much more abound."—John R. Rodman

SUNDAY: AUGUST THIRTEENTH

SERVICE OF WORSHIP

Sermon: What It Takes to Make Us See

TEXT: Matt. 13:10–17; John 9:35–41

One of the purposes of Jesus' coming was to teach us to see. The way of understanding what it means to a Christian is the new way of seeing all of the common experiences of life that come. One of the reasons Jesus came was to enable us to look at birth and marriage and work and daily life and suffering and death with new depth and appreciation in common everyday experiences.

The question becomes: how do we learn to experience life as Jesus did? What does it take to make us really see?

I. One clue permeates the Gospels. To see life as it really is, we have to look honestly at death. In a basic sense death reveals how to live a worthwhile life. When we admit that we do not have forever, we become a little more alert to the present moment.

(a) Most of us fail to see the reality of life. In our attempt to escape the reality of death, we tell ourselves that we have forever and that experiences today will be our experiences tomorrow. We live as though we have an unlimited amount of time and resources, and therefore any particular thing does not have to be viewed with intensity or seen in depth.

(b) Jesus was a man who lived with a consciousness of the limits of life and death. Jesus became aware of his impending death. He knew that his time was not unlimited. He said, "I must work the works of him that sent me, while it is day; the night cometh, when no man can work" (John 9:4). It is in light of the limits of life that he looked so carefully and so piercingly at everything and everyone.

Why don't we see as Jesus saw? Because we are trying to escape the reality that we do not have forever. The preachers of former times were good at telling deathbed stories. Their value was not in scaring people out of hell but in scaring people into living. Now! For we do not always have tomorrow.

II. We will see as Jesus saw when we take seriously the blinding power of our own self-centeredness.

(a) From Thornton Wilder's play *Our Town,* disillusioned Emily goes back to the grave. She is confronted by Simon Stimson—a man bitter in life and evidently clutching his bitterness even in death. To Emily he says: "Now you know! That's what it was to be alive. To move about in a cloud of ignorance; to go up and down trampling on the feelings of those about you. . . . To be always at the mercy of one self-centered passion or another. Now you know—that's the happy existence you wanted to go back to. Ignorance and blindness."

(b) In all of our vision there is a selectivity process going on. We see certain things, and we are blind to others. Perhaps the most blinding force of all is putting myself at the center of life and making everything else revolve around my presuppositions, preconceived ideas, and prejudices of life. Jesus' conflict with the Pharisees in New Testament days was at this point. Jesus said to them, "You are blind to things that are happening around you because you think you already understand. Seeing, you do not see; hearing, you do not hear; and being in the presence of the miracle of God's revelation, you continue without experiencing the redeeming love of God."

III. We will never see life as Jesus saw it until we recognize our inability to look at new truths.

(a) A young monastic student was working to understand the writings of Aristotle about the natural world and the heavens in light of his direct observations. Looking through a lens at the sun one day, he saw something he had not recalled reading in Aristotle's writings. Excitedly, in the joy of new discovery, he raced to his teacher to say, "I've found something. I've discovered some spots on the sun that are not mentioned in Aristotle's works." But he was quickly deflated when his teacher calmly said, "If the spots are not mentioned in Aristotle, then they are either on your lens or in your eye." And he would not look.

(b) We do not see because we assume we already know. We are content with our present position. Jesus was constantly inviting people to come and see. He encouraged persons to break out of their self-centered way of seeing things. Today he invites us to come and see if there is not some new thing that can come out of Nazareth. He invites us to some new discoveries that can be found in the common ventures of life from his perspective.

IV. We will not see until we realize that we have to look through the eyes of others.

(a) Humanity does not have to start over fresh with the birth of every new baby. We are the recipients of that great body of insight, knowledge, and culture that comes down to us. The critical question is: Through whose eyes will we look? Whose eyes do we choose to make our own? Whose experience will we share?

(b) This is the principle of revelation. It is the principle behind Jesus' coming to us and sharing himself and his understanding of God. He says to us, in effect: "Look at God, look at life, and look at your total experience through my eyes."

Christian discipleship involves seeing life through the eyes of Jesus. It means seeing nature as the arena of God's creative act, seeing people as beings in whom God's image dwells, seeing the infinite possibilities in every person, and perceiving the working of God for good even in the most tragic moments of life.

V. Many persons try to escape life. Others do not like the lives they are now living. They want to be someone else or they want to have something more or they want to do something different or they want to go somewhere they have never been. The gospel is not a ticket to escape from life, but rather it is the means of seeing life in a new way and affirming it with new meaning and hope.

Christian faith is the way of looking at the common experiences of life through the eyes of Jesus Christ.—M. Vernon Davis

Illustrations

GRACE AND HOPE. When we have exhausted all the available false repositories for our hope, it is possible that we will turn to God with a true sense of who we are, with an integrity that is both humble and confident, with a dignity that knows itself because it has met its limits (Luke 21:34).

Hope can sometimes be an elusive thing, and occasionally it must come to us with pain. But it is there, irrevocably. Like freedom, hope is a child of grace, and grace cannot be stopped. I refer once more to St. Paul, a man who, I am convinced, understood addiction: "Hope will not be denied, because God's love has been poured into our hearts" (Rom. 5:5).—Gerald G. May

A CHANGED VIEW OF LIFE. Early in his life Abraham Maslow, the outstanding psychologist, had a severe heart attack. Out of that crisis, which he survived, he came to a radically changed view of his own life. He spoke of what he called his "postmortem" life—life as he saw it in the face of death. He said, "One important aspect of the postmortem life is that everything gets doubly precious, gets piercingly important. You get stabbed by things, by flowers, by babies, and by beautiful things. Just the very act of living, of walking, of breathing and eating and having friends and chatting, everything seems to look more beautiful rather than less. One gets a much intensified sense of the presence of miracles."—M. Vernon Davis

Sermon Suggestions

ARE YOU READY? TEXT: Luke 12:32–40. (1) The final challenge—"the Son of man's coming." (2) The immediate requirements: (a) Generosity. (b) Alertness. (3) The comprehensive comfort—"to give you the kingdom."

ARGUING OUR CASE WITH GOD. TEXT: Isa. 1:1, 10–20 NRSV. (1) The offense—religious pretensions without true religion. (2) The result—divine rejection. (3) The ideal—reformation. (4) The promise—divine forgiveness.

Worship Aids

CALL TO WORSHIP. "The mighty God, even the Lord, hath spoken, and called the earth from the rising of the sun unto the going down thereof" (Ps. 50:1).

INVOCATION. O God, grant that we may greet each new day with gratitude that you own it and yet you permit us to share in its opportunities. And so may we worship you, as each occasion of worship begins to unfold before us.

OFFERTORY SENTENCE. "Ascribe to the Lord the glory due his name. Bring an offering and come before him" (1 Chron. 16:29 REB).

OFFERTORY PRAYER. O Spirit of the living God, who hast filled this place in times past, fill it now again that the people who come here may be strengthened and renewed to do thy will, enabled to surpass themselves and to share and show that love that belongs only to thee, the love of the perfect Father of all the children.—Theodore Parker Ferris

PRAYER. O divine love, who dost everlastingly stand outside the closed doors of our lives, knocking ever and again, give me grace now to throw open all my soul's doors. Let every bolt and bar be drawn that has hitherto robbed my life of air and light and love. Grant each of us grace to pray:

Give me an *open ear,* O God, that I may hear thy voice calling me to higher ground. Too often have I been deaf to the appeals thou hast addressed to me, but now give me courage to answer, Here am I, send me.

Give me an *open mind,* O God, a mind ready to receive and welcome such new light of knowledge as it is thy will to reveal to me. Let not the past ever be so dear to me as to set a limit to the future. Give me courage to change my mind when that is needed, that my life may be a continuing growth and maturing.

Give me *open eyes,* O God, eyes quick to discover you indwelling the world that you have made. Forgive all my past blindness to the grandeur and glory of nature, to the charm of little children, to the sublimities of human society, and to all the intimations of your presence that these things contain.

Give me *open hands,* O God, hands ready to share with all who are in want the blessings with which you have enriched our life. Deliver me from all meanness and littleness.

O Father, as thou art open to all the world in love, may we be open to one another as brothers and sisters. Bless all families in bereavement and strengthen us all as we share their sorrow. Encourage the sick with the experience of thy healing grace that ministers a wholeness that transcends physical illness and infirmity. May those facing new experiences not be intimidated but be open to receive the full blessing of their opportunity.

Called to the ministry of reconciliation, we pray not only for the overcoming of personal estrangements but for the healing of the nations. Forgive us provocations that only widen the gulf and grant to us the wisdom, the courage, the faith to be bridge builders, as we share bread and the Bread of life with which we have been so richly blessed.—John Thompson

LECTIONARY MESSAGE

Topic: The Power of a Prospect

TEXT: Heb. 11:1–3, 8–16

OTHER READINGS: Luke 12:32–40; Isa. 1:1, 10–20

I. The need for a goal. Abraham went out seeking. He was blessed by having a prospect to strive toward. Whatever goal a person strives for brings its fulfillment more in the striving than in the attaining. Too many people today are deluded by the material rewards they seek—they actually believe that life is at its best when riches, titles, and honors are received. Too many people would do anything to attain the trappings of such life, believing that the signs and signals—the incidentals—are the most important results of attainment, that they are really living. Their hopes are self-deceiving. Our passage records the glorious life of Abraham, not as one of possessing but as one of faithfulness following God's command.

(a) The true power of the prospect of material rewards is to urge one to keep on striving. The floods of 1993 could not drive true farmers from their prolific land or from lives of cultivation. Their lives consist in their faithful labors. A life of farming is more than crops and cash income, although these keep it possible. The best of every life is in the interest in living that one finds by following his prospects. It is in the joy of relationship with God and the discovery of his ways.

(b) One may be urged on to learn, work, and sacrifice by the prospect of better living, more comfort, better health, and recognition. But these bring their true rewards as goals rather than as possessions. One learns that possessing the earth is nothing compared with possessing the universe. "We live by faith, not by sight."

(c) The ascetics and the hermits may be said to have grasped a portion of the truth that life is not solely or even mainly of this world. But, in avoiding the life of worldly engagement, they missed the larger purpose; they neglected the discoveries of involvement and strife for which God has shaped us all. Love grows by attachment to those needing love; faith is enlarged by daring difficult deeds; spiritual strength is matured by defeats, disappointments, and doubts.

II. The life of promise. However much knowledge we may acquire, true wisdom is the gift of God. And true wisdom seems more and more to say that frustration with the achievements of worldly personal, national, or international goals or hopes is our constant condition. We shall always have a reach that exceeds our grasp, or, as Browning says, "What's a heaven for?"

(a) Byron said that life "is a vale of soul-winning." The souls of people are won through launching into life on faith, looking, as Abraham did, for a Promised Land, and persevering in that faith through years of desert sojourning. Every promise of God is a challenge to search and struggle. These bring a person close to God and to the realization that he is the fulfillment of his promises, the builder of that place of substance that fulfills hope, of that city that has foundations.

(b) Just as God led Abraham by promise, so we lead each other, and parents lead children. Some midcourse recognition reassures us of the validity of the promise, just as God gave Abraham and Sarah the promised offspring and other signs that their faith was not misplaced. Many question the advisability of paying a child money or giving other rewards for good grades in school. But a child cannot see far enough ahead to be moved wisely by seeing how much he or she will need an education for future needs or opportunities. Later, knowledge and understanding themselves are prospect enough to urge one on, even though completeness may never be realized.

(c) Perhaps our greatest frustration comes because we perceive the fulfillment of the promise in too individualistic terms, not as a "city" but as a "mansion." Our prospect must be broader if it is to be the one God has prepared for us. We may be limiting God too narrowly in facing the needs of our global community. But we shall reach our goal only by walking each step with God.—John R. Rodman

SUNDAY: AUGUST TWENTIETH

SERVICE OF WORSHIP

Sermon: More Than Meets the Eye

TEXT: Luke 13:1–9

Our passage this morning is perhaps one of the more obscure and less talked about discourses of Jesus. The matter that he gains to address is the commonly held belief at that time that when great tragedy and calamity come into someone's life it is generally an indication that they were guilty before God of something very grave. Whatever affliction one was faced with, the justice of God dictated that they were somehow deserving of it.

I. But there is a grave difficulty with this simplistic relationship between calamity and the displeasure of God or between good fortune and the happiness of God. And this difficulty is twofold.

(a) One, it simply does not answer an age-old question that has been pondered from the beginning of time: why is it that sometimes good and innocent people suffer, while evil and guilty people seem to prosper? Whether we look at the world situation in general, or even just at the life experiences of people right around us, it does seem evident at times that no one is completely immune to struggle, calamity, and misfortune, no matter how good a life they try to lead.

(b) The other difficulty with this simplistic notion is the problem of people becoming just a little self-righteous. In this passage Jesus cites certain historic events about which there is more speculation than actual written historical data. He hearkens back to a slaughter of certain Galilean worshipers by Pilate, the Roman curator who mixed the blood of his victims with the blood of their own religious sacrifices. He speaks also of the collapse of a tower in Siloam under construction, killing many in the tower as well as many on the ground. Through this kind of life perspective, such things must have seemed on the surface like the judgment of God against those with whom he was angry. Jesus, in no uncertain terms, dispels this commonly held philosophy and life view. He tells them the suffering and struggle of others are never reflections on your own superior goodness. There is none who has earned the right to feel more righteous than any other. "Do you think these were worse sinners than you because they suffered in this way?" asks Jesus. "No, I tell you, but unless you repent you too will all perish."

II. God's justice cannot be understood if we confine the measures of it only to the things that we see around us in this world. Tragedy and triumph may be the experience of either the believer or the nonbeliever, the good or the evil.

(a) Indeed there are many oddities that make it difficult for us to explain the justice of God. For the time being, we might have to be content to realize that his perfect justice cannot be understood in the confines of time and space. This seemed to be Paul's perspective when he said, "I believe that the things we suffer now will be nothing compared to the glory we will have in heaven." We must grant that if this life was all there was, such a view of the injustice of it all would have certainly been appropriate. But to the apostle, whose eyes had been open to the eternal dimension to which we as Christians attain, such a view was pitifully incomplete. For the justice of God is only eternally discerned, and it will ultimately prevail, righting the wrongs that the righteous have suffered, avenging the evil that they have endured, and comforting the sorrow that they have experienced, if not in this life, then in the life that has no end.

(b) Indeed, this discourse from Jesus appears to have a negative or accusatory tone to it. It is one of those times when we can almost visualize his finger pointing sharply at his audience. His warning to them and to us is that there is no cause ever to become convinced that we rank higher on God's list of favorite people. Nor should we ever fool ourselves into the natural and seemingly logical view that suffering in the world reflects the greater sin of its victims.

III. But this discourse could also be reframed in our understanding to demonstrate the transcendent and eternal nature of God's justice. In a sentence, Jesus is saying here, don't make the mistake of thinking we can have an accurate summation of God and his truth by looking only at the things that appear to be going on around us. Our eyes must be opened to his eternal dwelling place, where ultimately all things will be resolved in perfect harmony.—Richard Daggett

Illustrations

BEYOND COMPARISON. If a child tells his mother, "You are the most beautiful mother in the world; you are the only mother who ever was," he has not reached this conclusion by having all the mothers in the world pass by in review so that he can test which of them is the most beautiful and the best. The child, without having arranged that comparison, is bound to this one mother in love, looks to her in confidence, and risks himself and all that he is and has and longs for in the way of security on this one and only person whom he loves above all else. That is a paltry and thoroughly inadequate image of how we can also come to say to Jesus, "You are my only comfort in life and death. You are the first and the last, the Alpha and Omega; and you are the one and only person for whom we could wait."—Helmut Thielicke

GOD'S PARTICIPATION. It is the greatness and heart of the Christian message that God, as manifest in the Christ on the cross, totally participates in the dying of a child, in the condemnation of the criminal, in the disintegration of a mind, in starvation and famine, and even in the human rejection of himself. There is no human condition into which the divine presence does not penetrate. This is what the cross, the most extreme of all human conditions, tells us. The riddle of inequality cannot be solved on the level of our separation from each other. It is eternally solved through the divine participation in the life of all of us and every being. The certainty of divine participation gives us the courage to endure the riddle of inequality although our finite minds cannot solve it.—Paul Tillich

Sermon Suggestions

THE COST OF A CRY. TEXT: Isa. 5:1–7. (1) God births and nurtures his people with expectation of good. (2) God permits his people to go their self-defeating ways and bring judgment on themselves. (3) The clue to their misdeeds is in the cry of the oppressed, which God's people caused or ignored.

THE WORTHIES. TEXT: Heb. 11:29–12:2. (1) The triumph of faith, 11:29–35. (2) The suffering of the faithful, 11:35b–40. (3) The premier example, 12:1–2.

Worship Aids

CALL TO WORSHIP. "Turn us again, O God, and cause thy face to shine; and we shall be saved" (Ps. 80:3).

INVOCATION. We look to you, O God, in the midst of life's uncertainties and appeal to you from our personal pain. There are many who would and do help us, but after all the human resources that come to our side and offer us encouragement, we still look to you, for you are first and last the one who saves.

OFFERTORY SENTENCE. "All the Israelite men and women whose hearts made them will to bring anything for the work that the Lord had commanded by Moses to be done, brought it as a freewill offering to the Lord" (Exod. 35:29 NRSV).

OFFERTORY PRAYER. Accept these gifts, O Lord, some given with ease, others with difficulty, that all involved may know a closer walk with the Savior who never leaves or forsakes his own and waits with open arms the lost to enfold.—E. Lee Phillips

PRAYER. In this quiet moment of prayer, O Lord, we sincerely reach up to you. Help us to find that you are also reaching down to us. Help us to believe that when we are willing to listen, you will speak. Remind us that we often deny ourselves your blessing by bringing all our own plans and schemes to you and having the nerve to ask you to bless them. We know that some of the things we want and are tempted to do, you cannot and will never bless. Remind us that your aim is not to make our life easier by giving us everything we want. Your aim is to change us—to make us different. So, Father, begin changing us now by shaping our desires so that you may truly bless us in all we pursue.

Forgive us that we so often give our best to the wrong things. At times, we are far more enthusiastic about the thought and effort required by our trivial pursuits than we are about our daily work, our worship, and our service in your kingdom. We are guilty of saving our best behavior for strangers and our worst for our own homes. We admit that we often treat those who are nearest and dearest to us with a discourtesy and disrespect we never show to strangers. We get irritated, annoyed, and angry about things that in our more rational moments we know do not matter at all. Help us to know what is important and unimportant so that we will never forget the things that really matter and never allow the things that don't matter to matter too much.—Gary C. Redding

LECTIONARY MESSAGE

Topic: The Prince of Peace Declares War

TEXT: Luke 12:49–56

OTHER READINGS: Isa. 5:1–7; Heb. 11:29–12:2

All of us would like to believe the myth of painless Christianity. We would like to believe that the presence of Jesus in our lives will solve all our problems, smooth out all the rough places, and create a tranquil, peaceful existence. Does not the coming of Jesus promise "peace on earth" (Luke 2:14)?

The jarring words in this text disturb our image of the Prince of Peace and threaten our myth of a painless Christianity. In these words, Luke reminds us that peace comes through a reordering of relationships and loyalties. It threatens the status quo, and we are faced with the absolute choice.

I. Jesus longs to bring fire (vv. 49–50). Fire is the symbol of God's activity in judgment and purification. Jesus understands that the purpose of his ministry is to create a crisis on earth. Through his death (baptism), God will confront humanity with the moment of truth. The long-awaited "day of the Lord" will be initiated. Through the fiery presence of the Spirit, God will convict persons of sin, judge between those who repent and those who do not, and purge the disciples of their sinful dross. Even though this will mean suffering and death, Jesus anxiously desires to set this process in motion.

The passion of Jesus to create this crisis is startling. Despite the horror of the persecution and death that lay before him, Jesus knew that one enters the kingdom only through the fire of God's judgment and purification.

For the believer, the prospect of the coming fire is fearsome. Yet only by following Jesus through death to life will the disciple find true fellowship with God and one's true identity (Rom. 6:3–4).

II. Jesus' ministry divides (vv. 51–53). The disciples wanted Jesus to establish the kingdom but without pain and suffering. Jesus reminds them that suffering, rejection, and division are part and parcel of his mission, not an unfortunate result (Luke 2:34–35).

The use of family relations to illustrate the point is significant. Family relationship served to establish a person's identity as well as one's role and relationships in society. The loss of family brought the loss of one's primary economic, social, religious, and educational network. To choose to follow Jesus could cost a person dearly.

The Christian is confronted with the reality that those closest to him or her may not respond to Jesus, and that their choice will place them on the wrong side of God's judgment. One's family may even actively oppose one's choice.

The other side of this division in the human family is the reformation of human community in Jesus. As a follower of Jesus, the disciple will enter a new family, gain a new identity, and find the promised peace (Luke 8:19–21). While strife and division will characterize the disciple's relationship with the world, the angel's promise of peace will characterize the new humanity.

Eduard Schweizer said, "Jesus does not bring the peace and quiet we would expect, but in the ultimate and deepest sense, he is our peace."[4]

For centuries, the prophets had warned Israel that the "day of the Lord" was coming. That day would be one of mixed blessings. For the prepared, it would be a day of light, salvation, and peace. For the unprepared, it would be a day of darkness, death, and fear.

Jesus speaks to those who pretend to be able to read the ways of God. He warns them to open their eyes and see what is happening. God is preparing a scorching fire of judgment and purification. Will they be ready? Or will they be consumed by that which they refuse to see? Will they see the coming crisis, risk the right choice, and enter the new humanity? Or will they close their eyes and be swept away by the whirlwind (Hos. 8:7)?

The choice to follow Jesus comes with pain. It means death to an old way of life. It causes division between the believer and the world. In the end, however, it is the only life-giving choice we have. In Jesus we face a moment of truth. How will we choose?—Jim Holladay

SUNDAY: AUGUST TWENTY-SEVENTH

SERVICE OF WORSHIP

Sermon: Longing for the Shadow

TEXT: Job 7:1–7

Few of us would win any awards for optimism. More often than not, we lock horns with life. Too often, in fact, life feels like a fight to the finish. And—Lord knows!—the fight itself could finish us off!

And so, our guest this morning would seem to be in good company. I'm referring, of course, to Job. Now, I'm aware there are those of us who know the problems of poor Job—as though they were our own. Then there are others of us who think Job's only claim to fame was patience. So, for those who are yet unfamiliar with this man's misfortune, let me paint the picture.

I. Job, you see, was this wealthy landed gentry with gobs of goodies. He was not only prosperous, he was pious to boot! Job was a real stand-up guy.

(a) Well, one day, as fate would have it (or was it the hand of God?—that's Job's question, and ours as well), suddenly, his life came apart at the seams. He lost everything in a single day! Sheep, camels, cattle, servants, sons, daughters, crops, houses. The whole kit and caboodle! Lock, stock, and barrel! Gone. Dust.

So, what does Job do? Well, he decides to cash it all in. Let the chips fall where they may. Until his three friends come calling with some—well, what else? Some friendly advice. Just what you need when the chips are down—friends being all philosophical about *your* pain!

One blamed Job. Another simply nodded his agreement with that assessment. And a third suggested that Job had it coming—some good old-fashioned fire and brimstone!

(b) But poor down-and-out-on-his-luck Job had his own point of view.

In utter disgust, with the venom of vindictiveness dripping from his tongue, Job said: "Don't human beings have a hard service on earth, and aren't their days like the days of a laborer? Like a slave who longs for the shadow, and like laborers who look for their wages, so I'm allotted months of emptiness, and nights of misery are apportioned me. . . . " Pretty gruesome picture, wouldn't you say?

[4]*The Good News According to Luke,* p. 216.

II. But, at the risk of soiling our Sunday best, I'd like us to stand in this mess for more than a moment in time. Because sometimes I feel like we try to hide behind these holy mysteries that make us feel safe and secure. We hope that somehow—through magic, if perchance mystery can't get the job done—we hope that somehow the real world won't sneak in through those back doors.

(a) And yet, you and I both know that closing your eyes to the casket will not prevent your own death. And turning a blind eye to life's paradox and pain will make neither one disappear. At least to some degree we are forced to live life as it comes at us. There are some very real limits to our power and patience. Which all leads me to the conclusion that maybe Job has a point.

After all, "Don't human beings have a hard service on earth, and aren't their days like the days of a laborer? . . . allotted months of emptiness, and nights of misery . . . ?"

(b) Personally, I've seen Job in hundreds of names and faces. People who lost out on the scales of justice. People who wore their pain like a ball and chain. Entire families wiped out in the wink of an eye.

Dreams that died away. Sons and daughters, cut down in the prime of life. So, surely God knows that this world has far too many problems and pains to be fixed up with a little "possibility thinking."

(c) But I also think God knows that we humans have little patience with the paradox and pains of this life. I'm certain God's aware that, more often than not, we want a quick fix to a fuzzy future. Because it's hard to face the facts of life. Regardless of our age. Still, God is not in the business of denying life's down side or offering the quick fix!

III. And I suppose that's *exactly* why the Book of Job is in the Bible. God wants us to face the facts. There are forces about in this world that won't think twice about knocking us off our feet.

(a) So, God gives Job the soap box and lets him have his say: "Don't human beings have a hard service on earth, and aren't their days like the days of a laborer? . . . allotted months of emptiness, and nights of misery . . . ?"

(b) And as Job cries out, we listen. We listen because we hear an echo of where we've been and what we've felt. As more troops head for the Persian Gulf. As fewer jobs become available, with more people out of work. As the spot stares back at us from the X ray. As our memory slips and our body fails to follow our lead. And God knows. And God wants us to face the facts.

IV. But that's not all that God wants. Not by a long shot! Because there's really only one way to face the cold, hard facts—without a lame excuse or a cheap escape. And that's by *faith*. The faith that God creates, even from the midst of calamity. And when push comes to shove, that's what Job discovered, you know. Just that. Faith!

(a) Faith is a sense of being connected with God, in a way that allows us to be honest—even courageous—when facing hardships and limitations. Faith is trusting that God will be God and that we can be human. Faith acknowledges that we can't will God into existence—but that no one can will God out of existence, either!

(b) Faith recognizes that human life is *limited* to a span of years while confessing that God is *unlimited* in the power to heal, restore, and renew our lives, our world. And faith sees the presence of God in seemingly small and insignificant events: a relationship restored; a lost and lonely life redeemed; a wounded heart now healed. Faith sees beyond the brokenness to broader horizons of hope.

(c) "Don't human beings have hard service on earth, and aren't their days like the days of a laborer? . . . allotted months of emptiness, and nights of misery . . . ?" Well, yea, I guess they do. But God seeks to remind us that his power exceeds even our worst plight, and his Spirit will carry us through.

V. At the conclusion of his complaint, Job added a prayer. Imagine that, a prayer! But a prayer in the form of a petition.

(a) "Remember that my life is a

breath." A breath. A whisper in time. A faint breeze, blowing against the gale-force winds of an indifferent and often hostile world. A breath. Barely noticeable. A mere moment in time and space.

(b) And God remembers, doesn't he? God remembers and gives us a Redeemer—Jesus Christ. And Christ weaves his sacrificial love into the very fabric of this fractured world. Perhaps purposelessness seems to gain the upper hand just where God chooses to renew the promise that has held it all together from the beginning of time.—Albert J. D. Walsh

Illustrations

UNDER THE CIRCUMSTANCES. One Sunday morning, a woman met her friend in the narthex of their church. "How are you doing?" she asked.

"Oh," he said, "not bad under the circumstances."

And the woman said, "What are you doing under there?"

A colleague makes the point clearly: "As humans, we know that it's necessary for us to live in our circumstances. As Christians, however, we believe it's unnecessary for us to live under them!" God moves within our troubling circumstances, providing promise, power, and the purpose to transcend them.—Albert J. D. Walsh

BELIEFS THAT MAKE US BRAVE. Heroic souls have put up what we call lone fights. Back in the fourth century lived a great theologian, named Athanasius, who stood so alone against the popular religious trend that the saying arose, "Athanasius against the world." But if we could have looked behind the scenes, we should undoubtedly have found a coterie of friends whose sympathy sustained Athanasius in his struggle. Socrates was buoyed by the loyalty of his students when he defied to the death the authorities of Athens. Gethsemane is perhaps the loneliest spot of heroism in all history, for there on the night before his Crucifixion our Lord was left to pray alone while his disciples went to sleep; but even in Gethsemane, Jesus knew that he had the love of his disciples, wavering as they were at the time. Everyone who has enjoyed the love of another knows how it puts courage and nerve into the soul. To know that there is one whose heart waits for your coming after the trying toil of the day, to know there is one who keeps tryst with you in thought even when absent in person, to know there is one who believes in you when the crowd is howling you down, to know as you ride the seas that there is a light of love burning in a heart back home—those are thoughts that make you brave.—Ralph W. Sockman

Sermon Suggestions

HOW GOD SPEAKS—SOMETIMES! TEXT: Jer. 1:4–10. (1) The formation of a prophet, verses 4–8. (2) The task of a prophet, verses 9–10.

TWO MOUNTAINS AND HOW THEY DIFFER. TEXT: Heb. 12:18–29. (1) Mount Sinai—condemnation and vengeance. (2) Mount Zion—acceptance and forgiveness. (3) Our fitting response—thanksgiving with worship and awe.

Worship Aids

CALL TO WORSHIP. "In thee, O Lord, do I put my trust. . . . Be thou my strong habitation, whereunto I may continually resort: thou hast given commandment to save me; for thou art my rock and my fortress" (Ps. 71:1a, 3).

INVOCATION. Help us, O God, as we are overtaken by dangers and difficulties that are too deep for our understanding; grant that we may have no fear and that putting our trust not in ourselves but in thy power and thy love we may go forward to new victories through him who saved us, Jesus Christ, our Lord.—Theodore Parker Ferris

OFFERTORY SENTENCE. "Unto whomsoever much is given, of him shall much be required" (Luke 12:48b).

OFFERTORY PRAYER. Bring us to that point, O Lord, where we wish we could give more; then, if in thy providence we should have more, help us to give as generously and joyously as now we give from what is ours today.—E. Lee Phillips

PRAYER. Even though the course our lives have taken during the past week has occasionally led us away from your presence, Lord, we have nonetheless been drawn back to you today. Much as the needle of a compass cannot resist being always drawn toward the north, neither can we resist the steady pull of your grace. In the midst of the uncertainty and tension that fill our world and the confusion and indecisiveness that mark our lives, you remain at the center—calling us to hope, promising us life, giving us peace, and blessing us with your presence when we are willing to walk with you.

We know that the way to your kingdom is narrow and that few really find it. So be our guide, O Lord, that we may never lose our way or stray from the path. Give us strength to endure when the journey is more difficult—or takes longer—than we expected. Give us courage to face all the temptations and problems that frighten and perplex us. Give us wisdom to make the right choices in all our decisions. And give us humble spirits, ready to admit our helplessness, our sinfulness, our complete need of you.

Help us to be true followers of our Lord Jesus Christ, who taught us to live every day as if the kingdom were already here. Help us to live as he lived, sharing what we have with other persons and loving each other for no reason at all, except that you first loved us and Christ died to redeem us from our sin and to draw us into eternal fellowship with you. In his name we pray.—Gary C. Redding

LECTIONARY MESSAGE

Topic: Salvation Means Freedom

TEXT: Luke 13:10–17

OTHER READINGS: Jer. 1:4–10; Heb. 12:18–29

No one teaches in a synagogue unless invited to do so by the local rabbi. No rabbi would allow one to teach if he seriously believed that person would teach contrary to the rabbi's general religious perspective. The synagogue was not a place for an open-ended search for truth. It was a place where the Torah was taught, and its relevance to daily life worked out.

By inviting Jesus to teach, this particular rabbi was acknowledging the validity of Jesus' insight into the ways of God and was putting his own reputation on the line. The events recorded in this text indicate that the local rabbi had no problem with the words Jesus was speaking. He became indignant when Jesus stopped talking and began to demonstrate his understanding of God's way. Luke gives us little indication of what Jesus was teaching, but the context could imply a connection between what Jesus was teaching and the incident Luke records.

I. Jesus initiates liberation (vv. 10–13). As Jesus was teaching in a synagogue on the Sabbath, a woman caught his attention. For eighteen years she had suffered from a crippling disease. Normally women were not allowed in the synagogues, leading some to conclude that the incident occurred outside the worship setting. However, given Luke's flair for the dramatic, he intimates that Jesus interrupted his lesson to deal with the woman. (Perhaps Luke deliberately involves the woman in the story in order to point to another facet of Jesus' teaching about the kingdom, that is, in the new age, no distinction exists between male and female.)

When Jesus sees the woman, he calls her to come to where he is. The initiative in this healing encounter clearly belongs to Jesus. His words to her indicate Jesus' basic message about the kingdom. God seeks to liberate persons from that which oppresses them (Luke 4:18–19). "Woman," Jesus said, "you are set free . . . " (v. 12).

II. The rabbi objects (v. 14). The crux of the story rests with the rabbi's objection, for it gives Jesus the opportunity to reinforce his teaching on the kingdom of God. The rabbi's sensibilities are offended. Not only has Jesus contradicted the rabbi's teaching about appropriate

Sabbath activity, but Jesus has put the rabbi's reputation in danger.

The rabbi argues that this woman has suffered with this affliction for eighteen years. What difference would it make if Jesus waited one more day to cure her affliction? Then everyone would be satisfied. The woman would be healed, and the Sabbath would be preserved.

The issue for the rabbi centers around the work of healing on the Sabbath. He has missed entirely the point of what Jesus has said and done.

III. Jesus proclaims liberation (vv. 15–16). Jesus deals with the rabbi's objection on two levels. He starts with the issue the rabbi raised by asking if it is allowed to free an ox or donkey and lead it to water on the Sabbath. Rabbinic tradition allowed a person to relieve an animal's thirst. Without direct assault, Jesus points to the cruel irony of allowing animals more compassion on the Sabbath than people.

Then Jesus moves back to the real issue. Jesus argues that the issue is not the work of healing on the Sabbath. Rather, the issue is, "will a woman oppressed be set free?" This freedom from oppression cannot wait. It is more important that she be set free than that religious conventions be followed! To allow her to live in oppression one more day would be unconscionable in the eyes of God. The kingdom of God is about liberation.

For the rabbi, the issue was curing an illness on the Sabbath. For Jesus, the issue was the freedom of the kingdom of God, and what better day to enact freedom than on the day set aside to honor God's creative love.

IV. The crowd rejoices (v. 17). Luke intimates that Jesus' words and deeds were not lost on the people. They join the woman in celebrating the liberation Jesus proclaimed.

In this incident, Luke reminds us that the crux of Jesus' ministry is liberation. He comes to free persons from the various forms of bondage that diminish our created status. The salvation Jesus brings is more than healing. It is more than strength to cope with life's difficulties. Salvation liberates and creates a new person and a new community.—Jim Holladay

SUNDAY: SEPTEMBER THIRD

SERVICE OF WORSHIP

Sermon: Dealing with Falsehood

TEXT: Eph. 4:25–5:2; John 6:35, 41–51

How nice it would be if we could believe everything we see or hear. Imagine living in a world where politicians could be trusted to mean what they say, service people would show up at the set time, and an appointment at the doctor for 3:30 would mean he would see you at approximately that time.

Life would be simpler if the accepted standard in all things were truth rather than falsehood. It would be nice, but it is an unrealistic expectation.

Falsehood is a very complex condition in life. Some people fail to tell the truth simply because they do not know what is true. Some people tell lies for self-protection and even self-survival. Some people are just careless with their facts and others—for various reasons—stifle the truth by remaining silent when a falsehood is stated.

I. Paul had a strong concern for truth, perhaps because of his experience of assuming he knew the truth, which led him to oppose Jesus on the basis of that knowledge, and then later discovering he was wrong. But whatever the cause, he wrote to the Ephesians, "Therefore, putting away falsehood, let every one speak the truth with his neighbor, for we are members one of another" (Eph. 4:25).

(a) Notice the reason Paul gave for avoiding falsehood: we are members one of another. We are dependent upon one another for true life, for the full, abundant life. We need each other, just as the body needs all its parts for proper functioning.

(b) Sometimes we have to use more than one sense to get a true picture. I can feel a piece of paper and know what the material is, but I cannot tell what is on the paper unless I look at it. It may be a scrap of paper, or it may be a hundred-dollar bill. Without a true understanding of what I have in hand, I cannot respond properly. So also in the interrelationships of life; proper functioning together requires knowledge of what is true.

(c) John, in his Gospel, gives us a case in point. Jesus said, "I am the bread of life; he who comes to me shall not hunger, and he who believes in me shall never thirst" (John 6:35). Jesus came to provide proper nourishment for the inner, spiritual person. He came as bread from heaven; but the Jews could not comprehend that truth because all they saw was Jesus of Nazareth, the son of Joseph and Mary. Therefore, they were unable to connect in a meaningful way with the person who was "God with us" and to receive the truth he sought to state.

II. You see, it is essential in our relationship with God that we see Jesus as the revealer of the true knowledge about God. Without that belief, we can easily dismiss the truth he brings, which is exactly what the religious leaders did in his day.

(a) One of the problems we have as we try to deal with falsehood is that we often use the wrong standards. We use human assessments and accepted social values and worldly standards.

As Jesus taught, "Do not judge by appearances, but judge with right judgment" (John 7:24).

(b) This is another call for us to seek truth in life. One of the problems we face as we deal with falsehood is that we often fail personally to hold the truth in high regard. We tend to get upset and defensive when someone corrects us rather than thanking them for helping us to see the truth. We tell stories about people, and if we do not have all the facts, we add to what we know or we embellish what we have heard to make it sound better, for that is more important than stating the truth. The problem is not that we intentionally spread falsehood but that we are often careless about the truth.

(c) In addition to the problems we have in expressing ourselves correctly, we also recognize that there are some people who have no desire to know the truth. They have their set ideas, and that is all that matters.

Some people have no desire to see the truth when it goes contrary to what they hold as true. These people have no real regard for truth.

(d) There is one other way in which falsehoods are maintained. A person can stifle the truth by silence just as much as by twisting or embellishing the facts. Two people are talking about a third person. The other person knows that a statement made is not true, but rather than oppose the friend offers no correction. It is a difficult task to uphold the truth. It requires a great deal of strength and fortitude to do battle with falsehood. Therefore, we need to recognize that seeking after the truth in any situation will not come easy.

III. In our dealing with falsehood, in our search for the truth, our own unwillingness to act is one of the major obstacles we need to overcome. We need to be inspired if we are to overcome our laziness or indifference. We need to recognize the importance of matching our actions and our words.

The proper living of life requires us to deal with falsehood and to overcome it. We need to remember the guidance of the Bible: "Put away all falsehood, let every one speak the truth with his neighbor" (Eph. 4:25).

"Do not judge by appearances, but judge with right judgment" (John 7:24).

Jesus said, "If you continue in my word, you are truly my disciples, and you will know the truth and the truth will make you free" (John 8:31, 32).

As disciples of Jesus, let us become champions for the truth.—Kenneth Mortonson

Illustrations

FAKING IT. When I was in high school, I had a debate coach who taught us never to show our weaknesses. "If you go into a match, and the other team brings up something about which you know nothing, fake it," she would say. "Just get on your feet and start talking, and maybe the judges won't realize that you have no idea what is coming out of your mouth."—Charles B. Bugg

JUDGING BY EXTERNALS. T. E. Lawrence was a famous British soldier and writer. He was also known as Lawrence of Arabia. He was a close personal friend of the poet Thomas Hardy. Back in the days when Lawrence was serving in the Royal Air Force, he arrived for a visit with Hardy and his wife while in uniform.

It so happened that on that occasion, the mayoress of Dorchester was also visiting. The mayoress was bitterly affronted that she had to submit to meeting a common serviceman, for she had no idea who he was.

In French she said to Mrs. Hardy that never in all her born days had she had to sit down to tea with a private soldier. No one said anything until T. E. Lawrence said in perfect French: "I beg your pardon, Madame, but can I be of any use as an interpreter? Mrs. Hardy knows no French."

Sermon Suggestions

WHAT HAPPENS WHEN PEOPLE FORSAKE GOD. TEXT: Jer. 2:4–13, especially verse 13. (1) They cut themselves off from the sustaining and refreshing inflow of God's blessings. (2) They concoct failing schemes to substitute for what they lost from God.

WHEN MUTUAL LOVE IS AT WORK. TEXT: Heb. 13:1–8, 15–16. There will be (1) Christian hospitality, (2) care for the oppressed, (3) responsibility in matters sexual, (4) avoidance of greed, (5) respect for Christian leaders, and (6) praise to God in both worship and service.

Worship Aids

CALL TO WORSHIP. "But my people would not hearken to my voice; and Israel would none of me. So I gave them up unto their own hearts' lust: and they walked in their own counsels. Oh that my people had hearkened unto me, and Israel had walked in my ways!" (Ps. 81:11–13).

INVOCATION. Lord, as we come to call thy name and wait before thee, so fill us with the awe of thy mystery and the wonder of thy majesty that our lives will gladly conform to thy teachings and henceforth walk in thy counsels, to the glory of Christ, our Savior.—E. Lee Phillips

OFFERTORY SENTENCE. "Will a man rob God? Yet ye have robbed me. But ye say, Wherein have we robbed thee? In tithes and offerings" (Mal. 3:8).

OFFERTORY PRAYER. Grace us, O God, with a clearer vision and sharper understanding of thy will because we gave today when we did not have to but because we wanted to, for more like the Master we would ever be.—E. Lee Phillips

PRAYER. Father, in our self-sufficiency and pride, we so often forget whose we are. In our minds we remember that you have made us. In our saner moments we know that we could not exist but for your sustaining power and love and provision. Ye how often we forget and attempt to play God with the affairs of life. Especially do we try to play God with others. We need to somehow learn to live life in the humility of Jesus. To that end we come together before you in this sacred place. We are here to find ourselves in the light of Christ's truth and love. How we need to hear your Word spoken plainly in the very nature of our creation, that we may gain or regain perspective and direction for our lives. Let this be a high hour when great values are found! Tune our hearing to one who lived life out in the depths and to the heights and calls to us, saying, "What shall it profit a man or a woman if he or she shall gain the whole world and lose the soul?" "Or what shall persons give in exchange for their soul?" We know, Father, that you call us not to be gods but to be ourselves—to be the person you have created us to be. We know that it is in obedience to you in a relationship of trust, faith, and love that we are capable of becoming what you created us to be. Knowing ourselves and our many faults and failures amid our best intentions, it is consoling to know that even in our humanness we are made to be temples of your Holy Spirit.

As we discover who we are and dedicate our lives to being what you created us to be, make us aware of our responsibility to the weeping and sorrowing and sinful world through which we daily walk, Father. Open our hands to do the deeds that will lift the fallen. Open our hearts to embrace those who mourn. Open our minds to those who seek the truth that we have to share. In all relationships let the spirit of Jesus prevail, that we might ever look back without fear and regret at the life we have lived and the deeds we have done as we make our pilgrimage. For it is in Christ's name that we pray.—Henry Fields

LECTIONARY MESSAGE

Topic: Respectability in the Kingdom

Text: Luke 14:7–14

Other Readings: Ezek. 18:1–9, 25–29; Heb. 13:1–8

In Jewish society, meals were regular events that reaffirmed and cemented social roles and relations. Only those of similar social standing were invited to share table fellowship. Rare indeed were those occasions where persons of dissimilar tastes, interests, or social status shared a meal together. Mealtimes reflected the societal stratification of the day.

On this particular occasion, Jesus has been invited to a Sabbath meal with one of the leading Pharisees. By inviting Jesus to his table, the Pharisee acknowledged Jesus as his social, religious, and intellectual peer. Jesus was being accorded a great honor.

As the guests gather for the meal, they eye Jesus closely, observing how he conducts himself (v. 17). At the same time, Jesus scrutinizes the behavior of the guests as well as the composition of the party. What he observes provides the opportunity to share insights about the proper behavior and attitudes of the kingdom people. Once again, he uses an everyday situation to set kingdom righteousness over against accepted social norms.

I. When you . . . do not (vv. 7–9, 12). In his observations of the behavior of the assembled guests, Jesus notes their tendency to crawl over each other in order to claim the seats of honor. As is true within society as a whole, so in select groups, the persons closest to power are seen to be more important. Those allowed to dine at the Pharisees' table are privileged, but those allowed into the inner circle are esteemed indeed. Jesus observes how the guests engaged in self-seeking behavior in order to ensure they are acknowledged by the whole party as being particularly respectable.

Speaking to the guests, Jesus castigates their actions. Respectability and honor are not something to be earned or claimed. They are bestowed by those with the power to do so. All one's attempts to improve one's position can be undone by a word from the host. Jesus' rule of social relationships begins with, "Do not seek honor or respectability."

To his host, Jesus expresses disappointment with the guest list. He admonishes the Pharisee to consider a new type of guest list. By suggesting that those of equal or higher social standing be eliminated from the list of invitees, Jesus assails every social convention of his day. He encourages the Pharisee to avoid the game of social tag.

II. But when you . . . (vv. 10, 13). Jesus does not content himself with leaving the guests and host with negative impressions of life in the kingdom. He suggests alternative ways of seeing themselves, of ordering social relationships, and of relating to those of lesser standing. He presents to them a model of kingdom life.

To the assembled guests he suggests that rather than seeking places of honor, they should discipline themselves to resist the compulsion to be in first place and to compare themselves with others. The kingdom person sees social interaction as an opportunity for free, genuine interaction, rather than an opportunity to improve one's social standing.

To the host, Jesus suggests an entirely new guest list. Rather than inviting those who can cement or enhance his social standing, he should invite those who are nearest God's heart—the poor, the lame, the crippled. The kingdom person not only cares for the needs of the poor and disadvantaged but also accepts them as equals. In the kingdom, all sit together. Real love never seeks gain from those loved. Kingdom behavior means inviting to table those who have nothing to contribute.

III. And God will . . . (vv. 11, 14). Finally, Jesus reminds his hearers that their relationships with each other impact fellowship with God. Those who continue in their self-seeking ways will find that God is not impressed. They will climb the ladder of success only to find they have their reward (Matt. 6:2–6). Those who identify with the lowly will find themselves esteemed by God. It is God's honor they should desire, for only God can bestow the sense of honor, worth, and esteem they seek.

Jesus reminds the host that God will fellowship with those who fellowship with God's special people. Only fellowship with God satisfies. God will share the bounty of the kingdom's banquet table with those who practice a vulnerable hospitality in this world (Matt. 25:31–46).

While honor and status with God cannot be earned, Jesus reminds his hearers that God respects and blesses those who invest their lives in fellowship with the poor and dispossessed (Luke 4:18–19; 19:12–27).—Jim Holladay

SUNDAY: SEPTEMBER TENTH

SERVICE OF WORSHIP

Sermon: Open My Eyes!

TEXT: John 9

In taking the visual test to renew my driver's license a few years ago, I discovered I was blind—or at least I could not see things very well at a distance. When I got my glasses for driving, I soon discovered how blind I really was—how much of life I had been missing. As Jesus points out in our scripture lesson, our predicament may be not only that we are blind but also that we are blind and do not realize it.

I. We may have 20/20 vision but yet be blind to much of life.

(a) Jesus uses the incident of the healing of the man who was born blind for some of his most incisive teachings concerning *spiritual* blindness. His mission is not so much to open the eyes of the physically blind as to open the eyes of the soul. There is a blindness within. It is a blindness of the mind and the heart. Not sight but insight is man's deeper need.

(b) Our inner blindness takes many forms. There is the blindness of *fear,* of *prejudice,* of *hate,* of *self-righteousness.* Perhaps this latter malady is the most insidious. Jesus warns against trying to take the splinter out of our brother's eye when there is a plank in our own. The self-righteousness of religious people probably turns more people off to the faith than any other one thing. It is always so much more comfortable to condemn the Pharisees in Jesus' day than to exorcise the Pharisee that is in us.

II. Not only in scripture lessons but also often in the New Testament, conversion *is* represented as the "opening of the eyes." To look upon the world through the eyes of faith is as the difference between being blind and seeing, darkness and light, night and day, death and life.

"The greatest thing a human soul ever does in this world is to *see* something, and tell what it *saw* in a plain way. Hundreds of people can talk for one who can think, but thousands can think for one who can see. To see clearly is poetry, prophecy, and religion, all in one," is John Ruskin's evaluation of such an experience as he writes in his book *Modern Painters*.[5]

Christ's *mission* was to see, and his *ministry* is to help others to see. As he declares throughout his ministry, man's greatest need is not sight but insight. Perception—the apprehending of the nature of things—seeing things in depth—seeing things as they really are—seeing life in all of its originality. He is indeed the light of the world.

III. Could it be that often our blindness is that we do not see deeply enough—there is no perception? We move along on the surface of things. We see so much that we never see anything really.

(a) One day Jesus looks out upon his congregation; he senses their anxiety because they are not looking on life with eyes of faith. He invites us, with them, to take a good, long look at the bird flying by and a second look at the flower blooming at our feet and see the full orb of the Father's grace, in which "*we* live and move and have our being."

When one's eyes are opened from within, there is no place where one touches life—handles anything thoughtfully, carefully, contemplatively—that he does not find himself exclaiming, "God!"

(b) There is nothing much more common to our daily life than bread. When you hold the bread of Communion in your hand, handle it tenderly, for here are the meaning and mystery of seedtime and harvest, of life and death, of time and eternity. Here in this small piece of bread is the fullness of God's grace represented as no place else in the symbols of worship. In our coming to the sacrament, we are reminded that we are sinners saved by an amazing grace, and with the prodigal in Jesus' story we find ourselves exclaiming: "In my Father's house there is bread enough and to spare."

IV. What about your *worldview?* How do you see the world—through the eyes of Christ? Or are you blinded by fear, by prejudice, by suspicion? How we need to see the world as *God's* world—not something to be destroyed but something to be loved into fulfillment.

(a) "This is my *Father's* world"—we sing with gusto on Sunday—but is this the enthusiastic affirmation of our lives on Monday after reading the morning paper? I sense that there are *believers* who are withdrawing from accepting any responsibility for the world and its future, because they feel it is in such a hell of a mess. This is no time for God's people to relinquish their hold upon the world to sinister forces intent upon destroying it.

(b) We must not close our eyes to the world, for when we close our eyes, we close our ears—we become indifferent, even cynical. "Love," the love of God, the Apostle Paul declares, "*looks* for ways of being constructive." With eyes wide open, the believer embraces the good and confronts the evil. To love the world as God loves the world is to take its brokenness to oneself, to agonize over it, to pray and to work for its redemption, its reconciliation, its wholeness.

(c) When Jesus opens *our* eyes, it is not that we may see this or that more clearly but that we may see *all* things clearly. Reality comes strangely into focus. We see our self-righteousness, our prejudices, our fears for what they really are—how blind they have made us.

Open *my* eyes, O Father of all light, that *I* may *see*.—John Thompson

Illustrations

A CHANGED PERSPECTIVE. An American writer, a person of great talent, became bored with life. She even threatened suicide. In her desperation she turned to God. In telling of the change that came into her life as she began her journey of faith, she said: "Before, I dreaded to see another day come and would greet each dawn with a curse upon my lips, 'Good God, morning!'" After her conversion, the opening of her eyes, she could hardly wait for the morning, she was so anxious to be up and doing. She used the same words in greeting the dawn, but with a world of difference in meaning: "Good morning, God!"—John Thompson

[5]New York: Knopf, 1988.

A DIFFERENT WAY OF SEEING. When a man unites with the church, he should not come saying, "I am so holy that I think I must go in among the saints," but, "O brethren, I find I am so weak and wicked that I cannot stand alone; so, if you can help me, open the door and let me enter."—Henry Ward Beecher

Sermon Suggestions

BRINGING STUBBORNNESS TO AN END. TEXT: Jer. 18:1–11. (1) God is continuously at work to shape the lives and fortunes of his people. (2) God meets resistance in the stubborn will of his people. (3) God could cast his people aside forever. (4) But God gives his people opportunity to yield to him and be formed into vessels that honor God.

A POIGNANT APPEAL. TEXT: Philem. 1–21. (1) In gratitude. (2) In love. (3) In confidence.

Worship Aids

CALL TO WORSHIP. "O Lord, thou hast searched me, and known me. Thou knowest my downsitting and mine uprising, thou understandest my thought afar off. Thou compassest my path and my lying down, and art acquainted with all my ways. For there is not a word in my tongue, but, lo, O Lord, thou knowest it altogether" (Ps. 139:1–4).

INVOCATION. Slow us down, Lord, until in the deepest part of our souls we kneel quietly and reverently. Deliver us from the world with all its demands for these few moments we gather here this morning, and in the quiet of this sanctuary let us meet you without distraction, that the bond that binds us to you may be solidly confirmed. In your presence help us to reorder our minds and hearts, bringing before you the ones we love, our hopes, our fears, our joys, and our ill-admitted sins until we see with your eyes and love with your love.—Henry Fields

OFFERTORY SENTENCE. "I am not trying to relieve others by putting a burden on you; but since you have plenty at this time, it is only fair that you should help those who are in need. Then, when you are in need and they have plenty, they will help you" (2 Cor. 8:13–14a TEV).

OFFERTORY PRAYER. Lord, open our hearts and our eyes at the same time that we may be spiritually enriched and others may be blessed.

PRAYER. Mighty God: in Jesus Christ you dealt with spirits that darken minds or set men against themselves. Give peace to people who are torn by conflict, are cast down, or dream deceiving dreams. By your power, drive from our minds demons that shake confidence and wreck love. Tame unruly forces in us and bring us to your truth, so that we may accept ourselves as good, glad children of your love, known in Jesus Christ.—*The Worshipbook*

LECTIONARY MESSAGE

Topic: All to Jesus I Surrender

TEXT: Luke 14:25–33

OTHER READINGS: Ezek. 33:1–11; Philem. 1–20

In a culture of instant gratification, where status is determined by achievement, success, and possessions, how do Jesus' words sound? In a church culture attracted to user-friendly evangelism, what is to be done with Jesus' admonition to count the cost of discipleship?

Jesus' teaching and ministry had captured the imagination of a substantial number of people. A great many were so drawn to Jesus that they had begun to follow him from place to place. How does he respond to the crowds who adore him? How does he begin building his movement? The answer is shocking!

He turns to his adoring followers and, without garnish, outlines what is expected of those who would continue the journey with him. He states what is necessary to be a disciple.

I. The surrender of all relationships (v. 26a). Family relationships were crucial to one's well-being. First-century Judaism knew nothing of the individualism taken for granted in twentieth-century America. It was not the goal of children to grow up and leave home. One was defined by one's family. One's place in society was determined largely by one's family. Jesus' demand that the disciple must turn his or her back on family relationships threatened all that provided a person a sense of place.

Jesus places before the crowd a most radical choice—Jesus or family. To be a disciple, one must surrender one's claim to one's family of origin or marriage and submit oneself to Jesus and the new order he is creating.

Though family does not play the same role in modern, urban society, these words from Jesus still challenge us. He still asks us if we are willing to set aside all human relationships to follow him. The call to discipleship can call for radical and painful decisions.

II. The surrender of one's claim on life (vv. 26b–27). Jesus moves behind social relationships to the most basic relationship, that is, the relationship of a person to himself or herself. To be a follower of Jesus means to surrender one's claim on one's own life (1 Cor. 6:19–20). Like the call to subordinate family and social relationships to the claim of Christ, Jesus reminds his hearers that absolute subordination of one's own life to him is a necessity for discipleship. Jesus is not counseling self-hatred, but he is advocating a life of absolute obedience to the will of God.

Jesus' way of the cross serves as the example of what he means. Unless a person walks the way of the cross, that person cannot be a disciple (Matt. 10:37–39; Rom. 6:5–11).

III. Are you sure (vv. 28–32)? Jesus approaches the question of counting the cost indirectly. He does not stop and say, "Having heard all this, are you sure you want to be my disciple?" Nor does Jesus confront his hearers with, "Discipleship is costly; be sure going in this is what you want."

The parables of the builder and the king seem to appear out of nowhere and interrupt the flow of Jesus' admonitions. Their meaning is unmistakable. To paraphrase the words said in many weddings, "This relationship should not be entered lightly or unadvisedly but soberly and in the fear of God." So one does not enter into a relationship with Christ without mature self-examination. One must consider the absolute claim of God on one's life and how that will shape one's life and relationships before committing oneself to this way of life.

IV. The invitation to surrender all (v. 33). To those who are still with him, Jesus makes a startling statement. The disciple must come to Jesus empty-handed. This verse could aptly be stated, "So therefore, none of you can become my disciple if you do not say farewell to all you possess." The reference is not only to material things but also to anything we claim to own or control.

The condition for discipleship is to give up any claim of ownership over material goods, relationships, and one's own life. The life of discipleship consists of being totally claimed by God (Rom. 6:22). God is a jealous God who will tolerate no competition for the disciple's loyalty (Exod. 20:4–6).

So, the invitation to surrender is a paradox. Only by saying farewell to all one possesses can one be claimed by the love of God. To the crowds who are drawn to Jesus' teaching and ministry, to those seeking to find the answer to life, Jesus offers an invitation: surrender all you have and all you are to the love and will of God.—Jim Holladay

SUNDAY: SEPTEMBER SEVENTEENTH

SERVICE OF WORSHIP

Sermon: The Price of Glory

TEXT: John 12:20–36

A character in a contemporary novel confessed to her pastor, "There is just one reason, you know, why I keep dragging in there every Sunday. I want to find out if the whole thing's true. Just true," she said. "That's all; either it is or it isn't, and that's the one question you avoid like death." That may be a fictional situation but not a fictional question. It is our questioning with all its mixed motivations that we see in these Greeks who come to Jerusalem on a crowded festival day wanting to see Jesus. They, as we, come with images of who he might be: good man, prophet, miracle worker, God's chosen one. As the Jews seek a Messiah, the Greeks come seeking the truth.

I. Jesus, who has repeatedly said the hour has not yet come for him, changes all of that with this declaration: "The hour has now come for the Son of man to receive great glory."

(a) What could that mean? We know now in retrospect that he was at that moment preparing the way for the world to apprehend (experience, enjoy) the presence of God. If that is true, then we expect certain results of this glorification. We expect immediate ecstasy, a sense of being lifted up beyond the mundane, prosaic lives that we lead. Even a small dose of ecstasy would be cherished by most of us. After being with small children all day, just one adult conversation would be heaven. After hours falling into days of monotonous work, a small chance for creativity would be divine.

(b) Or if God is ready to show his glory, it should come in power. After another week of reading the newspaper, we want to say, "How long, O Lord?" How long before you show your power and defeat the forces of evil, injustice, and human stupidity? Week after week we say "thy kingdom" and "the power and the glory." Yet, when have we felt more powerless? We could see God's glory if his righteous power would crush such evil that surrounds us day and night.

(c) Some of us would settle for being caught up in the glory and majesty of God's Creation. That would be enough. But the problem with mountaintops is that it's difficult to stay there. The glory of God's Creation cannot save us and sustain us in the "dark nights of the soul."

II. No, Jesus gives us a picture of the other side of nature. It is the truth of the seed that must die before being reborn into fuller life. It's truth we see in all of life. Jesus gives up being "safe" and alone to die so that his glorified life can be lived out in the community he is creating. Through his Spirit, we are now identified with him to the point of eternal life . . . now!

(a) So it is that we meet here in this hour to remember his death. But it is not to glorify death. Here I see Jesus in all his humanity battling with the desire to avoid the cross. The temptation was always present in the desert, through Peter, within himself. Yet, his final prayer was not that he should be saved from that hour or that the bitter cup would be passed from him . . . but that his Father in heaven would be glorified. Now that's glory through agony, and we are not spectators. We are inextricably bound up in the drama, for it is the drama of life.

(b) Archbishop William Temple said, "It is my lust and selfishness that sends Christ to the cross, and in his agony he wins me from my lust and selfishness." That's it, isn't it? His victory becomes our victory, not just over sexual lust but also lust for power, for being right all the time. He wins us once and for all. Yet daily we are won from our shadow side, the darkness of our sin through the perfect sacrifice of his love.

III. This is the Jesus who is lifted up. For in his suffering, all men and women are drawn to the God who cares. The way to life is through the cross, and in dying daily to our own selfishness he promises that: where he is, we will be also. The glory of this promise is that we will know his presence not only in heaven but also upon this earth. The psalmist could cry, "If I made my bed in hell, thou art there. . . . " In our darkest night of the soul, in the depth of depression and despair . . . , the crucified one is there lifting us up into the presence of the Father . . . now and forever . . . world without end. . . . Amen.—Gary D. Stratman

Illustrations

THE PROBLEM OF EVIL. The contribution of Christian faith to the problem of evil has lain not so much in supplying a theory to explain it as in furnishing power to surmount it. Our English friend Maude Royden even says: "I never try to explain evil. If anybody asks me to explain suffering, I say I can't. I say I have a power that surmounts it." Jesus himself never said, "I have explained the world," but he did say, "I have overcome it."

Early Christianity certainly did not dodge trouble. It started with tragedy in its darkest form. It began with a cross and a man hanging on it, saying, "My God, my God, why—why hast thou forsaken me?" There never has been an adequate answer to that question. But one thing the cross made plain—that in this world now, and in ourselves if we will have it so, there is a power that can surmount such evil, rise above its tragedy, carry off a victory in the face of it, use it, transmute the symbol of the cruelest punishment that the ancient world knew into the symbol of salvation, until the miracle happens of multitudes singing: "in the cross of Christ I glory, towering o'er the wrecks of time."—Harry Emerson Fosdick

A YEAR LOST—A LIFE GAINED. Henry Drummond told of an American medical student in Edinburgh who tried to win an atheist. The two were great friends, but the American was a sincere Christian. Drummond himself had tried to win the atheist, but in vain. At last the American finished his course, packed his trunks, and got ready to return to the United States to start a practice.

"Then," he told Drummond later, "I wondered whether a year of my life would be better spent in starting as a doctor in America or staying in Edinburgh to win that man for Christ. I have decided to stay."

"Well," said Drummond, "it will pay you. You will get your man." It took eleven months, but after that time Drummond saw the two sitting together at a Communion service. Before the onetime atheist left the university, he came to Drummond's room. Drummond said: "What do you want?"

The man said: "I want to be a medical missionary."—Leslie D. Weatherhead

Sermon Suggestions

WHY SOME PEOPLE DON'T LIKE THE REAL JESUS. TEXT: Luke 15:1–10. (1) He goes looking for the losers. (2) His search may leave "the winners" in some ways vulnerable ("in the wilderness"). (3) Legalism is eternally at odds with grace.

AN EXAMPLE OF GRACE RECEIVED. TEXT: 1 Tim. 1:12–17 NRSV. (1) By a notorious sinner. (2) Who did not deliberately oppose God. (3) And received mercy. (4) So that he might, as the foremost of sinners, become "an example to those who would come to believe in [Jesus Christ] for eternal life."

Worship Aids

CALL TO WORSHIP. "The Lord is in his holy temple; the Lord's throne is in heaven. His eyes behold, his gaze examines humankind" (Ps. 11:4 NRSV).

INVOCATION. Eternal Spirit, you inhabit all ages and all worlds, yet you are pleased to come and dwell among us. Help us to worship you in spirit and in truth, that you may touch the lives of our friends and neighbors in special ways through us.

OFFERTORY SENTENCE. "But this I say, He which soweth sparingly shall reap also sparingly; and he which soweth bountifully shall reap also bountifully" (2 Cor. 9:6).

OFFERTORY PRAYER. Lord, grant that we will serve thee with our time as well as our substance, keeping thy kingdom as our foremost priority and thy will as the heartbeat of our faith.—E. Lee Phillips

PRAYER. O God, our true life, in whom and by whom all things live, thou commandest us to seek thee and art ready to be found; thou biddest us knock and openest when we do so. To know thee is life, to serve thee is freedom, to enjoy thee is a kingdom, to praise thee is the joy and happiness of the soul. We praise and bless and adore thee, we worship thee, we glorify thee, we give thanks to thee for thy great glory. We humbly beseech thee to abide with us, to reign in us, to make these hearts of ours holy temples, fit habitations for thy divine majesty. O thou Maker and Preserver of all things, visible and invisible! Keep, we beseech thee, the work of thine own hands, who trust in thy mercy alone for safety and protection. Guard us with the power of thy grace, here and in all places, now and at all times, forevermore.—Adapted from St. Augustine

LECTIONARY MESSAGE

Topic: Understanding God's Judgment

TEXT: Jer. 4:11–12, 22–28

OTHER READINGS: 1 Tim. 1:12–17; Luke 15:1–10

God's power to forgive should be the regular theme of every preacher and the joy of every believer. But the message of grace should not blind us to the reality of sin and its consequences. What is needed in preaching today is a renewed balance between the proclamation of divine grace and the reality of judgment for sin. If Jeremiah was the greatest prophet of hope for the future, he was also the most eloquent in describing coming judgment and the most constant in issuing calls to repentance. It was Jeremiah's program to help Judah avoid catastrophe through repentance, but failing that, to prepare people for life after tragedy when they could come to understand and appropriate the assurance of forgiveness. Deliverance may come after the tragedy rather than instead of it. What is remarkable is Jeremiah's ability to maintain balance in his preaching judgment and forgiveness.

I. Metaphors of judgment (4:11–12, 23–26). Coming judgment is likened to the blowing of the hot wind from the trackless wastes of the desert. Unlike the wind from the northwest, which could bring rain or welcome breezes in season, this dazzling wind refers to the sirocco, or east wind. The sirocco can blow in the intervals between spring and summer and between summer and autumn. It is a hot, dry wind that fills the atmosphere with dust, making life miserable for man and beast.

Coming judgment is also described in the most appalling terms: the return of chaos. What is envisioned in 4:23–26 is nothing less than Genesis 1 revisited, with important terms reversed. Order would give way to disorder, chaos and darkness would return to the earth, which would be denuded of men and animals.

This second depiction of judgment can be taken quite literally as a description of the natural order violated and ruined by human moral and spiritual failure. The prophets understood well the relationship of ecological concerns and the failure of human morality.

II. Judgment in context (4:18; 4:1–4). Jeremiah did not understand divine judgment as the work of a vengeful or capricious God. In the context of the judgment passages, one is able to discern the reason for the threat of judgment. Jeremiah 4:18 makes clear that judgment was threatened because "your ways and your deed" invited it. The abrogation of covenant initiated the built-in curse. Every evil deed has its judgment built into it. It is not that God delights to punish. Rather, it is that human failure sets in motion the appropriate consequences.

Also, Jeremiah did not announce the threat of judgment without extending the invitation to repentance. In the context, 4:1–4, the prophet calls for a return to covenant faithfulness so that the nations might glory in God. Repentance is described as breaking unplowed ground (a radical new departure) and as circumcising the heart (mind).

III. Life beyond judgment. Taking the reality of judgment seriously does not mean that judgment is the last word. Along with his calls to repentance, Jeremiah preached consistently about life and hope beyond tragedy. Jeremiah's letter to the exiles (Jer. 29) spoke of God's plans for their return, plans for their welfare to give them a future and a hope. When the Babylonian army had surrounded Jerusalem with siege works and it seemed that crushing defeat would come any day, Jeremiah bought a field that was located at Anathoth, beyond enemy lines (Jer. 32). He had no assurance he would ever see or enjoy the use of the property, but he put a down payment on the future with hard cash in order to say that houses and fields and vineyards would again be bought in the land.

If it is folly to ignore the judgment that our own bad choices make inevitable, it is equal folly to lose sight of the long-range plans of God to give a reason for hope and a basis for life beyond tragedy.—Thomas D. Smothers

SUNDAY: SEPTEMBER TWENTY-FOURTH

SERVICE OF WORSHIP

Sermon: Picture of Hope

TEXT: Ps. 107

The 107th psalm describes the joyous deliverance of people who have been through some terrifying, tumbling, battering experiences. Some of them had been through defeat in battle. Some of them had known imprisonment in the darkness of dungeons. Some of them had been through violent storms at sea. As they looked over their past experiences, they knew that they had not been alone. Out of the sharing of the experience of help in impossible situations they came to one great, overwhelming desire—it was to praise and give thanks to God. That is the way Psalm 107 begins. It is an invitation to authentic praise and gratitude.

As we hear the words of this psalm, we must see the faces of people—radiant, tear-filled, joyous faces. People utterly amazed and filled with wonder that they survived their ordeal.

I. Notice verse 4, "Some wandered in desert wastes, finding no way to a city to dwell in; hungry and thirsty, their soul fainted within them." In the first picture you see a desert. As far as the eye can see there is a sea of sand. There are no trees, no grass, or vegetation. There is only the sound of the wind, which moves the sand, and there is silence again.

(a) As we look at the picture more closely, we can see in the distance a tiny speck. It moves closer. We are able to see people. Clothes are dusty and ragged; hair is torn and wind blown, faces darkened and burned, eyes red, lips dry and cracked. They are weak from hunger and burning with thirst. They collapse in despair in the sand. They are lost. They have wandered in the desert until they cannot go on. They have given up all hope.

(b) Perhaps this picture represents a group of the exiles coming from Babylon after the time of Cyrus, king of Persia. Perhaps it represents the fact that some of them got lost on the way home. Verse 6 represents the turning point: "Then they cried to the Lord in their trouble, and he delivered them from their distress; he led them by a straight way, till they reached a city to dwell in."

II. We are led quickly now to see the second picture. We see the interior of a dungeon. It is a place of gloom and darkness. Prisoners are shackled and chained to cold, damp stone walls. The guards are cruel. They kick and beat the fallen. The turning point in this section is verse 13: "Then they cried to the Lord in their trouble, and he delivered them from their distress."

(a) Do you remember the picture of the young doctor in the news some time ago? He was buried in the rubble of the hospital in Mexico City. He thought that he was dead. People refused to give up hope. They kept working. Finally they found him. They cut the steel and lifted the heavy cement blocks that were on him. He lived because someone delivered him from his distress!

(b) Notice the words that describe God's action: "He brought them out of darkness and gloom, and broke their bonds asunder. Let them thank the Lord for his steadfast love, for his wonderful works to the sons of men!" Notice particularly verse 16: "For he shatters the doors of bronze, and cuts in two the bars of iron."

III. In the third picture we see a pitiful, sobering sight. There are people who are terribly ill. They are so sick they cannot stand the sight of food.

Look at verse 17: "Some are sick through their sinful ways, and because of their iniquities suffered affliction." I certainly do not believe that our illnesses are punishments for our sins. Still, we are learning more and more that there is a correlation between our life-styles and health. I do not think that God created the AIDS virus to punish people. Still the spread of the disease is related to a lifestyle. In verse 34 we read that wickedness transforms "a fruitful land into a salty waste." Our text is simply saying that sin has a wider impact than we sometimes realize.

Psalm 107 says in verses 18–20, "They loathed any kind of food, and they drew near to the gates of death. Then they cried to the Lord in their trouble and he delivered them from their distress; he sent forth his word, and healed them, and delivered them from destruction." We believe in the healing power of God in this congregation. We have no reservation about praying for healing for the sick. I believe that God heals some people immediately. I believe that he heals others in the Resurrection. Disease never wins! God heals and delivers his children.

IV. The fourth picture is in some respects the most dramatic and most powerful of all. Ancient sailing ships made their way across the sea on a routine voyage. In the distance storm clouds appear. A chilling wind begins to blow. The first drops of rain appear—the clouds darken. The wind increases. A driving rain begins. Waves mount. Whitecaps appear. At first no one on board is disturbed. Sailors go about their work with routine confidence. They have been through storms before.

Fear begins to spread. Experienced sailors see it in the faces of their mates. Men stumble and stagger like drunken men. At any moment the ship might break, sink, and be gone. "Their courage melted away in their evil plight; they reeled and staggered like drunken men, and were at their wits' end" (Ps. 107: 26–27).

(a) Once again there is the great verse that represents the central focus of the psalm. "Then they cried to the Lord in their trouble, and he delivered them from their distress; he made the storm be still, and the waves of the sea were hushed" (Ps. 107:28–29).

(b) The psalmist then adds his conclusion of his fourth picture. He says, "Let them thank the Lord for his steadfast love, for his wonderful works to the sons of men! Let them extol him in the congregation of the people, and praise him in the assembly of the elders" (Ps. 107:31–32).

V. Deserts, dungeons, sickbeds, and storm-tossed seas are real. They are all a part of our human experience, but they do not have the last word. The last word is not death and defeat. There is a way out of the desert, out of the dungeon, out of the bed of sickness, out of the storm. There is an oasis of cool water and shade. There is an open field with fresh air. There are calm water and a safe port. There is a God who brings us through!

That is what this great psalm is telling us. When we are facing life's impossible situations, we are not alone. So we conclude where we began, "O give thanks to the Lord, for he is good; for his steadfast love endures for ever! Let the redeemed of the Lord say so" (Ps. 107:1–2).—Joe A. Harding

Illustrations

AND YET—THE STARS! Leslie Weatherhead tells the story of a dreadful night in

London when enemy bombs were bringing death from the skies. A man and his wife were seated on their porch with their son and daughter when the danger signal pierced the air. They all started for the underground, the father with the son and the mother with the daughter. In the confusion that followed in the streets, the mother and daughter, because of the crowd, didn't even get to the underground in time. When the all-clear signal came, the father and son rushed out to find the mother and daughter. They found them, not too far from their home—dead. They had been crushed by a falling wall. The father gave way to grief as they returned to their home and found it completely destroyed. The boy, about five years old, had not quite comprehended all that had happened. In the gathering darkness, he wandered amid the wreckage of the home, seated himself on a pile of bricks, gazed into the sky, and saw the stars coming out. The father, momentarily left alone, cried, "Where are you, son?"

"Here I am, Dad," said the boy.

"What are you doing, son?"

"I'm watching God hang out the stars."

He is still hanging them out!—Gaston Foote

ASSURANCE FROM THE PAST. Dr. F. W. Boreham, a noted Australian minister, recalled an incident from his childhood. He told about a time when he and his brothers noticed their father looked anxious and worried and their mother's eyes were often red and swollen. Then one day, the atmosphere changed, and it seemed to have something to do with a piece of paper fixed to a wall. Printed on it was a verse from the Bible: "Hitherto hath the Lord helped us."

This tiny text made such a difference in the home that the boys decided to ask about it. Their mother made this response: "Your father and I have had a crushing trouble, and we feared a much heavier one. On Tuesday of last week, I was feeling dreadfully worried. I had to drop my work, pick up the baby, and walk up and down the kitchen feeling that I could endure it no longer. My burden was heavier than I could bear; it seemed to be killing me. In pacing up and down I paused for a second in front of the almanac on the wall. The only thing I saw was the text in the corner. I felt as if it had been put there especially for me. It was as if someone had spoken the words. 'Hitherto hath the Lord helped us.' I was so overcome that I sat down and had a good cry, and then I began again with a fresh start and trust. When your father came home I told him all about it, and he cut out the text with his penknife, had it framed, and hung it there where you now see it."

Writing about that incident fifty years later, Boreham said, "It was then that I made my discovery. Here was the secret! Here was the connection between religion and life."—Jerry Hayner

Sermon Suggestions

WHAT TO DO WITH YOUR MONEY. TEXT: Luke 16:1–13. (1) Be as clever as the dishonest manager in looking out for your future. (2) However, avoid getting enslaved by a master that can destroy you.

GOD'S UNIVERSAL LOVE. TEXT: 1 Tim. 2:1–7 NRSV. (1) God wishes us to pray for all people, good and bad. (2) Christ died for all and is the "one mediator between God and humankind." (3) God desires everyone to be saved.

Worship Aids

CALL TO WORSHIP. "Let us be grateful and worship God in a way that will please him, with reverence and fear" (Heb. 12:28b TEV).

INVOCATION. Still us, Lord. Wrap our hearts in thy quiet and pour thy peace over us that we may worship thee in humility and praise. Help us to be still and know that thou art God, for thou alone art our Creator and our God.—E. Lee Phillips

OFFERTORY SENTENCE. "Everyone is to give what he has made up his mind to give; there is to be no grudging or compulsion about it, for God loves the giver who gives cheerfully" (2 Cor. 9:7 MOFFATT).

OFFERTORY PRAYER. Lord, lift above the darkness of the valley and the mists of struggle all who believe in thee. Allow this offering to be part of that light that shines with healing in hearts of faith, through our conquering Savior, Jesus Christ.—E. Lee Phillips

PRAYER. O God of all grace and truth, without whom nothing is strong, nothing is pure, and nothing is holy, our hearts are lifted with glad expectation as we call upon thee in prayer. All nature around us witnesses to thy lively being, but only when thy Spirit moves in our quiet devotions and redeeming works do we know thee really as thou art. Thou art ageless in thy caring and living, and no one who has come to thee believing has ever been turned away unnoticed or unfed. Thy grace is sufficient for us, and to name thee truthfully and in sincerity is to qualify for the richest measure of thy concern. May we touch thee in faith as thy Spirit passes among us, and may the contagion of thy presence bind us together into a community of peace and love. Speak to us today a message above the noise and prattle of our careless tongues. Give us wisdom and patience to understand; and however hard the task or impossible the mission, lend us the courage and vision to accept. Hear our plea, O God, and in thy mercy give heed to our supplication. In the name of Christ, we pray.—Donald Macleod

LECTIONARY MESSAGE

Topic: The Cost of a Compassionate Ministry

TEXT: Jer. 8:18–9:1; 1 Tim. 2:1–7; Luke 16:1–13

In this passage one is able to observe some of the dynamics of a situation fraught with terror. The invasion by Babylonian forces was imminent. The people of Judah, now no longer able to shrug off Jeremiah's warnings, were terrified, trying to decide how to act in the face of the threat. The verses, which include the responses of the people, the Lord, and Jeremiah, give insight into the character of each in response to the threat.

I. The presumption of the people (Jer. 8:19b, 20). Jeremiah had detailed the moral and spiritual failings of the people. Especially serious were idolatry and susceptibility to falsehood. People trusted in the Temple as a guarantee of the Lord's presence among them, which they thought would safeguard them in any emergency. They thought that since the Lord, the divine king, was in Zion, they should not be under threat of invasion. Their question implies the Lord's failure.

Jeremiah had tried to disabuse the people of their one-sided trust in the Temple, which they had substituted for justice and covenant faithfulness. Their religion had become one of presumption, not one characterized by repentance. They lamented that harvest was past, summer had ended, and they were not saved. This is either a proverbial type of saying lamenting the absence of success or a complaint of a literal failure of crops to sustain them during siege. Their response reveals their lack of true religion and their inability to see reality by refusing to take responsibility for the consequences of their own deeds.

II. The divine challenge to presumption (8:19c, 22a). The Lord's reply to the people's question is first of all a direct challenge to their alleged piety. If the people thought that the Lord's presence was truly in Zion, why did they continue to pervert their religion with devotion to images and foreign idols? As Jeremiah 7:5–7 shows, the presence of the Lord among them was dependent upon their faithfulness to the covenant: if you practice justice and do not go after other gods, "then I will dwell with you in this place." The Lord's response then is more a call to a return to the covenant than simply an accusation.

In the second place, the Lord reminded the people that healing was still possible. Is there no balm in Gilead? Of course there was. Is there no physician there? Of course there was. The reference to healing balm may be a reply to the people's charge that the Lord had given them poisoned water to drink (8:14). In view of the resources available, in view of the Lord's wish to offer healing always, why had the diseased condition of the people not been healed? In the three questions in verse 22, one can sense not only disappointment but also a longing, a yearning on the part of the compassionate Lord, who, even at the last moment, was holding out the solution to the people's dilemma.

III. The anguish of the prophet (8:18, 21, 22b; 9:1). Jeremiah worked for nearly half a century to heal the breach between the Lord and the people. He was often confrontive, insulting, obstinate, and consequently he made many enemies. But he never forgot that he was one of the people and would likely have to share their fate, the guiltless along with the guilty.

Jeremiah learned the cost of compassion. Because he cared deeply for this wayward people, his personal anguish was profound. His reputation as the weeping prophet is based on these verses. Perhaps there are not enough weeping prophets today, not enough people with broken hearts over the hurt of the helpless and misguided. What one is willing to weep about is a good indication of the nature and depth of one's commitment.

Anyone who devotes one's life to the welfare of others soon learns the personal cost of compassion. Tears are but one way to express concern. The Christian will use every means available to meet the needs of others, no matter the cost. The life of the believer is not one's own and finds its sole meaning in ministering to others. The secret of such a life of compassion is expressed in being willing to complete the sufferings of Christ on behalf of others.—Thomas G. Smothers

SUNDAY: OCTOBER FIRST

SERVICE OF WORSHIP

Sermon: Praise in a Hurting World

TEXT: Ps. 146

On this World Communion Sunday we focus our attention on Psalm 146 and a theme, "Praise in a Hurting World." We are going to look briefly at what it means to praise and worship the God who cares for the whole world.

I. Notice that the psalm begins with a very positive, hopeful, healing word to the inner self.

(a) Listen again, "Praise the Lord, O *my* soul!" Verse 1 reminds us that we do, in fact, carry on a constant inner dialogue with ourselves, with our soul. Studies indicate that much of that inner dialogue is negative and hurtful. Many of us are soul beaters or batterers. We say, "You are stupid. You are a failure." Then we move ahead to actualize what we actually tell ourselves. Haven't you ever said to yourself, "I think that I will drop that"—and then dropped it? Young people, haven't you ever said to yourself, "I think that I am going to flunk this test," and you flunked it?

(b) In verse 1 we hear the great word: "Praise the Lord, O *my* soul!" The focus is clearly on God's goodness and adequacy and sufficiency. He doesn't begin by saying to himself, "Your problem, soul, is that you are so selfish. Your problem is that you don't really care about the poor or the homeless or you don't want to do anything about injustice." The way to create a great social conscience that brings about new action on the behalf of hurting people is to get a new "soul focus." That focus is upon God!

II. Notice next that the psalmist makes a great commitment. He says, "I will praise the Lord as long as I live."

(a) It is thrilling to remember that we have the capacity to say, "I *will*"—and then do it. God has given us freedom of choice—the capacity for life-changing commitments. Friends, you are not trapped! Perhaps you have your hands lifted up in praise. You go forward energized for ministry and mission. You are walking into the light because your focus is right. Each step you take there is an affirmation, "I will, I will"—not "I should" or "I ought" or "I might"—but "I will."

(b) Verse 4 describes the reality of all human leaders. "When his breath departs, he returns to his earth; on that very day his plans perish." The problem with the average American is that we have watched so much television—we have been deeply influenced by so many thousand commercials that we have actually come to believe that our salvation is going to be found in the purchase of certain products. The average American teenager has watched 350,000 television commercials before he or she leaves high school. We spend more money on advertisements than on all public institutions of higher education. No wonder that we begin to convince ourselves that Jesus was really wrong about the abundance of possessions.

III. Against the emptiness of our secular culture, the psalmist gives us a lasting word about authentic happiness. "Happy is he whose help is the God of Jacob, whose hope is in the Lord his God, who made heaven and earth, the sea, and all that is in them; who keeps faith for ever" (Ps. 146:5–7).

(a) Beginning with verse 7, we suddenly find ourselves reminded that God cares about his hurting world. He wants me to share his vision of healing and wholeness for hurting people. That means that God cares about people who are denied basic human rights in South Africa and in Poland. He cares about the dispossessed. He cares about the homeless in Mexico City. He cares about those who dwell in the terrible slums of Calcutta.

(b) The Scripture makes it clear that God rejects worship that separates us from human need. You remember the words of the fiery prophet Amos. Amos cried out, "I hate, I despise your feasts. I take no delight in your solemn assemblies. . . . But let justice roll down like waters, and righteousness like an ever-flowing stream" (Amos 5:21–24). That is why real praise can never be separated from social concerns and social responsibility. To worship is to be involved in action that seeks conversion, not just of persons but also of corrupt systems in society.

(c) I do not think that our task is to suggest a detailed solution for every problem. We are, however, to keep alive God's clear call for justice, compassion, and peace.

Our task is both to proclaim the Word of God and to be a part of the building of systems that will bring justice and peace and righteousness to God's hurting people.

IV. The psalm concludes with a great word about the certainty of the coming victory. "The Lord will reign for ever, thy God, O Zion, to all generations. Praise the Lord!"

(a) We may grow cynical or tired. God's victory is assured in the death and Resurrection of Jesus Christ. If we focus upon that victory, then we begin to understand that every action that furthers the cause of justice and peace and that helps meet the needs of hurting persons is ultimately and finally significant—and not lost! This is the reason we have confidence as a congregation to know that we can do something that can make a difference not only in our local community but also in the world. That is what our World Communion Sunday is really all about.

(b) When we take the bread and take the cup, we know that we are already beginning the celebration of God's justice, righteousness, and victory. We are nurtured and fed as a people—empowered and equipped for mission in God's hurting world.

In that transcendent moment as people share in the Holy Communion, there is a healing for the deepest pains. There is a crossing of barriers that we cannot cross. There is a dimension of wonder and of joy that no one understands. That is why today we take courage to praise the Lord! "Praise the Lord, O my soul! I will praise the Lord as long as I live; I will sing praises to my God while I have being" (Ps. 146:1b–2). In that wonder we come now to share communion.—Joe A. Harding

Illustrations

YOUR PRIVATE CHAPEL. The prophet Ezekiel in a vision was shown a secret door in the court of the Temple. Entering, he was amazed to find there, bowing down to representations of vile and repulsive things, the very same leaders of Israel whom he had seen worshiping in the Temple itself. As he looked in incredible and shocked surprise, his mysterious conductor whispered, "Do you see what the national and religious leaders do in the dark, every man in the private chapel of his own imagination?"

Here is mirrored a hideous possibility. For every man, in addition to the public Temple, where all actions and religious gestures are scrutinized, there is a hidden chapel where his altar of inner devotion stands. On the walls of this hidden chapel are the symbols of the affinities that draw his heart. Here both the saint and the sinner paint the things that reveal their ruling passions. Forever man is frescoing the walls of that hidden chamber with the representations of the things he really loves and admires, the deepest affinities of his heart.

The solemn thing is that this chapel may be God's or the devil's; it may be a shrine of love or a shrine of hate. But it is in every case the place of heart's desire.—Frederick Brown Harris

THE MEANING OF WORSHIP. To worship is to quicken the conscience by the holiness of God, to feed the mind with the truth of God, to purge the imagination with the beauty of God, to open the heart to the love of God, to devote the will to the purpose of God.—William Temple

Sermon Suggestions

EVEN IF ONE RISES FROM THE DEAD. TEXT: Luke 16:19–31. (1) The story: Jesus told a parable using contemporary pictures of the life to come to make his own point. (2) The meaning: (a) Judgment is now. (b) Death closes the books on one's opportunities. (c) There is ample truth in Scripture and faithful teaching and preaching to guide those who wish to know and follow truth.

AN ACT OF FAITH. TEXT: Jer. 32:1–3a, 6–15. (1) It may be an ordinary act with extraordinary significance. (2) It may set an example for the action of others.

Worship Aids

CALL TO WORSHIP. "He that dwelleth in the secret place of the Most High shall abide under the shadow of the Almighty. I will say of the Lord, He is my refuge and my fortress: my God; in him will I trust" (Ps. 91:1–2).

INVOCATION. Almighty God: from the ends of the earth you have gathered us around Christ's holy table. Forgive our separate ways. Forgive everything that keeps us apart, the prides that prevent our proper reunion. O God, have mercy on your church, troubled and divided. Renew in us true unity of purpose that we may break bread together and, with one voice, praise Jesus Christ our Lord.—*The Worshipbook*

OFFERTORY SENTENCE. "Give unto the Lord the glory due unto his name: bring an offering, and come into his courts" (Ps. 96:7).

OFFERTORY PRAYER. Almighty God, whose loving hand hath given us all that we may honor thee with our substance, and, remembering the account that we must one day give, may be faithful stewards of thy bounty, through Jesus Christ our Lord.—*Book of Common Prayer*

PRAYER. Our Father, your dwelling is in heaven, but whenever we hold dear your holy name, the eternal rule of love and grace becomes real among us. We are unhappy with things as they are, and we crave and yearn for a life shaped and supported by a will higher and better than our own. Heaven is to us a mystery, but our life becomes fairer when we catch glimpses of its light and feel the touch of an unseen hand enabling our steps and keeping our feet from stumbling. Our inner lives are hungry; feed us, we pray, with that bread your Word supplies and nourishes beyond our human sight. Help us to find our refuge in a personal commitment to your hopes for each of us, and in the security of that union may we be more forgiving and find ourselves forgiven. Safeguard us ever from a poor life outside your loving care, and through the ministries of your grace may our response to your call be made sure and strong. Lord of our lives, you are high and lifted up; grant that our service and sacrifice for others may expand and grow until wherever our journey takes us, your hand will direct and hold us fast. All things we ask in Jesus' name.—Donald Macleod

LECTIONARY MESSAGE

Topic: An Early Look at the End of Life

TEXT: 1 Tim. 6:6–19

It is never too early to take a long look at the probabilities for the duration of life and for its later conditions. In this text, Paul follows up his exhortations and instructions to Timothy on sound doctrine, sound social practices, and good preparation for spiritual leadership with a sobering look at the truth about what will really count at the end of one's life.

I. A time that is too late. We should begin with that look at the end of life, the last days of a life of hard work in which many pleasures have been sacrificed to the objective of being "successful" enough to make possible retirement and the enjoyment of the good things one has worked hard to acquire.

(a) Verse 9 promises temptation and a snare for those who would be rich. But we are familiar with the life—good schooling; part-time work while earning a college degree with honors; professional study or specialized learning for a promising career; long hours and careful day-in-day-out faithfulness to a company, a profession, or a trade, with little time to truly enjoy one's family; promotions or enlargement of work opportunities, usually meaning more hours and harder work; vacations spent sharpening skills instead of relaxing; finally receiving the income, recognition, and returns to enable a good home and, finally, retirement. But often, retirement comes when weakness, ill health, disruptions of family, and other changing circumstances of older life deprive one of the time or strength to reap the benefits looked for. Unless the life itself has been blessed, the results will be disappointing.

(b) A recently seen advertisement for a psychiatric hospital shows an older person crying, sitting and reflecting on childhood and youthful joys and mature responsibilities, accompanied by the song "Is That All There Is?" Then the ad offers treatment for depression, which often brings not a cure for the depression but a heightened consciousness of the reasons for it. Verse 17 offers the true cure for depression by preventing it absolutely, living in the light of God's riches and joys.

II. The wise course for early times. For the one who would avoid that syndrome, Paul has abundant successful strategies.

(a) "We brought nothing into this world, and it is certain we can carry nothing out." We are reminded of the answer given by a man who was asked how much a deceased friend had left. He replied, "Everything." We all know "there are no pockets in shrouds." So, Paul advises, first, contentment with food and raiment, the truly blessed condition afforded by God's grace. It seems to be life's business to make us discontented with enough—we feel we *must* have more. But if we come to love money, we have opened Pandora's box, tempted fate, and even "erred from the faith." Paul cautions against the "highmindedness" that comes from riches, lest we come to "trust in them."

(b) Therefore, we must discover the riches that will go before us into eternal life. Paul advises that we "flee these things and follow after righteousness, godliness, faith, love, patience, and meekness" and "lay hold on eternal life." Many great ones have sought to ensure eternal life by earthly means. Percy Shelley did more to immortalize an ancient king by writing the poem "Ozymandias" about him than the king did by having the statue built, the remnants of which are described in the poem. The days of our lives, no matter how good, are soon over.

A life spent keeping faith strong in Jesus Christ, "the blessed and only Potentate, the King of kings and Lord of lords," will be marked by richness in good works, distributing to those in need, making a "good foundation against the time to come."

III. Early wisdom is best. The point of Paul's advice to Timothy is to make *all* of life true to God's will and direction. But we should be remiss in our duty if we did not hold out the love and mercy of God to those who, even having trusted in uncertain riches, are still alive to hear the good news of Christ, "who only hath immortality," and thus, in Christ's grace, may still come professing error recognized in time. It is late, but never *too* late until death gives its final call.—John R. Rodman

SUNDAY: OCTOBER EIGHTH

SERVICE OF WORSHIP

Sermon: The Home Without a House

TEXT: John 14:21–29

What images come to your mind when I say the word *home?* The most common use of the word of course is to simply depict the place where you live. But the word *home* is invested with greater meaning than just *house.* When we talk about our home, we are talking about something that plays a very central role in our identity, both individual and family. Home is a place of family relationships; it is a place of personal development, socialization, a place where lifelong memories, both good and bad, are being made.

I. The home that we grow up in has an incredible impact and influence on who we become and on how we live the rest of our lives.

(a) A home is a very powerful thing in each of our lives. Ideally, it should be a place of solace and protection from the outside world. It should be the place where we go to heal the wounds that are inflicted upon us in our day-to-day lives. At times, it may seem like the only place where we are a somebody, where our lives have some real significance. I know for me, home is a place of protection and warmth, a place to kick back and be myself, sometimes even a place to hide from the pressures of the outside world.

(b) Whether we admit it or not, we tend to go through our entire lives never escaping the influence of the home that we grew up in. Our self-image, our idea of what we're here for, what our goals are, what we believe we should strive for, the way we get pleasure, the way we work and learn: all of these things have been influenced to a very significant degree by our growth years in the home, whatever that may be.

II. You might be thinking, well, I didn't have much of a home life. I didn't have parents, or I grew up in a foster home or in a very dysfunctional family.

(a) The most predominant memories of home for some are memories of abuse, pain, disappointment, constant tension, feelings of insecurity and low self-esteem, and so on. Many people go through life making decisions and choices that are unconsciously influenced by the inward drive to resolve unfinished issues from their home life.

(b) On the one hand, home can be an influence for the most profound good and the shaping of a constructive way of life and feeling, creativity, and security; on the other hand, it can be a force toward the deepest insecurities, poorest self-image, difficult and uncontrollable feelings, and so on. Home is something much bigger than we can articulate into words. Home life, parental and family relationships, have been a very important part of shaping who we are, how we feel and think, and what we consider important ever since the beginning of time.

III. So what does all this have to do with anything from our Scripture readings? In John 14:23 Jesus promises those who love and obey him: "We [that is, the Father, Son, and Spirit] will come to you and make our *home* with you."

(a) He speaks of God establishing a home life with each of us. "We will make our home with you." The seed of this idea begins to germinate into a new life of its own when we see it in the context of what this metaphysical phenomenon of home ideally means. God, who is perfection, is the perfect homemaker. This home, this family relationship, will be every bit as powerful and influential in your life as homes were meant to be, but the influence will be only for good. In this home, you will find true solace and protection. In this home you will find the kind of parental presence that exercises the perfect mix of liberty and discipline. In this home you will find acceptance of yourself as an individual made in the image of God. In this home you will find a family love that is based on giving and not receiving, on sharing for the mutual family benefit and not for any private agenda; a home where one can feel truly safe, truly loved, and truly important.

(b) No matter what your experience in life is of home, it is a word that God meant to be synonymous with love. To be at home with him is to come into the fullness of a positive and ideal family relationship. Such a home relationship is for all who, in love for Christ and obedience to his teaching, confess him as Lord and Savior and personally invite him into your life.—Richard Daggett

Illustrations

OUT OF WEAKNESS MADE STRONG. In 214 B.C. the authoritarian ruler of China, Emperor Shih Huang Ti, began to build the Great Wall of China. Work went on for generations until this rampart stretched for twelve hundred miles across the north of China, and it seemed as if everything were secure behind it. The wall would keep out the Mongol Tartar! But it did not do so, because the enemy finally bribed a gatekeeper and then just walked through the gate. Men may sit down behind a Maginot Line of apparent strength and security and find that after all it is not sufficient for their protection.—Jack Finegan

THE GOD WHO WAITS. There is a Jewish Hasidic story of a rabbi's son who came in drenched with tears from a game of hide-and-go-seek with some neighborhood playmates. When his father asked him what was the matter, his son told him that he had hidden as was expected but that no one had bothered to seek him. The rabbi drew his son to himself and tenderly told him that now, perhaps, he could for the first time know how the dear Lord felt who also hid himself in order to be sought and who was still waiting in vain for men to seek him.—Douglas V. Steere

Sermon Suggestions

GOD AND FAITH. TEXT: Luke 17:5–10. (1) The problem of faith. (2) The potential of faith, verse 6. (3) The focus of faith, Mark 11:22. (4) The prayer of faith, Mark 11:24.

DOWN AND OUT IN JERUSALEM. TEXT: Lam. 1:1–6. (1) Jerusalem can represent our dreams, our ideals, and our hopes. (2) This Jerusalem may suffer almost unbelievable misfortune. (3) Yet there is hope in the mercy of the God who reigns forever (see Lam. 5:19–22).

Worship Aids

CALL TO WORSHIP. "Though I walk in the midst of trouble, Thou wilt revive me" (Ps. 138:7a NAS).

INVOCATION. O Almighty God, who pourest out on all who desire it the Spirit of grace and of supplication: deliver us, when we draw near to thee, from coldness of heart and wanderings of mind, that with steadfast thoughts and kindled affections we may worship thee in spirit and in truth; through Jesus Christ our Lord.—*Book of Common Prayer*

OFFERTORY SENTENCE. "If you would enjoy ample rations in my House, then pay all your tithes into the treasury, and see what I will do, says the Lord of hosts; see if I will not then open the very sluices of heaven to pour a blessing down for you, a harvest more than enough" (Mal. 3:10 MOFFATT).

OFFERTORY PRAYER. O God, who has blessed us abundantly with inner joy and an outer supply of all good things, we bring you now our gifts in response to the message of your Word and in gratitude for your help in our poor attempts to do your will. May these offerings become streams of influence from this church to build and nurture your kingdom and to redeem our broken world; through Jesus our Lord.—Donald Macleod

PRAYER.

O God, our Father, we are helpless without your help.
Unless you help us,
we can see the ideal,
but we cannot reach it;
we can know the right,
but we cannot do it;
we can recognize our duty,
but we cannot perform it;
we can seek the truth,
but we can never wholly find it.
All our lives we are haunted by the difference between what we ought to do and what in fact we can do.
By your Holy Spirit,
Enlighten our minds,
that we may reach beyond guessing to knowing, and beyond doubting to certainty.
Purify our hearts,
that the wrong desires may not only be kept under control,
but may be completely taken away.
Strengthen our wills,
that we may pass beyond resolving to doing, and beyond intention to action.
By your Holy Spirit,
Break for us the habits we cannot break;
Conquer for us the fears we cannot conquer;
Calm for us the worries we cannot still;
Soothe for us the sorrows no human comfort can ease;
Answer for us the questions no human wisdom can answer.

O God, our Father, this day we rest our weakness in your strength and our insufficiency in your completeness. Take us, and do for us what we cannot do, and make us what we cannot be; through Jesus Christ our Lord.—William Barclay

LECTIONARY MESSAGE

Topic: Grace, Humility, and Courage

TEXT: 2 Tim. 1:1–14

I. The holy calling from God. Paul, in writing to his son in the faith, is intent on strengthening Timothy's practical work among his people. Paul's mention of *stirring up* the gift of God, of the *spirit of fear*, of *being ashamed* of the testimony of the Lord or of Paul's imprisonment, may indicate his concern that Timothy may be hesitant and unsure in his proclamation of a gospel powerful enough to command people's lives for God.

(a) The basis of both Paul's and Timothy's ministry, and also that of the whole Christian community, is that the calling is holy, coming from the heart of God for his own service. There is in the holiness of the calling a love for the whole earth's people, a life of service dedicated and set apart from the lures to sin and challenges to faith that life presents. The holiness of the calling is in the power, sacred in its nature, committed in its purpose, which God bestows. It is in the discipline of serious and orderly thought, convictions of truth that can uphold the spirit in the struggle with error. It is in the sense of victorious suffering, if need be, to see the faith professed by many.

(b) The holy calling is a claim on life, an appointment received by Paul and now transmitted through the Holy Spirit to Timothy, to be God's messenger, revealing the mystery of godliness as Christ has revealed it to the nations of the world. It is a commitment to the work of proclamation of God's loving redemption—no matter what the difficulties. It involves teaching, for, unless his subjects are aware of the meaning of life and its pitfalls and of the God who made it for his love, they will have no use for his gospel.

II. The purity of the grace of God.

(a) Paul declares that the calling is according to God's own purpose and grace, not according to our works. I take the "our" to include the works of all humankind, not just of Paul and Timothy, as in Titus 3:4–5: "the kindness and love of God toward *man* appeared, not by works of righteousness *we* have done, but according to his mercy."

(b) The meaning and intent here are not to apply to the controversy of works *vs.* grace but are to be taken as an emphatic statement of the positive purity and power of the grace of God, which reaches us in total absence of our qualification. It stresses that we have no merit deserving of God's favor and cannot have it, even if we present him the best of lives. Paul clarifies the basis for grace as being not in us but in God.

III. The eternal purpose of grace.

(a) The continuity of grace in the Old and New Testaments is clear in verse 9. Without that continuity, there would have been no chosen people; no salvation from the flood (Gen. 6:8); no covenant (Gen. 17:2); no exodus from Egypt (Exod. 15:13; "mercy" in the Old Testament is equivalent to "grace"); no protection in the wilderness (Deut. 7:7); no victory in the land of God's choice; no help in their struggles in Canaan; no plan of salvation revealed fully in the Lord Jesus Christ after being implicit in all God's dealings with Israel; no life and work—or death on the cross—of God's Son, Jesus Christ; no St. Paul; no setting aside the law's due punishment for sins (Rom. 3:21–24), now forgotten and overlooked; no personal victory over sin (Gal. 1:15); no individual salvation (our v. 9); no springing up of faith (Eph. 1:19); no holiness or sanctified living (1 Thess. 5:23).

(b) Some hold that God's grace is "irresistible." But whether it is or not, it works through a person's choice. One must take the action of confessing faith through grace. Grace certainly is "prevenient" in the process, but one's decision must follow for grace to find its home in the heart. It might be comparable to a concert for which a ticket is required but for which tickets are free for the asking. With God's grace, there will always be a reservation available. If a person is not aware of grace, he or she will emphasize human works; if aware of grace, he or she attributes all to it. Grace always proceeds from power to weakness, from greatness to the lesser, and from wealth to poverty.—John R. Rodman

SUNDAY: OCTOBER FIFTEENTH

SERVICE OF WORSHIP

Sermon: Guilt and Forgiveness

TEXT: Gen. 3:10

Annie Dillard tells about a little girl who was standing in a garden with her doctor, seeing for the first time in her life. She had been blinded by cataracts since birth, and a recent operation had cleared them from her eyes. In front of her was a peach tree, which she, seeing now, proceeded to touch and examine. The ripe peaches gleamed in the sunlight. Amazed by it all, the little girl named it "the tree with the lights on it."[6] That little girl sensed heaven as she looked and marveled.

My text is also about a garden and newly opened eyes. But these eyes were filled with tears from too much seeing. These were the eyes of Adam, a man who stood shaken, naked, and trying to hide himself. He was appalled by the ugliness

[6]"Sight into Insight," *Harper's,* February 1974, 45.

of himself as a sinner. He was shaken by the horrors of being guilty before God. Adam felt death at work inside him. Guilt usually gives that dread feeling.

I. One of the most painful experiences in life is to feel the awesome burden of being guilty before God. When Adam experienced guilt, he felt insecure. He felt naked before life. He felt exposed to death. Thus he made an attempt to hide himself. Adam did not want an offended God to see him. He did not even want to see himself. He knew he had "fallen." Adam knew that his life was not now on the high level he had previously known.

This man Adam began life on a high level indeed. His had been an unspoiled mind. He had known a native innocence. His conscience had been well informed, and his will was strong. But now he felt broken inside. He had fallen from the heights where he once lived. He had fallen in the sight of God. He had fallen in his own eyes.

The Fall is no strange subject to you, I am sure. We all know about it from our own sad experience of sin and guilt. Like Adam, we too can remember a time of lofty innocence. We too knew the beauty of an unspoiled mind and spirit. But we lost it, much to our sadness and shame.

Yes, Adam's Fall has an understood ring to it. It is no strange subject to us at all. We too fell for Satan's lie and dared to believe that God was trying to hold us back from having something good. If only Adam had believed God! If only we had not acted in our militant impatience with God's way of dealing with us! But selfishness goaded us to anxious thought. It inspired selfish planning. Selfishness led us to defiant decisions, and heavy guilt was the result. O how hard we fell! Like Adam, we knew that we were no longer what we once had been.

II. God intended that we should be figures of dignity. God gave us humans an exalted position in the world. We were given the needed capacities to handle ourselves and our ordained tasks. God made us with abilities to respond thoughtfully to life. God gave us freedom to affirm ourselves, reflect on our living, relate to each other, and walk and work with the Divine Being. This indeed is our dignity.

But what God gave to be our dignity has become our misery. Our freedom was given to be a power rightly understood and wisely used. But pride did its deadly work in us all, and we became guilty of sin. Søren Kierkegaard called pride the "arrogant satisfaction of standing alone."[7] The tragedy is that the sinner dares to stand alone even against God.

We are rightly appalled by heady tyrants, arrogant dictators, and, on a smaller scale, heedless bullies. But the greatest enemy to you and me is pride, with its arrogant satisfactions and selfishness. It is pride that lets us honor ourselves, misuse our freedom, and disregard God. Were it not for conscience and the guilt that comes when we sin and go our own way, we humans would keep on going our way—undisturbed, unheeding, uncaring, ungodly, unchanged.

But God has let us experience guilt. Through this painful inward look, God has let us see ourselves as he sees us—disobedient, fallen, unworthy, and needing forgiveness—and our dignity restored.

The experience of guilt is a sign that God is not through with us. Guilt is a token of God's continuing respect for our possibilities. Guilt reminds us of the red light we violated; it tells us why the siren of conscience is ringing so loudly within us. Guilt is an agent of God to remind us that we have moved beyond our limits.

Guilt also reminds us of our lost dignity. It is a call from God to help us reflect, repent, and seek forgiveness. Guilt is God's way to remind us that we were made for something higher and better than sin.

III. Writer Loren Eiseley recently explained how he began seriously to study human life and behavior. Something happened early in his boyhood years that

[7]*The Journals of Søren Kierkegaard,* ed. and trans. by Alexander Dru (London: Oxford University Press, 1938), 44.

made him want to know just how humans became such dangerous creatures in the world.

It all began when as a young lad Eiseley caught sight of a dead turtle beside a stream. He and his pal stopped and picked the turtle up to look at it. They discovered that someone had shot the turtle with a repeating rifle, stitching a row of bullet holes across the turtle's back. As young Eiseley finally lowered the dead turtle into the stream to be carried away by the water current, he and his pal headed for home, brokenhearted and asking why that rifleman had to do such a deed. Eiseley commented about it, "From that moment, I think, I began to grow up."[8]

When he reached home young Eiseley told his father about what he had seen. The two of them sat down together, and the father informed his son about the silliness and sinfulness of humanity; he tried to help his son understand that human beings are problem creatures.

Eiseley reports his father's advice as the discussion ended:

You will learn in time there is much pain here. Men will give it to you; time will give it to you; and you must learn to bear it all, not bear it alone, but be the better for the wisdom that may come to you if you watch and listen and learn. Do not forget the turtle, nor the ways of men. They are all orphans and they go astray; they do wrong things. Try to see better.[9]

Yes, "there is much pain here," and a lot of it comes from human failures, selfishness, and sins. "The ways of men" are silly and sinful. Humans do go astray. Yes, some act like orphans. People do wrong things.

The Bible tells us that it does not have to be that way. Guilt comes to prod us to seek forgiveness and a needed lift after a sad "fall." God has made it possible for us to rise from our failures and be forgiven for our sins.

[8]"The Cosmic Orphan: Reflections on Man's Uncompleted Journey Through Time," *Saturday Review/World,* February 23, 1974, 16.
[9]Eiseley, "Cosmic Orphan," 17.

We are not orphans. You and I have a heavenly Parent. Adam knew this, which is why he tried to hide. Adam felt unworthy of God's pure eyes. He had sinned and did not feel like a son. Adam was deep in guilt; he had failed God's trust. He had fallen from favor.

Adam had known, seen, felt, and enjoyed a status and relationship with God that were incomparably great, and now that he had lost them he felt like nothing when he remembered what he had lost. Thus his hiding and his deep fears. "I heard the sound of thee in the garden, and I was afraid, because I was naked; and I hid myself."

Are you burdened by guilt? Are you trying to hide from God? Are you appalled by your unworthiness? Do you need to be forgiven? Do you want another go at life as God intended it for you?

The gospel tells you that God wants you to have another go at life. All you need to do is return to God, confessing your sins and seeking his forgiveness. God still forgives. God still removes guilt. God still restores us to dignity.—James Earl Massey

Illustrations

WHERE LOVE MEETS SIN. In a home where love meets sin, if that love be a pure love, at the junction of that love and that sin suffering ensues, a cross is set up. And the purer the love, the more poignant the cross. This is not something extraneous and imposed on life; it is written in the makeup of our being and in the constitution of our relationships. It is the very nature of love to insinuate itself into the sins and sorrows of others. All loving goodness in moral natures has "the doom of bleeding upon it." It cannot be love and stay out; and if it gets in, it suffers.

This world is a human family; God is our Father. He is love, and when that love meets our sin—as it did in the Incarnation—at the junction of the two a cross is set up. That white love crimsons into a cross. God being what he is and we being what we are, the cross is inevitable. This is not something read into the account by loving hearts. It is written in the constitution of the nature of God and in the inner inevitabilities of our relationship with him.—E. Stanley Jones

THE CONVERSION OF C. S. LEWIS. You must picture me alone in that room in Magdalen, night after night, feeling, whenever my mind lifted even for a second from my work, the steady, unrelenting approach of him whom I so earnestly desired not to meet. That which I greatly feared had at last come upon me. In the Trinity term of 1929 I gave in, and admitted that God was God, and knelt and prayed: perhaps, that night, the most dejected and reluctant convert in all England. I did not then see what is now the most shining and obvious thing; the divine humility that will accept a convert even on such terms. The prodigal son at least walked home on his own feet. But who can duly adore that love that will open the high gates to a prodigal who is brought in kicking, struggling, resentful, and darting his eyes in every direction for a chance of escape? The words *compelle intrare,* compel them to come in, have been so abused by wicked men that we shudder at them; but, properly understood, they plumb the depth of the divine mercy. The hardness of God is kinder than the softness of men, and his compulsion is our liberation.—C. S. Lewis

Sermon Suggestions

THIS FOREIGNER. TEXT: Luke 17:11–19. (1) Then: It was a foreigner, a Samaritan, not one of the "chosen people," who saw the work of God in his life and praised God for it. (2) Always: God continues to surprise with unexpected gracious acts, for example, the calling of Moses, David, Jesus, Saul of Tarsus, Christians of every generation. (3) Now: God can be glorified today in (a) redeemed sinners, (b) simple believers, (c) all kinds of people who become instruments of God's power and love.

MAKING THE BEST OF IT. TEXT: Jer. 29:1, 4–7. (1) There is a sense in which we can understand injustice, persecution, and suffering as happening in the providence of God. (2) Life, however, must be lived as productively and meaningfully as possible under these less-than-ideal conditions. (3) In all circumstances, one may live with openness for the present and the future, for we always have to do with "the Lord of hosts, the God of Israel."

Worship Aids

CALL TO WORSHIP. "Make a joyful noise unto God, all ye lands: sing forth the honor of his name: make his praise glorious" (Ps. 66:1–2).

INVOCATION. Lord, our joy and praise are often muted, for our failures and our guilt depress our spirits. But we are told that there is forgiveness with you, that you may be revered and obeyed. By your cleansing love, blot out our transgressions and enable us to worship you in spirit and in truth—and with joy.

OFFERTORY SENTENCE. "Offer the right sacrifices to the Lord, and put your trust in him" (Ps. 4:5 TEV).

OFFERTORY PRAYER. Eternal God, from whom we have received generously all things whereof we are glad, we worship thee not only with our substance but chiefly with the offering of ourselves to thee in service. Bless these gifts, the symbols of our sacrifice and toil; enlarge them in spiritual usefulness for thy causes and our need throughout the world. In Christ's name we pray.—Donald Macleod

PRAYER. Eternal Father, whose care for your children is deeper than our poor human nature can ever know, we approach your mercy seat on bended knee and trusting firmly in the fullness of your grace. We turn to you in sincerity, but our story and our works are tinged with shame. Time and again our foolish thoughts and actions have broken our bond with our true home, where you are parent, Redeemer, and friend. We pledge ourselves and resolve to do good, but our bad habits are so ingrained we are unable by ourselves to break away. We promised you yesterday to be heroic servants of your will and truth today, but we find ourselves now disabled in our moral fiber and victims of our own caprice. Tomorrow will be another day, but we lack the stamina to put our lives on the line in faith, and we hesitate even to venture because we expect to fail you again. Come, O God, in your wisdom and convince us of our sin and at the same time lead us in our thinking and praying into the very secret of your love. Forgive us and cleanse us and give us another chance. Live within us and make us strong in the face of every temptation. May we accept Christ and his promise to plead for us before you, and in our daily surrender may our lives be an offering to his name.—Donald Macleod

LECTIONARY MESSAGE

Topic: The Life of Truth

TEXT: 2 Tim. 2:8–15

This passage contains the words that, in Greek, form the motto over the main entrance to Louisville's Southern Baptist Theological Seminary, "*Orthotomounta ton logon tes aletheias*" (rightly dividing the Word of truth). And these words ought indeed to guide and inspire all ministers of the Word of God, ought to form the ideals of their commitment and of their arduous hours of effort. The words have wide implications.

I. The minister must understand the truths of God's Word.

(a) As well as or more than every other Christian, the minister must have strong biblical knowledge. But knowledge of the Word, while basic, is not the final fulfillment of the purpose of God's Word. All Christians, especially ministers, must be deeply, personally conscious of the eternal essence of its offer of salvation and its timely office in the cleansing of their own soul and life and must accept Christ's grace revealed in it.

(b) Understanding the Word means to grasp in all its glory the significance of Christ's experience of being raised from the dead, when he, as a fully human person, of the lineage of David, becomes the exemplary reward of the promise for all who strive lawfully or labor diligently. The Gospel of Paul fully embodied both Christ's human lineage and his Resurrection from the common fate of humans.

(c) Understanding the Word means also discovering the relation of the gospel of Christ to all those faithful of old, who labored under the bondage of legalism, yet with the air of God's mercy and grace in their lungs and faith in their hearts. Just as Paul the prisoner knows the limitless, boundless freedom of God's Word for the world's redemption, so all his servants know release from the bondage of error, falsehood, myth, deceit, and perversion of truth in all its forms.

II. The minister must be an agent of the worldwide acceptance of the Word.

(a) If ministers are to handle aright the Word of truth, they must be hungry for the response of its intended beneficiaries, "enduring all things for the elect's sake," not only preaching in freedom but also explaining the earth-shaking and tradition-defying elements of the faith, its tenets and doctrines, which God has revealed only in his Word. They must write its meaning on their heart and spell it out in their life. Thus, the success of their work will be to them like the signs rewarding the good soldier (v. 3), the athlete (v. 5), and the farmer (v. 6).

(b) Ministers also need to see some fruit of their labors. Of course, the fruit is for eternity and will be enjoyed eternally, but it also needs to be seen while life yet lasts, for there is a beginning of eternal life evident while we are in the flesh. What a reassurance it is to know that God is abidingly faithful even if we suffer lapses. That is part of the confidence that keeps us loyal and strong.

(c) "Rightly dividing the word of truth" implies freedom from quarrels about words "to no profit." Of course, discussion may become heated when arguments arise because of incomplete understanding or even of doubt about the key words of our faith and life. And, indeed, our grasp of, our inferences from, and our attitudes toward the great words of Christianity determine the atmosphere and the direction of our lives. They do need to be as clear as possible and to be verified and revivified constantly. What the earnest minister must be careful of is not to fall into sophistries, formulary thinking, overly figurative language, or too easy interpretations of words about deep and eternal subjects. In their fulfillment of Paul's instruction, ministers are to be diligent in making the path of life as clear as possible to all those they can reach, so that they will have no cause for shame under the examination of their life's work.—John R. Rodman

SUNDAY: OCTOBER TWENTY-SECOND

SERVICE OF WORSHIP

Sermon: Can Love Be Legislated?

TEXT: John 13:31–35

Every society and culture needs its code of law. The laws of our land give us criteria by which to govern the behavior of its people toward one another. As complex as our legal system is, it can be basically reduced to a single definition of purpose, that being that it discerns acceptable behavior from unacceptable behavior.

We need our laws and rules. But there is a limit to what the law can accomplish. While it can dictate to us what we can and can't do, it is basically unable to dictate to us what we can or can't feel, or what we can or can't think. In effect, laws can only be used to directly influence matters of behavior, and while this may have an indirect effect on the way people think and feel, it is unable to legislate on this level.

Closer to home, we have an increasing number of antidiscrimination laws being put into effect each year. These laws govern the behavior of people toward others of a different race or gender or religious and political belief. But while you can legislate against prejudiced behavior, giving people a foundation on which to stand if they feel they have been discriminated against, the law is at a loss to directly affect the inward feelings of prejudice and superiority that some people continue to feel. At best we can only hope that these laws will affect the way future generations think and feel as they grow up in a society that takes legal action against the overt abuse of human rights.

I. This is the contrast that Jesus was drawing for us when he said, "You have heard the law: thou shalt not kill; but I say to you that whoever is angry is in danger of the judgment." In other words, while the laws of society govern the behavior of its people, God discerns very clearly on how the spirit of the law is honored. The laws of his kingdom have jurisdiction in matters of the heart.

(a) There is an unsearchable depth of power and meaning in Jesus' words when he said to his disciples: "A new commandment I give unto you, that you love one another." Commandment to the disciples meant "the law." It was not something to simply be agreed with; it was something to be obeyed, something for which there were consequences. When Jesus used the word *commandment* with these people, it was invested with the power of law and the expectation of its being upheld.

(b) Basic acceptable and legal behavior is quite clearly defined in the commandments. So what is this "new commandment," that we love one another? C'mon Jesus, give us something we can work with here. What new thing do we do to obey this commandment? What is the appropriate outward behavior that it dictates? But there was something much more holistic about this new commandment. To love one another went so far beyond acting and reacting to those around us. This law invaded the very depths of our beings; this law presumed to have jurisdiction over the way we think, the way we feel, over our opinions, our prejudices and biases, our concepts of superiority and our burden for need, over the way every fiber of our being, both inward and outward, responded to the world around us.

II. To those with only an earthly heart this must have been initially experienced as a commandment outside the realm of realism, outside the boundaries of possibility.

(a) But this is a new commandment. This is one that defines acceptability in the kingdom of God. This law doesn't only govern over your outward life; this law has dominion over your inward life, including your thoughts, your feelings. This is the commandment of holistic perfection. It clarifies the true parameters of the state of sinless perfection that God deems acceptable for life in his eternal presence. It clarifies to us that while religion and law may exercise lordship over our actions, over the way we live, Christ wants lordship over everything we are. It is the law of the spirit and not simply the law of the letter.

(b) The more that I contemplate this new commandment, the less I consider myself to be saved, and the more I consider myself as in the process of being saved. Behavior, the way we live, the rules we adhere to, the laws we live by—these are only the tip of the iceberg that represents our whole person. But the law of love, this new commandment, should demonstrate to us that Christ wants lordship over it all, above and beneath the surface.

III. As we contemplate the overwhelming fullness of this law, I encourage you to begin taking stock of the feelings that exist inside you toward others. Let us resolve to work with God as he works to change these hearts of stone. Let us begin to be sensitive to the lordship that sin has enjoyed over even our inner world and open up these areas of our lives to the healing and saving light of God's love that he may become Lord of all.

The law of love, the new commandment, is not fulfilled only in the realm of our actions and behaviors. To begin to fulfill this new commandment, we need a new life, we need a new heart, we need a new Lord, even Jesus Christ the Savior. In the process of our salvation, may we seek to give him lordship of all that we are, that we may love one another with the fullness by which he loved us and gave himself for us, that we might know life.—Richard Daggett

Illustrations

MARTIN LUTHER KING AND ROSA PARKS. Martin was prepared to lead, but it was not he who began the civil rights movement. It was Rosa Parks, a seamstress. Having been loved, she loved herself and all those who were yearning for home in our public household. One day they said to her, "You have to move to the back of the bus." And she said, "No, my feet are tired, and I'm not going to move." She could no longer be controlled by her guilt and her fear of death. And her act was experienced by millions of people as the love by which we could do justice.—M. Douglas Meeks

LOVE AND FREEDOM. Love for a friend takes away some of one's freedom, to be sure, but it gives one a greater freedom. A person grow, learns, and experiences more because he loves, all of which releases him for larger liberty. If he would not consent to be bound by his love, he could not taste the higher freedom.—Rollo May

Sermon Suggestions

THE LAW IN THE HEART. TEXT: Jer. 31:27–34. The New Testament shows how it works. (1) It is based on a love relationship (John 14:15). (2) It is the fruit of the Spirit (John 14:16; Gal. 5:16, 18, 22–25).

REQUIREMENTS OF THE SPECIALLY CALLED. TEXT: 2 Tim. 3:14–4:5, especially 4:2. (1) Proclamation. (2) Persistence. (3) Patience.

Worship Aids

CALL TO WORSHIP. "I have not departed from thy judgments: for thou hast taught me. How sweet are thy words unto my taste! yea, sweeter than honey to my mouth!" (Ps. 119:102–103).

INVOCATION. Almighty God, so stir in our souls that our voices will sing thy praise, our minds will ponder thy precepts, and our wills will embrace thy will, through the Spirit and the Son, who seal salvation in seeking hearts.—E. Lee Phillips

OFFERTORY SENTENCE. "Lay not up for yourselves treasure upon earth, where moth and rust doth corrupt, and where thieves break through and steal: but lay up for yourselves treasures in heaven, where neither moth nor rust doth corrupt, and where thieves do not break through nor steal: for where your treasure is, there will your heart be also" (Matt. 6:19–21).

OFFERTORY PRAYER. Lord, help us to understand what we do now in the presenting of our offerings to you: we are, all of us, participants in the preaching and teaching commanded by Christ for the purpose of bringing to maturity in him those who hear and learn. To that end, bless those of us who preach and teach, bless our schools for training ministers and missionaries and laypeople, bless those who facilitate the kingdom work of us all, and make these gifts useful to see your purpose accomplished.

PRAYER. Eternal holy love, God Most High, we seek to worship thee not only in words and outward form but also in the depths of our spirit and in truth. We have only one offering; it is our poor selves; we give thee but thine own. We know only one way to thee: the way of Jesus, the attitude of sonship and of childlike trust.

The perplexities of our strange natures drive us to thee. We cannot understand ourselves. Glorious gleams and darkest shadows chase across our hearts; conflicts rage there while we stand helpless aside; within is no rest, without is no hope. Unless thou canst rest us, O our God, we are exiles of eternity, homeless in infinite space.

The path to thee has been torturous and steep, our prayers fashioned in agony and moistened with tears. Help us to see that the path as well as the goal is thyself; the prayer thine, as the answer is thine. End our search by beginning thine. Steal upon us like the grace of summer evenings, like the dew on parched ground, like warm winds from sunnier lands. Lift our eyes to the hills, touch our aspirations, rest our longings in thyself, for thou hast made us.—W. E. Orchard

LECTIONARY MESSAGE

Topic: Faith Vindicated

TEXT: Luke 18:1–8 (Jer. 31:27–34; 2 Tim. 3:14–4:5)

In the parable of the persistent widow and the unjust judge, Jesus again argues from the lesser to the greater in order to illustrate the eschatological mercy of the heavenly Father toward his elect (cf. 11:13). The motive for the parable is literally stated "that it is necessary for them to pray and not to weary" (v. 1). Jesus gives assurance that God "will do the avenging of his elect," responding "in quickness" to their pleas (vv. 7–8).

I. Indifferent judge. As an impartial arbiter and advocate of fair play, a judge was expected to advance appropriate compensation for the poor and helpless. Apparently devoid of religious principle and public conscience, this particular office holder was esteemed by the community more for his authority than for his character. Unconcerned with the plight of an unimportant widow, the judge postponed justice in his court.

The judge represents the nightmare of the needy; he lacked respect for humanity and reverence for divinity. By design or accident, people of influence can obstruct holy purposes and confound the best intentions of human teaching into the narcissisms of cultural mythology (2 Tim. 4:2–4). Nevertheless, followers of Jesus must not allow themselves to be bound by such hindrances but should persevere with hopeful fidelity.

II. Persistent widow. The first-century world had few societal safeguards for a widow beyond familial care. In a legal battle without the weapons of bribery, coercion, or public opinion, this widow resorted to blatant nagging, ultimately "causing trouble" for the callous judge (v. 5; cf. 11:5–8). Born of despair, her strategy worked when the relenting official finally avenged her.

Although possibly culpable, the parable presumes the widow's innocence without expressly exonerating her manipulative method. Her perseverance, however, is more than a laudable facet of function, since it is analogous to the unyielding faith of followers. Disciples clamor, yet they are far more secure in the primary care of the Lord, who hears, cares, and responds.

III. Just God. In anthropomorphic comparison, the Lord judges in love and compassion, listening patiently and vindicating swiftly. Unlike the earthly counterpart, sovereign God is righteous, not subject to manipulation, but revered and respected by his prayerful and faithful elect. Their hope is the new covenant of the coming Lord, who is known by all, from the least to the greatest (Jer. 31: 27–34).

The concluding question haunts the heart of every hearer. The elect are accountable to serve in suffering. Such final vindication is superfluous for those who have avoided the struggle amidst the unrighteous, whose faith has not been purified by persecution. While the promised judgment by the Son of man brings certain justice against opponents of the kingdom, the presence of faith on earth is an unresolved matter.—Daniel E. Hatfield

SUNDAY: OCTOBER TWENTY-NINTH

SERVICE OF WORSHIP

Sermon: When Thanks Are Not Enough

TEXT: Luke 18:9–14

A missionary on furlough told me this story. He was home from the foreign mission field and spent his weekends speaking in churches about his work. One Sunday he dressed early and drove three hundred miles to preach morning and night at a little church far away. As he was leaving that evening, the church treasurer slipped an envelope into his hand and told him he hoped he would come back again. The preacher placed the envelope in his pocket and forgot about it. Hours later, when he finally arrived home and was getting ready for bed, he remembered the check. He pulled it out in the semidark bedroom and stared at it. Across the line where the amount was supposed to be had been scrawled: "A Million Thanks." In the corner was the name of the church and a Scripture verse. He thought he must be dreaming. So he took the check and the envelope into the lighted bathroom so he could see more clearly. He read it again. He held the envelope up to see if he had missed something. The only thing he had to show for that long Sunday's work was that silly check with "A Million Thanks" scrawled across it. Sometimes thanks are not enough.

I. Jesus understood this idea. We find it in a parable toward the end of his ministry. In those last pages of the Gospel you can almost feel the desperation as he tried to squeeze as much as he could out of his few remaining days. And in that setting of great urgency we find a warning about thanks.

Luke called the story a parable. It was addressed "to some who trusted in themselves that they were righteous and despised others." Two men went up to the Temple to pray. The first was a very good man, a Pharisee, which meant he was a keeper of the rules. He was respected, upright, and a pillar of the community.

As the parable opens, this good man is praying. "I thank thee that I am different from all those others, Lord. You wouldn't believe how they act. They extort, they are unjust in their behavior, more than a few of them have committed adultery. Lord, you know me. We've been friends a long time. I fast twice a week. I give tithes of all I get. I thank you, Father."

Jesus made the strangest response to these words. He said the prayer wasn't enough. He said the man's words did not matter. The whole thing was some kind of farce. Not enough, he said. Thanks, but no thanks.

What in the world could be wrong? Something may have been lost in translation. The Pharisee did pray. He thanked God right there in the Temple. He was correct in his evaluation of the others. They were extortioners, unjust, could not be trusted. And, of course, there were the lusty ones. He had always been faithful, at least in his own fashion. He did not lie. He fasted and gave a tithe of all he received. Sounds like a pretty good man. If we had been checking his references, he would get nothing but A's. So what was wrong? And what is the danger that can affect all of us that pray in some temple? When are thanks not enough?

II. Jesus gave a clue to understanding this story in the first verse. He told this parable to "some who trusted in themselves."

(a) *Thanks are not enough when the basis of our trust is only ourselves.* Phillips translates this verse: "He gave this illustration to certain people who were confident of their own goodness."

The target of his prayer was blurred. He trusted in himself. Note the pronouns. "*I* thank God . . . ," "*I* thank thee . . . , " "*I* am not like the others . . . ," "*I* fast . . . ," "*I* give tithes of all *I* have." Always watch the pronouns. They betray us every time. Thanks are not enough when the focus is on "me." Beating our chests, we betray our own ultimate allegiance.

(b) But trust is not the only problem here. Jesus told this parable to "some that were righteous. " *Thanks are not enough when we are confident of our own righteousness.* The Jerusalem Bible translates these words: "those who pride themselves on being virtuous." But the New English Bible may have it best: "They are sure of their own goodness."

But all this seems quite unfair. Isn't the result of our faith to make us good people? What's wrong with being righteous? The man in the Temple did seem to have a lot going for him. He fasted. He gave tithes. Surely that ought to count for something. But one translation reminds us that we can have "too high a regard for our own goodness."

Remember what Jesus told them in the Sermon on the Mount? "Except your righteousness exceed the scribes and Pharisees, you will never enter the kingdom of God." Do you see what he says? There is righteousness and there is righteousness. It's not all good.

Some of the meanest people claim to be Christian. Born again. They have never forgotten a single error somebody else committed. "Do you remember," they say, "back in 1954 when you. . . . " Or they say: "It reminds me of last time . . . ." "Last time?" you ask. "Yes, don't you remember what you did in February of 1965?" And people all over the community whisper: "Look what good Christians they are. The best people in this town." Real Christians? Their lips are pursed. Never having any fun. Looking for sin around every corner. *Real* righteousness, indeed.

The problem with these folk is that they are sure of their own goodness. *Dead* sure. But they have never seen through a glass darkly—they know everything! They have forgotten that there is a righteousness that is very much like filthy rags. Thank you, we need no one but ourselves.

But this Pharisee, this man of God, so confident that he could have written the book, had never heard Jesus say: "I am not come to call righteous but sinners to repentance." And he had never heard those terrible words of Paul: "There is none righteous . . . no, not one."

We're all the same. The ground at the foot of the cross is level. We all need. And so we don't come to church with our arms loaded with our own goodness. It is not enough. We simply come and stand in the silence and ponder the mystery until by some miracle we really know in our heart of hearts that it is all given. It really is grace after all.

(c) But there is more. "He also told this parable to some who trusted themselves that they were righteous and despised others." *Thanks are not enough when it cuts us off from our brothers and sisters.*

In Jesus' time, the pious Jews would pray: "O God, I thank thee that I am not a dog, a Gentile, or a woman." Our Lord told this parable to some who looked down on others.

One Sunday a Sunday school teacher was teaching her class of boys and girls this story of the Pharisee and the tax collector. She painted the Pharisee as such a mean man and the tax collector as a good person. And when she had finished the story, she said, "Now, boys and girls, let's get down on our knees and thank God we're nothing like that old mean Pharisee."

It is so easy to miss the point. "I thank God," he prayed, "that I am not like other men." His thanks built barriers and barricades so that his connections with the human family were minimal. Religion that isolates us from our brothers and sisters is a terrible thing. Carson McCullers once wrote: "It is a strange fact of the human race that we all need somebody to look down on."

Will Campbell has had an unusual ministry. For years he published a magazine called *Katallagete,* which means *be reconciled.* He spends most of his time visiting poor blacks and members of the KKK. He ministers to those behind bars and pushes for prison reform. He has been chaplain for some of the country music people. But underneath it all, in his own strange way, he is trying to deal with that larger thanks that makes us one with our brothers and sisters everywhere.

Jesus himself said that real religion ties us to those around us. And this is why he said if you leave your gift at the altar while they're singing the Doxology and go on back to your seat and act as if everything is right between you and somebody else when it is not—it won't count. And somebody spoke up and said, "Do you mean to tell me that large gift I left that could mean so much to so many hungry people won't count?" Jesus shook his head. "It won't count." "Do you mean all those times I starved myself and felt so bad from fasting—do you mean that won't count?" Jesus shook his head. "It won't count. Nothing counts," he said, "except going and getting reconciled as best you can and then coming back and leaving your gift." And Jesus said, "That's what counts."

Our Lord ended his parable by telling of a second man who went up to the Temple to pray. "But the tax collector, standing far off, would not even lift up his eyes to heaven, but beat his breast, saying, 'God, be merciful to me a sinner.' I tell you, this man went down to his house justified rather than the other; for everyone who exalts himself will be humbled, but he who humbles himself will be exalted."

Not chest beating—proud of his own accomplishments—but breast beating—whispering his confession and need to our understanding Father.

That, too, is what really counts. And that is when thanks are always enough.—Roger Lovette

Illustrations

PRAYER AT AN UPPER LEVEL. I suggest that we raise our prayer of thanksgiving to a high Christian level: "O God, I thank you that I *am* like the rest of humankind. I thank you that, like everyone else, I too have been shaped in your image, with a mind to know and a heart to love. I thank you that, like everyone else, I too was embraced by the crucified arms of your Son, I too have him for a brother. I thank you that you judge me, like everyone else, not by my brains or beauty, my skin tone or muscle power, my clothes or my color, the size of my pad or the roar of my Datsun, but by the love that is your gift to me, by the way I share in the passion of your Christ. I thank you that, for all our thousand differences, I am so remarkably like the people all around me.

"I thank you for letting me see that there is a little of the Pharisee in me, that I too have this very human yearning for something that sets me apart from the rest—if only because I am the only Jesuit theologian in residence! If I am to thank you for making me different, let it be because, through your mercy, I am different from what I would have been without you. Thank you, Lord, for making me so splendidly the same as everyone else, because it means I am that much closer to your Son, who became what all of us are: wonderfully and fearfully human. Keep me that way, Lord, and always 'be merciful to me, sinner that I am.' "—Walter J. Burghardt

WHO IS ON TRIAL? I heard once of a salesman who dated a preacher's daughter. He decided he wanted a full report on her, so he hired a private detective to give him a report. The report came back that she was of good reputation, gentle, refined, with many churchgoing friends. The only question mark was a salesman of doubtful reputation who had been seen with her lately.—James E. Carter

Sermon Suggestions

BETTER DAYS AHEAD. TEXT: Joel 2:23–32. (1) God's own people know suffering and loss, whether as a consequence of disobedience or unrelated causes, verse 25. (2) God promises a reversal of fortune, with overwhelming compensations, verses 23–24, 26–27. (3) What happens may be conditional upon repentance, verses 12–13.

ON GETTING FROM HERE TO THERE. TEXT: 2 Tim. 4:6–8, 16–18. (1) Paul's impending departure, verse 6. (2) Paul's strenuous persistence, verse 7. (3) Paul's expected reward, verse 8. (4) Paul's secret of success, verses 16–18.

Worship Aids

CALL TO WORSHIP. "Praise waiteth for thee, O God, in Sion: and unto thee shall the vow be performed. O thou that hearest prayer, unto thee shall all flesh come" (Ps. 65:1–2).

INVOCATION. God of Abraham, Isaac, and Jacob; God of prophets and martyrs: give us courage to obey your Word and power to renew your church, so that we may live in the Spirit, sharing faith with Jesus Christ our Lord.—*The Worshipbook*

OFFERTORY SENTENCE. "Those who are taught the word must share all good things with their teacher" (Gal. 6:6 NRSV).

OFFERTORY PRAYER. O God, we thank you that we are all of us in the ministry of teaching and preaching together. It is a common task. Grant that we may be aware of our stewardship in giving, in living, in teaching, and in receiving; and bless our work together, that in love and joy we may truly share.

PRAYER. O God, we who are bound together in the tender ties of love pray thee for a day of unclouded love. May no passing irritation rob us of our joy in one another. Forgive us if we have often been keen to see the human failings and slow to feel the preciousness of those who are still the dearest comfort of our life. May there be no sharp words that wound and scar and no rift that may grow into estrangement. Suffer us not to grieve those whom thou hast sent to us as the sweet ministers of love. May our eyes not be so holden by selfishness that we know thine angels only when they spread their wings to return to thee.—Walter Rauschenbusch

LECTIONARY MESSAGE

Topic: In Whom Do We Trust?

TEXT: Luke 18:9–14 (2 Tim. 4:6–8; Joel 2:23–32)

The express target of the parable are those who have trusted in themselves while negating the worth of others. These have convinced themselves of their righteousness and superiority over the rest.

With biting irony Jesus distinguished between false and true prayer, between the corruption of the impenitent and the humility of the vindicated. Divine mercy is bestowed upon the sinful seeker before the smug solicitor. In judgment, those esteemed may be condemned and those eschewed may be exalted.

I. Futile soliloquy. Simple grammar reveals the real audience of the Pharisee's prayer, since all five verbs are first-person singular: "I thank," "I am not like," "I fast," "I give," "I gain." The Pharisee prayed to himself, extolling his virtues and deeds by castigating the faults of others. The layman sought acclamation from humanity in the Temple instead of a word from the Lord in his soul (cf. Matt. 6:1–6). He trusted himself, and this spawned his concomitant disdain of others.

The Pharisee presumed himself to be a winner in a competition for good works. Since his legalism only honored results, motives did not matter. Indeed, the self-homage belied any joy of service. Although guilty of sin, he denied it, proud of his comparable merit.

The refusal to confess sin results from the sin of spiritual pride. Usually keynoted by disingenuous humility and capricious catalogs of negative virtues, self-congratulating testimonials evade the candor of truthful reflection. When prayer degenerates into a braggart's soliloquy, God denies justification.

II. Desperate prayer. In stark contrast to an articulate Pharisee stood an extortionist, perhaps unseen in the Temple corridors by a public more impressed with the trappings of piety. So guilty was he that words were inadequate. In simple eloquence the tax collector pleaded to God for mercy and confessed his sin.

The publican presumed his guilt—unscrupulous and unreformed, caught and condemned. With no worthy offering or sacrifice to submit, he humbled himself before God in posture and vocabulary. The sinner moved beyond the despair of self-recrimination and trusted the Lord as the only remedy. Thus, he was justified.

III. God's justification. Two men went to the Temple, but only one prayed. In spite of differences in status and background, both could have voiced genuine prayers, yet only one was willing to humble himself. The one who received exaltation had sought the Lord's mercy and had offered contrite confession. The one who was not justified was guilty of piety that pretended, reveling in futile testimonials.

The redeemed call upon the name of the Lord (Joel 2:32). Free from condemnation, the one who humbly follows Jesus will strive to keep the faith in an ongoing battle (2 Tim. 4:7). Exaltation is granted in grace to all who seek the Lord and his righteousness.—Daniel E. Hatfield

SUNDAY: NOVEMBER FIFTH

SERVICE OF WORSHIP

Sermon: The Love God Does

TEXT: 1 John 4:7–12

I. "God is love." The church believes that. Linda Owens believes that. You and I believe that. Yet the once extraordinarily popular Irish dramatist, poet, and wit Oscar Wilde once said there was enough suffering in any London lane to show God's love is fancy, not fact.[10] Could he be right and we wrong? When times are good it is easy enough to say it: "God is love." When times are tough, though—and times are tough right now for many—the words may stick in our throats and nearly choke us. Say it—"God is love"—when a loved one dies, after "the muffled drum's sad roll has beat the soldier's last tatoo."[11] Say it after "the snuffer [has lowered on some] shining mind to bow and chill the twisting wick of it,"[12] after Alzheimer's, that is. Say it after a young mother in Piscataway, New

[10]Paul Scherer, "The Gospel According to St. Luke: Exposition," in *The Interpreter's Bible,* ed. George Arthur Buttrick, vol. 8 (Nashville: Abingdon Press, 1952), 385.

[11]Theodore O'Hara, "The Bivouac of the Dead."

[12]Dorothy Thomas, "Far Echo."

Jersey, is kidnaped and knifed to death by a stranger and for no reason.

How can it be true that God is love when, in so many places in our world today, "famine, sword, and fire crouch for employment?"[13] How can it be true that God is love when in a land that used to love to sing, "give me your tired, your poor, your huddled masses yearning to breathe free,"[14] refugees from famine, sword, and fire are often neglected or harassed now, instead of helped, sent back to the places of terror and deprivation from which they have fled? No love for them? Shakespeare put it in a stark and chilling phrase when he said, "All our yesterdays have lighted fools the way to dusty death."[15] Life, good Lord, we pray; if there is no sense in it, there can be no love in it. First God must be sane; only then can God be love.

So it is possible to sit in the center of one's own universe daring God to explain the divine self, like the poet Robert Frost speaking to a distant star: "Use language we can comprehend, tell us what elements you blend," and like Frost's star, God may seem to give us "strangely little aid,"[16] no clear answers to our hardest questions, no settled way of salvation. And out there somewhere, far away from heaven's white light, "a grave for all [our] bright hopes with the heavy earth falling."[17] Is that it? And, if that is it, no wonder we wonder why, why anything? Why has this marriage soured? Why has learning lost its thrill? Why has love lost its value? Now we're at the bottom line, aren't we? If God is love, there ought to be some payoff for those of us who believe that he is.

II. Could it be that God will not define divine love in ways that suit us, in words and actions that appeal to our native instincts? Back in the sixties and seventies love was a "warm fuzzy." Now that's not much, but it does have some value. It's better than a "cold prickly." In the eighties love was romantic again; it was roses and candlelight, tuxedos and evening gowns, a limousine to take you to the prom. In the nineties love has to be made of sterner stuff. We all know that.

Love has to work hard to keep people from harm's way. In Florida people prayed that love would send them deliverance from wind and rain. Then the hurricane came bringing with it destruction such as never before has been seen in this country except, perhaps, during the human havoc of the Civil War nearly a century and a half ago. Then came the Nicaraguan tidal wave, the Hawaiian hurricane, the earthquakes of Egypt, and, through it all, starvation in Somalia and the Sudan, ethnic war in Bosnia-Herzegovina, and our own living and dying seemingly beyond our means. No heaven-sent deliverance from harm.

We plead for a logic to love, yet God fills love with the illogic of sacrifice, suffering, forgiveness, and death. Like the homeless and the dispossessed, it has nowhere to lay its head. "In this is love, not that we love God, but that God loved us." How? With a Christ and a cross, that's how, with a death wretched as any anyone has died, with a silence deep and lonely as human grief—deeper. God is love. God is love. And God loves us. That is the heart and soul of the gospel. God loves us not on our terms but on his own, not according to our wants but according to the measure of divine grace.

Often people ask for far less than God wants to give. They want an answer to the riddle of life. Instead they get life. They want deliverance from death, though there is no deliverance from it. Yet God brings people through death into the divine presence. So death, though inevitable, is not loveless. People want ease; God gives them adventure.

[13]William Shakespeare, *The Life of King Henry the Fifth,* prologue, lines 7–8.

[14]Emma Lazarus, "The New Colossus."

[15]*The Tragedy of Macbeth,* act 5, sc. 5, lines 22–23.

[16]Robert Frost, "Choose Something like a Star."

[17]Paul Scherer, "Let God Be God," in *The Word God Sent* (Grand Rapids: Baker Book House, 1965), 151.

They want the homeless housed and the hungry fed, refugees cared for at last and victims of human and natural disasters guarded from further harm. God gives them the chance to do it. They want things to make them happy. God gives them himself and each other. A great Presbyterian preacher of a generation ago, George Arthur Buttrick, expressed it memorably. He said: "We ask, 'What's the use of religion?' [But] God does not 'use' us, and we may not 'use' [God]. The 'use' is to save us from the utilitarian blasphemy of asking, 'What's the use of religion?' "[18] And, it must be added, "What's love's bottom line?"

In other words, love, as men and women often think of it today, and as you and I perhaps would have it if we could have our druthers, is not God. Instead, God made known to us in Jesus, the Christ, is love. God defines love. Our varied understandings of love do not define God. Love is something God does to us, among us, with us, for us. With love God makes us a divine possession—each of us and all of us together. Do you want to see God's love in action? Look around you. It is what has brought us all together and made us a church. God's love is not the private possession of any of us. It is God's public possession of all of us. For better or worse, for richer or poorer, in sickness and in health, though death us do part, God loves us.

III. Therefore we may love one another, not as well as God loves us, of course, for we are not God. We are very human beings, and our affections run hot and cold. Shakespeare said that "love is not love which alters when it alteration finds."[19] Our love does alter, however, doesn't it? Our caring for one another is not definitive. Now and then men and women have been known to take up their lives for their friends. They even have laid them down for their friends and enemies. But, when faced with such challenges, they also have been tempted to pray, "Not thy will, but mine be done." Was that really the last temptation of Christ? Who has not prayed and acted that way one time or another, wishing to know love, yet hoping to duck what love requires in order to be known: lifelong, life-deep devotion to the other's well-being?

Yet, despite it all, now and then, even when we have encased ourselves in a shell of self-concern, fearing to risk love, there seeps in a need that somehow cannot be neglected, a claim that cannot be refused, an offer of friendship that, for pity's sake, cannot be turned down, something that, instead of making life bearable, makes it inescapable,[20] and God has us, for God's own glory and our neighbor's good, however vacillating our affections. "If we love one another," even if we love one another just a little bit, "God abides in us, and God's love is perfected in us." Think of it: God perfects—or brings to completion—the circle of divine caring in you and in me, in the fellowship of the church, in the midst of the world, in flesh and blood and muscle, in what a poet somewhere has called "the clash and scratch of dirt." God's love is as close as the heartbeat of the person sitting next to you in that pew. It is as hearty as a handshake and the passing of the peace. It is as tight and tender as an embrace.

At the start of this sermon, you will recall, I indicated that Oscar Wilde once said there was enough suffering in any London lane to show that God's love is fancy, not fact. Yet toward that fancy Oscar Wilde himself came at last to stretch out his arms. In a poem, he wrote: "Come down, O Christ, and help me, reach thy hand, for I am drowning in a stormier sea than Simon on thy Lake of Galilee."[21] So Christ came down, not this time to calm the storm but to steady the man in the midst of it, for Oscar Wilde

[18]George Arthur Buttrick, *Sermons Preached in a University Church* (Nashville: Abingdon Press, 1959), 185–186.
[19]Sonnet 116.
[20]Peter S. Hawkins, *The Language of Grace: Flannery O'Connor, Walker Percy, and Iris Murdoch* (Cambridge: Cowley Publications, 1983), 98.
[21]Oscar Wilde, "E Tenebris."

was left to die, frankly, in exile, poverty, and disrepute for a breach of Victorian morality. No longer was he the extraordinarily popular Irish dramatist, poet, and wit.

So Christ comes down to where the most neglected, or abused, or disreputable, or grief-stricken hurt today, down to the streets of cities and towns like Sarajevo, Miami, and Los Angeles, Princeton, Piscataway, and Liberty Corner, down to places where people cry, "Why?" He comes to this sanctuary and to this pulpit, too, to speak to you and me with the rugged, wonderful words of Scripture and with the sometimes clumsy, sometimes eloquent words of us preachers. He comes in unspeakable joy, for he loves us, and in pain, for he loves us as we are, and with a peace that passes understanding. "In this is love, not that we loved God, but that God loved us." And, "if we love one another, God abides in us, and God's love is perfected in us."—Charles L. Bartow

Illustrations

SEMI-CHRISTIAN LIVING. Has your life since baptism been a constant conversion, a ceaseless turning to Christ? I am not suggesting that you have turned totally from him, that you are in a state of serious sin. Quite the contrary. My experience of Christians is very much my experience of myself. If Jesus Christ were to ask me: "Walter, do you love me?" I would respond: "Lord, you know everything; you know well that I love you." But I rarely live the logic of that love. So much of my life is superficial. I mean, so many of my human acts are not fully human, do not engage me as a total person. They do not enslave me to Satan, but neither do they commit me to Christ. The danger in such semi-Christian living was strongly stated in the last book of the Bible, where Christ warns a congregation of Christians: "I know your works: you are neither cold nor hot. Would that you were cold or hot! So, because you are lukewarm, and neither cold nor hot, I will vomit you out of my mouth" (Rev. 3:15–16).—Walter J. Burghardt

LOVE AND PEACE. Two neighbors have quarreled and parted company for some reason or other. Then it occurs to one of them that this situation is just not right. He writes a letter to his former friend suggesting that they make peace. He receives no reply. Come now, he thinks, I must try again. "Let us make peace and resume our former friendly relations." Still no reply. Then the man decides one evening—it is a bitterly cold winter's night with howling wind and snow—to undertake the long journey to the other man's house on foot. He arrives panting, snowed up, and petrified with cold. He repeats by word of mouth his invitation. And now it begins to dawn on his neighbor that he has before him a real human being, frozen, drenched with snow, and panting. Now his heart melts and he takes the invitation seriously. Now he says "Yes."—Emil Brunner

Sermon Suggestions

THE TRIALS OF A TAX MAN. TEXT: Luke 19:1–10. (1) He was despised because of his occupation: (a) working for the occupying power—Rome; (b) being suspect for his honesty. (2) The people would not give him a place for a view of Jesus. (3) However, Jesus was controlled by a higher agenda and treated him differently: (a) offering fellowship; (b) rejecting criticism of this action; (c) bringing salvation and acceptance.

WORTHY OF HIS CALL. TEXT: 2 Thess. 1:1–4, 11–12. Because of: (1) A growing faith. (2) An increasing mutual love. (3) Steadfast faith under persecution and suffering.

Worship Aids

CALL TO WORSHIP. "You are righteous, Lord, and your laws are just. The rules that you have given are completely fair and right" (Ps. 119:137–138 TEV).

INVOCATION. Draw close to us, Lord, as we draw close to you. Meet each of our deep needs and expand our faith. Bring us around to what you want us to see and lead us where you want us to be.—E. Lee Phillips

OFFERTORY SENTENCE. "You excel in so much already, in faith, in power of utterance, in knowledge of the truth, in devotion of every kind, in your loving treatment of us; may this gracious excellence be yours too. I say this, not to lay any injunction on you, but only to make sure that your charity rings true by telling you about the eagerness of others. You do not need to be reminded how gracious our Lord Jesus Christ was; how he impoverished himself for your sakes, when he was so rich, so that you might become rich through his poverty" (2 Cor. 8:7–9 KNOX).

OFFERTORY PRAYER. Merciful God, bless the gifts, the givers, and all who channel this offering into the kingdom's work that those who are the recipients may sense the love of God and recognize the stamp of eternal worth through the cross of Jesus.—E. Lee Phillips

PRAYER. Lord, make us instruments of your peace. Where there is hatred, let us sow love; where there is injury, pardon; where there is discord, union; where there is darkness, light; where there is sadness, joy. Grant that we may not so much seek to be consoled as to console; to be understood as to understand; to be loved as to love. For it is in giving that we receive; it is in pardoning that we are pardoned; and it is in dying that we are born to eternal life.—St. Francis of Assisi

LECTIONARY MESSAGE

Topic: The Place of Lament in the Life of Faith

TEXT: Hab. 1:1–4, 2:1–4

OTHER READINGS: 2 Thess. 1:1–4, 11–12; Luke 19:1–10

Lamentation was a characteristic part of worship in biblical days. About one-third of the psalms are laments. The psalmists were often bitter in their complaints and sometimes confrontive with God. It comes as a surprise today to observe that lament is seldom used in a typical worship service. It seems to be thought impious to question God. Yet hurting and bewildered people attend worship services and often are given no words in the ritual to help voice their hurt. They are given instead words of praise when their hearts are breaking. No wonder so many never return to church, feeling that their hurts have not been taken seriously. It is time to help people learn that it is all right to be honest in church about expressing their feelings.

I. The lament of the prophet (Hab. 1:1–4). Habakkuk lamented the apparent silence and inactivity of the Lord in a context of injustice and violence. Where was the Lord? Why did not the Lord help? What was even more mystifying was the Lord's seeming reluctance to act decisively, resulting in a numbing of the law and a perversion of justice. So far the prophet protests native injustice. But later he questions the Lord's ability to rule the cosmos with justice by asking why the Lord would choose to punish a wayward Israel by means of the ruthless Babylonians. "Why are you silent when the wicked swallows up one more righteous than he?" (1:13).

Of course, the prophet lamented out of his own anguish. But he dared to ask confrontive questions of the Lord because the Lord was a God of promise, the only one who could save and heal. Thus, confrontation may be seen as proof of the prophet's ultimate faith. Perhaps the Lord was more pleased by Habakkuk's probing questions than by any retreat to traditional theology, which would mute the divine-human encounter.

II. The expression of confidence (1:12–13). According to the pattern of the lament, the confrontive question is combined with a strong affirmation of confidence in the Lord's capacity to do what was needed. The statement of confidence is characteristic of the lament in the psalms and keeps the laments from being simply crybaby songs. In the same manner, because the strong confession of faith is combined with the confrontive lament, it is kept from being an unreflective, naive, traditional expression. It is crucial to recognize that because the prophet has such great faith in the Lord, he feels free to ask the hard questions. Such a role was in keeping with his prophetic office to be a mediator between the divine and human spheres.

III. The Lord's response (2:1–4). An important element of the lament was the record of the Lord's response, or at least a reference to an answering oracle. Habakkuk, like the watchman on the wall of the city, stationed himself to be ready for the divine response, which he confidently expected.

Already the Lord had informed Habakkuk about the work that the Lord was accomplishing with the power of the Babylonians (1:5–11), a plan that the prophet had confessed was for Israel's judgment (1:12). But was that all the Lord had in mind? And where was the justice in using a ruthless invader to punish one more righteous than he?

The prophet was not kept waiting for a reply. The Lord told him to write the vision plainly so that it might be read easily. The content of the vision is not given (unless 2:6–19 contain the vision), but it apparently concerned a promise from the Lord that would be the basis for continued faith. The fulfillment of the vision was near and should inspire faith. In that day the one whose life was not upright would fail, but the righteous person would have life because the vision was faithful.

It is the nature of faith that it walks where it cannot see clearly and that it trusts in promises not yet fulfilled. The person of faith is called to commit life fully before all the facts are known. In this context lament and expostulation with God have a proper place, provided the lamenter confesses confidence in God to fulfill the promises. Habakkuk's relationship with the Lord was the healthiest kind, asking probing questions about the divine intention while confessing fully the sovereignty of the Lord. The Lord responds with a faithful vision, making life possible in a troubling time.—Thomas G. Smothers

SUNDAY: NOVEMBER TWELFTH

SERVICE OF WORSHIP

Sermon: The Largest Giver—the Poor Widow

TEXT: Mark 12:43

I. The scene is the Temple of God in Jerusalem. The collection is being taken. Christ is present and is watching the proceedings with keen interest. He always does. He is abidingly interested in our conduct when the offering is taken. He watches with deep concern what we do when we face the collection plate.

(a) Christ is interested in the collection because money is power. Money is pent-up force. It can be used for the retarding of the progress of the kingdom of God. It can be used for the promotion of that kingdom.

(b) Christ is interested in the collection because what we do with our money is an index to our characters. The man who invests largely in the pursuit of pleasure is a pleasure seeker. The man who invests largely in the church of Jesus Christ is quite likely to be a Christian. What a man does with his money is a good indication of what he is.

(c) Not only do we judge ourselves in the presence of the collection plate, but Christ also judges us. He cannot help it. He sees what we give. We call forth either his commendation or his condemnation. We judge ourselves and are judged by our Lord by what we do with the wealth that he has put into our hands.

II. What did Jesus see as he sat over against the treasury?

(a) He saw much that was commendable. He saw many rich men cast their gifts into the treasury. That was fine. There were rich men in that far-off day that were interested in the church of God. Many of them are found in the church, and many of them give of their means to the support of the church.

(b) Not only were the rich men present with their gifts that day, but they were liberal in their giving. "Many that were rich cast in much." These men did not throw in pennies when they might have thrown in dollars. They gave liberally. "Many that were rich cast in much." It was a magnificent offering that was made for the Lord's cause on that day.

(c) But there was one giver who did not cast in much. She was a woman who had suffered. There was not the fraction of a penny in her humble little home. All she had in the world was in her hand. And that was so little that she was half ashamed to give it. And yet she could not withhold it. And so she cast into the treasury two mites, which make a farthing.

(d) Had you been by when this money was counted at the close of the day, you would not have heard any praise for the great gift of this widow. Christ alone could rightly estimate the full value of it. And when he had cast up the amount, he declared, "This poor widow hath cast more in than all they which have cast into the treasury."

III. What was there in this gift of the widow that made it more than all the gifts that the rich cast into the treasury? Certainly it was not more in amount.

(a) It was more because it represented more fidelity on the part of the giver. It was so little that this widow could give. "What are two mites worth toward the carrying on of God's work in the world?" she might have asked. The human thing, therefore, for her to have done was simply to have done nothing. How many take that position! Their name is legion. But what lies back of such conduct? Unfaithfulness. It is not a question of how much good your gift will do to the cause of God. It is a question rather of your fidelity in the handling of that gift for your Lord, however small it may be.

(b) This widow cast in more than all the rest in that her gift was more expensive to herself. There was more sacrifice in what she did.

The gift of the widow was costly. It cost her everything. If there is no sacrifice in our service, if there is no sacrifice in our giving, then it is not Christian. Costless giving may help after a fashion, but it is not beautiful either in the eyes of God or of men. Christ puts his stamp of approval only on the giving that costs. His gifts cost him something. Ours are to cost us something.

(c) This widow gave more than all the rest because there was more love in her giving. Her sacrifice would have gone for nothing had there been no love in it. The richest of gifts are but so much refuse in the sight of God if there is a sordid motive behind them. On the other hand, the smallest gift is beautiful beyond all words if it is given for love's sake.

IV. Now, since this poor widow made the largest gift that was brought to the treasury that day, her story is one full of encouragement for ourselves.

(a) It heartens us because it puts the very poorest of us on an equal footing with the richest. We who have the smallest gifts have exactly the same opportunity of winning God's approval as those who have the largest. Who will be the largest contributor to First Methodist Church this year? It will surely be the one who is most faithful and most sacrificing and most loving in the doing of what he can. The richest man in all the world cannot pass that mark. But the poorest in all the world can reach to it.

(b) This story heartens us because it tells us the very smallest gifts, if they are our best, are not despised. Men may despise them. But this is true only when they fail to understand. Our Lord never fails to understand. Therefore, he never looks upon them with contempt. If two mites are our best, his heart glows with gladness just as much as if we had given millions. And if it be so that we have not even that much, he will receive with gladness whatever we give. "He that giveth acup of cold water shall not lose his reward."

V. Therefore, since God does not despise our gifts, however small, let us see to it that nothing prevents us from offering them. But let us not become pitiful beyond our Lord. He had no hesitancy in accepting the last mite from this poor widow. He will take the last penny you have, and he will do it joyfully.

But this he will do not because he is grasping. He will do it because he knows that it is more blessed to give than to receive. The sureness of your giving conditions the sureness of your receiving. A hand that is wide open to give will be wide open to receive. Therefore our Lord does not hesitate to take our very last mite because such giving does not impoverish us but makes us rich forevermore. Let us therefore aspire to the place of the largest giver, for in so doing we will also win the place of the largest receiver.—Clovis G. Chappell

Illustrations

WHAT MATTERS. A young fellow beat the street car conductor out of his car fare in our city the other day. What said he in excuse for his dishonesty? This: "The street car company is a large corporation. It has ample means. It certainly will not miss the seven cents that I failed to pay it. It does not need an amount so insignificant." But that is not the question. The street car company can get on without his seven cents, but he cannot get on well without being honest.—Clovis G. Chappell

SELF-CENTEREDNESS. Our civilization teaches self-interest as the primary driving motive—"Every man for himself and the devil take the hindmost." But when you do that, the devil takes not only the hindmost but also us all, and especially the one who takes that attitude. And takes him first of all. For the self-centered are the self-disrupted. They are making themselves God, and they are not God, so the universe won't back their way of life.—E. Stanley Jones

Sermon Suggestions

ABOUT THE LIFE TO COME. TEXT: Luke 20:27–38. (1) Life in the age to come will be different from life in this age. (2) The God of both ages is the same gracious God.

HOLD FAST TO THE TRADITIONS. TEXT: 2 Thess. 2:1–5, 13–17 NRSV. (1) What to believe. (2) How to behave. (3) The way to worship (cf. *The New Oxford Annotated Bible,* p. 298 NT).

Worship Aids

CALL TO WORSHIP. "I will extol thee, my God, O king; and I will bless thy name for ever and ever" (Ps. 145:1).

INVOCATION. O God, your name is greater and more glorious than all we can imagine. We worship you, we praise you. Your very self is more than anything we could ask for or desire. We rejoice in only knowing you, the Eternal One.

OFFERTORY SENTENCE. "Give, and it shall be given unto you; good measure, pressed down, and shaken together, and running over, shall men give into your bosom. For with the same measure that ye mete withal it shall be measured to you again" (Luke 6:38).

OFFERTORY PRAYER. Gracious Lord, while knowing you is better than anything that you can give us, we do know that we receive many earthly blessings and material gifts and that there are surprising compensations for anything we do for others. We thank you for all gifts and blessings, but especially for your own self, our delight and our salvation.

PRAYER. Father, as we come to this special time of prayer, we come asking for deliverance. In so many subtle ways we fall into habits and situations that are not in keeping with your highest purpose for us. Hear us as in our feeble way we try to honestly look at our lives and relationships and seek to pinpoint those places where we need deliverance.

Deliver us from a spirit of domination that wants its way in every situation no matter what else may be the better way.

Deliver us from using people for our own benefit and promotion.

Deliver us from critical remarks and attitudes that are based on assumption more than fact and that would be better left unannounced in any manner.

Deliver us from looking for and expecting perfection in others when we know that such is impossible, even in ourselves.

Deliver us from assuming a posture of hurt feelings over little slights or even big ones as we see them to be.

Deliver us from being petty both in spirit and in action.

Help us to look upon others not as they momentarily are but as they can yet become.

Help us to love people, not just do good for them.

Help us to decide issues for the best interest of everybody, not just for our own wants and wishes.

Help us to be about the business of righting injustices that need our attention and help.

Help us to expect the best of others and to help others help themselves.

In all circumstances we encounter, help us to keep a good sense of humor and readily use the power of laughter like a good medicine.

And when we have experienced the wonder and power of your presence with us, may we, Father, walk in the glory of that experience as we make our pilgrimage in the everyday world apart from this sacred place.—Henry Fields

LECTIONARY MESSAGE

Topic: To Build or Not to Build?

TEXT: Hag. 2:1–9

OTHER READINGS: 2 Thess. 2:1–5, 13–17; Luke 20:27–38

In 538 B.C.E. the first contingent of Judeans was permitted to return to Jerusalem. In that year Sheshbazzar, the governor, laid a foundation for a new Temple, but apparently the work was soon discontinued. The people turned to more immediate and practical concerns, the building of their own houses. Haggai explained that the drought and hard times were the result of their skewed, selfish priorities. The enduring question presented by the book is: how can one justify the building of a grand sanctuary in the face of so much misery and privation? How can the people of God wisely set priorities for their activities when the needs of people are so pressing?

I. The call to complete the Temple (2:1–4a). In 520, eighteen years after the first attempt had failed, Haggai called leaders and people to get on with building the Temple. After an initial spurt of activity (1:14), the work lagged because the people became discouraged. They made the mistake of comparing their efforts with the remembered magnificence of the first Temple. To counter growing disappointment, Haggai called on leaders and people to take new courage and get on with the work.

II. The assurance of the divine presence (2:4b–5). But what could be a sufficient and convincing basis for a call to take courage? The answer is given in the Lord's assurance: "I am with you." Such assurance was actually a reminder, a summons to recall the whole history of the Lord's presence with the people since the days of the Exodus. The spirit of the Lord had always been present with them, even when they did their worst. And more recently the Lord's presence had been a reality during their foreign captivity. A people convinced that the Lord is truly with them can accomplish anything they are called to do.

Of course, the Lord did not need a Temple. The Lord's presence with the people had never been contingent on the existence of a building. But the people needed to build. In a time of weak commitment and selfish priorities, they needed a work that would focus their attention on the Lord and on the Lord's claims on their lives. Building the Temple was not only good in itself; it provided a cooperative effort for a disunited and discouraged people to take a first step on the road to moral and spiritual integrity.

III. The divine promise (2:6–9). The first Temple was remembered as a house of splendor. It was difficult for the people to see how their impoverished province could ever supply the means to build a Temple worthy of the Lord. Would not their efforts only inspire contempt among surrounding nations?

The Lord's response was that the Lord would see to the matter of splendor, rich appointment, and wealth. Their job was to build; the Lord would supply what they could not.

IV. Hearing the message today. Many congregations face the decision whether to build a new sanctuary. It is primarily a spiritual decision, because it concerns setting priorities that have an impact on so many needy people. In a time of pronounced world hunger, homelessness, joblessness, dislocation, and disease, a decision to spend large sums on brick and mortar can so easily become a misappropriation of funds to reach a less worthy goal.

Haggai's call to an impoverished people to build the Temple must be understood and evaluated in context. Even more important than the Temple was the need for a discouraged, disunited people to be summoned to a worthy project that would help them recapture a sense of unity, to overcome their apathy, and to focus their attention on the central place of the service of God. Haggai was not fixated simply on a building program, but on a means to help the people regain a sense of wholeness.

It follows, then, that every proposed building program must be judged in light of its particular context. Some congregations have built so ostentatiously that few resources remain to carry out their call to minister to a needy world. Other have built wisely and have found in the work a new sense of cooperative effort and a better basis for expanded ministry. It is not just the building that counts. What matters most are people and their needs, and whether a new building can help meet those needs.—Thomas G. Smothers

SUNDAY: NOVEMBER NINETEENTH

SERVICE OF WORSHIP

Sermon: The Little Things in Life

TEXT: Matt. 13:31

Few of us today escape the error of confusing size with significance. How many of us mistake quantity for quality! Our imaginations are so victimized by bigness that we are likely to think that bigness is equivalent to significance. We need to remind ourselves of the importance of the little things in life.

For want of a nail the shoe was lost,
For want of a shoe the horse was lost,
For want of a horse the rider was lost,
For want of a rider the battle was lost,
For want of a battle the kingdom was lost,
And all for the want of a horseshoe nail.

The little things in life have their own significance.

They were significant to Jesus, the little things in life. Notice the particularity of his ministry. Although he did proclaim general truths, yet so very often he gave attention to particular things—the fall of a sparrow, the growth of a seed, the cry of need in a noisy crowd of hundreds of people. The little things in life caught his attention and occasioned his comment. Read through the Gospels noticing how often his teachings, his parables are occasioned by some little thing, and you will understand anew how much attention he gave to the little things in life. A cup of water given in his name wins his praise. The widow's mite occasions a comment. The little things are not lacking in significance because they are little in size.

I. Modern scientists are learning the importance of the little. My scientist guide, as we discussed the classical physics versus the new physics, said, "The characteristic of the classical physics was that it dealt with the big world. It loved to use the telescope. It loved to talk in astronomical figures and great distances. It spoke of bigness of an expanding universe. Then came modern science, with its doctrine of relativity and the fission of the atom. Now the realm of nuclear physics has riveted our attention on the little, not the big."

I do not propose today to conduct a discussion of nuclear physics and chain reactions, nor could I do it any day! The amazing fact is that no one has seen an atom. Although our physicists, like my guide, can show us the cyclotron in which the atoms are bombarded and the reactions recorded, although they can use the great powers of these tiny particles, it still remains true that no scientist has ever seen an atom. A new age is centered in the discovery of the little things in life, things so little they cannot even be seen.

The power of a split atom defies all description. One can say that the energy released is a million times greater than any known explosive, and still one's mind cannot really grasp it. Let it suffice to say that the little things in life today have come into a significance that has nothing to do with size, and the energies that are being released now from these tiny things, so small that nobody has seen them, have power that can be employed by men either to destroy the world or to give the world a new era of hope.

II. One thinks of Jesus speaking about the mustard seed, so small in its beginnings, so large in its consequences.

(a) In the moral world, the mustard seed is the choice that is made by an individual. A little choice may have great consequences. Not just the dramatic deeds of moral heroism possess significance but also the individual choices of our daily life. Indeed, the individual choice is the matter of central importance in life for any person. Dante said that virtue is a habit of right choice. Picture it if you will—a person makes a right choice and then another and still another. Right choice becomes a habit. The habit weaves something good into the pattern of life, and we call it virtue. Dependability in the moral world is simply the habit of right choice. It begins with a free decision when a person chose something right when he had the power to choose something wrong, and then did it again and again. It is these little things that build gigantic moral strength into the life of the world. Conversely, if a person chooses wrong when he has the power to choose right, he then finds it easier the next time to choose wrong when he has the power to choose right. It is still easier to choose wrong the third time, and the sense of shame begins to disappear. So the habit of wrong choice becomes bad character. The cumulative consequence of the little choices is something big. The temptation, "Do it just this once," is seen to be a dangerous and terrible one, for it is the little things that build virtue or evil into the fabric and pattern of life. We might say that every decision is like coming to a crossroads where we must go one way or another. And if we go the right way we move toward our desired destination, but if we go the wrong way we go farther and farther away from it. How great the power of choice in the moral world!

There is an old Arabian legend about a sailor who has a genie in a bottle. His curiosity gets the better of the sailor, and one day he opens the bottle. The genie not only comes out of the bottle but goes up and up and up in the air, all the while getting bigger and bigger until the sailor is terrified at this black apparition as high as the sky and filling all his horizon. A wrong moral decision is like that, letting loose something whose blackness grows to terrible size, darkening the sky, filling all of our horizon with dread.

In contrast, a little deed of kindness goes farther than we can ever imagine.

> How far that little candle throws its beams
> So shines a good deed in a naughty world.

Yes, you can start a chain reaction of kindness, one good deed of kindness causing another. One good deed that shows goodwill will bring a response of goodwill. One good deed of love will bring a response in love. The power of moral chain reaction is greater than we imagine, because God's blessing is upon it. In the moral world, the little things, the little unremembered acts of kindness and love, are a power that we must never underestimate. It is the responsibility of Christians in their daily decisions, in their words, their thoughts, their purposes, their deeds to gather up in these little things of life the very quality of the Spirit of Christ so that they make the world a brighter and finer place because of the goodwill that they have released into it.

One time when I was on the West Coast as guest of a friend in British Columbia, we paused to look at the logs in the Fraser River, thousands and thousands of them. I said, "Is it true that a log in a wrong position can cause a jam? And if a man releases that one log from its position, the other logs will be freed and will then move on down the river?" He said, "Yes, it's true." A little thing—one log among so many thousand—but what great results for evil or good! One wrong decision can do so much harm; one good decision can do so much good!

(b) Again, in the spiritual world the little things of life are so very important. For instance, the way we are related to life and to our work is so much more important than we commonly understand. There are people who are doing right things in a wrong way. A wrong way of doing things is dangerous for mental and spiritual health. How important to be right with God! The Bible tells us to joy in the Lord. It tells us that God loves a cheerful giver, that is, a person who gives in the right spirit. It tells us to have courage and confidence and faith and enthusiasm and to rise above the constraints of law into the large liberty of God's world of love. How we are related to the obligations of the Christian life is very important, although it may seem a small thing. Do you say, "If I am a member of the church and do my duty that's enough"? It is not enough, by any means. Being a member of the church, important as it is, is but a symbol of your happy and free personal commitment to Christ as Lord and Savior. It is outward evidence of an inner spiritual loyalty. It is evidence that you are happily serving him and doing his will. But it is the spirit in which we do what we do that is important! Doing the right deed for the wrong reason may be the ultimate treason.

(c) Again, a person's relation to his work is so important. How many people in America today have a right relation to their work? Not as many as we would like. For some it is drudgery, and for others it is a perpetual holiday. To enter upon our work with eagerness and enthusiasm and a desire to be creative, to find joy in our work, to have a right relation to it, this is so important, although to many it seems a very little thing. If you talk like this to some groups, they will tell you how much money they make or how many benefits they have. But these are not the important things in life—how much money you make and how many benefits you have in your job. The important thing is your right relation to your work so that you love to be about it and have a high sense of God-given purpose in it. No small thing, the spirit of your work, but a thing of vast consequence for your happiness, your health, your peace of mind, your constructive contribution to the world and to the service of God.

(d) For the Christian whose life centers in worship, how true it is that the many little moments of consecration and devotion have such eternal significance—the moments of prayer that become wonderful habits of devotion, the moments of worship and praise that become such a custom in your life that without self-consciousness you sing God's praises and lift your prayers and find the strength you need for daily living. Let us remember Jesus' love of the particular, and each time that you sing a hymn and say a prayer, know that the blessing of Jesus is upon that particular experience. How he blessed the faith of the individual, spoken or unspoken! How he understood and answered the prayers of the heart, expressed or unexpressed, each particular instance having its own importance and its own significance! Let us not underestimate any particular moment of devotion, for it has an importance far greater than anything we can comprehend. Far greater than all the energies being released now from this mysterious universe in the realm of physics are the energies that can be released into this world through spiritual chain reaction as we give our attention to the little things in life. May God's blessing bring the mustard seed of faith in our life to greatness of loyalty, joy, and service. May we make this world a better place because we have lived in it, because we recognize the importance in God's plan of the little things in life!—Lowell M. Atkinson

Illustrations

FIRST STEPS. A Chinese engineer sat down with me and abruptly said: "What are you going to do with me? I am a man without any religion. The old is dead, and I haven't anything new to take its place. In America no church would take me, for I cannot believe in the divinity of Christ."

I could almost see him inwardly stiffen to meet my arguments to prove Christ divine. So I used none. Instead I asked: "What do you believe? How far along are you?"

"Well," he said, "I believe that Christ was the best of men."

"Then let us begin where you can. If he is the best of men, then he is your ideal. Are you prepared to act according to that ideal? To cut out of your life everything that Christ would not approve?"

He was startled and said, "But that is not easy."

"I never said the way of Christ is easy. Are you prepared to let go everything he will not approve?"

"If I am honest, I must," he quietly replied, "and I will."

"Then, whoever Christ turns out to be, man or more than man, wouldn't you be stronger and better if he were living with you, in you all the time?"

"Of course, I would be different."

"Then will you let him into your life?"

"I don't know how."

"Then pray this prayer after me, sentence by sentence."

He did. "This is different," he said as we arose, "for they always told me I had to believe first. Now at least here is something for me to begin on." The next day he came again, his face radiant. "I didn't know a man could be as happy as I have been today. All my questions and doubts as to who Christ is have gone. And, moreover, I have been talking to my wife, and she wants it too."—E. Stanley Jones

STEP BY STEP. We have become accustomed to thinking of the importance of a thing in terms of how much noise is made about it. If a thing is very important, then there ought to be streamers about it in the newspaper; there ought to be propaganda over the radio about it; we ought to have a billboard campaign; there ought to be a tremendous fuss made about the thing, and then we would believe it was important. But that isn't the way God gets his work done. There is no fanfare of trumpets when spring comes. Silently the drawing forces of the universe pull the sap, from down where it has been hibernating in the roots in the soil, up—step by step—into the tree, until finally one beautiful spring morning the miracle happens and the blossoms burst out. Spring is here! But there was no great to-do about it. Just so it is in the realm of spiritual life—the process is as silent and as invisible as what goes on in the ground when the seed is planted.—Paul Quillian

Sermon Suggestions

FOR A TIME OF TESTING. TEXT: Luke 21:5–19. (a) Then: Jesus discusses the signs preceding the destruction of Jerusalem. (2) Always: The story of God and his people has always dealt with catastrophic events that call for special courage, wisdom, and faith. (3) Now: (a) Expect difficulty. (b) Expect God's intervention.

WHILE WAITING FOR THE LORD'S RETURN. TEXT: 2 Thess. 3:6–13. (1) Do not coddle people who will not work. (2) Work quietly, responsibly, and untiringly.

Worship Aids

CALL TO WORSHIP. "Behold, God is my salvation; I will trust and not be afraid: for the Lord Jehovah is my strength and my song; he also is become my salvation" (Isa. 12:2).

INVOCATION. O Lord, our Lord, how excellent is thy name in all the earth. Draw close to us, that we may not only be aware of your presence but also rejoice in it. We have come here seeking you because we desire communion with you. Meeting you is not only our hope but also our prayer. As we worship together, make us obedient to your revelations, understanding of your truth, and committed to your calling.—Henry Fields

OFFERTORY SENTENCE. "If you are eager to give, God will accept your gift on the basis of what you have to give, not on what you don't have" (2 Cor. 8:12 TEV).

OFFERTORY PRAYER. Lord, if our circumstances are poverty, make our souls rich. If our circumstances are wealth, make our giving disciplined. Whether rich or poor, we would be found faithful. In the name of Jesus, who, owning little of earth's goods, gave everything that we might be saved.—E. Lee Phillips

PRAYER. Father God, even though you have made us from the dust of the ground, we know that it is your will that, through the power of our Lord Jesus Christ, we rise above our humble beginnings and ultimately claim our eternal inheritance in the heavenly home that you are preparing for us. We pray that our lives might always remain open to the transformation that only your redemption can bring about—the change required in us, from sons and daughters of the earth to the children of God.

We confess to you that our minds, our thoughts, our opinions, our attitudes, and our perspective most need to be changed by your power. Our minds are often filled with thoughts that make us feel ashamed and unworthy. We are frequently puzzled and sometimes even frightened by some of the images that flash across the screen of our mind. Our opinions and attitudes about life and toward others do not consistently reflect the Spirit of our Lord. We are far more negative, grudging, selfish, and judgmental than we really want to be. Our outlook is often gloomy and critical when we really should be full of your joy. Father, your Word reminds us that our thoughts reveal the kind of persons we really are, deep within ourselves. If that is indeed so, then our need for your forgiveness and for your transforming power is far greater than we have allowed ourselves to believe.

Father God, let the light of the world come now and shine in our hearts. Renew our minds. Replenish our strength. Restore our hope. Lead us from the darkness and the error of our ways. Fill us with your peace, which passes all understanding. And give us confidence that through Jesus Christ our Lord, you will deliver us from the evil we would do and that you will enable us to overcome the temptations that would cause us to stumble and fall. We ask this in the name of him who is able to make all things new, even Jesus, the Savior of the world.—Gary C. Redding

LECTIONARY MESSAGE

Topic: The Promise of a Glorious Future

TEXT: Isa. 65:17–25

OTHER READINGS: 2 Thess. 3:6–13; Luke 21:5–19

The Book of Isaiah is more than a book; it is a library of materials reflecting the experiences of Israel through three centuries and under the power of three great empires. It recounts oracles of judgment, catalogs Israel's sins, and reflects Israel's defeats and exile. But at every point the oracles of judgment are balanced with the most exquisite oracles of salvation, as though to say that while judgment is a reality, it is not God's final Word. Beyond the darkness of present reality, there is a promised new day, and the people of God live in the light of that promised day. Perhaps no oracle of salvation is more exalted or more complete than the one contained in this passage.

I. The Lord creates a new world of joy (Isa. 65:17–18). It was not enough to say that the Lord would cleanse or restore the old world. What the Lord intended was nothing less than a new creation. The Lord was prepared to start over again, to provide a new beginning, as though the whole history of human failure had never existed. Only the God of grace has a heart large enough to do this. The "former things," the old history with its catalog of Israel's sin, and even the countless expressions of divine forgiveness, would no longer be determinative. All things would be seen and judged in the light of the new creation of joy.

II. The reversal of fortunes (65:19–23). The promise of a new day signaled the removal of all sources of sorrow. For centuries the people of Israel had suffered not only the consequences of their own bad choices but also the depredations of conquerors. It was a history of weeping, devastation, dislocation, premature death, hunger, and homelessness. But no more would it be so. No longer would there be invasion, starvation, or injustice. Rejoicing would replace sorrow, peace would supplant war, and the cry of joy would drown out the old cries of mourning. There is not a word in this passage about restoration on the basis of repentance. This new thing was to be wholly a work of divine grace. It is not possible to explain God's grace; it is only possible to accept it and to live in its joy.

III. The assurance of divine presence (65:24). The people lived through many tragedies wondering if God had hidden from them or forgotten them. God had not forgotten them, but their unfaithfulness had constructed a wall against the inbreak of God's grace. But in the new world that is sung about in this poem, the people would be conscious of God's constant presence. Even before they could call on God for help, God would already have answered their prayer. This is divine action predicated not on human behavior but solely on the basis of God's will to bless and to bring all things to a good conclusion.

IV. A world of peace (65:25). The new creation would provide not only a world of joy for humans. All nature would be pacified. Replaying the description of the peaceable kingdom given in Isaiah 11:6–9, this poem also signals the end to all violence. There would be no one to hurt or to destroy in God's holy mountain.

V. Hearing the message today. While this text, along with others, holds forth the promise of a glorious future, it does not invite the believer to wait with folded hands. What is needed is active waiting filled with expectant work. Promise was never meant to cut the nerve of moral effort. The good news for today is about a God who is willing to start over with us in order that a new creation can come into existence. The gospel is about grace that is greater than all our sins and about the power of God to make all things new. We should work and serve as though that great day will never come and at the same time let the assurance of that promised day provide joy in our waiting for its arrival.—Thomas G. Smothers

SUNDAY: NOVEMBER TWENTY-SIXTH

SERVICE OF WORSHIP

Sermon: On Being in Two Places at the Same Time

TEXT: Rev. 1:9–10

We all have had the experience at some time of confronting conflicting claims upon our time and exclaiming, "I can't be in two places at the same time!" But you can!

I. In the Book of Revelation, John tells us that he "was on the island called Patmos" and "in the Spirit on the Lord's day." Patmos is an island in the Aegean; "in the Spirit," our experience of being in the kingdom of Jesus Christ. We *can* be in two places at the same time—in the place where we live and in the kingdom of Christ.

John was a prisoner of Rome on the island of Patmos, and he must have felt pain of frustration. He was an eager

Christian, but helpless against the massive power of pagan Rome. It was a time of persecution of the Christians, and John found himself a prisoner on Patmos—a frustrating experience. There is a tradition that John was a quarry slave there. When we first visited Patmos, we found it a mountain rising out of the Aegean. We rode donkeys to the top of the mountain, where we saw the cave traditionally associated with John. He lived in a cave of frustration, but at the same time in the glorious liberty of faith in Christ, the King of kings and Lord of lords.

II. The people of faith across the ages have learned this truth—that in the place of frustration may also be a place of spiritual freedom. The most popular book of the early Middle Ages was *The Consolation of Philosophy* by Boethius, and it was written in prison. Dante was in exile when he wrote his great poem of faith "The Divine Comedy." John Bunyan was in prison when he wrote that Christian classic *Pilgrim's Progress.* John Milton was blind when he did his greatest work, writing "Paradise Lost."

III. Again, John was in a place of persecution that was also a place of happiness. He rejoiced to be in the company of those who have been made priests and kings unto God. "To him who loves us and has freed us from our sins by his blood and made us a kingdom, priests to his God and Father, to him be glory and dominion forever and ever" (1:5–6). And so the trumpet call is sounded that is so characteristic of Revelation, a mighty message of encouragement to the Christians. No matter how distressful our experiences, we can look to God and find the foretaste of the joy of heaven bringing a glory into our life.

Every pastor has had the experience of calling upon a person who is suffering physical affliction yet is spiritually radiant. I shall long remember making a pastoral call in Torola, British Virgin Islands. I found myself talking with a Christian who had suffered greatly and had lost both his feet. He was in the place of affliction but at the same time in the place of promise. We repeated together the great words of St. Paul, "I consider that the sufferings of this present time are not worth comparing with the glory that is to be revealed to us" (Rom. 8:18). When we live in faith, the place of suffering can become a place of glory! We can in fact be in two places at the same time!

IV. But John was a prisoner, and he could not but feel the agony of defeat. It was his greatest trial. And it became his greatest triumph! For he found that he could be in the place of victory even while, as a prisoner, he was in the place of defeat. He trusted the uplook, not the outlook. The uplook revealed the glories of God's victorious purpose, giving new heart and new courage, which he could share with fellow Christians. So he wrote Revelation to encourage believers and give new hope.

He would put his message of hope in symbolic and grotesque form that the Roman authorities would dismiss as the work of an eccentric. But the churches would understand, and they would find new strength to keep on keeping on in tragic and difficult days. The place of defeat became the place of victory: "The kingdom of the world has become the kingdom of our Lord and of his Christ, and he shall reign forever and ever" (11:15). So the churches grew in spiritual strength in tragic days, and the place of defeat became the place of victory through faith in Christ, the King of kings and Lords of lords. The Lamb who was slain was the Lamb upon the throne. The great white throne (20:11), with its symbolism of heavenly power, gave hope and new heart to all who lived in the place of defeat.

Ours is the challenge and privilege and joy of being in the kingdom of Christ, even while in our own island of Patmos. Beyond frustration is freedom; beyond persecution is joy; beyond defeat is victory. We can be in two places at the same time, our place in this world and our place in the kingdom of Christ. Looking to God, we feel within us a new spirit, and no matter what happens to us, something wonderful happens in us, and glory fills the soul!—Lowell Atkinson

Illustrations

COME, LORD JESUS. Fundamentalists often speak as if their Lord were totally absent during the interim until the great day comes. Modernists often speak as if the presence of their Lord left no place or need for the coming of that day. Is the Lord absent or present? Could he be both absent and present? To be sure, in the prosaic language of everyday conversation, when a person is present we do not think of him as still to come. We quite readily apply this principle to Christ. If he is yet to come, he is not now present; if he is present, it is meaningless to speak of his coming. In the language of the Bible, however, this neat division of things breaks down. The Messiah can simultaneously be both present and absent; he can be here and yet be present as one who is to come.—Paul S. Minear

BUILDING A CATHEDRAL. The story says that a traveler from Italy came to the French town of Chartres to see the great church that was being built there. Arriving at the end of the day, he went to the site just as the workmen were leaving for home. He asked one man, covered with dust, what he did there. The man replied that he was a stonemason. He spent his days carving rocks. Another man, when asked, said he was a glassblower who spent his days making slabs of colored glass. Still another workman replied that he was a blacksmith who pounded iron for a living.

Wandering into the deepening gloom of the unfinished edifice, the traveler came upon an older woman, armed with a broom, sweeping up the stone chips and wood shavings and glass shards from the day's work. "What are you doing?" he asked.

The woman paused, leaning on her broom, and looking up toward the high arches, replied, "Me? I'm building a cathedral for the glory of almighty God."—Robert Fulghum

Sermon Suggestions

NOT DAILY BREAD ONLY. TEXT: John 6:25–35. (1) According to John, verse 35a, Jesus called himself the Bread of Life. (2) This bread is the indispensable spiritual substance without which we cannot live in the deepest sense, verse 32. (3) The bread endures and sustains through all seasons and circumstances, verse 27. (4) The bread is available to any and all who come to Jesus Christ, verse 35b.

WHEN YOU BRING YOUR OFFERING. TEXT: Deut. 26:1–11. (1) It should be a recognition of God's providence. (2) It should be of the choicest gifts. (3) It should betoken a total stewardship, as in the faithful payment of tithes. (4) It should be an occasion of celebration.

Worship Aids

CALL TO WORSHIP. "Enter into his gates with thanksgiving, and into his courts with praise: be thankful unto him, and bless his name" (Ps. 100:4).

INVOCATION.

We have gathered before you, O God,
Conscious of our sinfulness, our weakness, the times we have failed our neighbors,
Our families, ourselves,
occasions when we lacked justice and mercy.
United in faith we have come together,
Uplifted by the innocence of our children,
Who praise the God and Savior of us all,
Natives and immigrants, each one encompassed by divine love.
As we leave this assembly
Send us forth with your blessing.
We have shared this prayer of thanksgiving,
So may we share our food, our offerings,
That none of your chosen ones may be hungry or without shelter.

—Grace Donovan

OFFERTORY SENTENCE. "I will freely sacrifice unto thee: I will praise thy name, O Lord; for it is good" (Ps. 54:6).

OFFERTORY PRAYER. Gracious God, the earth is yours, and every wonder, season, and sunrise are signs of your concern and care; we offer now the fruits of our labor for the support and service of the common good. Add to these gifts the dynamic purpose of your kingdom so that their influence may be strong for the salvation and betterment of people both here and far away. And to your name be glory and dominion forever.—Donald Macleod

PRAYER. Almighty and everlasting God, Father of mercies and God of all comfort, we raise to thee our grateful praise.

For the life we have from thee, for the good earth yielding grain and fruits for our sustenance, for the cattle upon a thousand hills, and for the manifold gifts of the sea, we humbly thank thee.

For thy mercies bestowed through the nation to which we belong, and especially for the freedoms won of old by our fathers and cherished and preserved even until now, we humbly thank thee.

For thy prophets and saints whose vision of the eternal has lighted our path and strengthened our hearts; for valiant souls who, keeping faith and hope in the midst of adversity, shame our doubt and our discouragement; for those near to us and dear who share our joys and our sorrows, and whose love to us never fails; and for all those our brethren whose daily task on land or sea ministers to our good, we praise and bless thy glorious name.

Above all, we thank thee for thyself, O Lord, whose faithfulness is unto all generations. Give us grace, we beseech thee, to show forth thy praise not only in our words but in our lives, by committing ourselves wholly to thy service; through Jesus Christ our Lord.—Ernest Fremont Tittle

LECTIONARY MESSAGE

Topic: A Prescription for Inner Wellness

TEXT: Phil. 4:4–9

There seems to be an imbalance in contemporary preaching. While some preach a gospel of spiritual salvation, others proclaim a gospel of health and wealth. Preaching must be holistic. The gospel must be presented comprehensively enough that humankind is touched in all areas of its existence—physically, spiritually, mentally, and emotionally. Unquestionably, preachers are emphasizing the saving of people spiritually and physically. Not enough is being promulgated concerning the saving of people mentally and emotionally. Our Lord desired that God would be loved by us *holistically*—with all of our heart, soul, mind, and strength. In order to glorify our God with such love, a healthy heart, soul, mind, and body are needed. The text before us furnishes a prescription for the kind of inner wellness that will enable us as Christians to magnify the Lord and be edified within our own being. Inside the walls of a Roman prison, Paul, affected by the dampness of the elements and the distance of his friends, envisioned the private world of the Christian. Paul's conceptualization for inner wellness is seen in the following ideas.

I. An attitude of rejoicing (v. 4). There were problems in the church at Rome (Phil. 1:12–18). Paul informed the Philippian Christians that preaching had taken on a competitive spirit on the part of some of the ministers in the church at Rome. He was experiencing personal attacks from these preachers, who intended on increasing the pain of his imprisonment. There were problems in the church at Philippi (Phil. 1:28). Paul admonished the Philippian Christians not to be intimidated by their opponents. He also advised them to be aware of the false teachers in that community (Phil. 3:2). Additionally, internal division existed within the Philippian community and schism on the inside of the congregation. What does Paul advise the Christians in that city to do? *Rejoice in the Lord!* According to Galatians 5:22, joy is an ingredient of the fruit of the Spirit. When Christ enters into the life of a believer, he brings joy into that believer's life. The closer one walks with Christ, the greater the joy one experiences in Christ. Christians are not commanded to be happy. Happiness is dependent upon positive "happenings." Joy is an internal quality that is not dependent upon the outward circumstances of life. Rather, it is dependent upon the inner relationship with Christ. We are to rejoice *"in the Lord always."*

II. A spirit of gentleness (v. 5). The word for *gentleness* has been translated in various ways in different versions of the Bible. The multiplicity of the translations of this word provokes the possibility of Christians measuring themselves according to the definitions suggested by the translations. *Forbearance*—Christians need the ability to see others through rather than seeing through others. *Magnanimity*—saints are to be "rooms without walls." They are to possess a disposition of "sweet reasonableness" that is inclusive and inviting to those who are hurting. *Softness*—believers are to exhibit a tenderness in the way they minister to those who are in tough situations. This trait is not strictly a feminine characteristic—it is Christian. Paul lists it as a fruit of the Spirit in Galatians 5:22. Paul encourages the Philippian Christians to demonstrate this spirit in such an influential manner that they would be recognized for it outside of their own community.

III. An absence of worry (v. 6a). Depression is the number-one social problem in America today. People have a low tolerance for ambiguity and uncertainty. They cannot interpret the handwriting of the events on the walls of their lives. The uncertainty of the future dampens their spirits. Paul was not a stranger to depressing conditions. A catalog of pressures of persecution that Paul had faced is presented in 2 Corinthians 11:23–29. He instructs the Philippian Christians to refrain from worrying, which paralyzes and obstructs inner well-being and insults God. The most damaging effect of worry is not that it injures us. Rather, worry insults God. When we allow destructive worry to dominate us to the extent that we cannot function, we virtually say to God that even though he was able to create the world out of nothing, we have a problem that he cannot handle. Paul is echoing the words of Jesus from Matthew's Gospel: "Take no thought for tomorrow, what you will eat or drink" (Matt. 6:25).

IV. A practice of prayer (v. 6b). Paul's command to abstain from worrying is followed by his imperative to practice praying. The absence of worry must be accomplished by the presence of prayer. Three words are used to reflect the nature of prayer: *supplication, thanksgiving,* and *requests*. Christians must pray to God and believe that God will supply all of their needs (Phil. 4:19). Thanksgiving reminds us of past blessings and assures us that God provides for us in the future. Even though God knows what we are going to request prior to our asking, God still insists that we ask, seek, and knock, in order that the communication line remains open between heaven and earth and the relationship between God and us is strengthened.

V. The presence of God's peace (v. 7). After fulfilling the requirements of an attitude of rejoicing, a spirit of gentleness, an absence of worry, and a practice of prayer, Paul points us to the promise that is offered—*"the peace of God."* The promise of God's peace cannot be claimed without the fulfillment of the prerequisites in verses 4–6. This peace is not the peace that God gives at conversion when we experience justification. This is what Paul calls "peace *with* God" (Rom. 5:8). The peace *of* God is the actual presence of God within the life of the believer. It is more than a feeling—it is the actuality of the very being of God residing within the Christian. God's presence provides tranquility in the midst of turbulence and peace in the midst of a storm. God's peace "rises above every mind" and is superior to every intellectual effort to plan or strategize security. The peace of God is so profound that it "passes all understanding" or, in the modern vernacular, "blows the mind." Philippi was a military settlement. There was twenty-four-hour surveillance around the walls of the city. The best news that the residents could hear after a sentinel returned from his guard duty was that "all is well." The peace of God performs guard duty around the walls of our inner or private world. As Paul put it, "It keeps our hearts and minds." It braces us when our exterior world is coming apart at the seams and the bottom of life has fallen out.

VI. Right thinking and acting (vv. 8, 9). These verses constitute a single sentence in Greek. The rhetorical style and the lofty moral standards that emerge from the verses set forth the foundation that must characterize a Christian's attitude and actions. Paul is instructing the Philippian Christians to think and act in such a way that their witness will command the respect of people and the blessing of God. Since non-Christians embraced this kind of thought and action, how much more should they as Christians live up to these ideals! They are the light of the world and the salt of the earth.—Robert Smith, Jr.

SUNDAY: DECEMBER THIRD

SERVICE OF WORSHIP

Sermon: I Am Glad

TEXT: Ps. 122

An American tourist found himself in India on the day of the pilgrimage to the top of a sacred mountain. Thousands of people would climb the steep path to the mountaintop. The tourist, who had been jogging and doing vigorous exercise and thought he was in good shape, decided to join in and share the experience. After twenty minutes, he was out of breath and could hardly climb another step, while women carrying babies, and frail old men with canes, moved easily past him. "I don't understand it," he said to an Indian companion. "How can those people do it when I can't?"

His friend answered, "It is because you have the typical American habit of seeing everything as a test. You see the mountain as your enemy, and you set out to defeat it. So, naturally, the mountain fights back, and it is stronger than you are. We do not see the mountain as our enemy to be conquered. The purpose of our climb is to become one with the mountain, and so it lifts us up and carries us along."

I. Today is the first Sunday of Advent, the beginning of our journey toward the celebration of the birth of our Savior. No doubt you have at least thought about the preparations, where you will celebrate, with whom, gifts, food, and so on. We don't climb any mountains on this pilgrimage, but the preparations can become like a mountain of things to do.

Have you given some thought to how you will approach this season on a spiritual level? How will you get in touch with the reason for the season? What ways will you begin to prepare your soul? Will you approach it like the American tourist did the mountain, rushing, hurrying, pushing, forcing? Or will you embrace the spirit of this season and let it lift you up?

How do we prepare for Christmas? How do we prepare to celebrate the coming of the Lord among us? There are many ways, I suppose. If we jump ahead to what we commonly call the Second Coming, we find that our spiritual posture should be that of alertness and repentance. The day and the hour we do not know, but we live each day to its fullest, as if it were our last. If we follow the natural flow of this season, the true essence of our celebration, we find the opportunities of celebration in the joys of giving and sharing. We enjoy the exchange of gifts and the warm fellowship of family and friends.

For our journey together as a church, I have chosen a psalm that was meaningful for the people of God on a similar journey in another time. Found within a collection of songs known as the "Songs of the Pilgrimage," Psalm 122, much like our hymns, was an inspirational piece of music that also preserved theological meaning. Its words and images helped remind the people of God of the reason for their journey. They gave them strength along the way.

II. These songs were written and sung for and by the people of God as they journeyed from exile back to Jerusalem, the city of God's presence. The spirit of the contents can serve as an inspiration for us this Advent season.

(a) In our reading of the psalm we are struck first by the theme of *harmony*. Created by the writer's own vision of Jerusalem, the past and the future come together. Listen to some of the words of his song: "Jerusalem—built as a city that is bound firmly together. . . . Peace be within you." The memories for him were of a city of strength, security, and glory. Looking to the future, his prayers and hopes were for a city of peace, prosperity, and goodness. His memories and his visions of hope converged on the journey. What Jerusalem was like and the hope of the new Jerusalem as the tribes went up to the house of the Lord flowed together.

The Christmas season has a way of bringing together memories and hopes also. In the cartoon *Sally Forth,* Sally says to her mother after she has just viewed the large family Christmas tree with all the packages lying under it: "Have you ever noticed how one particular emotion gets real strong at Christmas?" Her mother answers: "I sure have, honey. I get very nostalgic at this time of the year. I especially like to think back to Christmas times when I was your age. My mind fills with memories of decorating the tree . . . singing carols . . . baking cookies. It's a big part of the holidays for me. I'm impressed that someone your age would recognize that nostalgia is such a strong emotion."

Sally goes back to the tree, looks at the huge pile of wrapped gifts, and thinks to herself: "Nostalgia? I was talking about *greed.*"

Oh, well, maybe for some the memories are a little misguided. At Christmas we rehearse the story of how God "dwelt among us in the flesh." We rehearse the memory of how a boy born in a manger becomes the King of kings and Lord of lords. We remember the story that God so loved the world that he sent Christ to save us from our sins.

But at the same time we look to the future because our story is also a story of hope. We look forward and work for a place where the first shall be last and the last first. We envision a world where all things become new. We pray for peace in Jerusalem, in Samaria, in Judea, and in the outermost parts of the earth. We rejoice and remember the past. We hope, pray, and work for the future.

(b) Yes, the theme of harmony catches our attention first, but another one decorates it. This is the theme of *gladness.* The beginning of the song says, "I was glad when they said to me, 'Let us go to the house of the Lord!' Our feet are standing within your gates, O Jerusalem." What should be our posture as we enter the Advent season? It should be a posture of joy and gladness for the things that God has done and will do!

When the things of God were mentioned, boredom, apathy, or cynicism did not surface. When the invitation to enjoy the goodness of God's presence was given, it was not ignored, squelched, or disregarded. When someone said to the writer, "Let us go to the house of the Lord!" he did not respond, "I've been there and done that!" He responded in an attitude of gladness and joy. He responded with a sense of readiness, alertness, and expectancy. He was standing, not slouching, within the gates. He was awake and not asleep in Jerusalem. In the presence of God, he was filled with energy and not weary.

Can you say this morning that you are glad to be in the house of the Lord? Can you say that you are standing within the gates? Can you say, "I am glad—let us go!"

This week we had the third of a series of neighborhood watch meetings. Getting this group off the ground has been difficult because of the fear. For some of you that don't know, these groups are a product of our work with the Lee-Moreland Owner's Coalition. Now that we have organized the owners, we are trying to organize the residents in this neighborhood to fight the drug dealing. In our first meeting, because of fear, no one came. In our second meeting, seven people came. Before our third meeting officers went to every household in this area to reassure the residents and rally support. Twenty people came this week. We had fewer complaints, and more thought was given to solutions. There was enthusiasm. There was a sense of unity. There was less fear.

I was glad. I was glad because I saw that the people were finally feeling unity and enthusiasm. I was glad because they found that in the house of the Lord. I was glad because next time when someone says to them, "Let's go to the house of the Lord," they themselves will be glad.

The birth of Jesus and his continual presence in our world is a time of great joy. Our preparation for his coming into our midst should be the same. I am glad. Are you?—Daniel N. Alejandro

Illustrations

JOYFUL PILGRIMAGE. The poet recalls in his song all the joyful events of the festival, which now lie behind him. He remembers first of all the pleasure of anticipation at home during the planning and preparation of the pilgrimage to Jerusalem, and then the fulfillment of the expectations that his sojourn in the city of God had brought and that he once more pictures to himself before he sets out on his homeward journey. His feet had been able to tread the sacred ground of the towering holy city, where the community of the people of God, grouped together according to the tribes to which they belonged, had assembled for the celebration of the festival in order to "appear before God's face" (cf. Exod. 23:17, 34:23) and to "testify to the name of their God" according to ancient sacred custom; he had been able to walk on the sacred ground of the holy city, where the rule of God, the heavenly King, and of his earthly representative is continually established anew on the basis of the order of law and is realized within the framework of the festival cult by means of divine judgment and salvation. The poet firmly impresses all these facts on his memory in his hymnic dialogue with Jerusalem in order to take these memories with him to his native country as the precious gift of the time spent at the festival.—Artur Weiser

JERUSALEM IS BUILT AS A CITY THAT IS COMPACT TOGETHER. There is not joy in going up to a church that is rent with internal dissension: the gladness of holy men is aroused by the adhesiveness of love, the unity of life; it would be their sadness if they saw the church to be a house divided against itself. Some bodies of Christians appear to be periodically blown to fragments, and no gracious man is glad to be in the way when the explosions take place: thither the tribes do not go up, for strife and contention are not attractive forces.—Charles Haddon Spurgeon

Sermon Suggestions

NOTES ON THE SECOND COMING. TEXT: Matt. 24:36–44. (1) Only God the Father knows when it will be. (2) It will be totally unexpected. (3) Therefore, everyone will be wise to be prepared at all times for this climactic and decisive event.

WHEN GOD HAS HIS WAY ON EARTH. TEXT: Isa. 2:1–5. (1) God's priority will be recognized and his blessing sought. (2) People will be willing to be instructed in the way of God. (3) War will cease.

Worship Aids

CALL TO WORSHIP. "I was glad when they said unto me, Let us go into the house of the Lord" (Ps. 122:1).

INVOCATION. Lord, sometimes when we come to your house we are overwhelmed by what we experience. We can understand your servant Jacob's feeling when he was afraid and said, "How awesome is this place! This is none other than the house of God, and this is the gate of heaven." But because of sins forgiven, assurance imparted, and work assigned, we rejoice as the doors of the sanctuary are opened, loving hearts welcome us, and your life-giving Word is read, sung, and proclaimed. So we are glad today and praise Father, Son, and Holy Spirit.

OFFERTORY SENTENCE. "And whatsoever ye do, do it heartily, as to the Lord, and not unto men; knowing that of the Lord ye shall receive the reward of the inheritance: for ye serve the Lord Christ" (Col. 3:23–24).

OFFERTORY PRAYER. Lord of all good gifts, open us to the deeper meanings of stewardship, that we might give with gratitude and share with compassion as did our Savior, Christ, the Lord.—E. Lee Phillips

PRAYER. O God of earth and altar, with whom the morning stars sing together to herald thy first creation, this is the season of joy, but our ideals are crying still for our world to be made new. Thy earliest voice declared, "Let there be light," but we have stood in its way and by our own willfulness have created shadows that enlarge the dark. Our days are clouded over by the threat of war, the decline of true religion, and the loss of clear meaning to life. So few give heed any longer to thy call to us to be just and kind and live in quiet fellowship with our God. In the words of the psalmist, then, we pray: "Turn us again, O God of hosts, and cause thy face to shine and we shall be saved."

We thank thee in this festive season that in the midst of the ages thou didst command a light to shine into our darkness that brought to us knowledge of thy divine being in the face of Jesus Christ. We bless thee that that light increased in and through him, and down the countless years ever since he has brought release and pardon from sin through his unfailing grace; healing to all our hurts through the touch of his tender love; and the hope and promise of a new age of goodwill and fraternity for the whole inhabited earth.

Lord, we praise thee for all these gracious benefits bestowed upon our common life, and we plead for help to prepare a wide room with us for the child of Bethlehem so that he may exercise his rule forever in our minds and hearts. Christmas is a time for deeper prayer and more costly devotion; challenge our will to cast off the easy ornaments of sentimentality and make this hour truly a celebration of the coming of eternal light to shatter the darkness and bring new life to all. May we hear again his voice, "I am the light of the world," and learn from the hope of his Second Coming that because he lives we "no more may die."

Blessing and honor and glory and power be unto thy name, for thou hast overcome our fears and assured us that "wherever meek souls will receive him, still the dear Christ enters in."—Donald Macleod

LECTIONARY MESSAGE

Topic: Waking to the Light

TEXT: Rom. 13:11–15

OTHER READINGS: Isa. 2:1–5; Matt. 24:36–44

Children frequently fight off sleep. They struggle not to miss any potentially new and exciting adventures. Too often adults face life with lethargy and boredom. For some, life is a travail to be endured rather than an adventure to be embraced. For the Christian, however, life is an invitation to an adventure with God. Despite life's inescapable sorrows and sufferings, the Christian lives under the canopy of a bright horizon. In Jesus Christ the long night of human sin has been broken. The present is suffused with the dawn of God's coming kingdom. Our lives are illumined not by the disappointment of what has been but by the light of what is to come. In the thirteenth chapter of Romans, Paul summons the church to actions appropriate for God's dawning kingdom.

I. Be alert to the time (v. 11). Ignorance may not only lead to vice; it can, itself, be one. Innocence is not identical with virtue. One fruit of the Spirit instrumental in yielding spiritual health is discernment. The maturing Christian needs to be alert not only to the events of the present but also to their significance. Biblical faith affirms that God acts and reveals himself in history. In the life, death, Resurrection, and coming consummation of Jesus Christ, the church has been given history's key. Christians are to understand the present not in isolation but in light of God's faithful actions and unfailing promises. Truthful reading of the present requires careful attention to our lives illumined by God's demonstration and revelation of his character. The church's calling is not to drift aimlessly but to offer an anchor for a time that has lost its mooring and has no compass.

II. Be awake to the hour (vv. 11–12). The imperative of Advent is to "watch!" Slumber represents forgetfulness of God. The "night" of life is where God's reign is obscured. Whoever is "awake" to the present hour is alive to the declaration of Christ's return. The same Christ who came—who is spiritually present now—is coming again. With each passing day that coming is closer. This is the "light" in which the Christian lives. Perhaps Paul thought that Christ's Second Coming was imminent. More to the point is the fact that after the first coming of Christ the decisive event of history has occurred. Because the end of history has already dawned in Jesus Christ, the church does not face a protracted future in which leisurely action is possible. There is a sense of urgency not only in light of Christ's future return but also because of the dawn in which his kingdom is already present. The opposite of love is not hate but apathy. Slumber represents the apathetic Christian life. Faith is life lived referring all things to the rule and reality of the present and coming King.

III. Put off the deeds of darkness (vv. 12a, 13, 14a). This present age, in which God's kingdom is still obscured, is represented by night. Christians know we live not in the twilight but in the gathering dawn. Consequently, we are to cast off conduct that makes no reference to God's reality and rule. Reinhold Niebuhr suggests that all sin falls into two categories: (a) sins of pride—thinking too much of the self, and (b) sins of sensuality—actions that by seeking to obliviate the self in sensate experience end up holding the self too little in esteem. Paul's list of the "deeds of darkness" embraces both these poles: orgies, drunkenness, sexual immorality are sins of sensuality; dissension and jealousy are sins of pride. All sin reflects forgetfulness of God. Deeds of the dark have no place for believers who know their lives are lived in the light of God's consciousness and care.

IV. Be clothed in Christ (vv. 12b, 14a). Important as "putting off the deeds of darkness" may be, more important still is the "putting on of the armor of light." Paul urges believers to "clothe" themselves with the Lord Jesus Christ. Here is union with Christ cast in intimate imagery. This may allude to the Christian's initial experience of baptism. The necessity to "put off" the old and to "put on" the new, however, is a continuing demand of the Christian faith. Our lives are to be covered, guarded, enveloped, and warmed by the Lord Jesus. Here are strength and power to live. Here is the love that truly brings the dawn of a whole new possibility for living.

Augustine, in his *Confessions,* speaks of this passage as occasioning his finding the resolve to break with his old life and to take up a new one. Through this text, the Spirit called one of the church's greatest voices to wake from slumber and live alive to the light of God. In these verses, Augustine heard both the conviction of his sin and the assurance of his salvation. By God's grace, so may they speak again, today.—John Shouse

SUNDAY: DECEMBER TENTH

SERVICE OF WORSHIP

Sermon: City Rainbows

TEXT: Gen. 9:8–17; Rev. 21:1–7

The first movie I saw as a child was *The Wizard of Oz*. I was probably five or six at the time, and I remember how frightened I was by the Scarecrow, the Tin Man, and the Cowardly Lion. In the movie Judy Garland plays the part of Dorothy, and she sings the familiar song that begins with the line "Somewhere over the rainbow."

The Wizard of Oz is a charming story full of rainbows, dreams, hopes, and longings for a better, happier world.

I. In a fascinating book, *Over the Rainbow,* Paul Nathanson[22] explores the enormous popularity and the countless interpretations of this story of Dorothy and her journey to the land of Oz. He calls it one of America's most influential secular myths. Among the many possible layers of meaning, it may be seen as offering a narrative of our national search for identity. Founded as a land of promise, America has fallen from its early innocence into political and commercial corruption. Dorothy's search for a dreamland over the rainbow takes her to Oz and the Emerald City, with all of its surface sophistication and glitter. Life in the Emerald City, however, proves to be disappointing and hollow, and Dorothy longs to return home to her small town in Kansas.

Perhaps Dorothy's and our nostalgia for a lost past rests on the assumption that our common life then was characterized by simplicity and homogeneity. Our little towns of yesterday, we suppose, were quiet, neat places, predominantly white, middle-class, and Protestant, with no poverty or pollution, or conflicts of race, gender, religion, or class. The story of *The Wizard of Oz* expresses America's ambivalence toward the big city, viewing it as exciting and alluring on the one hand, yet on the other hand, finally rejecting it in favor of a fantasy of rural or small-town America long ago. The land beyond the rainbow, we are told, is not in the future but in the idealized past of our personal and national childhood.

II. Like *The Wizard of Oz,* the Bible also contains a story of a rainbow.

(a) But the differences between the two stories are striking. In the biblical story, the rainbow is not a sign of human longing and hope; it is a sign of God's promise. Moreover, the biblical rainbow is not associated with going back home to the supposed security and innocence of a past world; it is the token of God's promise to be faithful to the creation as it moves beyond God's judgment toward a new future. Then too, the biblical story refuses to idealize a world marked by uniformity and simplicity; the rainbow of God's promise embraces all the riotous diversity of creatures that God blessed in the beginning and called good. Thus the biblical story of the rainbow gives in to neither the romantic nostalgia for the past that pervades *The Wizard of Oz* nor the bitter cynicism that tempts us when our hopes for a better world are dashed. As the sign of God's covenant with the whole creation, the rainbow gives testimony not to the power of human faith but to the resiliency of God's faithfulness.

(b) Also like *The Wizard of Oz,* the Bible tells the story of a beautiful city. Yet unlike the glitzy and fraudulent Emerald City, the new Jerusalem is God's city of the future, and its coming will be the consummation of God's promises. The New Testament drama that begins with the advent of Jesus Christ concludes with the vision of the advent of a new city where life will flourish and the peace of God will reign.

In this season of messianic expectation, does our hope also embrace our cities? Must we not admit that the promises of God's faithfulness, symbolized in the rainbow and in the new Jerusalem, seem far removed seriously if we do not be-

[22]Paul Nathanson, *Over the Rainbow: The Wizard of Oz as a Secular Myth of America* (Albany: State University of New York Press, 1991).

lieve that it also arches over our cities? Can we hope for the coming of the heavenly Jerusalem if we do not also pray and work for the renewal of our cities here and now?

Let us be clear. The Bible is far from being romantic about cities. It is fully aware of the injustice, violence, and desolation that often mark city life. We must not overlook the severity of God's judgment on the cities of Sodom and Gomorrah and Babel and Babylon and Rome. Still, the Bible is not indifferent or cynical about the future of the city. It never abandons hope for the city. Jesus does not simply condemn Jerusalem; he weeps over it. And according to the author of the Book of Revelation, the destiny of creation will be fulfilled in a city of the future, a city that is not "somewhere over the rainbow, way up high," but a city that by God's grace is coming to us and that will be firmly established on this earth. Here is indeed a stunning aspect of biblical hope: the promises of God, to which God is ever faithful, find their consummation in a new city.

(c) We must not forget that the early Christian movement was a missionary movement centered in the cities. The Apostle Paul did not seek to evade the cities of his time. He believed that God was present and at work in the cities. Paul took the gospel of God's promise in Jesus Christ to renew the whole earth into the metropolitan centers of antiquity—Corinth and Thessalonica and Philippi and the cities of Galatia and Athens and Rome. The cities of his time had their magnificent buildings and their wonderfully busy markets, as do the cities of our time. But they also had the poverty, the crime, the clashes of diverse peoples that afflict our cities today. Yet Paul believed that God's promise was for the cities, too. For the apostle of Christ crucified, the grace of God was present with renewing power in the cities even if only in germinal and hidden form.

Our society has just about given up on our inner cities. Protestant mainstream denominations are scarcely in a position to scold, since for some time they have been largely absent from the inner cities. They hardly seem equipped to help foster a new sensitivity to and solidarity with the poor of our urban centers. The world of the members of many congregations and the world of the inner-city poor are separated by a vast chasm. Given the minimal commitment of many Protestant denominations to the task, a calling to ministry in the inner city would understandably be considered by many seminarians as a ticket to despair and oblivion. So the dreamland over the rainbow has become for many of us the carefully manicured and thoroughly guarded stretches of American suburbia. Meanwhile, the cities and their abandoned millions repeat a litany of terrible misery and hopelessness, punctuated by occasional eruptions of fiery anger.

(d) Thus the nagging question will not go away: does God's promise embrace our cities? After many decades of neglect of the cities by our society and our churches, is God's grace still present there? Even after the fires of Watts and Detroit and Newark two decades ago, even after the Rodney King verdict and the ensuing burning of Los Angeles several months ago, is the church today still chasing Dorothy's rainbow, or does it really believe that the rainbow of God's promise arches over the run-down tenement buildings of our inner cities and shines over the staggering number of unemployed, homeless, and desperate people in our metropolitan centers? Does the vision of a coming new Jerusalem serve to strengthen our commitment to ministry in and renewal of our cities here and now?

This past summer I experienced an unexpected and unpretentious confirmation that God's promise and God's faithfulness are present in the city. I was give this assurance by a group of African-American children in the inner city of Trenton, New Jersey. Professor Kadi Billman, a friend who helped to organize a summer program for children in Trenton, invited me to take part in some of its activities. She suspected, I think, that I would receive as much as I gave to the children.

One day my assignment was to teach a

small class of nine- to ten-year-olds. Toward the end of our time together, three of the tired children asked me to read them a story from the Bible. I read the story of Noah and the rainbow. When I finished the story, I asked, "Where do you look to see a rainbow?" It was, I am afraid, the patronizing question of a professor of theology.

"On the streets," I was told. Thinking they had misunderstood me, I repeated the question.

"On the streets," came the reply again. "You can see rainbows in the oil slicks on puddles in the streets and parking lots."

These Trenton children had found God's promise of new life not up in the sky, not way up high (for city dwellers the view upward is often largely blocked by the tall buildings that line the streets and the smog that hovers overhead). Instead, they had found the sign of God's promise way down low, in the grimy puddles of their city streets.

God has not abandoned the cities. The rainbow of God's promise is present there, too. How could we ever have doubted it? Is not the promise of God always a surprise, always coming at unexpected times and in unexpected places? Not way up high but way down low. Not to the comfortable but to the afflicted. Not to the wise of this world but to little children.—Daniel L. Migliore

Illustrations

FANTASY AND UTOPIA. In Christianity this vision of the kingdom of God or the new Jerusalem has had a rich and stormy career. Sometimes it has acted as a catalyst stimulating the culture to transcend itself and its current values. At other times it has braked and deterred change. It is useful to examine the conditions under which religion operates in these different ways.

The power of the vision of a new world to spark change and innovation is undercut in at least three ways. One is to *postpone* the vision to an epoch beyond time and history. We merely wait for it, and patience becomes a primary virtue. Another way to destroy the catalytic power of a social vision is to *reduce* it to more "realistic" or "feasible" dimensions. We settle for less than we envision because anything more would be utopian. The tension is relaxed. A third is to *spiritualize* or *individualize* the radical hope so much that it becomes trivial, or at least socially inconsequential. The immortality of *my* soul takes the place of a new heaven and a new earth.—Harvey Cox

IS THIS LOVE ONLY FOR THIS LIFE? When once to a man the human face is the human face divine, and the hand of his neighbor is the hand of a brother, then will he understand what St. Paul meant when he said, "I could wish that myself were accursed from Christ for my brethren." But he will no longer understand those who, so far from feeling the love of their neighbor an essential of their being, expect to be set free from its law in the world to come. There, at least, for the glory of God, they may limit its expansive tendencies to the narrow circle of their heaven. On its battlements of safety, they will regard hell from afar and say to each other, "Hark! Listen to their moans. But do not weep, for they are our neighbors no more."—George MacDonald

Sermon Suggestions

MESSIANIC ANTICIPATIONS. TEXT: Isa. 11:1–10. (1) A promising birth in unpromising circumstances. (2) Service in the Spirit of the Lord. (3) A reign of righteousness. (4) Peace and harmony.

GOD'S WELCOME. TEXT: Rom. 15:4–13. (1) Where: promises in the Scriptures. (2) To whom: to the outsiders, specifically the Gentiles. (3) When: in the coming of Christ. (4) Why: because "Christ has welcomed you." (5) To what end: joy, peace, and hope.

Worship Aids

CALL TO WORSHIP. "Blessed be the Lord God, the God of Israel, who only doeth wondrous things. And blessed be his glorious name for ever: and let the whole earth be filled with his glory; Amen, and Amen" (Ps. 72:18–19).

INVOCATION. Father God, who has made all ages a preparation for the coming of your Son, make our hearts ready for the brightness of your glory as Christ comes to us in this sacred season. Awaken us from our slumbers amid the routines of life. Quicken us to the eternal dimensions of life. Revive and deepen our faith in spiritual realities. Kindle our affection for doing Christlike deeds and restore us to hope. In quietness we await the glorious and blessed dawn. Open our eyes that we may behold the coming of Christ in so many areas of life. Indeed, let us find the peace that only comes when we encounter the Prince of Peace as he comes to us even as he did to those who learned from him to pray: (LORD's PRAYER).—Henry Fields

OFFERTORY SENTENCE. "Verily, verily, I say unto you, He that believeth on me, the works that I do shall he do also; and greater works than these shall he do; because I go unto my Father. And whatever ye shall ask in my name, that will I do, that the Father may be glorified in the Son" (John 14:12–13).

OFFERTORY PRAYER. God of mystery and clarity, help us to be watchful and alert to the surprising ways you come to us and to the candle of your promises in the darkness of unwelcome events, for by that light, if we but be steadfast and faithful, your will may be made clear and your grace, like the Big Dipper, pour and pour from the night sky.

As we await your coming this holy Advent season, keep us purposeful and expectant, connected with your promises and with the deepest longings of your children, and especially the disheartened. Use these gifts to help prepare the feast that is to come. O come, O come, Immanuel.—Peter Fribley (adapted from the *Mission Yearbook 1993*)

PRAYER. Heavenly Father, in your Word you have given us a vision of that holy city to which the nations of the world bring their glory: behold and visit, we pray, the cities of the earth. Renew the ties of mutual regard that form our civic life. Send us honest and able leaders. Enable us to eliminate poverty, prejudice, and oppression, that peace may prevail with righteousness, and justice with order, and that men and women from different cultures and with differing talents may find with one another the fulfillment of their humanity; through Jesus Christ our Lord.—*Book of Common Prayer*

LECTIONARY MESSAGE

Topic: The Kingdom's Demand and Promise

TEXT: Matt. 3:1–12

OTHER READINGS: Isa. 11:1–10; Rom. 15:4–13

Sports events are regularly broadcast with dual announcers. The first reports "play by play" information, while the second adds "color" by setting events against their broader background. Our appetite for commentary affects the coverage of current affairs, arts, entertainment, sports, and politics. The human mind craves interpretation. Bare facts beg a context in which their significance can be viewed. We strain to hear those voices that promise accurately to orient our lives.

Through biblical prophecy God presents to his people his perspective on their lives. This Word is regularly spoken by the prophets in a twofold movement. First, the prophet lays bare the predicament of the present. To the devastation humanity has wrought upon itself, repentance is the only appropriate response. The prophet weeps. Then, the prophet dreams a new dream, opening the vista of a tomorrow different from any that could unfold independent of the gracious activity of God. The prophet laments the present and heralds the future. In both these actions the prophet is part of God's preparation for what he is bringing to pass in history.

I. An authentic voice appears (vv. 1–6). In hours of crisis, compelling figures sometimes arise who bring perspective and vision for their time. Abraham Lincoln may have done this later. Early in the first century a figure emerged from the Judean wilderness who wore the prophet's mantle. John spoke words of both demand and promise, but now the message seemed even more urgent, and God's coming action even more imminent.

Matthew records John's message of "repentance" as identical with the opening call of Jesus' ministry (4:17). Significantly, Matthew makes no mention of this as a "baptism of forgiveness" (Mark 1:4b). Forgiveness will not be a consequence of John's ministry but must wait upon the coming figure John is announcing as bringing both God's mercy and judgment. Forgiveness is not a possibility we can obtain on our own—even by repentance. If forgiveness comes, it will be an act of God . . . a gift of grace . . . the work of the Messiah.

John's voice came to his countrymen from outside the official channels of society. His clothing and diet—though not without precedent in his day—were severe. The word of challenge and renewal regularly comes from outside the societally sanctioned corridors of respect and power. The widespread response to John's call, culminating in confession, is evidence of a work of the Spirit. We are seldom so far from God as when we are unaware of our separation. One of the marks of the spiritual vacuum of our age is the relative ignorance of our people of our condition. The vocation of John in his day is the task of evangelism in ours: to sound an alarm that wakens people to their plight.

II. Penetrating pretensions (vv. 7–10). If any predicament is more disturbing than spiritual indifference, it may be spiritual arrogance. Pride presumes a status before God that is deserved rather than bestowed. Jesus reserved his sternest rebukes for the "professionally" religious. John's criticism of the religious establishment who seem initially to be answering his call is twofold. First, just as faith without works is dead, so words without actions are empty. Repentance unaccompanied by fruitfulness is blasphemy. Better to make no declaration of faith and show no interest in the things of God than to do so with an indifferent spirit. Presumption in the presence of holiness is intolerable. When we are casual in our attitude toward holy things, our spirits become callous to the things of God. No birthright, rank, position, or place in and of itself suffices to assure our relationship to God. We have no claim to God's favor independent of his grace. The Pharisees and Sadducees were proud of their Jewish lineage. John insists, however, we are not "born" into a relationship with God. We are not naturally "born" as Christians. We are "born again" as we receive God's gracious gift of himself through a repentance and faith that show their substance by the fruit of lives changed.

Authentic faith is often endangered by the impulse toward "magic." "Magic" attempts to control God and harness the power of the divine. John announces, by contrast, that God's judgment overtakes precisely those who presume upon God. John warns of pride based on status. God forgive the Christian church that exudes an air of self-righteousness! By definition, the church is a collection of people who have come to a point of public confession that their lives have been broken and that they are in need of a Savior. The church should be the soil in which self-righteousness is least likely to take root. John's message reminds that the way to God always involves humility, never presumption.

III. Baptized with spirit and fire (vv. 11–12). However appropriate repentance might be, by itself it has no power to save. John proclaimed the coming of one whose work would be powerful and decisive. Rather than carrying only the preparatory call for repentance, the coming one would cover human life with the Holy Spirit and fire. The Spirit is the Bible's language for God's intersection with his creation. Fire is used biblically to speak of both God's presence and his judgment. G. Campbell Morgan has made the intriguing suggestion that the fires of heaven and of hell might very well be the same. God's love, as well as his judgment, is a consuming fire. In its flames, the saint is energized and fulfilled, while the sinner is frustrated and in torment. The urgency of John's message can be seen in the consequences our actions will reap. There is to be a final accounting. Our deeds will be exposed. Our lives will be weighed. Wheat and chaff will be separated. The "wind" (or "Spirit") will carry away insubstantial lives to the unquenchable fire while the "wheat" of lives that have found nourishment by feeding deeply on the things of God will be gathered home. T. S. Eliot pictured our age as one filled with "hollow men." What Scripture promises to those who respond to the demand of the coming kingdom are lives of substance touched by the wind and fire of the Spirit of the living God.—John Shouse

SUNDAY: DECEMBER SEVENTEENTH

SERVICE OF WORSHIP

Sermon: A Word in the Wilderness

TEXT: Luke 3:1–6

Year in and year out, from Advent through Pentecost, we Christians can be found sharing the sacred story over and over again. Simply in the telling it touches the broken, and often barren, places of our lives—bearing a healing balm and a calming blessing.

Still in all, there are those contemporary skeptics who deem this sacred story little more than an idle tale.

But the Christian would never agree with such nonsense! We know that this story has planted hope in our aching hearts; it has given strength to waning faith; it has brought us back from despair and cynicism! "I love to tell the story because I know 'tis true, it satisfies my longings as nothing else can do."

I. Longings. We all have them, don't we? There are those of us who long to be freed from some sickness that has held our body captive to pain and our soul to grief. Maybe we long for the ache of loneliness to pass, and for real pleasure to once more make our heart its home.

(a) Some of us long for solace, others look for satisfaction, and others yearn for the compassion of someone who genuinely cares. We can long for success, or security, or a sense of well-being. But, regardless of the form they might assume, we all have longings.

(b) The world looks and longs for justice, and mercy, and the kind of lasting compassion that could eventuate in the upbuilding of world community. The Apostle Paul put it this way: "The whole created universe in all its parts groans as if in the pangs of childbirth!"

(c) Well, the people and the world at the time of Christ's public ministry were essentially no different. They too knew the desperations and discouragements of life. Because their children were also subject to serious—if not fatal—diseases.

Whenever their world threatened to collapse around their ears, they would tell the story of God as Creator, and that would put all of their fears in proper perspective.

II. Ironically enough, it was this same sacred story—so much of comfort and consolation to God's covenant community—which also sharpened the edge of their longing!

(a) Because, you see, the prophets—God's inspired interpreters of the story—proclaimed that there would come the glorious day of God's final deliverance.

(b) And it was this promise of the coming Messiah that created a holy restlessness among God's people. They looked with anxious and expectant hearts to that great day when God would make good on his promise to send them their deliverer.

(c) Isaiah, that great prophet of Israel's captivity in Babylon, expressed the breathtaking beauty of that coming day of deliverance. Do you recall his forceful imagery? He wrote:

> Then the eyes of the blind shall be opened,
> and the ears of the deaf unstopped;

then the lame shall leap like a deer,
and the tongue of the speechless sing for joy.
For waters shall spring forth in the wilderness,
and streams in the desert.

(d) So, the faithful now yearned for the advent of their Savior. They ached with all the longing of the parent kneeling at the bedside of the afflicted child; or the widowed spouse waiting for the grief to subside; or the AIDS patient, holding out for the cure; or the victim of a heart attack who pines for peaceful rest.

III. Luke proclaims that the fulfillment of God's promise of deliverance to his covenant people falls immediately in the arenas of political and religious realities. The herald, who is to prepare the way for God's Savior, has his feet planted squarely in the midst of this otherwise inglorious world.

(a) God's gospel, in all of its spiritual power, will confront the calamitous and insufferable experiences of human life and history. And will do so in and through those very avenues and arenas of this world in which we live and move and have our being! But always and everywhere to one end: to *exact* salvation!

(b) Luke tells us that both Christ's first Advent and the preparations for his coming, through the ministry of John the Baptist, are the initiative of our gracious God. And, as was true from the beginning of time, God's gracious and benevolent care and compassion permeate the very pores of human history. Do you understand the striking nature of that claim?

(c) It means that when you, or someone you love, lie languishing in a hospital bed, God, in the Spirit of Christ as Savior, is there to save you. It means that when you must wait in the silence of the surgical wing, God, in the Spirit of Christ as Comforter, is there to lend you courage. And it also means that whenever, wherever you and I must face trial, temptation, or deepening trouble, God's faithful power and presence will see us through.

IV. Beyond a shadow of a doubt, Luke wants us to hear this sacred story as "the truth, the whole truth, and nothing but the truth." Luke affirms that this story is no mere child's fable—fashioned to soothe our sores or to sweeten the sourness of life's mishaps.

(a) Because, with our God, all redemptive activity takes place smack dab at the heart of history's distortions, disconsolations, and divisions. Oh, I know! It's clearly *scandalous* to proclaim that God's presence is an *intimate* part of human history—personal and global. But it's this "scandal" that has *always* set our sacred story apart from all others.

(b) Well, the scandal drives even deeper that all of that, doesn't it? You remember, don't you? Luke also writes that "the Word of God came to John son of Zechariah in the wilderness." And while there's been much scholarly speculation over just what John was doing out there in the back woods of the Jordan, we needn't concern ourselves with such matters. Because we don't want to miss the essential!

(c) Which is just this: the Word of God came to John the Baptist while he was *in the wilderness*. Perhaps you already know that, according to the Bible, the "wilderness" represents several important—and I might add, painful—realities? And maybe your knotted stomach tells you that this "wilderness" is not so far removed from your own life experiences? We'll come back to that. But first, here's something of what the Bible means when it speaks of the "wilderness."

V. The wilderness was thought to be that place wherein the demons had dominion. It was, therefore, considered to be a place of abandonment, desolation, and devastation. In fact, the wilderness represents the whole sweeping panorama of godforsakenness!

(a) It's perfectly obvious, isn't it? We hear words like *abandonment* and *devastation,* and something inside our hearts begins to ache. We begin to understand where this biblical image of "wilderness" has a decisive bearing on realities engulfing us. And we already know that sense in which we too could speak of a "wilderness" in our common world—don't we?

(b) He's speaking of those places in the human heart where alienations, desperations, resentments, and feelings of forsakenness are to be found—isn't he? He's referring to our pain, our problems within this life, our emptiness, loneliness, and longings—isn't he? He's reading off our own hearts—isn't that so?

VI. Well, here's the gospel! God's redemptive Word comes to perform its wonder within the wastelands of this world—those places in which abandonment, discouragement, and death once reigned.

(a) God's Word can be heard even in the wilds where folks are lost, lonely—without love, and longing for release, redemption, and restoration. His Word is spoken in the wilderness of this contemporary world—where secularity so often threatens to devour our souls and the souls of our children.

(b) Our sacred story clearly proclaims that God's plan of salvation has been played out on the stage of world history and at the very center of the human heart.

(c) God chose to feel our pain and to heal our deepest wound from sin by being born in a manger. As someone once said, "God knew what to do with thorns; he made them into a crown. God knew what to do with a cross; he made it into a throne. God knew what to do with the place of Crucifixion; he made it into a garden of Resurrection!" And in doing so, God has filled our misery with his mercy!—Albert J. D. Walsh

Illustrations

THE UNATTRACTIVENESS OF JESUS. When I was a boy in Glasgow, there hung in our living room a large print of a painting by Sigismund Goetze entitled "Despised and Rejected." I know nothing about the artist. I know nothing about the merits of the painting. But I have never forgotten the picture. In the center was the Christ bound to a Roman imperial altar, overshadowed by an angel with the Gethsemane cup. On each side of the altar there streamed by a procession of men and women in modern dress. Here was the political agitator, and there a common laborer; here a sportsman with the pink edition of the paper, there a scientist with his test tube. A newsboy shouted the latest society scandal, and a woman went by in a widow's weeds. A soldier in uniform and a clergyman replete with clerical collar stalked by in unconscious company. Only one person had any look of surprise or wonder or sympathy for the Christ—a nurse.

What is the picture saying? For the artist, Christ is still "despised and rejected" by most folk in the everyday, workaday world—James T. Cleland

HOPE FOR THE HUNGRY. Advent is hope, but hope is far from the hungry of our world. The solution? It falls easily from our lips. The solution is . . . Christ. After all, he is the hope of *all* humankind; in him, as we shall sing at Christmas, "The hopes and fears of all the years are met." So, he will take care of the hungry in his own inimitable way. Not much *I* can do about it. And since I did not dry up the sub-Sahara, don't hang a guilt trip on me. Don't spoil my Christmas.

I'm afraid it will not wash; the solution is not that simple. The solution is indeed Christ, but not Christ in glorious isolation, at the right hand of the Father. Christ does not rain down manna from heaven on starving refugees; he no longer multiplies loaves and fishes. And it's a copout to mouth the Beatitude "Blessed are you that hunger now, for you *shall* be satisfied" (Luke 6:21). The problem is . . . now. There has to be "good news" for the hungry now.

The solution is the whole Christ, head and members. Unless *we* act, the most effective solution to hunger is our present solution: death. The hungry die. But for every one who dies, two will be born hungry. The hungry must have hope.—Walter J. Burghardt

Sermon Suggestions

TO THOSE OF A FEARFUL HEART. TEXT: Isa. 35:1–10. The words of encouragement to be spoken to disheartened exiles are relevant to disheartened people today. (1) You must be strong and fearless—an impossible task as one looks at one's problems and considers the weakness of human flesh, verse 4a. (2) The challenge is not impossible to meet, for God is present to make things right: "He will come and save you," verse 4b. (3) God will bring blessing upon blessing to make matters right for those who trust him, verses 5–9. (4) The outcomes of God's presence and providence are joy and more joy, verse 10.

HOW TO BE PATIENT. TEXT: James 5:7–10. (1) Take a lesson from agriculture, verse 7. (2) Consider what the coming again of Christ will mean, verses 8–9. (3) Follow the example of the prophets, verse 10.

Worship Aids

CALL TO WORSHIP. "He hath put down the mighty from their seats, and exalted them of low degree" (Luke 1:52).

INVOCATION. O God, in your strange reversals there is grace, that the proud may see more clearly our common humanity and all of us appreciate our worth in your sight. Only God is great, yet you have created us all in your image: so, help us all to worship you in spirit and in truth.

OFFERTORY SENTENCE. "May God, the giver of hope, fill you with all joy and peace because you trust in Him—so that you may be overflowing with hope through the power of the Holy Spirit" (Rom. 15:13 WEYMOUTH).

OFFERTORY PRAYER. Blessed Lord, through whom we live and move and have our being, so move in our offering this day as to comfort the sorrowing, strengthen the struggling, nurture the seeking, and save the lost. In the powerful name of Jesus.—E. Lee Phillips

PRAYER. During this beautiful season we gather from varied walks of life to join our hearts and voices in thanksgiving and praise to you, Father. When we ponder the blessings that are ours, we are overwhelmed by your providence and care. When we think of all the friendships that become more dear with the passage of time, we feel gratitude for such a wonderful gift as friendship. When we remember those who have stood by us in all seasons of life, who have encouraged and guided, chastised and cajoled and by so doing prodded us to be our best, we are forever thankful. Most of all, we are thankful for those who have given words of life, those who have stood as staunch examples of the highest values of life, those who have shown the virtue of sacrifice and the grandeur of selflessness, those who have learned from Christ the meaning of life and love and redemption. This morning help us to understand how we can incorporate his values in our lives even as we welcome him into our hearts.—Henry Fields

LECTIONARY MESSAGE

Topic: Living by Faith

TEXT: Matt. 11:2–11

OTHER READINGS: Isa. 7:10–16; James 5:7–10

Christians live in in-between times. We live in the "already" of Christ's appearance and the "not yet" of his consummation. The Book of Hebrews summarizes this dilemma: "At present we do not see everything subject to him. But we see Jesus" (2:8b–9a). From the gloom of a prison cell, John must have felt the pressure of his predicament and been anxiously watching the ministry of Jesus. He had anticipated that Jesus was the messianic figure coming with judgment and power he had been announcing. Now, in the darkness of a dungeon, facing imminent death at the hand of his enemies, and with Jesus pursuing a course he had not foreseen, John reaches out for assurance.

I. Breaking the mold (vv. 2–5). We are by nature idolaters. We take the God who has created us in his image and attempt to recreate him in ours. Christians frequently want Christ as their Savior but still want him on their terms. Jesus, however, never allowed himself to be a projection of the desires others placed upon him. He stands over against our expectations and offers us nothing other than his own authentic life.

John asks, "Are you the coming one, or are we to look for another?" Jesus' answer is dramatic and forceful, yet from the perspective of John's own anticipations for the ministry of the Messiah, ambiguous. Jesus' answer does not conform to the popular idea of the Messiah's work. From John's eyes, Jesus had not brought in the judgment of history's close, did not fast, and kept company a careful Jew would avoid.

Jesus answers John with unmistakable references to God's saving intentions in Isaiah 35:5–6, 29:18, and 61:1. Here is Jesus' own announcement of the work of the Messiah: the healing of affliction and the announcement of good news to the poor. Jesus demands we accept him on his terms, not ours. He sees himself as fulfilling the Old Testament prophetic promise while also remaining free to reinterpret the understanding of that promise. Jesus offers not so much to fulfill our hopes as to be our hope.

II. The Beatitude of acceptance (v. 6). The Apostle Paul understood the message of God's saving work through Jesus Christ to be a "scandal" to unbelievers (1 Cor. 1:23). The ministry of Jesus moves first to "low-pressure" areas—that is, areas of need rather than of contentment. Whoever we would look down upon, whoever we would think ourselves better than, the Spirit of God passes us over and seeks out first. Jesus shares a new "beatitude" aimed at those who are not "tripped up by" his ministry. This same verb is used in Matthew 5:29–30 ("If your right eye *causes you to sin*"). To accept Jesus on his own terms is to evidence a heart that has lowered its pretensions and defenses; it is to be open to the work and person of Jesus. Herein is blessing, indeed.

III. John's status and the believers' standing (vv. 7–12). One of the rarest achievements of human life is the emergence of an authentic self. We gravitate toward people who seem "centered"—who know who they are and where they are going. We hunger for words to help us understand our lives. We listen to songs, buy records, go to concerts, attend films, and read books in an attempt to gain insight into the mystery of our living. In any day, a voice that seems with credibility to carry a word of authenticity about our lives causes interest. In his own day John's authentic voice of judgment and prophecy caused a sensation. People flocked from the cities and towns to hear John's hard but penetrating word. Jesus forces his own hearers to focus on the reason for John's appeal: John was heard not because of the natural beauty of the wilderness where he spoke or because his was a frail and timid spirit ("a reed shaken by the wind," v. 7). Neither was he sought because he was "clothed in soft raiment" (v. 8) like those who occupy positions of prominence. No, in John people were presented with the truth about their lives and with a bold pronouncement for the future. In John's life the entire strain of prophetic tradition is brought to its climax. John's message embodied the double movement of the prophet—to lament the present and to reenvision the future. The coming hope that John foresees is consummated in the ministry of Jesus. Since the work of Jesus represents God's culminating act, no greater work could be imagined prior to Jesus than John's ministry of preparation for Jesus.

No greater than John has ever appeared on history's stage, for John stood on the threshold of the kingdom. Yet towering as this ministry was, greater still is the least of the disciples who follow Jesus, for theirs is the experience of the kingdom. What John announced, Jesus brings to pass. John is the last of the old order. Christian disciples stand in the face of a new one. Now all those who dare to heed the call and take the hand of Jesus are present at the beginning of a brave new world. The "greatness" of the Christian lies in this: it is the Christian's glory and honor to live as a citizen of and witness to the presence of the coming kingdom.—John Shouse

SUNDAY: DECEMBER TWENTY-FOURTH

SERVICE OF WORSHIP

Sermon: The Grace of God Has Appeared

TEXT: Titus 2:11–14

The words we'll be hearing are from a "pastoral epistle." One of those little known—seldom read—love letters in the New Testament.

"The Grace of God has appeared, bringing salvation to all, training us to renounce impiety and worldly passions and in the present age to live lives that are self-controlled, upright, and godly, while we wait for the blessed hope and the manifestation of the glory of our great God and Savior, Jesus Christ. It is he who gave himself for us that he might redeem us from all iniquity and purify for himself a people of his own who are zealous for good deeds."

That's pretty strong stuff, isn't it? And in particular for this, Christmas Eve!

I. I suppose that Paul used such forceful language because circumstances in his friend's congregation dictated that he do so.

(a) Look. Rumor has it that the older women in this Cretan congregation practiced gossip to the point of making it their profession. They could demolish a person's reputation, even before the morning coffee turned cold in the cup.

(b) And most of the men were no prize either. They were shiftless, abrasive, and altogether uncontrollable characters. Here's the upshot: these "Cretans" failed to relate the gospel of grace to anything going on in their daily lives.

(c) Well, don't look now, but that same temptation is hot on our heels also!

After all, you know as well as I do. The day will come when it's time to take down the decorations, burn the gift boxes, and pack away the bright lights.

Life—once again—resumes its regular, and for some, tedious, routines. It's bound to come, sooner or later. And with it come the colorless, and often wearisome, drudgeries of daily life.

II. And in that day-to-day, bread-and-butter existence—what impact will this gracious gospel have on us? What difference will it make in our daily living, and longing, and loving?

(a) You know, I've often heard it said that during this particular time of year people are more friendly, more gracious, even more generous. In fact, there's a commonplace observation—I'm sure we've all heard it said! "How wonderful this world would be if people had the 'Christmas spirit' all year round."

(b) That could well be true, if by the phrase "Christmas spirit" people *intended* to say something like, "living *in* and *under* the lordship of Christ's Holy Spirit" each and every day of the year. But I'm not sure that's what they mean. They mean something more sentimental.

(c) Unfortunately, I'm not even certain that people *are* "more friendly, more gracious, or more generous" at this time of year. It seems to me that we've all but lost the sacred—and therefore, *essential*—meaning of this holy season. And each year, we say *more* and do *less* about it! The secular celebration has all but swallowed up the spiritual—and we are all the poorer for it.

(d) Frustrated, because you failed to find the *right* gift. Provoked by the long lines at the cash register. Annoyed as that fourth batch of cookies burned on the bottoms. Bad tempered, because you spent two days untangling the tree lights—and the bulbs were burned out!

III. We all know how *frivolous* things soon *frustrate* us. We also know how quickly the sacred gets smothered by the secular. And the Apostle Paul steps forward to remind us, doesn't he?

(a) He reminds us of the real meaning of *redemption* and the *result* of God's grace.

(b) Even now someone, somewhere, languishes in a hospital bed. Perhaps she dies alone. Maybe he's surrounded by family and friends. Someone, somewhere, remembers—and weeps bitter tears. On some street, in some city, a family wonders where they'll get their next meal. It's all happening, right now, even as we make merry with music, and even as we sit—enthralled by candlelight and mystery. It's all happening. And it's called *real* life.

(c) And it's *this* life that God's love has entered, in order to redeem. So the genuine and unrelenting celebration of Christmas is soon discovered by those who place their lives in this Lord's compassion and care.

Only such *committed* saints discover that the deepest joy of this Christmas season can never be gathered up and celebrated in one solitary evening of candlelight and sacred song. Devoted disciples of the Lord will be filled with his glory and grace every day as they seek to follow his holy way and to worship him with commitment to his cause of compassion.

(d) Here's what we need to remember. God came in the person of his Son—as a tiny babe in a manger—not so as to provide us with a play script for a Christmas cantata! Paul says that "our great God and Savior, Jesus Christ . . . gave himself for us that he might redeem us from all iniquity."

IV. Now. Do you remember that "unavoidable" question? Well, it was this:

"What difference, if any, has this message of deliverance, mercy, and real redemption made in our lives? And what difference will it make?" I'll remind you once more of the importance, as the Apostle Paul sees it.

(a) He asserts that Christ redeemed us in order to "purify for himself a people of his own who are zealous for good deeds!"

The creation of a community of people, inspired by Christ, filled with his passion, who are "his own" and "zealous for good deeds." That's the sole, the sacred, the significant message and meaning of Christmas.

(b) God created a community—in Christ—to carry forward his compassion and grace into this wounded world. God creates and sustains a people of passion and power. The power to prevail over the enemies of God's grace, gospel, and goodwill!

There's the message of hope for the person dying in bed, or stricken with grief, or lonely, or haunted by the absence of familiar faces. God has not *forgotten* them—or us. God has not *forsaken* them—or us.

(c) God has graciously and lovingly created a covenant community of Christ-inspired lives, persons longing to join his mission of mercy to those in dire need. Perhaps we can be such a people!—Albert J. D. Walsh

Illustrations

THE FULLNESS OF TIME. At that time the saving act took place. Just why at that time, we do not really understand. But we know what God has done at that time for us, a humanity sick unto death. He has saved us. And the act by which he has done it is the coming of him whom the Bible calls the Son of God. That is, as everything that we say about God, a parable. God has no sons just as men have sons. But this parable expresses a truth that we can never completely grasp. It says: Jesus is he who comes forth from the heart and mystery of God, yes, who is God himself upon earth, without God having ceased to be in his eternity; he, in whom God himself is with us and wills to be with us, and in whom he himself speaks to us and deals with us; he in whom God himself encounters us and opens his heart, he through whom God has established the relation with himself.—Emil Brunner

CHRISTMAS. A recent television commercial for a particular fragrance says, "If you want someone's attention, whisper." Nothing captivates our attention like the soft, deafening sound of a whisper. When, in the midst of daily conversation, we suddenly hear someone whisper, our ears usually tune in. Of course, at times when we are so loud and so busy, everything that is soft and still escapes our notice. As I think about the birth of Jesus, God seems to have whispered his way into the history of man through that tiny babe in a manger. God often moves in quiet, soft ways. And he, in his infinite wisdom, has spoken to us in the soft, supple sounds of his Son, our Savior. More folks missed it than heard it. Their census season, like our Christmas season, was loud and fast. So not many heard God whisper his way into the world. If we are not careful, we will make the same mistake. And we will once again fail to hear the most important words ever whispered, written, or shouted: "For unto you is born this day in the city of David a Savior, which is Christ the Lord" (Luke 2:11).—Stephen Cloud

Sermon Suggestions

WHAT'S IN THIS NAME? TEXT: Isa. 7:10–16. Although the name Immanuel has a specific historical reference to a child to be born in Isaiah's time, it was applied to Jesus by Matthew. It means, *God is with us.* In what sense is it relevant for us? (1) In Isaiah's time, God gave a sign of his activity in the birth of a special child. (2) In the fullness of time, God declared and made visible his presence in the birth of Jesus of Nazareth. (3) In our own time, God makes his redeeming presence known in all that continues to point to Jesus Christ, "the same yesterday and today and forever."

SIGNIFICANT IDENTITIES. TEXT: Rom. 1:1–7. (1) Jesus Christ: (a) descendant of David; (b) Son of God, verse 3. (2) Paul: (a) bondslave of Jesus Christ; (b) apostle, verse 1. (3) Ourselves: (a) recipients of the gospel; (b) people called to believe in Jesus Christ and to belong to him, verses 5–6.

Worship Aids

CALL TO WORSHIP. "Turn us again, O God of hosts, and cause thy face to shine; and we shall be saved" (Ps. 80:7).

INVOCATION. Deepen our joy, O God, that we may go out to meet the difficulties and perplexities of life with untroubled spirits and quiet minds; take away our vain pleasures and superficial frivolities and give us that deep, abiding joy that comes to all who know thee.—Theodore Parker Ferris

OFFERTORY SENTENCE. "For God loved the world so much that He gave His only Son, so that everyone who believes in Him should not be lost, but should have eternal life" (John 3:16 PHILLIPS).

OFFERTORY PRAYER. Lord, allow what we give to reflect what we believe and let what we believe determine how we act through the life-giving love of our Savior.—E. Lee Phillips

PRAYER. O thou everlasting God from whom all blessings flow, hear our prayer as again we call to remembrance the birth of thy Son, the Prince of Peace. We thank thee for his coming among us as a little child and his making for himself a place among the diverse peoples of the earth where he could love and be loved. We think especially of the signs of his coming that the ages and sages set before us: thy sustaining providence through all the years as an ancient people awaited deliverance; the voices of prophets foretelling the direction and goal of human history; the shining star and the angel song in the heavens; and the wonder of that holy night when the whole creation hailed him in whom our human redemption had come near. With true believers everywhere we rise today to sing, "Joy to the world! the Lord is come: let earth receive its king."

We rejoice in this day of days, for wherever this Christian story has reached, the spirit of goodwill is manifest and has taken root. Multiply and magnify, we pray thee, the hymns and high thanksgiving of these festive hours, and may the purpose and sincerity of our heart's adoration not die out when the bells no longer ring. May the child of Bethlehem be truly reborn in all of us today. Capture our lives for him afresh so that he may rule with truth and grace in the common round of human service. Help us so to work and witness in union with his life that we shall prove before the world the integrity of thy righteousness and the exceeding loveliness of love. Make us more eager in this season in our resolve to reach others with the wondrous story of him who is now the king of glory. May every heart at worship in this house not fail to pray now and always that through the evercircling years will come an age

When peace shall over all the earth
Its ancient splendors fling,
And the whole earth give back the song
Which now the angels sing.
—Edmund H. Sears

Glory be to the Father, and to the Son, and to the Holy Spirit, now and forever.—Donald Macleod

LECTIONARY MESSAGE

Topic: The Birth of the Savior

TEXT: Matt. 1:18–25

OTHER READINGS: Isa. 7:10–16; Rom. 1:1–7

The medium, some say, *is* the message. Let us agree that content is inextricably bound together with the form through which it is conveyed. The Christian faith announces that in Jesus Christ God gave the world a fresh start and a new beginning. Into the unbroken cycle of our stumblings and failure—our birthings and dyings—God established a whole new possibility. Such a singular story would suggest a unique inception. Such a distinctive message would invite a surprising beginning. No wonder that Matthew's Gospel opens with the picture of a birth whose character was both startling and unanticipated.

I. Born of the Spirit (v. 18). Just as the Spirit is active at the foundation of the world (Gen. 1:2), so is the Spirit a part of God's first specific act of recreation. The new creation is appropriately inaugurated by a work of the Spirit. The old cycle of our beginnings and endings is decisively broken—as it could only be broken—by a new creative act of God. From its earliest years, the church has confessed that the Spirit is active in conceiving not just the work but the very person of the living Savior. The meaning of the Incarnation is connected to the Virgin Birth of Jesus. The birth of Jesus through the initiating act of the Spirit safeguards and communicates the significance of the Incarnation. According to Karl Barth, just as the Resurrection marks the distinctiveness of Jesus' life at its ending, so does the Virgin Birth mark the uniqueness of that life at its beginning. While the Virgin Birth of Christ is not the central mystery of the Christian faith, it is a potent witness to that mystery. Here is a sign that signals the entry of God's Son into the human condition while not subsuming him under it. Here is the inception not of a person but of the assumption by God of a new nature. Just as the empty tomb is a witness to the fact of the Resurrection, so the Virgin Birth gives testimony to the unique character of the Savior's birth.

II. Redirecting a "natural" response (vv. 19–21). God's ways are not our ways. When the Creator acts, our categories may well be insufficient to predict or comprehend. Every indication for Joseph was that Mary had been unfaithful to him during their time of engagement. As one "zealous for the law," Joseph took the most lenient and merciful route open to him, which was to "put Mary away quietly." The initiative of God in the events surrounding the birth of Jesus continue in the intervention wrought by the revelation of God in the guidance of Joseph's actions. God sent his Word to Joseph by angelic messenger in a dream. The kingdom of heaven will not be foreseen in or brought to pass by the best intentions or actions of the human spirit. It is a consequence of the movement of God's Spirit.

III. The Spirit gives a name (vv. 21–23). One of the gifts of God to humanity in Genesis is the authority to name the animals (Gen. 2:10–20). The ability to name embodies the position of dominion and stewardship. Significantly, the name of the Savior is conferred by God, not decreed by humanity. Jesus came to earth to be Savior and Lord, not a domesticated subject we, ourselves, have authority over. *Jesus* is the Greek form of the Hebrew *Joshua,* whose probable derivation is "Yahweh is salvation." If a name invokes the character of the one named, then from the outset the character of Jesus as Messiah is decisively interpreted. Popular Jewish piety sought a Messiah to deliver them from their circumstances. God sends a Savior who will deliver us from the bondage of our own actions.

IV. The promise fulfilled (vv. 23–25). The entirety of the Old Testament can be read against the background of God's promissory blessing. What God had only partially brought to pass now finds its fulfillment commencing in the birth of Jesus the Christ. Matthew is intent on showing how God's covenant promises are being fulfilled in the person of Jesus Christ. The Jewish hopes of a coming Messiah, evidenced in Isaiah 7:14, are clearly shown as continuous with the birth of Jesus. While the birth of Jesus is a new beginning, it also stands as the last stage in a long process of development.

In Isaiah 7:14, the prophet was promising deliverance to Judah. More than that, however, he was looking forward to the birth of Immanuel, "God with us," who would bring salvation to all peoples. Here is the Incarnation's wonder: that into our life came life's Author; that for love of you and me the Creator of the universe became as helpless and vulnerable as a babe. The bad news of the gospel is that we have experienced a spiritual death to all for which we had been made. The good news of the gospel is that in the birth of this child, Jesus, was born for human lives the possibility of a whole new life alive to God.—John Shouse

SUNDAY: DECEMBER THIRTY-FIRST

SERVICE OF WORSHIP

Sermon: The Fixing of Our Hearts

TEXT: Ps. 57

Bible reading is sometimes a strange experience. We read a verse of a chapter a hundred times, and then suddenly, when we least expect it, some passage will leap from the page and touch our hearts. This happened to me some time ago with the fifty-seventh psalm. In the very center of that psalm there is a beautiful phrase: "My heart is fixed, O God, my heart is fixed."

If you look at the beginning of the psalm, you will find some small print that describes what the editor felt was the setting of the psalm. David was on the run. Word came that King Saul was out to kill him. David was seen as a threat to the king, as David's popularity had grown year after year. Every Israelite knew the name of Jesse's son. They knew how he had, when only a small boy, killed the giant, and they had watched him carefully as he grew from boy to man. He was so popular that Saul had given him charge of his armies, but even that had backfired. One day King Saul stood on his balcony and watched as the villagers brought David in on their shoulders. As they marched, they shouted: "Saul has slain his hundreds; David thousands." It was more than the king could take. He sent for his top military attaché, and the order went out. This man David had to be stopped.

And so, as the psalm opens, David was on the run: frightened for his life, hiding in caves, cut off from his family, scared even to sleep. But by the seventh verse, we read words that do not seem to fit the setting at all. "My heart is fixed, O God, my heart is fixed." Even in hiding for his very life, David discovered a steadfastness and a great confidence.

These words are amazing. To have a will so set that nothing, even the anger of a great king, would turn you back? To know that whatever comes, the very worst the world can offer, your heart remains steadfast? To arrive at that point where you can say that underneath it all you find a strength that carries you through?

How does one finally come to say, with so much difficulty everywhere, *my heart is set?* The psalm can help us in our search.

I. *David began where he was.* Listen to his litany.

- He talked about "the storms of destruction" (v. 1).
- He talked of those who "trample on him" (v. 3).
- He talked of living "in the midst of lions that greedily devour the sons of men; their teeth are spears and arrows, their tongues sharp swords" (v. 4).
- He talked about those "who set a net for his steps" (v. 6a) and "how his soul was bowed down" (v. 6b) and "how his enemies had dug a pit for his downfall" (v. 6c).

This is no lead article in *Better Homes and Gardens* or *Southern Living*. Why, it all sounds like a scene from *As the World Turns* or *Knots Landing* or a page from the *National Enquirer*.

David understood his situation. Things were tough. He knew the king was out to kill him, and he did not know what to do.

Frederick Buechner called one of his early novels *Lion Country*. I never understood that title until I read the words from this psalm. His characters, much like you and me, find living hard most days. People they love die. Relationships are hard to keep straight and faithful. The struggle to hang onto integrity is a recurring problem. They stumble along, having kids, making money, trying to make do. And Buechner says it's lion country. There are so many things out there that can tear the heart out of it all.

We know about lion country. A forty-six-year-old man in the prime of his life takes his family to Disney World one week and is rushed to the hospital the next. He dies, unexpectedly, three weeks later. Down the street a fourteen-year-old is raped. A woman cannot get through the worship service without tears. Last week she placed her mother with Alzheimer's disease in a nursing home. A fifty-one-year-old man is bypassed for promotion yet another time and wonders how long he can hold out. We are no strangers to lion country. Life is hard for us all. And this is one of the reasons we ought to be gentle with all God's children. We all need some understanding and some kindness. Even the worst of us. In lion country, everybody is more than a little scared.

II. But the psalm does not stop there. *David took his troubles to God*. The raw honesty of this passage is striking.

Scholars call Psalm 57 a lament. There are personal laments and the laments of the community in the Scripture. The Bible is filled with the literature of lamentation. In the Book of Jeremiah we find six laments in which the prophet Jeremiah complained to God about his human condition. The Book of Lamentations was composed in the shadow of the destruction of Jerusalem by the Babylonians in 587 B.C. These lamentations were literally wailings and griefs lifted up to the Lord God in a painful encounter. We find the same kind of emphasis in much of the Book of Job. And when we come to the Book of Psalms, the laments of the individual or the group far outweigh any other kind of literature. They cried to God out of the depths of their all-too-human dilemmas. David was in a great tradition when he lifted up his agonies to the Almighty in Psalm 57. And I wonder if, when our prayer lives are so threadbare, it is because we do not bring the pain of our hearts to the throne of grace.

Sometimes people come to me with some heavy burden. Life has dealt them a bad hand. Or they have dealt themselves a bad hand. They feel cornered, boxed in, afraid—like David. A loved one suddenly dies. They lose a job. A child breaks their hearts. Physical pains come that do not stop.

Often I ask them: "Did you ever get so angry as a little child that you kicked your father in the shins?" They laugh and say: "Yes." And then I say something like, "Don't you think God can take your rage, your anger, your frustration? He will listen, and he will certainly understand."

Fiddler on the Roof is a wonderful play about the Russian Jews that were being driven out of their homeland. Everything around them was changing. And throughout the play, Tevye carries on a running complaint with the Lord God. One day someone brings him news that he doesn't particularly want to hear. He looks up to the heavens and says, "Dear God, did you have to send me news like that? Today of all days? It's true that we are the chosen people. But once in a while can't you choose someone else?"[23] Tevye understood his faith tradition well.

Years before, the great David had cried out to the Lord God in a terrible time, and he was heard.

III. But what was it that he found, there in that cave, where the wind howled and the lions roared? *David discovered that God was there.*

That incredible discovery flows throughout the entire psalm:

- "God will give mercy" (v. 1).
- "I will find refuge in the shadow of his wings" (v. 1).
- "He will fulfill his purpose" (v. 2).
- "He will save me" (v. 3).
- "He will put to shame my enemies" (v. 3).
- "God will send forth his steadfast love and faithfulness" (v. 3).

All this was the writer's way of saying what we find in verse 3 as summary: God is faithful. He can be counted on. In that cave, David discovered he was not alone. God was with him.

But someone protests, "I'm not at all sure that this applies to me. I have this physical problem, and I don't know if I can go on." *And we need to remember that God is mercy.*

Someone else protests, "I get so lonesome sometimes I could die. I don't know what to do." *And we need to hear these words again: God will give us refuge in the shadow of his wings.*

Someone else says that they are not sure. "Everything seems to be chance, a wrong throw of the dice, no purpose at all." *And we need to hear that God will fulfill the purposes he has for us all.*

Someone else says: "I am way over my head, and the water is cold, and I do not know where to turn. The work piles up, and the responsibilities just keep on coming." *And we need to hear the words of Psalm 57: "I will save you."*

In the late 1840s Joseph Scriven, on the eve of his wedding day, learned that his bride-to-be had been tragically drowned. With a heart full of grief, he left his beloved Ireland and moved to Canada. Once again he became engaged to be married, only to lose a second fiancee to a brief but fatal illness.

Scriven spent the rest of his life helping the physically handicapped. His days were lonely, he was poor, and his own health was precarious. So he lived out his days teaching and ministering to others in Ontario.

When he learned that his own mother back in Ireland was going through a distressing time, he sat down and wrote her a poem of consolation. They were the words that, in time, would ring around the world:

What a Friend we have in Jesus
All our sins and griefs to bear;
What a privilege to carry
Everything to God in prayer.
O what peace we often forfeit,
O what needless pain we bear;
All because we do not carry
Everything to God in prayer.[24]

Scriven had learned the hard way that God is always there.

IV. So we come to the heart of our text: "My heart is fixed, O God, my heart is fixed." Faith did not just happen for David. He found his steadfastness, his confidence, in his own personal struggles. There, in the darkness of that terrible cave, he began to see the stars. He railed out, and he was heard. His lamentations were not in vain. God heard those cries of his servant. He was not alone.

And so David learned an incredible lesson there in the darkness. *His heart could remain steadfast and fixed in a world where so little was fixed or steadfast.*

So, if you have a need for God, remember this psalm. Read it over and

[23]Joseph Stein, *Fiddler on the Roof* (New York: Pocket Books, 1971), 58.

[24]*Stories of Our Favorite Hymns,* Christopher Idle, compiler (Grand Rapids: Eerdmans, 1980), 60.

over again. You do not have to wait until the sunny days. You can bring to God even the dregs of your heart. He will listen, and he will care, and you will never be alone. Out of the depths of your own experience something will emerge—a confidence—an assurance that nothing can take away—ever. Isn't this the best news that ever was? "My heart is fixed, O God—my heart is fixed."—Roger Lovette

Illustrations

A PORTRAYAL OF REST. Two painters each painted a picture to illustrate his conception of rest. The first chose for his scene a still, lone lake among the far-off mountains. The second threw on his canvas a thundering waterfall, with a fragile birch tree bending over the foam; at the fork of a branch, almost wet with the cataract's spray, a robin sat on its nest. The first was only *stagnation;* the second was *rest.* For in rest there are always two elements—tranquility and energy; silence and turbulence; creation and destruction; fearlessness and fearfulness. This it was in Christ.—Henry Drummond

FOR THE SPIRIT OF HEAVINESS. Think of anyone at this moment whom the spirit of heaviness haunts. You think of a certain old woman. But you know for a fact that you can cure her. You did so, perfectly, only a week ago. A mere visit, and a little present, or the visit without any present, set her up for seven long days and seven long nights. The machinery of the kingdom is very simple and very silent, and the most silent parts do most, and we all believe so little in the medicines of Christ that we do not know what ripples of healing are set in motion when we simply smile on one another. Christianity wants nothing so much in the world as sunny people, and the old are hungrier for love than for bread, and the oil of joy is very cheap, and if you can help the poor on with a garment of praise it will be better for them than blankets.—Henry Drummond

Sermon Suggestions

SOMETHING LURKING WHILE GOD IS WORKING. TEXT: Matt. 2:13–23. (1) The story: the effort of Herod to destroy Jesus. (2) The meaning: God works out his purposes in the midst of and despite evil that threatens to destroy what God sets out to do.

CELEBRATING GOD. TEXT: Isa. 63:7–9 NRSV. (1) God's deeds, verse 7. (2) God's motive, verses 7b and 9b. (3) God's method—his presence, verse 9a.

Worship Aids

CALL TO WORSHIP. "Both young men, and maidens; old men, and children: let them praise the name of the Lord: for his name alone is excellent; his glory is above the earth and heaven." (Ps. 148:12–13).

INVOCATION. Almighty God, Creator of all things, as you established the rhythm of work and rest, so may we find in the different pace of this special day something of your wisdom. Cause our adoration, our confession of sin, our thanksgiving, our petitions, our intercessions, and our renewed commitments to prepare us for faithful labor in your world.

OFFERTORY SENTENCE. "Thanks be unto God for his unspeakable gift" (2 Cor. 9:15).

OFFERTORY PRAYER. O God, thou who hast given thine only Son to be our Savior, our largest gifts are but too small. Yet thou dost receive what we bring. Use our offerings, we pray, to spread abroad the good news of Christ Jesus.

PRAYER. Almighty God, our heavenly Father, we thank thee that thou hast set the star of hope in our life's sky, that in the darkness we can see thy brightness, that in times of shadow we can enjoy thy leading and thy guidance. We thank thee that even in the days of Herod, this earth could hear the herald angels sing the glory that comes only from the heavenly realm to bring a brightness and a glow to this earth. We pray that the ancient miracle may be renewed in our own experience.

Give us the star of hope to light, to lead, to guide. Give us a faith in dark days to look for thy bright stars. Give us a trust in that glory that lies beyond the things of earth and will bring transforming and transfiguring power even into the lives and experience of men. Wilt thou grant thy brightness to our minds, thy wholesomeness to our spirits, thy healing to our souls.

May we live for thee with intelligence and with zeal and with healthy habits and with holy ways of conduct. Grant thy presence in our hearts so that during this coming year we may live not only with new resolutions but also with high resolve and not in our own strength but in thy glorious sufficiency; not trusting our own goodness, but believing mightily in thy grace. Grant us thy leading through this year. Grant us thy strength for the facing of each day. And wilt thou give to our fellowship in this church the touch of thy glory.

Now we lift our prayer for the world's unfortunate, for those in our own community who have the sadness of sickness, for those who have the defection that comes of discouragement and disillusionment in life's circumstance. We pray for those in other lands who have tasted bitterly of the cup of suffering and sorrow, who have not had the proper sustenance to support body and spirit. For the suffering people of this world, we lift our prayer. And grant that this day we may so give in thought and prayer and offering the help that comes from the heart that it will bring consolation and strength to many in thy Spirit.

Now wilt thou enable us to rejoice with all who rejoice, to sorrow with those who sorrow. Wilt thou give to our hearts the inner glow of happiness of those who move in thy presence under thy guidance and in the glory of thy grace. For these mercies we ask through Jesus Christ our Savior.—Lowell M. Atkinson

LECTIONARY MESSAGE

Topic: The Path to Glory

TEXT: Heb. 2:10–14

OTHER READINGS: Isa. 63:7–9; Matt. 2:13–23

In his famous treatise *Why Did God Become Man? (Cur Deus Homo?),* Anselm answered the question posed in his title pithily by saying, "He became what we are that we might become as he is." Only what God has assumed, runs the argument, can he redeem. The mystery of the Incarnation is that without ceasing to be fully God, God became fully human. The church has long asserted the complete divinity and humanity of Jesus. In order for Jesus to be Savior, he must be divine. In order for him to be our guide and model, he must be human. The experience and testimony of the Christian church is that he is both. The Incarnation of God in Christ brings us face to face with the central mystery of the Christian faith.

I. Salvation through suffering (v. 10). According to our text all things are not only made *by* God, they are made *for* him. The author and destiny of all created life does not finally allow his creation to lapse away from him. God does not allow his purposes for life to be thwarted but in Christ brings many "sons" (and the created order with them) to glory. Because of the birth of Christ, God effects the joyful liberation and reintegration of the cosmos.

The author of our salvation was "completed" through suffering. Through the suffering of the cross, the life of Jesus was brought to its intended end. "Completion" is wrought by a purpose fulfilled. Humanity is bound together in suffering. Because suffering is both our common condition and the consequence of our sin, it is "fitting" that the author of our salvation, in sharing our lot, would not only experience suffering but by enduring it should effect our deliverance. There is a response to suffering that crushes. There is another response that ennobles. The greatest tragedy of all, perhaps, is not the fact of sorrow but a response to it that leaves life diminished rather than deepened. By his "completion" in suffering, Christ has forged a pathway to "glory" for all those who trust savingly in him.

II. Bound together in blood (vv. 11–14a). Genetically, no relationship is closer than that of siblings. The author of Hebrews uses the most vivid imagery to portray the extent to which God has gone in Christ to stand with us. He has shared in no less than our own flesh and blood (v. 14). Here is no "phantom" Jesus. Here is no supernatural "visitation" of a God who simply "appears" in human form. In Jesus Christ God shares our condition. The psalm whose beginning Jesus quotes as a cry from the cross ("My God, my God, why have you forsaken me?" Ps. 22:1) is used to show how Jesus' witness to the Father is anchored deeply in the community of his "brothers" and "sisters" (v. 12). That the brotherly analogy between ourselves and Jesus, however, is meant to be taken seriously but not precisely is shown by the shift from "brothers" to "children" in the quotation from Isaiah 8:18 (v. 13) that follows. Because of the miracle of Christmas, God has eternally joined himself to our condition and invited us to an intimate family relationship with him.

III. Through death to life (vv. 14b–18). Christmas is celebrated with the warm glow of twinkling lights. Our text reminds us, however, that Jesus was not born gently into the world. The forces that occasioned his birth were nothing less than the face and fact of evil itself. Here was a child literally born to die. Across Christ's cradle fell the shadow of Calvary. As Martin Luther put it, the cradle and the cross were created from the same wood. The birth made possible the death, whose victory was heralded in the Puritan work entitled *The Death of Death in the Death of Christ.* The "destruction" of the devil (v. 14) means literally "to render inoperative." The promise of "deliverance" (v. 15) means "to free from bondage." Humanity is bounded by death—both spiritual and physical. At the cross, Jesus defeated for his disciples death's penalty and power.

The Incarnation is the astonishing assertion that in Jesus Christ, God shared our condition. Its consequences are not just for time but for eternity. Theologians speak of the "eternal Incarnation" of Jesus Christ. The *Shorter Westminster Catechism* summarizes that Christ, "being the eternal Son of God, became man, and so was and continueth to be, God and man in two distinct natures and one person for ever" (question 21). This "humanity" of God means that there is no discouragement we might suffer, no temptation we might face, no defeat we might endure, no burden we might be forced to carry but that the God who has drawn near in Christ is able to understand. In Christ, God has literally gotten inside our skin. In Christ, God has shared our living at its deepest levels of joy and sorrow. Because of this, Christ has provided a path for us to intimately commune in the joy, fellowship, and love that are the life of God, our Father.—John Shouse

SECTION III. Messages for Communion Services

SERMON SUGGESTIONS

Topic: The Meaning of the Last Supper

TEXT: Luke 22:14–20

I. *Introduction.* Jesus' desire and purpose. Today we are going to observe the Lord's Supper. We do so following the instruction of Jesus in the same manner as he observed his last Passover with his disciples. This is a very special time for Jesus and the disciples. The traditional Passover question, "What makes this night different from other nights?" is truly appropriate for this evening, for Jesus and the Twelve. If we read this passage carefully, we get the impression that the supper is more significant to Jesus even than we can grasp. Why so?

Consider the sequence of events described in Luke 9. The first of these is the transfiguration. Jesus took Peter and James and John up to the mountain to pray. And while they were there they had a supernatural experience, unlike anything they had ever been a part of. They had a glimpse into another world. In the midst of this experience, we find a curious description—that Moses and Elijah were there with Jesus, and "they were speaking of his departure which he was about to accomplish at Jerusalem" (Luke 9:31). The three did not know what was going on. Dumbfounded, they said, "Let us make three tents for you," not knowing what they were saying.

Sometime later, Jesus said to his disciples, "Let these words sink into your ears; for the Son of Man is going to be delivered into the hands of men" (Luke 9:44). But just as it was on the mountain, they did not understand what he was talking about. It is very soon after this that Luke says of Jesus, "And it came about, when the days were approaching for his ascension, that he resolutely set his face to go to Jerusalem" (Luke 9:51).

It is clear here that Jesus, to a large extent, understood his destiny, he was committed to his Father's will, and he knew what it entailed. But the disciples did not understand; indeed, they were yet unable to comprehend what Jesus was about.

We find a similar description of events sometime later in the ministry of Jesus, in which he takes the Twelve aside and speaks to them about the suffering that awaits him in Jerusalem, according to what the prophets have said. But Luke tells us again, "They understood none of these things, and this saying was hidden from them, and they did not comprehend the things that were said" (Luke 18:34).

With these things in mind, we can hear differently Jesus' words when he says, "I have earnestly desired to eat this Passover with you before I suffer" (Luke 22:15). This is a very emphatic expression, which could be rendered, "I have desired with a great desire to eat this Passover with you."

Why is this night different from other nights? It is now the appropriate time, the appropriate season, for Jesus to explain the meaning of his life to the Twelve. This is the "teachable moment." The culmination of events has led up to this occasion, in which the most important observance in the Jewish calendar coincides with the most significant events in the life of Jesus. Jesus fully recognizes the import of the situation and intends to bring the Twelve into contact with the fullness of its meaning.

II. *The meaning of the Passover.* The Passover was the most important holiday or event in Jewish life. It was a prominent family tradition, a ceremony of great weight and with much symbolic meaning. At the end of the meal, one of the children, usually the youngest son, would ask: "What makes this night different from other nights?"

As we approach the Easter week, we might ask:

- What makes this holiday different from other holidays?
- What makes this group of people, these Christians, different from other people?
- What makes this way of life different from other ways of living?

In answer to the Passover question, the host would recount the story of the Exodus. Here with the disciples, Jesus does the same, but he speaks not of the Exodus but of the giving of his own life and what it means in God's plan for us.

III. *Jesus as fulfillment.*

(a) In the Exodus, the deliverance out of Egypt, God was keeping his promises, fulfilling his covenant with Abraham, Isaac, and Jacob, the promise to give them a home and make them a great people.

Jesus says, "This cup, which is poured out for you, is the new covenant in My blood" (v. 20). He is revealing to them a new basis for their hope and a new guiding promise in their life.

(b) The host would tell of the deliverance of the people from slavery in Egypt. They were not their own people. Rather, they belonged to the Egyptians and they served the Egyptians. This was the glory of the Passover experience—deliverance. This was their birth, and they no doubt remembered it with a depth of emotion similar to the experience of an African American in remembering the pivotal events of the civil rights struggle.

(c) The host would then speak of the blood of the Passover lamb, which was placed on the door post of the houses of the Israelite families, so that the plague of death would pass over their home.

In parallel fashion to this language of deliverance and the meaning of the blood of the lamb, Jesus speaks of the giving of his own self. Through Jesus' death we are able to be delivered from sin, just as the people were delivered from slavery in that day.

(d) Then the host of the Passover meal would explain the meaning of each of the elements. For example, he would explain that the unleavened bread signifies their readiness for travel. The bitter herbs remind them of the bitterness of slavery. Jesus explains that the elements of the new Passover indicate the giving of his own self. The language is striking: "This is my body which for you is given; . . . this is my blood which for you is poured out."

(e) The last thing the host would do is remind them to continue observing this Passover each year. Jesus did the same, urging the Twelve to continue to observe this supper in remembering him.

IV. *The hope of the new covenant.* What makes this night different from other nights?

This was the time that Jesus had waited for, the right moment, the fullness of the season, the moment of truth. Here the events were leading to a climax. Now he is able to help them understand who he is and what he is called to as God's Son, the Messiah.

And do they understand? Well, no. Is the event thus a failure? Do they still not get it? Was Jesus forever unable to get the disciples to comprehend the deeper meaning of his mission and the purpose, even the glory, of his suffering and death?

By no means. For the purpose and the glory in the cross lie not in knowing ahead of time that it is going to happen, or even knowing ahead of time what it is going to mean.

The grace to suffer or to live in the midst of suffering, and the hope by which it is overcome, lies not in knowing ahead of time that there will be suffering, or even in knowing that Jesus suffers.

The glory of this event is that there will be a supper in the kingdom, that there are a purpose and a promised redemption. There is a forthcoming "marriage supper of the Lamb." Jesus' words (vv. 16 and 18) assure them that he will eat the supper with them again in the kingdom; he will drink from the "fruit of the vine" when God brings the kingdom to fulfillment. It is true that the disciples do not yet understand, but there soon comes a time when they do understand. They learn that there is hope on the other side of the cross, which does not pass by the cross but takes it up and rests upon it.

When we observe the supper, we must recognize that there will come times when we will ask "Why?" And this "why" is not eliminated because we know ahead of time that there may be a cross. Rather, when we must walk through the garden, or when we must walk up that hill, we look for the hope and the glory of promised redemption. We are assured and upheld by our hope in the one who walks before us and who walks with us.

Let us now turn toward the observance of the supper.—Thomas H. York

Topic: A Time for Doxologies

TEXT: 1 Thess. 5:18

The Apostle Paul told the Christians in Thessalonica, "Give thanks in all circumstances." That's easy to do sometimes. It's easy to give thanks when a baby is born, when we're sick and get well, when a child does well, or when we get a job promotion. When the sun is shining, it's not so hard to sing, "Praise God from whom all blessings flow."

There are other times when it's not so easy: for instance, when the baby cries at two o'clock in the morning because he's hungry, or we get sick, and stay sick; the child turns out badly; or we don't get that job promotion, in fact, we get fired. In those moments, it's hard to find the words to sing a doxology to God.

But Paul said, "In every thing give thanks" (KJV). In all "circumstances" give thanks, that no matter what happens to us, we can give thanks. How can we do that? Maybe this supper can give us some indication of that, for here was something terrible, a very bad circumstance. A cross lifted on a lonely hill, a body broken and blood shed, Jesus killed. However, we come to celebrate that event today, not in despair but in joy and in hope because we know that even in that experience, God was working. This is why we can give thanks in all circumstances, because in any circumstance that happens to us, God is working in it to try to help us grow from it. He can take any circumstance and use that moment to help us become what we ought to be.

This is what this supper is trying to tell us. God is alive and well in our world and working in it to help us. What does it mean? When are the times for doxologies?

I. *We can give a doxology in difficult circumstances because God might be using that to surround us with his love.* If there's anything this tells us, it's of the intenseness of God's love for us. God created the world and put us in it to share its joy, but like rebellious children, we didn't want to live by his rules. We wanted to do it our way. We told God to get lost and walked away from him right into suffering, despair, emptiness, and pain. We deserved it, for that's what we chose to do. But the good news is that God did not let us stay there. Most fathers with such rebellious children would disinherit them, but not God. Instead, God came looking for his children who had turned away from him. "Where are you, Adam?" he asked.

Down through history, that has been the cry of God coming down upon the face of the earth, crying out our name, my name, "Where are you?" He wants to find us. He wants us to come home to where we need to be. He wants us to experience the joy of his love. When he climbed the cross and died on it, it was his supreme call to every one of us,

"Come home. I love you, and I want you to know that."

The Christian religion has a unique facet. In it, God comes looking for us. That's not the way it is in the other religions of the world. People have to go looking for God in those. But they will never be successful. Franz Kafka wrote in *The Castle* about a surveyor who was called to a distant town to work. The lord of the town lived in a castle on the hill, and it was hard to reach. The surveyor asked the villagers how he could reach it; and they were shocked that he wanted to go up to the castle, but never could, and he died frustrated. Not only was the surveyor unable to get up to the castle, but he was not able to discover what he was supposed to do in that town.[1]

Kafka wrote *The Castle* to try to point out how difficult it was for human beings to reach God. His opinion was that we can't, that God was too far removed from us to be reached, too disinterested in what we were doing to care about us.

Some religions say, "Look, this is what you've got to do. You've got to work your way back to God." But how do we do that? How do we work our way back to God? How do we get to be able to stand in his presence? How perfect do we need to be?

The Christian faith tells it this way: God comes down from the castle, as it were, looking for us. He can be found because he is around knocking on the doors of our lives. In anything we experience, however difficult it might be, God may be trying to speak to us. In that moment we may discover that the love of God is real. He is always after us. He is not willing to let us go. He does not want to let us go. He seeks us out.

Ralph Sockman, a Methodist preacher, told of the time he was riding on a horse and fell off. He hit his head, it stunned him, and he lost his sense of direction. He did not know where he was or how to get home. It was getting dark, but he felt one thing: that if he stayed where he was, probably the horse would find its way home. When his father saw the horse, Sockman knew his father would come looking for him. So he sat in the darkness, waiting for his father's voice—until it came.[2]

In the darkness, do we wait for God's voice? Sometimes in the difficult moments, we will discover that God is surrounding us with love, that God is there waiting for us, ready to help us. We can give thanks in all circumstances because God is seeking to surround us with his great love.

II. *We can raise a doxology in difficult times because he may be using these moments to forgive and remake us.* As the disciples came to celebrate the supper, they remembered how much they had changed. The disciples had to be forgiven a lot to become the disciples they were! Christ was willing to forgive, forget, and then use the experiences to help mold them the way he wanted.

This is the gospel for us. What Christ wants to do is to forgive us of our mistakes and to mold us into something new. In the difficult times as we realize mistakes that have led us to where we are, he is willing to come and forgive us. A young girl went into the pastor's office and told that she was going to have a child. She was afraid to go home again for fear of her father. The pastor went and talked to the father, and the father said in anger, "Never, never can she set foot in my house again." The minister simply said, "Be careful, now, because never is a long, long time."[3]

Fortunately, in that circumstance, the father forgave. It's not always that way. Sometimes "never" is said and meant. Sometimes reconciliation does not take place. Sometimes forgiveness does not happen. We may find forgiveness hard, but God is ready to forgive. Whatever we have done against him, he's ready to for-

[1]Andrew B. Smither, "Why Was I Born?" *The Pulpit* (July 1958): 21.

[2]Glen Edwards, "Preaching from the Book of Acts," *Southwestern Journal of Theology* (Fall 1974): 69.

[3]Ernest T. Campbell, "Times When NOT to Pray," *National Radio Pulpit*, n.d., 13.

give it, forget it, and put it in the past. Whatever that sin has been, forgiveness is available. In difficult times we may experience anew the presence of God in forgiveness.

A man working on one of the cathedrals in Europe was carving a piece of wood, a figure, and made a mistake with it. The master craftsman came and saw it and was very angry. Then he took his own tool and began to shape something out of that mess. He began to shape a new figure, a new picture. After he had done it, the master left it to the other man to finish the task. The workman was forgiven for his mistake, and something new happened because of it.[4]

This is what God does with you and me. Sometimes we are broken; then God takes our brokenness and uses it to shape us and make us something new. Have you become something new because of the forgiveness of God? When you left your sins behind, have you gone on to something better? We can give thanks because of the difficult moments when we leave our sins behind; God uses those moments to reshape us, to renew us.

III. *We can give a doxology because in the difficult times we discover a sure and certain hope*. This was what the disciples remembered when they came to celebrate the supper. They remembered the Crucifixion, and it caused despair because the one they loved had been killed; their purpose for living had been shattered. They knew the moment of despair and anguish that we do. When a loved one dies, we don't know how we're going to make it through. We feel so lost in despair. When difficulties of life, frustrations, and disappointment hit us, then we begin to wonder what life is about. Nothing seems to work; it all seems to fall to pieces. As we look at the tragedies that sometimes beset us, we wonder where the meaning is. What is it about anyway? We don't know. Life seems confusing and difficult. We can't understand it. We know those moments of despair.

We must never stop at the Crucifixion, for this supper celebrates the Resurrection. This was what the disciples came to know. That which seemed to be the worst that could ever happen was turned into something used to bring about the best that could ever happen. The redemption of all humankind. Christ could take the Crucifixion and turn it into a Resurrection. He could take that which looked bad and bring good out of it.

That's what the gospel is about. In all the difficult experiences of life, God is working to bring something good out of them. When we come to those moments of grief, when we stand at the graveside of those we love, somehow we can hear the voice of Christ crying to us, "Whoever loves me will not die but live forever." In the moments of life when we are disappointed and frustrated, and we don't know what it's for, we can hear his voice again saying, "He who loses his life for my sake will find it." To give yourself to love, to give yourself away to peace and justice, and to give yourself away to service is to find what you are here for. When life looks confusing, the voice comes to us: "Don't worry, I'm going to bring it out all right in the end. I'm working to accomplish my purposes. I'm building my kingdom."

Christ tries to take our lives and give them a sure and certain hope, to remind us that nothing can ultimately defeat him and, therefore, us, if we are his. When we keep our hands in his, he will never let us go.

F. B. Meyer, an English preacher of the last century, traveled miles on the train, preaching everywhere. He never forgot at the end of the trip to go seek out the engineer and thank him for getting him there safely.[5] This is why we can give thanks to God, because we know that, as we continue to hold onto him, one day he will get us safely through this experience of life. He will not let us be derailed if we continue to put our trust in him. Do we do that? Sometimes in the

[4]Allan J. Weenink, "The Cunning Craftsman: God," *The New Pulpit Digest* (September–October 1974): 53.

[5]W. B. J. Martin, *Little Foxes That Spoil the Vine* (New York: Abingdon Press, 1968), 114.

darkness, you see, we need to remember the light. That he is at work.

It's hard in all circumstances to give thanks. It's hard to sing, "Praise God from whom all blessings flow," when Christ hangs from a cross. But that's where we can sing it the most because, in that Crucifixion, he is expressing his love for us like never before. In that Crucifixion, he is sharing with us a forgiveness that we need. In that Crucifixion, he gave us the promise of hope with no cross, no death, no suffering, and no sin too powerful for God. He will take that cross and overcome it with a Resurrection.

So we remember today a body broken and blood shed. We remember a death for us, but we remember most what to be thankful for. God has brought himself to us through this, has offered himself to us through this, and whenever we put our lives in his hands, no matter what comes, he will always be with us. Since he is always with us, we can manage to keep on going. We can manage day in and day out to sing, "Praise God from whom all blessings flow." Life is a series of doxologies of praise to God because life has God in it—and with us!—Hugh Litchfield

Topic: Challenge to Dependability

TEXT: Luke 22:28

I suppose that I would have gone on missing it had I not read the printed wisdom of one of the most remarkable ministers I know anything about. Over thirty years ago, this individual chose a passage in Luke as the basis for thoughts on the Lord's Supper, thoughts intended to encourage followers of Christ in an extremely difficult stretch of the twentieth century. I had read the account in Luke many times; I have prepared numerous meditations for participation in the supper. But I had missed the full impact of one dramatic statement Jesus made to his disciples. Now when I read the passage, the sentence leaps out at me with all of its implications for me as a twentieth-century disciple—and for all of Christ's followers in a troubled time.

Luke gave a somewhat extended account of the institution of the Lord's Supper. Just as Mark before him, he gave details of a meal that Jesus arranged during the Jewish Passover celebration. Luke recorded Jesus' careful preparations for a private room in which he and his disciples could share a meal. He presented the stark drama of Jesus' actions as the group reclined at the table: giving the cup with suggestive words about its symbolic meaning; distributing the bread. And the dark note Jesus sounded about one who would betray him lingered in the room.

Then Luke alone recorded that, in the upper room setting, the disciples began to argue about who was number one in the group. See the scene, hear the words, feel the drama in your imagination. Time was running out in a hurry for Jesus. Added to the pressure of impending crisis was the imperative need to say some things to his disciples that would make a lasting impression on their minds—words that would draw their attention to their great responsibility. He wanted to give words that would assure, inspire, and instruct. He was thinking about the awesome task of redeeming people and about the terrible specter of death. His disciples were quibbling about rank in his company; they were concerned with settling the issue of greatness. Then, during a momentary lull in the claims and counterclaims of eminence, Jesus said softly: "Ye are they which have continued with me in my temptations" (22:28). I can imagine that all at once, things got quiet as those words began to sink in. The words would stay with them, even when they desperately wished that they could forget. The fact that Luke preserved this statement of Jesus, even though he was the only one to do so, says that the early church could not forget what Jesus said following the meal with his disciples.

The disciples' immediate reaction must have been shame, embarrassment, and discomfort. Previously, Jesus had spoken of his self-giving, the awesome cost of life for individuals and for his church; they had fallen to quarreling about rank in his company. "Ye are they which have continued with me in my temptations," Jesus said. And gentle rebuke was present: "You did not learn this overconcern about greatness from me; rather if you have paid attention, you have learned service from me."

Beyond this immediate reaction, the disciples must have remembered times when they had let Jesus down. James and John must have recalled the time when they had wanted to call down fire on some Samaritans who had refused to extend hospitality to Jesus and his men. The two brothers had been so slow to learn love for all people; they had added to Jesus' already heavy burden. Peter must have thought of the time he had confessed that Jesus was the Son of God and then immediately had disputed Jesus' statement that Jesus would suffer and die. Jesus had rebuked him sharply. Peter had intensified Jesus' anguish over the disciples' misunderstanding of him. The others could recall times when they had failed to support Jesus, to listen attentively, and to share his concern.

And later, after the Crucifixion and Resurrection, Jesus' men would remember how they had let him down—how three in the garden had failed to pray with him, how they all had deserted him, how confused and fearful and discouraged they had been before they knew that death had not conquered him. "You are the ones who stood by me in my trials," Jesus said in essence. And I can imagine that when they remembered his words, they bowed their heads in renewed repentance. Then they lifted their heads with a renewed determination to be the kind of people who were consistently responsive and faithful to the Lord, who still was present with them.

But something else made Jesus' words unforgettable, something that would offer encouragement and strength for dark days, when work for Christ would be difficult and trying. Something like a note of gratitude must have been in Jesus' voice as he said softly: "Ye are they which have continued with me in my temptations." As Harry Emerson Fosdick pointed out, these men were not much for which to be grateful, and they probably knew it. But they remembered what Jesus said and felt a lift to their spirits. They were ordinary people. They had been wrong; they had failed; they had been weak. But Jesus had chosen them. And at the last, he had thanked them for staying with him, no matter if they had stumbled frequently. They must have remembered this with the right kind of pride, the kind of pride that produces a happiness at being part of something good and worthwhile. They must have felt the kind of pride that moved them to make greater effort, to be better persons, to go on trying somehow to earn the gratitude that had been expressed for effort that they knew to be less than the best.

If we can comprehend the awesome truth, Christ is present in our celebration. And he says to those of us who are his: "Ye are they which have continued with me in my temptations." And in the moment of flashing honesty, we remember our failures, our wrongs, our moments of weakness. We know that we are those who have offered less than our best, and some of us have allowed ourselves to become discouraged, lazy, indifferent, or satisfied. And yet, the Lord of the church says to us: "Ye are they." That should cause many of us repentant embarrassment—and yet, a gratitude at being included that will cause us to be determined people.

As we participate in the Lord's Supper and thereby recreate the context in which Jesus said something remarkable and surprising to his disciples, we need to ponder his words. They are spoken to us at this time, in this place. We are the ones on whom he is counting to continue with him in all the crucial tests confronting the church for which he gave himself. *Are* we the ones on whom he can continue to depend? —Eli Landrum, Jr.

Topic: On the Occasion of the Holy Eucharist as Celebrated by Lutheran and Episcopalian Christians of Western Washington in St. Mark's Cathedral, Seattle

LECTIONARY FOR THE CELEBRATION: Deut. 26:5–11; Eph. 2:13–22; John 15:1–11. Psalms 122, 133, and 134 were sung.

In the name of Jesus. Amen.

Today on this happy occasion we are showered with images, an extravaganza of images. For a starter that wonderful text where, in the spirit of all the liturgical planning, the oil was running down Aaron's beard and spoiled the vestments (Ps. 133). And then it goes on and on and on. As you listen to the reading from the Epistle to the Ephesians, one image chases another, overwhelmingly, dizzyingly, as it often is in that Epistle. You feel it even more in Greek, for those verses are just one long sentence. Christ, our peace, making out of the two one; breaking down the barriers of the dividing wall; creating one new being; abolishing in his flesh the enmity; reconciling into one body through the cross, and so on . . . strangers and aliens; before, fellow citizens with saints (that's not bad); members of God's household . . . and then suddenly a building. It is similar to a modern movie where one image goes over into the other—you do not know quite how or when. And the building on the apostolic foundation with Christ as the cornerstone—one for the Episcopalians and one for the Lutherans—and then suddenly you are a temple, a dwelling place of God in the Spirit. We really are getting showered by images.

I think the point with such showers of images is that they are all images, so nobody should think that one of the images is really it. It is a little like the Trinity: when you have God the Father clearly in focus, the kaleidoscope of faith shifts to the Son, the Christ. When you have gotten used to looking at human images, there is a Spirit, which dissolves those images into pure presence of the divine. In the context of what we do here today, it could be said that one of the causes for divisions in Christendom is exactly arbitrary predilection for one's chosen images. But God showers us today so that nobody shall get stuck.

And now to the Gospel, the fifteenth chapter of the Johannine Gospel. The tree. The vine. The tree and the branches are beloved images when one speaks about ecumenism. It sounds so nice that it is one tree—Christendom, Christianity—and, of course, there are different branches. We like to have that both as a logo and a *Logos* so that the branches become respectable, and the image slows down the ecumenical process. But it does not say, "I am the oak." The oak tree, the beautiful tree, so symmetrical, so powerful, so awe-inspiring against the sky at both dawn and dusk while giving shade at noon. No, it is a vine. A vine really is nothing at which to look. It is not as aesthetically attractive as a tree. The least treelike of trees is the vine, and disorderly in its disposition of branches.

There is a tree in Israel that is called a pilpul tree. *Pilpul* is the complicated, intricate, Rabbinic discussion style, and this tree's branches twine into one another. The vine is like that. It is nothing at which to look. It is not impressive. The only thing it is good for is its fruit—a wonderful economy of the branchwork and fruit. It has been learned recently in agriculture how to make both the corn and the wheat grow on as little straw as possible, because it is better economy. God knew it already with the vine. It is all for the grapes—not to speak about the wine. It does not matter how it looks. Does it produce or not? That is the only reason to keep a vine. Jesus said, "I am the true vine; you are the branches." Does it produce good fruit?

So the first point is: it is not for looks; it is for fruit. If it does not bear fruit, it will be cut back, and even if it bears fairly decent fruit—a holding pattern in the statistics—it will be cut back so as to bear more fruit and better fruit. So this image of the tree, this image of the vine and the branches, is used by Jesus as an image of judgment. So the question about what we celebrate here this afternoon is whether these two branches of Christendom, the Lutherans and the Episcopalians. (Parenthetically, I note that we say "Episcopalian," not "Anglican." Anglican feels like having to be English or at least part of the British Commonwealth. We Lutherans have the same problem. It took a long time for us to become a church instead of a Swedish club. Or Danish. Or Norwegian. Or what might be. Actually we still have some way to go.)

As I began to say, the question is whether these two branches are healthy. If not, we might get closer together today, but little is gained if we both are proved rather irrelevant and obsolete, drying up faster than it takes to negotiate final agreements. Or perhaps we could ask when we get together, Lutherans and Episcopalians, do we busy ourselves with important questions about bearing fruit, or, when we come together at various levels, do our conversations bring out the worst in us? Our defensiveness and that caricature of faithfulness, which actually is fear of growth and newness in the Spirit? I am going to speak not for the Episcopalians but for the Lutherans. I have found that sometimes when Lutherans sit down with that wonderful insight from Luther, there is really very little that is important. Many of the things church people busy themselves with are *adiaphora,* as we say; that is, things that are not important enough to divide us, things about which we may have different opinions, while still living in full communion.

But when Lutherans get together with Episcopalians, they seem to think that not only should they say matters of polity are *adiaphora,* but they have to force the other to understand *adiaphora,* whereby they deny their conviction that it is *adiaphora.* There is a way in which an ecumenical approach brings out if not the worst, at least not the best, in people, because we get scared and our defensiveness comes. We are afraid of growth in the Spirit. But let us even so rejoice in our breaking bread together. It is an achievement, even if God smiles in surprise that it took us so long and we did not go further.

There is one thing more to note about our image of the vine. The imagery, yea, the whole language of the Gospel of John, and especially here about the vine, is organic. It is clearly biological or botanical. In the West, by and large, although the Episcopalians have been better at listening in on the wisdom of the Eastern Church (we Lutherans have not come that far yet), one has mainly thought one's theology; prayed one's faith; worked one's commitment with images of God either as lord or as judge, more recently stressing the word *father* to make it warm and familylike. It is as if the drama were either of God as lord and we as servants (especially true in Calvinism), or God as judge and we as sinners seeking desperately, and being mightily helped by Luther, to find the key to the gracious heart of God. But in the East and in the Gospel of John, there is not primarily the political language of lord and servants or the judicial language of judgment and forgiveness. It is all about life. Jesus came that they should have life and have it galore, it says in the Gospel of John (10:10). It is about life.

Life is an organic process, and this sacrament in the midst of our joint celebration is in that tradition called by Ignatius the *pharmakon athanasias*—the medicine of immortality (Ign. Eph. 20). The Episcopal Church has been enriched by often giving the bread and the cup with the words, "The body of Christ, the bread of Heaven. The blood of Christ, the cup of salvation." This is a move in the organic direction. Listen to how John uses that word "abide." Not "abide with me" but "abide in me," "abide in the vine and I will abide in you." The word means "remain," "rest in." And then the sap gives life.

I wanted to lift up this organic language, because getting closer together here this afternoon has no value in itself. It is only good if it leads to new growth, new mutual growth—if we together can find a new language instead of splicing old languages into some kind of Episcopal-Lutheran mixture. We need to find a new language. I think the language we will need is an organic language of organic, new insights. We should not just share with one another what we have seen. In the biological, biochemical process of mutuality, a new insight, new faith, a new Christian zeal and zest grow. We want not only to abide with one another, but to come into the lives of one another with love and joy of which the text speaks. From now on, it is uninteresting where and what we have been. The question is: what are we to become together? Strengthened and inspired by one another in the organic growth? It is said in the Epistle that through Christ we both have our access in one Spirit to the Father. And when we have that, the sky is the limit. But without renewal two branches will have come closer while in the process of drying up.

May God be good to us and we be good to ourselves so that we take to us all that energy, all that sap, all that power of life, which actually pulsates in the body of Christ, and which rises in the Spirit's springtime in the vine and all the trees. Amen.—Krister Stendahl © 1989

ILLUSTRATIONS FOR COMMUNION

HE IS THE ONLY ONE. On my pastor's desk is a plaque that reads, "God so loved the world that he did not send a committee." Instead, he gave his only begotten Son to bear our sins, griefs, and sorrows. —Herschel H. Hobbs

THE POWER OF THE CROSS. The cross is not merely the birthplace of my fears, or the birthplace of my shames, or the birthplace of my disgusts; it is the birthplace of the radiant and immortal hope. I like old John Nelson's words when he was preaching about the influence of John Wesley's preaching and its effect upon him. When he had done, he said, "This man can tell the secrets of my heart, but he hath not left me there, he hath showed me the remedy, even the blood of Christ. Then was my soul filled with consolation, through hope that God, for Christ's sake, would save me."—John H. Jowett

THE POWER OF HIS RESURRECTION. Commander Mitsuo Fuchida led the Japanese attack on Pearl Harbor, with its destructive and far-reaching effect. Hating Americans, Fuchida became more bitter after we dropped the atomic bombs on Hiroshima and Nagasaki. His hatred was further inflamed when he was led to believe that Americans, like Japanese, tortured their prisoners. But Fuchida had some positive exposure to Christians and Christian influence. One day when his anger and hatred were about to destroy him and he was in great desperation, he said to himself: "Maybe a Bible could help me." He began reading a Japanese translation. He later declared that when he came to Luke 23 and read Christ's prayer just before he died on the cross, then he understood. "I met Jesus that day. . . . He came into my heart and changed my life from a military officer to a warrior for Christ." Mitsuo Fuchida became a great preacher of the gospel of Christ.[6] —Chevis F. Horne

BLOOD. In the fall of 1945, Ernie Pyle, a famous war correspondent during World War II, was returning home from France on a ship that carried one thousand wounded American soldiers. About a fourth of them were terribly wounded, stretcher cases. Others were able to walk, although many had lost legs, arms, and eyes.

One hospitalized soldier was near death. He was wounded internally, and the army doctors were trying desperately to keep him alive until they got to America. They kept giving him plasma and whole blood until they ran out of the whole blood. Doctors quietly went about the ship typing blood specimens in search of suitable blood donors. They didn't want to make an announcement that a dying soldier needed blood because there would have been a stampede to the hospital ward by the other wounded men, offering their blood to this dying comrade. "Think of that," said Ernie Pyle, "a stampede of men themselves badly wounded, wanting to give their blood!"[7]

He, who "was wounded for our transgressions," said, "For this is my blood of the new testament, which is shed for many for the remission of sins" (Matt. 26:28). And by his blood we are healed. —Jack Gulledge

[6]Chevis F. Horne, *Dynamic Preaching* (Broadman Press, 1983), 40–41.
[7]Adapted from Ernie Pyle, "Challenge to Civilians," *Reader's Digest*, January 1945, 34.

THE MYSTERY OF HIS PRESENCE. Once at a simple and unforgettable Communion service at a historic little church on the banks of the Red River in Manitoba, the late Dr. Charles W. Gordon exclaimed as he stood at the Lord's Table, "The Lord is as real to me as he was to Peter, or James, or John!" Looking at his radiant face and recalling his own exploits for Christ's cause, we students knew that his testimony was true. So may all God's people know the mystery of his presence in the "mystery of consecration" to Christ.—David H. MacLennan

SECTION IV.
Messages for Funeral Services and Memorial Day

SERMON SUGGESTIONS

Topic: Feeling Grief

TEXT: John 20:11–15; 21:15–17

I have known people who seem to enjoy their sadness. They like life on the soap opera side; they know every sad thing that has happened to anyone; they spend their time telling sad stories.

I have known a few people who hang onto guilt like a prized possession. They complain about it but wouldn't know what to do without it. Sometimes they are guilty because of moral failure. Other times, it seems they can like themselves only when they feel a little guilty.

The two emotions we have discussed so far in this series are usually discouraging—if not downright depressing. But some people seem to be on friendly terms with both guilt and sadness. Today, our attention turns to grief, and unlike sadness or guilt, almost no one is on friendly terms with grief.

I. Grief is a bottom-of-the-barrel emotion. You can feel sadness and guilt on the way down—but at the bottom, when the cushion of hope is finally gone, there is grief. Some people know how to grieve better than others. Some people are required to grieve more than others. For all of us, grief is painful, hard work.

Most of us know the feeling of grief. Someone you loved has died, and you are getting ready to go to the first visitation at the funeral home. The loss will confront you in a casket, and you would give anything not to be facing what the next days will bring.

Grief is being fourteen, on the first Saturday of summer, working with your dad in the yard, when a poorly sighted man swerves off the road, hits your dad, and kills him instantly. Grief is going into the house to tell your mother there has been a terrible accident and then call an ambulance that will have no reason to speed away to the hospital.

Grief is standing by as you watch someone you love disintegrate with Alzheimer's disease into someone you hardly know and who does not know you at all.

Grief is watching your grown children make decisions that will have heartbreaking consequences and leave scars in them for the rest of their lives.

Grief is the feeling you get when something you loved is destroyed—and you know it will never—ever—be the same again.

Most of us have been to the funeral home or emergency room enough that even thinking about grief makes our mouths grow dry. A sense of foreboding settles in the pit of our stomachs. We may have grieved for different reasons, in different ways, but the feeling is common. It is a feeling that realizes something dear is lost, gone, dead, and will never be a part of our lives again.

Grief is taking two coffee cups from the cupboard and remembering you only need one.

Grief is running across an old wedding picture, after the divorce, and remembering all the good you dreamed would be a part of this marriage that ended the way no one thought it would.

Grief is going to work tomorrow and realizing the dream of what you could be vocationally, or what you could contribute professionally, is never going to be realized. The politics did not go your way. The breaks went another way. The career-making deal was close but fell through.

Grief is when you have scraped the bottom of the barrel, and nothing is there.

II. The Scriptures we read this morning confronted us with two deeply grieved people.

Mary had gone to the tomb, and the grief of Jesus' painful, humiliating death was intensified by what she assumed to be one more insult: the body had been stolen. The Jesus who had little peace in life couldn't even get peace in death. Grief and anger mixed their paths in her—as they do in almost all of us. Tears of grief mingled with tears of pain, and she could not see past the hurt. The person she had loved as source of life, hope for good, voice of comfort had been killed. It was all over. Everything she had put together as a way in the world had been crushed. She stands in this passage full of grief and tears. If she had hit bottom standing near the cross on Friday, she must have felt that the bottom had fallen out this early Sunday morning.

The other grieving person was Peter. He and the resurrected Christ are together, one more time. In the work of God, death had just been killed. The Christ of fulfilled promises was having a conversation with the Peter of denial oaths and broken intentions. Three times Jesus asks: "Do you love me?" And the echo of the three denials Peter made during that night of the arrest hang unbearably heavy. "Do you love me, Peter?" Jesus asks. "You know I do," Peter responds. But the response in no way hides the grief. He had wanted to be courageous but ran like a coward. He had wanted to be a supporter of Jesus but ended up claiming he didn't even know who Jesus was.

There would never be another time like that night. There was no way to go back to that moment and make it different. There was no way to return to that crisis and respond like a true follower. Peter could be faithful in the future, but that faithfulness could never undo the grief of being unfaithful on the one night Jesus most needed someone's steadfast companionship. The grief sat in the pit of his stomach like something swallowed that cannot be digested.

Mary and Peter are both quite literally in the presence of the resurrected Christ, and both are full of grief.

III. Even the Resurrection—the most dramatic and powerful act of God—does not keep us from grieving. To be Christian—to have loved like a Christian, to have dreamed like a Christian, to have failed as a Christian who refuses to surrender sin—is to know grief: tear-jerking, heart-wrenching, think-you-will-never-make-it-through grief.

When we dealt with guilt and sadness, we talked about feeling our way through those emotions in order to learn lessons of faith. I don't think we can feel our way through grief. The only way through it is to work. The temptation grief places on us is to give up. If you ignore grief or give in to it, you increase the odds that grief will win. And when grief wins in our lives, we die. However, if you work through it, if you work on it, over time, the grief will begin to dissipate; the fog will lift, the pain will ease.

Life comes in tragic proportions at times. Not just to others—but to us. We give our energy and love and best effort to something or someone that some random tragedy destroys. The tragedy is like a mountain caving in around us, and the only way through the grief is slowly to tunnel through the darkness, to move rocks one at a time, to pace ourselves, to adjust to the darkness so we can find our way to the light.

In the midst of our grief, it is important to keep the lessons of Scripture before us.

First. In both texts in John's Gospel, the grief is experienced in the presence of the risen Christ. It is no different for us. When we grieve, when we feel absolutely at the bottom, the Christ of comfort is present. This Christ does not wave a wand over us to make the grief evaporate. Rather, Christ is there to counsel, to help us see the hurt from a different angle of vision, to call us to look past our tears. Christ is there to accept us and to nurture us for another challenge.

All of us will face our days of grief, but none of us will have to face them alone. There is a Teacher, a Shepherd, a Christ, who in his own body has borne grief, dealt with sorrow, felt the pain.

Second. The God who has not spared us from grief has not spared God's self from grief either. Imagine. The God who could have lived safe, sacred, secure in a heaven somewhere chose in Jesus to be bruised, beaten, destroyed. This God has hit bottom—watching an only-one-of-a-kind Son die—hearing him scream about being forsaken and, in the scream, knowing profound abandonment. God has wept and weeps with us.

The God of the Bible is a God who is acquainted with grief, loss, tragedy, broken dreams, and death. And it is this God who comes close to us, in our tears, in our grief. Not as the outsider who must say, "I'm sorry, even though I cannot imagine how much it hurts." This God comes as one who has been through the same thing, and there is no need for words. You are embraced by one who has also grieved, and like the embrace of an experienced widow to the newest widow—there is healing.

IV. There is grief in the world, and there will be grief in your life. We cannot love and hope and not be pushed to the bottom by grief. And there, on the bottom, we discover the God who knows how it feels, shows us the entrance to the tunnel, and gives us the strength to do the work that grief requires.

It didn't take long for the early Christians to begin seeing a famous passage in Isaiah as a faithful description of Jesus.

> Surely he has borne our griefs
> and carried away our sorrows;
> Yet we esteemed him stricken,
> smitten by God, and afflicted.
>
> (Isa. 53:4)

It has been almost three decades since it became my Saturday morning job to call the ambulance and tell my mother my father had been in the accident. There are times as an adult I wish I had a father. Grief does not always go away. Our griefs, like God's, are borne. They are comforted. The God who has grieved never leaves any of us other grievers alone.

To be Christian is to make ourselves vulnerable to the feelings of grief. The Scriptures are clear that we do not grieve "as others do who have no hope" (1 Thess. 4:13). Our grief is not the grief unto despair. But it is grief. And, if we love and care, we will learn the lessons that only grief teaches and discover a part of the God who grieves with us. The Christian faith does not keep us from grief. We are blessed—happy—because our griefs have been borne, comforted.—Daniel Aleshire

Topic: When the World Tumbles in, What Then?

TEXT: Psalms 42, 43; John 14:1–6

Tragedy and catastrophe, sickness and disease, war, storm, flood, and earthquake stalk the world continuously. Even as this is being prepared, the memories of Hurricane Andrew are carried by thousands of persons, especially in southeast Florida. The cries of thousands of mourners in India are wailing in grief for the more than thirty thousand reported killed by the earthquake that hit so suddenly. And here we gather with friends for a memorial service in honor of a loved one and to glorify our Lord. We come as friends and neighbors to offer the warmth of Christian love, the touch of a hand reaching out to those caught up in their grief.

There is nothing beautiful about death. It marks the end of life on this earth. It is the break-off of relationships; it is our last great enemy. I never speak lightly of death.

In our grief we often feel anger, hurt, dashed hopes, loneliness, crushing emptiness, and a feeling that a part of ourself is gone. And it is so.

The death of a family member or close friend leaves one in shock and vulnerable to actions that otherwise would not be done.

Let us turn then to God's Word to see what it says to our needs. The writer of Psalms 42 and 43 feels the great need to draw closer to God. Evidently, he had missed worship at the Temple and was feeling the sting of criticism from his foes and had come to the place where he cried out, "My tears have been my meat day and night, while they continually say unto me, where is thy God?"

He continued as he remembered earlier days: "When I remember these things, I pour out my soul in me: for I had gone with the multitude, I went with them to the house of God, with the voice of joy and praise, with a multitude that kept holy day."

Then he cried, "Why art thou cast down, O my soul? and why art thou disquieted within me? hope thou in God: for I shall yet praise him for the help of his countenance."

Here is a word picture of one feeling the need for God and carrying a load of criticism being thrown at him by those who did not understand. And then came the answer: "Hope thou in God." It seems almost to be a command: "As for you, hope or place your hope in God." He had run until he was at the end of his rope and knew nowhere else to find relief.

So it is with you and me. Here gathered in this room are those who are feeling the deep grief of their lives and are asking, "Where is God?" and "How can I get closer to him?"

Three times the psalmist repeats those words in these two psalms, "Hope thou in God."

We turn to the New Testament. On the night before the Crucifixion of our Lord he had met with his disciples in an upper room somewhere in Jerusalem. There, after the incident of washing the feet of the disciples, and after Judas Iscariot had left the room, the Master began to talk very intimately to the eleven. He knew that his time was short and that within a few hours death would be coming. He knew, too, that his disciples were very much troubled, and he had special words for them. Listen:

"Let not your hearts be troubled." He knew that they were troubled even as he was, and he spoke to their hearts, their spiritual hearts. They needed him then at that hour, and they would need him even more during the hours ahead. He continued: "Ye believe in God, believe also in me." The two verbs in the Greek are the same; they can be indicative or an imperative. Perhaps he said, "Ye believe in God," an affirmation or indicative; "believe in me also," an imperative, a command for them to believe in him.

But he went on, "In my Father's house are many mansions" (dwelling places); "if it were not so, I would have told you. I go to prepare a place for you." Note that this is one of the most expressive descriptions of heaven found in the Bible. They were listening, even as you are listening to this word from his book. "And if I go and prepare a place for you, I will come again and receive you unto myself; that where I am, there you may be also."

It is enough that he is preparing a place for his children, that we may be with him forever. We do not know where that place is or what it is. We have some descriptions in the Book of Revelation, but that is figurative language, and the figure can never be as beautiful and meaningful as the object described.

Thomas then asked a question: "Lord, we know not where you are going; how can we know the way?"

Jesus replied, "I am the way, the truth, and the life: no man cometh unto the Father, but by me."

In these few words the Master gave them *hope,* promised his return, and told them of the home he would be preparing for all who believe and believed on him.

Thus, to the family, to the friends gathered here, to all who carry the load of anguish, the heartache and grief, the Master offers hope to you now and for the future. My prayer and my hope for each of you is that you will take these words and apply them to your lives. May the God of all comfort and grace be with you all. Amen.—G. Allen West, Jr.

Topic: The Resurrection and the Life

TEXT: John 11:1–44

INVOCATION. Our heavenly Father, we give thanks to thee for the long life thou has given to our loved one and friend, Dorothy A. We thank thee for the talents she had and used for thy service, and we thank thee for the influence of her life. Wilt thou take the words of thy servant and the expressions of love of friends to comfort the family and strengthen them for the days ahead. In Jesus' name. Amen.

INTRODUCTION. Our friend and loved one, Dorothy A., has lived a full and rich life among us and has left a treasure of rich memories of her life and service few can match. A graduate of George Peabody College in home economics, she became dietitian of the college for a number of years.

She was an artist with food and flowers. Not only could she prepare the foods to taste so good, she could prepare them to look beautiful for the table. The same could be said of her talent with flowers, growing them, arranging them, and teaching others how to do both with them.

She was an excellent Sunday school teacher of teenage girls. And she was a faithful wife to her husband, Fred P., who died many years ago, and a good wife to her second husband, who was blessing to her and blessed by her.

In the end she died of Alzheimer's disease, after having lived a rich and full life of a caring and loving friend.

A BRIEF MESSAGE FROM GOD'S WORD. In the Gospel of John there is a story of two sisters and their brother, Martha, Mary, and Lazarus. Many of you know the story, but I want to take part of it and share thoughts with you. They were close friends of Jesus, and evidently he would stop by their house when visiting the city of Jerusalem. A short time prior to his Crucifixion he was in Perea (modern Jordan) when Lazarus became ill and the sisters sent word to Jesus asking him to come to help Lazarus. But the Master did not go that very day. He delayed his going two days, which caused some consternation among his disciples with him. Then he said, let us go to Bethany, where the three lived.

As he and his disciples approached Bethany, word came to Martha, who left immediately to go and meet him. Note the dialogue that took place:

Martha: "Rabbi [Master or Teacher], if you had been here, my brother would not have died." What great faith she had in her friend Jesus.

Jesus replied: "Your brother shall rise again."

Martha: "I know that he shall rise again, in the Resurrection, at the last day." She thought of the Resurrection as an event in the far-off, dim future.

Then Jesus replied with one of the great statements found in the Bible: "*I* am the Resurrection and the life: he that believeth in me, though he were dead, yet shall he live: and whosoever liveth and believeth in me shall never die. Believest thou this?"

There are two references to death in these two verses. "Though he were dead," or die, refers to physical death. "Yet shall he live" refers to spiritual life. In the second instance, verse 26, Jesus restates the truth, "And he that liveth [spiritually] and believeth shall never die [spiritually]." It is our Lord's way of saying to his disciples that the life he gives is spiritual and eternal and transcends the physical life, which is affected by physical death; death then serves as the gateway into the greater life with the Father forever.

And then the Master makes it very personal: "Do you believe this?"

And Martha comes forth with one of the great confessional statements found in the New Testament: "Yes, Lord, I believe that you are the Christ, the Son of God, he who is coming into the world." Other confessions are found, of John the Baptist, Simon Peter, and Thomas. And I think that our friend, Dorothy, if here in the flesh, would rise up from her place and say with Martha, "That's my confession, too; God bless you, Martha!"

The scene changes, and Jesus finds Mary and she cries to him, and the friends wail in their sorrow, and the Master weeps, literally "bursts into tears," thus showing his own humanity but also decrying their failure to understand that he is the answer to their needs and the Comforter while with them.

He then commands someone to move the stone from the cave entrance and in a loud voice cries out, "Lazarus, come forth!"

The crowd is silenced by the authority of his voice and stands in silence. In a moment a man comes out of the cave with his face and legs still wrapped in the grave clothes with which he has been buried. The miracle of returning a grown man to life was the high-water mark of the "signs" done by Jesus up to that time, as John gives them to us.

When Lazarus came before Jesus, the Master said to those about him, "Loose him and let him go." For a while at least the friend and brother would live longer in the flesh to help and bless others. The rest of the chapter is given over to the effects of the miracle upon various groups.

But for us, the words and the sign speak for themselves.

There was the need for the Great Physician, but he waited in order that he might show forth a greater power than healing, the power of raising one from the dead, from the grave, and from the power of Satan!

We see Jesus caring for his friends, amazed at their wailing, grieving with them, and then moving to demonstrate the mighty power of God, even the Son of God.

And that same one is here among us today, in the person of the Holy Spirit, to bring his love and comfort to you all. He is here to say to you all, death cannot hold you captive. All that is needed is your trust in the Savior and Lord of life. Take comfort in these words and walk with him in high places.

May our heavenly Father be with you one and all, and may his grace be sufficient for you.—G. Allen West, Jr.

Topic: "He Was a Good Man"

TEXT: Acts 11:24

"For he was a good man, and full of the Holy Spirit."

This morning my message will be addressed particularly to the members of the family and to the close friends gathered in this place. Our friend and brother, Bill Echols, was a noble man of God, a faithful and loving husband, a caring and providing father to his four children, and a man devoted to the church. He was a leader.

He was called to his heavenly home suddenly and shockingly from his earthly life into the fellowship of the redeemed. His family is still trying to find answers but still must wait until God reveals them.

His death coming so quickly made all of us realize again the frailty of the human body and the mystery of death. It marks our humanity and causes us to remember the words of our Lord given almost two thousand years ago: "Watch therefore: for ye know not what hour your Lord doth come. . . . Therefore be ye also ready: for in such an hour as ye think not the Son of man cometh."

Bill was a handsome man, a man greatly beloved by his family and respected by his coworkers. He was an able leader in his company and served in Mexico City five years before returning to the States and becoming a member of our church. He was troubleshooter for his company and served in Lima, Peru; Buenos Aires, Argentina; Australia; and Jerusalem at different times.

He served our church as Sunday school teacher, Sunday school superintendent, deacon, and member of various committees. He was a true friend to his pastor, a veritable encourager. He was a short-wave radio operator (a ham), and frequently used it to keep in touch with missionaries. His other hobby was raising beautiful chrysanthemums. Above all, he loved God supremely and sought to honor our Savior and Lord in his daily walk.

I want to call your attention to several passages of Scripture that, I feel, describe him and his work. We turn to the first psalm.

"Blessed is the man that walketh not in the counsel of the ungodly, nor standeth in the way of sinners, nor sitteth in the seat of the scornful. But his delight is in the law of the Lord, and in his law doth he meditate day and night."

Such was our friend.

But we move to the New Testament and turn to a man named Barnabas and observe the descriptive words regarding him.

Acts 4:36, 37: "And Joseph, who by the apostles was surnamed Barnabas (which is, being interpreted, the son of consolation or encouragement), a Levite, and of the country of Cyprus, having land, sold it and brought the money and laid it at the apostles' feet."

These words indicate that Barnabas was a good steward and demonstrated his love both for God and for his church and its work of ministering to people in need.

It was Barnabas who stood up for the converted Saul of Tarsus when the latter had returned to Jerusalem more than two years after his conversion in Damascus. The leaders in the church at Jerusalem didn't want to receive Saul because of his former efforts to destroy the church, but Barnabas stood by him and pleaded with them to receive him.

Later, after Barnabas went to Antioch in Syria to help with the work, he found that he needed more help and left there and found Saul in Tarsus and brought him to Antioch to help with the witnessing and teaching. He stood up for John Mark when the Apostle Paul had refused to take him again on a mission trip. He was described as a man filled with the Holy Spirit and faith.

So my friend Bill, we believe to have been filled with the Spirit of Christ and a man of faith. He gave of his time, his talent, his means, and himself for the cause of Christ and the upbuilding of his family.

What is it that marks this father, this husband, this friend, and this servant of God? His dedication, his devotion, his readiness to help others, and his love for God and his fellowman.

As we come to the close of this service, a hymn comes to mind. Though saddened by his death and separation from us for a while, yet we go rejoicing in the memories he leaves with us and the heritage he leaves his wife and children.

Man of Sorrows

Man of sorrows, what a name
For the Son of God who came
Ruined sinners to reclaim!
Hallelujah, what a Savior!
Bearing shame and scoffing rude,
In my place condemned he stood,
Seal'd my pardon with His blood;
Hallelujah, what a Savior!
Lifted up was He to die,
"It is finished," was His cry,
Now in heav'n exalted high,
Hallelujah, what a Savior!
When He comes, our glorious King,
All His ransomed home to bring,
Then anew this song we'll sing,
Hallelujah, what a Savior!

(P. P. Bliss)

—G. Allen West, Jr.

Topic: The Shepherd's Care

TEXT: Ps. 1, 23

The funeral of brother W. E. Davidson, eighty-two.

Beloved members of the family and friends, we have come to this place this early morning to pay homage to one of God's true saints, William E. Davidson. Gathered here are his daughter, Miss Sue, with whom he lived, and his son, William L., and the son's family, who live away from Nashville. We come to his entrance into heaven. What a joy he was to all of us!

I was called early in the morning two days ago by Miss Sue, who said simply but with great tenderness, "Pastor, Father has just gone to be with our Lord. Can you come over?" Of course I could and quickly dressed and drove over to be with her during the hours ahead.

Some time after his wife's death he and his daughter moved here from Boston. Their neighbors, Mr. and Mrs. Bunch, invited them to church, and the two soon joined. He and she joined the choir and were two of the most faithful members.

He was a man of faith, a man of genuine piety and love. A man of gentle ways, he was beloved by the entire church family.

His faith was strong in the living Lord. When we would talk about his condition, he would always say, "Take care of my daughter." Quiet, loving, faithful, and always ready to help others were the grand qualities that marked his life.

We are the richer for having had him as friend and strong supporter of our Lord's work through his church.

One instance I want to relate to you. One of the highlights of the year was the early morning Thanksgiving service each year in the chapel. Each year the sun would break through on the east side of the chapel and stream through the panes of the various colors of the stained, seeded glass.

After the hymns and the prayers of thanksgiving were offered, the people were given opportunity to express their thankfulness.

On the year prior to his death, when the time came for such expressions, Brother Davidson stood in his place on the west side of the chapel, facing the pulpit, and gave thanks for his family, his church, and his pastor and friends. And then, in that beautiful tenor voice at that time eighty-one years young, he began to sing,

When He calls me, I will answer,
When He calls me, I will answer,
When He calls me, I will answer;
I'll be somewhere, listening—
I'll be somewhere, listening—
I'll be somewhere, listening
For my Lord!

That was the climax to the service, and there was no need to go on. Few if any of those present would forget that dramatically inspiring moment. For the next few minutes, I want you to hear God's Word.

In Psalm 1, "Blessed is the man who walketh not in the way of the ungodly, nor standeth in the way of the sinner, nor sitteth in the seat of the scornful. But his delight is in the law of the Lord, and in his law he meditates day and night."

And now let us consider the best known psalm, one that children and older persons love dearly, the twenty-third psalm. When I was younger, there were times when I thought David wrote this while still a young man. As I have grown older, I have to think he was an older person. Whatever his age, it was and is divinely inspired and has blessed millions who have read it and kept it close to their hearts through their lives. It is very personal. Notice how the writer of the psalm speaks in the pronouns used: "The Lord is *my* shepherd; *I* shall not want."

The beautiful metaphor "shepherd" was picked up by Jesus our Lord, who came and said, "I am the good shepherd." The good shepherd leads his sheep, knows his sheep, protects his sheep, and cares for his own. Thus, David followed that statement with this one: "I shall not want." As a child said, "And I don't need anything."

He goes further with the poem: "He maketh me to lie down in green pastures; he leadeth me beside the still waters."

It is as if David were thinking of the days of his youth, when he himself watched over his father's sheep. He knew what the sheep needed and what the shepherd lad had to do. In our time, we, too, come to the place where we lie down in green pastures of God's mercy and love, to feed on the riches of his grace, and we find the quiet stream of the water of life filling us daily and refreshing us.

I cannot deal with the entire psalm this day, but only parts of it. Note next, verse 4: "Yea, though I walk through the valley of the shadow of death, I will fear no evil."

Notice that he did not say "walk into the valley of the shadow," as if that were the end, but he said, "through" the valley. Death to the Christian becomes the gateway into the presence of God. It was so and is so for the person becoming a Christian. First, he must realize that he was dead in his sins, but then by dying to sin and accepting Christ as Savior and Lord, he can and does find life everlasting.

The Good Shepherd gave his life for us, and he gave us life eternal.

Listen again to the psalm: "For thou art with me; thy rod and thy staff, they comfort me."

Now let me read the rest of the psalm with no comment.

"Thou preparest a table for me in the presence of my enemies; thou anointest my head with oil; my cup runneth over. Surely goodness and mercy shall follow me all the days of my life, and I will dwell in the house of the Lord forever."

May we who have gathered here in this place be blessed by the words from our Lord's book and from this psalm, so rich and so meaningful for us at times like this. May the Holy Spirit of God and the Lord Jesus comfort you as family and friends.—G. Allen West, Jr.

Topic: "A Time to Mourn"

TEXT: Eccles. 3:1, 4

For everything there is a season,
and a time for every purpose under heaven:
a time to weep, and a time to laugh;
a time to mourn, and a time to dance.

There is a time to mourn. So often it is forced upon us. Someone close to us dies, and we are seized with grief. We and our community of family and friends gather together in the home, the funeral home, the church, and speak the words and perform the actions of a ritual that enables us to join together in mourning. Or some*thing* rather than some*one* dies in our life: a dream for the future, an ability of the past. We lose our job and cannot pursue our chosen career. We have a stroke and can no longer talk as we wish. In these tragedies we are often left to mourn alone. Family and friends speak only of what we still have, not of what is gone. No ritual helps us to mourn together. But still we mourn. We cannot help but mourn.

There is a time to mourn. Sometimes we must *choose* it. People have died; the ability to walk or to see has been lost; dreams for the future have been destroyed. Those who suffered were not our loved ones, and so we are not *forced* to mourn, but we have benefited from their tragic loss. A soldier went to war; he did not return. Another went and did come back—unable to play ball or build a house or watch a sunset. A family grieves; a veteran mourns. It was not our son who did not return, not our past and future that are suddenly cut off. But we have our freedom, our security, our prosperity. And we owe it to them to mourn with them. But mourning is not forced on us. We must choose it.

Memorial Day calls us to choose to mourn. When it was first established, the choice was not so difficult. The end of the Civil War was only three short years in the past. Many were living with the results of its devastation, with constant reminders of what they had lost. Today the choice is harder. We desperately need a few days away with the family instead. The Gulf War cost almost no American lives. The benefits of Vietnam are in no way clear. World War II, in which many died and did so clearly for the cause of freedom, is such a long time in the past. The need to mourn is not compelling. It requires a deliberate choice. Memorial Day calls to us: choose mourning!

And so we here turn to our public rituals. Parades and prayers and decorating graves with flowers direct us in our public mourning, the way a viewing, a funeral, and a card expressing sympathy guide us when we mourn with family and friends. Rituals can be empty, but they can also be very full. They invite us to come together. They direct our attention to the matter at hand. They spell out what people over the years have found it is helpful and proper to do on the occasion. And they direct us as we seek to speak and act as a group. Whether or not we fill them with meaning or find it there is largely up to us. They are there to guide us. We turn to them this Memorial Day.

Part of our ritual today is a passage from the Bible that helps us mourn. It is a song of lament for what is gone. David composed it and ordered that it should be taught to the people of Judah upon learning of the death in battle of King Saul, the first king of Israel, and Saul's son Jonathan, David's best friend.

Your glory, O Israel, lies slain upon your high places!
How the mighty have fallen! . . .
Saul and Jonathan, beloved and lovely!
They were swifter than eagles.
They were stronger than lions.
O daughters of Israel, weep over Saul,
who clothed you with crimson, in luxury,
who put ornaments of gold on your apparel.
How the mighty have fallen
in the midst of battle!
I am distressed for you, my brother Jonathan;
greatly beloved were you to me. . . .
How the mighty have fallen,
and the weapons of war perished!

(2 Sam. 1:19–27 NRSV: selections)

In David's words we can hear our own loss. Over the course of history as a nation, the glory of America has also been slain. Those we sent out mighty have fallen. They were beloved and lovely, swift and strong. They brought us freedom and prosperity. But they themselves have fallen in battle. And for some the distress is very great, because among the mighty was one whose love to us was wonderful. David's words help us to mourn.

But why dwell on what has been lost instead of what we have? No amount of mourning will bring it back! Because life is best enjoyed and preserved when lived in gratitude for what it cost.—Gilbert Bartholomew

ILLUSTRATIONS FOR FUNERAL SERVICES

HOW FAITH CAME. Faith came to me with the vision of Christ still alive in this world today. Christ means to me a living personality today who moves about in this world and who give us strength and power as we endure by seeing him who is invisible only to our fallible and finite human eyes, just as any other good comrade helps one to be brave and do the right thing.—Sir Wilfred Grenfell

THIS MOMENT. I remember hearing Sidney Montague of the Northwest Mounted Police tell of the thrill he felt when, in the midst of his explorations in the virgin forest of the Canadian Rockies, he came suddenly for the first time upon a breathtaking view, the grandeur of which was overwhelming, making him vividly aware that that moment was freighted with an unforgettable memory of splendor. It was then he said that he realized, as he had not realized before, that life is a matter of moments and that one only lives as one gets the most from each moment's experience. And later he wrote a poem that began: "This moment is your life."—Clayton E. Williams

AN ENDLESS SPLENDOR. All nature speaks the voice of dissolution. The highway of history and of life is strewn with the wrecks that time, the great despoiler, has made. We listen sorrowfully to the autumn winds as they sigh through dismantled forests, but we know their breath will be soft and vernal in the spring, and the dead flowers and withered foliage will blossom and bloom again. And if a man die, shall he, too, not live again? Is earth the end of all, and death an eternal sleep? Not so, but beyond the grave in the distant Aiden, hope provides an elysium of the soul where the mortal shall assume immortality, and life become an endless splendor.—D. W. Voorhees

IMMORTAL SYMPHONIES. Winter is on my head, but eternal spring is in my heart. The nearer I approach the end, the plainer I hear around me the immortal symphonies of the world to come. For half a century I have been writing my thoughts in prose and verse, but I feel that I have not said one-thousandth part of what is in me. When I have gone down to the grave, I shall have ended my day's work, but another day will begin the next morning. Life closes in the twilight but opens with the dawn.—Victor Hugo

THIS WORLD AND THE NEXT. Rabbi Jacob taught: "This world is like a vestibule before the world to come. Prepare thyself in the vestibule that thou mayest enter into the hall." He used to say: "Better is one hour of repentance and good deeds in this world than the whole life of the world to come. However, better is one hour of the blissfulness of spirit in the world to come than the whole life of this world."—Cited by William E. Silverman

LIFE EVERLASTING. A pastor in Portland, Oregon, learned from his physician that his life on earth was limited. Knowing how troubled his faithful flock would be at the news, he entered the pulpit the next Sabbath; and with his vibrant Christian faith, he shared the news with his people. Then he added:

> I walked out where I live, five miles out of this city, and I looked at the river in which I rejoice, and I looked at the stately trees that are always God's own poetry to my soul. Then, in the evening, I looked up into the great sky, where God was lighting his lamps, and I said: "I may not see you many times more, but river, I shall be alive when you cease running to the sea; and stars, I shall be alive when you have fallen from your sockets in the great downpulling of the universe.
>
> —Ernest J. Lewis

SECTION V.
Lenten and Easter Preaching

SERMON SUGGESTIONS

Topic: As We Forgive

TEXT: Matt. 18:23–35

In his letter to his friends at Ephesus, the Apostle Paul writes, "While we were yet sinners, Christ died for us." In this statement Paul is saying, "God's salvation, God's love is not something we have to or even can earn. In his wonderful grace, God just loves us. And because he loves us, he gives all that he has, spiritually, physically, and emotionally to us."

This is the real message of good news that the cross, the Lord's table, the Bible, and our faith teach us. God loves each of us, and in his love he gives each one of us the privilege of being one of his children.

This is what John meant when he said, "God so loved the world that he gave his only begotten Son."

If we pay attention to the stories of Lent and Easter, we find that such love is not easy either for God or for Jesus, because what they give is given though and even while we are not worth it.

The Bible's story of the last few months of Jesus' ministry shows us that the decision of the political and religious authorities to silence and do away with Jesus caused Jesus and his friends to accept a period of exile in the pagan, gentile areas of Tyre and Sidon northwest of Galilee.

After a brief stay in these unfriendly communities, they moved northeast to the resort city of Caesarea Philippi, a city built by the Romans as a place of rest and relaxation for their armies.

It was while they were here in this licentious, pagan army town that Simon Peter expressed the faith of all disciples when he said, "You are the Christ, the Son of the living God."

This confession of faith convinced Jesus that his disciples were beginning to grasp a true understanding of him and his mission. So Jesus set his face toward Jerusalem and the cross.

As Jesus hung there on the cross, he was without friends. Those who professed him to be the Son of God had run away.

The multitudes for whom he was giving his life were cursing him, mocking him, spitting upon him. Jesus was suffering the most painful death the human mind has ever devised, and those for whom he was dying were rejecting him and abusing him.

Needless to say, this was not a high or easy moment for Jesus. Yet he forgave them. Because of his love, because of God's love for them and for us, Jesus forgave them and died. God's grace required that nothing could be held back.

When God chose to love us as he loved Jesus, he set the condition for himself that his love had to be absolute, complete. From then, the gift of his Son on the cross was what God had to do!

There is Jesus' story about a man and his king. The king was a very great and rich king who lived thousands of years before the Magna Carta and our Bill of

Rights. And as such his power was absolute. He merely had to point at a person, say, "You live," or "You die," and it would happen.

That king went to his own treasury and gave this certain man stewardship over ten thousand talents of silver. In biblical times the going wage for a twelve-hour workday was a denarius—a silver coin one-fifth smaller than a quarter. A talent was a measure of silver that weighed five thousand times that much. Ten thousand talents would equal ten million pre–World War II silver dollars, or fifty million workdays' labor.

The man to whom the king gave this money must have been a prototype of some of our modern savings and loan managers. For all of the king's money was lost.

But the king who trusted this certain man with all his money forgave the man and the debt he owed to his king.

A short time later, this same man dealt with a neighbor who owed him money, one hundred denarii, one five-thousandth the loan the king had forgiven him.

He grasped the poor man by the throat and demanded instant payment. The poor neighbor begged for more time to pay, but the certain man called the authorities and had his neighbor cast into prison until the total debt was paid.

When the king heard of the certain man's deed, he called the man and said, "Because you would not show mercy to your fellowman, I will withhold my mercy; and you shall suffer the fate you gave to your fellowman."

When Jesus told his friends this story, he used a teaching method used daily by the rabbis and teachers of his day.

The king in those religious stories is always, always a symbol for God. Those who listened to these stories always, always knew that they represented the persons receiving special blessings from God!

God freely gives all of his blessings to us . . . light, life, his world, friendships and home, the ability to use and enjoy the beauty and wonders of creation. And above all, this is the special privilege of being created in God's image to live as his children in and for his kingdom.

And as "children," it is not uncommon for us to have more enthusiasm than wisdom. So that we make the choices and do the deeds that are less than the high hopes and the noble dream God has for us.

In this foolishness and self-will, we betray and sin against God. Yet again and again, and again, while and though we are sinners, God forgives us.

The point of Jesus' story is that we who have been forgiven by God are allowed to come home and, like the prodigal of Jesus' other story, enjoy the total joy and blessing of God's family.

The punch line of Jesus' story is: as those who are forgiven, we have no more important privilege than to share and give to others the forgiveness, the respect, and the care that we ourselves receive.

We are reminded of this every time we pray, "Forgive our debts as we also have forgiven our debtors."

This is not easy to do! It cannot be done unless we devote our *entire* heart, soul, strength, and mind to doing it.

The easy, sinful, wrong thought is to embrace the thought Satan places in our hearts, so that we say, "Nobody ever gave me anything!" If we pay attention, we hear others and we hear ourselves saying this much more often than it ought to be said.

Jesus' way, God's way comes when and only when we consciously say, "I must love and help others the same way I would act toward Jesus my Lord."

You see, we do need our brains in church, along with our heart, soul, strength, and love. It is not easy to live and love as Jesus did, but with him it can be done.—Raymond C. White

Topic: How to Handle Temptation

TEXT: Matt. 4:1–11

There is something delicious about temptation. It is full of promise—it offers pleasure, power, plenty. That is why some desserts have been playfully named "seduction," "temptation," and the like.

Oscar Wilde said, "The only way to get rid of temptation is to yield to it."

Even when the temptation is real and the stakes are high, we can indeed dismiss temptation by giving in to it, but we can't so easily get rid of the consequences. The consequences are not so beautiful as the promise. Some of us know that through painful personal experience.

We can suppose that when any rational person considers what unwanted results may follow yielding to temptation, then that person will want to deal with temptation in such a way as to produce the kind of results he or she wants. How can we handle temptation?

I. To begin with, don't be surprised by it. In the Scriptures, evil is personified by Satan, the devil. And that demonic force is compared to a ferocious predatory animal. We can be sure that a hungry animal on the loose prowls about looking for food. "Like a roaring lion your adversary the devil prowls around, looking for someone to devour" (1 Pet. 5:8 NRSV). The most stupid thing we could do would be to ignore the odds against us and be unprepared.

II. As we face temptation, it will help us to know Jesus' experience of it. We might say that Jesus' temptations were different from ours, that they were his messianic temptations and are not to be compared to ours. They *did* have to do with his fulfilling his mission as the Christ of God; however, the same dynamics were at work that press in upon us ordinary mortals. When Adam and Eve were tempted, they "saw that the tree was good for food, and that it was a delight to the eyes, and that the tree was to be desired to make one wise" (Gen. 3:6 NRSV).

There was something about each of Jesus' temptations to make it seem right. What would be wrong about Jesus' doing whatever was necessary to relieve his hunger after his long fast? Or what would be wrong with doing some death-defying feat that would compel God to rescue him and thus certify him as God's representative? Or what would be wrong with surrendering a bit to Satan if by that he could gain control over the whole world—wouldn't that good end justify the means? Jesus answered each temptation with God's counterpoint, as contained in Scripture.

III. When we are tempted, it is usually with some "good" in view: it may seem to be God's answer to our prayer for our daily bread or for greater influence over our fellow human beings or for some political coup that will advance even God's work in the world. All the while, we may be ignoring other considerations, factors that will, soon or late, hinder or make impossible the supposed good ends we seek. However, the wisdom to deal with such temptations and others is available if we seek it (James 1:5–8). Then we can savor the compensations that God gives to those who resist and overcome temptation. We are told that after Jesus successfully turned aside Satan's temptations, "The devil left him, and suddenly angels came and waited on him" (4:11 NRSV). William James's advice to people trying to establish good, healthy habits was this: never permit an exception to occur in the determination to do a right and good thing. One should garner moral successes as a veritable miser. B. F. Skinner, the behavioral psychologist, advised "positive reinforcement." God has many "angels" or messengers to wait on us today: the Scriptures, praying friends with helpful counsel, work in his kingdom to occupy us, and the Holy Spirit, who helps to make us "more than conquerors through him who loved us" (Rom. 8:37).—James W. Cox

Topic: Transfigured

TEXT: Matt. 17:1–9

No one who has followed the progress of a woolly worm to a hard cocoon to a beautiful butterfly can misunderstand the word for *metamorphosis* in verse 2. Although the changes come much more slowly from caterpillar to butterfly, the change is dramatic. How dramatic the instantaneous change in the appearance of Jesus! The Greek word from which *metamorphosis* is derived means simply *an outwardly visible change.* This they saw.

Almost a week after the confession at

Caesarea-Philippi, yet in that area, Jesus chose Peter, James, and John, something of an inner circle, and led them up a mountain. There he became "as the sun," and his garments "white as light." Then they noticed Moses and Elijah talking with him. How did they recognize Moses and Elijah? And what were they talking about? Luke (9:31) helps with the second question. They were talking about the "exodus" that he was about to make in Jerusalem. The Greek word is neatly transliterated. On the lips of these three, what would "exodus" mean? Note the relationships.

I. Law and prophecy and Jesus. What were the relationships? Some thought Jesus flew into the face of the law and completely fulfilled prophecy. Were they no longer important? Jesus himself had said of the law and the prophets: "Don't begin to think that I came to destroy them. I did not come to destroy, but to fulfill." Jesus respected both—and so does his church.

Here stood two of the greatest personalities in the Old Testament: Moses and Elijah. In his own ministry law and prophecy were transfigured but not destroyed. Remember how he interpreted the law in the Sermon on the Mount. Remember how he identified John the Baptist with the Elijah hope.

How would Peter, James, and John react? Peter "answered." Someone has reminded us that Peter was not addressed! Peter did not want to lose either Moses or Elijah. There may have been a popular belief that both Moses and Elijah would return in the last days . . . here they are: let's keep them.

Both law (legalism) and prophecy (millennialism) offer threats today to spiritual faith. The threats lie not in their transfiguration but in their perversion.

II. Jesus. To Peter's suggestion the heavenly voice spoke clearly: "This is my Son." All others fade away in the light of his countenance. The Father is well pleased with his ministry. It is the Father's testimony: neither law nor prophecy threatens him. "I am well pleased . . . hear him."

Listen to the developments immediately preceding: (1) at Caesarea-Philippi: he acknowledged the confession of his messiahship—and charged silence; (2) he spoke clearly and courageously about his Passion—and invited them to share; (3) he promised the coming of the kingdom of God in his own ministry.

This is light—as the sun—white as light. He is revelation.

III. Jesus and his friends. They were overwhelmed—"sore afraid." He ministered to their needs. They saw only Jesus now: "Be not afraid." What a lot they had to tell to the others! What a lot they had to tell to the crowds! "You just don't know who this is!"

Jesus spoke: "Tell the vision to no man." You don't understand it. You won't understand it until after the Crucifixion, after the Resurrection. And we remember the Father's words—Jesus is the focal person—"Hear ye him."

The understanding came in the Resurrection. But then all relations are transfigured in the Resurrection: with the Old Covenant, with Jesus, and with his followers.—J. Estill Jones

Topic: Passion Play

TEXT: John 19:17–42

Christ on the cross: when we look, what do we see? We know what a crucifix looks like, with the outstretched arms, the legs crossed at the ankles, the face laid to one side, and even in polished wood or gold that looks awful enough. But for a minute, imagine standing on the hill looking up at the cross, Jerusalem the holy city at your back and a crowd of spectators on either side of you. The man you see on the central cross looks like the other two and like every other criminal you have ever seen die this way, except that the fake wreath on his head makes him look a bit more pitiful. Words like "criminal" and "wretched" come to mind, but not in your wildest dreams would you call him "Messiah" or "Son of God" on that day.

Jump forward almost three-quarters of a century and look up at the cross again, as John tells the story; what do we see? An amazing transformation has taken place. The cross is still the cross, and the man on it is still dying, but the story is told from a different point of view. We hear now cries of anguish, no thud of hammers, not even the shouted taunts of the crowd. All is more serene, and the man on the central cross looks more divine.

I. Now the cross is a throne, and the man on it looks like a king. Pilate had tried to ridicule Jesus in his trial by putting the crown of thorns on his head and by draping a purple robe around his body, still bleeding from the beating he got from the soldiers. Yet when it came time to put him on the cross, Pilate wrote the sign out: Jesus of Nazareth, the King of the Jews. The Jews saw the irony in this and wanted the sign changed, but Pilate would not budge. Nope, it stays just as it was written: Jesus, the King of the Jews. Later, at the end of the story, Jesus got a king's burial. Criminals who died for their crimes were not permitted an honorable burial by Jewish law but were dumped unceremoniously into a common grave. Jesus, in contrast, got a private tomb. In normal burial, the preparer would mix a little of the pungent burial spices with oil and smear it on the corpse before they wrapped it in the burial cloth. Joseph and Nicodemus used an incredible amount of spices: one hundred pounds, enough for a whole town, or for the gaudy funeral of an emperor. Jesus died as a king dies, with a king's inscription over his head and a king's burial at the end.

The cross is a throne, and Jesus hangs upon it as a king. Isn't that appropriate? This man, as future Lord of Israel, rode in triumph into Jerusalem six days before—on a donkey, a pack animal. This man, as Lord and Teacher of the Twelve, washed their feet only the night before. If you want to be Lord, be a slave, he said, and so it is fitting that his throne is a cross. As you look up at it, remember that he is your King, and his cross is your throne. There is no gold on it, there are no armies to protect it, and it is unsupported by any territory. Turn aside from the cross and look back to Jerusalem or across the sea to Rome; they have armies and swords and money. They scrap because the strongest survive, and their king is the one who can claw to the top and hang on the longest. But if you are to belong to the one on the cross, it shall not be so among you. In this kingdom, the only way to rule is from the cross.

II. Scene change: as we watch John's drama progress, the throne is moved away for a little while, and a stone table moved onto center stage, the cross is an altar, and Jesus is dying on it as the Passover lamb.

Jesus died on the afternoon before the Passover meal, according to John. If you and I had been in Jerusalem that afternoon, we would have seen lots of fathers and husbands walking toward the Temple, crowding around the door that separated the big open area where any male Jew could stand from the smaller area into which only the priests could go. Inside the priests' court was a huge stone altar, and on this afternoon countless priests would be working steadily. Their bright knives flash in the sun, their robes are already stained and splattered, as they work steadily killing lambs, draining their blood into small golden bowls, and splashing them around the altar. Outside the city on the hill on the central cross another Lamb is dying, and soon his side is pierced by a bright spear and his blood is drained out. "Behold the Lamb of God, who takes away the sins of the world." John the Baptist said it first, when Jesus began to preach and heal; now the Evangelist says it again with the words he writes.

Jesus died as God's Passover, God's Lamb. In the original Passover God rescued a bunch of slaves and made them his people. In the new Passover he did it again, rescuing us from all the powers of evil. He rescues us—not out of the world, of course, for death is still death and temptation is still temptation. But we don't have to be afraid of them. One of the great reformers of the church was Ulrich Zwingli, who began the Reformation in Switzerland. In 1519 he was a pastor in Zurich when the Black Death hit the city. Hundreds died, and Zwingli himself caught the disease through his constant contact with the victims. In the midst of the illness he wrote a hymn of faith: "Death is at hand/my senses fail . . . Lo, Satan strains to catch his prey/I feel his grasp/must I give way?/He harms me not/I fear no loss/for here I lie/beneath thy cross." Can we sing with him, facing the cross of the Lamb of God? Can we sing of our victory over greed, over prejudice, over despair? Look up at the cross, beloved; the man dying on it has rescued you from all that.

III. The set changes again, and the prop men move away the altar, replacing it with a canopy: a big sheet of cloth held up at the four corners to make a tent open on all four sides. The cross is a canopy, and in it Jesus stretches open his arms to welcome his newly made family.

Sometimes all it takes to make a collection of individuals into a group is a canopy. Once a bunch of Boy Scouts on an overnight hike, sleeping out under the stars, woke up in the middle of a drenching rainstorm. One boy found a large piece of plastic from a refuse pile, and it was quickly stretched and nailed to some nearby trees. We had to scrunch, but we all got under it and had a great time telling stories until the rain quit.

Under the cross, looking up on this day were several people who felt that they had gone to sleep under the stars and woke up in a torrent. What must Mary have felt, to watch her son suffer so? How must John, "the disciple whom he loved," have wished he could do something to make his pain less? How could things have turned out so badly after they had started out so well? From the cross Jesus looked down at them and said, "You are family now; he is your son, and she is your mother." She would lose her son Jesus, but she would gain as a son a man who was closer to Jesus than anyone else. He would lose his friend, but from this day on he would be a member of his friend's earthly family. Jesus' death created the opportunity for a relationship that never would have existed otherwise.

What keeps us coming back to this place? There are other ways to find friends, you know. We could join a club for companionship. This place offers more than that; it offers the family of God. Jesus died to make us into a family that cares about and cares for each other. Brother, she is your sister; he is your brother; love each other, because you are family now.

John's Passion play is complete. The stage is empty now—the cross has been taken down, and the man on it is in the garden tomb. All is quiet, and yet you know that the story cannot end there. The King must return to reign, the Passover must be celebrated, and the community that he created must survive. Isn't it something how even a death such as this can be the sign of a happy ending yet to come?—Richard B. Vinson

Topic: First Word from the Cross: Forgiveness

TEXT: Luke 23:34

The Friday Jesus was crucified was our worst day, so how can we call it Good? One reason we call it Good Friday is that we overheard Jesus praying that day. Rising to heaven alongside the sound of hammer on nails was the prayer, "Father, forgive them; they don't know what they're doing." On our worst day, Jesus was praying for us. He was praying what he had always preached. As time ran out, as negotiations failed, in the last communique between holy parent and hostage child, the talk was of forgiving enemies, of pardon for persecutors.

This prayer was sent to break a seemingly unending cycle of domestic violence that began with Cain and Abel. The hostage Jesus was condemned by children of the parent to whom he prayed. At bottom, this prayer is a family affair, a child talking to his parent about sisters and brothers who are breaking his heart, taking his life. No wonder we call this a passion narrative.

Despite the line about not knowing, this prayer is not a defense of those brothers' and sisters' actions. It's true, they acted in ignorance, but ignorance is not innocence. This prayer is no expert testimony for plea bargaining with God: "Judge, we call to the stand one Jesus, specialist in human affairs, who advises a commuted sentence; after all, they didn't know what they were doing." The Jews could perhaps argue a measure of not knowing, lately among us called deniability: "I don't remember knowing he was the true Son of God." And the Romans could argue its equally popular corollary: "Don't blame us; we were just following orders from the top."

You and I understand this defense. We do our worst damage when we think we are doing right. Recently a review of documents revealed that a Nazi official in La Chambon, France, during World War II had secretly protected Jewish refugees. He didn't live to accept credit for this; Jewish members of the French resistance gunned him down just before the war ended. They didn't really know whom they were killing. Neither do we.

We all have bloody hands. In the play *2* Nazi leader Hermann Goering at Nuremberg defends himself by arguing that his death camps were no worse than the English saturation bombing of Dresden or the American holocaust that surprised Hiroshima. Our best defense doesn't prove us innocent and put us in the same camp with Jesus.

To plead insufficient knowledge won't do, not because it isn't true but because it isn't helpful. Such ignorance is not a shield against God's judgment; it is a locked gate separating us from God's love. Jesus pleads that we be forgiven, not because our ignorance acquits us but because it shuts off our escape. With forgiveness come knowledge and freedom. Jesus wasn't praying a legal argument; he was begging a thoroughly sympathetic judge to act mercifully toward the judge's own children. In the end we are dependent completely upon the tender mercies of God sought in Jesus' prayer.

What we need is forgiveness. In the movie *The Mission* an eighteenth-century slave trader who murdered his blood brother in a fit of jealous rage becomes a Jesuit in South America. In penance he drags through the mountainous jungle by a rope tied to his neck the heavy armor of his former life. He arrives in a Christian Indian village where in the past he had taken for profit by force children from their mothers, husbands from their wives. One of the Indians rushes toward him with a knife—and cuts the rope from his neck. The armor clangs down the mountainside; the forgiven murderer sobs with joyful repentance. This is the forgiveness we need; this is what Jesus prays for on Good Friday.

Received, this forgiveness looses more forgiving. The tender mercies that flow into the world from Christ on the cross create more mercy. Getting forgiveness is somehow all tangled up with giving it to others. The echoes of Jesus' prayer are heard sounding through the centuries from the lips of Christian martyrs. The spirit of "Father, forgive them; they know not what they do," is spoken by Stephen under a rain of stones; by James the Righteous just before the blow that killed him; by Sir Thomas More to his executioner; by the dying Anabaptist Michael Sattler with a tongue already cut by his pious torturers; and by Archbishop Romero as his blood spilled upon an altar in El Salvador.

Such mercy does not flow from the unforgiven. Like poor Simon the Pharisee, who had no tears with which to wash the feet of Jesus, the Inquisitor has no cleansing compassion. Never is this prayer heard from confident heresy hunters. This should be no surprise for us who so often pray: "Forgive us our debts as we forgive our debtors." It is the Inquisitor's hands that are tied, the forgiven who are free to offer forgiveness.

Once we do, we can move beyond forgiveness. Jesus wants more for us than the lifting of punishment; he died for reconciliation. The forgiving is the unlocking of the door that stands between the prisoner and return to family, if there is one. And there is. Jesus' final vision is a family reunited, a homecoming, a homecoming without anybody missing, a "Yes" answer to the song's question "Will the circle be unbroken?" Jesus knew that forgiveness is the only way to that end, so he prayed for it.

In *Places in the Heart* a drunken black man in a sleepy southern town shoots the local sheriff dead on a quiet Sunday afternoon. The killer is lynched by an angry mob. The sheriff's widow and two small children are left destitute. Hope appears in the form of a black sharecropper who tries to help her work her farm, but he is soon driven off by the Klan. The movie ends with the despairing widow trying to find solace at a small-town church service.

There we see her alone as she receives Communion from the minister. Then the scene shifts to show us the person sitting at her side, to whom she offers the bread and cup. It is the black sharecropper who had been run out of town. While we try to adjust to his entry into this sacred scene, the sharecropper turns and passes the Host to the dead sheriff, somehow resurrected. The revelation closes as the sheriff offers the broken body and the shed blood to his own murderer, sitting beside him, sober, clothed in his right mind. Jesus calls for us to be forgiven and for us to forgive, that such Communion may become reality. In this way the love of God makes our worst day a Good Friday.—William Loyd Allen

Topic: Sunrise Service: Easter

TEXT: Luke 24:1–11

How many of us remember other Easter Sundays when we have come to sunrise service, often shivering a bit, sometimes damp from a rain that still felt wintry to the skin, yet looking upward, hoping to see that splash of red in the sky, a sign that darkness was coming to an end, brightness and warmth beginning to dawn? From our morning vigil and early prayer we moved on to a festive breakfast, an indoor church service where we shared with other friends the tale of our early morning worship as Christians on God's good land, under skies open to all. The women who hastened to the place of Jesus' burial that first Easter morn had to watch their steps as they crossed the land before the dawn. If they stumbled, they might break the jars of ointment or spill the spices with which they sought to honor the dead body. They probably were remembering the goodness of Jesus, the forgiveness he had brought, the compassion he had shown, the healing of his outstretched hands, the hospitality he had accepted, even his weeping as he mourned with them the death of loved ones. But that morn they were remembering most vividly the horror of his death; they were bent over more from sorrow than from their linen cloths and fragrant balms.

Most likely, because they had not comprehended its meaning, what they failed to remember was the teaching of Jesus that his Crucifixion was not the end of his mission. The messengers at the empty tomb were able to penetrate their grief with the message that Jesus the Redeemer was alive; he had risen through the power of God the Creator.

With that reminder, how different was the rest of the day for those women. In their joy they may well have left their jars and spices at the spot where they had helped to lay the body of Jesus. With their generous spirit they wished to spread the good news to the other disciples. They were transformed, graced with instant acceptance and belief in the fulfillment of the prophecy of Jesus and the reality of the empty tomb. Then, as had happened to Jesus so often, they were also faced with doubt and scorn when they tried to communicate the Christ event to other disciples still in formation for faith and action. Yet we know the women did not wash their hands of these skeptical listeners.

Our reading from Luke this morning is incomplete; we need to reflect later today on the remainder of that chapter, to accompany Peter in seeing for ourselves, to sympathize with disciples on the road who were puzzling over what is ultimately a mystery of faith, to thank Jesus for his patience with unbelieving disciples, to humble ourselves with them when he graces us with his presence, to ask forgiveness of those who have tried so often to share with us the good news of Jesus.

The women left the empty tomb to become part of a pentecostal community, a new beginning, a new understanding of life. In remembering that first Easter morn, may we be open to letting Christ complete the good work already begun in us.—Grace Donovan

ILLUSTRATIONS FOR LENT AND EASTER

A SECOND BIRTH. Let it be remembered that a second birth necessitates proper attendance, same as the first birth. To be born the first time, we should be assisted into life by people who really want us to be born and are entirely sympathetic with our wish to be as they are.

If we want to be born again, we should avail ourselves of the kindly offices of persons who thoroughly approve of our wish to be born again. Some of them won't know anything else in the world but the importance of being born again. But, if they know *that much,* they can give valuable aid.—Lloyd C. Douglas

TRUE REPENTANCE. Repentance is not a "pious" word, at least not in our usual meaning of the word *pious.* It is not mere fear in crisis. It is not centrally remorse, even though it involves sorrow for our failures. It is never a morbid self-flogging. True repentance is an act of will, a "change of mind," as we review our whole life, in faith that our will is then held in a higher Will. It is a turning and returning: "Let him return unto the Lord." We turn our backs on the way of life that has brought our wars and delinquencies. We may not know where we are going, but at least we know then where we are not going: we are not going to selfish chaos and obscene death.—George A. Buttrick

THE NEW CREATION. I once heard the great mathematician and philosopher Lord Russell broadcast for the British Broadcasting Corporation. He described how lonely man is in this cosmos. As he once wrote (I quote freely), ultimately, when the universe runs down, "the whole temple of man's achievement must inevitably be buried in the debris of a universe in ruins." The cosmos is indifferent to man. But Lord Russell pleaded for two virtues even in such a cosmos—kindness and tolerance; these we must cling to in the cold world. But is not this a kind of whistling in the dark to keep up one's courage? Paul's call for obedience and forgiveness is different. He is appealing to a fact—the fact of Christ, in gratitude for whom the demand for obedience and forgiveness wells up in his breast. Where such obedience and such forgiveness break forth, there the world is being renewed, the new creation is in process. When we seek to obey and seek to forgive one another "in Christ," there *is* a new creation, even though its consummation lies in "what no eye has seen, nor ear heard, nor the heart of man conceived" (1 Cor. 2:9).—W. D. Davies

THE WAY THROUGH. A restless little daughter was disturbing her father, so to amuse her and keep her busy, he tore a map of the world from the newspaper he was reading and cut it into small pieces. "Here's a jigsaw puzzle, dear," he told the child. "Now run along and put it together."

The youngster, whose knowledge of geography was slight, went to work on the map and soon had it assembled. Her father, aroused by her clamor of triumph, was astonished at the feat, and asked, "How did you do it so quickly?"

"There's a picture of a man on the other side," she replied, looking up at him. "I put the man together and the world came out right."—Preston Bradley

NO OTHER LORDS. In our preaching we can still declare a risen Christ. What is more, we can still preach Christ in the full sense of the term *risen,* that is, raised to rule the world. In a world that seems to be controlled by raw power politics and multinationals, the exaltation of Christ is good news indeed. If Christ is Lord, then there are no other lords around. There are no absolutes in politics or in churches. Though we may not perceive the kingdom, we can affirm a risen "King," Jesus Christ. What we are saying is exactly what Paul says. Immediately after he has recited the Resurrection tradition, he speaks of Christ and announces, "He must reign until he puts all enemies under his feet . . . every rule, every authority, every power."—David G. Buttrick

SECTION VI.
Messages for Advent and Christmas

SERMON SUGGESTIONS

Topic: A Chronicle of Obedience

TEXT: Luke 1:25–56; Matt. 1:18–25

Obedience is not a soft, syrupy word. It is a gritty, tenacious one. It challenges us to do what God commands, to go where he leads, and to speak what he inspires. Mary and Joseph help us frame a picture of obedience in its full context and reveal to us the difficulty and delight of devotion to God.

I. Obedience in spite of circumstances. Nazareth was a small, obscure village nestled in the hill country halfway between the Sea of Galilee and the Mediterranean Sea. Nazareth had little to offer. Compared to Athens, Rome, Cairo, or even Jerusalem, it was merely a dull, monotonous dwelling place where nothing exciting ever occurred.

Mary lived in Nazareth. We have no indication of any personal looks that set her apart from other girls. To the human eye, she probably was an ordinary young teenager; but in the heart of God, she was an extraordinary person whom he chose to favor. The angel Gabriel called Mary "favored one" (Luke 1:28 NASB), meaning one who has been given grace. God's grace is always a result of his initiative, not our merit. Mary, having received God's grace and promise, embraced the consequences. She obeyed God in spite of the difficulties she inevitably would face.

Mary was a virgin. She kept her body pure as an expression of obedience to God, and she kept her mind alert with Scripture as a defense against sin. Mary heard from Gabriel what soon would happen, but she didn't know how it would happen. After all, how could a virgin give birth? We, like Mary, find ourselves facing circumstances that require obedience, even when we don't fully understand the details. Mary apparently considered the entire situation to be impossible, but Gabriel's final statement affirms that "nothing will be impossible with God" (Luke 1:37 NASB).

At the heart of obedience is faith that God can make the impossible possible. Mary did not demand an explanation. She did not complain that she had insufficient information. She simply obeyed. She said, "Be it done to me according to your word" (Luke 1:38 NASB).

Obedience for believers is not an option that depends on the circumstances. It is a duty in spite of the circumstances. If we obey only when we want to and believe only what is understandable, we do not trust God; we trust only ourselves.

Circumstances can throw long shadows over our lives. But we have the choice to shine in the shadows or to be engulfed by the darkness. We can spend our days living under the circumstances or above them.

An elderly woman I once knew had endured great personal sorrow and pain. Her circumstances were difficult. She was quiet and unpretentious, but she trusted the heart of God even when she could not trace the hand of God.

"Pastor," she said, "I choose to place my trust in a God whose plan does not require my approval."

Mary demonstrated confidence in God's method, although she did not fully grasp the total meaning.

II. Obedience in spite of conflict. Circumstances can make obedience perplexing, and conflict can make it painful. When Joseph learned that Mary was pregnant, the news must have been painful for him. He assumed the worst. He thought she had been unfaithful. According to the law, Joseph had two options: he could divorce Mary publicly and shame her in a court of justice, or he could "put her away secretly" (Matt. 1:19 NASB) by means of a private divorce. The fact that he did not want to "disgrace her" (Matt. 1:19 NASB) reveals the depth and tenderness of his love. In the midst of his own hurt, he was thinking of her feelings and welfare.

An interesting word play occurs in Matthew's description of Joseph's struggle. Joseph, whose inclination was based not on legalistic dogmatism but on loving devotion. In his head he knew the stature of the law, but in his heart he felt the greatness of love. Before Joseph could act on his inclination, an angel of the Lord informed him in a dream that Mary was pregnant by means of the Holy Spirit and that he should take her as his wife. Joseph obeyed the angel's message in the midst of conflicting feelings.

Obedience rarely is easy or convenient. Conflict, struggle, and agony frequently are present. Obedience is not a formula. It is an attitude in the heart of the person who says, "I want to follow God." The act that follows that attitude is one of faithfulness to God.

Joseph's obedience is a refreshing testimony to anyone who has experienced the distress of conflict. His action reminds us that obedience does not afford us the luxury of being neutral.

III. Obedience in spite of society. Mary and Joseph probably believed that the society in which they lived would not embrace the idea that she was going to give birth to the Messiah. Society can exert a powerful influence on people and hinder them from following the Lord. For example, several years ago in a revival, I was extending the invitation when a young woman came forward and said, "I want to become a Christian, but I don't want anyone to know it. What advice can you give me?" At first I thought she was kidding; unfortunately, she was serious. I told her if she was committed to Jesus Christ, others certainly would know it; but if she was not committed to Christ, all the advice in the world would not do much good.

If Mary and Joseph had waited for society to approve their faith, they never would have taken the first step toward obedience. If they had depended on the approval of religious priests and the socially elite, they would not have traveled the road to Bethlehem. A sad but certain commentary on some individuals today is that they raise the flag of conviction only after they have determined the prevailing wind of cultural opinion.

William Murray lived his adolescence in the presence of godlessness and oppression. He admitted that the only time he heard the word *God* was when his mother used it to curse someone or something. Williams was the fourteen-year-old plaintiff of record in the 1963 Supreme Court case that banned prayer in public schools. At age thirty-three, however, Murray rejected the atheism of his mother, Madalyn Murray O'Hair, and turned to faith in Christ. Despite an environment that fostered doubt, cynicism, bitterness, and strife, Murray obeyed the Lord.

Mary and Joseph submitted to God's purpose and accepted the embarrassment from a society that would spread despicable rumors and count the months from marriage to birth. They likely noticed the stares and overheard the whispers. They learned that obedience is a profound social battle concerning people's thoughts and actions as opposed to God's thoughts and ways. Mary and Joseph were willing to move against the current of society to honor God.—Dean Register

Topic: Direction and Decision

TEXT: Luke 3:1–18

I. He probably would be called the most unforgettable character anyone ever could meet. I am talking about the man known in the New Testament Scriptures as John the Baptist, or John the Baptizer. His colorful personality was the result of many factors. He was a man of the desert, to begin with, living by his wits in the Judean wilderness. His father was a Jewish priest, and so John was naturally disposed to religious thought and practice. But he possessed none of the graces of polite society. His words and deeds were rough and tumble; his patience was short; his perception of the judgment and righteousness of God, fearsome and unsettling.

For all of that, great crowds sought him out. Many people may have been attracted by the novelty of this "voice crying in the wilderness." Yet many of them also found their consciences seared and their ways of life called into question. John preached "a baptism of repentance for the forgiveness of sins." This meant that he challenged people to radically alter the direction of their lives, giving public evidence of their change of behavior through baptism in the waters of the Jordan River. You would not expect onlookers whom he called "a brood of vipers" to listen for long—but they did, and many responded to his moral and ethical demands. His fiery speech and surprising popularity caused the ruling king, Herod, to fear him. Eventually John's bold and unsettling ways cost him his life. His influence, though, could not be stopped, and the environment he created gave the one who followed him—Jesus of Nazareth—important help and focus.

The Bible explains that the mission and message of John the Baptist signaled the beginning of the gospel (or the good news) of Jesus Christ. To learn about Jesus, we start with John. John described himself as the forerunner, pointing not to himself but to the greater one who was to come after him.

Someone has said that John the Baptist brought his listeners to "the raw edge of excitement" when he addressed their life question, the question that asks, "What shall we do?" In their endless search for direction, human beings repeatedly raise that question. When a range of options is offered in response, human excitement is real—and that explains John's popularity; he presented the options. People forever want direction; you and I want to live purposefully, not aimlessly. We want a sense of movement that is not chaotic but stabilizing. "What shall we do?" is the question asked by serious people everywhere.

John's explanations were practical and to the point. "Whoever has two coats must share with anyone who has none," he said, "and whoever has food must do likewise." The prophet was specific and targeted needs as he saw them in relation to the people before him. His answers went a long way toward defining the changed lives his baptism represented. The crowds that followed John apparently were greatly helped by his teaching and direction.

II. Somehow, though, it was not enough. The repentance John insisted upon led to new ways of thinking and acting, yes. Ethical demands placed on newly baptized men and women were implemented gladly. But something still was missing. John the Baptist knew this, and that is why he said to the people, "One who is more powerful than I is coming; I am not worthy to untie the thong of his sandals." As significant as John's work was for those who responded to him, he could not meet the fullest and final expectations of the crowds. Another kind of question was needed for that purpose. John had been able to deal with the question of direction, the one that asked, "What shall we do?"

Beyond that discussion was an even more basic question, specifically, "To whom shall we go?" Who is there worthy of allegiance, able to meet the hurts and hopes of people, capable of mediating both forgiveness and renewal of the human soul? Can someone be found who will impart meaning to life—not just temporarily but eternally? These are some of the concerns caught up in that sweeping question, "To whom shall we go?" Implicitly John the Baptist understood this and without hesitation pointed others as well as himself to Jesus. "Here is the Lamb of God, who takes away the sin of the world!" John declared as Jesus approached.

Jesus is nothing less than the source of spiritual power into which we may dip and find strength, with whom we can commune, on whom we can draw. Visually and symbolically these things became plain to great numbers of people during the American influenza epidemic of 1918. During the height of that plague, churches and all public gathering places were ordered closed. Yet more than ever people needed hope and consolation. Burdened by his inability to reach out to people in their time of need, one resourceful pastor thought of the magnificent stained glass windows that graced the church he served. Those windows faced a major thoroughfare and were large and commanding in design. This pastor had numerous floodlights placed inside the church; illumination through the glass then gave passers-by the full effect of the windows' story.

There for all to see were matchless portrayals of Jesus: Jesus the good shepherd bearing a lamb on his bosom; Jesus the searching Savior rescuing the lone lost sheep while the ninety-nine rested safely in the fold; Jesus in Gethsemane; Jesus on the cross; Jesus triumphant in final Resurrection glory. These silent sermons in glass spoke their own eloquent messages. People who passed by tarried reverently, silently, before such testimonies of gracious, holy love. Some who looked were filled with new resolve and encouragement. They realized ever more clearly what the person of Jesus could mean to individuals caught in a crucible of human suffering. They found an unequivocal answer to that deepest of the heart's questions, "To whom shall we go?"

III. When the crowds asked John the Baptist, "What shall we do?" they were searching for direction. Whenever that second question is raised, "To whom shall we go?" there is an inescapable need for decision. We seek direction; we make decisions. When it comes to deciding about a guide and guardian for life's pilgrimage, deliberate commitment is required. To say we serve no masters, we have no guides, is a delusion, pure and simple. Inevitably, individuals align themselves with one or more overarching powers. It may be base or noble, bad or good. But we attach ourselves to those persons or forces that offer meaning to our lives. A decision to follow Jesus is the surest and soundest commitment that possibly can be made. Jesus is to be valued above all; his leadership is true and trustworthy altogether.

That is what this Advent season is all about. That is why we again turn our attention to Jesus' birth, to his entrance upon the human scene. "In the fullness of time" (as the New Testament says), God visited us in the person of Jesus, providing at last direction for our footsteps and enabling us to make the right decision about where our loyalties will lie.

We have the direction. Have we made the decision? Let every person be fully persuaded in his or her own heart and mind.—John H. Townsend

Topic: Carrying Christmas into Life

TEXT: Matt. 2:19–23

After we have sung the songs and worshiped at Christmas, after we have thought again of the meaning of Christmas, can we go back with indifference to our work not changed at all? Or has Christmas possibly burned a new fire and a new hope into our bones and we know somehow that life can't be the same? Is there any possibility for you and me to carry Christmas into life?

Mary and Joseph had to do it. The shepherds and the Wise Men and the angels and the star—all of that was wonderful, but there came that moment when they were all gone, and Mary and Joseph were left alone with their new child, left alone with a tremendous responsibility of having to take this child and help him to become what God wanted him to be. In a sense, they had the responsibility to take what they learned at Christmas and bring it into life. So do we. But how do we go about doing it? What does it mean to carry Christmas into life?

I. We must carry Christmas into the home.

Mary and Joseph had to do that. Parents of the Christ child! What a tremendous privilege and what an awesome responsibility! They had to help Jesus to grow up to understand the importance of God and of doing his will. That was not easy.

I am sure that Jesus was like any other baby and any other boy. I am sure he got sick in the night and cried and kept them up. I am sure there were times when he got into a little mischief. I'm sure he wiggled and squirmed in the synagogue services, like most children do. I'm sure there were probably those times when he didn't pick up his clothes or clean his teeth before he went to bed. Maybe there were those times when he didn't listen to them when they tried to tell him about God and about all that he meant in their lives.

But they tried. They tried to teach him. They took him to church. They read him the Scriptures. They told him what they knew. But more importantly, they lived their faith in the home. Through it all, Jesus heard. We read later in Scripture that he grew "in wisdom and in stature, and in favor with God and man" (Luke 2:52). Somewhere along the line, Christ understood what he was supposed to be and do. Christmas caught hold of Christ for one reason—because Mary and Joseph took that significant meaning of Christmas and lived it in the home.

We often talk about Christmas times of the past. Most of the time we talk about our families. We remember the good times when we were with the ones we loved and how nice it felt. This Christmas, many of your families got together again. You had reunions. How good it was, that feeling of togetherness, and how you wished you could keep it. But it won't be easy. In order for us to keep the spirit of love and joy and peace and hope that we feel at Christmas alive, we've got to keep it in the home. We've got to teach it to one another. We've got to live it in the home. It is no secret. If our children are to grow up to understand all that Christmas means, they're going to learn it first of all in the home.

The world's greatest theological school is the home. More is learned about God in the home than any other place. By what we teach our children, by our attitudes and the way we live at home, they will learn about God and how important or how unimportant he is. One of the tremendous responsibilities we have is to carry the Christmas spirit into our homes and live it.

What have we carried into our homes? We talk about the love of Christmas. Are we loving one another in the home? Are we treating each other there as persons or as things? We talk about hope. Are we hopeful persons, or are we very pessimistic about the way things are and about the way people are? We talk about the significance of God. How significant is he in our lives? Is worship something we do when we have nothing else to do? Do we involve ourselves in his ministry and in his service?

What concerns me as pastor is that many in our children's departments and many young people have parents who are not involved in the church at all. I think the sin of that will come home to roost one day. More often than not, they will grow up with a disinterest in the matters of faith. What are we teaching in the home? What are we living in the home? All that we celebrate at Christmas, all that we feel at Christmas—are we going to try to live it all year long?

What is the greatest hope we have for our children in our homes? That they may be successful in the eyes of the world? Beautiful or popular, rich? What is our greatest hope for our children? Is it that they know love and serve Jesus Christ? If Christmas has meant anything to us, our greatest desire should be that those we love most will know, love, and serve Jesus Christ. Christmas will never live in the world until we live it in our homes.

II. We must carry Christmas into our workaday worlds.

Mary and Joseph had to survive, and it wasn't easy for them. We know Joseph was a carpenter. That was hard work, and it didn't pay too much. They were poor, the parents of Christ. But somehow, they survived through the hard work they were able to do. Somehow, I feel that after Christmas, the work they did took on a new significance and a new importance. Now they knew that they were servants of God. He needed them. He was using them. They were important to him. They would provide Jesus an atmosphere in which he could grow up with a sense of security and love.

I feel that Joseph's hammer was not as heavy and his saw sawed a little bit easier. The clothes to wash and the meals to cook were not as hard for Mary to do. They both understood that they were offering service to God through their work. What they did was being used by God, every nail that he hammered, every pot that she cleaned. Jesus learned to be a carpenter, got blisters on his hands, brought honor and glory to human work, knowing that it could be used not only to serve others but also to serve God.

Most of us are looking toward going back to work after Christmas, but not with a sense of excitement and joy. It is routine and boring for many. But back to work we must go, back to the ships and the typewriters and the classrooms and the hammers and the saws. Soon the Christmas music and the Christmas hope will be lost as we struggle and sweat to survive. But does it have to be that way after we have listened again to the fact that God has come to dwell in the midst of this world? As we remember that this is his world and it is sacred, maybe, just maybe, we can begin to understand that what we do is important to God also.

All we do can be offered up to God as an offering. Maybe what we do he will take and use to better others and to make the world a better place in which to live. Maybe work doesn't have to be so boring if we understand that it is an offering to God. What will God do with it? I don't know. But would it make a difference in your life and work if the letters you typed, the truth you taught, the goods you sold, the hammers and the saws you used were offered to God? Unfortunately we often do work to make a living, and that is not the primary purpose of work. Work ought to be an offering to God, an offering that will help to contribute to the betterment of this world, to the betterment of others. God will be there to help you do that. He will use that.

I wonder if that would make any difference in your lives? If by you on the assembly line, sitting next to you in your classrooms, standing next to you and your typewriter, next to you on the ship, you imagine God there taking what you offer and using it? You see, Christmas is for all of life. It is for your work because in Bethlehem Christ was born.

III. We must carry Christmas into the area of our faith.

Mary and Joseph would need to remember Bethlehem often because there would be those moments in their lives when their faith in God would be sorely tested and tried. They would have to run for their lives to the strange land of Egypt. There were hard and difficult times in their lives when I'm sure they wondered where God was.

We know that Joseph died and Mary was left alone with the tremendous responsibility of bringing up their children. Had God deserted her then? There were surely those moments when she could have thought so, but one of our Scriptures reports the fact that Mary pondered all these things "in her heart."

Mary remembered the Christmas event. She needed to because when everything seemed to point to the fact that God had forgotten her, she would know that it was not so. She could remember there at Bethlehem God had not forgotten anyone, that he was at work in the world in ways that no one could really see. She didn't know how, but she lived by that faith and trusted that God was there.

There is no doubt that many of us will go away from this Christmas season and land in some "Egypt" where our faith will be tested. Maybe it will be sickness that will not go away. Maybe it will be a frustrating disappointment, a job we didn't get, a love that's rejected. Maybe we'll just find ourselves bored with the way life is. But life will come down hard on us, and in the middle of it we will begin to wonder, where's God anyway? All those songs we sang at Christmas about God being in the midst of the world, where is he?

That's when we'll need to remember Christmas. We'll need to remember that Christmas tells us that where he is is where we are. We are not forgotten. We're not alone. In the midst of our difficult, trying moments, we need to remember Bethlehem—that God has come. We must never give up on that; we must never lose hold of that. We must hold on to it with every ounce of faith we have in us. For that is what will keep us going on and on.

Christmas tells us that we can go on and on in the face of all our difficulties as long as we keep our eyes on the face of this Christ who has come to dwell with us. He knows the way. He is the way. Keep your eyes on him and never lose heart.

So the Christmas season is over. The decorations will be gone before too long. The trees will come down. But while the Christmas season is over and Christmas day is over, Christmas must never end. It must live, for Christmas is all about Christ helping us live at home and at work. We must never lose sight of him. If we don't, in the days ahead we will walk with a new step, a new hope, and a new joy because we will have once again been reminded that Jesus Christ is alive and in the world.—Hugh Litchfield

Topic: The Faith of Simple Folk

TEXT: Luke 2:22–38

I have an embarrassing confession to make. I realized only a few days ago what Luke is trying to do in this text. For years I had read it and made the unwarranted assumption that old Simeon was a priest. Simeon was a priest, and Anna was a prophetess—good balance and symmetry. But something about the text kept nagging me. And then I realized what it was. Simeon was not a priest at all. He was a simple old man—a layman—an ordinary person. And Anna was not an official prophetess. She was merely a devout old woman who came to the Temple a lot. Luke was only underlining a point he had begun to make by telling about the shepherds who were called from their fields and flocks to worship Christ: the coming of Christ was to simple folk! Luke, did you notice, doesn't even tell the story of the wise men; that's Matthew. Luke's whole concern, in the stories surrounding the birth of Jesus, is to emphasize one thing: Christianity is based on the faith of simple folk.

Come to think of it, that's what Luke's whole Gospel is about. It's what the Book of Acts is about. It wasn't the priests and Pharisees who received the kingdom of God, it was the laypeople, the untutored, the untrained, the unsophisticated. It was simple fishermen like James and John and Peter. It was unimportant public officials like Matthew. It was women like Mary and Martha and Mary Magdalene.

Christianity, my friends, has never been a religion of priests and theologians, ministers and teachers; from the very beginning it has been a religion of devout men and women with no claim whatsoever to professional expertise about their faith. This is important to remember.

God never intended for the church to be an organization of ministers. What he did intend for it to be is an organization of laypersons, all "righteous and devout" like old Simeon, all devoted to fasting and prayer like old Anna, and all ready, in simple faith, to receive his kingdom and rejoice in it. Ministers, in Christianity, are expendable; good, simple folk are not!

People expect ministers to have a lot of faith, and I suppose most of us do, at one time or another, or we wouldn't be in the ministry at all. But our faith is often beaten down or wrung out from having to deal with so many problems, from always being exposed to the seamy side of life. And at such times it is the faith of layfolks that does more than anything to restore us, to reinfuse in us a sense of hope and joy and expectation.

This is not to say that there is not a lot

of wrongheadedness among layfolks—a lot of spite and willfulness and confused theology. Any minister could write a book about the shortcomings of his or her congregation, and some have.

It is the faith of simple folk, nevertheless—folk uncontaminated by theological education and constant contact with the inner workings of the church—on which the church of Jesus Christ stands.

I. Look at them. Look at yourselves. *You take God at his word.* God says to Abraham, "Abraham, leave your home, go out into the wilderness. I want you to found a new dynasty, a new people that will be special"; and Abraham goes, just like that. God says, "Moses, go down to the pharaoh of Egypt and demand the release of my people." Moses says, "God, I'm not very good at that sort of thing." God says, "I know you're not, but I'll be with you." And Moses goes. God says, "Peter, go over to Greece and help those people over there to become Christians." Peter says, "Lord, they're not good Jews." God says, "You think I don't know that? I want you to go and help them to become Christians." And Peter goes. It's that way all through history. God says, "Go there, do this," and his simple folk say, "Yes, Lord, I will." You take God at his word; you do what he asks. No equivocation, no beating around the bush; you just do it.

I remember Sam Flynn, who was a member of the first church I ever pastored. Sam was a simple, uneducated man who eked out a small living for himself, his wife, and three little children out of a few hardscrabble acres of farmland. And when pledging time came at the church, Sam came in with a pledge far higher than he could afford. I said, "Sam, this is too much. God doesn't want you to short your family for the sake of the church." Sam said, "That's what God told me to give, and I have to do it. He'll take care of us. I know he will." He took God at his word.

II. Look again. *You build your lives around faith.* People build their lives around all sorts of things. Some build them around houses and some around racetracks and some around big bank accounts and some around social standing and some around education. God's good folk build them around faith.

In England's Winchester Cathedral, near the Lady Chapel, there is a pedestal bearing the brass figure of William Walker, a diver, who is credited with saving the cathedral with his own hands. In the early part of this century there was fear that the cathedral would collapse because of rotten underpinnings, and there was no money to replace them. From 1906 to 1912, working at night and on weekends, William Walker singlehandedly replaced all the underpinnings, working for no compensation and paying for the materials out of his own earnings. He did it because his whole life was built around the Christian faith. There were others who could have afforded to do the work much easier than he, whose lives were built around other things. But he did it because his life was built around faith.

Dame Edith Sitwell, one of the most famous intellectuals of our time, became a Christian because of the serenity she had seen on the faces of peasant women praying in the churches of Italy. What she saw—and envied—was lives built around faith.

III. And look once more. *You move toward death with unswerving acceptance.* I wish all of you could have known Norman Walker during the last months of his life. Norm suffered as painfully and ignominously as any person could: a vital, good-looking man in his fifties, hard worker, world traveler, attacked by cancer of the throat and jaw, operated on, treated with chemicals, got to the point where he couldn't eat anything, his body wasting away, his hair fallen out, his face distorted by the disease. But through it all, through all the horrible months of waiting and wasting away, his eyes glowed with softness and kindness and faith. "I've prayed about it," he said, "and made my peace." He knew he was going toward God, that the Father's arms would be there to receive him.

I've always liked G. K. Chesterton's description of the early Christian martyrs: "They went forward toward death as if they smelled a field of flowers afar off." Norm went that way. A lot of folks can't. They go like Dylan Thomas, cursing the darkness. But the simple folk of God know better. They may not want to leave their loved ones behind, but when the time comes they're not afraid. They know they go to something better, to a life of beauty and glory and riches this world only dreams of.

"Now let your servant depart in peace," said old Simeon. He had seen God's salvation in Christ. That was all he needed to see. He was ready to go. It's all any of us need, isn't it?

Christianity is based on the faith of simple folk. That's why this Sunday is so important, when we remember all those beautiful souls in the Lord who have gone before us and made such an impression on us that gifts have been made to the church and through the church in their names. Go home and read the list of them again. Dwell on the names and your memories of them. Ask God to help you to be like them and to be a witness to faith in your time as they were in theirs. It will do you good. It is faith like theirs that keeps this church alive.

Queen Victoria, against the advice of the Archbishop of Canterbury, once took Communion at the Church of Scotland in the little village of Crathie, near Balmoral, where the English monarchs have a home. The church register for the day quaintly records the attendance by profession. It reads: "Shepherds, 12; Servants, 11; Queens, 1." I thought I might start a Christmas sermon with that someday. Instead, I'd like to end this one with it. What it says is that the common folks are always the majority in church, and it is their faith that perpetuates everything. The queens may come and go; it is the shepherds and servants, year in and year out, who maintain the church.

"God bless us, every one."—John Killinger

Topic: The Light of Life

TEXT: John 1:4, 5

Every attentive reader must have been struck with the introduction to the Gospel of John. It is calculated and designed to give more correct and exalted conceptions of the dignity of him who became our Redeemer—that we may recognize his claims upon our love and obedience. Who can fail to take interest in the inspired account of such a subject? From the very nature of the subject, the passage contains much that is difficult—but without going beyond our depth, without wild and vain speculation, we may find our profit in dwelling upon the various parts of this introduction, which will come up in the process of explaining and commenting upon the verses read.

I. In *him.* Whom? The Word. Consider:

(a) The allusions to his preexistence and divinity. We may suppose (with reverence) that sacred writers often had great difficulty in finding suitable terms—never more than here. The term *Word* (*logos*) had come to be much used to denote an exalted being, supposed to have a very intimate relation to the Deity. Later Jewish writers identify or at least connect this *logos* with the Word of God—especially Philo, who is said to have employed the term frequently and to have referred to a peculiar use of it made by Plato. In the speculations that were already becoming rife in Asia Minor, the term was largely employed to express various ideas of divine being that were absurd and even blasphemous. Now the apostle adopted the term as coming nearest, not sanctioning these erroneous notions, but making such statements as were calculated to correct them—setting forth the real and true Word, in opposition to all false and fantastical notions.

(1) This exalted being existed in the beginning.

(2) He was with God—intimate communion, enjoyment of glory and blessedness.

(3) He was God. Plain, explicit, unambiguous. Numerous other statements like it.

(4) Repeated statements that he was with God seem to refer to the distinction of persons—the Word was God, and the Word was with God. How much the Scriptures explicitly declare concerning the divinity of the Father, the Son, and

the Holy Spirit, and yet that God is one. The terms *person* and *Trinity* are of human choosing, but the best perhaps that we can find.

(5) He was the Creator of all things.

(b) His Incarnation—"The Word was made flesh, and dwelt among us, full of grace and truth—and we beheld his glory." A real Incarnation—"forasmuch as the children were partakers of flesh and blood, he also."

II. "In him was life." Various terms employed in this introduction, which require and would repay a careful study, comparing especially the apostle's own use of them elsewhere. Besides *Word,* we have *life, light, darkness, grace, truth,* the *world,* and so on.

Life—Cf. John 5:26. "As the Father hath life in himself, even so." Also 1 John 1:1, 2—"Of the Word of Life; for the Life was manifested, and we have seen it, and bear witness, and shew unto you that eternal life which was with the Father, and was manifested unto us." Thus he is represented as the self-subsisting source of life, the fountain of life.

Again, as appointed to impart spiritual life. John 14:6—"I am the way, and the truth, and the life." Also 1 John 5:11—God hath given to us eternal life, and this life is in his Son. In him is life then, in the most extensive sense.

III. "And the life was the *light* of *men.*" The vitalizing, fructifying principle. Light used in Scripture is expressive of knowledge and happiness.

(a) Knowledge. As sight is the chief means of gaining knowledge of the external world, so very naturally light is the emblem of knowledge in general. He has given knowledge.

(1) Of immortality. So much more certainly and distinctly known.

(2) Of the attributes of God, and our relations to him.

(3) Of the way in which guilty man may be justified and saved. Notice this especially.

(b) Happiness. What a world of darkness is ours—not simply mental but also spiritual darkness! He is the sun of righteousness. Think of the happiness derivable from knowledge of the coming life. Still more happiness comes from knowledge and personal experience of the way of salvation.

The true light, which, coming into the world, lighteth every man. Not Jews alone, but "a light to lighten the Gentiles"—his mission is not restricted in its design, whatever may be true of its actual application.

IV. "And the light shineth in darkness, and the darkness comprehended it not" (received it not). Men are in the spiritual ignorance and misery that belong to sin.

(a) These received not the light. The world was made by him, yet knew him not. His own received him not. Often they who seem specially favored do most utterly reject the Savior. They loved darkness rather than light, because their deeds were evil.

(b) We may rejoice that the statement could be made without exception—there have always been some to receive him. To them he gave the right, privilege, to become the sons of God—to as many as received him, and not Jews alone. And these were not such by virtue of any natural birth, but by spiritual birth—born of God. Cf. "born of water and of the Spirit," the pure birth of the Spirit.

And now, my friends, do not wonder that I have failed to give any very clear and complete conceptions of these great truths; these are things the angels desire to look into—they shall be our study through eternity. Who can grasp the vast ideas here shadowed forth—who comprehend the mystery of the Trinity, the Incarnation—or appreciate all that is meant here by life, by darkness and light? A full comprehension and appreciation are reserved for the coming state, but we know enough for all the ends of life, all the wants of our spiritual being, if we will receive the light and act upon it. To which class shall we belong, those who receive or those who reject the light of the world, the only Savior?—John A. Broadus

IILLUSTRATIONS FOR ADVENT AND CHRISTMAS

THE WAY GOD CAME. That quiet insertion of himself into human history, which we celebrate at Christmas time, is not a piece of pious legend. It's a sober fact of history. Anyone with any imagination at all can think of some God of righteousness and power breaking through into the life of this sinful planet, in wrath and judgment, and displaying enough physical force to make the bravest tremble! But that was not the way of the God with whom we have to do. He came not to condemn but to save, and his humble means of entry is a strong clue to his character. No man's free will is interfered with; no man's personality is assaulted; no one is forced to do anything at all. God enters his world in humble circumstances; God lives life on the same terms as he expects all human beings to live it. God accepts no special privilege or protection, and in the end God is betrayed and executed, without any superhuman intervention. On the face of it, it seems a weak and feeble intrusion into human affairs, and it's that apparent weakness that we must never forget.—John Bertram Phillips

GOD AMONG US. The good news is that God came down into this world on the first Christmas morning. In his cosmic, sweeping mercy the infinite, everlasting God—not just a moral reformer, a religious poet, a gentleman of absolute integrity—broke into human history. He stooped beneath the lowest and least inviting roof in Bethlehem and clothed himself in the garment of our own frail flesh. It is not so astounding that God came down to earth; had he not visited "this vale of tears," spiritually, many times before? Of course he had! He once filled a desert shrub with the perfume of his presence and glory, and it flamed with fire. On another occasion he entered a great mountain, and it quivered and quaked with his presence. But the amazing fact is that "in the fullness of time" he shrank to the size of a small Son of man and limited himself to the loveliest of all earth's languages—the language of a newborn baby's cry! "The Word was made flesh, and dwelt among us, . . . full of grace and truth."—Johnstone G. Patrick

CHRIST—OUR STANDARD. More and more as we go along our way we assume that Christ does not mean to be unreasonable in this thing. Surely he does not expect us to go too far. Therefore let us insist that he was talking about things as they might be. He was using his Oriental imagery, not to be taken literally. Finally, we come to where our prayer, if we were honest, would be like the prayer in W. H. Auden's "Christmas Oratorio": "O God, put away justice and truth for we cannot understand them and do not want them. Eternity would bore us dreadfully. Leave thy heavens and come down to our earth of waterclocks and hedges. Become our uncle, look after Baby, amuse Grandfather, escort Madam to the opera, help Willie with his homework, introduce Muriel to a handsome naval officer. Be interesting and weak like us, and we will love you as we love ourselves." And if you think that is too bitter and too cynical, remember that we would not stand in this time uncertain about our future if we Christians had been willing to take the mind of Christ for our standard.—Gerald Kennedy

LIBERATION. To respond to this gospel does not imply that Christians must espouse every revolutionary cause in our world today or that everyone who talks about "liberation" is on the side of the angels. I cannot see either Jesus or his mother as members of the part of the Zealots of that day, with their program of revolutionary violence against the Romans. "My kingdom," said Jesus, "is not of this world; if my kingdom were of this world, then would my servants fight." Yet his disciples came to be called "those who turned the world upside down," for they were a disturbing and liberating force in that ancient world. One thing is clear. When Mary sang of the liberating power of God and rejoiced in the Savior she was about to bear, the world was being introduced to the revolution of love. There is no place for violence, for the fostering of hate, for the arrogance of the self-righteous in the Christian liberation movement. For the gospel according to Mary extols the humble heart and leaves the judgment to almighty God. But if you feel, as many do today, that the church is making grave mistakes on occasion in embracing very questionable movements that claim to stand for freedom and justice, you should remember that an even greater mistake would be to be found on the side of an oppressor.—David H. C. Read

SYMBOL OF JUDGMENT. Dear Abby made the mistake of asking her readers, "If you had it to do over again, would you have children?" She received ten thousand letters in response, and seven out of ten parents said no. Children were too much responsibility, was the reason, or they took too much time out of personal freedom. They disappointed their parents by the way they turned out, or they paid too little attention to those who raised them.

But that is not a judgment on the children as much as it is a judgment on the parents. And when we hear it all, we begin to get the feeling that something is terribly wrong. There is some sickness in this society we have made that is infecting our very offspring. Worse yet, there is some sickness in us that is making us warp and then hate our children. The child has become the symbol of judgment on our culture and on you and me. The child has become the instrument of our undoing.—Elizabeth Achtemeier

SECTION VII.
Evangelism and World Missions

SERMON SUGGESTIONS

Topic: The Quest for God

TEXT: Matt. 2:1–12

Of all the stories associated with the birth of Christ, none is more beloved than the story of the Wise Men who followed the star to Bethlehem to pay homage to the Christ child. We sing of it in our carols, picture it on our Christmas cards, and portray it in our manger scenes. But I wonder if in the midst of all our pageantry and celebration we haven't lost sight of the story's spiritual meaning. For the story of the Wise Men is, in the final analysis, the story of a quest, a quest for God that began in a far-off land, proceeded to Jerusalem, and culminated in Bethlehem. It's a story that contains in it the elements of every man and every woman's search for God.

The quest proceeded, as I see it, in three distinct stages: (1) awakening, (2) illumination, and (3) discovery. And what I propose to do in this sermon is to consider the quest of the Wise Men in light of these three stages. For in so doing, I think we shall see that there is a great deal we can learn about our faith journey from theirs.

I. Our story begins in a far-off land. And the reason I call this first stage of the journey an awakening is that the Wise Men's desire to undertake the quest was awakened within them by the appearance of the star.

The Wise Men, as the commentators tell us, were sages or holy men from the East. They were skilled in philosophy and natural science. They were soothsayers and interpreters of dreams. But above all, they were watchers of the sky—ancient astronomers and astrologers. Nothing was more fit to capture their attention, therefore, than the appearance of a great star.

No one really knows what the star was. Some say it was a comet, some say it was a conjunction of Saturn and Jupiter, some say it was a supernova or the birth of a new star, and some say it was a supernatural apparition. But regardless of what it was, the Wise Men recognized that it was a sign from God announcing the birth of a great king. I'm sure there were many others who saw the star. But what made the Wise Men wise was this: they understood that God was beckoning them in and through this star, and, as a consequence, they set forth on a long and arduous journey.

From this we learn that no one is beyond the reach of God's grace. There is a star for everyone, a star sent by God to awaken us, a star that beckons us to undertake a journey of faith even as did the Wise Men of old.

Sometimes it's not so much *a* star as it is *the* stars. The heavens above beckon us with their serene and silent voices, which seem to be saying: "God is real! God is calling you!" Sometimes it's the birth of a child, a baby whose smile and whose tiny hands say to us as if by some mysterious sign language: "God is real! God is calling you!" Sometimes it's a providential deliverance from an accident or misfortune, an answer to prayer in whose aftermath we seem to hear a still, small voice saying: "God is real! God is calling you!" Sometimes it comes to us shrouded in darkness in the form of a great ordeal. And yet, in and through the sufferings that afflict us, we cannot escape the awareness of that insistent voice that says: "God is real! God is calling you!"

I have no doubt that God has sent some such star, some such token of his presence, to every one of us in whatever far-off land we may find ourselves. The only question is, having seen the star, are we willing to undertake the quest? Some see the star but don't recognize it as a sign from God. Others recognize it as a sign from God but never begin the quest. We may well ask ourselves, therefore, "Have I seen my star rising in the east? Have I set out on the quest, faith's journey to God?" After all, that's what made the Wise Men wise—having seen the star, they undertook the quest.

II. According to our story, the star in itself was unable to lead the Wise Men directly to Bethlehem. Where it led them instead was to Jerusalem, where they entered the second stage of the quest, illumination.

Jerusalem, of course, was the home of the Temple, the city of God. It was in Jerusalem that the Wise Men had access to the source of illumination they needed if the quest was to be completed—the sacred Scriptures. For through Herod and the chief priests, the Wise Men learned of the following words spoken by the prophet Micah: "And you Bethlehem, in the land of Judah, are by no means least among the rulers of Judah; for from you shall come a ruler who is to shepherd my people Israel."

What the star couldn't tell them, what natural reason and philosophy couldn't tell them, the Scriptures could: the Messiah was to be born in Bethlehem. And thus illumined by the Scriptures, they were enabled to continue the quest.

Isn't it the same for us? The most natural thing for a person on a quest to do is to ask *quest*ions. And the place to find the answers to life's most profound questions is in the Scriptures, the Word of God written.

The heavens may tell us of the glory of God. The earth may declare his handiwork. But neither nature, reason, nor experience can tell us where to find Christ, where to find the forgiveness of sins, or where to find the key that unlocks the secret of our destiny. For this we must journey to Jerusalem, to the church, and to the Scriptures. There we will find the writings of the apostles and prophets. There we will find the accumulated wisdom of the ages. There we will find the testimony of multitudes who have made the journey before us and can point us to the place where we, too, can find Christ. So, you see, this is what made the Wise Men wise—having begun their quest under the guidance of the star, they continued it by the illumination they received from the sacred Scriptures. And if your heart's desire is to make progress in the quest, my advice to you is: seek illumination from the Word of God.

III. The final stage of the quest is discovery. For having received illumination from the Scriptures, the Wise Men were then led by the star to Bethlehem, where they discovered the Christ child. When they found him, we're told the Wise Men were overwhelmed with joy and that, kneeling down before the child, they opened their treasure chests and offered him gifts of gold, frankincense, and myrrh.

The word *Bethlehem* means "the house of bread." Bethlehem, therefore, is the place where God meets us and feeds us the Bread of Life, Jesus Christ. Some people stop short and end the quest in Jerusalem. They have some knowledge of the church and the Scriptures, but they've never tasted the Bread of Life for themselves. They've never been nourished within by the grace of God. They've never known the joy of discovery. They've never experienced that wondrous moment of faith and consecration when they have knelt before the Christ child and offered him their gold, frankincense, and myrrh—their lives and the very best that they have to offer. But don't you see? That's what made the

Wise Men wise—they followed the star, they received the Scriptures, and they pressed on to Bethlehem where they discovered the Christ child for themselves.

The story of the Wise Men, then, bids us to ask ourselves the following questions: are you still in that far-off land content with a mere vision of a star, a mere token of grace? Have you stopped short in Jerusalem, thinking you could find peace of mind among the church and her traditions? Or are you among that company of wise men and women who, having come to Bethlehem, have made the great discovery? Have you knelt before the Christ child and, kneeling, offered him the very best you have to give? After all, that's what made the Wise Men wise. And so it shall be for all those who, having seen the star, undertake the quest.—Neil Babcox

Topic: On Being a Christian

TEXT: Acts 11:26

A prominent eye physician died some years ago and left a will that caused some distress, both in the immediate family and beyond it. An avid Christian, that physician had willed a large portion of income from his estate to support Christian causes. His stipulation was that the willed funds must be distributed to "persons who believe in the fundamental principles of the Christian religion and in the Bible and who are endeavoring to promulgate the same." When the doctor's wife died ten years later, anxious nephews and nieces started a lawsuit to break the will. Motivated by selfish concern, they argued that there is no common agreement on the "fundamental principles of the Christian religion." The court proceedings continued for some time, and several preachers and professors of religion were summoned to define and explain the Christian faith. After all the views were heard, the presiding judge, himself a Methodist, took several weeks more to prepare and announce his decision about the case.[1]

[1]"What Is a Christian?" *Time*, October 22, 1951, p. 15.

What *is* a Christian? Why was there such a dilemma about definition? Why such confusion over the deceased doctor's terms? Can a clear answer be given about this matter of being a Christian? My answer is: yes.

I. A challenged term. What *is* a Christian? There was a time when nearly everybody we knew could immediately and rightly answer this question. But it is not so now. Actually, many questions are being raised in our time about things we used to know quite well. Our time has witnessed such change, such revolution in thought and morals, such disarray in ethics and social patterns, such breakdown of tradition, and such religious insecurity that everything is being questioned. The fact is that these crucial changes have placed organized Christianity (or better, Churchianity) in their shadow. Traditional Christian faith is fighting for its life against secularism and revolutionary concerns. But all of this only makes the question more vital and the right answer more strategic. What is a Christian? What does it mean to be one?

A dictionary answer is inadequate. It is not enough to say that a Christian is one who professes the religion of Christ because profession can be mere talk or sterile belief. It is not enough to use the term *Christian* to distinguish so-called civilized persons from so-called savages. It will not do to use that term *Christian* to describe those who belong to a country or nation in which Christianity is the prevailing religion. Being Christian involves far more than what any country or nation in Western civilization reflects or represents. What does it mean to be a Christian? The dictionary cannot tell us in full, but the New Testament can and does.

II. An all-important description. The early believers used the term *Christian* as a distinctive word about themselves. It was for them an all-important description of the life they were called to live. *Christian* was no mere general term; it was a governing word, a crown upon the head.

Interestingly, the first believers did not coin that word to describe themselves. Some believe that the word *Christian* was at first a term of jest against followers of

Jesus, that it was a pun, a nickname used by their opponents to ridicule them. The text credits the people of Antioch with coining the word. Perhaps the people of Antioch heard followers of Jesus constantly using his name in their talk and witness. They might have noticed the strong concern among the disciples to be like Jesus, so those who watched them finally used a Latinized word to describe the believers. Whether they did this in admiration or out of spite we do not know. It is entirely possible that some who spoke it used the word with admiration, and that they considered it a good description of those who were serious about the spiritual, ethical, and social demands of Jesus Christ upon them.

Whatever the exact spirit behind the use of the word, we do know that the believers finally accepted *Christian* as a title of honor. It became for them an apt character reference. It marked them as persons intent to "copy" Jesus and imitate his example. The name spread across the empire and was commonly used among Romans and others as the church grew. Acts 26:28 records its use by Agrippa II during a conversation with Paul, and 1 Peter 4:16 repeats the word as a recognized and regular part of church talk.

The early believers had long used other terms to describe themselves—disciples, brethren, friends, saints, believers, followers of the Way, but *Christian* finally became the great label. What might have begun in Gentile jest had now become a glorious title. The early disciples of Jesus had lived out the highest meanings of the term.

III. Doing Christ's business. What is a Christian? A Christian is a person whose life and living are under the direction of Jesus Christ; a Christian is someone whose concern in life is to do the business of Christ himself.

Acts 11:26 tells us that the disciples were "called Christians." The Greek word used there for "called" was used originally to explain or label some business being transacted. We should understand this: we "call" or label someone who bakes a baker, someone who makes shoes a shoemaker, someone who drives a driver. It is logical to call or label someone a Christian who is busy living like Christ and promoting his work.

The only persons who should be called Christians are those who believe that Jesus is the Christ and are fully identified with him in the business of his life. And what was the business of his life? The business of Jesus was disclosing the character of God, identifying with human need, sharing the love of God, and gathering people into the fellowship of care.

Christ life is life lived in loyalty to Jesus Christ. It is life lived in his service and to his honor. The Book of Acts shows us this in grand measure. Those early believers committed themselves to Christ and lived their way into the higher meanings of his name and nature. Only those who live by his name and honor his claims are worthy of being called *Christian*.

What is a Christian? A Christian is someone who believes that Jesus is the Christ, God's anointed Son, and lets that anointing influence all aspects of life and living. A Christian is someone who so identifies with Jesus that Jesus also identifies with them.

A traveling journalist tells of seeing a group of soldiers during wartime set a church building afire. They did so to dislodge enemies who had fired on them from the church belfry. The journalist watched to see the outcome. Some of the soldiers rushed into the smoke-filled building and soon hastily emerged, not with the enemies, but carrying a statue of Jesus! Someone asked those soldiers why they did that. They replied, "[Because] he is one of [us]."[2] Even revolutionaries have tried to claim kinship with Jesus. The problem is not so much our claiming identification with him but whether Jesus claims and verifies his acceptance of us. The Christian is someone loyal to Jesus Christ, someone to whom Jesus is readily identified as Master and friend.

IV. Honoring the charge. Becoming a Christian begins with repentance toward

[2]Pierre van Paassen, *Why Jesus Died* (New York: Dial Press, 1949), 24.

God and faith in Jesus for salvation and forgiveness of sins. Remaining a Christian calls for a settled will to live as Jesus requires. The true Christian will honor the change Christ makes possible in us and will share the testimony about grace with others. Remaining a Christian is by commitment to Jesus and constancy in following him.

Let the world change, but the Christian must not! Let others close their eyes to moral concerns, but we Christians must not! Let us live with conviction, commitment, and constancy!

Some will not view us in friendliness. Not all will honor Christ the way we do. Some will hurl epithets against us in jest, intent to scorn, scare, or injure us. Peter has warned and advised us about such times: "Yet if one suffers as Christian, let him not be ashamed, but under that name let him glorify God" (1 Pet. 4:16).

Some will speak the name "Christian" in honor and with hope, complimenting us on some value we have helped to preserve or some change we have helped them to have in their lives. There is still "something in a name," and it is our privilege to show it. A committed Christian always does.

Stephen did, and when subjected to the meanest acts of terror against him, he died showing what he had found in the name of Jesus Christ! So did James, killed by decree with a sword, as Acts 12:2 reports. But James knew Christ and honored his name to the death. Full belief leads to committed behavior, even under the direst threat and severest strain.

Polycarp, disciple of John the apostle, grew strong on stories of such faithful Christians as Stephen and James. When he was apprehended and told that he must die, Polycarp only requested time alone to pray. When told by the judge that he could be released because of his old age if he would renounce Christ, Polycarp refused repeatedly, and the proconsul let his wrath fall heavily upon that sainted bishop. The gray-haired Christian shouted his testimony while being led to the funeral pyre: "Eighty and six years have I served Christ and he has never done me wrong; how can I blaspheme my King and Savior?'"[3]

About to be nailed to the torture post, Polycarp asked that no spikes be used; he promised to stand steady in the flames: "He who gives me strength to bear the fire will also give me power to remain unmoved without being bound by spikes." Overwhelmed by his spirit, the enemies did not nail him to the stake but did bind his hands behind him with rope. Polycarp died praying, "I bless thee that thou hast thought me worthy of the present day and hour, to have a share in the number of the martyrs and in the cup of Christ . . . wherefore, on this account, and for all things I praise thee . . . through the eternal High Priest, Jesus Christ, thy well-beloved Son."

Having lived in faith and labored in love, Polycarp died in honor. He had walked with Christ, and his confession had deepened his resolute trust.

Polycarp was a Christian—born again, committed to Christ, constant in obedience, and of contagious faith. That is what being a Christian is all about. It is a life to which we all are called and a privilege from which no one is excluded.

If you are a Christian, live up to the name. If you are not a Christian, you ought to be one. It all begins with repentance toward God and faith in Jesus Christ. And this can happen for you right now if you desire it.—James Earl Massey

Topic: The Question of All Ages

TEXT: Matt. 21:10

One of the things a reader of the New Testament will notice at once is how the question of the identity of Jesus often arose. Even his own disciples often wondered who he was. Although other men had arisen, presenting some unique claim or manifesting some special quality or ability, these were soon classified by their fellowmen and their true worth assessed. Some gifted rabbi would arise and teach

[3]Eusebius, *Ecclesiastical History,* vol. 3, trans. C. F. Cruse (London: George Bell and Sons, 1897), 134f.

in the synagogue of one town, but men would soon grasp his teaching and the rabbi would move on to another town. Unique individuals were always appearing on Mars Hill among the cultured Greek philosophers, and whilst these ancient scholars were always delighted to hear some new thing, they soon had the worth of a man and he would move into new territories to make the best of his limited powers of rhetoric, or debate, or whatever his particular ability may have been. With Jesus it was different. From the beginning of his earthly life and ministry to the end, he was always arousing curiosity and intense interest. He always made people ask questions about him, and the most common of these was: "Who is this?" This identity was a puzzle to them. He was a man like themselves, and yet somehow he was different. He couldn't be classified. And if any did think that he was another Judas of Galilee, to whom Gamaliel referred—a one-day wonder—then they found they were mistaken, for this man could confound the wisest and most intellectual among them, and at his death he still had men wondering as to his true identity.

"Who is this?" Both friends and foes alike asked this question. The question was asked by the scribes and Pharisees, the exponents of law, ethics, and morality: "Who is this that forgiveth sins?" By the representative of royalty, King Herod: "Who is this of whom I hear such things?'" By the representative of politics, Pontius Pilate: "Who art thou? Art thou the king of the Jews?" By the leaders of religion at the religious trial of Jesus: "Art thou the Son of the Blessed?"

It is the same today. When the teaching of Christ is applied to the immorality and loose living going on today, the question comes, "Who is this?" When the spiritual teaching of Jesus is brought to bear upon the nominal, official leaders of established institutional religion, the cry again goes up, "Who is this?"

Jesus knew that this question of his identity was always on people's lips, and he became curious about the various conclusions they were arriving at, so one day he asked his apostles, "Whom do men say that I am?" and they replied, "Some say thou art John the Baptist risen from the dead, others say Elias, and others say one of the prophets." But Jesus turned the question back to them: "But whom say ye that I am?" and Peter confessed, "Thou art the Christ, the Son of the living God"; and Jesus told Peter that this truth had been revealed unto him not by his own human wisdom and insight but by God himself.

Note that the revelation of the truth wasn't found in the sphere of religion, law, politics, ethics, or in the king's palace but in the heart of a simple fisherman from Galilee. The great question of the day—"Who is this?"—doesn't find its answer in the mighty glory of the Roman empire or in the shining splendor of Greece, nor in the great elaborate and honorable religion of the Jews, but on the lips of an ignorant fisherman. "God hath chosen the foolish things of the world to confound the things that are mighty." If you are in the same position as so many who wondered who Jesus was in the days of his flesh, the answer for you is not, "This is the prophet from Galilee," but is found in Peter's great reply, "Thou art the Christ, the Son of the living God." If you seek the answer to your question from those who have never been enlightened as to the true nature of Christ's person, whose eyes have never been opened to observe Christ as the Redeemer of men, who have never seen the glory of God in the face of Jesus Christ, whose hearts have never been regenerated by the Spirit of God, then you will be disappointed, and you must turn sorrowfully away. The answer as to who this is can only be given by those whose hearts have been set on fire by the warmth of his love, by those who have been changed by his matchless grace, by those who have thrilled to the music of his name, by those who know his risen power pulsating in their veins. This man whom we preach is not merely a prophet of God. He is the Son of God, the Savior of mankind, the Savior of your soul. This man is the answer to your great quest in life. This man, in his person, is the very essence of the Christian gospel. This man, who rides down the long corridors of time and across our path to where we are in history, is the way, the truth, and the life, and he wants to turn our question, "Who is this?" into the glorious and triumphant answer, "Thou art the Christ!"

Christianity has never sought or claimed to give men cast-iron, mathematically demonstrated proof of its claim. What it does do is offer men and women evidence, and I have three pieces of evidence to offer you now.

I. First, I believe that Jesus Christ is the Son of God and the Savior of mankind because of the *miracle of the Bible.*

The miracle of the Bible? Isn't the Bible on the same level as other great religious books? Haven't the modern critics explained the processes by which our Bible was composed and how it came to us? Modern criticism may have explained certain problems, but it has also done a great deal of harm, and the extreme critics, of course, have robbed the Bible of many of its miraculous elements and of its verbal inspiration. But the results of modern critical research are incomplete, and whilst we welcome anything that is going to clarify some of the so-called problems of the Scriptures, we cannot accept the contention that the Bible can be explained adequately in human terms. One cannot escape the miraculous elements of the Bible. The Scriptures themselves declare that they are given by inspiration of God and that this inspiration came as holy men spake by the Holy Ghost.

Thousands of years before Christ, men like David, Isaiah, Jeremiah, and Ezekiel prophesied about the coming Messiah, gave some details of his life, and gave exact details of his death. Joel the prophet prophesied concerning the Pentecostal outpouring of the Holy Spirit recorded in Acts 2 hundreds of years before the event. And is it not miraculous that there are events recorded in the Old Testament concerning the Jewish nation that are taking place at the present time? How do you explain all this in human terms? How do you explain, in human terms, the fact that the Bible has been preserved all down the long centuries? It has been preserved from the wrath of ungodly men, from the fury of hell, from the flames to which it has been committed time and time again. Manuscripts and fragments carried by early Christian scribes have been preserved from the effects of long journeys by early pilgrims across desert sands and from long, dusty roads throughout Asia and Syria. Many others have endured the devastating effects of the dampness and dirt of old Roman dungeons. At a later time, a succession of scholars worked laboriously translating New Testament manuscripts, which had miraculously come together to form one complete whole, and many of these men, just prior to the Reformation, suffered great persecution and even death. John Wycliffe was severely persecuted for his part in the translation of the Bible into English. William Tyndale was strangled as an old man and then burned for his part. When the Reformation dawned, the Reformers built the new faith upon what Gladstone called the "infallible Rock of Holy Scripture," and they said, in effect, "This book is the one that reveals the Christ who is the answer to every man's need"; and John Knox took the pulpit from the side of the church in St. Gile's Cathedral in Edinburgh and placed it in the center, symbolic of the centrality of the Word of God, the central message of the written Word being the Christ, the living Word.

The Bible is a miracle! It was banned and burned, and many of its translators suffered death, but it has emerged as the world's best seller and the most influential of all books. Men thought so highly of this book and were so convinced of its miraculous nature, so convinced that it was the Word of God to man, that many of them were prepared to die for it. Men don't die for something fake, for an invention, for a book of fairy tales, myth, or legend. Men don't die for the works of Homer, Milton, Shakespeare, or Shaw. Yet men died for the preservation and promotion of the Bible as the Word of God. This, then, is my first piece of evidence: the miracle of the Bible.

II. The second piece of evidence I wish to offer is the *miracle of the church.*

Here again, as in the case of the Bible, the fury and onslaught of hell have lashed against the bulwarks of the faith. Jesus foretold it would, and it wasn't long before the ferocious forces were unleashed. Satan, through the agency of evil men, sought to strangle the church in its infancy. Herod killed James with the sword. The leaders of religion stoned Stephen, the first Christian martyr, urging them on with fury and hatred. So there was wholesale slaughter. Christians were flung to lions in the Roman sporting arenas. Some were wrapped in the skins of wild animals so that they would be more savagely attacked by dogs. Some were crucified, others were smeared with pitch and set on fire, and these living torches were used by the Emperor Nero to illuminate his gardens. You don't die like that for a fable, a fabrication, a fallacy. The attempt was made to stamp out the church at its birth.

The attempt was made to stamp out the church at the dawn of the Reformation. Hundreds died at the stake, from loyal archbishops to lowly peasants. Who is this? Go and ask the question of Stephen, and he will reply, as the stones are breaking every bone in his body: "I see Jesus standing at the right hand of God." Who is this? Address your question to the early Christian martyrs as they are enduring unspeakable agonies under Nero, and they will reply: "This is Jesus, the Redeemer of our souls," or take your question to sixteen-year-old Mary Wilson, who was drowned on the shores of the Solway Firth in Scotland, and she will sing to you "The Lord's My Shepherd" as the waters rise to overwhelm her. Who is this? Take your question to Archbishop Latimer, and you will hear him say to Archbishop Ridley as they are both about to be burned at the stake, "Be of good cheer, Master Ridley: we shall this day, by God's grace, light such a torch in England as will never be put out." Or take your question to the members of the underground church in China, Russia, Hungary, and they will reply: "This is Jesus, the Son of the living God!"

The triumph of the Christian church! The miracle of the Christian church! Is the miracle of the church's survival after almost twenty centuries of such scorn, criticism, and persecution a substantial piece of evidence?

III. My third piece of evidence is the *miracle of changed and transformed lives.*

This is undeniable evidence for Christ and his religion. You may argue about the trustworthiness of the Bible if you so wish; you may find some justifiable criticism of the church and its organization, but you can never deny the evidence of a godly life. No one can explain *that* away.

The multitudes were amazed when they saw the disciples of Christ, who previously were timid and afraid, speaking with a power and a boldness that were supernatural. The pagans of the first century could hardly believe that so many could give up their pagan and immoral practices to suffer and die so courageously for this Jesus. Indeed, it was the changed lives of men and women that won the greatest amount of converts to Christianity in those days. The ancient world was shattered when Saul of Tarsus—one of the greatest intellectuals of his day—was transformed from a blasphemer and a proud, haughty Pharisee and persecutor into a follower and disciple of the despised Jesus. When Christ confronted Saul on the road to Damascus, Saul naturally asked, "Who art thou, Lord?" but toward the close of his life many years afterward, he expressed his years of proven experience concerning Jesus in these words: "The Son of God who loved me and gave himself for me."

All down through the centuries Christ has been transforming human lives, not only the lives of intellectuals but also the lives of thousands of ordinary men and women. Alan Redpath, John Stott, Billy Graham, and others tell us in their books of the most despicable characters in every country of the world, apparently beyond all human aid, who have been completely transformed by the reception of Christ into their lives. This is the miracle of changed and transformed lives.

Perhaps you are a more "respectable" person. You have planned your own future, and at present you are enjoying life to the full, but Christ has come across your path sometime in the past or perhaps even at this moment, and you are confronted with the challenge of his message and its claims. Perhaps you see him as a threat to the settled course of your life, and you are crying out with a nod of apprehension: "Who is this?" Many have been in your position. Those who have yielded to his claims have been changed from selfish aspiration and ambition to unselfish and fruitful service for the one who is the Christ, the Son of the living God.

"Who is this?" We have considered, briefly, some of the evidence. Has it been in any way convincing? Have you reached your verdict? Are you satisfied with such evidence? If not, what kind of evidence are you looking for?—Robert A. Penny

Topic: The Church on Mission

TEXT: John 1:6–8; Matt. 28:16–20

We have defined missions too narrowly. We think "foreign mission"—exotic and faraway. Missions include overseas work, but it begins at home. We think "money," special appeals, and offerings. Funds are essential, but that's only one fact of mission. We may think "prayer" (at least the women of the church know how vital this is to missions), but mission is more than prayer. Actually we think of missions as vicarious—something done by someone else who goes in our place. But mission should be incarnational, personal. It begins with us and is as broad as life, and a world in need of the gospel.

A seminary professor said, "Missionary concern is far more than recruiting missionaries and raising money for their support. Mission is the purpose of God, through the church, to bring all people to faith." The church is the people of God on mission. We represent the continuing incarnation:

His tongue telling the Good News;
His hands sharing and helping;
His feet going with the Gospel.

Emil Brunner wrote: "The church exists by mission as fire exists by burning." Elton Trueblood called us "the incendiary fellowship." His hymn contains these lines:

Thou whose purpose is to kindle:
Now ignite us with Thy fire.

I. Mission is important. It is not an elective but a divine command. Jesus said, "As you go make disciples, baptize them . . . teach them." Missions make the church great. It is the cement that holds us together, as well as being our driving force.

There has long been an antimission spirit in the land. Some people oppose missions because of their theology. They believe Christ died only for the "elect," and God will save the heathen if he wants them saved. There is nothing we can do about it. In 1835 two women were turned out of a church in Illinois. They were charged with "harboring a missionary and trying to start a Sunday school." Both activities were forbidden. (The missionary was John Mason Peck, who began home mission work in this country among Baptists.) Missions and Sunday schools were opposed by many pastors in earlier years.

An antimissionary attitude is found today among some intellectuals. Their cool logic contends that it is an *insult* to send missionaries to other countries. After all, they have their cultures and religions. Why disturb them? They consider missions a form of religious imperialism.

Let me point out that U.S. business interests have no such hesitancy. They've managed to send our products into every nook and cranny of the world: soft drinks and fast foods, sewing machines and American automobiles are found in many nations. Since World War II, the largest economic force in Europe has been American business. Why do you suppose those nations got together to form a Common Market? Business is not timid about promoting its goods.

Neither is the U.S. government bashful. Why do you suppose we reestablished diplomatic relations with China? Could it be because China, with a large population, is the largest market on earth?

Mission is important. We need not

apologize for being obedient to Christ's command to share the faith.

II. Our mission field is the world. There are some three billion unsaved persons on earth—"without God, without hope in the world."

It is true. We have had some marvelous successes in carrying out the mission of the church. The United Nations indicates that the population of Africa will be 818 million by A.D. 2000, and 500 million will be members of Christian churches. I wonder if that's not a higher percentage of believers than we have in America today.

We have had mission work in Brazil and Nigeria for more than one hundred years. Did you know that the church there has grown until they now send missionaries to neighboring countries?

Our mission field is the world, but that also includes the United States. We are seeking to win America to Christ. We have ministries working among ethnic groups, in the great urban centers, and are constantly starting new churches.

Many churches send lay and clergy volunteers as short-term missionaries to strengthen the work of indigenous believers and professional missionaries in meeting human needs and evangelism.

Our hometown is also our mission field. There are many who have never been confronted with the claims of Christ where we live. Many would respond to an invitation to worship and Bible study. We can reach out to these friends with the gospel.

There are business and professional persons where we live. Many of them function in a cold, impersonal world; for some, it is brutal. It can chew people up, with an eye on profits more than persons. These friends face hard decisions. The church offers them ethical guidance, inspiration, and encouragement.

There are senior adults who lack a Christian quality of life. Some are lost and close to eternity without Christ. The church offers them the gospel of hope.

III. You have a mission—a ministry. Begin to see missions as incarnational. It involves persons: *us*. The church has ministers who are enablers, playing coaches. But the ministry belongs to the membership, to all believers. We can never hire enough ministers to win the world to Christ. That is every Christian's task.

You are God's minister. You may serve within the church through teaching, singing, serving on a committee, visiting newcomers. An accountant gave outstanding leadership as chairman of a committee. When I commended him, he said, "I'm happy for an opportunity to use my training and gifts in the Lord's service."

You are a minister where you work. Don't check your religion along with your hat and coat. Set an example of honesty and consideration there. You may be the only Bible someone will read, the only authentic Christian someone knows. Be God's minister on the street where you live.

Mission means money, yes, but money is not enough. Money can be a way of escaping involvement, sort of missions in absentia. God wants *you* on mission. "There was a man sent from God whose name was John." What is your name?

There are missions hungry, some for food, all to know Christ. A man named Rudd told what it's like to live at the North Pole during three months of darkness. You never see the sun. He said, "I ached and hungered to see the dawn." Then one morning in February he climbed atop the wind-swept ridge and sat quietly, facing east; the sky was a gray sheet. Then it became a pale blue, which deepened. There was a silent rush of color as the sun rose. Rudd stood blinking with frozen tears on his cheeks.

Many hunger for they know not what. They "ache and hunger for the dawn," for the Son rise!

We have been called out of the darkness into his marvelous light to be the light of the world. Mission is a call to become and a call to share. Won't you discover your mission for God?—Alton H. McEachern

Topic: Good Shepherd Day

TEXT: John 10:1–18

If I had our pastor's courage, I would

ask you to close your eyes, to say softly the words "Jesus Christ of Nazareth," then to echo the phrase "we shall see God as God is" and gently let an image of God appear under your darkened eyelids. Unfortunately, I do not have the confidence that you would stay awake. Yet, probably some of you within these few seconds have envisioned God. I doubt that many, unless very much struck by today's scripture, pictured God as a stone or as a rural shepherd.

Whatever sign helps us to be receptive to the love of God, to the mission of Jesus, should manifest the quality "good." The first tale of the Bible, that of Genesis, repeats over and over God's evaluation of the heavens and earth, water and land, day and night, living creatures of sea and earth, man and woman, procreation of new generations: "God saw everything that he had made, and indeed, it was very good."

So, in John, Jesus says, using an image with which his listeners could identify, "I am the good shepherd, the good shepherd who lays down his life for the sheep." Of course, the disciples did not realize Jesus would actually lay down his life on the coming Good Friday. His use of power to restrain himself from calling for war against his persecutors and judges was incomprehensible. Easter and Pentecost would have to come before the first followers of Christ could comprehend the goodness of nonresistance, of forgiveness, for those responsible for the Passion and death of Jesus.

If we sought an image to signify ourselves as believers in Jesus Christ, as members of the Christian community, I doubt that "sheep" would be our choice. Yet, even in our technological society I do not think we wish to think of ourselves as computers or disks at the whim of programs and batteries. We are the summit of good creation; we are the sons and daughters of God; we have the power to listen to the call to a good life, to choose to make life good for others, to realize that light will still come as to what we shall become, shall be.

From Jesus' contacts we do know whom he considered the flock that he knew and cared for and those who were still to be added to the fold. The grazing meadows and hillsides had no fences, no stone walls. His closest friends were fishermen, an unappreciated tax collector, and a family consisting of a sickly brother and two faith-filled women. He challenged the rigidity of legalism to heal the sick, the crippled, the blind, even the dead; to bring back dignity to women used and abused by men, to accept hospitality from those held in contempt by the town leaders, to teach by story and signs ordinary people confused by the dialogue and circumlocutions of the rulers of the people and the elders.

There were no limits to his care and concern. Yet, if he had a preference, it seemed to be for the outcasts, those we would call in our time the underclass. The image of Jesus most often represented in text, portraits, and hymns, particularly when we are in need of strength, comfort, and compassion, is that of a good shepherd—an occupation, like that of fishermen, low on the economic and social ladder.

At times, perhaps, there can be overemphasis that the ultimate test of goodness is laying down one's life for others. Certainly, that is a reason why a friar who died in a concentration camp in World War II was formally declared a saint. Maximilian Kolbe stepped forward to replace one of the ten men marked for execution in a town captured by the Axis powers. Yet the most revered saint in the church, Mary the mother of Jesus, is so because she said "Yes" to a life beyond the conception, birth, raising, and death of her son. While witnessing and supporting Jesus in his sacrifice on Calvary, she accepted the commission to become mother to the first disciples, to go on living in the struggling infant community of Christians after the glory of Easter and the successful rally of Pentecost.

On Good Shepherd Day the entire Christian community in general, we of our assembly in particular, are called to open ourselves to awareness, discernment, and response to God's call to each of us in our adult life. Most of us test the waters before determining the direction of our lives. A brief weekend in urban plunge followed by personal and communal reflection can affect the rest of our lives. Play, excursions, tutoring inner-city children can fill us with the joy that comes from revealing to others there is beauty in the world. Spending a spring break in Appalachia rather than Cancún can surprise us with the revelation of goodness as well as deprivation among inhabitants of the "hollers." A period of volunteer service and simple living can determine our priorities in the years that follow.

Eventually, many of us will make the mutual promise, "I do." Some of us will present ourselves before a bishop or representative of a religious community and say simply, "Here I am." Still others will live a life outwardly independent but marked by thoughtfulness and understanding of the lonely and needy.

Though for most in our assembly it does not yet appear what we shall be, we are reminded that we will know, when the inspiration comes, to what we are destined. May we pray for one another that we use our power of response to become building stones for our generation and future ones. May we also have the good sense to consult, to inquire, to spend time with those whose life-style, commitment, and actions lead us to say, "M-m-m, that is a good life," and to risk finding out, "Is that the life for me?" Let us seize this moment, this period in our lives, to listen, to observe, to test, possibly even to determine to what way of life we will say, "Yes."

Whatever it is, may God be able to observe and declare, "That is good. [A few first names], like my son, are good shepherds."—Grace Donovan

ILLUSTRATIONS OF EVANGELISM AND MISSIONS

MOTIVATION. Charles Ludwig, in his book *Mother of an Army,* the biographical novel of Catherine Booth, cofounder of the Salvation Army, writes of William Booth's passion to reach the lost:

Doing the unexpected was a part of Booth's personality. Aboard a ship in a South Sea port, Kipling was drawn to the rail by a spectacular scene. Peering through his heavy glasses, he noticed that General Booth was about to board the ship. He wrote, "I saw him walking backward in the dusk over the uneven wharf, his cloak blown upward, tulip fashion, over his gray head, while he beat a tambourine in the face of the singing, weeping, praying crowd who had come to see him off." Disturbed, the future Nobel Prize winner for literature told Booth he didn't like it. He never forgot the General's reply: "Young feller," he said, bending great brows at him, "if I thought I could win one more soul to the Lord by walking on my head and playing the tambourine with my toes, I'd learn how."

The famous author was momentarily shocked. But overwhelmed by Booth's sincerity, he admitted, "He had the right of it, and I had the decency to apologize."[4]

—Scott Moody

UNDYING FLAME. Elton Trueblood tells of a ship of Quakers headed for the new colonies in the eighteenth century that had to pull into Plymouth, England, for repairs. The ship's log records that while the ship was being repaired, the Quakers went up and down the streets of that town telling the inhabitants about Jesus. The ship's log continues: "They gathered sticks, kindled a fire, and left it burning behind them."

MISSION. Jacob Walker was a lighthouse keeper on Robbin's Reef, off the rocky shore of New England. After years of faithfully minding the light, he became ill and died. His wife buried his body on the hillside above the shore on the mainland, in view of the lighthouse.

Later she applied for and received the appointment as the keeper of the lighthouse. For twenty years she carried on

[4]Charles Ludwig, *Mother of an Army* (Minneapolis: Bethany House, 1987).

alone, and then a New York reporter went out to get her story. She told him this: "Every evening I stand in the door of the lighthouse and look across the water to the hillside where my husband's body is buried. . . . I always seem to hear his voice saying, as he often said when alive, 'Mind the light! Mind the light!' "

"Minding the light" is at the heart of our mission as a church.[5]—Joe Trull

SALVATION. An old legend tells about a man who had a very stupid servant. The master often became exasperated with the servant. One day in a fit of frustration, the man said to the servant, "You have to be the stupidest man I have ever met. Look, I want you to take this staff and carry it with you. And if you ever meet a man stupider than you are, give him the staff."

Years passed as the servant carried the staff. One day he came back to the castle and was ushered into his master's bedroom, where his master lay sick.

The master said to the servant, "I'm going on a long journey."

The servant asked, "When do you plan to be back?"

The master said, "This is a journey from which I'll not return."

The servant asked, "Sir, have you made all the necessary preparations?"

The master said, "No, I have not."

The servant asked, "Could you have made preparations?"

[5]"The Pastor's Desk," North Vista Baptist Church, Buena Vista, California.

The master said, "Yes, I guess I've had my life to make them, but I've been busy about other things."

The servant asked, "Master, you're going on a long journey from which you'll never return, and you could have prepared for it but just didn't?"

The master said, "Yes, I guess that's right."

The servant took the staff he had carried so long and said, "Master, take this with you. At last I've met a man more stupid than I am."

Do not be so foolish as to make necessary preparations for everything else and fail to make preparation for your journey into eternity.—Greg Potts

CONFESSION. Many revolutionary statements of truth have changed history. Nikolaus Copernicus in the sixteenth century angered the church by affirming that the earth was not the center of the universe but revolved around the sun.

Two centuries later the Declaration of Independence asserted that "all men are created equal," refuting the notion of an aristocracy.

Albert Einstein's theories of relativity changed forever the way physicists view the cosmos.

The most revolutionary statement of truth ever uttered was made not by a scientist or statesman. It was made by a simple fisherman. Simon Peter confessed to Jesus: "Thou art the Christ, the Son of the living God" (Matt. 16:16).—Douglas G. Denton

SECTION VIII. Preaching from Galatians: Luther on Liberty

BY CHARLES J. SCALISE

Contemporary Christians need a fresh encounter with the vibrant reality of Christian liberty proclaimed in Paul's Epistle to the Galatians. Perhaps no Christian in the West can serve as a more experienced guide than Martin Luther.

One of the limitations of the education preparation received by many Christian ministers in our time is its fascination with novelty in biblical interpretation and its corresponding neglect of the classics of the past. Relegated to the dustbin labeled "precritical interpretation," the great commentaries in which Christians documented their struggles with the Word of God are rarely read by today's all-too-busy preachers. Isn't there some way in which a few gems of biblical insight may be mined from these quarries of the Christian past and made available to Christian preachers today?

The following suggestions for preaching from Galatians are largely my adaptation of selections from Martin Luther's commentary on the epistle. They represent an attempt to merge my own efforts to read Galatians with Luther's strenuous exertions in this regard. The goal is a deeper appropriation of the Word of God through Paul's letter.

Of course, today such an enriched understanding of Galatians presupposes the sort of critical engagement with the text and with Paul's social and cultural world afforded by current New Testament studies. (Recent commentaries that may be of help include those of Betz [1979], Cousar [1982], Bruce [1982], Ebeling [1985], Krentz [1985], Longenecker [1991], and Matera [1992].)

The difficulty that I have observed, however, is that many ministers are unable to navigate their way back from the ancient Mediterranean to the secularized modernity of their congregations. Luther may have some "premodern" light to shed upon the dark night of our postmodern souls. "For the Germans are not much unlike to [the Galatians] in nature."

Luther's commentary is based on lectures he delivered at the University of Wittenberg in 1531. It was first published by some of his students in 1535—with his blessing and preface. Luther gave these lectures on his favorite epistle because he felt the religious and political controversies in which he was involved were distracting attention away from the center of the Bible's message. Through rediscovering Paul's teaching of justification by faith, Luther hoped he could keep the Reformation on a steady scriptural course.

Quotations from and references to Luther's commentary are taken from Philip S. Watson's revised and completed translation, based on the "Middleton" edition of the English version of 1575.[1]

"But these thoughts of mine on this Epistle are being published not so much against these people [Luther's enemies] as for our people, who will either thank me for my pains or pardon my weakness

[1]Cambridge: James Clarke, 1953.

and temerity. . . . I produced them (with much toil) only for such as those to whom St. Paul himself wrote his epistle—the troubled, afflicted, and tempted (who alone understand these things), wretched Galatians in the faith."

Topic: The Astonished Apostle

TEXT: Gal. 1:1–10

Maintaining a healthy Christian community centered in the gospel is a fragile task. Experienced church leaders know the astonishment of waking one morning to discover that their carefully nurtured gardens of faith are overgrown with weeds. We can identify with Jerome's struggle with the powerful false teachers of his day: "The whole world groaned and marveled to find itself Arian." Paul's apostolic astonishment at the Galatian apostasy is unfortunately not just an ancient phenomenon.

I. Commissioned by God (vv. 1–5). Paul holds himself up as an example for every Christian to make sure of his or her calling to ministry. It is particularly important that those who teach and preach the Word of God be certain of their calling.

At the end of the very first verse Paul bursts out and asserts Christ's Resurrection, the basis of the gospel that Paul is called to proclaim. Only as we hear the gospel and cling to God's Word of grace will our consciences find the peace they seek (v. 3). As Luther declares, "There is no other god besides this man Christ Jesus."

Jesus' giving himself for *our* sins is the heart of the gospel (v. 4). Luther warns that "it is a very hard thing that thou which judgest thyself unworthy of this grace, shouldest from thy heart say and believe that Christ was given for thine invincible, infinite, and horrible sins." God is not angry with us but loves us so much that the Son gave himself for us "according to the will of our God and Father."

II. Confronting the confused deserters (vv. 6–10). Paul omits the usual and expected thanksgiving for the Galatians (v. 6; cf., for example, Rom. 1:8f.). He instead immediately expresses his astonishment: "Whereby he signifieth both that it grieved him and also displeased him, that they had fallen away from him."

Luther carefully points out that Paul does not rage at the confused Galatians like he does at their accursed false teachers (vv. 8–9; cf. also 6:1). More than one minister in the midst of a church conflict can identify with Luther's picture of pastoral frustration:

"[One] may labor more than half a score years ere he shall get some little church to be righteously and religiously ordered; and when it is so ordered, there creepeth in some mad brain, yea and a very unlearned idiot, which can do nothing else but speak slanderously and spitefully against sincere preacher of the Word, and he in one moment overthroweth all."

Those who are confusing the Galatians come claiming to build upon the teaching of Paul, but they are "making a cloak" to cover their sinful intentions (v. 7). As a German proverb put it, "In God's name beginneth all mischief!" So, the Galatians are "wavering hither and thither, as uncertain and doubtful to which part they may lean, or whom they may safely follow."

Luther observes that Paul's curses upon the false teachers change person from the gospel "*we* have preached" (v. 8) to what "*you* have received" (v. 9), seeking to rule out the idea that the Galatians didn't understand Paul's gospel correctly the first time. Furthermore, the false teachers "picked out of [Paul's] preachings and writing certain contradictions (as our adversaries at this day do out of our books) and by this means they would have convinced him that he had taught contrary things."

Unlike the false teachers, Paul is not a "people pleaser" but a servant of Christ (v. 10). His honest, caring confrontation may help us deal effectively with our own astonishment at the contemporary failings of the Christian community.

Topic: Paul's Pilgrimage

TEXT: Gal. 1:11–24

Who is the most unlikely Christian convert you've ever known? C. S. Lewis, the Christian-baiting Oxford skeptic who became a leading evangelical apologist for the faith, might be a likely candidate. Perhaps Charles Colson, the Watergate conspirator turned prison ministry organizer, might be an outstanding political example. The biblical role model for all of these unlikely converts is the Apostle Paul. Like the persecutor transformed into the "apostle to the Gentiles," unlikely converts see their experience as a proof of the power of God.

I. From religion to revelation (vv. 11–12). Paul's Damascus road experience (Acts 9:1–30) involved a blinding apprehension of the power of God "through a revelation of Jesus Christ" (v. 12). Luther argues that Paul is making this claim "to put away the slander of the false apostles," who were claiming that Paul was their inferior. They asserted they had received their gospel from the apostles. Paul's reply is that his gospel is "not of human origin" (v. 11). It is based upon revelation, not religion. As Luther proclaims, "My doctrine is such that it setteth forth and preachest the grace and glory of God alone, and in the matter of salvation, it condemneth the righteousness and wisdom of all men."

Luther reminds us of how easily we can lose our vision of the divine revelation of the gospel. "For I know in what hours of darkness I sometimes wrestle. I know how often I suddenly lose the beams of the gospel and grace, as being shadowed from me with thick dark clouds." Since the Galatians were so easily deceived by false teachers, they are in great danger, for "there is nothing more dangerous than to be weary of the Word."

II. From persecutor to proclaimer (vv. 13–16). Paul the persecutor had advanced ahead of his peers on the ladder of Jewish piety. Luther compares his own preconversion zeal to Paul's:

"I was zealous for the papistical laws and traditions of the fathers, as ever any was, most earnestly maintaining and defending them as holy and necessary to salvation. . . . Whatsoever I did, I did it with a single heart, a good zeal, and for the glory of God. But those things which were then gainful unto me, now with Paul I count to be but loss for the excellency of the knowledge of Jesus Christ my Lord."

Paul was called from his "cruel rage" to God's "inestimable grace." Do we like Luther see the same destructive anger in ourselves? Can we see our sinful blindness and admit that "if you compare publicans and harlots with these holy hypocrites, they [the former] are not evil"?

III. From withdrawal to witness (vv. 17–24). Luther believes that Paul's activities in Arabia (v. 17) were evangelistic. "For what else should he do but preach Christ?" Others have understood the journey to Arabia as a period of withdrawal for retreat and prayer. In any case, the process is part of the development of Paul's identity as "apostle to the Gentiles" (cf. v. 16).

Paul's brief visit with Peter and James in Jerusalem (vv. 18–19) was to "see" them, not to become their student. Meeting some of the leaders of the Jerusalem church might help to allay doubts about the genuineness of Paul's conversion and the validity of his ministry. Luther observes that suspicion of Paul was so great among the Gentiles that Paul felt he needed to swear an oath (v. 20) to guarantee he was speaking the truth.

Paul wanted his witness to be endorsed by "the churches of the Jews" as well as the Gentile churches. As an unlikely convert, Paul's goal was that his life-transforming experience would enable others to glorify God (v. 24).

Topic: Encountering the Ecclesiastical Establishment

TEXT: Gal. 2:1–10

Christians throughout history have experienced a continuing tension between the church as an ecclesiastical institution and the church as a gospel-created community. The church is not one or the other. The church is both institution and community. Boundary-crossing mission efforts regularly run into conflict with boundary-setting church establishments. If we are going to be engaged in creative gospel ministry, then we must come to terms with the realities of the organized church without losing our integrity.

I. Returning to Jerusalem (vv. 1–3). Luther emphasizes that, after fourteen busy years away, Paul returns to Jerusalem "not for his own cause, but for the people's sake." He is not forced or compelled to go back to Jerusalem but travels under God's leadership "in response to a revelation" (v. 2). Paul seeks to stop the rumors of his opponents that his preaching is in vain because he frees the Gentiles from observing the law. Paul tries not to offend the Jewish Christian leaders, treating them as weaker brothers and sisters who are dependent upon the law. For example, he neither condemns circumcision nor demands that the Jews stop its practice. Luther adds, "So we at this day do not reject fasting and other good exercises as damnable things, but we teach that by these exercises we do not obtain remission of sins."

According to Luther, the "principal question" is the necessity of observing the law for salvation (justification). Christian teachers who maintain that human "traditions cannot be omitted without peril to salvation" provide false examples of faith, for "there is but one experience of faith, which is to believe in Jesus Christ."

II. Resisting the spies (vv. 4–6). The false teachers challenged "the truth of the gospel" (v. 5), defined by Luther as the insight that "our righteousness cometh by faith alone without the works of the law." In contrast, the false gospel is "that we are justified by faith, but not without works of the law." In other words, the false gospel adds a condition (works of the law) to God's unconditional gift of faith.

Faith grasps "this precious pearl," "Christ alone." Luther affirms, "Here I must take counsel of the gospel, I must hearken to the gospel which teacheth me, not what I ought to do (for that is the proper office of the law), but what Jesus Christ the Son of God hath done for me."

III. Receiving the right hand of fellowship (vv. 7–9). Luther carefully distinguishes between "matters of divinity," in which "God shows no partiality" (v. 6) to recognized leaders, and "matters of polity," in which the "outward veil" of leadership should be respected and honored.

Paul uses the acceptance of his ministry by the leaders of the Jerusalem church to turn the argument of the false teachers on its head. They argued that Paul lacked apostolic endorsement of his ministry, while he shows that "the apostles are on [his] side."

Using a part for the whole (the literary figure of synecdoche), Paul distinguishes between "the gospel for the uncircumcised" and "the gospel for the circumcised" (v. 7). He is seeking to establish the legitimate difference between his ministry and that of Peter and the Jewish church.

Luther portrays the "acknowledged pillars" (v. 9) of the Jerusalem church, confirming their harmony with Paul: "We conclude here that neither uncircumcision nor circumcision ought to hinder our society and fellowship, since it is but one gospel which we both preach." Peter expresses his approving confirmation of Paul's ministry, "not as a superior and ruler, but as a brother and witness."

IV. Remembering the poor (v. 10). The special injunction to "remember the poor" calls Luther to point to the special relationship between the gospel and the poor (Matt. 11:5):

"After the preaching of the gospel, the office and charge of a true and faithful pastor are to be mindful of the poor. For where the church is, there must needs be poor, who for the most part are the only true disciples of the gospel."

We see Christ in the needs of the poor.

As we face our own inevitable encounters with the ecclesiastical establishment, may we be guided by Paul's example of a wise return to Jerusalem. May we resist whenever necessary, receive wherever possible, and remember those who are needy.

Topic: Cephas Circumcised or Christ Crucified?

TEXT: Gal. 2:11–21

The externals of religion so easily distract us from the heart of the Christian faith. The materialism of contemporary American society drives us to focus upon the physical practices of piety rather than upon the spiritual realities of faith. Peter's preoccupation with the politics of circumcision comes into conflict with Paul's proclamation of the power of the crucified Lord. How easily we are tempted to replace Christ crucified with Cephas circumcised!

I. Self-condemned by hypocrisy (vv. 11–14). Luther observes that Paul's conflict with Peter is "not a matter done in a corner, but in the face of the whole church." Luther challenges us to view the matter from a God-centered perspective: "For what is the creature in respect to the Creator? . . . Even as one drop of water in respect to the whole sea. Why then should I so highly esteem Peter, which is but a little drop, and set aside God, which is the whole sea?"

Peter's fallibility reminds us of the sinfulness of all saints. We should take "great comfort" from the realization that "even the saints, which have the spirit of God, do sin. . . . If Peter fall, I may likewise fall. If he rose again, I may also rise again." It is God's help, not all of our gifts, that ultimately matters.

Luther claims that it is the *purpose* of Peter's withdrawal, "not the act itself," that was wrong. Peter doesn't "live as the Jew"; he acts to "play the Jew." Peter's hypocrisy is the problem.

Luther expresses amazement (perhaps autobiographical) that "God preserved the church . . . and the gospel itself, by only one person." Even when Paul loses Barnabas (v. 13), Paul stands up for the truth.

Christians must beware of the deceptive power of the reason of the law: "Now, as soon as the law and reason join together, faith loseth her virginity." The Christian's faith must rest upon grace. Luther's liberty, however, is not antinomian. He argues that "the conscience must be free from the law, but the body must be obedient to the law." Alluding to Genesis 22:5ff., Luther illustrates, "the ass [like the body carrying the burden of the law] remain[eth] in the valley, but the conscience ascendeth with Isaac into the mountain, knowing nothing of all the law."

Luther believes that, after receiving Paul's rebuke, Peter "gladly acknowledged his offense." Peter's great error lies in his attempt to "compel the Gentiles to live like Jews" (v. 14) rather than in the freedom of the gospel. Luther proclaims, "This word, 'Thou compellest,' containeth all those perils and sins, which Paul urgeth and amplifieth throughout all this epistle."

II. Justified by faith (vv. 15–21). Luther argues that "children circumcised in the faith of Abraham are not saved for their circumcision, but for their faith." Works of the law may be done "before justification" (e.g., by "good men even amongst the pagans") or "after justification" (by Christians). Works only become dangerous if we believe they justify us, "for without faith all things are deadly." The Scriptures thus describe the "schoolmasters of the law and works" as "oppressors and tyrants," who "drive [us] into spiritual and most miserable bondage of soul." The person who believes he or she is justified by works is "such a holy and bloody hypocrite as Paul was when he went to Damascus."

Justifying faith is not a form that must be infused with love (*caritas*), as the medieval scholastics taught. Rather, "true faith . . . is a sure trust and confidence of the heart, and a firm consent whereby Christ is apprehended." Faith possesses "this treasure," the presence of Christ. Faith grasps Christ like the setting of a ring holds a "precious stone."

Luther advises, "If thou feel thy sins and the burden thereof, look not upon them in thyself, but remember that they are translated and laid upon Christ, whose stripes have made thee whole." Through Christ we are liberated from the law. Once we have been justified by faith, then "good works . . . flow out of this faith."

When Paul speaks of being "crucified with Christ" (v. 19), he is referring not to mere earthly "imitation or example" but to "that high crucifying, whereby sin, the devil, and death are crucified in Christ." By faith the Christian participates in this spiritual reality, "so that all these things are crucified and dead." Luther encourages the reader of verse 20: "print this '*me*' in thy heart." He testifies, "This faith doth couple Christ and me more near together, than the husband is coupled to his wife."

As we scrutinize our lives and examine our hearts, what pattern do we see at the center—politics or Passion? circumcision or Crucifixion?

Topic: Foolish Bewitchment or Baptized Faith?

TEXT: Gal. 3:1–29

The many shades of gray that characterize decision making in our society make it difficult for us to choose clear-cut alternatives. There is always another version of the story, another angle of vision, another perspective to consider. Christian faith instead confronts us with an "either-or." Faith summons us to a life-changing decision.

I. Works or faith (vv. 1–14)? Why does Paul reprimand the Galatians so sharply? Calling one's readers "foolish" and "bewitched" is not exactly gentle pastoral demeanor! Luther analyzes Paul's sharp reproof as stemming from reasons of either "zeal or compassion," or "both may be true." In any case, Paul seeks not their "destruction" but their "profit and welfare" (cf. Prov. 27:6).

Luther warns that "to seek to be justified by the law or by works is nothing else . . . but the illusion and enchantment of the devil," which makes people "so bewitched, that in no wise they can acknowledge the benefits of Christ." No one should think that only the Galatians "were bewitched of the devil: but let every man think that he himself might have been and yet may be bewitched."

A person "is made a Christian, not by working but by hearing" the gospel. Luther pictures Paul as "a cunning physician" who places responsibility upon "the false apostles, the authors and only cause of this deadly disease" that afflicts his "sickly and scabbed children," the Galatians.

Paul moves from the experience of the Galatians (vv. 1–5) to the example of Abraham (vv. 6–10) to show that faith, not works, makes us righteous before God. "Christian righteousness" has two parts: "faith of the heart" and "God's imputation." Luther sees our faith as only "a little spark," which begins "to render unto God his true divinity." Our little faith must be joined with God's powerful imputing of righteousness through Christ.

Christians are children of "the believing Abraham," not "the begetting Abraham." The "spiritual Abraham" possesses the promises of God; he "is not born of Adam, but of the Holy Ghost." The doctrine of justification teaches us that "whatsoever is without the faith of Abraham is accursed" (vv. 10ff.).

Although Christians are not justified by the law, Luther asserts that the law has two important roles: "the one politic[al] and the other spiritual"—to restrain civil transgressions and to convict of sin. As Paul declares in Romans 8:4, "The just requirement of the law" will "be fulfilled" in us. "To do the law" is, first of all, to believe in Christ. "For Christians are not made righteous in doing righteous things, but being now made righteous by faith in Christ, they do righteous things." After our justification, then "we go forth into the active life."

II. Law or promise (vv. 15–22)? Luther observes that in verse 15 Paul argues "from the things of man to the things of God," basing his argument upon God's promise to Abraham. This promise is God's "last will and testament," which has been confirmed by the death of Christ.

The law comes 430 years after God's promise to Abraham, so the law cannot abolish or annul the promise (v. 17). The law marks the time of waiting, due to "transgressions" (v. 19), until the promise can be fulfilled in Christ, who is the one true "offspring" (vv. 16, 19) of Abraham. Luther compares the law to "seals" added to a letter until the time has arrived for the letter to be opened. The law lacks the blessing of the promise and so cannot justify humanity before God.

As the law convicts people of their transgressions, it fosters "a special hatred of God," which prepares "the way unto grace." Luther comforts those with troubled consciences: "Now is the time not to see the smoking and burning Mount Sinai, but the Mount Moriah [cf. 2 Chron. 3:1], where is the throne, the temple, the mercy-seat of God."

The covenant that Christ the Lord brings is "a far better testament" than that which comes "through angels" by the human "mediator" Moses (v. 19). Luther pictures the process like that of parched soil desiring the rain; "even so the law maketh troubled hearts to thirst after Christ."

III. Slavery or freedom (vv. 23–29)? Luther describes two different ways in which the law keeps people in bondage: "civilly and spiritually." The civil bondage of the law operates out of fear and punishment. As Luther sarcastically comments, "Look how heartily the thief loveth his prison and hateth his theft: so gladly do we obey the law." The spiritual bondage of the law, however, is the most fearful—"The law is also a spiritual prison, and a very hell." Luther confesses that "the spiritual prison is a trouble and anguish of mind, and he that is shut up in this prison cannot enjoy quietness of heart and peace of conscience."

Luther takes Paul's picture of the law as "disciplinarian" (vv. 24–25; Greek: *paidagogos*) to resemble a stern German schoolmaster. "Although a schoolmaster be very profitable and necessary to instruct and to bring up children, yet show me one child or scholar which loveth his master." In contrast, "now that faith has come" (v. 25), we experience liberty in Christ.

Luther emphasizes that clothing ourselves with Christ through baptism (v. 27) is "a new birth and a new creation." As a result of this salvation, "in Christ Jesus all states . . . even such as are ordained of God, are nothing" (cf. v. 28).

So, where do we stand as we confront the great "either-ors" of Christianity: works or faith? law or promise? slavery or freedom? Are we bewitched fools or faithful believers?

Topic: Perplexed Parenthood

TEXT: Gal. 4:1–20

Growing up in Western culture almost guarantees that the adolescent years will be a lively and stormy time. Teenagers are seeking independence from parental authority and rigidly conforming to the expectations of their peer groups. Parents are baffled to find themselves simultaneously loved and hated by their children.

Growing up in the Christian life is also a challenging and often frustrating experience. In this passage Paul calls the Galatians to remember that they are God's spiritual children and not slaves. Paul then reveals some of his own agonized perplexity over his relationship with his children in the faith, the Galatians.

I. The Galatians: spiritual slaves or adopted children (vv. 1–11)? Like the members of our video society, Luther remarks that the Galatians "will rather behold an image well painted, than a book well written." So, in verses 1–2 Paul uses again (cf. 3:24–26) the image of "the little heir," who is not yet of age to receive the inheritance.

Luther understands Paul's reference to "the rudiments [Greek: *stoicheia*] of the world" (v. 3) to refer to the law. In particular, Luther point to the ceremonial laws (vv. 9–10) rather than seeing a reference to cosmic powers ("elemental spirits") or to the material "elements" of the universe. Since Christ has paid such a great price "to deliver the conscience from the tyranny of the law," Christians must not allow the law to rule their consciences. Luther exclaims, "Therefore, feeling thy terrors and threatenings, O law, I plunge my conscience in the wounds, blood, death, Resurrection, and victory of Christ."

Because of Christ's redemption, we have been freed from spiritual slavery under the law and now have received "free adoption" with the gift of the Holy Spirit. Paul uses the word "crying" (v. 6), rather than just "calling," to describe the Spirit's intercession because Paul wants to depict "the temptation of a Christian which yet is but weak and weakly believeth."

Luther asserts that "this little word 'Father,' conceived effectually in the heart," is far more eloquent than the speeches of the world's greatest orators. In this cry there "is no exacting, but only the childlike groaning that apprehendeth a sure hope and trust in tribulation."

In Luther's view, for the Galatians to return to their slavery "to the weak and beggarly rudiments" (v. 9) is a fall into idolatry. He maintains, "Whosoever is fallen from the article of justification is ignorant of God, and an idolater." Whether one worships physical idols or the law ultimately makes no difference.

True knowledge of God does not consist in the performance of external religious observances. People who seek to be saved by keeping the rules resemble the proverb that says, "One man milketh the he-goat, while the other holdeth the sieve under [it]" (cf. Mark 5:25–26). To use a more classical example, "The poets tell of Sisyphus, which rolled the stone to the top of the mountain in hell, and as often as it reached the top, is rolled down again."

II. Paul: welcomed messenger or despised enemy (vv. 12–20)? Luther portrays Paul as caring so much for the Galatians that he is now worried that his strong reproofs might do more harm than good. So, Paul now shows "that this sharp chiding proceedeth of a fatherly affection and a true apostolical heart." Luther affirms that "all pastors . . . ought to bear a fatherly and motherly affection, not toward ravening wolves, but toward the poor sheep."

Perhaps autobiographically, Luther remarks that "it is a dangerous thing for a man to defend his cause by letter against those which are absent, and have now begun to hate him, and are persuaded by others that his cause is not good."

In contrast, Luther notes that Paul's "commendation" of the Galatians' initial reception of him (vv. 13–14) is distinctive among all his epistles. Paul pleads with the Galatians to accept both his rebuke and his ministry: "Judge me not to be your enemy in rebuking you so sharply, but rather think that I am your father." Paul's sharp reproofs were expressive of his love for his spiritual children, the Galatians, and his trust that he was "beloved" by them.

Luther pictures himself as suffering "the same temptation" as Paul, since both of their ministries resulted in conflict and sectarian divisions. Yet Paul "was not discouraged, he forsook not his vocation, but went forward."

Paul's image of being "again in the pain of childbirth" (v. 19) describes the role of the apostles as similar to that of parents. "For as parents beget the bodily form, so [the apostles] beget the form of the mind. Now, the form of a Christian mind is faith." Paul is in travail *again* because he is seeking to "repair the form of Christ in the Galatians," which has become "disfigured" through the teaching of the false apostles.

Paul keenly feels the inadequacy of a letter—"a dead messenger"—to carry his affection and deep concern for the Galatians. Any perplexed parent today writing to a teenager in trouble away from home can certainly identify!

Topic: Who's Your Mother?

TEXT: Gal. 4:21–5:1

P. D. Eastman's children's classic *Are You My Mother?* tells the story of a little bird, recently hatched, who goes searching for his mother in the big, wide world. Finally, a steam shovel returns him to his nest. The story ends with the following dialogue: "Just then the mother bird came back to the tree. 'Do you know who I am?' she said to her baby. 'Yes, I know who you are,' said the baby bird. 'You are not a kitten. You are not a hen. You are not a dog. You are not a cow. You are not a boat, or a plane, or a Snort [steam shovel]! You are a bird, and you are my mother.' "

The last part of the fourth chapter of Galatians show us that baby birds aren't the only ones who need to discover the identity of their real mother. As children of promise, the Galatians are called to come home to their real mother, who "corresponds to the Jerusalem above" (v. 26).

I. The slave woman. Although Luther is suspicious of the use of allegory to interpret Scripture, he admires Paul as "a marvelously cunning workman in [the] handling of allegories," which are applied to teach the doctrine of faith, not works. Paul uses allegory "to give beauty to all the rest" of his arguments and examples.

The slave woman's son, Ishmael, "was born after the flesh, that is to say without the promise and the word of God." Ishmael's birth is based upon the words of Sarah (Gen. 16:2) rather than the Word of God. Ishmael shows us that one may be a child of Abraham and yet not be the child of promise.

Hagar symbolizes the Old Covenant (Testament) of Mount Sinai. "So, the law given in Mount Sinai . . . begetteth none but servants." Luther emphasizes, however, that we must not underestimate the number and power of these servants who are children of the law (v. 27). "For men of all ages, not only idiots, but also the wisest and best (that is to say all mankind, except the children of the free woman) do neither see nor know any other righteousness than the righteousness of the law."

II. The free woman. In Genesis 17:19 God specifically promises Abraham, "Your wife Sarah shall bear you a son." So, Isaac "was not only born of the free woman, but also according to the promise." Isaac shows us that "they that will be the children of Abraham, besides their carnal birth, must also be the sons of promise, and must believe."

The free woman, Sarah, symbolizes the New Covenant (Testament). Therefore, the promise given in the heavenly Jerusalem results in "a spiritual and a free people."

Luther admires Paul's daring freedom in using this allegory. Nevertheless, Luther candidly admits, "I would not have been so bold to handle this allegory after this manner, but would rather have called [the earthly] Jerusalem Sarah."

Against medieval scholastic interpretation of this passage, Luther argues that "the heavenly Jerusalem is the Church, which is now in the world, and not the city of life to come." The key distinction is between things that are "spiritual" and things that are "earthly." "The spiritual things are 'above,' the earthly are beneath." The church bears children by preaching and teaching the gospel.

Paul uses Isaiah 54:1 (v. 27) to underline the contrast between Sarah (who was once childless) and Hagar. In Luther's view, the difference between Sarah and Hagar is finally "the difference between the law and the gospel."

Luther points to his experience ("so it is now also"—v. 29) to confirm that the children of the free woman should expect to be persecuted by the children of the slave woman. He asserts: "Whoso will not suffer the persecution of Ishmael, let him not profess to be a Christian."

Warning that "liberty is a very spiritual thing," which carnal humanity cannot understand, Luther urges Christians to obey Paul's exhortation (5:1) to stand fast in their liberty of conscience. The choice is between "everlasting liberty or everlasting bondage."

So, who's your mother? Are you a child of the slave woman or of the free woman? Christians are the children of "the Jerusalem above; she is free, and she is our mother" (v. 26).

Topic: Liberated for Love

TEXT: Gal. 5:2–15

The opportunities and options offered in a free society create confusion. Many people today proclaim that they are liberated. If you ask, they will tell you at great length from what they have been liberated—tradition, racism, oppression. But if you ask *why* and *for what purpose* they have been liberated—by God's love and for God's love.

I. What really counts (vv. 2–6)? Paul declares that "the only thing that counts is faith working through love" (v. 6). Luther explains this process: "Paul . . . setteth forth the whole life of a Christian . . . namely, that inwardly it consisteth of faith toward God, and outwardly in charity [love] and good works toward our neighbor."

The problem is that the Galatians believe that other good works—like circumcision—also count. Luther observes that we should not think that the "works of themselves are nothing," for "the law and circumcision were ordered by God himself." Rather, the difficulty lies in "the use of the work, that is to say, of the confidence and righteousness that is annexed to the work." To trust in our good works rather than in Christ is to "cut [ourselves] off from Christ" (v. 4). "Wherefore let us learn with all diligence to separate Christ far from all works."

Luther's zealous life as a monk confirms the truth of Paul's teaching: "The more I went about to help my weak, wavering and afflicted conscience by men's traditions, the more weak and doubtful and the more afflicted I was." While granting that Christians should read and study the law of Moses, Luther warns that we should not let Moses "have dominion over our conscience." There's a good reason why Deuteronomy 34:6 tells us that nobody knows "where his grave is"!

The Galatians "have fallen away from grace" (v. 4) and are drowning in sin, just like a person who falls off a ship and perishes in the sea. "He therefore that will be justified by the law hath mad shipwreck and hath cast himself into the danger of eternal death."

Luther pictures faith (v. 5) like a teacher, instructing and judging. Hope is imaged "like a general or captain of the field" exhorting the troops. When we find ourselves in "great and horrible terrors," we must learn "not to follow the sense and feeling of our own [terrified] heart, but to stick to the Word of God."

II. Who really hinders (vv. 7–12)? Luther paints a vivid portrait: "The false apostles were jolly fellows, and in outward appearance far passing Paul in both learning and godliness." Their false show of piety and wisdom deceived the Galatians. Like many of Luther's hearers, they "were seduced" by the appearances of the religious establishment. Rather than being led astray by the cunning display of Satan, Christians must hold fast to Christ, who is set forth in the Scriptures as a "gift" and "an example to be followed."

When the false prophets accuse Paul of making a mountain out of a molehill, he responds with the proverb of the leaven (v. 9). Luther asserts that "doctrine ought therefore to be a golden circle, round and whole, wherein there is not breach; for when there is the very least breach, the circle is no longer complete." Luther reminds us that the true teaching of the gospel will be followed by "the cross . . . and offense . . . or else truly the devil is not rightly touched but slenderly tickled."

Luther wonders whether Paul's cursing the Galatians (v. 12) makes it "lawful for Christians to curse." He concludes that in cases where God is blasphemed, "we must turn this sentence and say: Blessed be God and his Word, and whatsoever is without God and his Word, accursed be it."

III. Who's really important (vv. 13–15)? Liberty should be not an occasion to serve ourselves but an opportunity to serve our neighbor. Luther, remembering Jesus' parable of the good Samaritan (Luke 10:25–37), affirms "my neighbor is every man [and woman]," especially those who need help. Luther invites us to look into our own hearts and discern how we love ourselves. That examination will show us how we should love our neighbors.

How do all of these good works of neighbor love fit with Paul's teaching "that we are made righteous without works"? Luther admits "it is a hard and dangerous matter," but urges that both salvation by faith alone and the requirement of good works "must be diligently taught."

Saving faith means that in Christ we are both liberated by God's love and liberated for neighbor love.

Topic: Comparing Catalogs

TEXT: Gal. 5:16–26

Our consumer-driven culture is filled with catalogs. Not only can we receive catalogs in the mail, but we can view catalogs on the screens of our computers. Just purchase a modem and the right interactive software, and you can shop in your living room.

The catalogs in the Bible use word pictures rather than video graphics. So, it takes more effort than pushing a few buttons to enter into their content. But, for almost two thousand years, Christians reading Galatians have found the struggle to be worth the effort.

I. The catalog designers: flesh and Spirit (vv. 16–18). Luther contends that there are "two contrary captains in you, the Spirit and the flesh." Paul urges us to obey and follow the captain of the Spirit, against the captain of the flesh. Luther point out that the flesh is more than sexual lust; our sinful desire (concupiscence) includes "all other corrupt affections." Different temptations characterize different ages of life.

Paul does not require that Christians "should utterly put off or destroy the flesh: but that they should bridle it, that it might be subject to the Spirit." We can only reach this goal if the "perfect righteousness" of Christ is "our ground and anchor hold."

Although Christians continue to commit sin after they have "received the knowledge of Christ," they are protected from the accusation of the law by the power of the Spirit (v. 18). The Scriptures teach that "all they which faithfully believe in Christ are saints." Luther confesses that he has suffered "very vehement and great" temptations, but "so soon as I have laid hold of any place of Scripture, and stayed myself upon it as my chief anchor hold, straightaways my temptations did vanish away."

II. The works of the flesh catalog (vv. 19–21). Luther observes that Paul does not attempt to list all the works of the flesh in this catalog. Rather, "Paul reckoneth up the kinds of lust"; he uses illustrations of categories. Paul employs the term *flesh* to encompass sins of lust, anger, and false understanding.

Luther stresses that Paul's catalog of the works of the flesh does not just include the obvious kinds of "carnal lust" (cf. v. 19), but a great range of other vices (vv. 20–21). Some of these, like idolatry, are often mistaken for true spirituality. Luther emphasizes that the text does not say that eating and drinking are works of the flesh, but gluttony and drunkenness, "which of all other vices are most common at this day."

III. The fruit of the Spirit catalog (vv. 22–26). Luther notices that Paul does not describe these Christian virtues as "*works* of the Spirit" but uses the more attractive name of "fruit." Love takes first place on the list "to admonish Christians that before all things they should love one another."

Luther contends that the virtue of faith listed here (v. 22) refers not to "faith in Christ" but to the "fidelity or sincerity" that one person has toward another. Since Christians put their trust in God alone, Luther wisely maintains that a person with the virtue of faith "giveth credit to all men, but he putteth not his trust in any man."

Luther warns that walking in the Spirit (v. 25) does not lead along a path of "praise, reputation, and glory." Those who teach the gospel are "subject to the cross and to all kinds of afflictions."

The fruit of the Spirit does not make distinctions of vocational status. "Therefore a poor artificer [skilled worker] faithfully using the gift which God hath given him, pleaseth God no less than a preacher of the Word; for he serveth God in the same faith and with the same Spirit." If we receive praise for our service, we should remember that it is "Christ to whom all praise is due."

The virtues Paul lists in the fruit of the Spirit catalog are not for sale—unlike many of the works of the flesh. Yet Christians who gradually acquire the fruit of the Spirit in their lives know that they have found the greatest treasure of all.

Topic: The Marks of Jesus

TEXT: Gal. 6:1–18

If someone claims to be a follower of Jesus, what kinds of things might make you think he or she really is a disciple? What signs are there that should help me to discern whether I myself am following the Lord? Given the prevalence of hypocrisy and deception in the world, in the church, and in ourselves, what marks are there to help us become imitators of Christ?

I. Marks of community (vv. 1–10). Luther remind Christians who have leadership responsibilities in churches to display "the fatherly and motherly affection which Paul here requireth of those that have charge of souls." Those who guide and correct others must always remember that "we stand on a slippery ground."

Mutual support (v. 2) should characterize the Christian community, for "the law of Christ is the law of love." Christians take responsibility for themselves and "test their own work" (v. 4); they do not hide behind "the praise of other [people]."

Luther remarks that those who truly profess the gospel commonly find themselves to "be as rich as [once] Christ and his apostles were." Luther decries the danger of rich, upper-class parishioners who "make their pastors subject unto them like servants and slaves." Paul's exhortation to spiritual liberality (vv. 7–8) provides an occasion for Luther to lament, "But what a misery is it, that the perverseness and ingratitude of men should be so great, that the churches should need this admonition?"

The well-doing of the Christian community must be more than tokenism. It is "easy . . . to do good once or twice," but "to continue and not to be discouraged" is the challenge. Christians are called to give "alms to all such as have need," but there is a particular obligation to support the need of the Christian community. Paul uses the term *household of faith* (v. 10), which, Luther observes, represents "a new kind of speech" to denote this special responsibility.

II. Marks of the cross (vv. 11–18). The false teachers, who "want you to be circumcised so that they may boast about your flesh" (v. 13), are doing "an injury unto Christ." Luther imagines Paul indignantly declaring, "This carnal glory and ambition of the false apostles is so dangerous a poison, that I wish it were buried in hell, for it is the cause of the destruction of many."

Christians can glory in the cross because "our cross and suffering is the suffering of Christ." The cross of Christ is not "that piece of wood which Christ did bear" but "all the afflictions of the faithful." If a person hurts "the little toe," the face immediately shows the pain. "So Christ our head maketh all our afflictions his own and suffereth also when we [his Body] suffer."

Following our crucifixion with Christ (v. 14), we become a new creation through "the work of the Holy Ghost, which cleanseth our heart by faith." The marks of Jesus that Paul bore "branded on [his] body" (v. 17) are also his physical sufferings for the cause of Christ. Luther confesses, "These marks we choose not of any sweet devotion, . . . but because the world and the devil do lay them upon us for Christ's cause." Though forced to bear these physical marks of suffering, "we rejoice with Paul in the spirit . . . for they are a seal and most sure testimony of true doctrine and faith."

As you think about your church and your life, do you see the marks of Jesus? Where are the marks of community in our relationships? Where are the marks of the cross in our hands, in our feet, . . . and in our hearts?

SECTION IX.
Preaching Doctrinal Themes of the Life of Jesus

BY LEE MCGLONE

Doctrinal preaching has a bad name. Some will say that, due to the very diverse cultural milieu of our day, preachers should shy away from talk of specific doctrines. Others are offended at any talk of dogma for fear that it may stifle our quest for freedom in Christ. Still others judge the preaching of doctrines as boring and uneventful. In short, doctrinal preaching is too often viewed as extraneous and ephemeral, often separated from the "real" issues of life.

It is true that doctrinal preaching can be all of the above—but it does not have to be. When a biblical doctrine is addressed to the modern audience and related explicitly to a specific text, it takes on life—and vitality. After all, the Bible's doctrinal themes are a recounting through persons of God's interaction with the Creation. The church has for twenty centuries proclaimed the central themes of Christian faith. As we make the transition into the twenty-first century, the church must once again stand firm with our heritage. A portion of our preparation can be the resounding word of eternal truth spoken boldly from the pulpits of our land.

Three great doctrinal themes emerge from the study of Scripture: Creation, Incarnation, and consummation. These themes describe, in a broad and general sweep, the entirety of the biblical story. They involve hundreds of individual stories, men and women, the great and small, the faithful and the sinful. They involve us. Creation declares an intention behind our existence, Incarnation the identification of the Creator with us, and consummation the direction toward which our existence is headed. Preachers will do well to keep these themes in mind, at least in part, as every sermon is prepared and preached.

It is the second of these great themes the following sermon series seeks to address. The five sermons relate to five specific doctrines drawn from events in the life of Jesus: Incarnation, described in the birth narratives and celebrated during Advent and Christmas; Crucifixion, remembered from the events of Good Friday; Resurrection, the celebration of Easter Sunday; Ascension, forty days after the Resurrection; and the Second Coming, not calendared but celebrated in every remembrance of the Lord's Supper.

Since these themes are so central to our proclamation, the preacher will find great reward in this concentrated five-week journey. It will be especially meaningful for our congregations if they are encouraged to read ahead some suggested material dealing with the various doctrines. Planning the Lord's Supper for the last sermon of the series is also a way of bringing to life the doctrinal themes.

Topic: Incarnation: A Word for the World

TEXT: John 1:1–14

Almost everyone has something to say about the way things are in our world today. Opinions, notions, causes, and cures flow nonstop on everything from the economy to public education. With so many words bombarding us from all sides, do we dare ask, "Does God have a Word for us?" John, the Gospel writer, says that God does—and that God says it through his Son, Jesus Christ, the Word made flesh.

Theologians call the doctrine of God's Word to us the Incarnation. We celebrate it annually during Advent and Christmas. It is central to our faith. It is a Word that we need sorely to hear once again just now.

I. Of first importance, God is saying forcefully, though not loudly, "I love you." The ancients wanted to know. Who is out there? What is out there? Be ye friend or be ye foe? The bold answer to their yearning, and ours, came in the proclamation of John, "In the beginning was the Word, the Word has taken on human flesh, and we know him as Jesus." Through him, God spoke his highest message to the world: "I love you."

Time and again in the life of Jesus, we are made aware of God's love. A poor widow cast her money into the treasury, and Jesus was glad. The rich stood by and boasted pridefully of their wealth, and Jesus was sad. But the truth is that he loved the rich as well as the poor. A penitent publican begged humbly for forgiveness, and Jesus was glad. A self-righteous Pharisee gloried in his goodness, and Jesus was sad. But the truth is that he loved the Pharisee as well as the Publican. The black militant, the Klan member, the male chauvinist, the angry feminist—God loves them all.

We look today to the central event in all history—to a life eternal in the heavens but come to live among us. God said through him, "World, one and all, I love you."

II. What else is God saying in the Incarnation? Surely that God loves us, but this too: "I want the best for you." Look at what we are promised. "In him was *life,* and the life was the light of men." We are promised life that is more than physical or material. What God wants for us is the best, and the best is a life of intimacy. If we save our lives, that is, if we choose to live selfishly, a kind of death takes over. If, however, we lose ourselves in following Christ, life will take on a new and meaningful existence. Because of his life, the light that he brought into the world, we have the power to become the "children" of God.

Our deep belief is that life lived through faith in God is the best life of all. Deep living, with thoughts and attitudes raised infinitely above the best of human potential, with every day a new challenge and a new opportunity, every day lived in vital communication with the eternal: this is the best life of all.

III. But another word may be the most important for us today. I hope you can hear God say to you, "I love you," and, "I want the best for you," but also hear God say, "I am with you!" John put it this way: "And the Word became flesh and *dwelt* among us, full of grace and truth." God came to be one of us in the person of Jesus. The promise of memory is that God is still with us and that we will never be alone.

But having God with us doesn't mean that life will be free from trouble. The truth is that sad circumstances arise, quite beyond our control, that leave us fearful and uncertain. Life is not always smooth sailing on calm and easy seas. At times it is more like riding out a raging ocean, its waves rising higher and higher, and we try our best to keep our heads above water. It happens to all of us, at some time and in some way.

Yet the promise of God through Christ is that, even in the worst of times, we are never alone. God is with us. He is "Immanuel" to all who believe. He is our high priest, already "touched by the feelings of our infirmities, yet without sin."

When David Livingston first sailed for Africa, he was met at the pier by a number of friends, fearful for his safety, seeking to persuade him not to go. Livingston opened his Bible and read to them the final words of Matthew's Gospel: "Lo, I am with you always, even to the end of the age." Turning to his friends, he declared, "That, my friend, is the word of a gentleman. Let us be going."

Does God have a Word for the world? Indeed! It is God's divine, eternal communication to the world—embodied in the person of Jesus. God spoke his Word clearly but not loudly. He spoke it plainly but quietly. It was spoken in humility but would profoundly affect the whole world. If, my friend, you are waiting for the shout, you may miss the whisper. It is God's Word—to you!

Topic: Crucifixion: The Power of God

TEXT: 1 Cor. 2:1–5

Some years ago the *New York Times* printed the results of a survey in which respondents were asked to rank one hundred historical events in order of their importance. First place went to Columbus's discovery of America. Three events tied for fourteenth place: the discovery of X rays, the Wright brothers' first airplane flight, and the Crucifixion of Jesus.

What are we to think of the Lord's Crucifixion? Is it simply another of the significant events in human history that caught the attention of many people? Or is it as central as Paul declares, who decided to "know nothing among you except Jesus Christ and him crucified." Is the Crucifixion a unique event that changed the course of human history or only an ancient symbol that has gained support in the church? Is it foolishness—or is it the power of God?

We must admit that our thinking about the Crucifixion is clothed in mystery. We stand here on holy ground—and tremble. Its imagery may well be gruesome and offensive to human sensibilities. Yet we are assured that when our minds linger around the cross, we are very near the heart of God. While the finite mind is unable to comprehend the mystery, we *can* experience it. It is power to those who believe.

I. The Crucifixion powerfully portrays the awfulness of the human condition. It reminds us that we are everyone sinners. It wasn't the Jews and the Romans who stood behind the execution of Jesus. Surely there was a corrupt political system in that day. Surely there was a spiritually bankrupt religious system in that day. Yet the Crucifixion's cause was neither of these. It was the malady of human sin that crucified our Lord.

It is difficult to look at the scene on Golgotha. There is much agony there, tears there, betrayal and denial there. There is much blood there. There is death there. And because I, too, am a sinner, I see myself there—hammer in hand, pounding nails, raising a beam into the sky. And when I see it, I tremble.

II. There is just as powerfully portrayed in the Crucifixion the love of God. From the beginning, God chose to be involved in the Creation. That involvement was brought to fulfillment in Jesus' birth and life. But in no place was it as personal as in his Crucifixion. He who descended from the heavens to take on the form of human flesh was obedient unto death, even death on the cross (Phil. 2:7–8). It wasn't just a life, but love poured out.

The essence of such love is captured in the verse of Scripture we know the best and quote the most: "For God so loved the world, he gave . . . " (John 3:16)—and he gave the best he had so that we who believe might not come to nothing but instead would know the fullness of life.

Love like this has drawing power. It attracts us and calls from us commitments deeper than any that the threat of punishment could coerce.

III. The Crucifixion portrays the most powerful of lives—the life poured out for others. Most of our thinking, and preaching, on the Crucifixion never moves to this point. We do exactly what the Scripture says for us not to do. We speak with words of human wisdom. We define, we defend, we explain, but when all is said and done we go out into a secular world and live as if the Crucifixion had meaning only once a year. We would do better to heed the text's advice, to go out into our world "in demonstrations of the Spirit and of power." Here is the wisdom of God. It is the Crucifixion put into action: our lives poured out for others.

When viewed this way, the Crucifixion is no longer only a historical remembrance. It is a way of life. It is life removed from the rule of self-love and placed under the rule of self-denial. When the Crucifixion becomes a way of life for us, Christianity begins to make a difference. This is the wisdom of God that changes the world.

Consider the lives of those who most influenced us. Some may have been persons known far and wide, like Mother Theresa, Martin Luther King, or Billy Graham. Others may have been lesser known persons, like parents, ministers, friends, whose names never made it to the newspaper. Yet one thing they hold in common: they were persons who gave themselves to us. They poured themselves out for our sake. They believed the Crucifixion—but they also lived it. So ought we!

So what are we to say about the Crucifixion? It is easy to be captured by the emotion of Jesus' dying, to envision the gruesome scene, and to be overcome by it. And when we do, tears may come to our eyes. But is it tears that are needed? Not really. What then? "Drops of grief can ne'er repay the debt of love I owe." If not, what then? "Here, Lord, I give *myself* away, 'tis all that I can do."

Topic: Resurrection: Victory Assured

TEXT: Luke 24:1–12

The heart of Christianity is proclaimed boldly in the resurrected Christ. Christians everywhere gather Sunday by Sunday to celebrate anew the Resurrection of our Lord. For believers, every Sunday is Easter morning. Because of what happened that blessed morning, we face every day with profound hope.

It all began, in Luke's account, with an encounter at the tomb between the women and two men in dazzling apparel: " 'Why do you seek the living among the dead? Remember what he told you . . .' and they remembered."

I. The day began with the desire by disappointed followers to get on with life. Any hope of lasting good from Jesus' ministry seemed lost. Despair was more the order for the day. The women are Luke's examples here. On their way to the tomb, they had in their minds the need to complete proper burial rituals. Spices were prepared. Ointments were readied. They were reverting to reality, or as some would say, "doing the next thing." It was a way of coping with their loss—but it wasn't the answer to their real need.

We can understand their behavior, for we have our own ritual burial patterns. Ours include death certificates, funeral homes, visitation times, food prepared for family, and memorial services. All these are quite proper. They are ways of dealing with our sense of loss. They help us deal with tragedy and then to move on to the rest of our lives. Yet the customary patterns of behavior are not enough for us either. We need more to have answered our real need. There must be more—and there is!

II. There follows an interruption of the women's reality. Their intention was only to prepare the dead body of Jesus. What happened was an alteration of life. Surprise stepped in and caught them off guard. The stone was removed from the tomb's entry, and the body of Jesus was gone. They stood absolutely astonished.

Someone has said that God's last name ought to be surprise. Maybe so. Just when we think we have life figured out, something else comes along that opens us to even deeper levels of contemplation. For most of us, life is rather routine. We pretty well know what each day holds for us. There will be certain meals, appointments, work schedules, school calendars, family gatherings, evening activities, sleep. We even know what Sunday worship is going to be and feel like. But it's just here, on a predictable day like today, that our God may just step out of the ordinary and say "surprise!" You never know.

C. S. Lewis said it was that way with him. Never was there anyone so surprised as he, when there in his own room, alone in the darkness of night, he bowed and humbly acknowledged the reality of the one he had so long denied. You just never know.

III. The angel's query stands before us now: "Why do you seek the living among the dead?" It's almost as if he said, "You should have known better! Only death abides here. If you truly seek Jesus, you'll have to go among the living. That's where he always is."

How very sad that too often we continue our search for Jesus in places where he can't be found. The living Lord will never be found bound and gagged in cultural restraints, strangled by any man's creeds, not in pious and sometimes empty ordinances, not in "holy places made with hands, which are the figure of the true" (Heb. 9:24).

Jesus is found in the hope that arises from faith. It is an assurance that because Jesus lives, so do we. His victory over death is ours. I'm not sure that the agnostic Robert Ingersoll fully understood what that means to us—or that he fully misunderstood it either. This is what he said standing at the grave of his brother: "Life is a narrow vale between the cold and barren peaks of two eternities. We strive in vain to look beyond the heights. We cry aloud. The only answer we receive is the echo of our wailing cry. From the voiceless lips of our unreplying dead no voice comes to the world. But in the night of death hope sees a star and listening love can hear the rustle of a wing."

IV. A final word is spoken that calls us to victorious faith. "Remember what he told you . . . and they remembered." There is obvious power in memory. It is a resource for great living. A recollection, drawn deeply from the wells of faith and experience, has within it a certain assurance. It says that God has been this way before. I am not, nor are you, the first to walk this path. Another has gone this way, and that one has prepared the way.

Here is the memory that stands supreme in the life of every believer. Spoken earlier by Jesus, the angel at the tomb recalls it for us: "The Son of Man must be delivered into the hands of sinful men, and be crucified, and on the third day rise." The early church laid down its life for this memory. It has been, and continues to be, the brightest beacon of light to shine in our often darkened world. And so, when we come to our own Good Fridays and the sun gives way to night, we must remember that Easter Sunday is only three days away—and we shall rise again.

The world that looms so large grows incredibly small on this first day of the week, very early in the morning. All the earthly vanity for which we strive, and its attendant pain, is pushed aside for the time being. Here life overcomes death. Here our victory for life and for eternity is complete.

Topic: Ascension: Christ Above All

TEXT: Luke 24:44–52; Acts 1:6–11

The accounts of Luke and Acts describe a moving and inspiring departure of Jesus from the world. For forty days after the Resurrection, Jesus walked and talked with the disciples. The kingdom of God was the major topic of consideration (Acts 1:3). The apostles' eschatological hopes were clarified. Commands were given that they become "witnesses" in the world. With these thoughts completed, Jesus ascends into the clouds. No interpretation of the event is given in the text itself—simply the awe-inspiring image of the apostles' longing gaze into the heavens to which their Lord had gone. The sight of the risen Savior, ascended into the realms of glory and ready to return at the appointed day, gave both encouragement and direction to the church in its pivotal early days. A close look at this event can do the same for us twenty centuries later.

I. The Ascension is a demonstration that God's salvation is available to all people. The scope of Jesus' ministry was not limited to a certain place, to a certain people, in a certain era of history. The work of salvation extended beyond all of the limitations often imposed on it. The Ascension placed Jesus at a place of preeminence. There, high above the distinctions that too often divide the world, Jesus sits viewing the whole of humanity. His loving gaze and strengthening hand reach to the most remote of places.

In an almost mundane way, we experience the same phenomenon. When one rises high, either literally or figuratively (in lofty thoughts or in a jet airplane), the boundaries that set distinctions at a lower level are erased. From the vantage point "on high," there is a oneness that binds all things together. Jesus' mission upon the earth was to prepare the way for the whole of creation to become children of God (Rom. 8:18–20).

The universal aspect of Jesus' salvation is demonstrated over and again in Luke and Acts. In the birth narratives, the angelic chorus described a "good news of great joy that will come to *all* people." When accused of eating with tax collectors and sinners, Jesus pleaded guilty and then declared that "they will enter the kingdom of God before you!" On the day of Pentecost, people of varied backgrounds, Parthians and Medes and Elamites and dwellers of Mesopotamia, were gathered in Jerusalem, and the Spirit descended on them all. Later, an unnamed eunuch from Ethiopia and a Roman soldier named Cornelius helped clarify the mission of the early church. The good news of Jesus was never to be, and never could be, contained. It was directed to all people. And aren't we glad! "I am so happy in Christ today . . . when the Lord said, whosoever, he included me."

II. The Ascension declares, in a closely related way, that all people stand equal before God. There are no elevated planes upon which selected people stand. There is before God no place of privilege.

Now the apostles had a problem with such a thought. It left little place for their well-documented national and religious heritage. It was surely this longing that lay behind their plea, "Lord, will you now restore the kingdom to Israel?" Such a question seems utterly amazing, especially since the apostles had followed Jesus for three years and had just spent an intense forty days in conversation about the kingdom of God. Some presuppositions are difficult to overcome, especially those of a religious kind.

Parallels with the twentieth century are easy to identify but just as difficult to alter. Not many thinking Christians would dispute that Paul had the mind of God when he wrote that within the church "there is neither Jew nor Greek, slave nor free, male nor female; for you are all one in Christ Jesus" (Gal. 3:28). We can read these inspired words, know that they are true, and still fail to allow their spirit to change our behavior.

In the Lukan text it is said that before Jesus ascended he "opened their minds to understand the Scriptures." The word *opened* is a surgical term. It images the use of a scalpel in corrective surgery. Flesh is "opened" so diseased tissue can be removed or damaged tissue can be rebuilt. Here Jesus "opened" their minds so they could understand what had before been a mystery. Such surgery is not without pain. Some long-held and cherished personal opinions may have to be cut away. Not a few unseemly epithets, spoken about individuals we know precious little about, may need to go. If the spirit of Jesus is to rule in the inner person, some changes must take place. One obvious change is the demolition of any notions of superiority. We all stand before the ascended Christ on equal ground.

III. The Ascension placed the ongoing work of God's saving plan in the care of God's people. One cannot miss, even by a cursory reading of these passages, this emphasis. Instead of centering attention on the restoration of Israel's kingdom, surely a short-sighted endeavor, the apostles were to become "witnesses" of Jesus to people everywhere. Jerusalem, Judea, Samaria, the ends of the earth—these were the new fields of endeavor.

The word *witnesses* translates the Greek *marturia,* from which we also derive the word *martyr.* The verse could well read, "And you will become my martyrs." Our image of the martyr depicts one who has died for the faith during times of persecution. But it means more. One man has written that Christians are martyrs long before hard times come. Persecution simply locates them. Surely this is what Jesus meant when he said that to be his followers we must first die to ourselves.

Standing before every Christian is the call to be a part of this expanding endeavor. When Jesus was on the earth, his ministry was limited to one place at one time. When in Jerusalem, he could not be in Capernaum. But after his Ascension, his followers could. His earthly life was thirty-three years, and his ministry only three. But after his Ascension, his followers could be active in every generation throughout the ages. Our Lord's earthly ministry was located in a certain small portion of the world during what we call the first century. The church, however, is not limited by geography or time. Others have gone before us, our spiritual forefathers and foremothers, and by faith have shown us the way. We are the inheritors of their spiritual labors. But now, today, it is our turn. We cannot let the calling pass us by.

The Ascension of Jesus is recorded at the ending of Luke's Gospel and at the beginning of the companion Book of Acts. This seems not to be by accident. In one way, the Ascension was the closing scene in the greatest story ever told. It brings to an end our earthly knowledge of Jesus. But it only seems like an ending. In reality, it is the beginning. A new thing, invigorating, stimulating, pulsating with life, was on the rise. And so we stand here today awestruck, dumbfounded, mouths wide open, like the apostles of old, overcome by the grandeur of it all. And the angel said, "Why are you so amazed? What he began, he will finish!"

Topic: Second Coming: Already but Not Yet

TEXT: 1 Thess. 3:11–13

What comes to your mind when you hear the phrase "the Second Coming of Christ"? Possibly fear that accompanies judgment? Or maybe the mindless dating of the end of the world by an unscrupulous prophet? The image of tanks lumbering across the valley of Megiddo? Or maybe a sigh? After all, how is this relevant to me? Your response may be any of these. Let me suggest that our guide for faith, the Bible, paints a different image than any of these.

How about hope? How about the deep belief that the God of creation still holds the world in his hands and guides its destiny? How about a faith stance that says that the God in whom we trust will finally punctuate with a period the sentence he began? How about the assurance that the Christ who came in the person of Jesus two millennia ago, who walks now by our sides, will someday come in power to fulfill his kingdom? Are these relevant themes? Indeed they are—for now and forever!

There is a great deal of fascination with the Second Coming of Christ. Scores of books are written on the subject. A number of authors, and their followers, have attracted much attention with their "predictions" of an imminent return. Our generation is no different than others. Dating back to the first century, believing Christians, even Paul himself, have proclaimed their belief in the hurried return of Christ.

The Thessalonian Christians were no different. In both letters to the church there, the theme of the Second Coming rises to the surface as a major concern. Some, apparently believing the end was near, quit their jobs and waited in idleness. Paul suggested that if such people refused to work, neither should they eat. His concern was that we make the most of our time between now and then.

So what are we to think of the Second Coming of Christ? Let me suggest that we think about it in seemingly contradictory terms: that Christ is with us now but not with us; he is here already but not yet.

I. Christ is with us now. We have to go no further than the final words of Jesus' great commission: "And, lo, I am with you always." In our moments of struggle and loneliness, this promise becomes amazingly real. Often we can stand through life's greatest crises with this promise—and at times little else.

But it's not just in crisis moments that we acknowledge the present reality of our Savior. Christ is with his church now in the everyday expressions of faith. In the benediction that serves as our text, three times the apostle affirms the active involvement of Jesus with the Thessalonian Christians. He prays that the "Lord Jesus" would "clear the way for us to come to you," would "make your love increase and overflow for each other and for everyone else," and would "strengthen your hearts that you will be blameless." There is no mistaking Paul's intention. The Lord Christ is not absent from his church.

When viewed this way, the Second Coming of Christ is not the faithful's last ditch effort to find a way out of a wicked world. Instead, it is our way of making the most of life while we are in the world. We are not of the darkness but of the light (4:4). Instead of fretting away the possibilities of witness, we are to be vigilant, making the most of our time.

II. But while Christ is here now, he is not here. That is, he is not here now as he will be here in some future day. How that day will come and when it will come are not significant. All our human efforts to qualify the event fall short of their goal—and often very close to blasphemy. Sufficient for us is the sense of mystery Scripture places over these themes. Faithful unknowing may well represent our stance. Yet there is also the absolute certainty our faith provides. There is a direction toward which our world is headed. The universe is not haphazard, without intent or purpose. We are going somewhere.

Our text lends itself to no hesitancy. The living Christ is here now "clearing our way," "increasing our love," and "strengthening our hearts." But the level of intensity is raised when Paul connects the present day with the day when "our Lord comes with his holy ones." Suddenly, the stakes are higher. We are moved from concerns about temporal matters to things of eternal consequence. All of life means more when placed in the light of that day.

The Second Coming of Christ is God's clear Word to us about hope. In a world that seems at times filled only with malice and sadness, headed quickly toward its own self-destruction, the believing community says, "Look up—your redemption draweth nigh." Jesus himself prayed concerning a day when God's will would be done on earth even as it is done in heaven. On another occasion, he sat at table with his followers and declared that he would not eat with them again until his kingdom came in fullness. It is that day toward which we look with anticipation.

"Are you sure," someone will ask, "that Christ will come again?" The believing community says, "Yes, we are sure. Either Christ will come someday soon and receive us unto his own, or we will, very soon, go to be with him. Of that we are sure—dead sure. Our Savior keeps all his promises."

SECTION X.
Children's Sermons and Stories

January 1: Happy New Year Noises

Did any of you stay up last night until midnight? Many people do. They stay up until that time so that they can welcome in the new year. And very often, people welcome in the new year with noise makers like these. (Share whatever noise makers you can find. Let them make noise together.) This is a very old custom. It goes back to the time when people thought that there were bad spirits about and these bad spirits could cause them all kinds of trouble. It was also thought that by making a lot of noise, they would scare the bad spirits away and they would not enter the new year with them. It was a way of asking for good things to happen to them in the coming year. Now, it may be fun to make a lot of noise on New Year's Eve, but we believe that good fortune comes to us not by keeping bad spirits away but by living with God.

We believe that all things work together for good to those who love God. So, the important thing in the new year is for us to love God and to ask him to be with us every day.

Let's do that together in a prayer.—Kenneth Mortonson

January 8: Tell Mother It's Bill

Off the coast of the Pacific Northwest there was a terrible storm, and a crowd gathered to see a storm-tossed vessel not far offshore being pounded to pieces on the rocks. Sturdy men launched a lifeboat and pulled at the oars to rescue the imperiled seamen who clung to that fast-disintegrating ship.

As the small lifeboat came struggling back to shore, those who waited cried out, "Did you get them?"

Those in the lifeboat answered through the storm, "All but one! We had to leave him."

And when those on shore heard that, one stalwart boy stepped from the group and said, "Who will join me in rescuing that man who remains behind on the ship?"

Just then an old woman with gray hair cried out, "Oh, Jim, my son, don't go! Please don't risk your life. You are all I have left. Your father was drowned in the sea, and your brother William sailed away, and we've never heard from him; and now, if you are lost I shall be left alone! Please don't go!"

But that son replied, "I must go, Mother! It's my duty! I must go!"

Then he and a small group of brave souls launched the lifeboat and pulled for the wreck, risking their lives with every tug at the oars. Anxiously that mother waited on the shore for that boy to return—waited with tears on her cheeks and prayers in her heart.

At last they saw the lifeboat pull away from the wreck and start for the shore. They saw that small, frail craft lifted to the top of a huge wave and then smashed into the trough of that wave. At every drop it looked as if it would be crushed like an eggshell.

But finally, after an hour's struggle,

the boat got near enough to hail, and those on the shore called out, "Have you got your man?"

And a voice rang out, high, clear, and triumphant above the roar of the surf, "Yes—and tell Mother it's Bill!"—William Stidger

January 15: Super Sunday

There is a special event on television. Not everyone watches, but most people who are interested in football watch it. Do you know what it is called? (The Super Bowl.) This year's Super Bowl is the twenty-ninth one. That's a lot of Super Bowls. For most of us they kind of run together. No one game seems that important, but for the players this feels like the most important day in all of their lives. They will always remember what happens tonight.

There are days for everybody that they will never forget. Your mother will never forget the day her doctor told her you were on the way. People remember the day they got their first car, the day they graduated from high school, the day they moved here.

This day may not seem so important to us, but if we decide today to do what God wants us to do, then this day is very important, because there is nothing more important than being God's helper.—Brett Younger

January 22: Riding a Train

Have any of you ever ridden on a train? It is an interesting experience. Long ago, when a person rode on the train, they bought a ticket from a person in the station, and when they got on the train, they gave the ticket to a conductor. This is not the case with many trains today. In Philadelphia, for example, the people boarding the train never see anyone who has anything to do with the operation of the train. At the train station, there is a machine that takes a five-dollar bill and returns five silver dollars. Then there is another machine into which the rider puts some of these silver dollars, and out comes a plastic ticket. The rider then uses the plastic ticket to unlock a gate that lets him or her into the station to get the train. When the train stops, the rider boards the train, and when it stops again at the desired place, the rider gets off and uses the plastic ticket to open a gate to get out of the station. During the ride, the people on board will hear a voice announcing the different stops, but outside of that, they have no contact with the people operating the train. There is no one there to check up on them, but if you want to ride the train, you have to follow the rules.

That is a lesson that applies to life also. If you want to get the most out of life, you need to follow the rules. To have a friend, be a friend. Do unto others as you would have them do unto you. Part of growing up is to learn about the rules of life that work, and Jesus is the best teacher in that regard. Jesus can open the gateway to true life.—Kenneth Mortonson

January 29: Blessing and Promise

TEXT: Matt. 5:1–12

"Blessed are those who hunger and thirst for righteousness, for they will be filled" (v. 6).

Object: a banana (or the fruit of your choice)

Good morning, boys and girls. I brought a banana with me this morning. I love to eat bananas. When I am hungry for a snack, I can eat a banana, and it will fill me up. Do you like bananas? (Let them answer.)

One day Jesus was teaching people. Many people were listening to him. Jesus talked to the people about many important things. One of the things he talked about was a word called *righteousness*. That's a big word. It means being good. It also means doing the right thing, or the correct thing. Jesus said that if you hunger to be a good person, you will be a good person. You will be filled.

Have you ever been with some of your friends? Maybe one of them did something that you felt was wrong? Maybe you knew it was wrong at the time, but you did it anyway. After it was over, you might have wished that you didn't do it. If you've ever felt that way, you are a good person—you are a righteous person. You want to do the right thing. You want to do what is good. Sometimes it is hard to do the right thing. Sometimes it is hard to know what the right thing is. Many people, even adults, have a hard time knowing what the right thing is. Jesus said that anyone (point to children and call them by name) who tries to be good will be a happy person. Have you ever felt happy after you did something good? (Let them answer.) Jesus said if you want to be a good person, it is like eating your favorite food. If you are hungry for something and you eat enough of it, you will be filled. If you hunger to be a good person, God will help you. God will bless you. That means to me that when I eat my favorite fruit I will be filled. If I want to be a good person, with God's help I will be. You will be, too.—*Children's Sermon Service Plus!*

February 5: Salt of the Earth

TEXT: Matt. 5:13–20

"You are the salt of the earth; but if salt has lost its taste, how can its saltiness be restored?" (v. 13).

Object: a container of table salt

Good morning, boys and girls. I brought some salt with me this morning. (Show the salt.) What do we use salt for? (Let them answer.) We use it for flavoring food. How many of you put salt on your popcorn? (Let them answer.) What else do we use salt for? (Let them answer.) We put salt on the sidewalks in the winter to keep us from slipping. We put salt in water softeners to soften our water.

In this morning's lesson Jesus said that we are the salt of the earth. What do you think he meant by that? (Let them answer.) In Jesus' time salt was very important. It was used to keep food from spoiling or tasting bad. It was used in religious services. It was an example of something that was very pure and valuable. Like today, salt in Jesus' time was also used to give flavor to food. Without salt, popcorn doesn't taste as good, does it?

When Jesus said that we are the salt of the earth, he meant that being a Christian gives flavor to our lives. So, without salt in our food, our food might become dull tasting. It wouldn't have flavor. Without Jesus in our life, our life might become dull and meaningless. Our life wouldn't have flavor. But, since Jesus is in our life, our life is exciting. When we show others that Jesus gives our life flavor, other people who don't know Jesus as we do will want to know about him. That's why we are all the salt of the earth. This week, see if you can show other people that you have flavor in your life. That flavor is because you know Jesus.—*Children's Sermon Service Plus!*

February 12: Loving Care

A friend of mine sent me a poem that was written by a girl in his Sunday school. The teacher of that class had wisely offered a prize for the best poem to be written, and this little girl handed in her poem. Here it is:

Friendship is like a garden
or flowers rich and rare;
It cannot reach perfection
Without much loving care.

To me that poem is one of the most beautiful I have ever read, not only because of the unusual fact that a child wrote it but also because of the eternal truth that is contained within its brief four lines. Within those lines lies the greatest truth on what to do with friendship, how to preserve it, how to make it rich and beautiful.

Now and then I see beautiful friendships broken for the simple reason that one party to that friendship does absolutely nothing to cultivate it. He simply accepts that friendship watered, cultivated, and beautiful. I have seen hundreds of friendships wither and die for the simple lack of attention. I have seen many homes break up simply because one partner in that marriage did not take the trouble to try to keep it going, to speak a friendly, appreciative word that would be as water to a thirsty flower in that home. "The soul too must be fed and watered," I have heard some wise person say.—William L. Stidger

February 19: Trusting God

I need a volunteer to play a game. This game will not sound like much, but it might be fun. The victim, excuse me, volunteer, will lean back and fall down. I will do my best to catch this brave girl or boy. Who's feeling courageous?

Stand right here. Go very slowly, because if I miss you, I am going to be very embarrassed. (Make sure you catch the child.) Wasn't that great? It is a little bit scary, but it is fun. The hardest part is believing that you will be caught.

Trusting another person to catch you is a little like trusting God. The Bible tells us that sometimes we have to do scary things and trust God to care for us. We are to try to be friends with people who may not want to be our friends. That can be scary. We need God's help. We are to tell others about Jesus. That can be scary. We need God's help. We can learn to do new and scary things for Jesus, knowing that God will catch us if we fall.—Brett Younger

February 26: Hungry for Righteousness

TEXT: Matthew 5:6

(This children's sermon requires a partner planted nearby.)

I would like to talk about one of the Beatitudes, one of Jesus' teachings, but I am really hungry. Do any of you have anything to eat? How many of you had breakfast? I didn't have breakfast. When I left home I was in a hurry, so I didn't get any breakfast. I really do feel hungry. Do any of you have a hamburger or an apple? Wait here a second.

Preacher: Do you have any food?
Partner: This is embarrassing.
Preacher: I'm hungry.
Partner: Here's a tic-tac.
Preacher: No, that's no good.
Partner: Here's a cracker. Now leave me alone.
Preacher (eating): It's pretty good. Do you have anything to drink?
Partner: Eat your cracker and finish the children's sermon.

I am sorry about that interruption, but when you're really hungry, it is hard to think of anything else. Jesus understood that. Once Jesus said that what we should hunger for most of all is to do what God wants us to do. There are lots of things that we want. We want toys, friends, good grades at school, and good food. What we should want more than anything else is to do what Jesus wants us to do.—Brett Younger

DISCIPLES AND DECISIONS

"Disciples and Decisions" is a series of children's sermons designed to introduce children to the apostles and the concept of discipleship as well as guide them along in the development process of decision making. Visual aids throughout this series might include a picture of Jesus and the disciples, a flannelgraph display, and name tags that would allow children to role play as disciples. Additional specific props would include a fishing net, introduction name tags, props representing different professions, a solid rock, and a crumbling stone. Throughout sermons one should always allow time for feedback and follow through with appropriate responses from children.

March 5: Who Are Disciples?

Today we are going to begin talking about disciples. Can anyone tell me who or what are disciples? According to the dictionary, a disciple is a pupil, a student who decides to follow the teachings of a special teacher. A disciple also helps share those teachings with other people. When Jesus started his ministry, he chose a small number of people to be his special students, and these people decided to become followers of Jesus, his disciples.

The Bible tells us the names of some of these early disciples. Can any of you tell me the names of these disciples? Generally we think of twelve special disciples whom we call the apostles. The word *apostle* means someone sent out as a special messenger. In the Bible there are several different lists of these disciples' names. Most of the lists agree on eleven names: Simon Peter, his brother Andrew,

James and John the sons of Zebedee, Philip, Bartholomew, Matthew the tax collector, Thomas the twin, James the son of Alphaeus, Simon the Zealot, and Judas Iscariot who betrayed Jesus. The Gospels of Matthew and Mark list Thaddaeus, while Luke and Acts list another Judas, the son of James. The Gospel of John also mentions a disciple named Nathaniel.

Perhaps some of the disciples were known by different names, but more important than coming up with a list of twelve names to remember is the fact that many people, men and women, girls and boys, made decisions to follow Jesus to share the good news of his teachings with others. People continue to make that decision today. Your Sunday school teachers have decided to follow Jesus. That is why they come every Sunday to teach you about Jesus. Perhaps your parents and grandparents or uncles and aunts have as well. Maybe you have older sisters and brothers who have decided to accept Jesus as their Savior and follow his teachings. A long time ago I decided to follow Jesus and share his good news through teaching and preaching. It is a very important decision.

Now, we make decisions every day. We decide what clothes to wear, what toy to play with, what we want to eat, what we want to be when we grow up. But one of the most important decisions we make is whether or not to become disciples of Jesus. Over the next several weeks we are going to share stories about some of the first disciples and their decisions to follow Jesus and how those decisions changed their lives. This week I want you to see how many people you can find who have decided to follow Jesus and ask them what that has meant to them.—Ronald L. Loughry

March 12: Fishers of People

Remember last week we began talking about disciples? Did you find some followers of Jesus this past week? Today we are going to talk about some of Jesus' first disciples. (Hold up fishing net.) Can any of you tell me what this is? This is a fish net. Fishermen back in the Bible days would go out in boats and toss their nets into the water, then pull them back in full of fish. Several of the disciples were fishermen. Simon Peter and his brother Andrew were fishing when Jesus called out and told them to come and follow him. James and John, the sons of Zebedee, were also out fishing when they decided to follow Jesus. Jesus told these fishers that if they followed him he would make them fishers of people. Jesus meant that he would teach them about God's good news so they could share this with others and gather them into God's net of love. Simon Peter, Andrew, James, and John decided to leave their fishing jobs and become disciples. It was a decision that changed their lives. Remember last week when I asked you to find some people who had decided to follow Jesus? This week I want you to ask them how that decision changed their lives.—Ronald L. Loughry

March 19: The Gift of Introduction

Does everyone here know each other? (If answer is yes: Good, then you have all been introduced. If answer is no: Well, let's introduce each other. Each of us will tell our name and something about ourselves; then we will all know each other.) Introductions are very important. When we introduce someone, we tell others about that person.

We have been talking about Jesus' disciples over the last couple of Sundays. Among the disciples there were some whom we know made special efforts to introduce others to Jesus. In the Gospel of John, we read of how Andrew told his brother Simon Peter about Jesus. Then when Jesus came and told them to follow him, Simon Peter already knew who Jesus was. Andrew was also the disciple who introduced Jesus to a little boy who was willing to share his small lunch of fish and bread with a huge crowd of over five thousand people. Because of that introduction, all the people soon had plenty to eat. Along with the disciple named Philip, Andrew also brought a group of Greek people to meet Jesus. These people were able to ask Jesus some very important questions.

Besides helping Andrew, Philip also brought Nathaniel to meet Jesus. Philip even asked Jesus to introduce him to God the Father. Even though he may not have understood everything that Jesus taught him, Philip recognized how important it was to know God. Perhaps you can use the gift of introduction this week. Tell someone what you know about Jesus or ask someone to tell you more about Jesus.—Ronald L. Loughry

March 26: What Do You Want to Be?

What do you want to be when you grow up? How about a (use props such as hats, clothing, tools to represent different professions) firefighter, or a doctor, or a dancer, or a carpenter, or a secretary, or a teacher? Over the past few weeks we have been talking about Jesus' disciples. We mentioned that some of the disciples were fishermen. Do you remember?

Other disciples had different jobs. One of the disciples, named Matthew (he might also have been known as Levi), was a tax collector. Not many people liked the tax collectors. During the New Testament days, a foreign government forced people to pay a lot of taxes. Tax collectors were offered a share of all the taxes they could collect. Tax collectors were not well liked because they often cheated people in order to make more money for themselves. A lot of people looked down on tax collectors and would not have anything to do with them.

But guess what Jesus did? Jesus went to see Matthew at work and told him to come and follow him. Matthew left his job and went with Jesus. Jesus even went and had dinner with a group of tax collectors. Do you know the story of Zaccheus? Zaccheus was a tax collector who had probably cheated a lot of people, and he wasn't very well liked. Jesus went and visited with Zaccheus, and Zaccheus decided to follow Jesus. It really changed his life. He repaid all the money he had forced people to give. Even still, some people continued to dislike tax collectors.

Earlier I asked you what you wanted to be when you grow up. What I want you to remember is this: what job you have is not the most important thing in life. It is important that you like what you are doing. It is important that you not hurt anyone; it is even better if you can help someone. Whether you wear a suit or a dress, jeans or a uniform isn't important. And even if you make some mistakes, remember, you can always change and do better. What is most important is the decision we make to follow Jesus. When Matthew and Zaccheus decided to follow Jesus, they stopped doing things that might have hurt people and began to treat people more fairly. Jesus had showed them that who they were and what was in their hearts and how they lived was what was most important. I hope that someday, as you get older, you all will decide to be disciples and follow Jesus.—Ronald L. Loughry

April 2: Sons of Thunder

Do we have any brothers or sisters here today? If you remember from our recent discussions about Jesus' disciples, some of Jesus' special followers were brothers. Remember, Simon Peter and Andrew were brothers. Also, Thomas was sometimes called Thomas the twin, so he must have had a brother or sister.

There was also another set of brothers. Do you remember James and John, the sons of Zebedee? I want to talk about these two today. James and John were fishermen; they were very close to Jesus. They were both with Jesus almost all the time and shared some really important experiences with Jesus. But James and John were also nicknamed "the sons of thunder." Most people think this was because they tended to be loud and boastful. And in spite of all their love for Jesus, they sometimes got mixed up about some very important decisions. When Jesus talked about his kingdom and power, James and John decided they wanted to hold important positions. Perhaps one way of putting it would be to say they wanted to be bigshots.

Even though they had misunderstood what Jesus was trying to teach them, Jesus still loved them. Jesus tried to explain that the best way to be close to God was to help other people, to put others first, to love other people just as God loves us.

I want you to think about that this week. I want you to watch how people help other people. I want you to find a way you can help someone. It may be as simple as holding a door for someone or playing with someone who doesn't have anyone to play with. You may not be the first in line or the first through the door. You may not come in first in a game or a race, but if you are helping others, if you are putting others first, then in God's sight you're a real winner!—Ronald L. Loughry

April 9: The Rock

Today we are going to conclude our talks about Jesus and his disciples. I hope we have all learned some very important lessons over the past few weeks. There is still something else, very special, that I want you to remember. There is one disciple whose name is usually at the top of all the lists. His name was Simon Peter. Actually his name was Simon, but Jesus nicknamed him Peter, which means rock. Perhaps Jesus wanted everyone to know that Simon Peter would set a good example of what it means to be a strong, faithful follower of Jesus. A faithful disciple is someone who believes in Jesus so strongly that nothing can turn him or her away.

We need to be strong and solid like a rock, but for a while it seemed like Simon Peter wouldn't live up to his new name. Simon Peter was very close to Jesus. Simon Peter was the first to proclaim that Jesus was the Messiah, the Savior, the special chosen one of God. But Simon Peter was also often the first one to get into trouble. One day when he saw Jesus walking on the water, Simon Peter jumped out of the boat and tried the same thing, but he became afraid, took his eyes off of Jesus, and began to sink until Jesus saved him. Simon Peter also tended to brag about how much he loved Jesus and how he would stick with Jesus no matter how tough or how dangerous things would get. But on the night Jesus was betrayed, Simon Peter ran away and hung back, hiding in the crowd. Three times that night people asked Simon Peter if he knew Jesus. They asked him if he was not one of Jesus' disciples. Peter lied and denied even knowing Jesus.

It seemed like Simon Peter's faith was nothing at all like a solid rock. (Hold up solid rock.) It seemed, instead, that Simon Peter was more like a crumbling rock (hold up crumbling rock), but Jesus knew differently. Jesus knew that Simon Peter would learn from his mistakes, and indeed Simon Peter did learn. He became a leader of the disciples and shared Jesus' story and teachings with thousands of people. Many people decided to become followers of Jesus because of Simon Peter. Simon Peter even used his own story to help others realize that we all can be rock-solid disciples with Jesus' help.

Do you remember when we first started learning about the disciples? We said disciples are people who decide to become followers of Jesus. Disciples try to live the way Jesus teaches us to live and share the good news of God's love for all people. Some of you may be too young to understand all this, but I hope you remember some of what we have talked about. I hope you will talk about Jesus and being a disciple of Jesus with your parents, grandparents, aunts and uncles, older brothers and sisters, or your Sunday school teachers. I want you to know that you can always come and talk with me and ask me questions about Jesus and his teachings. Most of all, I hope and pray that someday each and every one of you will make the decision to be a disciple and follow Jesus.—Ronald L. Loughry

April 16: Symbols of Easter

Look at the people who are in church today. This must be a special day with so many people here. And so it is. This is Easter. Now, you may have noticed that Easter comes on a different day each year. That is because the time of Easter is set by the moon. Once it is spring, Easter is the first Sunday after the full moon.

There are some special symbols in that fact. When we have a full moon, it is a bright light shining in the darkness. On that day, it is as bright as it can be at night. Now, we say that Jesus is the light of the world. Spring is the time when life returns to our earth, as things start to grow again. And Jesus is the true light of life that shines in the darkness and helps us to grow into the type of person God wants us to be. As we celebrate today, we have new life in Jesus.—Kenneth Mortonson

April 23: Forgiving Others

TEXT: Matt. 18:23–35

Narrator: Jesus told this story. Once there was a king who had a servant who owed him a million dollars.

King: You owe me a million dollars.

First servant: I don't have a million dollars. Please, please, please, please, please, please with sugar on top, don't throw me in jail.

Narrator: The master felt sorry for him, so he let him go. The man went out and found a fellow servant who owed him two dollars. He grabbed him and started shaking him.

First servant: You owe me two dollars. Pay it back now.

Second servant: I don't have two dollars. Please, please, please, please, please, please with sugar on top, don't throw me in jail.

Narrator: But the first servant had him thrown in jail. When the king found out what had happened, he was very upset.

King: You should have been as kind to him as I was to you. You are the one who belongs in jail.

Narrator: And Jesus said, there's a lesson in this for all of us. We need to treat each other with kindness and forgiveness.

King: When someone hurts your feelings, remember the times you have hurt other people, and forgive them.

First servant: When a friend needs your help, remember the times you have been helped, and help them.

Second servant: When your parents make a mistake, remember the good things they have done, and let them off the hook.

Narrator: Because that is how God treats us.

—Brett Younger

April 30: The Mirror

Have you ever wondered what God looks like? (Give a moment for children to respond.)

Would you agree that we know what each other looks like more than we can describe God's appearance? The Bible tells us that we are created in the image of God. What do you think of that? We must be very special for God to create us in his image.

Have you ever looked in a mirror? (Hold up a small mirror and let the children look at themselves.) What do you see? That's right, a picture of yourself.

Imagine how much pleasure it gives God to look at us and see a reflection of himself. That's why God wants us to be the best we can be.

Frederick Buechner in his book *The Magnificent Defeat* tells the story of a motherless tiger cub who was adopted by goats. After years of living in this strange setting, the tiger learned to sound like the goats, to eat like them, and in general to act like a goat, for that is what the tiger thought he was. One day a king tiger came along, and all the goats ran for their lives. The young tiger, however, remained unafraid. He began to bleat and to nibble the grass. The king tiger couldn't understand why he was playing this masquerade, so he took the young tiger to a pool, where the two of them stood side by side observing their reflections in the water. After this act did not convince him, the king tiger offered him a piece of raw meat. At first the taste turned his stomach, but the more he ate the more the young tiger felt his blood flow increasingly warmer. Buechner says, "Lashing his tail and digging his claws into the ground, the young beast finally raised his head high, and the jungle trembled at the sound of his exultant roar."

Yes, you are special. God created you. No one can be you like you can. What a wonderful gift.—Ron R. Blankenship

May 7: Musical Instruments

Preparation: Review the stories of David playing for King Saul in 1 Samuel 16:14–

23, David bringing the Ark of the Covenant to Jerusalem in 1 Chronicles 15, and Gideon and his army in Judges 7.

Look through teaching pictures in children's Sunday school departments and find pictures of musical instruments referenced in the stories listed above.

Prepare the children: After the children are comfortably seated in front of you, ask, "What musical instruments have you heard played today at church?" (Give the children time to respond.) Continue, "What musical instruments other than the piano and organ have you heard played at church?" (Children may need some help in remembering. If so, ask something like, "Do you remember the musical instruments that were used at Christmas?")

Say: "Today, we will learn how musical instruments were used in Bible times to help people worship and to do other things. Listen to discover what musical instruments were used and why they were used."

Sermon: Musical instruments have been used for many, many years in the worship of God. Musical instruments were used in worship in Bible times and as a part of everyday living, as well as on special occasions. Although in Bible times musicians did not have pianos and organs to play, they did have a variety of instruments to use. Some musical instruments were played by plucking strings. Others were played by blowing wind into them, while others had to be struck or hit together in order to play.

An interesting Old Testament story is about the time when King David brought the golden box called the Ark of the Covenant into the city of Jerusalem. It was a happy time—a time for great celebration and worship. David got musicians to sing and play musical instruments as the men carried the Ark into the city. The musicians dressed in white linen robes. They played horns and trumpets, harps and zithers, as well as crashing cymbals. (Show picture and identify the instruments.)

In fact, David himself was a good musician. He played a stringed instrument called a harp. He probably played the instrument and sang songs while he watched his father's sheep. Do you remember the story about David playing his harp for King Saul in order to help the king feel better? (Show picture.)

The loudest of the wind instruments (instruments played by blowing into them) was called the shofar. It was made from a ram's horn. The shofar was also called a trumpet. Many times this horn was used in battle. One Old Testament story tells about a soldier named Gideon. He gave each of his soldiers a trumpet and a clay jar with a torch in it. At his command, all the soldiers blew their trumpets and broke their clay jars. The torches hidden in jars shone into the night. All the noise and light confused the enemy, and Gideon and his army won the battle. (Show picture.)

Response: Ask: "Are you glad for musical instruments that we can use to help us worship and praise God?" (Response.) "I am too. Let's thank him for them."

Prayer: God, thank you for musical instruments we use to help us think about and praise you. In Jesus' name, amen.—Leon W. Castle

May 14: You Belong

This morning I have a special picture I want to show you. (Use whatever family group picture you might have. Identify the people in your picture and tell when the picture was taken.)

Now, suppose something nice happens to one of the people in the picture. What effect do you think it would have on the other people in our family? (They would be happy.) And suppose something unpleasant happened to one of the people in this picture. What effect do you think that would have upon the other people in the family? (They would be sad.)

You see, we sometimes forget that we belong to a family and what happens to us affects the other people in that family. Also, since we are part of a group, we should be concerned about the things that happen in that group. For example, if you like to live in a nice clean house and you see a piece of paper on the floor that you did not drop, what should you do? (If you want a clean house, and you are part of that family, you should pick it up.)

Remember, you are a part of the family that lives in your home, and also you are a part of this church family. We want you to do your part to make your home and your church a happy place for all who are in that house.—Kenneth Mortonson

May 21: No Two Alike

I was hoping to find two of you just alike. Let's start by having all the girls raise their hands. Keep your hand up if you are a girl who is eight years old. Keep your hand up if you are an eight-year-old girl with blond hair. Keep your hand up if you are nine years old. Keep your hand up if you are a nine-year-old boy with brown hair. Keep your hand up if you are a nine-year-old boy with brown hair who is good-looking. Several of you have you hands up, but you don't really look alike.

No two of us are exactly the same. Even twins, who can look a lot alike, are not exactly the same. The Bible tells us that God has made each one of us special. God loves each one of us as though there were only one of us to love.—Brett Younger

May 28: God's Strength

TEXT: Ps. 46:1

"God is our refuge and strength, a very present help in trouble."

Main truth: God gives us strength when we need it.

Interest object: One metal rod and several (eight to ten) sticks about the same length as the rod. I used an automobile jack handle for the rod and cut up a cane pole for the sticks. Any old rod and sticks will do, however.

I'm holding a stick. I could break it in two very easily. What if I add another stick? I can still break them with no trouble.

When I add several more sticks, I can still break them, but not as easily. Look at what happens when I add a whole bunch of sticks. They would be very difficult to break.

Now, what if I put a steel rod into the middle of all these sticks? There's no way I could break them, ever. Strength has been added beyond my own.

Let's say the single stick represents you or me. There are a lot of things that could happen in life to break us—to hurt us—and make us feel all broken up inside. Like when someone you love dies. Or when you have to move and leave all your friends. Or when you do something that hurts those you love and you feel rotten about it. Or when you fail in something you really wanted to do well in.

These are things that make us feel broken. It's easy to break when you're all alone. We need other people to give us strength. We need family and friends. That's like adding these sticks. It makes it harder to break. We need the support and fellowship of the church. This makes the sticks even stronger.

But still, they're pretty fragile. Is there anything or anyone who can make us so strong nothing can break us?

Yes! There's God. He can be a steel rod of strength within us when we call on him for help and trust him.

The psalmist wrote, "God is our refuge and strength, a very present help in trouble" (Ps. 46:1).

That means God gives us strength when we need it. And we all need it. Let God be your strength, and troubles can never break you!—Roy E. DeBrand

June 4: Why Do We Do This?

This morning I want to ask you a question. It may be one that you ask yourself each week as you come up here. The question is this: why do we do this? Why do we have you boys and girls come up here each week to spend a little time together? The question may be hard for you to answer, so let me help you. We do this because you are very important to our church. You help us to make this church a family. You remind us of the fact that if we do not have young people like you in our church, in a short time there might not be any church here. You are very important to us, and that is why I have this microphone in my hand.

This morning I would like you to introduce yourself so that all the people here will know who you are. Line up and speak right into the microphone and tell us your name and where you live, and anything else you would like us to know about you. . . . Thank you for sharing that with us this morning.—Kenneth Mortonson

June 11: Slippers

Do you know what these are? (Slippers.) How many of you have slippers? And where do you keep your slippers? I keep mine in the bedroom, but in some countries, like Austria, people keep their slippers by the front door. The reason for this is that they have the practice of taking their shoes off and putting on their slippers as soon as they enter the house. They do this for a very practical reason: it helps to keep the house clean. Any dust or dirt on the shoes is not carried through the whole house. I like that idea, for it shows that you care about the place where you live. I am not saying that you should do the same thing in your house, but the lesson is important for us all. Be it your own room, or your house, or even your church and school: helping to keep it clean is an important job for everyone. So, the next time you put on your slippers, remember what they do in Austria and remember to do what you can to keep your living space looking nice.—Kenneth Mortonson

June 18: Father's Day

This is the day when we celebrate all kinds of fathers. There are tall fathers and short fathers, thin fathers and not-so-thin fathers, fathers who run fast and fathers who look funny when they run, young fathers and mature fathers, good-looking fathers and normal fathers.

In the Bible, the name Jesus uses most for God is Father. Jesus understood that there are all kinds of fathers, so he tried to make it clear exactly what kind of father he meant. Some fathers don't let their children do anything, but God the Father lets his children make lots of decisions. Some fathers really do not care much for their children, but God the Father adores his children. Some fathers are forever getting angry, but Jesus' Father is always forgiving.

If you can imagine the best father in all the world, you can know that God loves you like that and even more.—Brett Younger

June 25: When We Rob Ourselves

TEXT: Matt. 16:26

"For what is a man profited, if he shall gain the whole world, and lose his own soul?" (KJV).

Main truth: We rob ourselves when we put anything ahead of spiritual values.

Interest object: A toy gun that looks very much like a real gun.

The newspaper carried a funny but sad story the other day about a man who went into a large bank to rob it. He handed the teller a note and a bag. The note instructed the teller to put all her money into the bag.

"I have a gun," the man said as he pulled one out. The only problem was, it was a toy gun. Though it looked very much like a real gun, the teller recognized it as a toy gun and called a guard.

The man was arrested and convicted for bank robbery and sentenced to twenty years in prison!

Now, I want to ask you something. Whom did the man really rob? He didn't rob the bank. He got caught! Whom did he rob?

He robbed himself! He robbed himself of twenty years of freedom. He robbed himself of whatever name and influence for good he may have had. Look at all he gave up just to try to steal a little money!

Boys and girls, we sometimes rob ourselves. You may think not, but we do. We rob ourselves when we put anything ahead of being like Jesus.

We rob ourselves when we think only of ourselves and not of others.

We rob ourselves when we do wrong instead of right.

We rob ourselves when we seek less for ourselves than what God wants for us.

We rob ourselves when we love things more than people.

Anytime we put anything ahead of God, of loving and serving him, it's like the man with a toy gun. We rob ourselves.

Jesus talked about this when he asked, "For what is a man profited, if he shall gain the whole world, and lose his own soul?" (Matt. 16:26 KJV). And the answer to his question is: *nothing!*

You only rob yourself if you lose your soul over anything. Don't rob yourself. Invest yourself by putting your faith in God and your interest in spiritual values. Anything else is self-robbing!—Roy E. DeBrand

July 2: Freedom

Does anyone know what a straight jacket is? It is a special kind of jacket that has long arms that can be tied behind a person so that that person's arms are crossed in front of them like this. This morning I would like you to see what it would feel like to be in a straight jacket. Put your arms around yourself like this. Now, keep them there. Could you open a door? If your nose itched, could you scratch it? If I offered you a piece of wrapped candy, could you take it? You might pick it up out of my hand with your teeth, but then how would you get it unwrapped?

How easy it is to lose some of our freedom. And when we do lose it, then we begin to understand what a precious gift freedom is. I hope you boys and girls will always be thankful that you live in a country where people are free. Now, I have a bowl with some wrapped candy in it, and you are free to take one before you return to your seats. Thank you for coming up here today.—Kenneth Mortonson

July 9: A Joyful Noise

Visual introduction: A small replica of the Liberty Bell.

Sentence summary: Let us celebrate and never keep quiet about Jesus.

Scripture text: "Make a joyful noise to the Lord, all the lands!" (Ps. 100:1).

Here is a little replica of the original Liberty Bell, which still hangs in Philadelphia, Pennsylvania. Something special happened in that city on the Fourth of July in 1776. Wise and courageous leaders decided to declare our country's independence from the king of England. So they wrote what we now call the Declaration of Independence. Then, after signing it, they all rushed outside to shout and rejoice.

Perhaps a few of them had firecrackers, but most people back then made noise with bells. All the church bells rang that day. But the bell that we best remember ringing in celebration was that big Liberty Bell on the courthouse square in Philadelphia.

The Fourth of July is still a happy holiday, not a time to keep quiet. When we are excited, we want to make a joyful noise to celebrate. So bring out the bells and celebrate our freedom and independence. No foreign armies march in our land. That's good news.

When we come to church for worship, we ought to be just as excited. The psalmist urged us to "make a joyful noise to the Lord." This is no time to lean back in your pew and sleep. Let us celebrate how Jesus Christ came to earth revealing God's love for us. That's good news worth shouting about. Ring those bells.—C. W. Bess

July 16: The Lesson of "O"

Today I would like you to do a few things with the figure "O." (Place a large O on a poster or form the letter O with your fingers.) This figure can represent several things. Can you tell me what they are? (The letter O and zero. It is also called a circle.)

Now, let's see what happens to the word *Good* if you take "God" out of it. (Suggestion: put words *Good* and *O* on front and back of a poster board.) What is left? (Zero. Nothing.) Without God we cannot know what is good.

Now, let's call our figure a circle. When we have a circle, it surrounds everything that is inside the circle. (You may let the children form a circle around you.) The circle reminds us that we need to include other people in our lives. When we like someone, sometimes we put our arms around them. We need to reach out to people and let them be a part of our lives. Again, we have two words that help us to remember this. First, what does this letter "I" stand for? (Again, use a poster board to show the I.) It represents a person whom we call "I."—Kenneth Mortonson

July 23: Somebody Special Loves Us

What is your favorite Bible verse? Different people have different favorites. I am not sure that it was his favorite verse, but a great Christian leader, Martin Luther, thought that it was very important. He thought it tells us in one verse what the whole Bible means. He called it "the little Bible." How many of you can say John 3:16 with me? "For God so loved the world, that he gave his only begotten Son, that whosoever believeth in him should not perish, but have everlasting life."

That one verse tells us several important things. It tells us that God loves us, for we are a part of the world that God made. It tells us that God sent his special Son, Jesus, into the world to bring God close to us, so that we can know how much God cares for us. It tells us that by believing in Jesus and following him we are doing what God wants us to do and that Jesus shows us the way to heaven, where we will live forever with God.

John 3:16 is a wonderful verse, isn't it? Why is it special to you?—James W. Cox

July 30: When Jesus Cried

Another favorite Bible verse just says, "Jesus wept." What do you think of when you hear the words "Jesus wept"? Yes, Jesus cried. Jesus came from God, and he was God's special Son, and he showed what God is like. But Jesus was human, too. He got tired and hungry and sleepy. In those ways and others he was just like us. But in other ways he was different. The Bible tells us that he was "without sin." That means that he did not do bad things. Satan tried to get him to do bad things, but he wouldn't do them. He always did what his heavenly Father wanted him to do.

The reason some people like this verse, "Jesus wept," is that it is short. It really may be the only Bible verse that some people can say. But it is very important, for it helps us understand how God feels when people die and are sad and don't have enough faith in God. Jesus must have cried because others were crying and were sad. We can be sure that when we are hurting and sad God cares and shares. We can be sure that God's heart is broken when people do not believe in him and refuse to believe his promises to be with them and help them and make them happy.

There is a story about a little girl who was late getting home and explained to her mother that her friend's doll was broken and that she stopped to help her. "Did you help her fix the doll?" "No, we couldn't fix it, but I helped her cry." The Bible tells us, "Be happy with those who are happy, weep with those who weep" (Rom. 12:15 TEV).—James W. Cox

August 6: Making Choices

Sometimes it is hard to make up our mind. People have already started asking what you will be when you grow up. Will you be a firefighter or a lawyer or a teacher? Those kinds of choices are hard to make.

Baskin Robbins drives some of us crazy. That's the ice cream store with thirty-one flavors—butter brickle and rocky road and double double chocolate. It is hard to choose.

We all have to make choices all the time. You have to decide whether you are going to do your homework or clean your room or play with your brother or watch television or help your parents. The choices go on and on.

Jesus was always telling people to choose carefully. Choosing the best thing is choosing what Jesus wants you to choose. You have lots of choices. You may be firefighters, lawyers, or teachers, but the most important thing you can be is someone who chooses like Jesus wants them to.—Brett Younger

August 13: Don't Worry

This morning I want you to look at something that I am sure you have seen before. (Show them an egg.) What comes out of this egg? If it is allowed to hatch in a normal way, a chick will come out of it.

And the way it comes out is to break through the shell from the inside, when the time is right.

Now, if you were to see the chick trying to break out of the shell and you said, "Maybe that chick will not get out, I will help him," that would be the wrong thing to do, for the work of getting out of the shell helps to strengthen the little chick. Sometimes you may have trouble with something, and you worry about doing it right, and your first thought is to ask for help. Because you are worried, you are unwilling to try. And sometimes, the person whom you asked to help will not help right away. Because that person cares about you, they want you to keep on trying because that is the best thing for you. So, when you have a problem, don't worry. Remember the egg, and do all you can to take care of your problem; and then, when you have done all you can, then you can ask for help if it is still needed.—Kenneth Mortonson

August 20: We Are Like Clay

TEXT: 1 Pet. 5:6–1, verse 6: Humble yourselves therefore under the mighty hand of God, that in due time he may exalt you.

Object: Clay or crazy putty. You may find some in your Sunday school nursery.

Good morning, boys and girls. How are you on this lovely God's day? Isn't it wonderful the way God made the world and then put all sorts of things in it? Do you know when I was a little boy I used to love to make things out of a special material called clay? How many of you have ever worked with clay? Isn't it fun? I think so, too.

But have you ever really looked at clay? (Show them the clay.) It's just a big gray blob. That's right. There is nothing very pretty about a lumpy old piece of gray clay. As a matter of fact, to look at that lumpy, old, slimy gray piece of clay kind of make you feel sorry for it. Poor old clay. What good is anything that looks like this? I'm sure I don't know.

However, if you pick that piece of clay up in your hands and begin to roll it and twist it and make it soft and workable, you can do a lot of things with it. Men have made statues that look so real they remind you of people. Some others have made flowers and trees out of clay, and after they were painted they looked almost as beautiful as real flowers and trees. (You might press the clay against something to show how an image can be made in the clay.)

Well, you know, boys and girls, we are like that clay in the sight of God. If God just left us alone and never cared for us or loved us, we would not be very pretty or strong or happy. If God just left us alone, we would look like that lump of clay before we worked with it. Now, who wants to be like an old lump of clay when we can look as beautiful as a flower or as strong as a tree? So remember who it is who makes you what you are. It's God! God loves you and can fill you full of love. God cares for you, and you care about others.

It's nice to know that God thinks so much about us that we never have to worry about being old lumps of clay. He will make us into something that he needs and something that we will want to be.—Wesley T. Runk, *Growing Up in God*

August 27: I Can Tell the Truth

Preparation: Read John 9 and become familiar with the story of the man born blind.

Prepare the children: "Is telling the truth always easy? Have you ever been in a situation when you wanted to tell the truth but were afraid to do so? Have you ever known that something bad would happen to you if you told the truth?

"Listen to the story I will tell you and discover what one person did when he had to decide whether or not to tell the truth."

Sermon: One Sabbath day, as Jesus and his disciples walked, they saw a man who had been blind from birth. The disciples began to ask questions. "Master," they said. "Why was this man born blind? Did he or his parents sin?" People thought that bad things happened to persons who had sinned or whose parents had sinned.

Jesus' response probably surprised the disciples. "Neither," he said. Then he spit on the ground, made some mud, picked it up, and smeared the mud on the blind man's eyes.

"Go wash in the Pool of Siloam," Jesus instructed. Feeling his way through the city, the blind man found the pool and washed. Then a wonderful thing happened. The man who was blind was able to see.

His neighbors and those who knew him could not believe it.

"Is this our neighbor—the one who could not see?" they asked.

"Sure it is," some said, while others responded saying, "No, it can't be." Still others said, "He sure looks like the blind beggar."

The beggar spoke for himself. "I am he," he said.

"How, then, can you see?" the neighbors questioned.

"A man called Jesus spit on the ground, made mud from the dust, smeared it on my eyes, and told me to wash in the Pool of Siloam. I obeyed, and now I can see."

Not being able to find Jesus, they took the man to some Pharisees. Learning that Jesus had healed the blind man on the Sabbath greatly disturbed the Pharisees. They considered what Jesus had done work. No one was to work on the Sabbath.

After arguing among themselves, the Pharisees asked the man who had been blind, "Who was the man who healed you?"

"He must have been a prophet sent from God," the man responded.

Still finding this event hard to believe, the Pharisees brought in the man's parents. "Is this your son?" they questioned. "Was he born blind? And now can he see?"

His parents were afraid. They feared that if they said that it was Jesus who had healed their son, they would not be allowed to worship anymore in the synagogue.

"Yes, this is our son," his parents said. "Yes, he was born blind. But how he is now able to see we cannot explain. Ask him. He is old enough to speak for himself."

Again the Pharisees questioned the man who had been blind. They pressured him to deny the fact that Jesus had healed him. But the man who had been blind could only tell the truth. He said, "This I know. Once I was blind, but now I can see. Jesus, the man from God, healed me."

The Pharisees became so angry that they threw him out.

Response: Ask: "Do you think it was easy for the man born blind to tell the truth, knowing that if he did bad things could happen to him?"

Continue: "Boys and girls, sometimes you will find it hard to be truthful. But always remember, one way you can worship God is by telling the truth."—Leon W. Castle

September 3: What Is Work?

Tomorrow is a special day in our country. Do you know what it is called? (Labor Day.) Do you know why we have a Labor Day? It is to honor all the people who work. On your feet are shoes that I assume your parents bought for you at the store. Now the people in the store did not make those shoes; someone else did. That was their work, just as the people in the store work to help you buy things. Working is a very important part of our life together. It is what people do to accomplish something that needs to be done.

One of the difficult lessons of life that boys and girls have trouble learning is that there is joy in working to accomplish something. Coloring a picture with crayons is work, but it is also fun when you feel the pleasure of having a finished picture that is nicely colored. Learning to ride a bike is hard work; but once it is accomplished, it helps you travel fast and far. Cleaning up your room is hard work, but when it is done, it looks nice and usually you are able to find your things better when you need them. Every day we all have work that needs to be done, and we should be thankful that we have things to do, and we should be thankful for those who have done things for us.—Kenneth Mortonson

September 10: Things You Know

One of the best things about being your age is that you are learning all the time. You go to school and learn to read and write and add and subtract. You learn history and science. You learn every day at school.

You come to church and learn about the Bible. You learn the stories of Jesus and his disciples, about David and Moses and Paul. You learn every Sunday.

You learn in all kinds of ways. If you are on sports teams, you learn to play your game. If you are in a choir, you learn to sing. If you are in a scouting group, you learn about the outdoors.

Some of the most important things you will ever learn are not things you have to be old to understand. You already know some good rules that will last all of your life. Be kind. Share. Return what you borrow. Smile. Be a friend. Listen to your parents. Say nice things. Tell the truth. Do your best. One of the smartest things you can do is not forget the good things you have already learned.—Brett Younger

September 17: Our Shepherd

Object: A picture of a shepherd and his sheep.

Many people love the twenty-third psalm more than any other part of the Bible. Why? Because it tells us how much God loves us and cares for us all through our life—from the time we are born until we die. The psalm says, "The Lord is my shepherd, I shall not want." What does that mean? Does it mean that we will never wish for anything—a toy, new clothes, pizza, ice cream, or a wonderful trip? No. All of us wish for things like these, and that is OK. What it really means is that because God cares for us as a shepherd cares for his flock, his sheep, God will give us what we really need—not everything we wish for. What we need more than anything in all the world is God's love, and we can count on God's love, for God is love. So we have that for sure! And because God loves us he gives us people to love us and care for us. He gives us friends. And all of the good things we enjoy in life we have because the Lord—God—is our shepherd. —James W. Cox

September 24: How to Give Gladly

Visual introduction: A pair of boxing gloves and an offering plate.

Sentence summary: God loves us to give in a glad spirit.

Scripture text: "Each one should give, then, as he has decided, not with regret or out of a sense of duty; for God loves the one who gives gladly" (2 Cor. 9:7 GNB).

Today, we have an offering plate that looks very familiar in church. It belongs in church. But what are these boxing gloves doing here today? When we come to church, we expect the offering plate will be passed. People who love God just want to give to God. They are generous and happy in giving.

Boxing gloves are for people who wish to fight. When the big boys at school get mad at one another and threaten to fight, the coach may say: "All right, boys, put on the boxing gloves. If you want to fight, then go ahead and fight."

Some people do not like to give. They are very stingy. When the offering plate appears or the preacher begins talking about money, they act as if they are angry. Perhaps the only thing they want to give is a punch in the nose to the usher who passes the offering plate by them.

Of course, we are only joking. Boxing gloves have no place in church. The pastor does not use boxing gloves on his members who may not wish to give. Neither can church members use boxing gloves to beat up the ushers or the pastor.

The Bible says that each one of us must decide how much he will give to God. This is our decision to make. No one forces us to donate. And when we give, we do so gladly. We ought not give in an angry spirit. God wants us to give gladly. We should be happy to give without any regrets or sorrow.

Then what happens? God loves everyone who gives gladly. He loves to see us happy, and we are really happy when giving freely to God.—C. W. Bess

October 1: Stability

(For use at the start of a new church school year.)

This morning, I would like each one of you to stand up. Now, stand on one foot, and as soon as you lose your balance and have to touch the floor with the other foot, sit down. Some people find that they can stand for a long time on just one foot, but such people usually have to concentrate on what they are doing to keep their balance. It is much easier for us to stand or move about when we use both feet. Our feet give us a special stability in life when we use them properly.

Today marks the beginning of a new church school year. All of you are expected to go to public school or some other type of school that will teach you the things you need to learn to be an educated person. But in the church family, we believe that to be a complete person, you also need to learn the things that are offered to you in the church school program. That is like the second foot that gives stability to your life. So, I hope you will remember how important it is to come to Sunday school and that you will pay attention so that you can learn those important things that you need for life. And I hope all the people here this morning will remember that Christian education is important no matter how old you are and that they also will take advantage of the opportunities offered to them to keep on learning. Thank you for coming up here this morning.—Kenneth Mortonson

October 8: On Doing Good

A group of men sat in a smoke-filled club room. They were young men, and after discussing politics, women, and war, they finally fell into more serious themes of conversation, each of them telling what he would most like to do and be in the life that was ahead.

Finally a tall, sunburned, distinctly good-looking lad bluntly gave his testimony by saying: "I want to be a millionaire."

The others smiled; some laughed out loud.

"Who doesn't?" asked one young blonde.

"No! I mean it!" the tall, dark boy responded. "No, not for what the money could do for me. Not that at all. But imagine what good a rich man could do if he so desired. I've seen some of the desperate poverty of the slums, and I have felt just as young King Edward did when he said, 'Something's got to be done about this!' I think of friends I could help, members of my own family, a young sister who is married and paying for a home. I want to help her get some of the things she wants. I know people who, if they had a little help right now, could change their whole lives."

The crowd was silenced by the boy's apparent sincerity, and one friend said: "I can add nothing to that wish of yours, but I can think of something even more thrilling, and that is to give without others knowing about it; and something even more thrilling than that—to give without even knowing it yourself."—William L. Stidger

October 15: The Great Party

Narrator: Jesus told a story that went something like this. Once a man threw a big party. There were going to be food and music and all kinds of games. It was going to be the best party that town had ever seen. When everything was ready he invited his friends. It's time for the big party. Are you ready?

First invitee: I am sorry. I just bought a car, and I have to go see it.

Narrator: You bought a new car?

First invitee: It's a little used. I think it's a 1974 or a 1975.

Narrator: But it's in good shape.

First invitee: The salesman said it was in the best shape of any car with 125 thousand miles he had ever seen. Or was it 150?

Narrator: Is it a Honda? Is it a Corvette?

First invitee: I think he said it was a Pinto.

Narrator: A Pinto.

First invitee: Maybe it's a Gremlin.

Narrator: You bought a used 1974 or 1975 with 125 or 150 thousand miles. It is a Pinto or a Gremlin. You have not driven or seen this car.
First invitee (happily): Isn't it great?
Narrator: Are you ready for the party?
Second invitee: I have so much to do I'm not going to make it.
Narrator: What is so important that you would miss the best party ever?
Second invitee: My hair is such a mess. I need to wash it.
Narrator: Your hair looks great. Come to the party.
Second invitee: I really need to change the water in my goldfish bowl.
Narrator: Your goldfish can make it another day.
Second invitee: I need to catch up on my coupon clipping. I'm going to have to miss.
Narrator: Are you ready for the party?
Third invitee: I have a new girlfriend, so I won't be able to come.
Narrator: She can come. Everyone is invited.
Third invitee: She's going to be out of town.
Narrator: You should come by yourself.
Third invitee: I would love to, but she told me I couldn't. She's very jealous.
Narrator: That's silly. Ask her again.
Third invitee: I really don't want to make her mad. I'm sure it will be a great party without me.
Narrator: It was a great party. Even without the ones who made excuses, the party was crowded. There were food and music and games. Everyone had a great time. Sometimes we miss the best times for no good reason. Sometimes we waste our time when we should be smiling and laughing.

—Brett Younger

October 22: What Do You Do When You Are Lost?

(Blindfold a child.) Now, you cannot see, so I do not want you to move, because you could get hurt. Our blindfolded person knows where (he/she) is at but cannot get back to the place where (he/she) was seated. It is up to one of you to help (him/her). What could you do? Take (his/her) hand and lead (him/her) back. Tell (him/her) how to walk and when to turn. That would take longer, but it could be done. And if (his/her) parents would help talk (him/her) back at the other end that would help too. (Take off blindfold.)

There is an important lesson for us here. The blindfolded person is like someone who is lost. He or she cannot get back to where they want to be. In that condition, what does a person need? They need someone to guide them or to tell them what to do. Now, a person could mislead the one who is blindfolded or who is lost. So, the one they receive help from must be someone they can trust. So, if the time ever comes that you feel lost, turn to someone you trust for help. And you should be able to find such a person at home or in your church home.—Kenneth Mortonson

October 29: Saints in Shining Armor

When Earl Marlatt published his book *Protestant Saints,* he was asked by a small friend, Philip Fox, six years old, "Uncle Earl, what's your book about?"

Uncle Earl hesitated a moment before he answered: "I'm afraid, Phil, it's about something you never heard of—saints. Do you know what saints are?"

Phil's eyes lit up, as if he were remembering a room full of rainbows at Sunday school.

"Sure," he said. "I know what saints are. They're the men the light shines through."

And so they are, and so they have been from the time when the early Christians saw martyrs die in winding sheets of flame and spoke of it as "shining armor." One of the greatest of them, St. Paul, knowing the glow that sacrificial service can give to any life, advised his friends to "put on the whole armor of God, that ye may be able to stand against the wiles of the devil."—William Stidger

November 5: Being a Friend

Take three-by-five cards to groups of children and adults before the worship service. Ask them to write "one good rule for being a good friend." Encourage creativity. Both children and adults should be invited to give answers both serious and silly. Each answer should be signed. You should tell everyone that they are helping you with the children's sermon.

Go through your stack of answers and choose the ones to share during the children's sermon. You may want to share the humorous ones you have chosen first, and then move on to the more serious answers. You can also move from prohibitions of unacceptable behavior to positive affirmations of how to build friendship. Duplications should be skipped. The larger your sampling, the more selective you can be in which answers you present. After having explained the question you have asked and shared the answers you have chosen, close with a reminder of the importance of friendship.

Not many things are as important as being a good friend. We need to work to be good friends by avoiding the mistakes we should not make and doing the good things that build friendship.—Brett Younger

November 12: Our Church Home

(Show a key.) Do you know what this is? What is a key used for? Why do people lock up a car or a house or anything else that is important to them? (To protect it, that is, to take care of what they have.) The key is a good symbol of a very important lesson we all need to remember. It is part of what we call stewardship. We are to take care of what we have, and this is especially important in our church, for what we have here we have received from others. They took care of it and passed it on to us, and we are to do the same.

Now, how do you think you boys and girls can help do this? If you came into the church with dirty shoes, would that be taking care of the church? If you made crayon marks on the tables in the Sunday school rooms, would that be taking care of the church? If you took a pencil and scribbled in the worshipbook, would that be taking care of the church? So, remember, you are part of the church family, and we want you to do all you can to take care of our church home, just as we expect your parents and these other adults to help take care of this church for you and for others who will come after us all.—Kenneth Mortonson

November 19: The Importance of Giving Thanks

Do any of you have a dog at home? Do you do anything special when you feed your dog? In our house, we have the dog do a trick, like sitting up, before she is fed. And you know what she does when we put the food down? She eats it right away. And you know what else? She never says thank you. No, of course, I don't expect her to say thank you, because she is a dog. But I do expect people like you who can talk to say thank you when someone gives you something or does something nice for you. When you say thank you to someone, you are showing them that you like what they have done for you, that you are happy to have received their special gift. And when you are happy with what has been done for you, then the person doing it shares your happiness, and that is good. Yesterday I made some cookies, and I'd like to share them with you this morning. You may take one as you return to your seats. (Hopefully, they will all say thank you.)—Kenneth Mortonson

November 26: Raise Your Right Hand

TEXT: John 18:33–37

"For this I was born, and for this I came into the world, to testify to the truth" (v. 37).

Object: a Bible

Good morning, boys and girls. I brought a Bible with me today because we're going to talk about truth. How many of you have ever been in a courtroom or seen a courtroom on television? (Wait for show of hands.) What do they use this Bible for? (Let them respond.) Some of you have seen them ask a person to raise his or her right hand, put their left hand on the Bible, and swear to tell the truth, the whole truth, and nothing but the truth, so help you God. This means the person is asking God to help them to promise to tell the truth. Do you think people always tell the truth when they put their hand on the Bible and make that promise? (Let them respond.) Some of them do tell the truth, but sometimes not all of them do even when they promise to.

Our lesson today is about a time when Jesus was in a courtroom. People were saying Jesus was a king, and Jesus said his kingdom was not of this world. Many people thought Jesus was going to be their earthly king to rescue them from the Romans. But Jesus said in our verse for today that his whole reason for being born was to tell the truth. What did Jesus come to tell the truth about? (Let them respond.) He came to tell us to trust that God loves us and that we should love ourselves and take care of each other. Jesus didn't come to be a king on earth. Jesus' kingdom was a special place where people loved each other and cared for each other and didn't hurt each other and everyone lived in peace. When Jesus told the truth, not everyone believed him. But Jesus didn't lie; he told the truth. We can all live in love and peace, and that's the truth, the whole truth, and nothing but the truth, so help me God. (Put your hand on the Bible.)—*Children's Sermon Service Plus!*

December 3: Advent

How many of you have a baby brother or sister? Do you remember some of the things you did to get ready before the baby came? You had to get the bed, diapers, pacifiers, and toys. Sometimes expectant mothers have parties for you before you are born.

Christmas is a time to get ready for a baby. The baby whose coming we celebrate at Christmas is Jesus. For many years the church has used the four Sundays before Christmas to get ready. The Advent wreath marks each Sunday as we get closer to Christmas.

At church we get ready for Christmas by singing songs about Jesus' coming. The tree reminds us of the first Christmas. We read the story of Jesus' birth from the Bible. We do all these things to remember that Christmas is about Jesus coming to tell us to love each other.—Brett Younger

December 10: Peacemaking

If I say the word *peace* (*piece*) to you, what comes to your mind? You might think of a piece of cake, or if you have had a fight with someone, you might long for peace with them. Just by hearing the word *peace* or *piece,* you cannot tell what is meant. There is a big difference between these two words. P-i-e-c-e refers to a part of something. This half of a cookie is a piece of the cookie. P-e-a-c-e can have the meaning of being complete. A peaceful situation is when things are as they should be, when life is complete and full and everything is working as it should. This is the peace that we are to help to bring into our world as Christians. As peacemakers for God, we are to do all we can to make things work as they were intended to work out. That means helping people get along with one another and be at peace. It means showing love for one another, for God is love. It means trying to live as God wants us to live and sharing that good life with others.

As a reminder of that meaning of peace, as being as it should be, being complete, I'd like to give you a complete cookie for your enjoyment. Thank you for coming up today.—Kenneth Mortonson

December 17: The Secret Is Out!

TEXT: Rom. 16:25–27

"According to the revelation of the mystery that was kept secret for long ages but is now disclosed" (vv. 25b–26a).

Object: A Christmas present with a manger scene and Jesus inside.

Good morning, boys and girls. I brought a present with me this morning that was under our tree. This present is a bit of a mystery. There is no one's name on it. Have any of you ever found a present under your tree with no one's name on the outside? (Let them answer.)

I want to tell you a story of a little girl about your age. Like you, she was getting ready for Christmas. She was waiting patiently until it was time to open presents.

She liked to make things for members of her family. As she made things, she would wrap them and put them under the tree as presents for different family members. Do any of you do that? (Let them answer.) She would draw pictures and then wrap them and put them under the tree. She wrote a poem and wrapped it. She even had a gift for her cat that she wrapped and placed under the tree.

Every time she placed a gift under the tree, she would look at the other gifts already under the tree. She noticed a gift like this one—with no name on it. (Hold up your gift.) As Christmas came nearer and nearer, this gift became more and more of a mystery. She didn't know who it was for or whom it was from. Finally it was time to open the presents. When all were passed around, the mystery gift was still under the tree. Now it's time to open the mystery gift to see what it is. (Select someone to open it.) It is baby Jesus.

The Bible tell us that for many, many years God had a secret for us. Jesus is the mystery that God kept secret. But, when Jesus was born, God's secret was no longer a secret. Jesus told everyone of the love of God. Jesus told everyone that we are all children of God. That is the secret, or the mystery gift, that came to us at Christmas.

When you unwrap your presents later this week, remember the secret gift of God. That gift is Jesus. Jesus is the reason we celebrate Christmas.—*Children's Sermon Service Plus!*

December 24: What's an Angel?

TEXT: Heb. 1:1–9

Of the angels he says, "He makes his angels winds" (v. 7).

Object: an angel ornament or Christmas card

(Note: This lesson has more questions for children than other lessons. The lesson is designed for children to give their thoughts about angels. If you use a microphone, have it ready for children to give their responses so that worshipers may hear these responses.)

Good evening, boys and girls. Can anyone tell me what an angel is? (Let them answer.) Has anyone ever called you an angel? (Let them answer.) What does an angel look like? (Let them answer.) If you could be an angel for one day, would you? (Let them answer.) Angels are important at Christmas time, aren't they? I have one example of what an angel might look like. (Show your example.) I think that the reason we think angels have wings is from tonight's scripture. It says that God makes the angels God's winds. Winds make me think of flying.

If I were an angel, I think I'd like to be an angel at Christmas time. How many of you remember that it was the angel Gabriel who told Mary that she would have a baby named Jesus? Another angel, whose name we don't know, was important on Christmas Eve. It was an angel who told the shepherd about the baby Jesus.

Angels are very important to God. The angels that appeared to Mary and to the shepherds were God's messengers. The Bible says that angels are spirits in God's service. Angels are very important to God. But there is one other person more important to God than angels. Who do you suppose that person is? (Let them answer.) That person is Jesus. Our Bible story tonight says that Jesus is more important than angels. It says that all God's angels worship him.

This weekend you will see angels on your Christmas tree, on Christmas cards, and even on wrapping paper. Remember that angels are God's messengers. Remember that, like all Christians, angels worship Jesus.—*Children's Sermon Service Plus!*

December 31: God's Time

Does anyone know what this is? (Show them a sun dial or a picture of one.) It is used to tell the time by the position of the sun in the sky and the shadow that is cast on the plate. But if the sun is not shining, it will not work. So most of us use a clock or a watch. (Show them a clock or watch.) What time is it on this clock? Is it nighttime or daytime? Can you tell that by looking at the clock? (No, you need to think about time in the setting of the day.) And as time passes, we call each twenty-four hours a day, and the days make up the weeks, and the weeks become months and then years. And all of time is a gift from God. But as with all gifts, their true meaning is found in the use of the gift. Time is like an ever-flowing stream that carries us through life. We all have the same amount of time each day. And a wise person is one who learns to make good use of time. That is a lesson you are never too young to learn.—Kenneth Mortonson

SECTION XI.
A Little Treasury of Sermon Illustrations

ADVENTURE. I remember the time our younger son broke his leg while skiing, at the age of fourteen. My wife and I were naturally very upset. But he said to us: "You know, I'm quite glad, because I've had a personal experience at last. My life was so normal and sheltered! Something's happened to me at last!" Alas! Since then he has had plenty of adventures of a more serious kind and on one occasion escaped death by a miracle. But, thank God, he has kept his spirit of adventure. Like our elder son also, he has preserved an inexhaustible capacity for enthusiasm. Woe betide those who no longer feel thrilled at anything, who have stopped looking for adventure!—Paul Tournier

THE COMING JUDGMENT. Even the coming judgment of the living and the dead is a subject for *hope*, for longing and the prayer "Come soon, Lord Jesus!" For who is the judge? It is the same Christ who gave himself up to death for sinners and who has borne our griefs and sicknesses. How should we not trust ourselves joyfully to his judgment? What will the crucified Jesus judge us by? The law or his own gospel? Our own acts or his sufferings for us? How should we not hasten joyfully to meet the universal judge when he is the one who was crucified for us?—Jürgen Moltmann

SIGN OF THE KINGDOM. In the New Testament it is clear that the only sign of the kingdom is Jesus himself. The central task of the church, as it prays "Your kingdom come!" is to bear witness to him in whom the kingdom *has* come, to call all men to the U-turn in the mind that we call conversion so that they may acknowledge him as King and join his whole church in the prayer "Come, Lord Jesus!"—Lesslie Newbigin

THE SOCIAL GOSPEL. Walter Rauschenbusch ranks as one of the most outstanding representatives of the social gospel in the United States, and it is worth recalling that he wrote: "We have a social gospel. We need a systematic theology large enough to match it and vital enough to back it." For him, it could not be a case of choosing one at the expense of the other, for he saw that they need each other and that it is only when they are woven together that they are strong and alive. "The social gospel needs a theology to make it effective; but theology needs the social gospel to vitalize it."—John Macquarrie

GOD'S GUIDANCE. God guides us, despite our uncertainties and our vagueness, even through our failings and mistakes. He often starts us off to the left only to bring us up in the end to the right; or else he brings us back to the right, after a long tour, because we started off by mistake to the left in the belief that we were obeying him. He leads us step by step, from event to event. Only afterward, as we look back over the way we have come and reconsider certain important moments in our lives in the light of all that has followed them, or when we survey the whole progress of our lives, do we experience the feeling of having been led without knowing it, the feeling that God has mysteriously guided us.—Paul Tournier

FEAR. One does not need to be afraid of anything. To achieve the complete absence of fear is, of course, difficult. But it can almost be done if one vigorously challenges the neurotic idea that we ought to be afraid of things because they are unpleasant and the idea that events happening outside of our lives have the ability to upset us. When my clients insist they are not neurotic just because they express a fear or a worry over something that is happening or may happen, I point out to them that in every case they are ignoring a hundred other dangers around them that are a great deal worse than the ones they are presently focusing upon. If they are to be consistent about their fears, then they will worry about airplanes dropping on them or atomic bombs going off, about being poisoned by botulism, or being shot or robbed on the street.—Paul A. Hauck

BELIEVING. Making war over beliefs is surely a sign of how important the activity of believing has always been to human beings; it is a tragedy, however, when this elementary human inclination is shriveled and scorched by the unknowing flames of controversy. Putting belief in a vise is a mistake because it goes against what we understand about all other human functions. There is nothing locked in about man, no way in which he will ever hear or utter the last word on any issue in his life. Believing will always retain notes of searching in the healthy person who feels constrained and crippled if his spontaneous response is choked by too many rigid or irreducible formulations.—Eugene C. Kennedy

FAITH AND LIFE. A couple who wants to grow in their love knows that they cannot shut themselves off from questions nor from the experiences of change that are bound to occur because of illness, aging, or other processes. They live by a kind of faith that is enhanced by the explorations of self that are demanded of a man and woman who must continually find new answers together. They experience life through their belief in each other and through their willingness to risk change and hurt in pursuit of greater truth and depth together. It is the same way for the questioning believer; the search keeps him alive and responsive even though it asks him to live on the quivering edge of doubt and self-exploration.—Eugene C. Kennedy

GOODNESS OF GOD. During my earliest ministry I was given a sermon by an old preacher who stopped dying long enough to give me a sermon of just three words. When I met Daddy Bishop, he was paralyzed and on his deathbed in an El Paso hospital. He called me over to his bed and looked up into my face. "You are just a boy," he said. "I am old and will never preach again. Let me preach through you. Say God is good—always." He closed his eyes. I never saw Daddy Bishop alive again, but I have felt his presence while I have preached for almost fifty years.—Harold E. Dye

IDOLS. Great twentieth-century dictators such as Lenin, Mussolini, and Hitler, to mention only the departed, not only had all the somewhat repulsive qualities usually needed for success in democratic politics; they owed their rise to democratic processes. In due course, all such dictators fall, though not usually before they have brought incalculable human suffering in their train. Idols of the people who admire them for their power and invest them with a still larger panoply of it, they turn out in the end to be powerless for the task entrusted to them because they have so abused their power that it has turned in upon themselves and destroyed them.—Geddes MacGregor

THE TRINITY. Through the Son, God creates, reconciles, and redeems his creation. In the power of the Spirit, God is himself present in his creation—present in his reconciliation and his redemption of that creation. The overflowing love from which everything comes that is from God is also the implicit ground for God's readiness to endure the contradictions of the beings he has created. And here too is already the source of his will toward reconciliation and the redemption of the world through the suffering patience of his hope.

The Son, the eternal counterpart within God himself, becomes the wisdom, the pattern, through which creation is made. The Son in whom the world is created becomes flesh, and himself enters into the world in order to redeem it. He suffers the self-destruction of creation in order through his sufferings to heal it. What is not assumed by God in this way in his creation cannot, either, be healed.

God the Spirit is also the Spirit of the universe, its total cohesion, its structure, its information, its energy. The Spirit of the universe is the Spirit who proceeds from the Father and shines forth in the Son. The evolutions and the catastrophes of the universe are also the movements and experiences of the Spirit of creation. That is why Paul tells us that the divine Spirit "sighs" in all created things under the power of futility. That is why the divine Spirit transcends himself in all created beings. This is manifested in the self-organization and the self-transcendence of all living things.—Jürgen Moltmann

REPENTANCE. When a man undertakes to repent toward his fellowmen, it is repenting straight up a precipice; when he repents toward law, it is repenting into the crocodile's jaws; when he repents toward public sentiment, it is throwing himself into a thicket of brambles and thorns; but when he repents toward God, he repents toward all love and delicacy. God receives the soul as the sea the bather, to return it again, purer and whiter than he took it.—Henry Ward Beecher

EXPLOITING GOD. I read a fine sentence the other day that puts in condensed form what I have often preached about as a symptom of the present age: "Instead of placing themselves at the service of God, most people want a God who is at their service." These two tendencies represent in the end two different religions. The man who is exploiting God for the purposes of his own soul or for the race has in the long run a different religion from the man who is putting his own soul and race absolutely at the disposal of the will of God in Jesus Christ.—P. T. Forsyth

ON HEARING VOICES. Occasionally, in my care of profoundly psychotic persons, one of them will tell me, "I hear these voices that terrify me." I ask, "Are these voices the voice of one particular person?" They reply, "Yes. The devil tells me to kill myself." Such extreme commands also appear in other patients' reports. As their pastoral counselor, I respond with the question, "Do you know what Jesus said the devil is?" The answer is usually no. I respond, "Jesus said the devil is a liar. The truth is not in him. He is the father of lies." I encourage them to say this aloud when they hear voices. They tend to remember this godly admonition, use it, and be comforted as they do so. It is a workable admonition for all of us when we are tempted to blame our own desires on the devil.—Wayne E. Oates

SHORTSIGHTEDNESS. Many years ago Colonel Low, a professor at St. Joseph's College in Bardstown, Kentucky, was fired by the trustees of the college. Why? Because he wrote a pamphlet advocating a railroad to the West Coast. You will know that he wrote a long time ago and that the trustees were shortsighted men when I tell you that Low was fired "on the ground of insanity." The trustees knew that anyone who wrote about the possibility of a train going to the West Coast had to be insane.—David W. Richardson

PUT TO THE TEST. In a remarkable book chronicling two South Pole expeditions, those of Amundsen and of Scott—Admundsen the Norwegian, Scott the

Englishman—the record shows that whereas the English went in, all *Rule Brittania* arrogance and minds set to conquer the cold, with ponies no less, than which there were few beasts less practical—the Norwegians went in to cooperate with the elements and to survive. In the end, Scott sat in his tent, writing his last lines, a penned pity party for the misfortune of wretched weather—where he should have expected it! Amundsen's team, on the other hands, went in with dogs (too unmanly for the English) and their best skiers. When the weather was particularly foul, the Norwegians simply holed up and saw the occasion as an opportunity to rest, repair the dogs' harness, and in general catch their breath. At one point they butchered some of the dogs, with each man having to kill one of his own team. (Some of the faithful beasts would be slain, but they would be loved to the last.) Thus armed with fresh meat, they avoided the scurvy that laid the English low.—Peter Fribley

A QUESTION OF VALUES. Leith Anderson, a pastor, shared an experience that throws light upon this truth. As a boy, he grew up outside of New York City and was an avid fan of the old Brooklyn Dodgers. One day his father took him to a World Series game between the Dodgers and the Yankees. He was so excited, and he just knew the Dodgers would trounce the Yankees. Unfortunately, the Dodgers never got on base, and his excitement was shattered. Years later he was engrossed in a conversation with a man who was a walking sports almanac. Leith told him about the first major league game he attended and added, "It was such a disappointment. I was a Dodger fan and the Dodgers never got on base." The man said, "You were *there?* You were at the game when Don Larsen pitched the only perfect game in all of World Series history?" Leith replied, "Yeah, but uh, we lost." He then realized that he had been so caught up in his team's defeat that he missed out on the fact that he was a witness to a far greater page of history.—Dean Register

KINDS OF BELIEF. There are two kinds of unbeliever: those who say something is not true *because* they *wish* it were not true and those who say something is not true because they wish that it were. This latter kind is curable. After eight days of the gloom that comes from doubt, the Savior appears to the doubter and says: "Let me have thy finger; see, here are my hands. Let me have thy hand; put it into my side. Cease thy doubting and believe" (John 20:27). Thomas casts himself at Jesus' feet, saying: "My Lord and my God" (John 20:28).—Fulton J. Sheen

PRIVILEGE OR DUTY. Beverly Sills had just given an outstanding matinee performance, and according to the program, she would give another performance that evening at eight o'clock. Backstage she was being congratulated by one of her fans. He said, "You must rest now, because I see that you have to give another performance tonight."

"No," said Beverly Sills. "I don't have to give another performance tonight."

"Well," said the fan, "it says here in the program that you have an eight P.M. performance. Did you forget?"

"I do have a performance tonight," she said, "but I don't have to give it. I get to give it."—Thomas Hilton, *Church Management—The Clergy Journal*

A SENSE OF JUSTICE. I met a delightful three-year-old going on twenty-one. Her parents keep pecan twirls in the pantry for breakfast and snacks. One day she went to the pantry to get one to eat but found they were all gone.

"Daddy!" she cried. "You and Mommy have been eating my pecan twirls. That's not fair. You've been eating them for years; now it's my turn."

A child's wronged sense of justice may seem funny and illogical to us, but it may tell us something of the resentment we may feel toward others or that others may feel toward us. Holley's parents had been eating pecan twirls for years, and she thought it only fair for her to have a chance to catch up. They had already eaten plenty; now it was her turn.

When will our turn come? It isn't hard to look around and see people who seem to have had more than their share. And resentment may encourage us to think they have part of our share, too. The next time that sort of resentment begins to build up toward someone else, you might stop to wonder whose pecan twirl *you* have been eating.—Hal Poe

UNRECOGNIZED SUCCESS. I read somewhere (I can't recall where) about a perfunctory funeral service. It was only old Thomas who used to sit up in the gallery of some undistinguished church and nod during the sermon. No one troubled overmuch about old Thomas. And for the funeral, it was scarcely worth the expense of a coach for mourners because there were only two, his daughter and her husband. But after the pathetically small procession had left the church, the funeral ended, and a large resplendent car joined on behind. It followed to the cemetery. From it stepped a general in full uniform. He saluted at the graveside. Afterward the story was disclosed why he came. "I had to come," he said, "I saw the announcement in the local paper. You see, he was my Sunday school teacher years ago. He used to pray for me. I laughed at him and made fun of him. But the Bible he gave me I still possess. That is all, but I should never have found my way to God without him." A pretty story? But I would like to add, I hope old Thomas knew. I am sure sometimes he thought his life a failure.—D. W. Cleverley Ford

TRUSTING GOD. God still sustains his servants in times of trial. When TWA flight 847 was hijacked by the Muslim extremists in June 1985, the terrorists brutalized passengers and repeatedly threatened to blow up the plane with everyone aboard. But, even though he was convinced that at any moment his plane would be destroyed and he and his passengers killed, Captain John Testrake found comfort in the thought, "If I die, I'll get to see Jesus." With half-crazed hijackers waving live grenades in his face and pointing guns at his head, Testrake said to himself, "I have trusted God for many years. I am trusting strongly in the Lord now."—Lucien Coleman

A WORTHY CREED. I *believe* in the supreme worth of the individual and in his right to life, liberty, and pursuit of happiness.

I *believe* that every right implies a responsibility; every opportunity, an obligation; every possession, a duty.

I *believe* that the law was made for man and not man for the law, that government is the servant of the people and not their master.

I *believe* in the dignity of labor, whether with head or hand; that the world owes no man a living, but that it owes every man an opportunity to make a living.

I *believe* that thrift is essential to well-ordered living and that economy is a prime requisite of a sound financial structure, whether in government, business, or personal affairs.

I *believe* that truth and justice are fundamental to an enduring social order.

I *believe* in the sacredness of a promise, that a man's word should be as good as his bond, that character—not wealth or power or position—is of supreme worth.

I *believe* that the rendering of useful service is the common duty of mankind and that only in the purifying fire of sacrifice is the dross of selfishness consumed and the greatness of the human soul set free.

I *believe* in an all-wise and all-loving God, named by whatever name, and that the individual's highest fulfillment, greatest happiness, and widest usefulness are to be found in living in harmony with his will.

I *believe* that love is the greatest thing in the world, that it alone can overcome hate, that right can and will triumph over might.—John D. Rockefeller, Jr.

A SPRINKLING RELATIONSHIP. The late Bishop Pike used to refer to some of his fellow Episcopalians (and I am sure to people of all denominations) as having a "sprinkling relationship" to the church. "They are sprinkled with water at baptism, sprinkled with rice at marriage, and sprinkled with earth at death."—Fred W. Andrea

PAYING COMPLIMENTS. Blessed is the couple who remembers: praise is like manna. It lasts only one day.

But the daily praise was only part of this covenant. Every week we paid each other a new compliment, something we'd never said before. Multiply fifty-two by the years you've been married. Does your mate know that many things you like?

Promise: if you will begin today (one compliment daily, one new compliment weekly), your marriage will take on a wonderful new glow. No small part of life's well-being comes from feeling that we're doing well. And nothing brings the heart more gladness than to know we're doing well with the person we love best. The Bible tells it like it is: "Love rejoices not a wrong but rejoices in the right" (1 Cor. 13).—Charlie W. Shedd

STEWARDSHIP. Bertrand Russell said, "It is the preoccupation with possession, more than anything else, that prevents men from living freely and nobly."—C. Neil Strait

A DISTINCTION. Dwight L. Moody recognized the difference between those who've had a true encounter with Christ and those who have not. The story is told that he was preaching on a street corner when he was interrupted by a drunken man, shouting, "Mister Moody! Mr. Moody! D'you 'member me? Mr. Moody! D'you r'member me?"

Moody finally stopped preaching and said, "I'm sorry, sir, but I do not."

"Why, Mr. Moody!" the drunk admonished. "You oughta 'member me! I'm one of yer converts!"

Moody was said to reply, "You *must* be one of mine. Apparently you're *not* one of *his*."—Robert Don Hughes

VISION LOST. Don't ever be content with having reached a goal; don't rest on your laurels. History is filled with examples of people who, though they had accomplished great things, lost sight of their vision. When Alexander the Great had a vision, he conquered countries; when he lost it, he couldn't conquer a liquor bottle. When David had a vision, he conquered Goliath; and when he lost his vision, he couldn't conquer his own lust.—John C. Maxell

WHAT WE CAN KNOW. If we want to know something about the first ascent of a mountain peak, the incomplete and fragmentary report of a simple mountain guide who survived a fatal accident during the expedition is infinitely more valuable than the thrilling presentation by a great poet who has pictured the adventure only in his poetic imagination. For the important thing to us in this vital question is not a comprehensive system or an aesthetically satisfactory overall picture. The question on which our eternal destiny depends is too serious for that. The only thing that matters is whether the little that we can know really does come from the authority that cannot only utter guesses concerning the ultimate things, as all human thinkers and poets do, but has God's mandate to instruct us on them.—Karl Heim

PATIENCE AND DILIGENCE. When people become members of our church, there are some we think will be strong, vital, working members and others we figure won't last two weeks. How often we are wrong. Often we look at marriages and think, "This marriage does not have a chance." It lasts and lasts and lasts. We look at another and say, "This marriage was surely made in heaven and will last forever." And we are wrong. We look at young people and say, "There's a young person who is going to accomplish things, and there's one who is going to get into trouble." How often we are wrong.—Robert C. Shannon

VISIBLE SIGN. A lady in a Connecticut village told her pastor that all she remembered of a minister who preached there fifty years before, and who since rendered distinguished service as a bishop of the Methodist Church, South, was that two little beads of perspiration always formed on his brow when he preached. Her pastor replied that he would be willing to have every sermon of his forgotten if the impression of earnestness and sincerity were strong enough to span half a century.—Halford E. Luccock

THE RIGHT TO SPEAK. When death darkened the home of Thomas Carlyle, a friend took out a Testament and read these familiar words of the Fourth Gospel: "Let not your heart be troubled. . . . In my Father's house are many mansions."

"Aye," muttered the brokenhearted Carlyle, "if you were God, you had a right to say that; but if you are only a man, what do you know any more than the rest of us?"—G. Ray Jordan

FREEDOM. Last October I spoke to the men at the Maryland Penitentiary, the Maryland jail. It was the feast of their patron saint, St. Dismas, the thief who was crucified at the right hand of Christ on Calvary, the thief who heard Christ whisper: "This day you will be with me in paradise." That morning I asked one of the prisoners what in prison life he found hardest to take. He was a very sensible young fellow, intelligent, and he answered: "Father, for the most part it's not too bad. They're quite kind to me here: I'm learning a trade; I have friends; I have some time to myself; even the food could be worse. But the one thing I don't have is the one thing I want: I don't have freedom; I'm not free."—Walter J. Burghardt

PROBLEMS. Henry J. Kaiser predicated his remarkable career on the premise that "*problems are only opportunities in work clothes.*" Challenged by the need for greater water reserve in the production of electricity, he put together a company that constructed Hoover Dam. During World War II, when the government desperately needed ships, he organized a company that built nearly one-third of the U.S. freighters. Needing steel for these ships, he started a company in California, later adding an aluminum operation. Mr. Kaiser's orbital achievements (sixty companies operating 180 plants with assets totaling $1.7 billion) were launched by problems that had to be solved, needs that had to be met.—G. Othell Hand

OPEN TO OUR HELP. There are many people round about us—far more probably than we suppose—who in secret are not satisfied with the life that they are leading, and who, perhaps unknown to themselves, are lying open to the first genuine religious influence that they shall encounter. It may even be that some of them have quite sincerely begun the Christian life. Their strength is not yet very firm; their faith has not yet become settled; they have no experience of the religious life to draw upon for any special moment of danger. For such people—people in whose hearts the higher life is just beginning to take root—the world today is a perilous place.—John A. Hutton

THE NATURALNESS OF STEWARDSHIP. Stewardship is the life-style of a steward, just as swimming is the life-style of a fish. The fish does not stop and think and decide it will swim. Swimming is so natural it does not have to think about it. When things are such a natural part of us that we don't have to stop and think about them, they have become part of our nature. Jesus said that giving should be such a natural part of living that our left hand would not know what our right hand was doing (Matt. 6:3). Giving is a natural part of life in Christ. For the Christian, living is giving.—Hal Poe

BIGGER THAN LIFE. On national television an art dealer explained his success this way: "People are searching for anything to prove that they are not dead. Their lives are so thin. I connect them with something bigger."—David W. Richardson

WHEN RIGHT IS WRONG. Carlyle has a grim parable of an orator at a street corner, crying out to the passers-by that everything was upside down, men, trees, houses, everything. Whereupon one of his hearers went forward and turned *him,* the speaker, upside down, that is to say, planted him on his feet! For it was he who had been standing on his head!

That is amusing enough; but I can imagine a parable infinitely more powerful of a man standing at a street corner assuring everybody who passed by that everything as it is today is just about all right. And I can imagine Christ coming by, whereupon, as they look at each other, Christ and that tame approver of this present world, the terrible idea dawns upon him that if Christ standing there is right, most things are wrong.—John A. Hutton

IMMORTALITY. Imagine that you are standing at the end of a long, narrow corridor. Looking down the corridor, you see part of a large room opening at right angles to the corridor. On the farther wall of that room you discern clearly the pattern in the wallpaper. You see certain large figures appearing at regular intervals, certain small figures emerging in a definite sequence, certain lines diverging and converging and forming a coherent design. Do you know anything about the parts of that room that at present are cut off from your vision? There are some things about them you do not know, but there is at least one thing that seems certain. The design on the wallpaper will continue beyond the point at which your view is cut off. The same figures, large and small, will be there. The same line will continue to form the same coherent pattern. Why do we Christians believe in personal immortality? Why do we think God's final gift to all his children is another chance to live and work, help and love and grow? Because this is the pattern of existence seen in the part of the room of life now visible to us. In a scheme of things as consistent as this one seems to be, that pattern will—we are confident—be present in the part of the room of life now hidden from us.—James Gordon Gilkey

THE VICTORY. To be able to say at any stage in life, "I have everything that God can give," is to have the victory that overcomes the world. But distinguish this from saying, "I have everything that a heart can wish." There are things you cannot have now because you are not ready for them and because of the exigencies of the kingdom of God.—P. T. Forsyth

GOD'S VOICE. One of the most successful missionaries in India at the turn of the century was an ex-convict, a Norwegian called Skrefsrud. After a bad school record and an apprenticeship to a blatant atheist, he was thrown into prison by the army for his appalling behavior. It was there, however, in the prison, utterly wretched, that he began to read the Bible. No more unlikely Bible student could be imagined. But God spoke to him. It was so decisive that when he was finally discharged he sought to be a missionary. But no society would accept an ex-convict. Undeterred, he set off for India alone, and so successful were his labors that he toured America and Europe raising funds for his work. And when on those fund-raising tours he watched the crowds streaming in to hear him speak, often and again he saw in his mind's eye that terrible prison cell where reading the Bible in his time of need he heard the voice of God speaking to him.—D. W. Cleverley Ford

HE PROMISED. A father and his daughter drifted far from the shore while swimming. Suddenly the girl, near exhaustion, realized that she could not swim back to safety. Her father had only strength enough to return and was unable to tow her in. He instructed her to float and remain as calm as possible until he could return with help. Later, when he returned, he found her calmly waiting. When someone remarked concerning her composure in the midst of such danger, she replied, "He said he would come for me, and that I could float all day, so I swam and floated, because I knew he would come."—Hugh R. Horne

OH, HAPPY DAY! A few weeks ago an eleven-year-old boy was baptized at our 9:15 service. After the service he came up to me and extended his hand. He had an olive wood cross around his neck. He had a sparkle in his eyes, an enormous smile on his face. He was radiant. He was so enthusiastic. His father and mother had completed the pastor's seminar and had just been received into membership. His brother had been baptized with him. He said, "This is wonderful. This is the happiest day of my life!" What had happened? A child had welcomed Jesus into his heart and life.—Joe A. Harding

STICK-TO-IT-IVENESS. We all know some Christians who display a charming reality of experience, a freshness of faith, and a capacity to "keep on keeping on" that marks them off from others. I should like to name this elusive quality of spiritual life that abounds in power and devotion right through to the finish as "stick-to-it-iveness."

"Stick-to-it-iveness" is a word rather like "ain't," as the farmer discussed it. "You ortenta use 'ain't!' " he scolded his schoolboy son. "It 'ain't' a proper word; it 'ain't' right grammar; and it 'ain't' fittin' to be used because it 'ain't' even in the dictionary. 'Ain't' that right, son?" I know all the arguments against using a word like "stick-to-it-iveness," but I still want to do it because it seems to express exactly what I mean. It means that tenacity of purpose that gives power to a Christian race at the end as well as when the runner began at the beginning.—Craig Skinner

SALVATION. Every loving word that God speaks to us acts back again and makes music in his heart. He never says, with a scowl, "Here comes that poor, limping sinner again." The path of the sinner back to God is brighter and brighter all the way up to the smile of the face and the touch of the hand; and *that* is salvation.—Henry Ward Beecher

TWO DIFFERENT WORLDS. On a New York City television talk show, a producer appeared to promote a television special on Mother Theresa of Calcutta. The producer talked about the grim human conditions that were a part of Mother Theresa's daily life. Throughout the interview, commercials were interspersed with the subjects discussed in the following sequence: lepers ("bikinis for sale"); mass starvation ("designer jeans"); agonizing poverty ("fur coats"); abandoned babies ("ice cream sundaes"); the dying ("diamond watches"). These topics and the commercials that followed represent two different worlds—the world of the poor and the world of the affluent. In James 2:2, the world of affluence is symbolized by the "man with gold rings and in fine clothing."—Lucien Coleman

THE USE OF THEOLOGY. When C. S. Lewis wanted to show the nature of theology, he recognized the point of view of the hard-bitten old officer who said he had no use for theology, but that he had felt God out alone in the desert at night. Lewis then goes on:

> Now in a sense I quite agreed with that man. I think he'd probably had a real experience of God in the desert. And when he turned from that experience to the Christian creeds, I think he *was* really turning from something quite real to something less real. In the same way, if a man has once looked at the Atlantic from the beach, and then goes and looks at a map of the Atlantic, he also will be turning from something more real to something less real: turning from real waves to a bit of colored paper. But here comes the point. The map *is* only colored paper, but there are two things you have to remember about it. In the first place, it is based on the real Atlantic. In that way it has behind it masses of experience just as real as the one you could have from the beach; only, while yours would be a single isolated glimpse, the map fits all those different experiences together. In the second place, if you want to go anywhere, the map is absolutely necessary. As long as you're content with walks on the beach, your own glimpses are far more fun than looking at a map. But the map's going to be more use than walks on the beach if you want to get to America.
>
> Well, theology's like the map.—Ronald E. Sleeth quoting C. S. Lewis

ORDINARY PEOPLE. The picture conjured up in my mind is that of an old baronial hall in an English mansion. You walk around it under the direction of a guide, and to the right and left of you there are oil portraits, which become the objects of the guide's comments. You are surprised as you stop before a portrait or two—as your mind wanders off, and you hear the sonorous sounds of the guide's voice recalling some of the highlights of their careers—and you are surprised to discover what ordinary men and women they were. You get the same feeling when you read the famous eleventh chapter of Hebrews. You wonder why some of those people were ever included among the heroes and heroines of faith—Abraham, for example, a dreamer, a young adventurer, who set out "not knowing whither he went" in response to a largely undefined call to become an immigrant in a strange land!—Elam Davies

TAKING A MODEL. It is right to take so absolute a model as Christ, but it is sure that we cannot "grow up in all things into him" in a hurry. Von Hugel spoke of "the mysterious yet very certain truth that we can actually hamper our advance by trying too directly, too vehemently, too much by absolute recipes or models." And Fenelon said, "It is an excess of self-love that would become perfect in a moment, rather than by slow degrees." Seeking quick perfection, we fail and become discouraged, and give up.—Sam Shoemaker

SLAVERY TO SUCCESS. We associate the name of Admiral Robert E. Peary with the North Pole, for he was the first white man to reach the North Pole. Peary thought maltreatment of his men unimportant if only he could be the first to reach the Pole, which he did April 6, 1909. Peary was so pushed by the wrong motives that he took with him on that final trek Matthew Henson, a black man, because supposedly a black man did not count as a person. Peary said, "After a lifetime of effort I dearly wanted the honor for myself." It did not make him happy. At the Pole Peary said, "What a cheerless spot to have aroused the ambition of man for so many ages." Even when Peary returned victorious, he was never as happy as he thought he would be.—David W. Richardson

DOUBT. There may be points of faith that we do not yet accept: let us not swallow them simply "on authority" but seek to work them out with our minds plus God's inspiration. There is the mood of doubt that may be caused by indigestion or a bad liver, and there is the mood of doubt that sweeps us now and then when evil presses hard. Faith does not dispel doubt by making us fear to admit or face it; faith dispels doubt by winning out over it in an honest duel.—Sam Shoemaker

TRUTH AND DEED. Christianity is founded on the historical fact of the union of truth and deed: "The Word became flesh." Wisdom became incarnate; God became man; knowledge passed into act; oughtness became isness, and theory became practice. He not only gave the theory that the greatest of all his followers should be the least, but he washed the feet of his own disciples. This order of first the Word of truth, then the truth in the flesh, was changed by Goethe into: "In the beginning was the deed"—first, you live, then you rationalize. First you act, then you think of a way to justify your action. First you seize property, then you write a law to sanction the theft. From this primacy of the act over truth have come all the moral disorders of the present day, as men no longer fit their lives to a creed, but a creed to the way they live.—Fulton J. Sheen

WELCOMED AND VALUED. Churches grow where there is warm and welcoming "body language" that is perceived as authentic and genuine. I learned as district superintendent in Seattle some years ago that churches have personalities as varied as the personalities of people. Many churches, suffering a crisis of low self-esteem, send signals of indifference or hostility to outsiders. Congregations that feel loved and valued, that experience health and vitality, tend to attract undiscipled persons by their congruent messages of interest and concern. People tend to join groups where they perceive they are genuinely welcomed and valued.

How is a member of the congregation or a visitor helped to know he is loved and valued? Primarily by being "listened to." Listening is one of the most loving things we can do for another person. Listening says, "You matter. I value you."—Joe A. Harding

BREAD, ALSO! C. H. Spurgeon used to preach only once each year "for his orphans." At that great meeting many would come to hear the famous preacher, and an offering would be received for his orphanage. After one of these meetings he is reputed to have been leaving the building where the service had taken place when one of those "superspiritual," narrow-minded, nitpicking individuals accosted him with the charge, "Why, Mr. Spurgeon, I thought you preached for souls and not for money!"

The story relates that Spurgeon gravely replied, "Why, Mr. So-and-So, normally I do preach for souls and not for money. But my orphans can't eat souls! And if they could, my brother, it would take at least four the size of yours to give one of them a square meal!"—Craig Skinner

LOVE COSTS. Love then is the giving of self, and as long as we have a body and are working out our salvation, it will always be synonymous with sacrifice, in the Christian sense of the word. Love sacrifices naturally just as the eye sees and the ear hears. That is why we speak of "arrows" and "darts" of love—something that wounds. The bridegroom who loves will not give to his bride a ring of tin or of brass, but one of gold or of platinum, because the gold or platinum ring represents sacrifice—it *costs* something. The mother who sits up all night nursing her sick child does not call it hardship but love.—Fulton J. Sheen

DISCOVERY. Christ never told his disciples he was Messiah till it was borne in on them by contact with him. He never told them till, by the working of the actual messiahship upon them, they found it out. Revelation came home to them as discovery. It burst from experience. So gracious is God with his revelation that he actually lets it come home to us as if we had discovered it. That is his fine manner—so to give as if we had found.—P. T. Forsyth

ACQUIESCENCE. It was Dr. Edward Livingston Trudeau, the American physician who spent virtually his entire adult life adjusting to tuberculosis. At the end of the years he wrote these profound words: "To cease to rebel, to stop fighting back, to be content with half a loaf when you cannot have a whole one—these are hard lessons, but all of us must learn them. I have found that the great word is *acquiescence*." You are trying to make adjustments? You find it hard to do so? Remember what the great word is. It is not protest. It is not rebellion. It is not even struggle. It is *acquiescence*.—James Gordon Gilkey

A LIGHT TO WALK BY. The man who carries a lantern in a dark night can have friends all around him, walking safely by the help of its rays, and be not defrauded. So he who has the God-given light of hope in his breast can help on many others in this world's darkness, not to his own loss but to their precious gain.—Henry Ward Beecher

NAPOLEON'S LAMENT. In his isolation at St. Helena, he reflected upon the vanity of his own life and that of Louis XIV, of whom he said, "That great king is long dead, and even now he is alone in his room at Versailles, abandoned by the courtesans and perhaps the object of their scorn. He is no longer their master; he is a cadaver, a coffin, and a horror. Not long now and it shall be my lot too. That is what will happen to me. What an abyss between my profound misery and the reign of Jesus Christ, preached, loved, adored, and living in all the universe."—Fulton J. Sheen

FAULTY PREDICTION. In the early 1920s, D. W. Griffith said, "Speaking movies are impossible. When a century has passed, all thought of our so-called speaking movies will have been abandoned. It will never be possible to synchronize the voice with the picture."—Robert C. Shannon

JESUS' GIFT. Celsus was the first great skeptic. He once asked, "What has Jesus given to the world that no one else has given?" Someone answered, "Himself!" Yes, that's Jesus' magnificent, stunning gift to the world. He gave himself! He gave himself not only in submission upon the cross but also in power at the Resurrection.—Robert C. Shannon

FRIENDSHIP. However much friendship has been made to play second to romantic love in modern Western culture, it continues to exist as a significant form of love between people. Social and geographic mobility have made it an especially hard relationship to sustain over a long period of time, but it is such an important way in which human beings find life worth living that it deserves careful consideration in its own right. Like romantic love between a man and woman, friendship requires *agape* as an ingredient. Even though friendship and romantic love are very different, they have one thing in common: the need to love our neighbor as we love ourselves. If they lack that as an integral part, then both of them lack what they need to sustain themselves. They will fail to be a proper realization of themselves and because of that failure can even become destructive. They can all too easily become, for example, dominated by possessiveness and jealousy.—Diogenes Allen

WHATEVER BECAME OF TEMPTATION? As I began gathering materials for writing this book, I was immediately struck by the scarcity of contemporary books and serious articles on temptation. I discussed this with a colleague of mine, Douglas P. Hobson, M.D., a psychiatrist with the U.S. Diplomatic Corps. In a letter to me he wrote, "Perhaps the absence of material on temptation reflects the permissive and promiscuous society in which we live, where there are fewer temptations because there are fewer sins, or at least less talk about sin."—Wayne E. Oates, *Temptation*

LOVE AND PRAYER. Love and prayer belong indissolubly together. If you want to pray in a way that can be answered, you must have the spirit of love. A doctor who is about to perform an important operation takes sufficient time—about twenty minutes on the average—to cleanse his hands thoroughly. He does his utmost to ensure that his work on the patient will bless and not harm, heal rather than infect. If a doctor prepares himself so thoroughly in order to help a man's body, how much more should we take time to cleanse ourselves inwardly before bringing others help for their souls.

This examination of our emotions and thoughts is not a vain self-reflection; it is rather a necessary cleansing so that nothing evil will settle down in us—no germs of hate, resentment, jealousy, envy, or impurity that could have a contagious and devastating effect. This also corresponds to the admonition of the Apostle Paul, "Do not be hasty in the laying on of hands" (1 Tim. 5:22). There is an infection of the soul. Only the person who is cleansed and infused by the spirit of love is protected against such infections and is so healthy that he does not bring harm to others.

Love for our brothers in Christ has still another decisive meaning. It is a wonderful measure of my love for God. Besides, this love—to use a common illustration—is like the draft of a fireplace or coal stove. The more I open the flue, the more oxygen comes in to the wood or coal and the more flame is produced. When I practice loving my brother and my sister, I produce a greater flame of love for God.—Wilhard Becker

STRENGTH WHEN NEEDED. I remember an occasion as a young man when I felt as though I were undergoing an unfair experience. I resented very greatly that all this should be happening to me, for it seemed so much greater than anything my peers had to suffer. I cried out, "Why me, Lord?" I read the verse from 1 Corinthians 10:13, and it dawned upon me that if God would not allow temptations beyond our strength, then my strength must be above average, since my test was above average. I came to see it as a backhanded compliment and actually felt comforted by the thought. Looking back, I can see how much my ego was involved in the incident—even in the experience of comfort. Today I understand more clearly that the strength I had at the time was just a temporary loan to me from above and was not my innate strength. Nevertheless I believe all the more firmly today that if another experience like that comes along, I shall again be strengthened to bear it. You truly may not be able to bear some trials with the strength you now have, but when that heavy trial comes, sufficient strength will come along with it.—Charles D. Bass

WE ARE DEBTORS. What shall we say of the multitude who owe the peace and purity of their homes, the whole core of their life's happiness and security, to the gospel and the church, and who think to cancel the obligation by a few patronizing words?

What an irresistible force the church would have did it not have to carry so many who merely ride and do nothing else! We hear much good advice about keeping out of debt. St. Paul has something better to offer. Get in debt! Give your life the impetus of a realization of that love so amazing, so divine that the whole realm of nature could never repay it. Only such an acknowledged obligation can redeem our lives from tawdriness and selfishness. "I beseech you, brethren, by the mercies of God." "I am debtor to the Greeks and to the Gentiles."—Halford E. Luccock

INDIFFERENCE. Why customers quit:

- 1 percent die
- 3 percent move away
- 5 percent other friendships
- 9 percent competitive reasons (price)
- 14 percent product dissatisfaction
- 68 percent because of an attitude of indifference toward them by some employee

—John Maxwell

A HEART TO HELP. William Gladstone, the great English statesman, suffered many heartaches and reverses during his useful career. Yet it is known that even though the affairs of state pressed him sorely, he was in the habit of calling on the most humble in London. When he heard of sickness and sorrow—perhaps from the corner policeman or the street sweeper—he would go to the home of the one in trouble and there he would offer his help, and invariably he would also read the Bible and pray before leaving. It is said that once while on his way to Parliament, he stopped to greet a street sweeper with whom he was accustomed to passing the time of day. On this occasion the man told Gladstone that he had lost his wife, who was a good woman. The great statesman placed his arm around the man and wept with him as he attempted to comfort him in his grief. He had learned to share his light with others, and as a result his own spiritual resources were multiplied.—Hugh R. Horne

TIME FOR LIVING. People who knew Justice Louis D. Brandeis recognized that he was a tireless worker. However, he believed in taking periodic vacations. He was convinced that these intervals of relaxation made it possible for him to increase his workload.

A colleague once chided him for going on a trip when he had an important trial coming up. Brandeis explained, "I need this period of change. I can do a year's work in eleven months, but not in twelve."—Franklin Segler

LIGHTS AND SHADOWS. An essay, thought to be among the last expressions that came from the pen of H. E. Dana, was entitled "Lights and Shadows on the Canvas of Life." One of his daughters was an amateur artist. Looking at one of her unfinished pictures, he remarked to her that it was not as good as she usually painted. She answered, "That picture is not yet completed. I haven't put the shadows in it yet. No picture is complete without both lights and shadows."

He saw in this a marvelous parable of life. It takes both lights and shadows to make life's picture complete. We may think of life as a vast canvas on which an unseen hand is painting. Dana said some would call that hand fate; he insisted upon calling it providence. "It is the very hand of God. For the portrait he is painting there to be best, the various colors must be properly blended. The picture must carry upon it both lights and shadows. Upon the canvas of every life there are both the lights and the shadows, and the shadows are just as necessary as are the brighter hues," my teacher affirmed.—Franklin Segler

WISDOM OF FRIENDS. God has as many avenues of approach to the heart of a man or woman, as they have friends who are friends of Christ. We bear our glad witness to the fact that God speaks to us constantly without any intermediary at all—but we bear witness also to our need of his voice through the fellowship. The sins we are strangely blind to, he can show us by a friend. The tasks he is pressing on us but that, by reason of sloth or modesty or dullness of understanding, we are leaving undone, he can call us to through the group. The doubts that fill the mind at times when our personal guidance is not clear can be resolved in the fellowship and our path confirmed or corrected by the common mind.—W. E. Sangster

GOD'S PRESENCE. In the midst of our most pressing temptations, the presence of God provides sustenance and direction. In fact, as a very young granddaughter of one of my good friends says, we are met by God's providence in our temptations "right in the middle of now."—Wayne E. Oates

ACKNOWLEDGMENTS

Acknowledgment and gratitude are hereby expressed to the following for kind permission to reprint material from the books and periodicals listed below.

BROADMAN PRESS: Each of the following is used by permission. Excerpts from Hugh Litchfield, "Longing for Egypt," in *Award Winning Sermons,* Vol. 1, pp. 129–136, © 1977, Broadman Press; Excerpts from Joe E. Trull, "Thomas: Locked Out by Doubt," in *Award Winning Sermons,* Vol. 3, pp. 120–127, © 1979, Broadman Press; Excerpts from James E. Carter, "It's Dynamite," in *Award Winning Sermons,* Vol. 2, pp. 11–18, © 1978, Broadman Press; Excerpts from Alfred L. Miller, "God's People in God's World," in *Award Winning Sermons,* Vol. 4, pp. 113–118, © 1980, Broadman Press; Excerpts from James W. McClendon, "Lydia," in *More Southern Baptist Preaching,* © 1964, pp. 56–62, Broadman Press; Excerpts from M. Vernon Davis, "What It Takes to Make Us See," in *Award Winning Sermons,* Vol. 3, pp. 37–42, © 1979, Broadman Press; Excerpts from Richard Groves, "Sin as a Loss of Perspective," in *Award Winning Sermons,* Vol. 2, pp. 55–62, © 1978, Broadman Press; Excerpts from Hugh Litchfield, *Sermons on Those Other Special Days,* pp. 134–140, © 1990, Broadman Press; Excerpts from Eli Landrum, Jr., *More Than Symbol,* pp. 106–109, © 1983, Broadman Press; Excerpts from Hugh Litchfield, *Preaching the Christmas Story,* pp. 47–53, © 1984, Broadman Press.

SUNDAY SCHOOL BOARD OF THE SOUTHERN BAPTIST CONVENTION: Each of the following is used by permission. Excerpts from William Richard Ezell in *Proclaim,* July–September 1993, pp. 20–21, © 1993, The Sunday School Board of the Southern Baptist Convention; Excerpt from Stephen Cloud in *Proclaim,* January–March 1992, p. 26, © 1991, The Sunday School Board of the Southern Baptist Convention; Excerpts from Dean Register in *Proclaim,* October–December 1993, pp. 4–6, © 1993, The Sunday School Board of the Southern Baptist Convention; Excerpts from Scott Moody in *Proclaim,* October–December 1992, pp. 27–28, © 1992, The Sunday School Board of the Southern Baptist Convention; Excerpt from Joe E. Trull in *Proclaim,* April–June 1988, pp. 34–35, © 1988, The Sunday School Board of the Southern Baptist Convention; Excerpt from Joe E. Trull in *Proclaim,* October–December 1991, p. 31, © 1991, The Sunday School Board of the Southern Baptist Convention; Excerpt from Greg Potts in *Proclaim,* October–December 1993, p. 40, © 1993, The Sunday School Board of the Southern Baptist Convention; Excerpt from Douglas G. Denton in *Proclaim,* October–December 1993, pp. 37–38, © 1993, The Sunday School Board of the Southern Baptist Convention; Illustration from Harold E. Dye in *Open Windows,* October–December 1990, for November 18, © 1990, The Sunday School Board of the Southern Baptist Convention; Illustration from *Advanced Bible Study,* October–December 1990, p. 22, © 1990, The Sunday School Board of the Southern Baptist Convention.

HARPERCOLLINS PUBLISHERS, INC.: Excerpts from Karl Barth, *Deliverance to the Captives,* © 1961 Harper & Brothers; Excerpts from Harry Emerson Fosdick, *A Book of Public Prayers,* © 1959, Harper & Brothers; Excerpts from Harry Emerson Fosdick, *On Being Fit to Live With,* © 1946, Harper & Brothers; Excerpts from Helmut Thielicke, *Christ and the Meaning of Life,* © 1962, Harper & Brothers; Excerpts from D. W. Cleverley Ford, *An Expository Preacher's Notebook,* © 1960, Harper & Brothers; Excerpts from Samuel H. Miller, *Prayers for Daily Use,* © 1957, Harper & Brothers; Excerpts from David H. C. Read, *Unfinished Easter,* © 1978, Harper & Row; Excerpts from Harry Emerson Fosdick, *What Is Vital in Religion,* © 1955, Harper & Brothers; Excerpts from Nels F. S. Ferre, *God's New Age,* © 1956, 1958, 1960, 1962, Harper & Brothers; Excerpts from Halford E. Luccock, *Marching Off the Map*, © 1952, Harper & Brothers; Excerpts from Gerald Kennedy, *Fresh Every Morning*, © 1966, Harper & Row; Excerpts from Paul Scherer, *The Word God Sent*, © 1965, Harper & Row; Excerpts from Charles R. Brown, *Being Made Over*, © 1939, Harper & Brothers; Excerpts from Clovis G. Chappell, *Sermons on New Testament Characters*, © Harper & Brothers, 1924; Excerpts from Vernon L. Stanfield, ed., *Favorite Sermons of John A. Broadus*, © 1959, Harper & Brothers; Excerpts from James W. Cox, ed., *Best Sermons 1*, © 1988, Harper & Row.

INDEX OF CONTRIBUTORS

SERMON TITLE INDEX

(Children's stories and sermons are identified as **cs**; *sermon suggestions as* **ss**)

SCRIPTURAL INDEX

INDEX OF PRAYERS

INDEX OF MATERIALS USEFUL AS CHILDREN'S STORIES AND SERMONS NOT INCLUDED IN SECTION X

INDEX OF MATERIALS USEFUL FOR SMALL GROUPS

TOPICAL INDEX